Praise For Richard Deal's CCNA Study Guide

As a CCIE and instructor, I can personally assure you that the importance of learning the fundamentals cannot be stressed enough. I have instructed certification candidates who were preparing for every level of Cisco certification, from CCNA up to CCIE. Those individuals who took the time to learn the essential technologies have always had a much greater chance of success, both in pursuing certifications and working "real life" in the field. This book is a wonderful tool to truly learn about Cisco networking.

In the years I have known Richard Deal, he has repeatedly impressed me with his technical knowledge and teaching ability. Every time we work together on a project, Richard takes complex subjects and presents them in a way that is understandable. He has a unique ability to enable people to understand complex technical content. Richard has found a way to impress me again by efficiently covering Cisco's large list of exam topics for the new CCNA exams.

This book is much more than the bound paper you are holding in your hands. It contains the McGraw-Hill NetSim Learning Edition and corresponding labs that are included for critical hands-on experience. The practice exam included on the CD by Richard Deal uses the Boson Test Engine with the latest in simulation technology. I would recommend taking advantage of the discounted NetSim upgrade and additional practice tests prior to your exam date. This will give you maximum exposure to the new topics.

In summary, this book and its enclosed CD-ROM will be a great resource to those preparing for Cisco certification and to those who want to master essential technologies. It will remain accurate reference material about Cisco networking for years to come.

Stephen Marcinek
CCIE 7225

Praise For Richard Deal's CCNA Study Guide

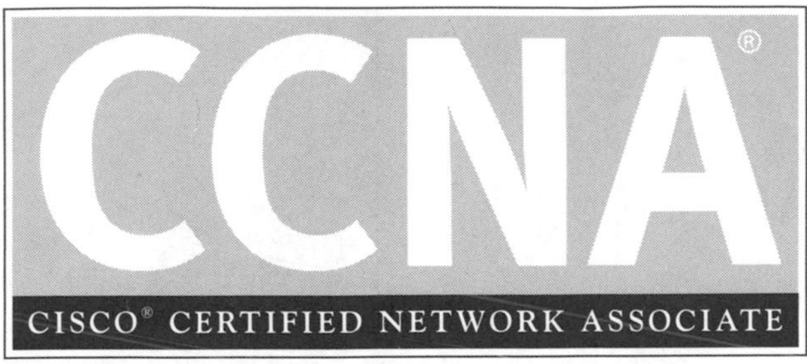

CCNA® Cisco® Certified Network Associate Study Guide (Exam 640-801)

CCNA® Cisco® Certified Network Associate Study Guide (Exam 640-801)

Richard Deal

McGraw-Hill/Osborne

New York Chicago San Francisco Lisbon London Madrid
Mexico City Milan New Delhi San Juan Seoul Singapore Sydney Toronto

The McGraw-Hill Companies

McGraw-Hill/Osborne
2100 Powell Street, 10th Floor
Emeryville, California 94608
U.S.A.

To arrange bulk purchase discounts for sales promotions, premiums, or fund-raisers, please contact **McGraw-Hill**/Osborne at the above address. For information on translations or book distributors outside the U.S.A., please see the International Contact Information page immediately following the index of this book.

CCNA® Cisco® Certified Network Associate Study Guide (Exam 640-801)

567890 CUS CUS 01987654

Book p/n 0-07-222935-7 and CD p/n 0-07-222936-5
parts of
ISBN 0-07-222934-9

Publisher
Brandon A. Nordin

Vice President & Associate Publisher
Scott Rogers

Editorial Director
Gareth Hancock

Associate Acquisitions Editor
Timothy Green

Project Editor
Elizabeth Seymour

Acquisitions Coordinator
Jessica Wilson

Technical Editor
Steve Marcinek

Copy Editor
Robert Campbell

Proofreaders
Paul Medoff, Mike McGee

Indexer
Valerie Perry

Composition
Apollo Publishing Services

Illustrator
Sue Albert

Series Design
Roberta Steele

Cover Design
Regan Honda

This book was composed with Corel VENTURA™ Publisher.

ABOUT THE AUTHOR

For the past six years, Richard Deal has operated his own company, The Deal Group Inc., in Oviedo, FL, east of Orlando. Richard has 17 years experience in the computing and networking industry including networking, training, systems administration, and programming. In addition to a B.S. in Mathematics from Grove City College, he holds many certifications from Cisco and has taught many beginning and advanced Cisco classes. Richard is the author of *Cisco PIX Firewalls*, an in-depth book on Cisco's PIX firewalls and their implementation, published by McGraw-Hill/Osborne. Richard is also the author of *CCNP: Remote Access Exam Prep*, *CCNP: Switching Exam Cram*, and *CCNP: Cisco LAN Switching Configuration Exam Cram* (The Coriolis Group), and also developed CD questions and tutorials for The Coriolis Group. Richard also authored *CCNA Secrets Revealed!* (Boson Software, Inc.), an electronic book. Richard is actively writing Cisco tests for Boson and QuizWare (Boson's Practice Test software can be purchased from www.boson.com—QuizWare's Practice Test software can be purchased from www.quizware.com) and has written computer-based tests for many of Cisco's certification exams, including the CCNA, in addition to developing various courses on networking and networking security.

Richard periodically holds bootcamp classes, which provide hands-on configuration of Cisco routers and switches. More information on his bootcamp classes, as well as a current schedule, can be seen at http://www.quizware.com/dealgroup/.

To Natalie, my loving wife, and
to our soon-to-be-born first child.

CONTENTS AT A GLANCE

CONTENTS

FOREWORD

From Boson Software, Inc.

The Cisco CCNA certification requires you learn and master a number of skills. As you read this book, incorporating the Boson NetSim™ into your learning process will help you successfully complete the CCNA certification track. The Boson NetSim LE (learning edition) included with this book will get you started on your way, with additional capability from the Standard Edition after purchasing an upgrade.

One of the most common ways to use the Boson NetSim™ is in conjunction with a book or in an instructor led class. Whether you are using this study guide or studying from the published Cisco objectives, learning Cisco routers and switches involve two fundamental tasks: learning and mastering the theory of routers and switches, and applying the hands-on practical implementation of that theory by configuring and testing the networking devices in a lab.

The theory portion of the education can be taught by reading books or by listening to an instructor. The purpose of the Boson NetSim™ is to help you with the practical hands-on portion of your education, and it ensures that you not only understand the concepts of routing and switching, but that you can actually configure and implement routing and switching on Cisco devices. Once you feel you have mastered both the theory and the practical labs, you can test your knowledge using the exams included with this book and the CD. You may also purchase additional Practice Tests from Boson, available at www.boson.com, which support and contain the industry's newest testing methods. Boson's advanced testing methods include: hands-on simulated lab questions, router and switch mini-configuration questions, drag and drop questions, and other operating system simulation questions.

The Boson NetSim™ is the most advanced simulator product on the market for learning how to configure a Cisco® router and Catalyst® switch. The Boson NetSim™ will not only help you become CCNA® certified, it will actually help you learn and understand how to configure routers, switches, and networks.

At any time, you can (and are encouraged to) install both editions of the Boson NetSim™ at the same time—the Learning Edition included with this CDROM, in addition to the standard demo version available at http://www.boson.com/netsim.

After registration, this Learning Edition of the Boson NetSim™ permits enough functionality for the LE labs within this book to be completed free of charge.

The Boson NetSim™ Learning Edition can be upgraded to the Standard Edition v5.0 for CCNA at any time for the special price of 50% off the normal $249.95 USD price (with a valid book code unique serial number from your qualifying McGraw-Hill/Osborne® book). Upgrading enables all other Boson NetSim™ labs, commands, telnet, and advanced features such as drag-and-drop custom network design. In addition, once upgraded, the Boson NetSim™ LE upgrade license also works for the Boson NetSim™ Standard Edition v5.0 for CCNA, which may be downloaded at any time from http://www.boson.com/netsim. Thank you very much, and best wishes in your future studies!

Boson Software, Inc.
www.boson.com

ACKNOWLEDGMENTS

We would like to thank the following people:

- This book would not have been possible without the support of my wife, Natalie. A book of this size is very time-consuming, especially when you have to balance a book, a job, and, most importantly, a family. My wife provided endless encouragement to keep me writing when I was pressed to meet deadlines for the book.
- A special thanks to Steve Marcinek for providing excellent feedback and encouragement on the technical content of this book. I have worked with Steve and his company, Boson Software, on numerous occasions and know of no one more knowledgeable in this field. I would also like to thank David Rajala and John Swartz, co-owners of Boson Software for their assistance and the use of their wonderful router simulator product and test engine included on the CD. Another special thanks to Chad Altman for all his hard work testing the simulator. Throughout the work on this book, I have had the opportunity to work with many wonderful people at Boson and would like to thank all of them for their assistance: Jon, Stacy, Jeremy, Martin, and the rest of the crew.
- The team at McGraw Hill, especially Tim Green, Jessica Wilson, and Elizabeth Seymour. I owe a debt of gratitude to you three, especially in pulling all of the pieces together for the CD-ROM material and the final proofing—thanks for your help!

Best wishes to all! And cheers!
Richard A. Deal

PREFACE

The primary objective of this book is to help you achieve the Cisco Certified Network Associate (CCNA) certification so that you can enhance your career. I believe that the only way you can increase your knowledge is through theoretical and practical learning. In other words, this book provides the book learning as well as basic hands-on experience that you'll need to pass the exam. However, once you pass the CCNA exam, your journey is just beginning: you'll need to enhance your newly acquired skills with additional reading and a lot of hands-on experience.

It is important to point out that there are two ways of achieving your CCNA certification:

- Pass the CCNA (640-801) exam, or
- Pass both the INTRO (640-821) and ICND (640-811) exams

The CCNA 640-801 exam includes the same topics that the INTRO 640-821 and ICND 640-811 exams cover. Cisco developed the second approach more for individuals who are just beginning their journey into networking, especially for people taking the CCNA curriculum at a Cisco Network Academy. The two-test approach is better suited for this environment since it takes a year to two years to go through Cisco's CCNA curriculum at the Network Academies. With this approach, you take the INTRO 640-821 exam half way through the curriculum and the ICND 640-811 exam at the end of the curriculum.

If you already have networking experience, especially if that experience includes configuring Cisco devices, you are better off taking the single CCNA 640-801 exam. The main advantage of this approach is that you only have to pay for one exam. Currently, most Cisco exams cost $125 US to take (at the time of the printing of this book), but Cisco has changed their pricing scheme in the past and will probably do so in the future.

This book was primarily written for those individuals wishing to pass the CCNA 640-801 exam. However, this book contains ALL of the information that you would need in order to pass both the INTRO 640-821 and ICND 640-811 exams. Therefore, it is really up to you which testing approach you wish to take in order to achieve your CCNA certification.

In This Book

This book covers all of the exam objectives posted on Cisco's web site concerning the CCNA 640-801 exam as well as the INTRO 640-821 and ICND 640-811 exams. Each of the chapters cover one or more of the main objectives in this list, especially as it relates to how things work and how to configure them on Cisco's routers and switches.

In Every Chapter

I've created a set of chapter components that call your attention to important items, reinforce important points, and provide helpful exam-taking hints. Take a look at what you'll find in every chapter:

- Every chapter begins with the **Certification Objectives—**what you need to know in order to pass the section on the exam dealing with the chapter topic. The Objective headings identify the objectives within the chapter, so you'll always know an objective when you see it!
- **Practice Exercises** are interspersed throughout the chapters. These are step-by-step exercises that allow you to get the hands-on experience you need in order to pass the exams. They help you master skills that are likely to be an area of focus on the exam. Don't just read through the exercises; they are hands-on practice that you should be comfortable completing. Learning by doing is an effective way to increase your competency with a product. These exercises are directly tied to the McGraw-Hill NetSim Learning Edition simulator, produced by Boson Software, included on the CD. These exercises will always work with the simulator product. Please note that Cisco's real exams contain simulation questions, so it is very important that you practice your skills with either this simulator or with real routers and switches!
- **On The Job** notes describe the issues that come up most often in real-world settings. They provide a valuable perspective on certification- and product-related topics. They point out common mistakes and address questions that have arisen from on the job discussions and experience.
- **Exam Watch** notes point out important information you should learn when preparing for your exam.

- Multimedia Demonstrations, called **CertCams**, are included on the CD. If you want to see ***actual*** configurations of Cisco routers and switches in action, you can view these multimedia demonstrations. Throughout each chapter involving configurations, there are multiple multimedia demonstrations with a pointer to the CD where you can locate and run them. You will need to read the instructions included on the CD in order to run the multimedia demonstrations.
- The **Two-Minute Drill** at the end of every chapter is a checklist of the main points of the chapter. It can be used for last-minute review.
- The Chapter **Self Test** section at the back of each chapter offers questions similar to those found on the certification exams. The answers to these questions, as well as explanations of the answers, can be found at the end of each chapter. By taking the Practice Exams after completing each chapter, you'll reinforce what you've learned from that chapter while becoming familiar with the structure of the exam questions.
- The **Exam Readiness Checklist** section at the end of the Introduction and in Appendix B is a list of the official exam objectives, presented exactly as the Vendor specifies them, cross-listed with the exam objectives as they are presented in the book along with page and chapter references. You should work with this list as you study, noting your familiarity with the objectives by checking off the appropriate box before you review each chapter. The table in the Introduction covers exam 640-801. Appendix B covers the objectives for the INTRO and ICND exams.

Some Pointers

Once you've finished reading this book, set aside some time to do a *thorough* review. You might want to return to the book several times and make use of all the methods it offers for reviewing the material:

1. *Re-read all the Two-Minute Drills*, or have someone quiz you. You also can use the drills as a way to do a quick cram before the exam.
2. *Re-read all the Exam Watch notes*. These are important items you should know for the exam. In other words, don't be surprised to see these topics appear on the real exam.
3. *Re-take the Self Test sections at the Back of each chapter*. Taking the tests right after you've read the chapter is a good idea, because the questions

help reinforce what you've just learned. However, it's an even better idea to go back later and do all the questions in the book in one sitting. Pretend that you're taking the live exam. (When you go through the questions the first time, you should mark your answers on a separate piece of paper. That way, you can run through the questions as many times as you need to until you feel comfortable with the material

4. *Use the Exam Test Engine on the CD.* Did you use the test engine on the CD to test your knowledge? There are 400 questions in the test engine covering all of the topics in the book. The test engine is provided by Boson Software and allows you to test yourself by choosing questions from one or more categories. Each category matches a chapter in the book. Therefore, whenever you finish a chapter in the book, make sure that you test yourself with these questions from the corresponding category in the test engine! You can also purchase additional tests from Boson Software at their web site (www.boson.com). I even have my own versions of test for the INTRO, ICND, and CCNA exams, with different questions than what are included in this book and CD. These exams can be purchased at www.quizware.com.
5. *Use the Flashcard program on the CD.* This program has 300 flashcards with a basic question and answer format. The flashcards cover important topics on the CCNA exams that you should be very familiar with. The flashcards can be used on a Windows-based PC or a PDA. Please see the CD for PDA requirements.
6. *Do all the Practice Exercises in each of the chapters.* There will be some simulation questions on the real CCNA exams. In the simulation questions, you'll be required to perform basic configuration *and* troubleshooting tasks on a Cisco router and/or switch. Therefore, it is important that you have good configuration skills. Use the Practice Exercises to hone your configuration skills! I have developed two types of simulation questions in this book. All of them have to do with configuring Cisco routers and Catalyst switches; however, some of them also have you troubleshoot networking problems, where two or three configuration errors are introduced into the network and it is your job to track down these configuration errors, using the tools you learned about throughout this book, and fix them.

Practice Exams and the Simulator

As I mentioned earlier, it is important that you have hands-on experience not only for the exam, but also to prepare you for working with Cisco equipment in a real network. A lot of time and effort has been devoted in the creation of the Practice Exercises in this book. I have developed two figures which display the network topology used with the simulator.

As you can see from these figures, you have four PCs, two routers (a 2600 and a 2500), two Catalyst 2950 switches, and two Catalyst 1900 switches. Throughout the chapters that have Practice Exercises, they will refer you to this part of the book

FIGURE 1 Basic network topology for the Practice Exercises.

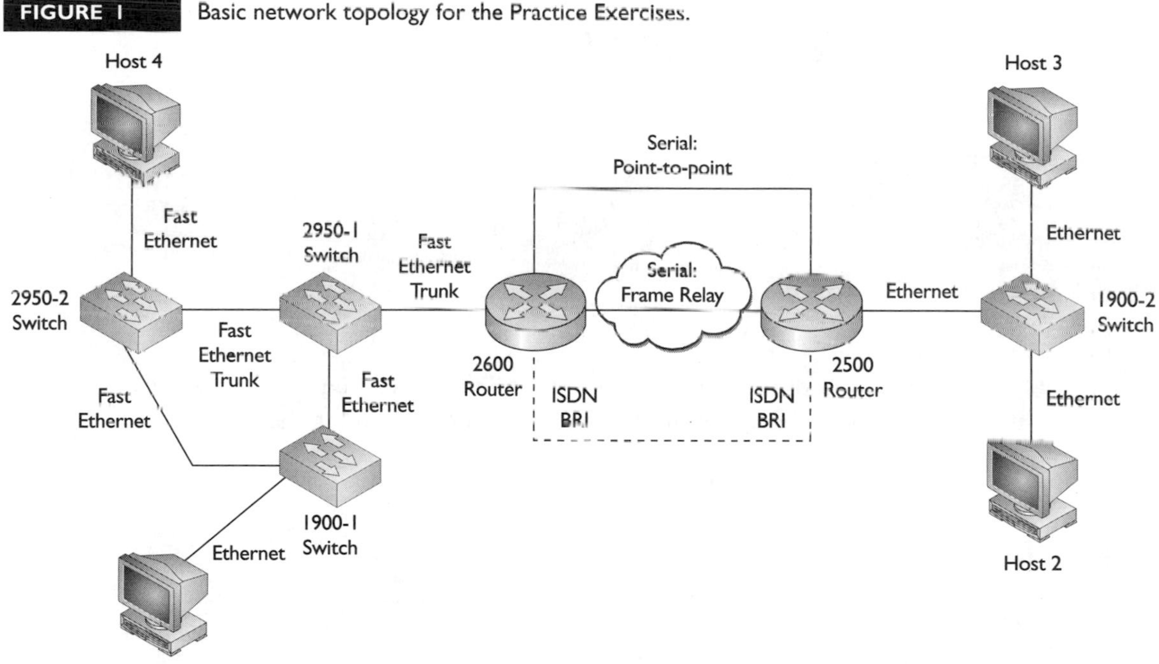

FIGURE 2 Addressing for the network topology used for the Practice Exercises.

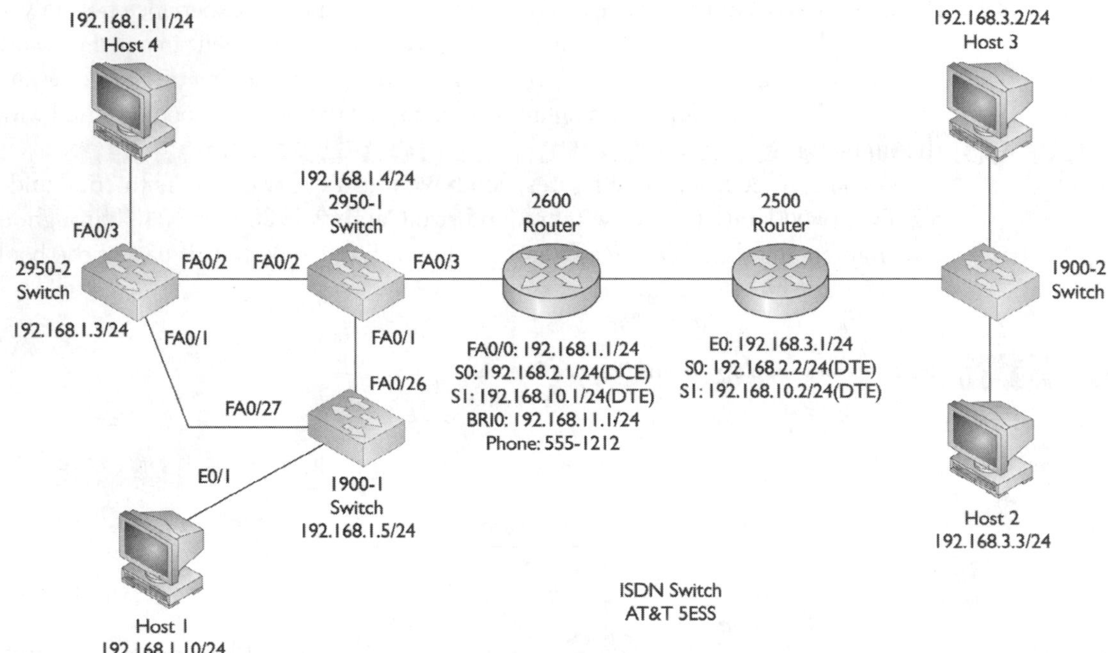

for the layout of the network topology and the addressing assigned to the devices in the topology. Please refer to these figures when performing the exercises.

INTRODUCTION

How to Take a Cisco Certification Examination

This introduction covers the importance of your CCNA certification and prepares you for taking the actual examination. It gives you a few pointers on methods of preparing for the exam, including how to study and register, what to expect, and what to do on exam day.

Catch the Wave!

Congratulations on your pursuit of Cisco certification! In this fast-paced world of networking, few certification programs are as valuable as the one offered by Cisco.

The networking industry has virtually exploded in recent years, accelerated by nonstop innovation and the Internet's popularity. Cisco has stayed at the forefront of this tidal wave, maintaining a dominant role in the industry.

The networking industry is highly competitive, and evolving technology only increases in its complexity, so the rapid growth of the networking industry has created a vacuum of qualified people. There simply aren't enough skilled networking people to meet the demand. Even the most experienced professionals must keep current with the latest technology in order to provide the skills that the industry demands. Cisco certification programs can help networking professionals succeed as they pursue their careers.

Cisco started its certification program many years ago, offering only the designation Cisco Certified Internetwork Expert (CCIE). Through the CCIE program, Cisco provided a means to meet the growing demand for experts in the field of networking. However, the CCIE tests are brutal, with a failure rate of over 80 percent! Fewer than 5 percent of candidates pass on their first attempt! As you might imagine, very few people ever attain CCIE status.

In early 1998, Cisco recognized the need for intermediate certifications, and several new programs were created. Four intermediate certifications were added: CCNA (Cisco Certified Network Associate), CCNP (Cisco Certified Network Professional), CCDA (Cisco Certified Design Associate), and CCDP (Cisco

Certified Design Professional). In addition, several specialties were added to the professional and CCIE certification levels.

exam watch ***I would encourage you to take beta tests when they are available. Not only are the beta exams less expensive than the final exams (some are even free!), but also, if you pass the beta, you will receive credit for passing the exam. If you don't pass the beta, you will have seen many of the questions in the pool of available questions, and can use this information when you prepare to take the exam for the second time. Remember to jot down important information immediately after the exam. You will have to do this after leaving the exam area, since materials written during the exam are retained by the testing center. This information can be helpful when you need to determine which areas of the exam were most challenging for you as you study for the subsequent test.***

Why Vendor Certification?

Over the years, vendors have created their own certification programs because of industry demand. This demand arises when the marketplace needs skilled professionals and an easy way to identify them. Vendors benefit because it promotes people skilled in their product. Professionals benefit because it boosts their careers. Employers benefit because it helps them identify qualified people.

In the networking industry, technology changes too often and too quickly to rely on traditional means of certification, such as universities and trade associations. Because of the investment and effort required to keep network certification programs current, vendors are the only organizations suited to keep pace with the changes. In general, such vendor certification programs are excellent, with most of them requiring a solid foundation in the essentials, as well as their particular product line.

Corporate America has come to appreciate these vendor certification programs and the value they provide. Employers recognize that certifications, like university degrees, do not guarantee a level of knowledge, experience, or performance; rather, they establish a baseline for comparison. By seeking to hire vendor-certified employees, a company can assure itself that not only has it found a person skilled in networking, but also it has hired a person skilled in the specific products the company uses.

Technical professionals have also begun to recognize the value of certification and the impact it can have on their careers. By completing a certification program, professionals gain an endorsement of their skills from a major industry source. This endorsement can boost their current position, and it makes finding the next job even easier. Often a certification determines whether a first interview is even granted.

Today a certification may place you ahead of the pack. Tomorrow it will be a necessity to keep from being left in the dust.

exam watch

Signing up for an exam has become easier with a Web-based test registration system. To sign up for the CCNA exams, access Prometric's site (http://www.2test.com to locate a test center, or http://www.prometric.com to register) or Vue's site (http://www.vue.com), and register for the Cisco Career Certification path. You will need to get an Internet account and password, if you do not already have one for these sites. Just select the option for first-time registration, and the Web site will walk you through that process. The registration wizard even provides maps to the testing centers, something that is not available when you call Prometric or Vue on the telephone.

Cisco's Certification Program

Cisco now has a number of certifications for the Routing and Switching career track. While Cisco recommends a series of courses for each of these certifications, they are not required. Ultimately, certification is dependent upon a candidate's passing a series of exams. With the right experience and study materials, you can pass each of these exams without taking the associated class.

Cisco has recently changed the certification track for the CCNA and CCNP exams. They have updated the exam tracks to accommodate changes in Cisco technology.

Cisco recommends that any new candidate planning to achieve Cisco certification follow the current 801 exam track. Any candidate who is currently pursuing CCNP status and who has already taken exams under the 2.0 path may continue to take the 2.0 exams to achieve the CCNP. You have one year after starting your certification track to finish all the exams. You may mix-and-match exams, however, between the different versions. For instance, if you started your CCNP with an earlier version of the exam, but Cisco discontinued these tests, you can still finish your CCNP by completing the remaining exams that you have left to take from the most current version of the exam. For more information about Cisco exams visit Cisco on the web at http://www.cisco.com/.

exam watch

In addition to the technical objectives that are being tested for each exam, you will find much more useful information on Cisco's Web site at http://www.cisco.com. You will find information on becoming certified, exam-specific information, sample test questions, and the latest news on Cisco certification. This is the most important site you will find on your journey to becoming Cisco certified. The Career and Certification sections of the web site change periodically, so be sure to check for updates regularly.

Computer-Based Testing

In a perfect world, you would be assessed for your true knowledge of a subject, not simply how you respond to a series of test questions. But life isn't perfect, and it just isn't practical to evaluate everyone's knowledge on a one-to-one basis. (Cisco actually does have a one-to-one evaluation, but it's reserved for the CCIE Laboratory exam).

For the majority of its certifications, Cisco evaluates candidates using a computer-based testing service operated by Prometric or Vue. This service is quite popular in the industry, and it is used for a number of vendor certification programs, including Novell's CNE and Microsoft's MCSE. Thanks to Prometric's and Vue's large number of facilities, exams can be administered worldwide, generally in the same town as a prospective candidate.

Cisco no longer allows you to mark questions for later review—once you answer a question, you cannot go back and change your answer!

For the most part, Prometric and Vue exams work similarly from vendor to vendor. However, there is an important fact to know about Cisco's exams: They use the traditional test format, not the newer adaptive format. This allows Cisco to choose an appropriate number of questions on each objective in order to test your knowledge.

To discourage simple memorization, Cisco exams present a different set of questions every time the exam is administered. In the development of the exam, hundreds of questions are compiled and refined, using beta testers. From this large collection, a random sampling is drawn for each test. Plus, Cisco has developed simulation questions that require you to place basic configurations on Cisco devices and troubleshooting an existing network topology. These types of questions require a candidate to have hands-on, and not just book learning, experience.

Each Cisco exam has a specific number of questions and test duration. Testing time is typically generous, and the time remaining is always displayed in the corner of the testing screen, along with the number of remaining questions. If time expires during an exam, the test terminates, and incomplete answers are counted as incorrect.

At the end of the exam, your test is immediately graded, and the results are displayed on the screen. Scores for each subject area are also provided, but the system will not indicate which specific questions were missed. A report is automatically printed at the proctor's desk for your files. The test score is electronically transmitted back to Cisco.

In the end, this computer-based system of evaluation is reasonably fair. You might feel that one or two questions were poorly worded; this can certainly happen, but you shouldn't worry too much. Ultimately, it's all factored into the required passing score.

Question Types

Cisco exams pose questions in a variety of formats, most of which are discussed here. As candidates progress toward the more advanced certifications, the difficulty of the exams is intensified, through both the subject matter and the question formats.

True/False

The classic true/false question format is not used in the Cisco exams, for the obvious reason that a simple guess has a 50 percent chance of being correct. Instead, true/false questions are posed in multiple-choice format, requiring the candidate to identify the true or false statement from a group of selections.

Multiple Choice

Multiple-choice is the primary format for questions in Cisco exams. These questions may be posed in a variety of ways.

Select the Correct Answer This is the classic multiple-choice question, in which the candidate selects a single answer from a minimum of four choices. In addition to the question's wording, the choices are presented in a Windows radio

exam watch

In order to pass these challenging exams, you may want to talk with other test takers to determine what is being tested, and what to expect in terms of difficulty. The most helpful way to communicate with other CCNA hopefuls is the Cisco Network Professional Connection. With this bulletin-board system, you can ask questions from other members, including employees of Cisco. These discussions cover everything imaginable concerning Cisco networking equipment and certification. Go to http://forum.cisco.com/eforum/servlet/NetProf?page=main to learn how to access this source of a wealth of information. Note that at the time of publication, this information was correct. Please contact Cisco directly for the most up-to-date information about Cisco's forums.

button format, in which only one answer can be selected at a time. The question will instruct you to "Select the best answer" when they are looking for just one answer.

Select the Three Correct Answers The multiple-answer version is similar to the single-choice version, but multiple answers must be provided. This is an all-or-nothing format; all the correct answers must be selected, or the entire question is incorrect. In this format, the question specifies exactly how many answers must be selected. Choices are presented in a check box format, allowing more than one answer to be selected. In addition, the testing software prevents too many answers from being selected.

Select All That Apply The open-ended version is the most difficult multiple-choice format, since the candidate does not know how many answers should be selected. As with the multiple-answer version, all the correct answers must be selected to gain credit for the question. If too many answers or not enough answers are selected, no credit is given. This format presents choices in check box format, but the testing software does not advise the candidates whether they've selected the correct number of answers. Cisco's CCIE exams have questions like this. You probably won't see any questions like this on the CCNA exam.

Freeform Response

Freeform responses are prevalent in Cisco's advanced exams, particularly where the subject focuses on router configuration and commands. In the freeform format, no choices are provided. Instead, the test prompts for user input, and the candidate must

exam watch

Make it easy on yourself and find some "braindumps." These are notes about the exam from test takers, which indicate the most difficult concepts tested, what to look out for, and sometimes even what not to bother studying. Several of these can be found at http://www.dejanews.com. Simply do a search for CCNA and browse the recent postings. Another good resource is at http://www.groupstudy.com. Beware, however, of the person that posts a question reported to have been on the test and its answer. First, the question and its answer may be incorrect. Second, this is a violation of Cisco's confidentiality agreement, which you, as a candidate, must agree to prior to taking the exam. Giving out specific information regarding a test violates this agreement and could result in the revocation of your certification status.

type the correct answer. This format is similar to an essay question, except the response must be specific, allowing the computer to evaluate the answer.

For example, the question

Type the command for viewing routes learned from an IP routing protocol.

requires the answer:

show ip route

For safety's sake, you should completely spell out router commands, rather than use abbreviations. In this example, the abbreviated command **SH IP ROU** works on a real router, but it is counted as wrong by the testing software. The freeform response questions almost always are answered by commands used in the Cisco IOS. As you progress in your track for your CCNA you will find these freeform response questions increasingly prevalent.

Fill in the Blank

Fill-in-the-blank questions are less common in Cisco exams. They may be presented in multiple-choice or freeform response format.

Exhibits

Exhibits, usually showing a network diagram or a router configuration, accompany many exam questions. These exhibits are displayed in a separate window, which is opened by clicking the Exhibit button at the bottom of the screen.

Scenarios

While the normal line of questioning tests a candidate's "book knowledge," scenarios add a level of complexity. Rather than asking only technical questions, they apply the candidate's knowledge to real-world situations.

Scenarios generally consist of one or two paragraphs and an exhibit that describes a company's needs or network configuration. This description is followed by a series of questions and problems that challenge the candidate's ability to address the situation. Scenario-based questions are commonly found in exams relating to network design, but they appear to some degree in each of the Cisco exams.

Simulations

The CCNA exam will have a handful of simulation questions. With a simulation question, you will be prompted to put a basic configuration on a Cisco router or switch. This will require you to access the CLI of the router or switch, access the appropriate mode on the router or switch, put a basic configuration, and possibly test the configuration. Some simulation questions will already have a pre-configuration on existing Cisco devices, with configuration errors. You will be required to find the configuration errors, fix them, and then test the corrections. While working with the router or switch simulator, you will have the context-sensitive help feature available to you. Before you actually start the exam at a Prometric or Vue site, you are offered the chance to become more familiar with the look-and-feel of a simulator question. I highly recommend that you NOT skip this part, especially since the time you spend on this tutorial is NOT counted against you. For a demonstration of what the simulator is like, you can also visit: http://www.cisco.com and browse to the certification section to find the demo. This example is very similar, but not exactly the same, as the simulator that you would see on the real exam. For additional simulation questions that are similar in concept to the actual exam, please be sure to investigate the McGraw-Hill Practice Tests for CCNA including on the CDROM.

Studying Techniques

First and foremost, give yourself plenty of time to study. Networking is a complex field, and you can't expect to cram what you need to know into a single study session. It is a field best learned over time, by studying a subject and then applying your knowledge. Build yourself a study schedule and stick to it, but be reasonable about the pressure you put on yourself, especially if you're studying in addition to your regular duties at work.

One easy technique to use in studying for certification exams is the 30-minutes-per-day effort. Simply study for a minimum of 30 minutes every day. It is a small but significant commitment. On a day when you just can't focus, then give up at least 30 minutes. On a day when it flows completely for you, study longer. As long as you have more of the flow days, your chances of succeeding are extremely high.

Second, practice and experiment. In networking, you need more than knowledge; you need understanding, too. You can't just memorize facts to be effective; you need to understand why events happen, how things work, and (most important) how and why they break.

The best way to gain deep understanding is to take your book knowledge to the lab. Try it out. Make it work. Change it a little. Break it. Fix it. Snoop around "under the hood." If you have access to a network analyzer, like Network Associate Sniffer, put it to use. You can gain amazing insight to the inner workings of a network by watching devices communicate with each other.

Unless you have a very understanding boss, don't experiment with router commands on a production router. A seemingly innocuous command can have a nasty side effect. If you don't have a lab, your local Cisco office or Cisco users' group may be able to help. Many training centers also allow students access to their lab equipment during off-hours. There are many router and switch simulator products also available on the market. The simulator included on the CD of this book is a stripped-down version of Boson's NetSim™ simulator product. It can simulate many router and switch commands for various models of Cisco products. The version included on this CD includes a 2600 and 2500 series router as well as 1900 and 2950 switches. It comes with a pre-set topology that includes Ethernet, Fast Ethernet, serial point-to-point connections, Frame Relay, and ISDN. If you want the full functionality of the simulator product, a voucher is included that gives you a steep discount over buying the product retail. By purchasing the full product, you have access to all of the commands within the product as well as being able to create your own topologies! For hands-on experience, this is a great bargain for the money that you would spend.

Another excellent way to study is through case studies. Case studies are articles or interactive discussions that offer real-world examples of how technology is applied to meet a need. These examples can serve to cement your understanding of a technique or technology by seeing it put to use. Interactive discussions offer added value because you can also pose questions of your own. User groups are an excellent source of examples, since the purpose of these groups is to share information and learn from each other's experiences.

The Cisco Networker's conference is not to be missed. Although renowned for its wild party and crazy antics, this conference offers a wealth of information. Held every year in cities around the world, it includes four to five days of technical seminars and presentations on a variety of subjects. As you might imagine, it's very popular. You have to register early to get the classes you want.

Then, of course, there is the Cisco Web site. This little gem is loaded with collections of technical documents and white papers. As you progress to more advanced subjects, you will find great value in the large number of examples and reference materials available. But be warned: You need to do a lot of digging to find the really good stuff. Often your only option is to browse every document returned by the search engine to find exactly the one you need. This effort pays off. Most CCIEs I know have compiled six to ten binders of reference material from Cisco's site alone.

Scheduling Your Exam

The Cisco exams are scheduled by calling either Prometric or Vue directly. For locations outside the United States, your local number can be found on the Prometric Web site at http://www.prometric.com and on Vue's Web site at http://www.vue.com. Prometric and Vue representatives can schedule your exam, but they don't have information about the certification programs. Questions about certifications should be directed to Cisco's education division.

The Prometric telephone number is specific to Cisco exams, and it goes directly to the Cisco representatives inside Prometric. These representatives are familiar enough with the exams to find them by name, but it's best if you have the specific exam number handy when you call. After all, you wouldn't want to be scheduled and charged for the wrong exam.

Exams can be scheduled up to a year in advance, although it's really not necessary. Generally, scheduling a week or two ahead is sufficient to reserve the day and time you prefer. When you call to schedule, operators will search for testing centers in your area. For convenience, they can also tell which testing centers you've used before.

Prometric and Vue accept a variety of payment methods, with credit cards being the most convenient. When you pay by credit card, you can even take tests the same day you call—provided, of course, that the testing center has room. Prometric and Vue will mail you a receipt and confirmation of your testing date, although this generally arrives after the test has been taken. If you need to cancel or reschedule an exam, remember to call at least one day before your exam, or you'll lose your test fee.

When you register for the exam, you will be asked for your ID number. This number is used to track your exam results back to Cisco. It's important that you use the same ID number each time you register, so that Cisco can follow your progress. Address information provided when you first register is also used by Cisco to ship certificates and other related material. In the United States, your Social Security number is commonly used as your ID number. However, Prometric and Vue can assign you a unique ID number if you prefer not to use your Social Security number.

You will also be required to give a valid email address when registering. If you do not have an email address that works, you will not be able to schedule the exam. Once you are registered, you will receive an email notice containing your registration information for your scheduled exam. Examine it closely to make sure that it is correct.

In addition to the regular Prometric and Vue testing sites, Cisco also offers facilities for taking exams free of charge or at a greatly reduced rate at each Networkers Conference in the United States. As you might imagine, this option is quite popular, so reserve your exam time as soon as you arrive at the conference.

Arriving at the Exam

As with any test, you'll be tempted to cram the night before. Resist that temptation. You should know the material by this point, and if you're too groggy in the morning, you won't remember what you studied anyway. Instead, get a good night's sleep.

Arrive early for your exam; it gives you time to relax and review key facts. Take the opportunity to review your notes. If you get burned out on studying, you can usually start your exam a few minutes early. On the other hand, I don't recommend arriving late. Your test could be canceled, or you might be left without enough time to complete the exam.

When you arrive at the testing center, you'll need to sign in with the exam administrator. In order to sign in, you need to provide two forms of identification. Acceptable forms include government-issued IDs (for example, passport or driver's license) and credit cards. One form of ID must include a photograph.

Aside from a brain full of facts, you don't need to bring anything else to the exam. In fact, your brain is about all you're allowed to take into the exam. All the tests are closed book, meaning that you don't get to bring any reference materials with you. You're also not allowed to take any notes out of the exam room. The test administrator will provide you with paper and a pencil. Some testing centers may provide a small marker board instead.

Calculators are not allowed, so be prepared to do any necessary math (such as hex-binary-decimal conversions or subnet masks) in your head or on paper. Additional paper is available if you need it.

Leave your pager and cell phone in your car—you are not allowed to take them into the actual testing room. Purses, books, and other materials must be left with the administrator before you enter. While you're in the exam room, it's important that you don't disturb other candidates; talking is not allowed during the exam.

In the exam room, the exam administrator logs onto your exam, and you have to verify that your ID number and the exam number are correct. If this is the first time you've taken a Cisco test, you can select a brief tutorial for the exam software. Before the test begins, you will be provided with facts about the exam, including the duration, the number of questions, and the score required for passing. Then the clock starts ticking, and the fun begins. Please note that Cisco does not officially publish the number of questions on their exams or their passing rate. Cisco changed this philosophy to allow them to dynamically adjust the number of questions and pass rates in order to either create a harder or easier exam based on past scores of test-takers. Typically, you'll have about 60 questions with about 75 minutes to complete the exam. But as I just mentioned, Cisco can change this at any time!

The testing software is Windows-based, but you won't have access to the main desktop or to any of the accessories. The exam is presented in full screen, with a single question per screen. Navigation buttons allow you to move between questions. In the upper right corner of the screen, counters show the number of questions and time remaining. Make sure you periodically look at the question you are on and the time remaining—you'll want to budget your time appropriately. Also remember that the two or three simulation questions will probably take you about 5 minutes to complete each one. And once you answer a question and go to the next one, there is no way of going back to previous questions!

The Grand Finale

When you're finished, the exam will automatically be graded. After what will seem like the longest ten seconds of your life, the testing software will respond with your score.

This is usually displayed as a bar graph, showing the minimum passing score, your score, and a PASS/FAIL indicator. With some of Cisco tests, the score is actually not displayed on the screen, but only on the printed version of your test results.

If you're curious, you can review the statistics of your score at this time. Answers to specific questions are not presented; rather, questions are lumped into categories, and results are tallied for each category. This detail is also given on a report that has been automatically printed at the exam administrator's desk.

As you leave the exam, you'll need to leave your scratch paper behind or return it to the administrator. (Some testing centers track the number of sheets you've been given, so be sure to return them all.) In exchange, you'll receive a copy of the test report.

This report will be embossed with the testing center's seal, and you should keep it in a safe place. Normally, the results are automatically transmitted to Cisco, but occasionally you might need the paper report to prove that you passed the exam. Your personnel file is probably a good place to keep this report; the file tends to follow you everywhere, and it doesn't hurt to have favorable exam results turn up during a performance review.

Retesting

If you don't pass the exam, don't be discouraged—networking is complex stuff. Try to have a good attitude about the experience, and get ready to try again. Consider yourself a little more educated. You know the format of the test a little better, and the report shows which areas you need to strengthen.

If you bounce back quickly, you'll probably remember several of the questions you might have missed. This will help you focus your study efforts in the right area. Serious go-getters will reschedule the exam for three days after the previous attempt, while the study material is still fresh in their minds—you must wait three days before taking the same exam again.

Ultimately, remember that Cisco certifications are valuable because they're hard to get. After all, if anyone could get one, what value would it have? In the end, it takes a good attitude and a lot of studying, but you can do it!

CCNA 640-801

Exam Readiness Checklist

Official Objective	Study Guide Coverage	Ch #	Beginner	Intermediate	Expert
Planning and Designing					
Design a simple LAN using Cisco technology	Networks Topologies Network Types Hierarchical Network Model	1 1 1 2			
Design an IP addressing scheme to meet design requirements	IP Addressing Introduction Subnetting Planning IP Addressing Variable Length Subnet Masking Route Summarization	3 3 3 12 12			
Select an appropriate routing protocol based on user requirements	Types of Routes Static Routes Dynamic Routing Protocols	9 9 9			
Design a simple internetwork using Cisco technology	Networks Topologies Network Types Hierarchical Network Model Cisco's Networking Products	1 1 1 2 4			
Develop an access-list to meet user specifications	Access-List Overview Types of Access-Lists Placement of Access-Lists	13 13 13			
Choose WAN services to meet customer requirements	Network Types Wide Area Networking Overview	1 15			
Implementation and Operation					
Configure routing protocols given user requirements	IP Routing Protocol Basics IP RIP IP IGRP OSPF EIGRP	10 10 10 11 11			

Exam Readiness Checklist

Official Objective	Study Guide Coverage	Ch #	Beginner	Intermediate	Expert
Configure IP addresses, subnet masks, and gateway addresses on routers and hosts	Basic Switch Configuration	5			
	Basic Router Configuration	5			
Configure a router for additional administrative functionality	Basic Router Configuration	5			
	Address Translation Overview	14			
	Address Translation Configuration	14			
	Dynamic Host Configuration Protocol	14			
Configure a switch with VLANS and inter-switch communication	VLAN Overview	8			
	VLAN Connections	8			
	VLAN Trunk Protocol	8			
	1900 and 2950 VLAN Configuration	8			
Implement a LAN	IOS Basics	5			
	Basic Switch Configuration	5			
	Basic Router Configuration	5			
	1900 and 2950 Configuration	7			
Customize a switch configuration to meet specified network requirements	Basic Switch Configuration	6			
	1900 and 2950 Configuration	7			
Manage system image and device configuration files	Router Configuration Files	6			
	Router IOS Image Files	6			
Perform an initial configuration on a router	Basic Router Configuration	5			
Perform an initial configuration on a switch	Basic Switch Configuration	5			
Implement access-lists	Basic Access-List Configuration	13			
	Wildcard Masks	13			
	Types of Access-Lists	13			
	Placement of Access-Lists	13			
Implement simple WAN protocols	HDLC	15			
	PPP	15			
	Frame Relay Configuration	16			
	Non-Broadcast Multi-Access	16			
	ISDN Interface Configuration	17			
	Legacy Dial-on-Demand Routing	17			
	Dialer Profiles and DDR	17			

Exam Readiness Checklist

Official Objective	Study Guide Coverage	Ch #	Beginner	Intermediate	Expert
Troubleshooting					
Utilize the OSI model as a guide for systematic network troubleshooting	OSI Reference Model	2			
	Data Link Layer	2			
	Network Layer	2			
	Transport Layer	2			
	IOS Troubleshooting	6			
Perform LAN and VLAN troubleshooting	IOS Troubleshooting	6			
	1900 and 2950 Configuration	7			
	1900 and 2950 VLAN Configuration	8			
Troubleshoot routing protocols	IOS Troubleshooting	6			
	Static Routes	9			
	IP RIP	10			
	IP IGRP	10			
	OSPF	11			
	EIGRP	11			
Troubleshoot IP addressing and host configuration	IOS Troubleshooting	6			
Troubleshoot a device as part of a working network	IOS Troubleshooting	6			
	1900 and 2950 VLAN Configuration	7			
Troubleshoot an access list	IOS Troubleshooting	6			
	Types of Access-Lists	13			
	Placement of Access-Lists	13			
Perform simple WAN troubleshooting	IOS Troubleshooting	6			
	HDLC	15			
	PPP	15			
	Frame Relay Configuration	16			
	Non-Broadcast Multi-Access	16			
	Legacy Dial-on-Demand Routing	17			
Technology					
Describe network communications using layered models	OSI Reference Model	2			
	Transferring Information Between Computers	2			
Describe the Spanning Tree process	The Spanning Tree Protocol	7			

Exam Readiness Checklist

Official Objective	Study Guide Coverage	Ch #	Beginner	Intermediate	Expert
Compare and contrast key characteristics of LAN environments	OSI Reference Model	2			
	Data Link Layer	2			
	Network Layer	2			
	Transport Layer	2			
	Bridges and Switches	7			
	Functions of Bridges and Switches	7			
Evaluate the characteristics of routing protocols	Types of Routes	9			
	Static Routes	9			
	Router-on-a-Stick	9			
	Dynamic Routing Protocols	9			
	Problems with Distance Vector Protocols	9			
Evaluate TCP/IP communication process and its associated protocols	Transferring Information Between Computers	2			
	TCP/IP Protocol Stack	3			
Describe the components of network devices	Chassis Information	4			
	Connections	4			
	Cables	4			
Evaluate rules for packet control	Access-List Overview	13			
Evaluate key characteristics of WANs	Network Types	1			
	Wide Area Networking Overview	15			

1

Networking Technologies

CERTIFICATION OBJECTIVES

1.01 Networks

1.02 Topologies

1.03 Network Types

✓ Two-Minute Drill

Q&A Self Test

This chapter offers a brief introduction to networking and some basic networking terms and concepts. This material should be a review of many already known concepts. You should be familiar with the various networking topologies used in networks, as well as different types of networks, such as local area networks (LANs) and wide area networks (WANs).

CERTIFICATION OBJECTIVE 1.01

Networks

A *network* is basically all of the components (hardware and software) involved in connecting computers across small and large distances. Networks are used to provide easy access to information, thus increasing productivity for users. This section covers some of the components involved with networking, as well as the basic types of topologies used to connect networking devices, including computers.

Components

One of the main components of networking is applications, which enable users to perform various tasks. Many applications are *network-aware*. These applications allow you to access and use resources that are not located on your local computer. Some of the more common networking applications include e-mail (sending mail electronically), FTP (transferring files), and WWW (providing a graphical representation to information). The number of networking applications ranges in the thousands, but those listed are the most commonly used.

To build a network, you need three types of devices or components: computers, networking devices, and cabling. Computers—devices such as PCs and file servers running Microsoft Windows, Macintosh OS, Unix (including Linux), or other operating systems—are responsible for providing applications to the users. Networking devices—such as hubs, bridges, switches, routers, firewalls, modems, NT1s (an ISDN network termination device), and channel service units / data service units (CSU/DSUs)—are responsible for moving information between computers. Cabling, such as copper or fiber cabling, is needed to connect the computers and networking devices so that information can be shared between components. Wireless communication also falls in this category.

TABLE 1-1 Networking Locations

Term	Definition
Small office/home office (SOHO)	Users working from a home or small office (a handful of people)
Branch office	A small group of users connected in a small area, called a LAN, geographically separated from a corporate office
Mobile users	Users who can connect to a network from any location, LAN, or WAN
Corporate office	The location where most users in an organization and their resources are located

Locations

Network components can be located in various locations. Table 1-1 shows some common terms used to describe the location of network components.

CERTIFICATION OBJECTIVE 1.02

Topologies

When you are cabling up your computers and networking devices, various types of topologies can be used. A topology defines how the devices are connected. Figure 1-1 shows examples of topologies that different media types use.

A *point-to-point* topology has a single connection between two devices. In this topology, two devices can directly communicate without interference from other devices. These types of connections are not common when many devices need to be connected together. An example of a point-to-point topology is when you connect two routers across a dedicated WAN circuit.

In a *star* topology, a central device has many point-to-point connections to other devices. Star topologies are used in environments where many devices need to be connected. An example of a media type that uses a star topology is 10BaseT Ethernet. When connecting devices together, you connect your computers to a hub or switch (the center of the star). An extended star topology is basically multiple star topologies interconnected.

A *bus* topology uses a single connection or wire to connect all devices. Certain media types, like 10Base5 and 10Base2 Ethernet, use a bus topology. Typically, special

FIGURE 1-1 Network topologies

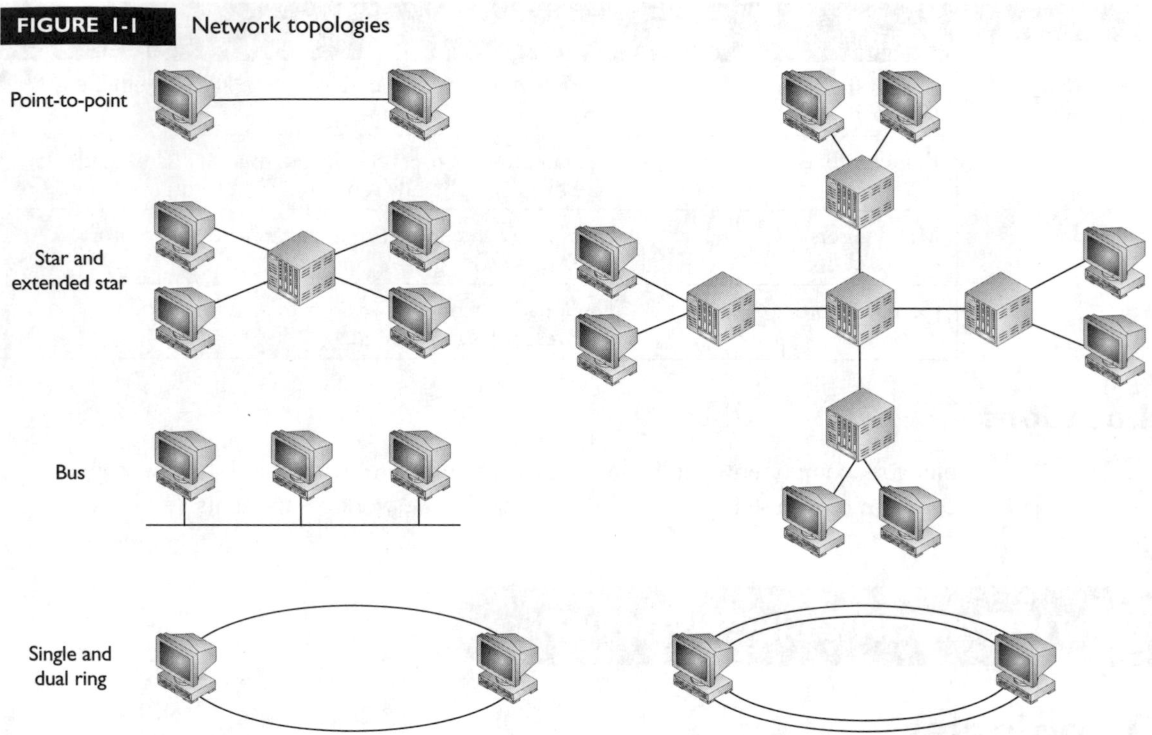

types of connectors or transceivers are used to connect the cables in order to provide the bus topology. In 10Base5, for example, each device connects to a single strand of coaxial cable via a vampire tap. This device taps into the single strand of coaxial cable and provides the physical connection from a networking device to the single strand of cable.

In a *ring* topology, device one connects to device two, device two connects to device three, and so on to the last device, which connects back to device one. Ring topologies can be implemented with a single ring or a dual ring. Dual rings are typically used when you need redundancy. For example, if one of the devices fails in the ring, the ring can wrap itself, as shown in Figure 1-2, to provide a single, functional, ring. Fiber Distributed Data Interface (FDDI) is an example of a media technology that uses dual rings to connect computer devices.

FIGURE 1-2 Dual rings and redundancy

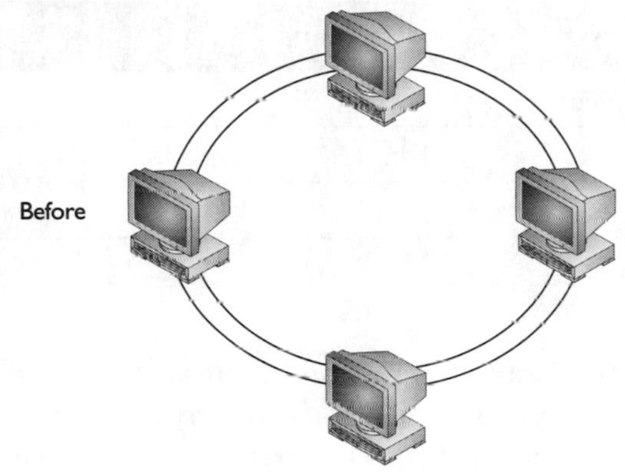

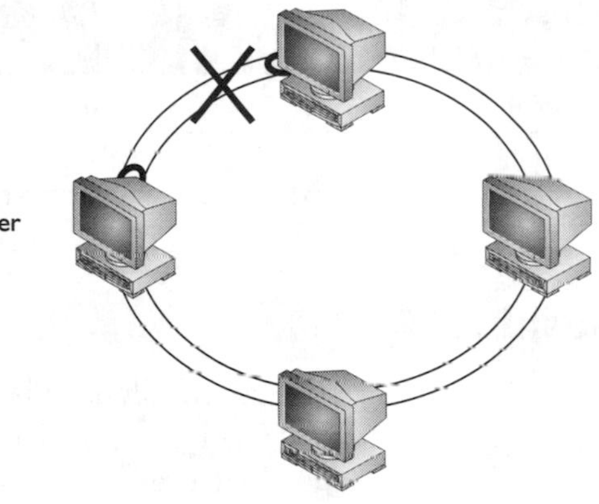

Physical vs. Logical Topologies

A distinction needs to be made between physical and logical topologies. A *physical* topology describes how devices are *physically* cabled together. For instance, 10BaseT has a physical star topology and FDDI has a physical dual ring topology. A *logical* topology describes how devices communicate across the physical topology. The physical and logical topologies are independent of each other. For example, any variety of Ethernet uses a logical bus topology when devices communicate. This means that in Ethernet, you might be using 10BaseT with a physical star topology to connect devices together; however, these devices are using a logical bus topology to communicate.

The information listed in Tables 1-1 and 1-2 is important to know for the exam.

Token Ring is actually a good example of a media type that has a different physical topology from its logical one. Physically, Token Ring uses a star topology, similar to 10BaseT Ethernet. Logically, however, Token Ring devices use a ring topology to communicate. This can create confusion when you are trying to determine how devices are connected together and how they communicate. FDDI, on the other hand, is straightforward. FDDI's physical and logical topologies are the same: a ring. Table 1-2 shows common media types and their physical and logical topologies.

TABLE 1-2 Examples of Physical and Logical Topologies

Media Type	Physical Topology	Logical Topology
Ethernet	Bus, star, or point-to-point	Bus
FDDI	Ring	Ring
Token Ring	Star	Ring

Meshing

Meshing generically describes how devices are connected together. There are two types of meshed topologies: partial and full. In a partially meshed environment, every device is *not* connected to every other device. In a fully meshed environment, every device *is* connected to every other device. Figure 1-3 shows examples of these two types of topologies.

Note that like the topologies in the preceding section, partial and full mesh can be seen from both a physical view and a logical one. For example, in a physical bus topology, all the devices are fully meshed, since they are all connected to the same piece of wire—this is both a physical and logical fully meshed topology. This is common in LAN topologies. WANs, on the other hand, because of their cost, commonly use partially meshed topologies to reduce the cost of connected devices. For example, in the partially meshed network shown in the left part of Figure 1-3, the top, left, and bottom devices can all communicate via the device on the right-hand side. This communication introduces a delay in the transmission, but it reduces the cost, since not as many connections are needed.

FIGURE 1-3 Partial- and full-mesh topologies

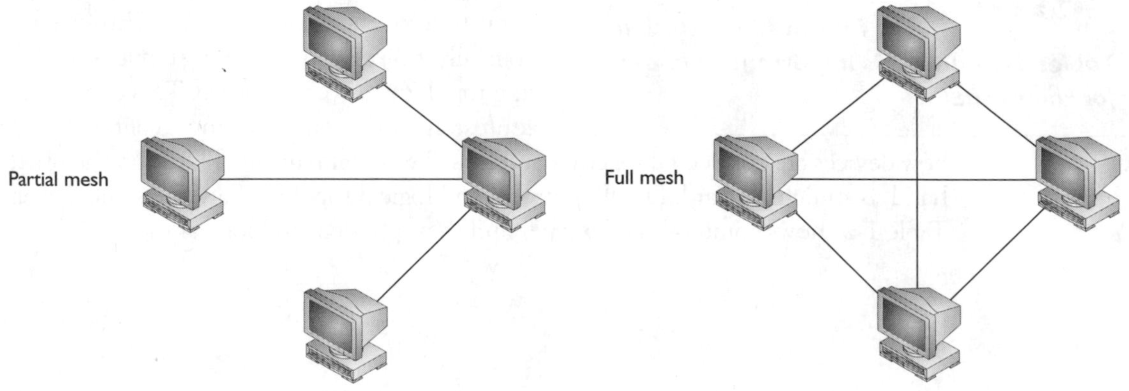

CERTIFICATION OBJECTIVE 1.03

Network Types

Networks come in a wide variety of types. The most common are LANs and WANs, but there are many other types of networks, including metropolitan area networks (MANs), storage area networks (SANs), content networks (CNs), intranets and extranets, VPNs, and others. The following sections provide a brief overview of each of these network types.

Local Area Networks

Local area networks (LANs) are used to connect networking devices that are in a very close geographic area, such as a floor of a building, a building itself, or a campus environment. In a LAN, you'll find PCs, file servers, hubs, bridges, switches, routers, multilayer switches, voice gateways, firewalls, and other devices. The media types used in LANs include Ethernet, Fast Ethernet (FE), Gigabit Ethernet (GE), Token Ring, and FDDI. Today, most networks use some form of Ethernet. Ethernet is discussed in Chapter 2.

Wide Area Networks

Wide area networks (WANs) are used to connect LANs together. Typically, WANs are used when the LANs that must be connected are separated by a large distance. Whereas a corporation provides its own infrastructure for a LAN, WANs are leased from carrier networks, such as telephone companies. Four basic types of connections, or circuits, are used in WAN services: circuit-switched, cell-switched, packet-switched, and dedicated connections.

A wide array of WAN services are available, including analog dialup, ATM, dedicated circuits, cable, DSL (digital subscriber line) Frame Relay, ISDN, Switched Multi-megabit Data Services (SMDS), and X.25. Here, analog dialup and ISDN are examples of circuit-switched services, ATM and SMDS are examples of cell-switched services, and Frame Relay and X.25 are examples of packet-switched services.

Circuit-switched services provide a temporary connection across a phone circuit. These are typically used for backup of primary circuits and for temporary boost of bandwidth. A dedicated circuit is a permanent connection between two sites where the bandwidth is dedicated. These circuits are common where you have a variety of services, such as voice, video, and data, that must traverse the connection and you are concerned about delay issues with the traffic and guaranteed bandwidth.

Cell-switched services can provide the same features that dedicated circuits offer. Their advantage over dedicated circuits is that a single device can connect to multiple devices on the same interface. The downside of these services is that they are not available at all locations, they are difficult to set up and troubleshoot, and the equipment is expensive when compared to using dedicated circuits.

Packet-switched services are similar to cell-switched services. Whereas cell-switched services switch fixed-length packets, called cells, packet-switched services switch variable-length packets. This feature makes them better suited for data services, but they can nonetheless provide some of the Quality of Service (QoS) features that cell-switched services provide. All of these service types are discussed in more depth in Chapter 15.

exam watch

Circuit-switched connections, like analog and ISDN are typically used for temporary or backup connections. Dedicated circuits, like leased lines, are used to provide guaranteed bandwidth for applications across short distances. Cell-switched and packet-switched services are used when you only want to use a single connection to the WAN, but provide a partially or full-meshed network. Cell-switched services, like ATM and SMDS, can provide a granular level of quality of service (QoS) for an application and are typically used to provide voice and video connections. Packet-switched services, like Frame Relay and X.25, provide a more cost-effective solution than cell-switched services, but not with the same level of QoS support.

Two newer WAN services that are very popular in the U.S. are cable and DSL. DSL provides speeds up to 2Mbps and costs much less than a typical WAN circuit from the carrier. It supports both voice and video and doesn't require a dialup connection (it's always enabled). Cable access uses coaxial copper connections—the same medium used to provide television broadcast services. It supports higher data rates than DSL, but like DSL, it provides a full-time connection. However, it has one major drawback: it is a shared service and functions in a logical bus topology much like Ethernet (discussed in Chapter 2)—the more customers in an area that connect via cable, the less bandwidth each customer has.

Examples of networking devices used in WAN connections include cable and DSL modems, carrier switches, CSU/DSUs, firewalls, modems, NT1s, and routers.

Metropolitan Area Networks

A metropolitan area network (MAN) is a hybrid between a LAN and a WAN. Like a WAN, it connects two or more LANs in the same geographic area. A MAN, for example, might connect two different buildings or offices in the same city. However, whereas WANs typically provide low- to medium-speed access, MANs provide high-speed connections, such as T1 (1.544Mbps) and optical services.

The optical services provided include SONET (the Synchronous Optical Network standard) and SDH (the Synchronous Digital Hierarchy standard). With these optical services, carriers can provide high-speed services, including ATM and Gigabit Ethernet. These two optical services (covered in Chapter 2) provide speeds ranging into the hundreds or thousands of megabits per second (Mbps). Devices used to provide connections for MANs include high-end routers, ATM switches, and optical switches.

Storage Area Networks

Storage area networks (SANs) provide a high-speed infrastructure to move data between storage devices and file servers. A storage device, sometimes referred to as a storage unit, includes disk drives, disk controllers, and any necessary cabling. This infrastructure can be dedicated to just these devices or can include other devices. Typically, fiber channels are used for the connections. A *fiber channel* is an optical cable that connects the file servers, disk controllers, and hard drives at rates exceeding 1 gigabit per second (Gbps). The advantages of separating the storage device from the file services are more flexibility and centralization of storage, which eases management.

SANs are becoming very popular in LAN environments, and some ISPs and carrier companies are starting to offer these services in MAN environments. However, SANs are not currently being used in WAN environments, because of the connection types and access speeds required.

Since optical connections are used, you gain the following advantages over normal storage techniques (keeping the data local to the server):

- Performance is fast.
- Availability is high because of the redundancy features available.
- Distances can span up to 10 kilometers.
- Management is easy because of the centralization of data resources.
- Overhead is low (uses a thin protocol).

The main disadvantage of SANs is their cost. If you are using fiber channels, you must buy special disk controller cards for your file servers and buy a SAN storage unit, and you must lay down the necessary fiber. Of course, if you are using your own network infrastructure, you only need to buy a storage unit and lay down any necessary cabling for it. Plus, if you are concerned about redundancy, your cost will increase because you'll need to ensure that your network infrastructure has redundant paths between your servers and the SAN storage unit(s).

Content Networks

Content networks (CNs) were developed to ease users' access to Internet resources. CNs are aware of layers 4–7 of the OSI Reference Model (discussed in Chapter 2) and use this information to make intelligent decisions about how to obtain the information for the user or users. CNs come in the following categories: content distribution, content routing, content switching, content management, content delivery, and intelligent network services, which include QoS, security, multicasting, and virtual private networks (VPNs).

Companies deploy basically two types of CNs:

- Caching downloaded Internet information
- Distributing Internet traffic loads across multiple servers

For the first item, CNs are used to reduce the amount of bandwidth that you need for your users' Internet connections. When users download content, it is cached on a local server. And then when a user makes another request, that request is first checked with the local server to determine if the content exists there. If it does, the local server sends the information to the user, thus providing higher data rates, since the client is acquiring its information from the LAN instead of having to download it again from the Internet. If not, the local server will obtain the information from the Internet resource. Because many items, especially GIFs and JPEGs, are included on every page from a web site, this information doesn't have to be repeatedly downloaded. The main problem with this solution, however, is that all traffic to and from the network must go through a CN device, commonly called a proxy server, which can reduce your throughput.

CNs are also used to reduce the overhead for external users that want to access internal resources in your network. In the old days of networking, if your web server was overwhelmed with requests, your only solution was to upgrade its processor, memory, disk drive, and interface card to larger sizes or faster speeds. And if you have ever upgraded a server, you know that this is not always an easy process. With the introduction of CNs, you can distribute the traffic load from external users across multiple internal servers, thus reducing network congestion to the servers and reducing the resources required to handle the external users' requests.

Because of the advantages that CNs provide, they are commonly used in LAN environments. Customers use them to access external resources more efficiently and to provide better throughput and redundancy for local resources. ISPs also commonly use CNs in their LANs to help reduce some congestion by providing caching services for commonly accessed web pages.

Intranets, Extranets, and Internets

Now that you have a basic understanding of various types of networks, let's discuss some other terms that are used to describe locality: intranet, extranet, and internet. An *intranet* is basically a network that is local to a company. In other words, users from within this company can find all of their resources without having to go outside of the company. An intranet can include LANs, private WANs and MANs, and SANs.

An *extranet* is an extended intranet, where certain internal services are made available to *known* external users or external business partners at remote locations. The connections between these external users and the internal resource are typically secured via a firewall and a VPN, a feature that is briefly discussed in the next section.

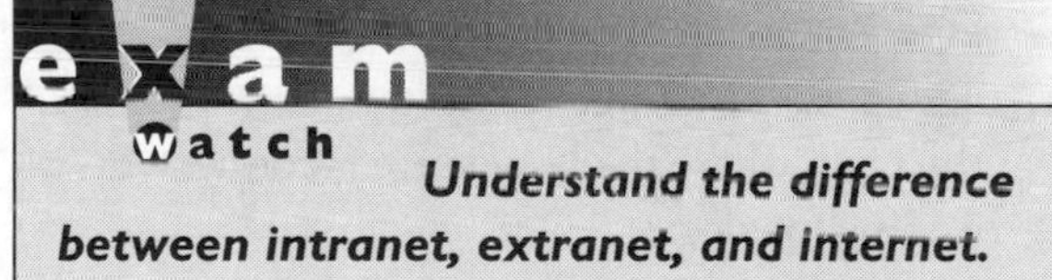

Understand the difference between intranet, extranet, and internet.

An *internet* is used when *unknown* external users need to access internal resources in your network. In other words, your company might have a web site that sells various products, and you want any external user to be able to access this service.

There is a difference between the terms *internet* and *Internet*. The lowercase *internet* refers to any type of network connection where external users access publicly available resources. The *Internet* is the main public network that most companies and people use when accessing external resources. Typically, a firewall is used to secure your internal resources from external users.

Virtual Private Networks

A virtual private network (VPN) is a special type of secured network. A VPN is used to provide a secure connection across a public network, such as an internet. Extranets typically use a VPN to provide a secure connection between a company and its known external users or offices. A VPN typically provides authentication, confidentiality, and integrity to create a secure connection between two sites or devices. *Authentication* is provided to validate the identities of the two peers. *Confidentiality* provides encryption of the data to keep it private from prying eyes. And *integrity* is used to ensure that the data sent between the two devices or sites has not been tampered with.

TWO-MINUTE DRILL

Networks

- A network includes all of the hardware and software components to connect computers across a distance in order to provide easy access to information and increase productivity. To build a network, you need computers, networking devices, and cabling (or wireless connections).
- A SOHO describes people working from home or a small office. A branch office describes a small group of users connected in a small area. Mobile users connect to a network from any remote location, including LANs, MANs, and WANs.

Topologies

- A point-to-point topology uses a single connection between two devices and is typically used in WAN environments. In a star topology, a central device makes many point-to-point connections to other devices. A 10BaseT hub is an example of a central device in a star topology. A bus topology uses a single connection between all devices; Ethernet 10Base5 is an example of this topology. A ring topology connects one device to the next, where the last device is connected to the first. FDDI is an example of a ring topology.
- A physical topology defines how the computing devices are physically cabled together. A logical topology describes the method by which devices communicate across a physical topology. The two topologies can vary with the media type used.
- Meshing generically describes how devices are connected. A partially meshed network is one where not every device has a connection to every other device. In a fully meshed network, each device has a connection to all other devices.

Network Types

- LANs are used to connect networking devices in a very close geographic area. Media types used include varieties of Ethernet, Token Ring, and FDDI. WANs are used to connect LANs across large distances. WAN services include analog dialup, ATM, dedicated circuits, cable, DSL, Frame Relay, ISDN, SMDS, and X.25. MANs are hybrid networks used to connect two

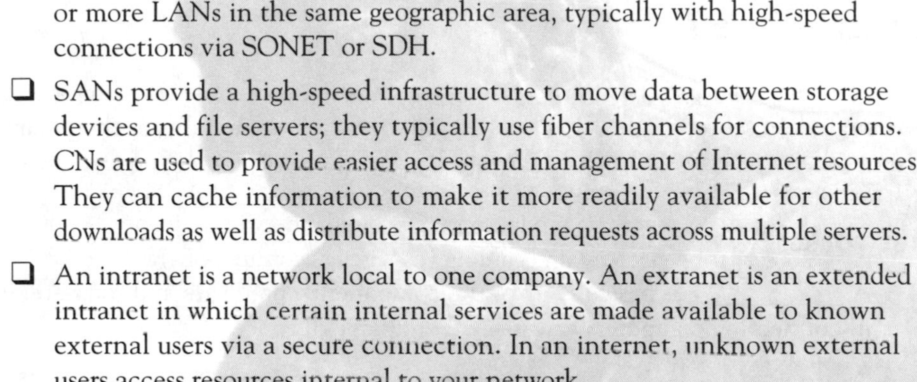

or more LANs in the same geographic area, typically with high-speed connections via SONET or SDH.

- SANs provide a high-speed infrastructure to move data between storage devices and file servers; they typically use fiber channels for connections. CNs are used to provide easier access and management of Internet resources. They can cache information to make it more readily available for other downloads as well as distribute information requests across multiple servers.
- An intranet is a network local to one company. An extranet is an extended intranet in which certain internal services are made available to known external users via a secure connection. In an internet, unknown external users access resources internal to your network.

SELF TEST

The following Self Test questions will help you measure your understanding of the material presented in this chapter. Read all the choices carefully, as there may be more than one correct answer. Choose all correct answers for each question.

Networks

1. A __________ is basically all of the components, hardware and software, involved in connecting computers across small and large distances.
   - A. LAN
   - B. WAN
   - C. Network
   - D. SAN
2. __________ describe(s) users working from home.
   - A. SOHO
   - B. Branch office
   - C. Regional office
   - D. Corporate office
3. __________ describe(s) users that can connect to a network from any location.
   - A. SOHO
   - B. Branch office
   - C. Mobile users
   - D. Corporate office

Topologies

4. A __________ topology uses a single connection to connect all devices together.
   - A. Bus
   - B. Star
   - C. Point-to-point
   - D. Ring

5. ___________ has both physical and logical ring topologies.

   A. Ethernet
   B. FDDI
   C. Token Ring

6. Ethernet ___________ has/have both a physical and logical bus topology.

   A. 10BaseT
   B. 10Base2 and 10Base5
   C. 10BaseT and 10Base2
   D. 10BaseT, 10Base2, and 10Base5

7. A _______ topology describes how devices communicate with each other.

   A. Physical
   B. Logical

8. _________ has a physical star topology but a logical ring topology.

   A. Ethernet
   B. FDDI
   C. Token Ring
   D. FDDI and Token Ring

Network Types

9. A _________ is used to connect networking devices that are in a very close geographic area, such as a floor of a building, a building itself, or a campus environment.

   A. WAN
   B. LAN
   C. MAN
   D. LAN and MAN

10. A _________ uses Gigabit Ethernet as a media type

    A. WAN
    B. LAN
    C. MAN
    D. LAN and MAN

11. A ________ connects two or more LANs in the same geographic area.

    A. LAN
    B. WAN
    C. MAN
    D. SAN

12. A ________ provides a high-speed infrastructure to move data between storage devices and file servers.

    A. SAN
    B. LAN
    C. CN
    D. SAN and CN

13. Which of the following is a disadvantage of SANs?

    A. Distance limitation
    B. Cost
    C. Overhead
    D. Management

14. A ________ looks at OSI Reference Model layers 4–7 to make intelligent decisions about how to obtain information for a user.

    A. SAN
    B. LAN
    C. CN
    D. SAN and CN

15. A ________ is a network that provides a secure connection from a company to other business partners.

    A. Intranet
    B. Extranet
    C. Internet

SELF TEST ANSWERS

1. ☑ **C.** A network is basically all of the components, hardware and software, involved in connecting computers together across small and large distances.
☒ **A** is true for small, but not large, distances. **B** is true for large distances only. **D** describes how a file server accesses remote storage devices.

2. ☑ **A.** The term SOHO describes users working from a home or small office.
☒ **B** is a small group of users connected via a LAN at one location. **C** is users that can dynamically connect from either a LAN or a WAN. **D** describes the central site, where most of the users and resources are located.

3. ☑ **C.** Mobile users are users that can dynamically connect from either a LAN or a WAN.
☒ **A** describes users working from home or a small office. **B** is a small group of users connected via a LAN at one location. **D** describes the central site, where most of the users and resources are located.

4. ☑ **A.** A bus topology uses a single connection to connect all devices together.
☒ **B** uses a central device, which has point-to-point connections to other devices. **C** is a single connection between two devices. **D** is where one device is connected to another and so on until the last device is connected to the first device, forming a ring.

5. ☑ **B.** FDDI has both physical and logical ring structures.
☒ **A**, depending on the type, uses a physical star or bus topology, but all types use a logical bus topology. **C** uses a physical star topology and a logical ring topology.

6. ☑ **B.** Ethernet 10Base2 and 10Base5 have physical and logical bus topologies.
☒ **A** has a physical star topology and a logical bus topology. **C** and **D** are incorrect because 10BaseT has a physical star topology and a logical bus topology.

7. ☑ **B.** A logical topology describes how devices communicate with each other.
☒ **A** defines how devices are connected to each other.

8. ☑ **C.** Token Ring has a physical star topology but a logical ring topology.
☒ **A** uses a logical bus topology. **B** uses a physical ring topology. **D** is incorrect because FDDI uses a physical ring topology.

9. ☑ **B.** A LAN is used to connect networking devices together that are in a very close geographic area, such as a floor of a building, a building itself, or a campus environment.
☒ **A** connects LANs together across large distances. **C** connects two or more LANs together in a small geographic area, such as between two buildings in a city. **D** is incorrect because it includes MAN.

10. ☑ **D.** LANs and MANs use Gigabit Ethernet media types for connections.
☒ **A** typically uses lower-speed connections. **B** is incorrect because it omits MAN, and **C** is incorrect because it omits LAN.

11. ☑ **C.** A MAN connects two or more LANs in the same geographic area.
☒ **A** connects networking devices together that are in a very close geographic area, such as a floor of a building, a building itself, or a campus environment. **B** connects LANs together across large distances. **D** connects storage devices to file servers.

12. ☑ **A.** A SAN provides a high-speed infrastructure to move data between storage devices and file servers.
☒ **B** connects networking devices together that are in a very close geographic area, such as a floor of a building, a building itself, or a campus environment. **C** looks at OSI Reference Model layers 4–7 to make intelligent decisions about how to obtain information for a user. **D** is incorrect because it includes CN.

13. ☑ **B.** The main disadvantage of SANs is cost.
☒ **A**, **C**, and **D** are advantages.

14. ☑ **C.** A CN looks at OSI Reference Model layers 4–7 to make intelligent decisions in order to obtain information for a user.
☒ **A** provides a high-speed infrastructure to move data between storage devices and file servers. **B** connects networking devices that are in a very close geographic area, such as a floor of a building, a building itself, or a campus environment. **D** is incorrect because it includes SAN.

15. ☑ **B.** An extranet is a network that provides a secure connection from a company to other business partners or known external users.
☒ **A** is a network local to one company. **C** is where unknown external users access internal resources in your network.

2

Networking Concepts

CHAPTER OBJECTIVES

Before considering how to configure Cisco routers and switches, you must be introduced to basic networking concepts you'll need to understand in order to grasp the advanced concepts discussed in later chapters. The OSI Reference Model is the best place to start, since it will help you understand how information is transferred between networking devices. Of the seven layers in the OSI Reference Model, be especially sure to understand how the bottom three layers function, since most networking devices function at these layers. This chapter discusses information flow, as well as Cisco's three-tiered hierarchical model, which is used to design scalable, flexible, and easy-to-troubleshoot-and-maintain networks.

CERTIFICATION OBJECTIVE 2.01

OSI Reference Model

The International Organization for Standardization (ISO) developed the Open Systems Interconnection (OSI) Reference Model to describe how information is transferred from one machine to another, from the point when a user enters information using a keyboard and mouse to when that information is converted to electrical or light signals transferred along a piece of wire or radio waves transferred through the air. It is important to understand that the OSI Reference Model describes concepts and terms in a general manner, and that many network protocols, such as IP and IPX, fail to fit nicely into the scheme explained in ISO's model. Therefore, the OSI Reference Model is most often used as a teaching and troubleshooting tool. By understanding the basics of the OSI Reference Model, you can apply these to real protocols to gain a better understanding of them as well as to more easily troubleshoot problems.

Advantages

ISO developed the seven-layer model to help vendors and network administrators gain a better understanding of how data is handled and transported between networking devices, as well as to provide a guideline for the implementation of new networking standards and technologies. To assist in this process, the OSI Reference Model breaks the network communication process into seven simple steps. It thus

- Defines the process for connecting two layers, promoting interoperability between vendors

- Separates a complex function into simpler components
- Allows vendors to compartmentalize their design efforts to fit a modular design, which eases implementations and simplifies troubleshooting

A PC is a good example of a modular device. For instance, a PC typically contains the following components: case, motherboard with processor, monitor, keyboard, mouse, disk drive, CD-ROM drive, floppy drive, RAM, video card, Ethernet card, etc. If one component breaks, it is very easy to figure out which component failed and replace the single component. This simplifies your troubleshooting process. Likewise, when a new CD-ROM drive becomes available, you don't have to throw away the current computer to use the new device—you just need to cable it up and add a software driver to your operating system to interface with it. The OSI Reference Model builds upon these premises.

Layer Definitions

There are seven layers in the OSI Reference Model, shown in Figure 2-1: application, presentation, session, transport, network, data link, and physical. The functions of the application, presentation, and session layers are typically part of the user's application. The transport, network, data link, and physical layers are responsible for moving information back and forth between these higher layers.

Each layer is responsible for a specific process or role. Remember that the seven layers are there to help you understand the transformation process that data will

FIGURE 2-1

OSI Reference Model

Layer 7	Application
Layer 6	Presentation
Layer 5	Session
Layer 4	Transport
Layer 3	Network
Layer 2	Data link
Layer 1	Physical

undergo as it is transported to a remote networking device. Not every networking protocol will fit exactly into this model. For example, TCP/IP has four layers. Some layers are combined into a single layer; for instance, TCP/IP's application layer contains the functionality of the OSI Reference Model's application, presentation, and session layers. The following sections go into more detail concerning the seven layers of the OSI Reference Model.

Application Layer

The seventh layer, or topmost layer, of the OSI Reference Model is the *application* layer. It provides the interface that a person uses to interact with the application. This interface can be command-line-based or graphics-based. Cisco IOS routers and switches have a command-line interface (CLI), whereas a web browser uses a graphical interface.

> **exam watch** ***The top (seventh) layer of the OSI Reference Model is the application layer. It provides the user interface. Examples of TCP/IP applications include telnet, FTP, HTTP, and SMTP.***

Note that in the OSI Reference Model, the application layer refers to applications that are network-aware. There are thousands of computer applications, but not all of these can transmit information across a network. This situation is changing rapidly, however. Five years ago, there was a distinct line between applications that could and couldn't perform network functions. A good example of this was word processing programs, like Microsoft Word—they were built to perform one process: word processing. Today, however, many applications—Microsoft Word, for instance—have embedded objects that don't necessarily have to be on the same computer. There are many, many examples of application layer programs. The most common are telnet, FTP, web browsers, and e-mail.

Presentation Layer

The sixth layer of the OSI Reference Model is the *presentation* layer. The presentation layer is responsible for defining how information is presented to the user in the interface that they are using. This layer defines how various forms of text, graphics, video, and/or audio information are presented to the user. For example, text is represented in two different forms: ASCII and EBCDIC. ASCII (the American Standard Code for Information Interchange, used by most devices today) uses seven bits to represent characters. EBCDIC (Extended Binary-Coded Decimal Interchange Code, developed by IBM) is still used in mainframe environments to represent characters. Text can also be shaped by different elements, such as font, underline, italic, and bold.

exam watch *The presentation layer determines how data is represented to the user. Examples of presentation layer protocols and standards include ASCII, BMP, GIF, JPEG, WAV, AVI, and MPEG.*

There are different standards for representing graphical information—BMP, GIF, JPEG, TIFF, and others. This variety of standards is also true of audio (WAV and MIDI) and video (WMV, AVI, and MPEG). There are literally hundreds of standards for representing information that a user sees in their application. Probably one of the best examples of applications that have a very clear presentation function is a web browser, since it has many special marking codes that define how data should be represented to the user.

The presentation layer can also provide encryption to secure data from the application layer; however, this it not common with today's methods of security, since this type of encryption is performed in software and requires a lot of CPU cycles to perform.

Session Layer

The fifth layer of the OSI Reference Model is the *session* layer. The session layer is responsible for initiating the setup and teardown of connections. In order to perform these functions, the session layer must determine whether data stays local to a computer or must be obtained or sent to a remote networking device. In the latter case, the session layer initiates the connection. The session layer is also responsible for differentiating among multiple network connections, ensuring that data is sent across the correct connection as well as taking data from a connection and forwarding it to the correct application.

The session layer is responsible for setting up and tearing down network connections. Examples include RPCs and NFS.

The actual mechanics of this process, however, are implemented at the transport layer. To set up connections or tear down connections, the session layer communicates with the transport layer. Remote Procedure Call (RPC) is an example of an IP session protocol; the Network File System (NFS), which uses RPC, is an example application at this layer.

Transport Layer

The fourth layer of the OSI Reference Model is the *transport* layer. The transport layer is responsible for the actual mechanics of a connection, where it can provide both *reliable* and *unreliable* delivery of data. For reliable connections, the transport layer is responsible for error detection and correction: when an error is detected, the transport layer will resend the data, thus providing the correction. For unreliable connections, the transport layer provides only error detection—error correction is left up to one of the higher layers (typically the application layer). In this sense, unreliable connections attempt to provide a best-effort delivery—if the data makes it there, that's great, and if it doesn't, oh well!

exam watch ***The fourth layer, the transport layer, provides both guaranteed data delivery and no guarantee of data delivery. Examples include IP's TCP and UDP protocols.***

Examples of a reliable transport protocol are TCP/IP's Transmission Control Protocol (TCP) and IPX's SPX (Sequenced Packet Exchange) protocol. TCP/IP's User Datagram Protocol (UDP) is an example of a protocol that uses unreliable connections. Actually, IPX and IP themselves are examples of protocols that provide unreliable connections, even though they operate at the network, and not transport, layer. In IPX's case, if a reliable connection is needed, SPX is used. For IP, if a reliable connection is needed, TCP is used at the transport layer. The transport layer together with its mechanics is discussed in more depth in the section "Transport Layer" later in this chapter.

Network Layer

The third layer of the OSI Reference Model is the *network* layer. The network layer provides quite a few functions. First, it provides for a logical topology of your network using logical, or layer-3, addresses. These addresses are used to group machines together. As you will see in Chapter 3, these addresses have two components: a network component and a host component. The network component is used to group devices together. Layer-3 addresses allow devices that are on the same or different media types to communicate with each other. Media types define types of connections, such as Ethernet, Token Ring, or serial. These are discussed in the section "Data Link Layer" later in this chapter.

exam watch ***The network layer provides a logical topology and layer-3 addresses. Routers function at the network layer. Layer-3 protocols include TCP/IP, IPX, and AppleTalk.***

To move information between devices that have different network numbers, a *router* is used. Routers use information in the logical address to make intelligent decisions about how to reach a destination. Routing is discussed in more depth in Chapters 9, 10, and 11.

Examples of network layer protocols include AppleTalk, DECnet, IPX, TCP/IP (or IP, for short), Vines, and XNS. The network layer is discussed in much more depth in the section "Network Layer" later in this chapter.

Data Link Layer

The second layer in the OSI Reference Model is the *data link* layer. Whereas the network layer provides for logical addresses for devices, the data link layer provides for physical, or hardware, addresses. These hardware addresses are commonly called Media Access Control (MAC) addresses. The data link layer also defines how a networking device accesses the media that it is connected as well as defining the media's frame type. This includes the fields and components of the data link layer, or layer-2, frame. This communication is only for devices on the same data link layer media type (or same piece of wire). To traverse media types, Ethernet to Token Ring, for instance, typically a router is used.

The data link layer is also responsible for taking bits (binary 1's and 0's) from the physical layer and reassembling them into the original data link layer frame. The data link layer does error detection and will discard bad frames. It typically does not perform error correction, as TCP/IP's TCP protocol does; however, some data link layer protocols do support error correction functions.

Examples of data link layer protocols and standards for local area network (LAN) connections include IEEE's 802.2, 802.3, and 802.5; Ethernet II; and ANSI's FDDI. Examples of WAN connections include ATM, Frame Relay, HDLC (High-Level Data Link Control), PPP (Point-to-Point Protocol), SDLC (Synchronous Data Link Control), SLIP (Serial Line Internet Protocol), and X.25. Bridges, switches, and network interface controllers or cards (NICs) are the primary networking devices functioning at the data link layer, which is discussed in more depth in the section "Data Link Layer" later in this chapter.

exam watch

The data link layer defines hardware (MAC) addresses as well as the communication process that occurs within a media type. Switches and bridges function at the data link layer. Examples of data link layer protocols and standards include IEEE's 802.2, 802.3, Ethernet II, HDLC, PPP, and Frame Relay.

Physical Layer

The first, or bottommost, layer of the OSI Reference Model is the *physical* layer. The physical layer is responsible for the physical mechanics of a network connection, which include the following:

- The type of interface used on the networking device
- The type of cable used for connecting devices
- The connectors used on each end of the cable
- The pin-outs used for each of the connections on the cable

The type of interface is commonly called a NIC. A NIC can be a physical card that you put into a computer, like a 10BaseT Ethernet card, or a fixed interface on a switch, like a 100BaseTX port on a Cisco Catalyst 1900 series switch.

The physical layer is also responsible for how binary information is converted to a physical layer signal. For example, if the cable uses copper as a transport medium, the physical layer defines how binary 1's and 0's are converted into an electrical signal by using different voltage levels. If the cable uses fiber, the physical layer defines how 1's and 0's are represented using an LED or laser with different light frequencies.

Data communications equipment (DCE) terminates a physical WAN connection and provides clocking and synchronization of a connection between two locations and connects to a DTE. The DCE category includes equipment such as CSU/DSUs, NT1s, and modems. Data terminal equipment (DTE) is an end-user device, such as a router or a PC, that connects to the WAN via the DCE device. In some cases, the function of the DCE may be built into the DTE's physical interface. For instance, certain Cisco routers can be purchased with built-in NT1s or CSU/DSUs in their WAN interfaces. Normally, the terms DTE and DCE are used to describe WAN components, but they are sometimes used to describe LAN connections. For instance, in a LAN connection, a PC, file server, or router is sometimes referred to as a DTE, and a switch or bridge as a DCE.

Examples of physical layer standards include the following cable types: Category-3, -5, and -5E; EIA/TIA-232, -449, and -530; multimode and single-mode fiber (MMF and SMF); Type-1; and others. Interface connectors include the following: AUI, BNC, DB-9, DB-25, DB-60, RJ-11, RJ-45, and others. A hub and a repeater are examples of devices that function at the physical layer.

exam watch

The physical layer defines physical properties for connections and communication, including wires (UTP and fiber) and connectors (RJ-45 and DB-9). A hub and a repeater are examples of devices that function at the physical layer. A repeater is used to physically extend a single segment, while a hub, which is also a repeater, connects many segments together.

Fiber Cabling LANs typically use either copper or fiber-optic cabling. Copper cabling is discussed in more depth in the section "Ethernet" later in this chapter. Fiber-optic cabling uses light-emitting diodes (LEDs) and lasers to transmit data. With this transmission, light is used to represent binary 1's and 0's: if there is light on the wire, this represents a 1; if there is no light, this represents a 0.

> **exam watch**
> ***Fiber cabling is not affected by electromagnetic interference (EMI), whereas copper cabling is.***

Fiber-optic cabling is typically used to provide very high speeds and to span connections across very large distances. For example, speeds of 100Gbps and distances of over 10 kilometers are achievable through the use of fiber—copper cannot come close to these feats. However, fiber-optic cabling does have its disadvantages: it is expensive, difficult to troubleshoot, difficult to install, and less reliable than copper.

Two types of fiber are used for connections: multimode and single-mode. Multimode fiber transmits 850 or 1,300 nanometer light (light in the infrared spectrum; you can't see it with the naked eye). The thickness of mulimode fiber is 62.5/125 microns and the light signal is typically provided by an LED (light-emitting diode). When transmitting a signal, the light source is bounced off of the inner cladding (shielding) surrounding the fiber. Multimode fiber's relatively large core diameter supports the propagation of multiple longitudinal modes (i.e., different light paths) at a given wavelength; thus the term multimode is used. These multiple modes cause dispersion (signal spreading), which effectively limits the data speeds carried on the fiber to the hundreds-of-Mbps range. Single-mode fiber transmits 1,300 or 1,550 nanometer light and uses a laser as the light source. Because lasers provide a higher output than LEDs, single-mode fiber can span over 10 kilometers and have speeds up to 100Gbps. Due to single-mode fiber's very small core diameter, only a single longitudinal mode is propagated at a given wavelength—hence the term single-mode. Since only a single mode is propagated, single-mode fiber exhibits less dispersion (i.e., signal spreading) than multimode fiber, and therefore can support much higher data speeds than multimode fiber (100+Gbps).

The last few years have seen many advances in the use and deployment of fiber. One major enhancement is wave division multiplexing (WDM) and dense WDM (DWDM). WDM allows more than two wavelengths (signals) on the same piece of fiber, increasing the number of connections. DWDM allows yet more wavelengths, which are more closely spaced together: more than 200 wavelengths can be multiplexed into a light stream on a single piece of fiber.

Obviously, one of the advantages of DWDM is that it provides flexibility and transparency of the protocols and traffic carried across the fiber. For example, one wavelength can be used for a point-to-point connection, another for an Ethernet connection, another for an IP connection, and yet another for an ATM connection. Use of DWDM provides scalability and allows carriers to provision new connections *without* having to install new fiber lines, so they can add new connections in a very short period when you order them.

Let's talk about some of the terms used in fiber and how they affect distance and speed. First, you have the cabling, which provides the protective outer coating as well as the inner cladding. The inner cladding is denser to allow the light source to bounce off of it. In the middle of the cable is the fiber itself, which is used to transmit the signal. The index of refraction (IOR) affects the speed of the light source: it's the ratio of the speed of light in a vacuum to the speed of light in the fiber. In a vacuum, there are no variables that affect the transmission; however, anytime you send something across a medium like fiber or copper, the media itself will exhibit properties that will affect the transmission, causing possible delays. IOR is used to measure these differences: basically, IOR measures the density of the fiber. The more dense the fiber is, the slower the light travels through the fiber.

The *loss factor* is used to describe any signal loss in the fiber before the light source gets to the end of the fiber. *Connector loss* is a loss that occurs when a connector joins two pieces of fibers: a slight signal loss is expected. Also, the longer the fiber, the greater the likelihood that the signal strength will have decreased when it reaches the end of the cable. This is called *attenuation*. Two other terms, microbending and macrobending, describe signal degradation.

Microbending is when a wrinkle in the fiber, typically where the cable is slightly bent, causes a distortion in the light source. *Macrobending* is when there is leakage of the light source from the fiber, typically from a bend in the fiber cable. To overcome this problem over long distances, *optical amplifiers* can be used. They are similar to an Ethernet repeater. A good amplifier, such as an erbium-doped fiber amplifier (EDFA), coverts a light source directly to another light source, providing for the best reproduction of the original signal. Other amplifiers convert light to an electrical signal and then back to light, which can cause a degradation in signal quality.

Two main standards are used to describe the transmission of signals across a fiber: SONET (Synchronous Optical Network) and SDH (Synchronous Digital Hierarchy). SONET is defined by the Exchange Carriers Standards Association (ECSA) and American National Standards Institute (ANSI) and is typically used in North America. SDH is an international standard used throughout most of the world (with the exception of North America). Both of these standards define the physical layer framing used to transmit light sources, which also includes overhead for the transmission. There are three types of overhead:

- **Section overhead (SOH)** Overhead for the link between two devices, such as repeaters

- **Line overhead (LOH)** Overhead for one or more sections connecting network devices, such as hubs
- **Path overhead (POH)** Overhead for one or more lines connecting two devices that assemble and disassemble frames, such as carrier switches or a router's fiber interface

Typically, either a ring or point-to-point topology is used to connect the devices. With carrier MAN networks, the most common implementation is through the use of rings. Autoprotection switching (APS) can be used to provide line redundancy: in case of failure on a primary line, a secondary line can automatically be utilized. Table 2-1 contains an overview of the more common connection types for SONET and SDH. Please note that SONET uses STS and that SDH uses STM to describe the signal.

Wireless Wireless transmission has been used for a very long time to transmit data by using infrared radiation, microwaves, or radio waves through a medium like air. With this type of connection, no wires are used. Typically, three terms are used to group different wireless technologies: narrowband, broadband, and circuit/packet data. Whenever you are choosing a wireless solution for your WAN or LAN, you should always consider the following criteria: speed, distance, and number of devices to connect.

Narrowband solutions typically require a license and operate at a low data rate. Only one frequency is used for transmission: 900 MHz, 2.4 GHz, or 5 GHz. Other technologies—household wireless phones, for instance—also use these technologies. Through the use of spread spectrum, higher data rates can be achieved by spreading the signal across multiple frequencies. However, transmission of these signals is typically limited to a small area, like a campus network.

TABLE 2-1 Fiber Connection Types

Common Term	SONET Term	SDH Term	Connection Rate
OC-1	STS-1	–	51.84Mbps
OC-3	STS-3	STM-1	155.52Mbps
OC-12	STS-12	STM-4	622.08Mbps
OC-48	STS-48	STM-16	2,488.32Mbps
OC-192	STS-192	STM-64	9,953.28Mbps

The broadband solutions fall under the heading of the Personal Communications Service (PCS). They provide lower data rates than narrowband solutions, cost about the same, but provide broader coverage. With the right provider, you can obtain national coverage. Sprint PCS is an example of a carrier that provides this type of solution.

Circuit and packet data solutions are based on cellular technologies. They provide lower data rates than the other two and typically have higher fees for each packet transmitted; however, you can easily obtain nationwide coverage from almost any cellular phone company.

exam watch

Narrowband solutions provide a low data rate. This can be overcome using spread spectrum, which spreads a signal across multiple frequencies and therefore increases your bandwidth over short distances. Cisco's Aironet products use spread spectrum. Broadband solutions, such as PCS, provide low data rates but can provide a large coverage area. Infrared solutions provide high data rates over very small distances, while satellite connections provide international coverage but have high latency and cost.

Wireless is becoming very popular in today's LANs, since very little cabling is required. Three basic standards are currently in use: 802.11a, 802.11b, and 802.11g, shown in Table 2-2.

Of the three, 802.11b has been deployed the most, with 802.11g just introduced as a standard. One advantage that 802.11b and 802.11g devices have over 802.11a

TABLE 2-2 Wireless Standards

	802.11a	802.11b	802.11g
Data Rate	54Mbps	11Mbps	54Mbps
Frequency	5 GHz	2.4 GHz	2.4 GHz
Compatibility	None	With 802.11g	With 802.11b
Range	25–75 feet	100–150 feet	100–150 feet

Be familiar with the contents of Table 2-2, especially the data rates. The 802.11b standard is commonly called *Wi-Fi*, even though the term applies to all 802.11 standards.

is that 802.11b and 802.11g can interoperate, which makes migrating from an all-802.11b network to an 802.11g network an easy and painless process. Note that 802.11g devices are compatible with 802.11b devices (but not vice versa) and that 802.11a devices are *not* compatible with the other two standards. Also note that the speeds listed in Table 2-2 are optimal speeds based on the specifications—the actual speeds that you might achieve in a real network vary according to the number of devices you have, the distance that they are from the base station, and any physical obstructions or interference that might exist.

One of the biggest problems of wireless networks is security. Many wireless networks use Wired Equivalency Privacy (WEP) for security. This is an encryption protocol that uses 40-bit keys, which is weak by today's standards. Many vendors use 128-bit keys to compensate this weakness; however, weaknesses have been found in this protocol, and WEP is used with other security measures to provide a more secure wireless network. The 802.1x/EAP (Extensible Authentication Protocol) is used to provide authentication services for devices: it authenticates devices to an authentication server (typically a RADIUS server) before the device is allowed to participate in the wireless network. Cisco has developed an extension to this called LEAP, or lightweight EAP. LEAP centralizes both authentication and key distribution (for encryption) to provide scalability for large wireless deployments.

Devices

Table 2-3 is a reminder of the devices that function at various OSI Reference Model layers.

TABLE 2-3 Devices and the Layers at Which They Function

Layer	Name of Layer	Device
3	Network	Routers
2	Data link	Switches, bridges, NICs
1	Physical	Hubs

CERTIFICATION OBJECTIVE 2.02

Data Link Layer

Layer-2 of the OSI Reference Model is the data link layer. This layer is responsible for defining the format of layer-2 frames as well as the mechanics of how devices communicate with each other over the physical layer. Here are the components the data link layer is responsible for:

- Defining the Media Access Control (MAC) or hardware addresses
- Defining the physical or hardware topology for connections
- Defining how the network layer protocol is encapsulated in the data link layer frame
- Providing both connectionless and connection-oriented services

Normally, the data link layer does not provide connection-oriented (i.e., reliable) services (ones that do error detection *and* correction). However, in environments that use SNA (Systems Network Architecture) as a data link layer protocol, SNA can provide sequencing and flow control to ensure the deliver of data link layer frames. SNA was developed by IBM to help devices communicate in LAN networks (predominantly Token Ring) at the data link layer. In most instances, it will be the transport layer that provides for reliable connections.

Make sure to remember that the primary function of the data link layer is to regulate how two networking devices connected to the same media type communicate with each other. If the devices are on different media types, the network layer typically plays a role in the communication of these devices.

Data Link Layer Addressing

The data link layer uses MAC, or hardware, addresses for communication. For LAN communications, each machine on the same connected media type needs a unique MAC address. A MAC address is 48 bits in length and is represented as a hexadecimal number. Represented in hex, it is 12 characters in length. To make it easier to read, the MAC address is represented in a dotted hexadecimal format, like this: FFFF.FFFF.FFFF. Since the MAC addresses uses hexadecimal numbers, the values used range from 0–9 and A–F, giving you a total of 16 values for a single digit. For example, a hexadecimal value of A would be 10 in decimal. There are other types of data link layer addressing besides MAC addresses. For instance, Frame Relay uses Data Link Connection Identifiers (DLCIs). I'll discuss DLCIs in more depth in Chapter 16.

The first six digits of a MAC address are associated with the vendor, or maker, of the NIC. Each vendor has one or more unique sets of six digits. These first six digits are commonly called the *organizationally unique identifier* (OUI). For example, one of Cisco's OUI values is *0000.0C*. The last six digits are used to uniquely represent the NIC within the OUI value. Theoretically, each NIC has a unique MAC address. In reality, however, this is probably not true. What is important for your purposes is that each of your devices has a unique MAC address on its NIC within the same *physical* or *logical* segment. A logical segment is a virtual LAN (VLAN) and is referred to as a broadcast domain, which is discussed in Chapter 8. Some devices allow you to change this hardware address, while others won't.

exam watch

The first six hexadecimal digits of a MAC address form the OUI. MAC addresses only need to be unique in a broadcast domain, which includes all layer-2 connected collision domains. You can have the same MAC address in different broadcast domains (virtual LANs).

Each data link layer frame contains two MAC addresses: a source MAC address of the machine creating the frame and a destination MAC address for the device or devices intended to receive the frame. There are three general types of addresses at the data link layer, shown in Table 2-4. A source MAC address is an example of a unicast address—only one device can create the frame. However, destination MAC addresses can be any of the addresses listed in Table 2-4. The destination MAC address in the data link layer frame helps the other NICs connected to the segment to figure out if they need to process the frame when they receive it or to ignore it. The following sections covers each of these address types in more depth.

TABLE 2-4 Data Link Address Types

Address Type	Description
Unicast	Represents a single device on a segment
Broadcast	Represents every device on a segment
Multicast	Represents a group of devices on a segment

Unicast

A frame with a destination unicast MAC address is intended for just one device on a segment. The top part of Figure 2-2 shows an example of a unicast. In this example, PC-A creates an Ethernet frame with a destination MAC address that contains PC-C's address. When PC-A places this data link layer frame on the wire, all the devices on the segment receive it. Each of the NICs of PC-B, PC-C, and PC-D examine the destination MAC address in the frame. In this instance, only PC-C's NIC will process the frame, since the destination MAC address in the frame matches the MAC address of its NIC. PC-B and PC-D will ignore the frame.

Multicast

Unlike a unicast address, a *multicast* address represents a group of devices on a segment. The multicast group can contain anywhere from no devices to every device on a segment. One of the interesting things about multicasting is that the membership of a group is dynamic—devices can join and leave as they please. The detailed process of multicasting is beyond the scope of this book, however.

FIGURE 2-2

MAC address types

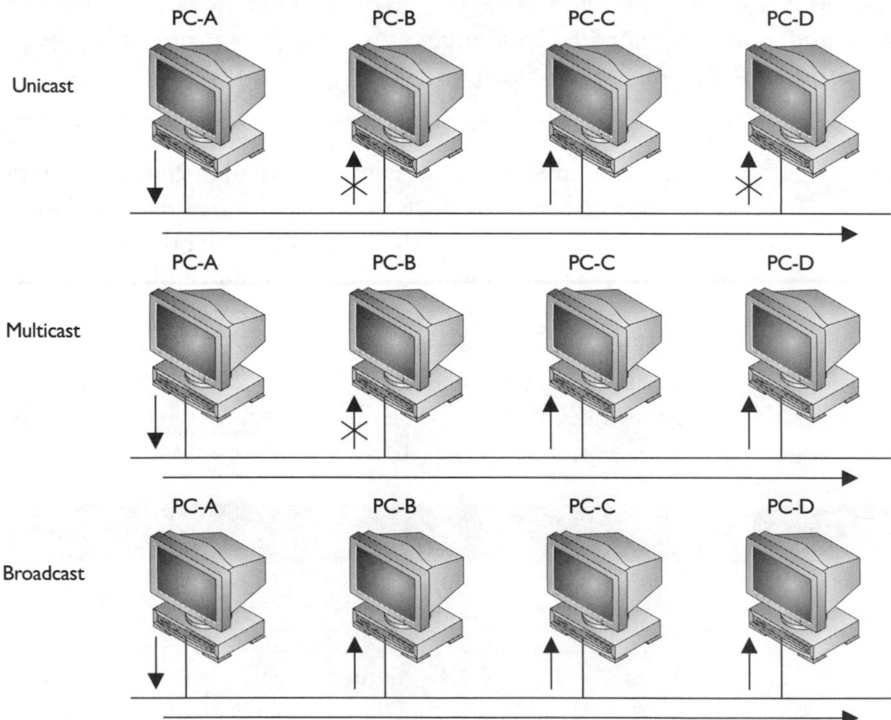

The middle portion of Figure 2-2 shows an example of a multicast. In this example, PC-A sends a data link layer frame to a multicast group on its segment. Currently, only PC-A, PC-C, and PC-D are members of this group. When each of the PCs receives the frame, its NIC examines the destination MAC address in the data link layer frame. In this example, PC-B ignores the frame, since it is not a member of the group. However, PC-C and PC-D will process the frame.

Broadcast

A *broadcast* is a data link layer frame that is intended for every networking device on the same segment. The bottom portion of Figure 2-2 shows an example of a broadcast. In this example, PC-A puts a broadcast address in the destination field of the data link layer frame. For MAC broadcasts, all of the bit positions in the address are enabled, making the address FFFF.FFFF.FFFF in hexadecimal. This frame is then placed on the wire. Notice that in this example, when PC-B, PC-C, and PC-D receive the frame, they *all* process it.

Broadcasts are mainly used in two situations. First, broadcasts are more effective than unicasts if you need to send the same information to every machine. With a unicast, you would have to create a separate frame for each machine on the segment; with a broadcast, you could accomplish the same thing with one frame. Second, broadcasts are used to discover the unicast address of a device. For instance, when you turn on your PC, initially, it doesn't know about any MAC addresses of any other machines on the network. A broadcast can be used to discover the MAC addresses of these machines, since they will all process the broadcast frame. In IP, the Address Resolution Protocol (ARP) uses this process to discover another device's MAC address. ARP is discussed in Chapter 3.

Ethernet

Ethernet is a LAN media type that functions at the data link layer. Ethernet uses the Carrier Sense Multiple Access/Collision Detection (CSMA/CD) mechanism to send information in a shared environment. Ethernet was initially developed with the idea that many devices would be connected to the same physical piece of wiring. The acronym CSMA/CD describes the actual process of how Ethernet functions.

In a traditional, or hub-based, Ethernet environment, only one NIC can successfully send a frame at a time. All NICs, however, can simultaneously listen to information on the wire. Before an Ethernet NIC puts a frame on the wire, it will first *sense* the wire to ensure that no other frame is currently on the wire. If the cable uses copper, the NIC can detect this by examining the voltage levels on the wire. If the cable is fiber, the NIC can also detect this by examining the light frequencies on the wire. The NIC must go through this sensing process, since the Ethernet medium supports *multiple access*—another NIC might already have a frame on the wire. If the NIC doesn't sense a frame on the wire, it will go ahead and transmit its own frame; otherwise, if there is a frame on the wire, the NIC will wait for the completion of the transmission of the frame on the wire and then transmit its own frame.

If two or more machines simultaneously sense the wire and see no frame, and each places its frame on the wire, a *collision* will occur. In this situation, the voltage levels on a copper wire or the light frequencies on a piece of fiber get messed up. For example, if two NICs attempt to put the same voltage on an electrical piece of wire, the voltage level will be different than if only one device does so. Basically, the two original frames become unintelligible (or undecipherable). The NICs, when they place a frame on the wire, examine the status of the wire to ensure that a collision does not occur: this is the *collision detection* mechanism of CSMA/CD.

If the NICs see a collision for their transmitted frames, they have to resend the frames. In this instance, each NIC that was transmitting a frame when a collision occurred creates a special signal, called a jam signal, on the wire, waits a small random time period, and senses the wire again. If no frame is currently on the wire, the NIC will then retransmit its original frame. The time period that the NIC waits is measured in microseconds, a delay that can't be detected by a human. Likewise, the time period the NICs wait is random to help ensure a collision won't occur again when these NICs retransmit their frames.

The more devices you place on a segment, the more likely you are to experience collisions. If you put too many devices on the segment, too many collisions will occur, seriously affecting your throughput. Therefore, you need to monitor the number of collisions on each of your network segments. The more collisions you experience, the less throughput you'll get. Normally, if your collisions are less than one percent of your total traffic, you are okay. This is not to say that collisions are *bad*—they are just one part of how Ethernet functions.

Because Ethernet experiences collisions, networking devices that share the same medium (are connected to the same physical segment) are said to belong to the same *collision*, or *bandwidth, domain*. This means that, for better or worse, traffic generated by one device in the domain can affect other devices. Chapter 7 discusses how bridges and switches can be used to solve collision and bandwidth problems on a network segment.

Make sure you understand the mechanics of Ethernet: CSMA/CD. No device has priority over another device. If two devices transmit simultaneously, a collision occurs. When this happens, a jam signal is generated and the devices try to retransmit after waiting a random period.

IEEE's Version of Ethernet

There are actually two variants of Ethernet: IEEE's implementation and the DIX implementation. Ethernet was developed by three different companies in the early 1980s: Digital, Intel, and Xerox, or DIX for short. This implementation of Ethernet has evolved over time; its current version is called Ethernet II. Devices running TCP/IP typically use the Ethernet II implementation.

The second version of Ethernet was developed by IEEE and is standardized in the IEEE 802.2 and 802.3 standards. IEEE has split the data link layer into two components: MAC and LLC. These components are described in Table 2-5. The top part of the data link layer is the LLC, and its function is performed in software. The bottom part of the data link layer is the MAC, and its function is performed in hardware.

The LLC performs its multiplexing by using Service Access Point (SAP) identifiers. When a network layer protocol is encapsulated in the 802.2 frame, the protocol of the network data is placed in the SAP field. When the destination receives the frame, it examines the SAP field to determine which upper-layer network layer protocol should process the frame. This allows the destination network device to differentiate

TABLE 2-5 IEEE Ethernet Components

Data Link Layer	Name	IEEE Standard	Description
Top part	Logical Link Control (LLC)	802.2	Defines how to multiplex multiple network layer protocols in the data link layer frame. LLC is performed in *software*.
Bottom part	MAC	802.3	Defines how information is transmitted in an Ethernet environment, and defines the framing, MAC addressing, and mechanics as to how Ethernet works. MAC is performed in *hardware*.

between TCP/IP and IPX network layer protocols that are being transmitted across the data link layer connection. Optionally, LLC can provide sequencing and flow control to provide a reliable service, as TCP does at the transport layer. However, most data link layer implementations of Ethernet don't use this function—if a reliable connection is needed, it is provided by either the transport or application layer.

IEEE 802.3 As mentioned earlier, IEEE 802.3 is responsible for defining the framing used to transmit information between two NICs. A frame standardizes the fields in the frame and their lengths so that every device understands how to read the contents of the frame. The top part of Figure 2-3 shows the fields of an 802.3 frame.

Table 2-6 shows the fields found in the 802.3 frame. The field or frame check sequence (FCS) value is used to ensure that when the destination receives the frame, it can verify that the frame was received intact. When generating the FCS value, which is basically a checksum, the NIC takes all of the fields in the 802.3 frame, except the FCS field, and runs them through an algorithm that generates a four-byte result, which is placed in the FCS field.

When the destination receives the frame, it takes the same fields and runs them through the same algorithm. The destination then compares its four-byte output with what was included in the frame by the source NIC. If the two values don't match, then the frame is considered bad and is dropped. If the two values match, then the frame is considered good and is processed further.

IEEE 802.2 IEEE 802.2 (LLC) handles the top part of the data link layer. There are two types of IEEE 802.2 frames: Service Access Point (SAP) and Subnetwork Access Protocol (SNAP). These 802.2 frames are encapsulated (enclosed) in an 802.3 frame when being sent to a destination. Where 802.3 is used as a transport to get the 802.2 frames to other devices, 802.2 is used to define which network layer

FIGURE 2-3

Ethernet 802.3 and Ethernet II

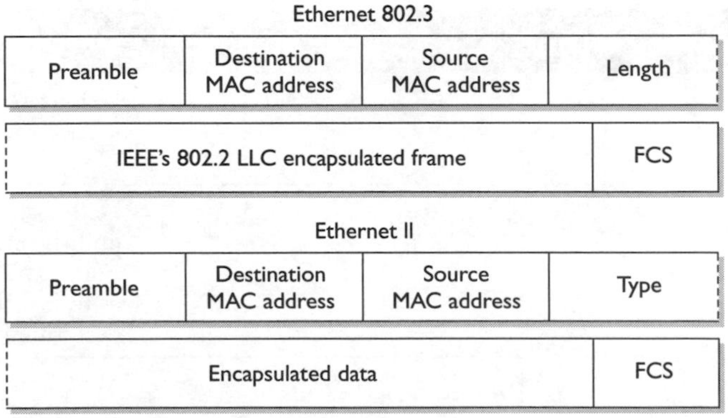

TABLE 2-6 Fields in the 802.3 Frame

Field	Length in Bytes	Description
Preamble	8	Identifies the beginning of the 802.3 frame
Destination MAC address	6	Is the MAC address that the frame is to be sent to
Source MAC address	6	Is the MAC address of the source of the frame
Length	2	Defines the length of the frame from this point to the checksum at the end of the frame
Data	Variable	Is the 802.2 LLC encapsulated frame
FCS (Field Checksum Sequence)	4	Is a checksum (CRC, cyclic redundancy check) that is used to ensure that the frame is received by the destination error-free

protocol created the data that the 802.2 frame will include. In this sense, it serves as a multiplexing function: it differentiates between TCP/IP, IPX, AppleTalk, and other network-layer data types. Figure 2-4 shows the two types of 802.2 frames.

Table 2-7 lists the fields found in an 802.2 SAP frame.

When a destination NIC receives an 802.3 frame, the NIC first checks the FCS to verify that the frame is valid and then checks the destination MAC address in the 802.3 frame to make sure that it should process the frame (or ignore it). The MAC sublayer strips off the 802.3 frame portion and passes the 802.2 frame to the LLC sublayer. The LLC examines the destination SAP value to determine which upper-layer protocol should have the encapsulated data passed to it. Here are some examples of SAP values: IP uses 0x06 (hexadecimal) and IPX uses 0x0E. If the LLC sees 0x06 in the SAP field, it passes the encapsulated data up to the TCP/IP protocol stack running on the device.

FIGURE 2-4

SAP and SNAP

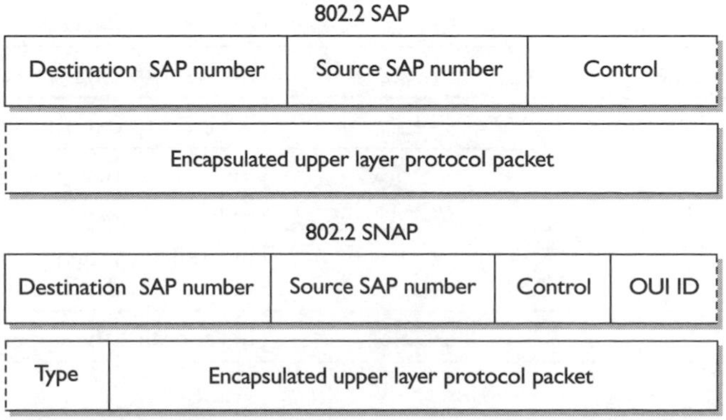

TABLE 2-7 802.2 SAP Fields

Field	Length in Bytes	Description
Destination SAP number	1	Identifies the network layer protocol that this is to be sent to
Source SAP number	1	Identifies the network layer protocol that originated this data
Control field	1–2	Determines the fields that follow this field
Data	Variable	This contains the upper-layer network layer packet

The second frame type supported by 802.2 is SNAP, which is shown in the bottom portion of Figure 2-4. As you can see from this frame, there is one additional field: *type*. Table 2-8 explains the 802.2 SNAP fields.

One of the issues of the original SAP field in the 802.2 SAP frame is that even though it is eight bits (one byte) in length, only the first six bits are used for identifying upper-layer protocols, which allows up to 64 protocols. Back in the 1980s, there were many more protocols than 64, plus there was an expectation that more protocols would be created. SNAP overcomes this limitation without having to change the length of the SAP field.

To indicate a SNAP frame, the SAP fields are set to hexadecimal *0xAA*, the control field is set to *0x03*, and the OUI field is set to *0x0*. The *type* field identifies the upper-layer protocol that is encapsulated in the payload of the 802.2 frame. Since a SAP frame can identify only 64 protocols, the type field was made two bytes in

TABLE 2-8 802.2 SNAP Fields

Field	Length in Bytes	Description
Destination SAP number	1	This is set to **0xAA** to signify a SNAP frame
Source SAP number	1	This is set to **0xAA** to signify a SNAP frame
Control field	1–2	This is set to **0x03** to signify a SNAP frame
OUI ID	3	This value varies by vendor but is set to **0x0** to signify a SNAP frame
Type	2	This indicates the upper-layer protocol that is contained in the data field
Data	Variable	This contains the upper-layer network layer packet

802.2 uses a SAP or SNAP field to differentiate between encapsulated layer-3 payloads. With a SNAP frame, the SAP fields are set to 0xAA and the type field is used to indicate the layer-3 protocol.

length, which theoretically allows the support of up to 65,536 protocols! AppleTalk is an example of a protocol that uses an 802.2 SNAP frame.

Note that concerning 802.2 there are other data link layer protocols for the LAN besides Ethernet, including Token Ring and FDDI. IEEE's 802.2 standard supports these sublayer standards at the MAC layer. Token Ring is specified in IEEE's 802.5 standard, and FDDI is specified in an ANSI standard. This book only focuses on Ethernet.

Ethernet II's Version of Ethernet

Ethernet II is the original Ethernet frame type. Ethernet II and 802.3 are very similar: they both use CSMA/CD to determine their operations. Their main difference is the frames used to transmit information between NICs. The bottom part of earlier Figure 2-3 shows the fields in an Ethernet II frame. Here are the two main differences between an Ethernet II and IEEE:

- Ethernet II does not have any sublayers, while IEEE 802.2/3 have two: LLC and MAC.
- Ethernet II has a *type* field instead of a length field (used in 802.3). IEEE 802.2 defines the type for IEEE Ethernet.

Be able to compare and contrast the two versions of Ethernet: Ethernet II and 802.2/3.

If you examine the IEEE 802.3 frame and the Ethernet II frame, you can see that they are very similar. NICs differentiate them by examining the value in the type field for an Ethernet II frame and the value in the length field in the IEEE 802.3 frame. If the value is greater than 1500, then the frame is an Ethernet II frame. If the value is 1500 or less, the frame is an 802.3 frame.

Both versions of Ethernet can coexist in the same network. However, because of the frame differences between the two types, a NIC running only 802.3 will discard any Ethernet II frames and vice versa.

Ethernet Physical Layer Properties

Many physical layer standards define the physical properties of an Ethernet implantation. One of the most common is IEEE's 802.3 10Mb. Table 2-9 shows some of the 10 Mb standards.

Ethernet supports a bus topology—physical or logical. In a bus topology, every device is connected to the same piece of wire and all devices see every frame. For example, 10Base5 uses one long, thick piece of coaxial cable. NICs tap into this wire using a device called a vampire tap. With 10Base2, the devices are connected together by many pieces of wire using T-taps: one end of the T-tap connects to the NIC and the other two connect to the two Ethernet cables that are part of the bus. With 10BaseT, all devices are connected to a hub, where the hub provides a logical bus topology. All of these 10Mb Ethernet solutions support only half-duplex: they can send or receive. They cannot do both simultaneously. Duplexing is discussed in more depth in Chapter 7.

exam watch

Half-duplex connections allow devices to either send or receive and experience collisions. Full-duplex connections require a point-to-point connection between two devices. With this type of connection, both devices can simultaneously send and receive without any collisions occurring.

Ethernet 10Base2 and 10Base5 haven't been used in years because of the difficulty in troubleshooting network problems. And many 10BaseT networks have been supplanted by higher-speed Ethernet solutions, like Fast Ethernet and Gigabit

TABLE 2-9 10Mb Ethernet Properties

Ethernet Type	Distance Limitation	Cable Type	Interface Type	Physical Topology	Logical Topology
10Base5	500 meters	Thick coaxial cable—50 ohm *(thicknet)*	AUI	Bus	Bus
10Base2	185 meters	Thin coaxial cable *(thinnet)*	BNC	Bus	Bus
10BaseT	100 meters	Unshielded twisted pair (UTP) cabling (CAT-3, -4, -5)	RJ-45	Star (Hub)	Bus

TABLE 2-10 100Mb Ethernet Properties

Ethernet Type	Distance Limitation	Cable Type	Cabling	Physical Topology	Logical Topology
100BaseTX	100 meters	UTP CAT-5	RJ-45	Star (Hub)	Bus
100BaseFX	400 meters half-duplex, 2,000 meters full-duplex	MMF 62.5/125 micron with SC and ST connectors	RJ-45	Star (Hub)	Bus
100BaseT4	100 meters	UTP CAT-3,4,5	RJ-45	Star (Hub)	Bus

Ethernet. Fast Ethernet and Ethernet use the same frame types and support the same CSMA/CD operation. However, there are two main differences between the two: Fast Ethernet supports 100Mbps speeds and the physical layer is implemented differently. Table 2-10 shows the different implementations of Fast Ethernet. Fast Ethernet supports both half- and full-duplex connections. With full-duplex connections, a device can send *and* receive simultaneously but requires a point-to-point connection that doesn't involve a hub.

Gigabit Ethernet is defined in IEEE 802.3z. To achieve 1Gbps speeds, IEEE adopted ANSI's X3T11 Fiber Channel standard for the physical layer implantation. The physical layer is different from Ethernet and Fast Ethernet in that it uses an 8B/10B encoding scheme to code the physical layer information when transmitting it across the wire. Table 2-11 shows the different implementations of 1Gbps. There is also a 10Gbps implementation of Ethernet that only runs across fiber. This standard is currently in the development process.

Table 2-12 compares the different cable types.

TABLE 2-11 1Gbps Ethernet Properties

Ethernet Type	Distance Limitation	Cable Type
1000BaseCX	25 meters	Shielded twisted pair (STP) copper
1000BaseLX	3–10 kilometers	SMF
1000BaseSX	220 meters	MMF
1000BaseT	100 meters	CAT-5E and CAT-6 UTP
1000BaseZX	100 meters	SMF

TABLE 2-12 Cable Type Comparisons

Cable	Distance	Data Rates	Comparison
UTP	100 meters	10–100Mbps	Is easy to install but is susceptible to interference
STP (Shielded Twisted Pair)	100 meters	10–100Mbps	Is difficult to install
Coaxial	500 meters	10–100Mbps	Is easy to install but is difficult to troubleshoot
Fiber	10 kilometers	10Mbps–100Gbps	Is difficult and expensive to install, difficult to troubleshoot, but can span very long distances and is not susceptible to interference

Data Link Devices: Bridges

Bridges are data link layer devices that switch frames between different layer-2 segments. They perform their switching in software, and their switching decisions are based on the destination MAC address in the header of the data link layer frame.

Bridges perform three main functions:

- They learn where devices are located by placing the MAC address of a device and the identifier of the port it is connected to in a port address table.
- They forward traffic intelligently, drawing on information they have in their port address table.
- They remove layer-2 loops by running the Spanning Tree Protocol (STP).

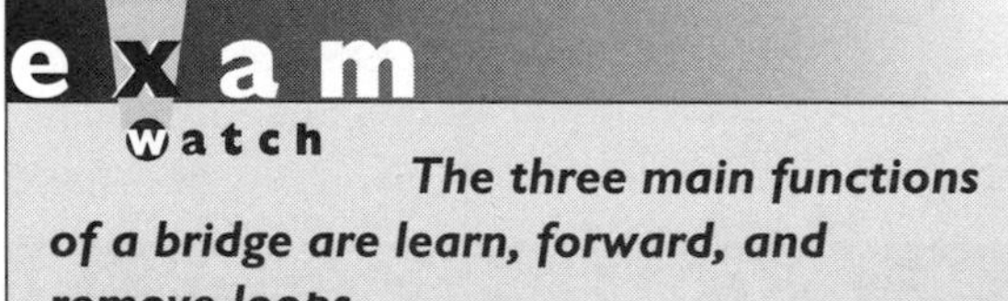

The three main functions of a bridge are learn, forward, and remove loops.

Actually, these three functions are implemented in bridges that perform transparent bridging. There are other types of bridging, including translational bridging, source route bridging, source route transparent bridging, and source route translational bridging. However, this book only focuses on transparent bridging. The following sections introduce you to bridging; Chapter 7 goes into more depth about this subject.

Learning Function

One of the three functions of a bridge is to learn which devices are connected to which ports of the bridge. The bridge then uses this information to switch frames intelligently. When a bridge receives a frame, it reads the source MAC address in the frame and compares it to a local MAC address table, called a port address table. If the address is not already in this table, the bridge adds the address and the port identifier on which the frame was received. If the address is already in the table, the bridge resets the timer for the table entry. Entries in the table remain there as long as the bridge sees traffic from them; otherwise, the bridge ages out the old entries to allow room for newer ones.

Forwarding Function

The second function of a bridge is to intelligently forward traffic. In order to do this, the bridge uses the port address table to help it find where destinations are located. When a frame is received on a port, the bridge first performs its learning function and then performs its forwarding function. The bridge examines the destination MAC address in the frame header and looks for a corresponding entry in the port address table. If the bridge finds a matching entry, the bridge forwards the frame out of the specified port. If the port is the same port on which the frame was received (the source and destination are connected to the same port), the bridge drops the frame. If the bridge doesn't find an entry, or if the destination MAC address is a broadcast or multicast address, the bridge *floods* the frame out all of the remaining ports.

exam watch

Remember that these three types of traffic are always flooded: unknown unicast addresses, broadcasts, and multicasts.

Removing Loops

The third function of a bridge is to remove layer-2 loops. To see the problem that layer-2 loops can cause, consider Figure 2-5. One advantage of using two bridges to connect two segments together, as is shown in Figure 2-5, is that you have redundancy.

But these loops also create problems. For instance, a bridge always floods traffic that has a destination address that is an unknown unicast, broadcast, or multicast address. And this traffic will continually circle around the loop—possibly forever. For example, in Figure 2-5, assume that a PC generates a broadcast on Segment1. When BridgeA and BridgeB receive the broadcast, they flood it out all of their remaining ports. This means that the same broadcast will appear twice on Segment2. Each bridge sees the other's broadcast on Segment2 and forwards this to Segment1. And this process will go on ad infinitum. This process not only wastes bandwidth on your LAN segments but also affects the CPU cycles of all devices on these segments, since all NICs will accept the broadcast and pass it up the protocol stack for further processing.

FIGURE 2-5

Layer-2 loops and redundancy

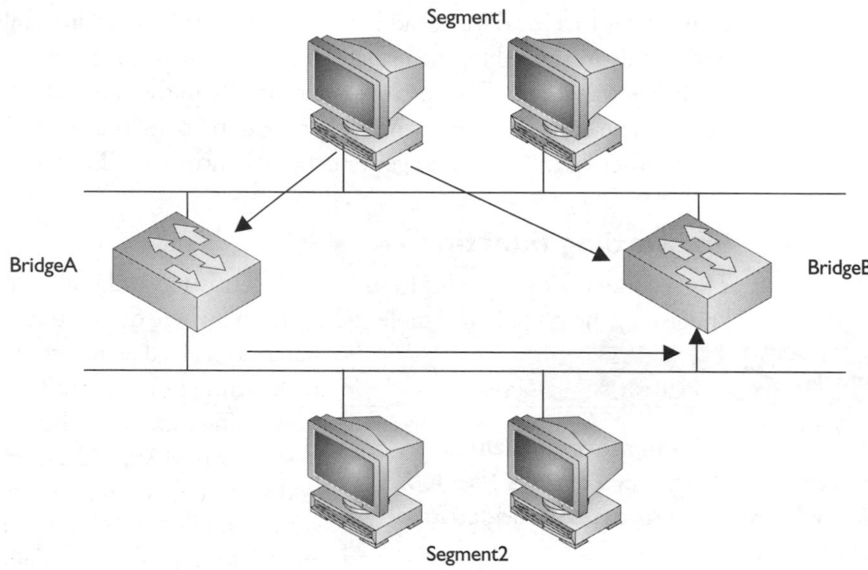

The Spanning Tree Protocol (STP) is used to remove loops in your layer-2 network. When STP runs, one of the ports of the bridges in a loop is disabled in software. In Figure 2-5, this is the port on BridgeB that is connected to Segment2. Any user traffic is ignored if it is received on this port and is not forwarded out of this port. Going back to our broadcast example, if a PC on Segment1 generated a broadcast, both bridges, again, would receive it. BridgeA would flood the broadcast to Segment2, but BridgeB would not, since the port is in a *blocked* state. STP is discussed in much more depth in Chapter 7.

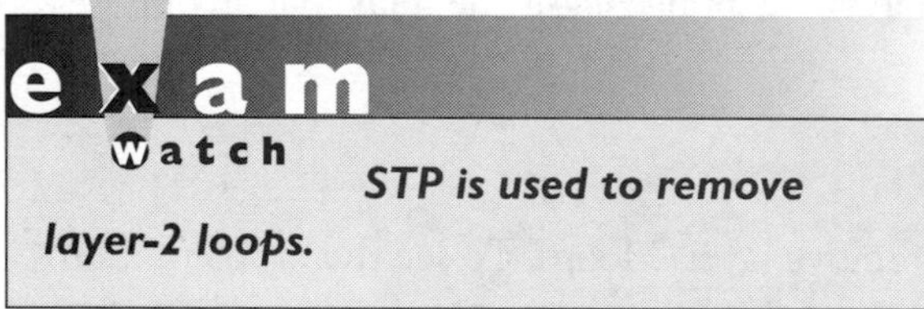

STP is used to remove layer-2 loops.

Problems That Bridges Solve

Bridges are used to solve collision and bandwidth problems. Each port connected to a bridge is a separate collision domain. When a frame is pulled into a port on a bridge, the bridge checks the frame's FCS, and if the FCS if valid, the frame is forwarded out of a destination port or ports. Basically, the bridge is creating the illusion that all the physical segments that it is connected to are actually one large logical segment. All devices connected to this "logical" segment are in the same broadcast domain—this makes sense because bridges flood broadcasts. Note that if you are having problems with large amounts of broadcasts, bridges will not solve these problems.

Data Link Devices: Switches

Switches, like bridges, operate at the data link layer. The three main functions of a bridge are also true of a switch: they learn, forward, and remove loops. However, switches have many more features than bridges; for instance, they make their switching decisions in hardware by using application-specific integrated circuits (ASICs). ASICs are specialized processors built to perform very few specific tasks. Because they do only a few things, ASICs are much more cost-effective than a generic processor, like the one found in your PC. Cisco, like most networking vendors, extensively uses ASICs throughout its switching products. Chapter 7 continues the discussion of the differences between bridges and switches.

Bridges, as well as switches, are used to solve bandwidth and collision problems. Routers, at the network layer, can also perform this function, but they cost more than bridges or switches.

CERTIFICATION OBJECTIVE 2.03

Network Layer

Layer-3 of the OSI Reference Model is the network layer. This layer is responsible for three main functions:

Memorize the three main responsibilities of the network layer.

- Defines logical addresses used at layer-3
- Finds paths, based on the network numbers of logical addresses, to reach destination devices
- Connects different data link types together, such as Ethernet, FDDI, Serial, and Token Ring

The following sections cover the network layer in more depth.

Layer-3 Addressing

Many protocols function at the network layer: AppleTalk, DECnet, IP, IPX, Vines, XNS, and others. Each of these protocols has its own method of defining logical addressing. Correct assignment of these addresses on devices across your network allows you to build a hierarchical design that can scale to very large sizes. This provides an advantage over layer-2 addresses, which use a flat design and are not scalable.

All layer-3 addressing schemes have two components: network and host (or node). Each segment (physical or logical) in your network needs a unique network number. Each host on these segments needs a unique host number from within the assigned network number. The combination of the network and host number assigned to a device provides a unique layer-3 address throughout the entire network. For example, if you had 500 devices in your network that were running IP, each of these devices would need a unique IP layer-3 address.

This process is different with MAC addresses, which are used at layer-2. MAC addresses need to be unique only on a physical (or logical) segment. In other words, within the same broadcast domain, all of the MAC addresses must be unique. However, MAC addresses do *not* need to be unique between two *different* broadcast domains.

To understand the components of layer-3 addresses, let's look at a few examples. TCP/IP addresses are 32 bits in length. To make these addresses more readable, they are broken up into four bytes, or *octets*, where any two bytes are separated by a period. This is commonly referred to as dotted decimal notation. Here's a simple example of an IP address: 10.1.1.1. An additional value, called a *subnet mask*, determines the boundary between the network and host components of an address. When comparing IP addresses to other protocols' addressing schemes, IP is the most complicated. IP addressing is thoroughly covered in Chapter 3.

Most other protocols have a much simpler format. For example, IPX addresses are 80 bits in length. The first 32 bits are always the network number, and the last 48 bits are always the host address. IPX addresses are represented in hexadecimal. Here's an example: ABBA.0000.0000.0001. In this example, ABBA is the network number and 0000.0000.0001 is the host number. Every protocol has its own addressing scheme. However, each scheme always begins with a network component followed by a host component.

Routing Tables

Routers are devices that function at the network layer; they use network numbers to make routing decisions: how to get a packet to its destination. Routers build a *routing table*, which contains path information. This information includes the network number, which interface the router should use to reach the network number, the metric of the path (what it costs to reach the destination), and how the router learned about this network number. Metrics are used to weight the different paths to a destination. If there is more than one way to reach the destination, the metric is used as a tie-breaker. The router will put the best metric paths in its routing table.

There are many different types of metrics, such as bandwidth, delay, and hop count. Each routing protocol uses its own metric structure. For instance, IP RIP uses hop count, while Cisco's EIGRP uses bandwidth, delay, reliability, load, and frame size (MTU). Routing and routing metrics are discussed in Chapters 9, 10, and 11.

Routers make routing decisions based on the network numbers in layer-3 addresses, like IP addresses. Locations of networks are stored in a routing table.

When a router receives an inbound packet, it examines the destination layer-3 address in the packet header. The router then determines what the network number is in the address and then compares this network number to its routing table entries. If the router finds a match, it forwards the packet out of the destination interface. However, if the router does not find a match, the router *drops* the packet. This is unlike bridges and switches at layer 2: with these devices, unknown unicast destinations are flooded, not dropped.

Advantages of Routers

Because routers operate at a higher layer than the data link layer and use logical addressing, they provide many advantages over bridges and switches, including:

- Logical addressing at layer-3 allows you to build hierarchical networks that scale to very large sizes. This is discussed in Chapter 12.
- They contain broadcasts and multicasts. When a broadcast or multicast is received on an interface, it is *not* forwarded to another interface, by default. Routers are used to solve broadcast problems. (Actually, routers also create separate bandwidth and collision domains, but bridges and switches provide a cheaper solution.)
- Routers can typically find a better path to a destination than bridges, since routing protocols support a rich metric structure.
- Routers allow you to connected different media types together, like Ethernet and Token Ring or FDDI and PPP, without any conversion issues.

- Routers can switch packets on the same interface using VLANs. (VLANs are discussed in Chapter 8.)
- Routers have advanced features that allow you to implement Quality of Service using queuing or traffic shaping, filtering traffic using access lists, or protecting traffic using encryption. (Access lists are discussed in Chapter 13.)

Study the preceding bulleted points and know the advantages that routers provide over switches.

By using logical addresses, routers can create a hierarchical network that supports thousands of devices. Bridges and switches, on the other hand, do not support hierarchical addressing: MAC addresses support a flat addressing space. In other words, you can't typically change MAC addresses to fit a specific network layout. Also, since routers use logical addresses, it is much easier to implement policy decisions, such as traffic filtering or quality service, since the decisions are made on logical, more easily handled addresses than the physical addresses that bridges and switches use. For example, since logical addresses support a network component, you could filter an entire network number. To accomplish this with a bridge, you would have to filter each individual device's MAC address within the network segment.

Another problem with layer-2 devices is that they don't operate very well when connecting different media types, Ethernet and Token Ring, for instance. At layer-2, this process is called *translational bridging*. There are many reasons why layer-2 devices have issues translating media types, but the main reason is that since both topologies are layer-2, the bridge has to translate the layer-2 information from the different media types. This is very process-intensive and can create many problems.

For example, Ethernet supports frame sizes up to 1,500 bytes, while Token Ring supports frame sizes up to 16KB in size for 16Mbps speeds. Therefore, if a large Token Ring frame had to be sent to an Ethernet segment, the bridge would have to fragment the information into multiple Ethernet frames. There might also be a speed difference between the media types: Ethernet supports 10Mb while Token Ring supports 4Mbps, 16Mbps, and 100Mbps, and this difference could cause congestion problems on a bridge or switch.

Also, the translation process between frame types is not always easy. For example, some media types order their bits from low-to-high, while others order them high-to-low, which can create translation issues. Fortunately, routers provide a clean solution to this translation process. Routers don't actually translate between different frame or media types; instead, they strip off the layer-2 frame, make a routing decision on the layer-3 packet, and then encapsulate the layer-3 packet in the correct layer-2 frame type for the interface the packet needs to exit. This process is described more thoroughly later in this chapter, in the section "Transferring Information Between Computers."

Another advantage routers have over layer-2 devices is that they contain broadcast problems. When a router receives a broadcast, it processes that broadcast, but by default, it will not forward the broadcast out any of its other ports. This is different from bridges and switches, which flood broadcast traffic. If broadcasts are affecting the bandwidth and performance of your network, you should break up your network into multiple broadcast domains and use a router to route between the different domains. Each broadcast domain in a network needs a unique layer-3 network number.

CERTIFICATION OBJECTIVE 2.04

Transport Layer

The fourth layer of the OSI Reference Model is the transport layer. The transport layer has four main functions:

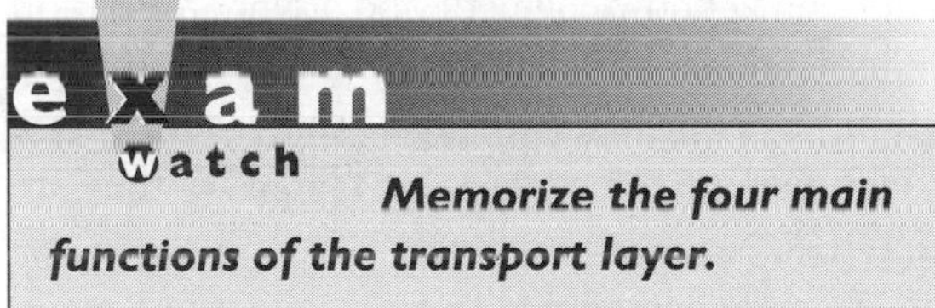

Memorize the four main functions of the transport layer.

- It sets up and maintains a session connection between two devices.
- It can provide for the reliable or unreliable delivery of data across this connection.
- It can implement flow control through ready/not ready signals or windowing to ensure one device doesn't overflow another device with too much data on a connection.
- It multiplexes connections, allowing multiple applications to simultaneously send and receive data.

The following sections cover these processes.

Reliable Connections

The transport layer can provide reliable and unreliable transfer of data between networking devices. TCP/IP's Transmission Control Protocol (TCP) is an example of a transport layer protocol that provides a reliable connection. When implementing a reliable connection, sequence numbers and acknowledgments (ACKs) are used. For example, when information is sent to a destination, the destination will acknowledge to the source what information was received. The destination can examine the sequence numbers to determine if anything was missing, as well as put the data back in the correct order, if it arrived out of order, before passing it on to the upper-layer application. If a segment is missing, the destination can request the source to resend the missing information. With some protocol stacks, the destination might have the source resend all of the information, or parts of the information, including the missing parts.

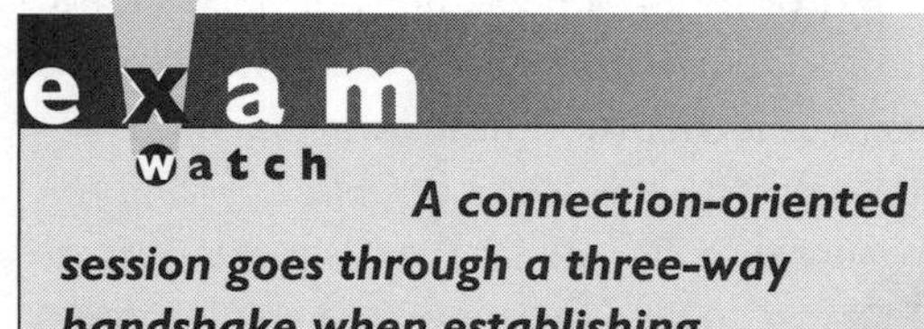

A connection-oriented session goes through a three-way handshake when establishing a session.

With reliable connections, before a device can send information to another device, a handshake process must take place to establish the connection. Figure 2-6 shows the steps involved. Let's assume that this is TCP setting up a reliable IP connection. In this example, PC-A wants to send data reliably to PC-B. Before this can take place, PC-A must set up a reliable connection to PC-B. The two devices go through a *three-way handshake* to establish the connection. Here are the three steps that occur:

1. The source sends a synchronization (SYN) message to the destination, indicating that the source wants to establish a reliable connection.
2. The destination responds with both an acknowledgment and a synchronization message. The acknowledgment indicates the successful receipt of the source's SYN message, and the destination's SYN message indicates that a connection can be set up. Together, these messages are referred to as SYN/ACK; they are sent together in the same data transfer.
3. Upon receiving the SYN/ACK, the source responds with an ACK message. This indicates to the destination that its SYN was received by the source and that the connection is now complete.

Once the three-way handshake has taken place, data can be transferred across the connection. Because the connection was established first, this type of service is referred to as *connection-oriented*. Remember that this type of connection always goes

FIGURE 2-6

Setting up a reliable connection: three-way handshake

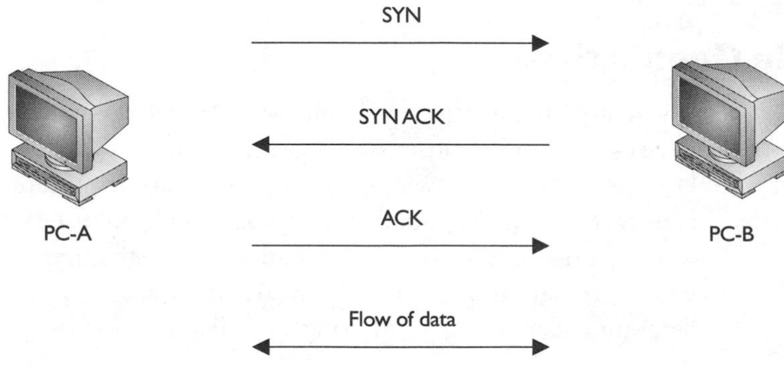

through a three-way handshake before one device can start sending and receiving information from another. Connection-oriented connections provide a reliable service, whereas a connectionless service doesn't.

Unreliable Connections

One of the issues of connection-oriented services is that they must always go through a three-way handshake before you can transfer data. In some instances, like file transfers, this makes sense, because you want to make sure that all data for the file is transferred successfully. However, in other cases, when you want to send only one piece of information and get a reply back, going through the three-way handshake process adds additional overhead that isn't necessary.

A DNS query is a good example where using a connection-oriented service doesn't make sense. With a DNS query, a device is trying to resolve a fully qualified domain name to an IP address. The device sends the single query to a DNS server and waits for the server's response. In this process, only two messages are generated: the client's query and the server's response. Because of the minimal amount of information shared between these two devices, it makes no sense to establish a reliable connection first before sending the query. Instead, the device should just send its information and wait for a response. If a response doesn't come back, the application can send the information again or the user can get involved. Again, with DNS, you can configure two DNS servers in the Microsoft Windows operating system. If you don't get a reply from the first server, the application can use the second configured server.

Because no "connection" is built up front, this type of connection is referred to as a *connectionless* service. The TCP/IP protocol stack uses the User Datagram Protocol (UDP) to provide unreliable connections.

Connection Multiplexing

Another function of the transport layer is to set up and maintain connections for the session layer. The information transferred to devices at the transport layer is called a *segment*. Because multiple connections may be established from one device to another device or devices, some type of multiplexing function is needed to differentiate between the various connections. This ensures that the transport layer can send data from a particular application to the correct destination and, when receiving data from a destination, get it to the right application.

To accomplish this feat, the transport layer assigns a unique set of numbers for each connection. These numbers are called *port* or *socket* numbers. There is a source port number and a destination port number for each connection. The destination port numbers assigned by the source device are referred to as well-known port numbers.

The source device uses an appropriate port number in the destination port field to indicate to the destination which application it is trying to access. For example, the TCP/IP protocol stack gives each application a unique port number.

Here are some well-known port numbers used by TCP/IP applications: FTP (20 and 21), telnet (23), SMTP—e-mail (25), DNS (53), TFTP (69), WWW (80), and POP mail (110). With TCP/IP, port numbers from 0–1,023 are well-known port numbers. However, some applications have port numbers higher than these numbers. Actually, TCP/IP uses a 16-bit field for the port number, allowing you to reference up to 65,536 different numbers. Port numbers above 1,023 are used by the source to assign to the connection. Each connection on the source has a unique source port number. This helps the source device differentiate its own connections.

Let's look at an example, shown in Figure 2-7, that uses TCP for multiplexing connections. In this example, PC-A has two telnet connections between itself and the server. You can tell these are telnet connections by examining the destination port number (23). When the destination receives the connection setup request, it knows that the process it should start up is telnet. Also notice that the source port number is *different* for each of these connections (2,000 and 2,001). This allows both the PC and the server to differentiate between the two separate telnet connections. This is a simple example of multiplexing connections.

Of course, if more than one device is involved, things become more complicated. In the example shown in Figure 2-7, PC-B also has a connection to the server. This

FIGURE 2-7

Multiplexing connections

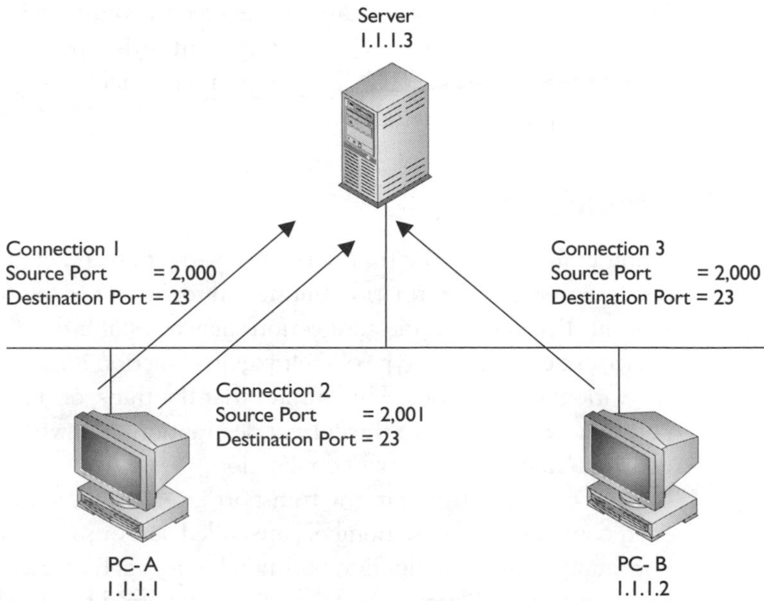

connection has a source port number of 2,000 and a destination port number of 23—another telnet connection. This brings up an interesting dilemma. How does the server differentiate between PC-A's connection that has port numbers 2,000/23 and PC-B's, which has the same? Actually, the server uses not only the port numbers at the transport layer to multiplex connections, but also the *layer-3* addresses of the devices connected to these connections. In this example, notice that PC-A and PC-B have *different* layer-3 addresses: 1.1.1.1 and 1.1.1.2 respectively.

exam watch ***The transport layer uses source and destination port numbers and layer-3 addresses to perform multiplexing of connections.***

As you can see from this example, no matter where the connections are coming from, or how many connections a device has to deal with, the device can easily differentiate between the connections by examining the source and destination port numbers as well as the layer-3 addresses.

Flow Control

Another function of the transport layer is to provide optional flow control. Flow control is used to ensure that networking devices don't send too much information to the destination, overflowing its receiving buffer space, and causing it to drop the sent information. Overflow is not good because the source will have to resend all of the information that was dropped. The transport layer can use two basic flow control methods:

exam watch ***The purpose of flow control is to ensure the destination doesn't get overrun by too much information sent by the source.***

- Ready/not ready signals
- Windowing

Reading/Not Ready Signals

With *ready/not ready signals*, when the destination receives more traffic than it can handle, it can send a *not ready* signal to the source, indicating that the source should stop transmitting data. When the destination has a chance to catch up and process the source's information, the destination responds back with a *ready* signal. Upon receiving the ready signal, the source can resume the sending of data.

There are two problems with the use of ready/not ready signals to implement flow control. First, the destination may respond to the source with a not ready signal when its buffer fills up. While this message is on its way to the source, the source is *still sending* information to the destination, which the destination will probably have to drop because its buffer space is full. The second problem with the use of these signals is that once the destination is ready to receive more information, it must first send a ready signal to the source, which must receive it before more information can be sent. This causes a delay in the transfer of information. Because of these two inefficiencies with ready/not ready signals, they are not commonly used to implement flow control.

Windowing

Windowing is a much more sophisticated method of flow control than using ready/not ready signals. With windowing, a window size is defined that specifies how many pieces of information can be sent before the source has to wait for an acknowledgment (ACK) from the destination. Once the ACK is received, the source can send the next batch of information (up to the maximum defined in the window size).

Windowing accomplishes two things. First, flow control is enforced, based on the window size. In many implementations, the window size is dynamically negotiated up front and can be renegotiated during the lifetime of the connection. This ensures that the most optimal window size is used to send information without having the destination drop anything. Second, through the windowing process, the destination tells the source what was received. This indicates to the source if any information was lost along the way to the destination and allows the source to resend any missing information. This provides reliability for a connection as well as better efficiency than ready/not ready signals provide. Because of these advantages, most connection-oriented transport protocols, like TCP/IP's TCP, use windowing to implement flow control.

The window size chosen for a connection impacts its efficiency and throughput in defining how many segments (or bytes) can be sent before the source has to wait for an acknowledgment. Figure 2-8 illustrates the importance of the size used for the window.

The top part of the figure shows the connection using a window size of 1. In this instance, the source sends one segment with a sequence number (in this case 1) and then waits for an acknowledgment from the destination. Depending on the transport protocol, there are different ways the destination can send the acknowledgment: it can send back a list of the sequence numbers of the segments it received, or it can send back the sequence number of the next segment it expects. The acknowledgment from the destination has a number 2 in it. This tells the source that it can go ahead and send Segment2. Again, when the destination receives this segment, since the

FIGURE 2-8

Window sizes affect efficiency.

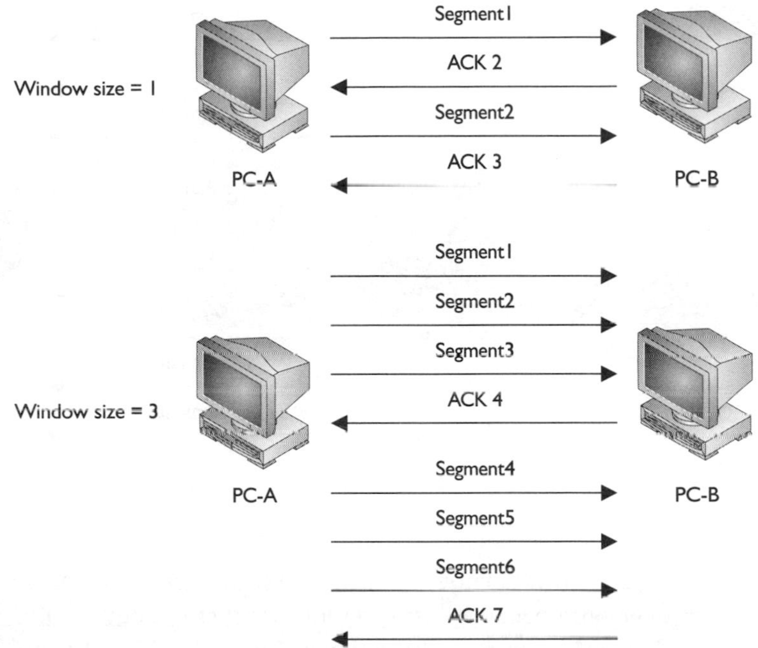

window size is 1, the destination will immediately reply with an acknowledgment, indicating the receipt of this segment. In this example, the destination acknowledges back 3, indicating that Segment3 can be sent.

As you can see, with a window size of 1, the flow control process is not very quick or very efficient. Let's look at an example where the window size is 3, as is illustrated at the bottom of Figure 2-8. With a window size of 3, the source can send three segments. Once they are sent (each with its own unique sequence number: 1, 2, and 3), the source must wait for an acknowledgment. In this instance, the destination sends an acknowledgment back with the number 4 in it, indicating that the fourth segment is expected next. The source can then proceed to send Segments4, 5, and 6 and then wait for the destination's acknowledgment. In this instance, having a larger window size is more efficient: only one acknowledgment is required for every three segments that are sent. Therefore, the larger the window size, the more efficient the transfer of information becomes.

However, this is not always the case. For example, let's assume that one segment gets lost on its way to the destination, as is shown in Figure 2-9. In this example, the window size is 3. PC-A sends its first three segments, which are successfully received by PC-B. PC-B acknowledges the next segment it expects, which is 4. When PC-A

FIGURE 2-9

Lost segments and retransmissions

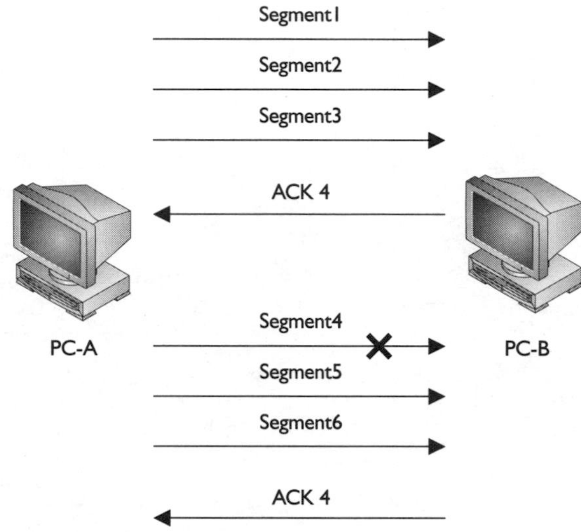

receives this acknowledgment, it sends Segments4, 5, and 6. For some reason, Segment4 becomes lost and never reaches the destination, but Segments5 and 6 do. Remember that the destination is keeping track of what was received: 1, 2, 3, 5, and 6. In this example, the destination sends back an acknowledgment of 4, indicating that Segment4 is expected next.

At this point, how PC-A reacts depends on the transport layer protocol that is used. Here are some possible options:

- PC-A understands that only Segment4 was lost and therefore resends Segment4. It then sends Segments7 and 8, filling up the window size.
- PC-A doesn't understand what was or wasn't received, so it sends three segments starting at Segment4, indicated by PC-B.

Of course, if two segments are lost, the first option listed won't work unless the destination can send a list of lost segments. Therefore, most protocol stacks that use windowing will implement the second option. Given this behavior, the size of the window will really affect your performance. You would normally think that a window size of 100 is very efficient; however, if the very first packet is lost, some protocols will have *all* 100 packets resent! As mentioned earlier, most protocol stacks use a window size that is negotiated up front and can be renegotiated at any time. Therefore, if a connection is experiencing a high number of errors, the window size can be dropped to a smaller value to increase your efficiency. And once these errors disappear or drop down to a lower rate, the window size can be increased to maximize your throughput.

What makes this situation even more complicated is that the window sizes on the source and destination devices can be *different*. For instance, PC-A might have a window size of 3, while PC-B has a window size of 10. In this example, PC-A is allowed to send ten segments to PC-B before waiting for an acknowledgment, while PC-B is allowed to send only three segments to PC-A.

Flow control through the use of sequence numbers and acknowledgments is covered in more depth in Chapter 3, where TCP is discussed.

Ready/not ready signals and windowing are used to implement flow control. Ready/not ready signals are not efficient, causing drops in unnecessary traffic and delays in the transmission of traffic. Windowing addresses these issues. With windowing, a window size is established, which defines the number of segments that can be transferred before waiting for an acknowledgment from the destination.

CERTIFICATION OBJECTIVE 2.05

Transferring Information Between Computers

Before delving into the mechanics of how information is transferred between computers, you must grow familiar with the terminology used to describe the transmitted data. Many of the layers of the OSI Reference Model use their own specific terms to describe data transferred back and forth. As this information is passed from higher to lower layers, each layer adds information to the original data—typically a header and possibly a trailer. This process is called *encapsulation*.

Generically speaking, the term *protocol data unit (PDU)* is used to describe data and its overhead. Table 2-13 describes the terms used at the various layers of the OSI Reference Model. For instance, as data is passed from the session layer to the transport layer, the transport layer *encapsulates* the data PDU in a transport layer segment. For TCP and UDP in the TCP/IP protocol stack, the transport layer only adds a header. As the PDU information is passed down, each layer adds its own header and, possibly, trailer.

TABLE 2-13 PDU Terms

Term	OSI Reference Model Layer
Data	Application, presentation, and session layers
Segment	Transport layer
Packet	Network layer (TCP/IP calls this a *datagram*)
Frame	Data link layer
Bits	Physical layer

It is vital to know the information given in certain tables in this chapter. Pay particular attention to Tables 2-3, 2-4, 2-9, and 2-13.

Once the physical layer is reached, the bits of the data link layer frame are converted into a physical layer signal—a voltage, light source, radio wave, or other source according to the type of physical medium that is employed. When the destination receives the information, it goes through a reverse process of *de-encapsulating* information—basically stripping off the headers of the PDU information at each layer as the information is passed up from layer to layer of the OSI Reference Model.

Figure 2-10 shows an example of the process used for encapsulating and de-encapsulating PDUs as data is passed down and back up the OSI Reference Model. In this example, you can see how the application, presentation, and session layers create the data PDU. As this information is passed down from layer to layer, each layer adds its own header.

The next few sections are to help you better understand the process that devices go through as information is transmitted between computers. The next section covers the details as to how information is encapsulated and sent down the protocol stack and then placed on the wire to the destination. The section following that covers the reverse process: how the information is de-encapsulated at the destination and delivered to the application at the application layer. The third section looks at a more complex environment, where bridges, routers, and hubs are involved in the communication process to get information from the source to the destination.

Going Down the Protocol Stack

This section covers the basic mechanics as to how information is processed as it is sent down the protocol stack on a computer. I'll use the diagram shown in Figure 2-10 to illustrate this process as PC-A sends information to PC-B. In this example, assume that the data link layer is Ethernet and the physical layer is copper.

FIGURE 2-10

Encapsulation and de-encapsulation process

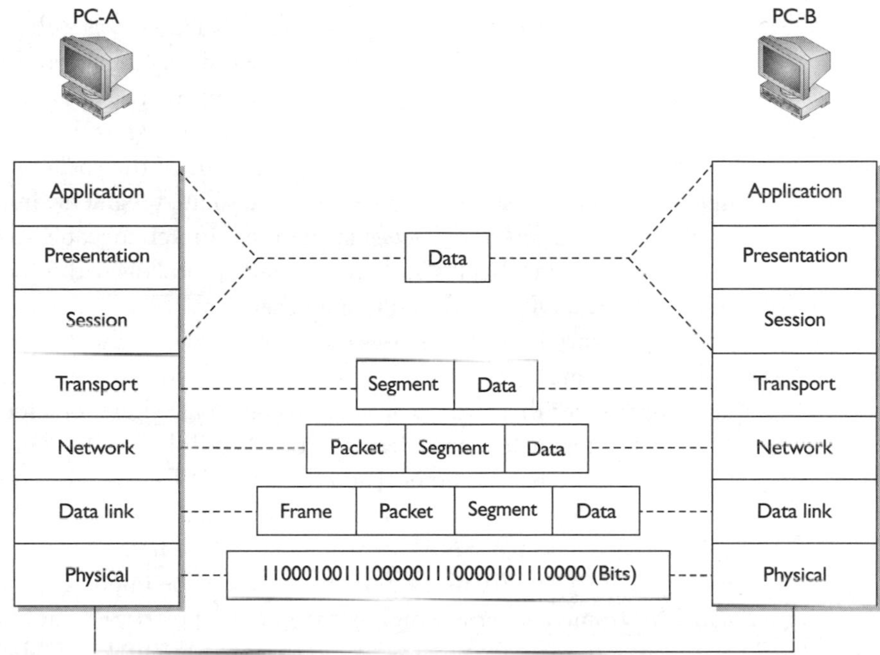

The first thing that occurs on PC-A is that the user, sitting in front of the computer, creates some type of information, called *data*, and then sends it to another location (PC-B). This includes the actual user input (application layer), as well as any formatting information (presentation layer). The application (or operating system), at the session layer, then determines whether or not the data's intended destination is local to this computer (possibly a disk drive) or a remote location. In this instance, the user is sending the information to PC-B. We'll assume that the user is executing a telnet connection.

The session layer determines that this location is remote and has the transport layer deliver the information. A telnet connection uses TCP/IP and reliable connections (TCP) at the transport layer, which encapsulates the data from the higher layers into a *segment*. With TCP, as you will see in Chapter 3, only a header is added. The segment contains such information as the source and destination port numbers. As you may recall from the section "Connection Multiplexing", the source port is a number above 1,023 that is currently not being used by PC-A. The destination port number is the well-known port number (23) that the destination will understand and forward to the correct application.

The transport layer passes the segment down to the network layer, which encapsulates the segment into a *packet*. The packet header contains layer-3 logical addressing information (source and destination address), as well as other information, such as the upper-layer protocol that created this information. In this example, TCP created this information, so this fact is noted in the packet, and PC-A places its IP address as the source address in the packet and PC-B's as the destination. This helps the destination, at the network layer, to determine if the packet is for itself and which upper-layer process should handle the encapsulated segment. In the TCP/IP protocol stack, the terms *packet* and *datagram* are used interchangeably to describe this PDU. As you will see in Chapter 3, there are many protocols within the TCP/IP protocol stack—TCP, UDP, ICMP, OSPF, and others.

The network layer then passes the packet down to the data link layer. The data link layer encapsulates the packet into a *frame*. If you are using IEEE for the data link layer, remember that two encapsulations take place here: one for LLC and one for MAC. This example uses Ethernet as the data link layer medium, and there are two versions of Ethernet: Ethernet II and IEEE 802.3. To make this more complex, assume the data link layer is based on IEEE's Ethernet implementation. At the LLC sublayer, either an 802.2 SAP or SNAP frame is used. (These frame types were shown previously in Figure 2-4.) TCP/IP uses a SAP frame type. The important information placed in the SAP frame header is which network layer protocol created the packet: IP. The 802.2 SAP frame is then passed down to the MAC sublayer, where the 802.2 frame is encapsulated in an 802.3 frame. The important components placed in the 802.3 frame header are the source and destination MAC addresses. In this example, PC-A places its MAC address in the frame in the source field and PC-B's MAC address as the destination.

The data link layer frame is then passed down to the physical layer. At this point, remember that the concept of "PDUs" is a human concept that we have placed on the data to make it more readable to us, as well as to help deliver the information to the destination. However, from a computer's perspective, the data is just a bunch of 1's and 0's, called *bits*. The physical layer takes these bits and coverts them into a physical property based on the cable or connection type. In this example, the cable is a copper cable, so the physical layer will convert the bits into voltages: one voltage level for a bit value of 1 and a different voltage level for a 0.

Going Up the Protocol Stack

For sake of simplicity, assume PC-A and PC-B are on the same piece of copper. Once the destination receives the physical layer signals, the physical layer translates the voltage levels back to their binary representation and passes these bit values up to the data link layer.

The data link layer takes the bit values and reassembles the original 802.3 frame. The NIC, at the MAC layer, examines the FCS to make sure the frame is valid and examines the destination MAC address to ensure that the Ethernet frame is meant for itself. If the destination MAC address doesn't match its own MAC address, or is not a multicast or broadcast address, the NIC drops the frame. Otherwise, the NIC processes the frame: it strips off the 802.3 frame and passes the 802.2 frame up to the LLC sublayer. The LLC sublayer examines the SAP value to determine which upper-layer protocol at the network layer should process the encapsulated packet. In this case, the LLC sees that the encapsulated packet is a TCP/IP packet, so it strips off (de-encapsulates) the LLC frame information and passes the packet up to the TCP/IP protocol stack at the network layer. If this were an encapsulated IPX packet, the LLC would pass the encapsulated IPX packet up to the IPX protocol stack at the network layer.

The network layer then examines the logical destination address in the packet header. If the destination logical address doesn't match its own address or is not a multicast or broadcast address, the network layer drops the packet. If the logical address matches, then the destination examines the protocol information in the packet header to determine which protocol should handle the packet. In this example, the logical address matches and the protocol is defined as TCP. Therefore, the network layer strips off the packet information and passes the encapsulated segment up to the TCP protocol at the transport layer.

Upon receiving the segment, the transport layer protocol can perform many functions, depending on whether this is a reliable or unreliable connection. I'll just focus on the multiplexing function of the transport layer. In this instance, the transport layer examines the destination port number in the segment header. In our example, the user from PC-A was using telnet to transmit information to PC-B, so the destination port number is 23. The transport layer examines this port number and realizes that the encapsulated data needs to be forwarded to a telnet application. If PC-B doesn't support telnet, the transport layer drops the segment. If it does, the transport layer strips off the segment information and passes the encapsulated data to

exam watch

Be familiar with the process of going down (encapsulation) and back up (de-encapsulation) the protocol stack when transferring data between devices, including when the transfer occurs between devices separated by a switch or a router (described in the next section).

the telnet application. If this is a new connection, a new telnet process is started up by the operating system.

Note that a logical communication takes place between two layers of two devices. For instance, a logical communication occurs at the transport layer between PC-A and PC-B, and this is also true at the network and data link layers.

Two Segment Example

As you can see from the encapsulation and de-encapsulation process, *many* things are occurring on both the source and destination computers to transmit and receive the information. This can become even more complicated if the source and destination are on different segments, separated by other networking devices, such as hubs, bridges, and routers. Figure 2-11 shows an example of this process.

In this example, PC-A wants to send data to PC-B. Notice that each device needs to process information at specific layers. For instance, once PC-A places its information on the wire, the bridge connected to PC-A needs to process this information. Recall from the section "Data Link Layer" of this chapter that bridges function at layer-2 of the OSI Reference Model, making switching decisions based on the destination MAC address found in the frame. Therefore, the bridge's physical layer will have to convert the physical layer signal into bits and pass these bits up to the data link layer, where they are reassembled into a frame. The bridge examines the destination MAC address and makes a switching decision, finding the port the frame needs to exit. It then passes the frame down to the physical layer, where the bits of the frame are converted into physical layer signals.

The next device the physical layers encounter is a router. Recall from the section "Network Layer" of this chapter that routers function at layer-3 of the OSI Reference Model. The router first converts the physical layer signals into bits at the physical layer. The bits are passed up to the data link layer and reassembled into a frame. The router then examines the destination MAC address in the frame. If the MAC address doesn't match its own MAC address, the router drops the frame. If the MAC address matches, the router strips off the data link layer frame and passes the packet up to the network layer.

At the network layer, one of the functions of the router is to route packets to destinations. To accomplish this, the router examines the destination logical address in the packet and extracts a network number from this address. The router then compares the network number to entries in its routing table. If the router doesn't find a match, it drops the packet; if it does find one, the it forwards the packet out the destination interface.

FIGURE 2-11 Multi-segment communications

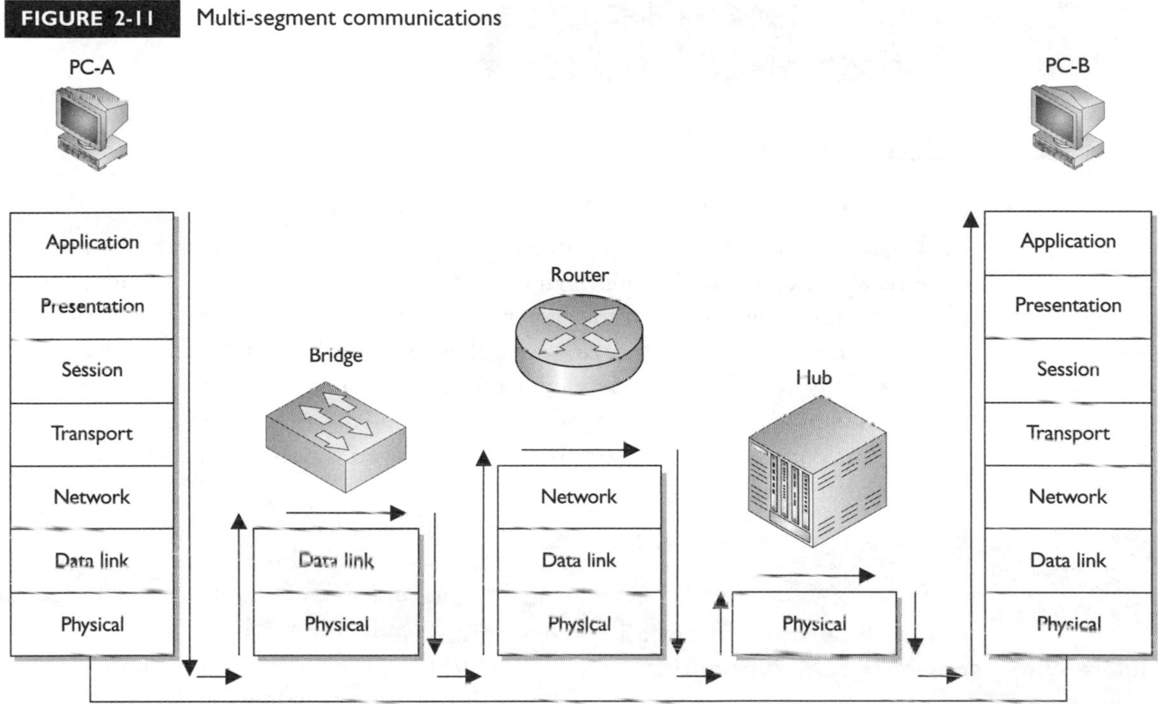

To accomplish this, the router passes the packet down to the data link layer, which encapsulates the packet into the correct data link layer frame format. If this were an Ethernet frame, for this example, the source MAC address would be that of the router and the destination would be PC-B. At the data link layer, the frame is then passed down to the physical layer, where the bits are converted into physical layer signals.

Note that routers separate physical or logical segments, while bridges (and switches) don't. Therefore, if PC-A wants to send traffic to PC-B, PC-A uses the router's MAC (or layer-2) address to get traffic to the exit point of the segment, but it uses PC-B's logical (or layer-3) address to tell the router that this traffic is not for itself but for a machine on a different segment. This process is discussed in more depth in Chapter 3.

The next device that receives these physical layer signals is the hub. Recall from the section "OSI Reference Model" that hubs and repeaters operate at the physical layer. Basically, a hub is a multiport repeater: it repeats any physical layer signal it receives. Therefore, a signal received on one interface of a hub is repeated on all of its other interfaces. These signals are then received by PC-B, which passes this information up the protocol stack as described in the preceding section.

CERTIFICATION OBJECTIVE 2.06

Hierarchical Network Model

Cisco has developed a three-layer hierarchical model to help you design campus networks. Cisco uses this model to simplify designing, implementing, and managing large-scale networks. With traditional network designs, it was common practice to place the networking services at the center of the network and the users at the periphery. However, many things in networking have changed over the past decade, including advancements in applications, developments in graphical user interfaces (GUIs), the proliferation of multimedia applications, the explosion of the Internet, and fast-paced changes in your users' traffic patterns. Cisco developed the three-layer model to accommodate these rapid changes.

The three layers in Cisco's hierarchical design are core, distribution, and access.

Cisco's hierarchical model, shown in Figure 2-12, contains three layers: core, distribution, and access. A well-designed network typically follows this topology. The following sections cover the functions of the three layers, including the devices that function at the various layers.

Core Layer

The *core* layer, as its name suggests, is the backbone of the network. It provides a high speed connection between the different distribution layer devices. Because of the need for high-speed connections, the core consists of high-speed *switches* and will not, typically, perform any type of packet or frame manipulations, such as filtering or Quality of Service. Because switches are used at the core, the core is referred to as a layer-2 core. The traffic that traverses the core is typically to access enterprise corporate resources: connections to the Internet, gateways, e-mail servers, and corporate applications.

The core provides a high-speed layer-2 switching infrastructure and typically does not manipulate packet contents.

FIGURE 2-12

Cisco's hierarchical model

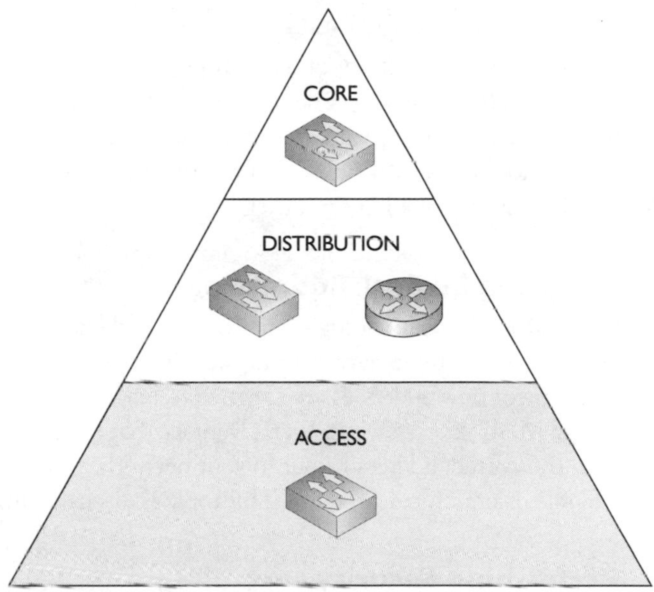

Distribution Layer

Of the three layers, the *distribution* layer performs most of the connectivity tasks. In larger networks, routers are used at the distribution layer to connect the access layers to the core. For smaller networks, sometimes switches are used. The responsibilities of the distribution layer include the following:

- Containing broadcasts between the layers
- Securing traffic between the layers
- Providing a hierarchy through layer-3 logical addressing and route summarization
- Translating between different media types

As mentioned in the section "Network Layer," routers give you by far the most flexibility in enforcing your company's networking policies, since routers deal with logical addresses. And because routers are used at the distribution layer, the implementation of your policies, at least most of them, is done here.

Containing Broadcasts

One of the main functions of the distribution layer is to contain broadcast and multicast traffic that the access layer devices create. If a broadcast storm is created in one access layer, or there is a large amount of multicast traffic from a real-time video stream, the distribution layer, by default, confines this traffic in the access layer and thus prevents it from creating problems in other areas.

Providing Logical Addressing

Routers also provide for logical addressing of devices in your network. This makes it much easier to implement your networking policies, including filtering and QoS since you control how addresses are assigned to machines: it is very difficult to do this with layer-2 MAC addresses. Another advantage that logical addressing provides is that, again, with the correct address layout in your network, you should be able to create a highly scalable, hierarchical network. This topic is discussed in Chapter 12.

Performing Security

Another function of this layer is to enforce your security policies. Because switches are used at the core and access layers, security is not typically implemented at these layers, given the issues of filtering MAC addresses. Since routers deal with logical addresses, however, they make it much easier to implement your policies. In Chapter 13, you'll see how you can use access lists to implement your security policies.

Connecting Different Media Types

If you have two different media types that you want to connect, Token Ring and Ethernet, for instance, a router is the best solution; and since routers are used at the distribution layer, this is where this conversion takes place. As mentioned in the section "Data Link Layer," bridges are not very good at performing translations between different media types. However, routers do not have this problem, as you saw in the section *Two Segment Example*. Routers don't translate between media types. Instead, they perform a de-encapsulation and encapsulation process. From layer-2, the router strips off the frame and passes up the packet to layer-3. At layer-3, the router makes its routing decision and queues the packet on the outbound interface. Once again, at layer-2, the packet is encapsulated in the frame type for the corresponding media type the interface is connected to.

The distribution layer provides a boundary between the access and core layers. It contains routers and switches. Routers are used to provide the logical boundary--broadcasts are contained within the access layer and filtering policies can be implemented to restrict traffic flows.

Access Layer

The bottom layer of the three-layer hierarchical model is the *access* layer. Actually, the access layer is at the periphery of your campus network, separated from the core layer by the distribution layer. The main function of the access layer is to provide the user's initial connection to your network. Typically, this connection is provided by a switch, or sometimes, a hub. Sometimes if the user works at a small branch office or home office, this device can also be a router. But in most cases, the connection is provided by a switch.

The access layer provides the user's initial access to the network, which is typically via switches or hubs.

Connections

Remember that the three-layer hierarchical model is a logical, not a physical, representation. For example, sometimes the distribution layer device might contain both switches and routers. You might, say, use a Catalyst 5000 switch with a route switch module (RSM) in its chassis—this combination of devices can provide both layer-2 and layer-3 functionality at the distribution layer. This kind of setup is common at the distribution layer: sometimes the routing function sits inside the chassis of the switch, like the MSM card for a Catalyst 6000 switch, and sometimes the routing function is in a separate chassis, like a 3600 series router. No matter what configuration is used, it is important that you configure the layer-3 device correctly to create a boundary between the access and core layer devices. The switching function that can be provided by the distribution layer is used to connect departmental services that the access layer devices commonly access.

Remember that, since this is a hierarchical model, connections should always be made in the upward direction: access-to-distribution and distribution-to-core. You should never cross-connect layers: access-to-access or distribution-to-distribution. If you do this, you'll be creating a non-scalable flat network. Cisco's CCDA, BCMSN, and ARCH exams cover this process in more depth.

CERTIFICATION SUMMARY

The OSI Reference Model defines the process of connecting two layers of networking functions. The application layer provides the user's interface. The presentation layer determines how data is represented to the user. The session layer is responsible for setting up and tearing down connections. The transport layer is responsible for the mechanics of connections, including guaranteed services. The network layer provides a logical topology and layer-3 addresses: routers operate here. The data link layer defines MAC addresses and how communication is performed on a specific media type: switches, bridges, and NICs operate here. The physical layer defines physical properties for connections and communication: repeaters and hubs operate here. Wireless solutions are defined at the physical layer. The 802.11 services define wireless access. Wi-Fi is defined by 802.11b.

The data link layer defines hardware addressing. MAC addresses are 48 bits in length in hexadecimal. The first 24 bits (6 digits) are the OUI. MAC addresses only need to be unique on a logical segment. A unicast is where one frame is sent to a single device. A multicast is where one frame is sent to a group of devices. A broadcast is where one frame is sent to all devices.

CSMA/CD is used to implement Ethernet. Ethernet is a shared medium. When a device wants to transmit, it must first listen to the wire to determine if a transmission is already occurring. If two devices try to simultaneously send their transmissions, a collision occurs. When this happens, a jam signal is created and the two devices back off a random period before trying again. There are two versions of Ethernet: IEEE 802.2/3 and Ethernet II (or DIX). 802.2 defines the LLC (software) and 802.3 defines the MAC (hardware). 802.2 uses a SAP or SNAP field to designate the layer-3 encapsulated protocol. Ethernet II doesn't have any sublayers and doesn't have a length field; instead, it has a type field.

Half-duplex connections allow a device to either send or receive at a time, while full-duplex allow simultaneous sending and receiving. Full-duplex require a point-to-point connection.

The three main functions of a bridge and switch is to learn where devices are located, forward traffic using their port address table, and remove loops using STP. Unknown unicast addresses, broadcasts, and multicasts are flooded by a bridge and switch. Bridges and switches are used to solve bandwidth and collision problems.

The network layer defines logical addresses, finds paths to destinations based on the network component of the address, and connect different layer-2 media types together. Routers are used to contain broadcasts. Routers use their routing table, which has a list of destination network numbers, to assist them when finding a destination. If a destination is not found in the routing table, traffic for this destination is dropped.

The transport layer sets up and maintains a session layer connection, provides for reliable or unreliable delivery of data, flow control, and multiplexing of connections. Reliable connections go through a three-way handshake to establish a connection: SYN, SYN/ACK, and ACK. Acknowledgments are used to provide reliable delivery. Port or socket numbers are used for connection multiplexing. Ready/not ready signals and windowing are used to implement flow control. Windowing is more efficient than ready/not ready signals.

A PDU describes data and its overhead. A PDU at the application layer is referred to as data; the transport layer PDU is called a segment, the network layer PDU is called a packet or datagram, the data link layer PDU is called a frame, and the physical layer PDU is called bits. As traffic goes down the protocol stack, each layer encapsulates the PDU from the layer above it. At the destination, a de-encapsulation process occurs.

Cisco uses a hierarchical model to help with designing networks. The core layer provides a high-speed layer-2 infrastructure and typically doesn't manipulate packet contents. The distribution layer separates the access and core layers, typically through a layer-3 process. It uses routers and switches. The access layer provides a user's initial connection to the network, typically done by a switch.

TWO-MINUTE DRILL

OSI Reference Model

- The OSI Reference Model provides the following advantages: it promotes interoperability, defines how to connect adjacent layers, compartmentalizes components, allows a modular design, serves as a teaching tool, and simplifies troubleshooting.
- The application layer (7) provides the user interface. The presentation layer (6) defines how information is presented to the user. The session layer (5) determines if a network connection is needed and initiates the setup and teardown of connections. The transport layer (4) handles the mechanics of reliable or unreliable services. The network layer (3) creates a logical topology with logical addresses. Routers function at this layer. The data link layer (2) assigns physical (MAC) addresses and defines how devices on a specific media type communicate with each other. Bridges, switches, and NICs operate at this layer. The physical layer (1) handles all physical properties for a connection. Hubs and repeaters function here.

Data Link Layer

- The data link layer defines MAC addresses, the physical or hardware topology, and the framing used; it provides for connection-oriented and connectionless services.
- MAC addresses are 48 bits in length and are represented in hexadecimal. The first six digits are the OUI (vendor code), and the last six digits represent the NIC within the OUI.
- A unicast is sent to one destination on a segment, a multicast is sent to a group of devices, and a broadcast (FFFF.FFFF.FFFF) is sent to all devices.
- Ethernet uses Carrier Sense Multiple Access/Collision Detection (CSMA/CD) for its operations—a collision is when two devices try to send a frame at the same time. There are two versions of Ethernet: DIX (Ethernet II) and IEEE 802.3. Ethernet II has a type field, and IEEE 802.3 has a length field. IEEE breaks the data link layer into two components: LLC (software, 802.2) and MAC (hardware, 802.3). LLC has two frame types: SAP and SNAP (the SAP fields are set to AA).

- ❑ Ethernet uses a bus topology (physical or logical). 10BaseT has a 100 m distance limitation, 10Base5 reaches 500 m, 10Base2, 185 m, 100BaseFX half, 400 m and full, 2 km.
- ❑ Bridges have three functions: learn where devices are located, make intelligent forwarding decisions, and remove layer-2 loops with STP. Bridges place address information in a port address table. Bridges solve bandwidth and collision problems.

Network Layer

- ❑ This layer defines logical addresses, finds paths to destinations using the network number in the logical address, and connects different media types together.
- ❑ Routers function at the network layer. A routing table contains information about destination network numbers and how to reach them. Routers contain broadcasts, allow for scalability through hierarchical designs, make better decisions to reach a destination than bridges, can switch packets on the same interface using VLANs, and can implement advanced features such as QoS and filtering.

Transport Layer

- ❑ The transport layer sets up and maintains a session connection, provides for reliable or unreliable transport of data, implements flow control, and multiplexes connections.
- ❑ Reliable connections use sequence numbers and acknowledgments. TCP is an example. TCP uses a three-way handshake to set up a connection: SYN, SYN/ACK, and ACK. Unreliable services don't use a connection setup process. UDP is an example.
- ❑ Multiplexing of connections is done with port or socket numbers.
- ❑ Flow control can be implemented with ready/not ready signals or windowing. Windowing is more efficient. The size of the window affects your throughput. Depending on the size, a source can send X segments before having to wait for an acknowledgment.

Transferring Information Between Computers

- ❑ A protocol data unit (PDU) describes data and its overhead. As data is sent down the protocol stack, it is encapsulated at each layer by additional information. The destination de-encapsulates the data as it goes back up the protocol stack.
- ❑ The transport layer PDU is a segment, the network layer PDU is a packet or datagram, the data link layer PDU is a frame, and the physical layer PDU is bits.

Hierarchical Network Model

- ❑ There are three layers of the Cisco hierarchical model: core, distribution, and access. This model is used to design highly scalable networks. It is recommended that connections always be made upward and not across: access-to-distribution and distribution-to-core are acceptable connections.
- ❑ The core layer, the backbone of the network, provides high-speed connections between the different distribution layers. It is typically composed of switches. The distribution layer contains broadcasts, secures traffic, and provides a hierarchy with layer-3 addressing and route summarization. It consists of routers and/or switches. The access layer provides the user's initial connection to the network. Typically switches are used, but hubs and routers can also be used.

SELF TEST

The following Self Test questions will help you measure your understanding of the material presented in this chapter. Read all the choices carefully, as there may be more than one correct answer. Choose all correct answers for each question.

OSI Reference Model

1. Put the following in the correct order, from high to low: session (a), presentation (b), physical (c), data link (d), network (e), application (f), transport (g).

A. c, d, e, g, a, b, f
B. f, a, b, g, d, e, c
C. f, b, g, a, e, d, c
D. f, b, a, g, e, d, c

2. Which of the following standards or protocols are used by the session layer?

A. JPEG
B. NFS
C. TCP
D. Ethernet

3. The ________ layer provides for hardware addressing.

A. Transport
B. Network
C. Data link
D. Physical

Data Link Layer

4. MAC addresses are _________ bits in length and are represented in a ___________ format.

5. CSMA/CD stands for ________.

A. Collision Sense Multiple Access/Carrier Detection
B. Carrier Sense Multiple Access/Collision Detection
C. Collision Sense Media Access/Carrier Detection
D. Carrier Sense Media Access/Collision Detection

6. Ethernet ________ uses a type field.
   A. II
   B. 802.3
   C. 802.2
7. Which component of the data link layer for IEEE specifies network protocols?
   A. LLC
   B. MAC
   C. 802.5
   D. 802.3

Network Layer

8. The network layer solves all of the following problems except __________.
   A. Broadcast problems
   B. Conversion between media types
   C. Hierarchy through the use of physical addresses
   D. Collision problems
9. If a router has a packet it needs to route, and it can't find the destination network number in the routing table, the router ________ the packet.
   A. Drops
   B. Floods

Transport Layer

10. ________ are used to provide a reliable connection.
    A. Ready/not ready signals
    B. Sequence numbers and acknowledgments
    C. Windows
    D. Ready/not ready signals and windowing
11. Connection multiplexing is done through the use of a ________ number.
    A. Socket
    B. Hardware
    C. Network

D. Session

12. Reliable connections go through a three-way handshake. Place the following in the correct order: ACK (1), SYN, (2), SYN/ACK (3).

A. 2, 1, 3
B. 3, 2, 1
C. 2, 3, 1
D. 1, 2, 3

Transferring Information Between Computers

13. The network layer transmits ________ PDUs.

A. Datagram
B. Segment
C. Bits
D. Frame

Hierarchical Network Design

14. The ________ layer uses high-speed switches to provide high-speed connections.

A. Core
B. Access
C. Distribution

15. The ________ layer contains broadcasts.

A. Core
B. Access
C. Distribution

SELF TEST ANSWERS

OSI Reference Model

1. ☑ **D.** From high to low, the OSI Reference Model has the following layers: application, presentation, session, transport, network, data link, and physical.
   ☒ **A** doesn't begin with the application layer. **B**'s second from the top layer is presentation. **D** switches the session and transport layers.

2. ☑ **B.** NFS is a session layer protocol.
   ☒ **A** is a presentation layer standard. **C** is a transport layer protocol. **D** is a data link layer standard.

3. ☑ **C.** The data link layer provides for hardware addressing.
   ☒ **A** uses port numbers for multiplexing. **B** defines logical addressing. **D** doesn't have any addressing.

Data Link Layer

4. MAC addresses are 48 bits in length and are represented in a hexadecimal format.

5. ☑ **B.** CSMA/CD stands for Carrier Sense Multiple Access/Collision Detection. It defines how Ethernet functions.

6. ☑ **A.** Ethernet II uses a type field.
   ☒ **B** uses a length field. **C** is not an Ethernet standard.

7. ☑ **A.** The LLC uses SAPs to define network layer protocols.
   ☒ **B** defines hardware addresses. **C** is Token Ring, and **D** is Ethernet.

Network Layer

8. ☑ **C.** The network layer creates a hierarchy through the use of logical, not physical addresses.
   ☒ **A**, **B**, and **D** are true and thus incorrect.

9. ☑ **A.** If a router has a packet it needs to route, and it can't find the destination network number in the routing table, the router *drops* the packet.
   ☒ **B** is true of switches, not routers.

Transport Layer

10. ☑ **B.** Sequence numbers and acknowledgments are used to provide a reliable transport layer connection.
☒ **A**, **C**, and **D** are used for flow control.

11. ☑ **A.** Connection multiplexing is done through the use of a socket or port number.
☒ **B** references the data link layer. **C** references the network layer. **D** is a nonexistent number type.

12. ☑ **C.** Reliable transport layer connections go through a three-way handshake process: SYN, SYN/ACK, ACK.
☒ **A**, **B**, and **D** are incorrect because they specify the wrong order.

Transferring Information Between Computers

13. ☑ **A.** The network layer transmits packet or datagram PDUs.
☒ **B** is true for the session layer. **C** is true for the physical layer. **D** is true for the data link layer.

Hierarchical Network Design

14. ☑ **A.** The core layer uses high-speed switches to provide high-speed connections.
☒ **B** provides the users' initial connection to the network. **C** provides a boundary between access and core and allows you to implement your policies.

15. ☑ **C.** The distribution layer contains broadcasts and multicasts.
☒ **B** provides the users' initial connection to the network. **A** provides a high-speed switching infrastructure to connect different distribution layers.

3

IP Addressing

CERTIFICATION OBJECTIVES

3.01 TCP/IP Protocol Stack

3.02 IP Addressing Introduction

3.03 Subnetting

3.04 Planning IP Addressing

3.05 Figuring Out IP Address Components

✓ Two-Minute Drill

Q&A Self Test

The Transmission Control Protocol/Internet Protocol (TCP/IP) is a standard that includes many protocols. It defines how machines on an internetwork can communicate with each other. It was initially funded by and developed for DARPA (Defense Advanced Research Protects Agency), which is a conglomeration of U.S. military and government organizations. Developed initially for the government, it was later made available to the public, mainly seen on Unix systems. First specified in RFC 791, it has become the defacto standard for networking protocols. The Internet uses TCP/IP to carry data between networks, and most corporations today use TCP/IP for their networks. This chapter will provide an overview of TCP/IP, including some of its more important protocols, as well as IP addressing.

exam Watch

It is VERY important that you understand ALL aspects of IP addressing. Therefore, spend a lot of time on this chapter. If you don't understand IP addressing when taking the exam, you will have a difficult time in passing it. This Exam Watch goes for all three exams: INTRO, ICND, and CCNA.

CERTIFICATION OBJECTIVE 3.01

TCP/IP Protocol Stack

To help articulate how data is moved between devices running TCP/IP, a model was developed that resembles the OSI Reference Model discussed in Chapter 2. Table 3-1 compares the two models. Even though you can see five layers here, TCP/IP treats the physical and data link layers as one logical layer. Therefore, TCP/IP, from most people's perspectives, has four layers, even though there is much debate about this. The following sections will cover the layers of the TCP/IP Protocol stack.

Application Layer

One main difference between the OSI Reference Model and TCP/IP's model is that TCP/IP lumps together the application, presentation, and session layers into one layer, called the application layer. Here are some common TCP/IP applications Cisco devices support: DNS, HTTP, SNMP, telnet, and TFTP.

TABLE 3-1 Comparison of the OSI Reference Model and the TCP/IP Protocol Stack

Layer	OSI Reference Model	TCP/IP Protocol Stack
Layer 7	Application	
Layer 6	Presentation	
Layer 5	Session	Application
Layer 4	Transport	Transport
Layer 3	Network	Internet
Layer 2	Data link	Data link
Layer 1	Physical	Physical

Transport Layer

The TCP/IP transport layer is responsible for providing a logical connection between two devices and can provide these two functions:

- Flow control (through the use of windowing and acknowledgments)
- Reliable connections (through the use of sequence numbers and acknowledgments)

exam watch

TCP/IP's transport layer can provide for flow control and reliable connections.

The transport layer packages application layer data into *segments* to send to a destination device. The remote destination is responsible for taking the data from these segments and forwarding it to the correct application. TCP/IP has two transport layer protocols: Transmission Control Protocol (TCP) and User Datagram Protocol (UDP). These protocols are discussed in the following sections.

TCP

TCP's main responsibility is to provide a reliable connection-oriented logical service between two devices. It can also use windowing to implement flow control so that a source device doesn't overwhelm a destination with too many segments.

exam watch

Here are some examples of applications (and their ports) that use TCP: HTTP (80), FTP (21), SMTP (25), and telnet (23).

TCP Segment TCP transmits information between devices in a data unit called a segment. Table 3-2 shows the components of a segment.

TABLE 3-2 TCP Segment Components

TCP Field Name	Length (in bits)	Definition
Source Port	16	Identifies which application is sending information
Destination Port	16	Identifies which application is to receive the information
Sequence Number	32	Maintains reliability and sequencing
Acknowledgment Number	32	Used to acknowledge received information
Header Length	4	Number of 32-bit words that comprise the header
Reserved Field	6	Currently not used (set to all zeroes)
Code Bits	6	Defines control functions, like synchronization
Window Size	16	Indicates the number of segments allowed to be sent before waiting for an acknowledgment from the destination
Checksum	16	CRC of the header and encapsulated application data
Urgent Field	16	Points to the any urgent data in the segment
Options	0-32	
Data	Variable	Application data (not part of the TCP header)

The segment is composed of a header, followed by the application data. Without any options, the TCP header is 20 bytes in length.

TCP's Multiplexing Function TCP, and UDP, provide a multiplexing function for a device: This allows multiple applications to simultaneously send and receive data. With these protocols, port numbers are used to differentiate the connections. Port numbers are broken into two basic categories: well-known port numbers (sometimes called reserved port numbers) and source connection port numbers. Each application is assigned a well-known port number that is typically between 1 and 1,023. Any time you want to make a connection to a remote application, your application program will use the appropriate well-known port number.

exam watch ***Be familiar with the TCP field names, especially the fact that a TCP segment contains a sequence and acknowledgment number as well as a window size.***

As you saw in Table 3-2, however, there happens to be two port numbers in the segment: source and destination. When you initiate a connection to a remote application, your operating system will pick a currently unused port number greater than 1,023 and assign this number as the source port number. Based on the application that you are running, the application will fill in the destination port number with the well-known port number of the application. When the destination receives this traffic, it looks at the destination port number and knows which application this traffic should be directed to. This is also true for returning traffic from the destination. This process was discussed in Chapter 2.

Port numbers are assigned by the Internet Assigned Numbers Authority (IANA). When a vendor develops a new commercial application and wants a reserved (well-known) port number, he applies for one to this organization. Here are some common TCP applications with their assigned port numbers: FTP (20 and 21), HTTP (80), SMTP (25), and telnet (23).

TCP's Reliability TCP provides a reliable connection between devices by using sequence numbers and acknowledgments. Every TCP segment sent has a sequence number in it. This not only helps the destination reorder any incoming frames that arrived out of order, but it also provides a method of verifying if all sent segments were received. The destination responds to the source with an acknowledgment indicating receipt of the sent segments.

Before TCP can provide a reliable connection, it has to go through a synchronization phase, called a *three-way handshake*. Here are the steps that occur during this setup process:

1. The source sends a synchronization frame with the SYN bit marked in the Code field. This segment contains an initial sequence number. This is referred to as a SYN segment.
2. Upon receipt of the SYN segment, the destination responds back with its own segment, with its own initial sequence number and the appropriate value in the acknowledgment field indicating the receipt of the source's original SYN segment. This notifies the source that the original SYN segment was received. This is referred to as a SYN/ACK segment.
3. Upon receipt of the SYN/ACK segment, the source will acknowledge receipt of this segment by responding back to the destination with an ACK segment, which has the acknowledgment field set to an appropriate value based on the destination's sequence number.

Here is a simple example of this three-way handshake:

1. Source sends a SYN: sequence number = 1

2. Destination responds with a SYN/ACK: sequence number = 10, acknowledgment = 2
3. Source responds with an ACK segment: sequence number = 2, acknowledgment = 11

TCP uses a three-way handshake to set up a reliable connection: SYN, SYN/ACK, and ACK.

In this example, the destination's acknowledgment (step 2) is one greater than the source's sequence number, indicating to the source that the next segment expected is 2. In the third step, the source sends the second segment, and, within the same segment in the Acknowledgment field, indicates the receipt of the destination's segment with an acknowledgment of 11—one greater than the sequence number in the destination's SYN/ACK segment. This process was described in Chapter 2.

Windowing TCP allows the regulation of the flow of segments, ensuring that one device doesn't flood another device with too many segments. TCP uses a sliding windowing mechanism to assist with flow control. For example, if you have a window size of 1, a device can send only one segment, and then must wait for a corresponding acknowledgment before sending the next segment. If the window size is 20, a device can send 20 segments and then has to wait for an acknowledgment before sending 20 additional segments.

The larger the window size is for a connection, the less acknowledgments that are sent, thus making the connection more efficient. Too small a window size can affect throughput, since a device has to send a small number of segments, wait for an acknowledgment, send another bunch of small segments, and wait again. The trick is to figure out an optimal window size: one that allows for the best efficiency based on the current conditions in the network and on the two devices.

exam watch

TCP employs a positive acknowledgment with retransmission (PAR) mechanism to recover from lost segments. The same segment will be repeatedly resent, with a delay between each segment, until an acknowledgment is received from the destination. The acknowledgment contains the sequence number of the segment received and verifies receipt of all sent prior segments. This eliminates the need for multiple acknowledgments and resending acknowledgments.

A nice feature of this process is that the window size can be dynamically changed through the lifetime of the connection. This is important because many more connections may come into a device with varying bandwidth needs. Therefore, as a device becomes saturated with segments from many connections, it can, assuming that these connections are using TCP, lower the window size to slow the flow of segments coming into it. TCP windowing is covered in RFC 793 and 813.

UDP

Where TCP provides a reliable connection, UDP provides an unreliable connection. UDP doesn't go through a 3-way handshake to set up a connection—it just begins sending its information. Likewise, UDP doesn't check to see if sent segments were received by a destination; in other words, it doesn't have an acknowledgment process. Typically, if an acknowledgment process is necessary, the transport layer (UDP) won't provide it; instead, the application itself, at the application layer, will provide this verification.

exam watch ***UDP is more efficient that TCP because it has less overhead. Here are some examples of UDP applications, along with their assigned port numbers: DNS queries (53), RIP (520), SNMP (161), and TFTP (69).***

Given these deficiencies, UDP does have an advantage over TCP: it has less overhead. For example, if you only need to send one segment, and receive one segment back, and that's the end of the transmission, it makes no sense to go through a 3-way handshake to first establish a connection and then send and receive the two segments: this is not very efficient. DNS queries are a good example where the use of UDP makes sense. Of course, if you are sending a large amount of data to a destination, and need to verify that it was received, then TCP would be a better transport mechanism.

Table 3-3 contains the components of a UDP segment. Examining this table, you can notice a lot of differences between a UDP and TCP segment. First, since UDP

TABLE 3-3 UDP Segment Components

UDP Field Name	Length (in bits)	Definition
Source Port	16	Identifies the sending application
Destination Port	16	Identifies the receiving application
Length	16	Denotes the size of the UDP segment
Checksum	16	Provides a CRC on the complete UDP segment
Data		Application data (not part of the UDP header)

is connectionless, there is no need for sequence and acknowledgment numbers. And second, since there is no flow control, there is no need for a window size field. As you can see, UDP is a lot simpler, and more efficient, than TCP. Any control functions that need to be implemented for the connection are not done at the transport layer—instead, these are handled at the application layer.

Internet Layer

Layer-3 of the TCP/IP protocol stack is called the *Internet* layer. The corresponding layer in the OSI Reference Model is the network layer. The *Internet Protocol* (IP) is just one of the protocols that reside at this layer. It is very common in the industry to hear people refer to TCP/IP as just "IP"; however, this is a misnomer, since IP is just one of many protocols within TCP/IP. Other IP protocols include ARP, RARP, ICMP, OSPF, and others. The next few sections explain the components of an IP packet and some of the protocols that function at the Internet layer.

> **exam watch**
>
> ***IP provides an unreliable, connectionless connection to other devices. If reliability and flow control are required, TCP (transport layer) can provide this.***

IP Datagram

Where the transport layer uses segments to transfer information between machines, the Internet layer uses datagrams. Datagram is just another word for *packet*. Table 3-4 shows the components of the IP datagram. Without any options, the IP header is 20 bytes in length.

The main function of the IP datagram is to carry protocol information for either Internet layer protocols or encapsulated transport layer protocols. To designate what protocol the IP datagram is carrying in the data field, the IP datagram carries the protocol's number in the Protocol field of the datagram.

> **exam watch**
>
> ***IP uses a TTL field to limit the number of hops a packet can travel. Here are some common protocols and their protocol numbers: ICMP (1), IGRP (9), IPv6 (41), TCP (6), and UDP (17).***

ICMP

The *Internet Control Message Protocol* (ICMP) is used to send error and control information between TCP/IP devices. ICMP, defined in RFC 792, includes many different messages that devices can generate or respond to. Here is a list of these messages: Address Reply, Address Request, Destination Unreachable, Echo, Echo Reply, Information Reply, Information Request, Parameter Problem, Redirect, Subnet Mask Request, Time Exceeded, Timestamp, and Timestamp Reply.

TABLE 3-4 IP Datagram Components

IP Field Name	Length (in bits)	Definition
Version	4	IP version number, like IPv4
Header Length	4	Length of the IP header in 32-bit word values
Priority and TOS (Type of Service)	8	Defines how the IP network should treat the datagram
Total Length	16	Length of the IP datagram, including the header and encapsulated data
Identification	16	
Flags	3	Is set if the datagram is a fragment; also used for other purposes
Fragment Offset	13	Defines information about the datagram if it is a fragment
TTL (Time-To-Live)	8	Sets the number of allowed layer-3 hops the datagram is allowed to traverse
Protocol	8	Identifies the protocol (like TCP, UDP, ICMP, OSPF, etcetera) that was used to encapsulate payload information
Header Checksum	16	Checksum on just the IP header fields
Source IP Address	32	IP address of the source device
Destination IP address	32	IP address of the destination device
Options	0–32	
Data		Protocol information (like an encapsulated UDP segment or ICMP information)

exam watch

Two common applications that use ICMP are ping and traceroute (trace). Ping uses an ICMP echo message to test connectivity to a remote device.

One of the most common implementations using ICMP is ping. Ping uses a few ICMP messages, including echo, echo request, and destination unreachable. Ping is used to test whether or not a destination is available. A source generates an ICMP echo packet. If the destination is available, it will respond back with an echo reply. If it isn't available, a router will respond back with a destination unreachable message. Trace is an application that will list the IP addresses of the routers along the way to the destination, displaying the path the packet took to reach the destination.

ARP and RARP

The *Address Resolution Protocol* (ARP) is an Internet layer protocol that helps TCP/IP devices find other devices in the same broadcast domain. ARP uses a local broadcast to discover neighboring devices. Basically, ARP resolves an IP address of a destination to the MAC address of the destination on the same data link layer medium. Remember that for two devices to talk to each other in Ethernet, the data link layer uses MAC addresses to differentiate the machines on the segment. And that when devices talk to each other at the data link layer, they need to know the destination's MAC address.

The top part of Figure 3-1 shows an example of the use of ARP. In this example PC-A wants to send information directly to PC-B. PC-A knows PC-B's IP address, however, it doesn't know PC-B's Ethernet MAC address. To resolve the IP to MAC address, PC-A generates an IP ARP. In the ARP datagram, the source IP address is 10.1.1.1 and the destination is 255.255.255.255—every device on the segment. PC-A includes PC-B's IP address in the data field of the ARP datagram. This is encapsulated into an Ethernet

FIGURE 3-1 ARP and RARP examples

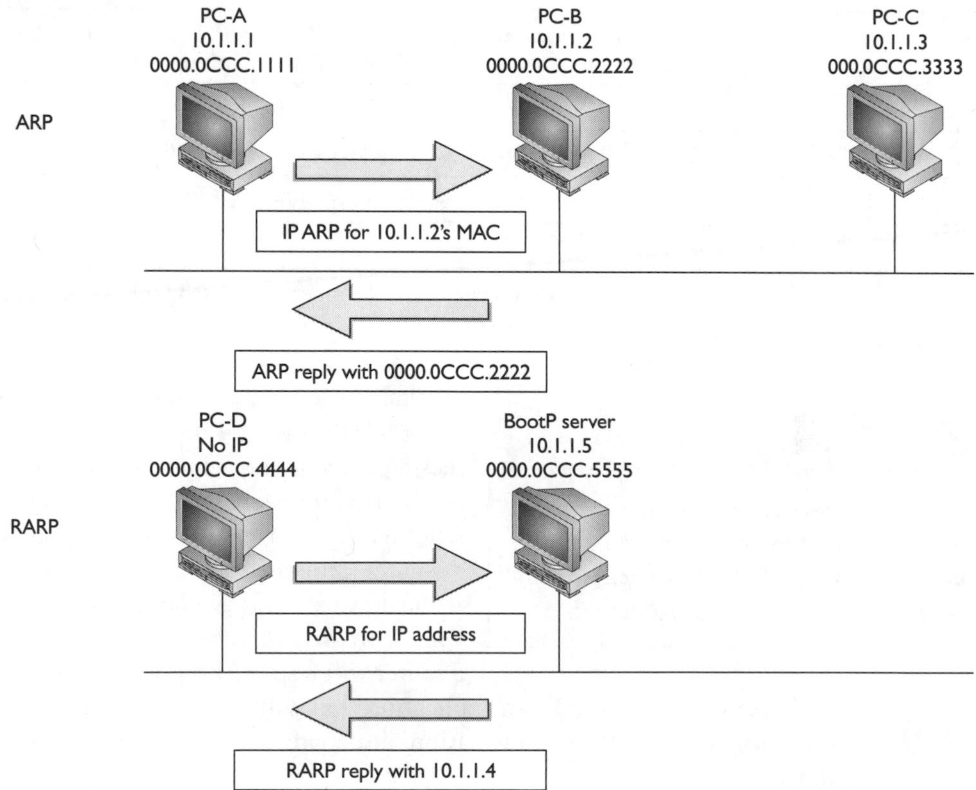

frame, with a source MAC address of 0000.0CCC.1111 and a destination MAC address of FFFF.FFFF.FFFF and is then placed on the wire. Both PC-B and PC-C see this frame. Both devices notice the data link layer broadcast address and assume that this frame is for them, so they pass it up to the Internet layer. Again, there is a broadcast address in the destination IP address field, so both devices examine the data payload. PC-B notices that this is an ARP and that this is its IP address, and therefore responds directly back to PC-A with PC-B's MAC address. PC-C, however, sees that this is not an ARP for its MAC address and ignores the datagram.

Figure 3-2 shows a more detailed example of the use of ARP. In this example, PC-A wants to connect to PC-B using IP. The source address is 1.1.1.1 (PC-A) and the destination is PC-B (2.2.2.2). Since the two devices are on different networks, a router is used to communicate between the networks. Therefore, if PC-A wants to send something to PC-B, it has to be via the intermediate router. This communication does not occur at the network layer using IP; however, it occurs at the data link layer. I'll assume that Ethernet is being used in this example.

The first thing that PC-A will do is to determine if the destination is local to this subnet or on another subnet (I'll discuss this process when I cover IP addressing and subnetting later in this chapter). In this example, it's a remote location, so PC-A will ARP for the default gateway's MAC address—note that one thing you must configure

FIGURE 3-2 ARP Example with a router

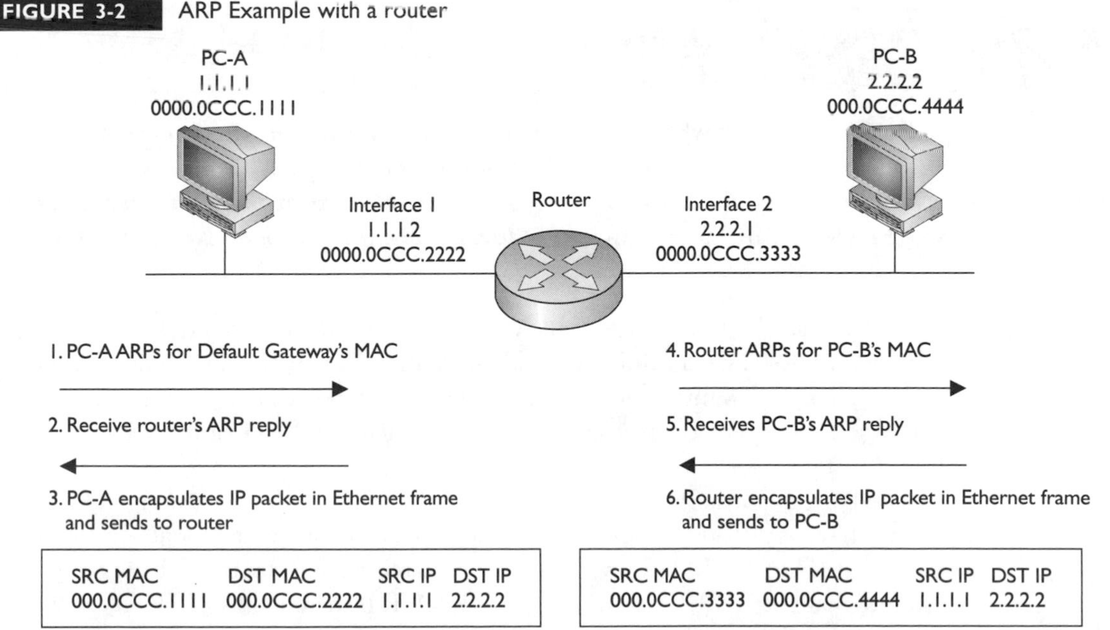

on PC-A, besides it's own IP address and subnet mask, is the default gateway address. This is shown in step 1 of Figure 3-2. In step 2, the router responds back with the MAC address of the interface connected to PC-A. In step 3, PC-A takes the IP packet with the source and destination IP addresses (the source is 1.1.1.1 and the destination is 2.2.2.2) and encapsulates this in an Ethernet frame, with the source MAC address of PC-A and the destination MAC address of the router.

When the router receives the Ethernet frame, it compares the frame to its own MAC address, which it matches. The router strips off the Ethernet frame and makes a routing decision based on the destination address of 2.2.2.2. In this case, the network is directly connected to the router's second interface, which also happens to be Ethernet. In step 4, the router ARPs for the MAC address of 2.2.2.2 (PC-B) and receives the response in step 5. The router then encapsulates the IP packet in an Ethernet frame in step 6, placing its second interface's MAC address, which is sourcing the frame, in the source MAC address field and PC-B's MAC address in the destination field. When PC-B receives this, it knows the frame is for itself (matching destination MAC address) and that PC-A originated the IP packet that's encapsulated).

Note that in this example, the IP packet was not altered by the router, but two Ethernet frames are used to get the IP packet to the destination. Also, each device will keep the MAC addresses in an ARP table, so the next time PC-A needs to send something to PC-B, the devices will not have to ARP each other again.

exam watch

Be familiar with what device talks to what at both layer-2 and layer-3. With a router between the source and destination, the source, at layer-2, uses its own MAC address as the source but the default gateway MAC address as the destination. Note that the IP addresses used at layer-3 are not changed by the router.

RARP is sort of the reverse of an ARP. In an ARP, the device knows the layer-3 address, but not the data-link layer address. With a RARP, the device doesn't have an IP address and wants to acquire one. The only address that this device has is a MAC address. Common protocols that use RARP are BOOTP and the Dynamic Host Configuration Protocol (DHCP).

The bottom part of Figure 3-1 shows a RARP example. In this example, PC-D doesn't have an IP address and wants to acquire one. It generates a data-link layer broadcast (FFFF.FFFF.FFFF) with an encapsulated RARP request. This example assumes that the RARP is associated with BOOTP. If there is a BOOTP server on

DHCP allows devices to dynamically acquire their addressing information. This information can include a client IP address and subnet mask, a default gateway, DNS, TFTP, and WINS server addresses, a domain name, and the length of the lease of the client address.

the segment, and if it has an IP address for this machine, it will respond back. In this example, the BOOTP server, 10.1.1.5, has an address (10.1.1.4) and assigns this to PC-D, sending this address as a response to PC-D.

CERTIFICATION OBJECTIVE 3.02

IP Addressing Introduction

Probably one of the most confusing aspects of the TCP/IP protocol stack is the addresses used at the Internet layer, referred to as IP addresses. The remainder of this chapter will focus on IP addressing, its components, and how to plan for addressing. Please note that there are two different versions of TCP/IP: IPv4 and IPv6. Only IPv4 is covered in this book.

IPv4 addresses are 32 bits in length. However, to make the addresses readable, they are broken into four bytes (called octets), with a period (decimal) between each byte. So that the address is understandable to the human eye, the four sets of binary numbers are then converted to decimal. Let's look at a simple example: 11111111111111111111111111111111, which is 32 1's. This is broken up into four octets, like this: 11111111.11111111.11111111.1111111. Then each of these octets are converted into decimal, resulting in 255.255.255.255. The format of this address is commonly called *dotted decimal.*

Bit Values

Before you can begin to understand the conversion process, you need to understand binary mathematics. Computers and networking devices process everything in binary. In a byte (octet), there are eight bits. Each bit, when enabled, represents a specific decimal value. Table 3-5 shows the conversion of a specific bit position when it is enabled. In this table, the bit positions are labeled from left-to-right, where the left-most bit is the most

TABLE 3-5 Binary to Decimal Conversion for Byte Values

Bit Position	8	7	6	5	4	3	2	1
Decimal Value	128	64	32	16	8	4	2	1

significant and the right-most bit is the least significant. A bit can contain one of two values: 0 or 1. If it is enabled (set to 1), then that equates to a particular decimal value, shown in the second row of Table 3-5. If it is disabled (set to 0), then this equates to a decimal value of zero. Higher-order bits are the ones with a higher-numbered bit position (like 8) while lower-order bits are the ones with a lower-numbered bit position (like 1). To convert the binary byte value to a decimal value, you look at all the bits that are turned on and add up the equivalent decimal values.

exam watch

Remember how to convert a binary 8-bit value to a decimal number and vice versa.

For example, assume that you had a byte with a value of 11000001. Bits 8, 7, and 1 are on, so add up the associated decimal values to get the corresponding decimal equivalent of the byte value: 128 + 64 + 1 = 193. If you had a byte value of 00110011, the decimal value would be: 32 + 16 + 2 + 1 = 51. If all the bit positions where set to 0, then the decimal value would be 0. If all the bit positions were set to 1, the equivalent decimal value would be: 128 + 64 + 32 + 16 + 8 + 4 + 2 + 1 = 255. Given this, a byte value can range from 0 to 255.

Hexadecimal Conversion

Even though IP addressing deals with octal, decimal, and binary notations, you might be required to perform decimal to hexadecimal conversion and vice versa. Therefore, since part of this chapter deals with numeric conversions, I'll briefly cover the process of performing decimal/hexadecimal conversion.

First, as you already know, binary has two possible values in a bit position and octal has 8 bit positions, allowing you to represent numbers from 0–255 in a byte (8 bits). And in decimal, you have values that range from 0–9 (10 values). Hexadecimal has a range of 16 values: 0, 1, 2, 3, 4, 5, 6, 7, 8, 9, A, B, C, D, E, and F. As an example, a decimal 10 is equivalent to A in hexadecimal. A decimal 17 is equivalent to 11 in hexadecimal. When dealing with hexadecimal, a hex digit is represented in four bits. Table 3-6 lists a handy conversion chart.

exam watch

You should be familiar with converting binary to both decimal and hexadecimal, as well as hexadecimal to decimal and vice versa.

TABLE 3-6

Binary to Decimal to Hexadecimal Conversion for Bit Values

Decimal	Binary	Hexadecimal
0	0000	0
1	0001	1
2	0010	2
3	0011	3
4	0100	4
5	0101	5
6	0110	6
7	0111	7
8	1000	8
9	1001	9
10	1010	A
11	1011	B
12	1100	C
13	1101	D
14	1110	E
15	1111	F

For example, if you had an 8-bit value of 10000001, break this up into two 4-bit values, since a hexadecimal value is represented in 4 bits: 1000 and 00001. In hexadecimal, this value would be 8 and 1, or 81. If you had an 8-bit value of 11011001, this would be D9 in hexadecimal.

Classes of Addresses

Recall from Chapter 2 that logical, or layer-3, addresses, have two components: a network and host number. The network number uniquely identifies a segment in the network and a host number uniquely identifies a device on a segment. The combination of these two numbers must be unique throughout the entire network. TCP/IP uses the same two components for addressing, but does add a twist by breaking up network numbers into five classes: Class A, B, C, D, and E. Each of these classes has a predefined network and host boundary:

- With a Class A address, the first byte is a network number (8 bits) and the last 3 bytes are for host numbers (24 bits)
- With a Class B address, the first two bytes are a network number (16 bits) and the last 2 bytes are for host numbers (16 bits)
- With a Class C address, the first three bytes are a network number (24 bits) and the last 1 byte is for host numbers (8 bits)
- Class D addresses are used for multicasting and Class E addresses are reserved

Remember the 5 classes of IP addresses, and the fact that Class A addresses have, by default, 8 network bits, Class B 16 bits, and Class C 24 bits.

Distinguishing Between Classes of Addresses

Given the above distinction, it would seem that addressing for IP is easy. However, what distinguishes the different classes of addresses are what the first bit to 5 bits is set to:

- Class A addresses always begin with a "0" in the highest order bit
- Class B addresses always begin with "10" in the highest order bits
- Class C addresses always begin with "110" in the highest order bits
- Class D addresses always begin with "1110" in the highest order bits
- Class E addresses always begin with "11110" in the highest order bits

exam watch

Remember the binary values that IP addresses begin with and be able to determine, by looking at the first binary byte, whether the address is a Class A, B, C, D, or E address.

When talking about the highest-order bit or bits, this includes *all* 32 bits. Therefore, this would be the very first bit on the *left* of the address (the most significant bit). If the first octet contains 1000001, this represents 129 in decimal, which would be a Class B address.

Network Numbers and Classes of Addresses

Given the above distinctions with the assigned high-order bit values, it is easy to predict, for a given address, what class of network numbers it belongs to:

- Class A addresses range from 1–126: 0 is reserved and represents all IP addresses; 127 is a reserved address and is used for testing, like a loopback on an interface: 00000001–01111111.
- Class B addresses range from 128–191: 10000000–10111111.
- Class C addresses range from 192–223: 11000000–11011111.
- Class D addresses range from 224–239: 11100000–11101111.
- Class E addresses range from 240–254: 255 is a reserved address and is used for broadcasting purposes.

Given the above restrictions with beginning bit values, it is fairly easy to predict what address belongs to what class.

exam watch

Class A addresses range from 1–126, Class B from 128–191, Class C from 192–223, Class D from 224–239 and Class E from 240–254. 127 is reserved for the loopback interface (internal testing). Also remember the ranges in binary.

When you are dealing with IP addresses, there are always two numbers reserved for a given network number: the first address in the network represents the network's address, and the last address in the network represents the broadcast address for this network, commonly called a *directed broadcast*. When you look at IP itself, there are two IP addresses reserved: 0.0.0.0 (the very first address), which represents all IP addresses, and 255.255.255.255 (the very last address), which is the local broadcast address (all devices should process this datagram).

exam watch

Remember the list of private networks, which cannot be used in public networks: 10.0.0.0, 172.16.0.0–172.31.0.0, and 192.168.0.0–192.168.255.0.

Within this range of addresses for Class A, B, and C addresses, there are some reserved addresses, commonly called *Private Addresses*. All the other addresses in these classes are called public addresses. Anyone can use private addresses; however, this creates a problem if you want to access the Internet. Remember that each device in the network (in this case, this includes the Internet) must have a unique IP address. If two networks are using the same private addresses, then you would run into reachability issues. In order to access the Internet, your source IP addresses must have a unique Internet public address. This can be accomplished through address translation. Here is a list of private addresses, which are assigned in RFC 1918:

- Class A: 10.0.0.0–10.255.255.255 (1 Class A network)
- Class B: 172.16.0.0–172.31.255.255 (16 Class B networks)
- Class C: 192.168.0.0–192.168.255.255 (256 Class C networks)

Private and public addresses, as well as address translation, are discussed in Chapter 14.

IP Address Components

As was mentioned earlier, there are two components to addressing: network and host. The host portion is actually broken into three subcomponents: network address, host addresses, and directed broadcast address.

The very first address in a network number is called the network address, or *wire number*. This address is used to uniquely identify one segment from all of the other segments in the network. The last address in the network number is called the directed broadcast address, and is used to represent all hosts on this network segment. A directed broadcast is similar to a local broadcast. The main difference is that routers will not propagate local broadcasts, but can propagate directed broadcasts. Any address between the network address and the directed broadcast address is a host address for the segment. You use these middle addresses to assign to host devices on the segment, like PCs, servers, routers, and switches.

exam watch

Each network has two reserved addresses: a network number (the first address) and a directed broadcast (the last address). Any addresses between these two values can be assigned to networking devices on the segment.

Network and Directed Broadcast Addresses

When dealing with a network address, all of the host bits in the host portion of the address are set to zeros. If all of the host bits in a network number are set to ones, making it the very last address, then this is the directed broadcast address. Any combination of bit values between these two numbers in the *host* portion of the address is considered a host address.

As example, 192.1.1.0 is a Class C address and is also a network number. If you recall from earlier in this chapter, the Class C addresses range from 192–223 in the first byte and the network number is three bytes long. Therefore, "192.1.1" is the network number. The last byte is the host address. This byte is 0, which is the very first address in the network. Therefore, the network address is 192.1.1.0. If you would set the last 8 bits to all ones (the host bits), which is equivalent to 255 in decimal, this would be the directed broadcast (192.1.1.255) for the network.

Host Addresses

Any number between the network address and the directed broadcast address is a host address. In the previous example, any number between 0 and 255 is a host address for the network 192.1.1.0: 192.1.1.1–192.1.1.254.

An important item to point out about this process is that for any given network number, you *lose* two addresses. The first address in a network is reserved for the network itself and the last address is reserved for the directed broadcast address. There is a formula that defines the number of available host addresses, assuming that you know the number of bits that are reserved for host numbers: $\mathbf{2^N - 2}$. At the beginning of this formula, **2** is raised to the power of **N**, where **N** is the number of host bits. When figuring out a power of a number. You take the number and multiply it by itself based on the power it is being raised to. As an example, 2^4 would be 2 * 2 * 2 * 2 = 16. The "**– 2**" part of the formula represents the loss of the first and last addresses. Table 3-7 represents the powers of 2, up to 32.

So, as an example, a Class C network has a 24-bit network number component and an 8-bit host component. Therefore, for a Class C network, the lowest address in this fourth octet is 0 and the last address in this octet is 255 (all 8 bits are set to 1). All numbers between 1–254, are host addresses for the Class C network. Using the addressing formula, you can easily show a Class C network has 254 host addresses:

TABLE 3-7 Powers of 2

2^1 = 2	2^9 = 512	2^{17} = 131,072	2^{25} = 33,554,432
2^2 = 4	2^{10} =1,024	2^{18} = 262,144	2^{26} = 67,108,864
2^3 = 8	2^{11} = 2,048	2^{19} = 524,288	2^{27} = 134,217,728
2^4 = 16	2^{12} = 4,096	2^{20} = 1,048,576	2^{28} = 268,435,456
2^5 = 32	2^{13} = 8,192	2^{21} = 2,097,152	2^{29} = 536,870,912
2^6 = 64	2^{14} =16,384	2^{22} = 4,194,304	2^{30} = 1,073,741,824
2^7 = 128	2^{15} = 32,768	2^{23} = 8,388,608	2^{31} = 2,147,483,648
2^8 = 256	2^{16} = 65,536	2^{24} = 16,777,216	2^{32} = 4,294,967,296

Remember that each network loses two addresses for host assignments. Also remember the $2^N - 2$ formula, which you can use, based on number of host bits, to determine the number of hosts a network will support.

$2^N - 2 = 2^8 - 2 = 256 - 2 = 254$. For a Class B network, the number of host addresses is 65,534: $2^N - 2 = 2^{16} - 2 = 64,536 - 2 = 65,534$. And for a Class A network, the number of host addresses is 16,777,214: $2^N - 2 = 2^{24} - 2 = 16,777,216 - 2 = 16,777,214$.

CERTIFICATION OBJECTIVE 3.03

Subnetting

One of the problems with the original IP addressing scheme was that for Class A and B networks, address efficiency was an issue. In other words, how many hosts can you physically put on a network segment? Even with the advent of VLANs, this number did not increase dramatically. With IP, you can get between 300–500 devices in a single broadcast domain before experiencing broadcast problems. This is 1–2 Class C networks. If you would assign a Class B network for this broadcast domain, you'd be wasting over 65,000 addresses.

To overcome this deficiency issue, subnetting was introduced. Subnetting allows you to take some of the higher-order ***host*** bits in a network number and use them to create more networks. In the process of creating more networks, each of these additional networks has a lesser number of hosts. These smaller networks are commonly called *subnets*. One disadvantage of subnetting is that you are losing more addresses—each of these subnets has a network and broadcast address. However, the advantage of subnetting is that you now can more efficiently use your addressing.

Let's look at an example. A Class C network has 8 host bits, giving you a total of 256 addresses. Of these 256 addresses, you can only use 254 for host devices, like PCs, routers, and servers. Let's assume that you use the highest-order bit to create more networks, leaving 7 bits for host addresses. With this example, you are creating two subnets: $2^1 = 2$. In this formula, the 1 is the number of subnet bits. In each of these subnets you have 126 host addresses: $2^7 - 2 = 126$. Originally, you lost 2 addresses in a Class C network. Now that you have two subnets, you are losing a total of 4 addresses. However, you now have two networks.

For example, you might have two segments in your network with 100 hosts each on them. You could assign a separate Class C network to each of these segments, but this would be a very inefficient use of your addresses. By using subnetting, you can more efficiently use your addresses. In this example, one Class C network, subnetted with one subnet bit, created two subnets with 126 host addresses each. In this example, you are wasting a smaller number of addresses.

Subnet Masks

TCP/IP is unique amongst most layer-3 addressing schemes. When dealing with TCP/IP addresses, there are actually three components to the address: A network component, a host component, and a *subnet mask*. The function of the subnet mask is to differentiate between the network address, the host addresses, and the directed broadcast address. Subnetting is defined in RFC 950.

Like an IP address, the subnet mask is 32 bits long. In binary, a 1 in a bit position in the subnet mask represents a network component and a 0 in a bit position represents a host component. One restriction of subnet masks is that all the network bits (1s) must be contiguous and all the host bits (0s) are contiguous. This is true not only in a single octet, but across all the bits in all four octets. A subnet mask of 11110000.00001111.11111111.11111111 (240.31.255.255) would be invalid, since all the 1s are not contiguous. A subnet mask of 1111111.11111111.11111111.11111000 (255.255.255.248), however, is valid.

There are actually four methods that you can use to represent a subnet mask. Here is a list with a demonstration using a Class C network:

- Dotted-decimal: 192.168.1.0 255.255.255.0
- Number of networking bits: 192.168.1.0/24
- Hexadecimal: 192.168.1.0 0xFFFFFF00
- Binary: 192.168.1.0 11111111111111111111111100000000

The most common of these formats is the dotted-decimal and number of networking bits. The last two are not commonly used.

Subnet mask values, binary 1s and 0s, must be contiguous in order to be considered as a valid subnet mask. When representing subnet masks, be very familiar with both the dotted decimal and number of networking bits nomenclature.

Subnet Masks Values

Given the fact that subnet mask values must have all 1's contiguous and all 0's contiguous, Table 3-8 shows some valid decimal numbers for subnet masks in an octet.

For a Class A network, the default subnet mask is 255.0.0.0: the first octet is the network number and the last three octets are the host numbers. For a Class B network, the default subnet mask is 255.255.0.0: the first two octets are the network number and the last two octets are the host numbers. For a Class C network, the default subnet mask is 255.255.255.0: the first three octets are the network number and the last octet is the host numbers.

One important item to point out is that the subnet mask, in and of itself, means nothing without the context of the IP address associated with it. For example, most people would assume that when you see a subnet mask of 255.255.255.0, you are dealing with a Class C address. However, remember that you can perform subnetting on any class address. So this mask can also be used for Class A and B addresses. Therefore, the IP address and subnet mask have a symbiotic relationship. The following sections will show you the valid subnet mask values for Class A, B, and C networks.

Subnet Masks for A-Class Networks

Table 3-9 shows valid subnet masks for Class A networks. In this table, the number of networking bits is the total number of bits used in networking, including both the network and subnet bits. This is also true with Tables 3-10 and 3-11.

Subnet Masks for B-Class Networks

Table 3-10 shows valid subnet masks for Class B networks.

Subnet Masks for C-Class Networks

Table 3-11 shows valid subnet masks for Class C networks.

exam watch

You will need to be very familiar with subnet masks for a given address and the number of networks that a subnet mask creates, as well as the number of host addresses for each network.

As you can see from Tables 3-9, 3-10, and 3-11, you can't just choose any subnet mask and apply it to any class of addresses: Some masks are valid for some classes, but not valid for others. For instance, 255.255.0.0 is a valid mask for Class A and B networks, but is an *invalid* mask for Class C networks.

TABLE 3-8 Valid Subnet Mask Values

00000000 = 0	11100000 = 224	11111100 = 252
100000000 = 128	11110000 = 240	11111110 = 254
110000000 = 192	11111000 = 248	11111111 = 255

TABLE 3-9 Class A Subnets

Subnet Mask	Networking Bits	Number of Networks	Number of Hosts
255.255.255.252	/30	4,194,304	2
255.255.255.248	/29	2,097,152	6
255.255.255.240	/28	1,048,576	14
255.255.255.224	/27	524,288	30
255.255.255.192	/26	262,144	62
255.255.255.128	/25	131,072	126
255.255.255.0	/24	65,536	254
255.255.254.0	/23	32,768	510
255.255.252.0	/22	16,384	1,022
255.255.248.0	/21	8,192	2,046
255.255.240.0	/20	4,096	4,094
255.255.224.0	/19	2,048	8,190
255.255.192.0	/18	1,024	16,382
255.255.128.0	/17	512	32,766
255.255.0.0	/16	256	65,534
255.254.0.0	/15	128	131,070
255.252.0.0	/14	64	262,142
255.248.0.0	/13	32	524,286
255.240.0.0	/12	16	1,048,574
255.224.0.0	/11	8	2,097,150
255.192.0.0	/10	4	4,194,302
255.128.0.0	/9	2	8,388,606
255.0.0.0	/8	1	16,777,216

TABLE 3-10 Class B Subnets

Subnet Mask	Networking Bits	Number of Networks	Number of Hosts
255.255.255.252	/30	32,768	2
255.255.255.248	/29	8,192	6
255.255.255.240	/28	4,096	14
255.255.255.224	/27	2,048	30
255.255.255.192	/26	1,024	62
255.255.255.128	/25	512	126
255.255.255.0	/24	256	254
255.255.254.0	/23	128	510
255.255.252.0	/22	64	1,022
255.255.248.0	/21	32	2,046
255.255.240.0	/20	16	4,094
255.255.224.0	/19	8	8,190
255.255.192.0	/18	4	16,382
255.255.128.0	/17	2	32,764
255.255.0.0	/16	1	65,534

TABLE 3-11 Class C Subnets

Subnet Mask	Networking Bits	Number of Networks	Number of Hosts
255.255.255.252	/30	64	2
255.255.255.248	/29	32	6
255.255.255.240	/28	16	14
255.255.255.224	/27	8	30
255.255.255.192	/26	4	62
255.255.255.128	/25	2	126
255.255.255.0	/24	1	254

exam watch

When subnetting, depending on the device, the first and last subnet in a network, referred to as subnet 0, might or might not be valid. For the exam, remember this, since the exam doesn't tell you one way or the other. However, when looking for an answer, you'll never see both as a valid answer, either the answer will include the first and last subnet or it won't.

CERTIFICATION OBJECTIVE 3.04

Planning IP Addressing

When it comes to addressing, dealing with protocols like AppleTalk, IPX, and XNS is easy: each has a distinct network and host component. With these protocols, there is no such thing as a subnet mask, which can change the boundary between network and host numbers. When I started out with TCP/IP, one of the most difficult tasks I've faced in my networking career was tackling and understanding how to handle subnetting and IP addressing. To make matters worse, IP addressing has its roots in binary mathematics, since this is how computing devices deal with numbers. And considering that I have a degree in Mathematics, and that I had trouble with IP addressing, imagine how strange IP addressing must be to the layman?

Through my years of experience dealing with TCP/IP and teaching Cisco-related courses, I've developed a six-step approach to help students plan for their IP addressing needs in their networks. Here are the six steps:

1. Figure out network and host requirements
2. Satisfy host and network requirements
3. Figure out the subnet mask
4. Figure out the network addresses
5. Figure out the directed broadcasts for your networks
6. Figure out the host values for your networks

The following sections will cover the six steps in depth.

Step 1: Figure Out Network and Host Requirements

In this step, you need to do two things:

- Determine the number of hosts that do, or will, exist on the largest segment in your network.
- Determine the maximum number of segments that you have in your network—this will tell you how many networks, or subnets, you'll need.

If you already are dealing with an existing network, then you have a lot of analysis ahead of you. You'll need to perform the above two tasks, counting hosts on each segment, and the number of segments that you have. Remember that when you are counting hosts, each device with a connection to the segment needs to be counted—this includes PCs, routers, servers, printers, and other devices. Remember that a segment could be used in a logical sense, like all the ports off of a switch, or a VLAN. Switching is discussed in more depth in Chapter 7 and VLANs in Chapter 8. You might even want to leave some room for growth by taking your final numbers and adding to them.

To assist with the remaining 5 steps, I'll create an imaginary network. This network has 14 segments and the largest segment has 14 devices on it. You've been assigned a single Class C network number (192.168.1.0). Now you're ready to proceed to step 2.

Step 2: Satisfy Host and Network Requirements

In the second step, you'll use three formulas:

1. 2^X => number of networks you need (**X** represents subnet bits)
2. $2^Y - 2$ => number of hosts on your largest segment (**Y** represents host bits)
3. **X** + **Y** <= total number of host bits

In the first step, you need to figure out how many bits you need to steal from the host bits to create your subnets. In the second step, you need to figure out how many host bits you need to accommodate your host requirements. And last, you need to make sure that when you add up the bits that you stole for subnets, and the bits that you need for your hosts, that you didn't exceed the original number of host bits that you started out with, based on the Class A, B, or C network.

As an example, if you had a Class C network and were subnetting it and needed 5 bits for subnets and 4 bits for hosts, this would total 9 bits. Unfortunately, Class C networks only have 8 host bits to begin with, so this wouldn't work. In this situation,

Remember that the exam might not allow you to use subnet 0. Therefore, in Step 1 preceding, you might need to subtract 2 from the total valid number of networks in order to come up with a valid value. In this chapter, I'm assuming that subnet 0 is valid in all of the examples.

you would either need a Class B network or 2 Class C networks. As an other example, if you had the same Class C network and were subnetting it, and you needed 3 bits for subnets and 4 bits for host addresses, this would total 7 bits. In this situation, the Class C network as 8 bits, and you only need 7. This gives you some flexibility—you could use the extra bit to either create more subnets, or to have more hosts with your 3 bits of subnets.

Let's go back to our original example of 192.168.1.0, where you need 14 subnets with a maximum of 14 hosts on each:

1. 2^X => 14 subnets; in this example, **X** needs to be 4, which would result in 16 subnets.
2. $2^Y - 2$ => 14 hosts; in this example, **Y** needs to be 4, which would result in 14 hosts.
3. **X + Y** <= 8 (Class C network); in this example 4 + 4 is less than or equal to 8.

Let's break this down step-by-step. In the first step, you need to find a power of 2 that will give a number that is either equal to or greater than the number of subnets that you need. In our example, the power of 2 needs to be 4: $2^4 = 16$. This meets our subnet requirements, since we only need 14 subnets (there are only 14 segments).

Next, you need to figure out your hosts bits by using this formula: $2^Y - 2$ => 14 required hosts; where **Y** is the necessary number of host bits. In this example, $2^4 - 2 =$ 14, so you need 4 host bits to get your required 14 hosts.

And last, since we are dealing with a Class C network, we only have 8 original host bits. We need to make sure that the total of our subnetting and host bits does not exceed this original value. In our case, 4 + 4 = 8, so we're okay. If the number of bits totaled higher than 8, then we would need two Class C networks, or a Class B network. If the number of bits were less than 8, then we could allocate the extra bit or bits to either create more subnets and/or hosts. Remember that if you are ever in this situation where you have extra bits to deal with, then you need to closely examine your network and figure out, based on future growth, whether you should create more subnets, or allow for more hosts on a subnet.

Step 3: Figure Out the Subnet Mask

Now that the hardest part is over, the rest of the four tasks is easy. At this point, you now know the number of subnet bits you need. However, when dealing with networking and subnet masks, a subnet mask's network portion contains both network *and* subnet bits. Here's a reminder of the default number of networking bits for a class address: A is 8, B is 16, and C is 24.

Given this, just add the class address bits to the subnet bits, and this gives you the total number of *networking* bits. In our example, this would be 24 + 4 = 28. To make the remaining three steps easier, I recommend that you convert the number of bits of the subnet mask to a dotted decimal mask. Tables 3-8, 3-9, and 3-10 have the lists of subnet masks if you need help. However, this is not too hard of a process. First, remember that a subnet mask, just like an IP address, is represented in a dotted decimal format, where there are 8 bits in each octet. That means, for a Class C mask, the first 24 bits are set to 1. In other words, the mask at least begins with 255.255.255. Our job is to figure out the mask in the last octet. Remember that the four highest bits are for subnetting, so just add up these decimal values: 128 + 64 + 32 + 16 = 240.

exam watch

Remember how to convert a binary subnet mask value to a dotted-decimal format: add up the host bit values in decimal and subtract them from 255.

There is actually a short cut that I always like to use. If you recall from our example, the number of host bits that are used are the four lower-order bits. Add up these values: 1 + 2 + 4 + 8, which equals 15. The largest number represented by a byte is 255. Since we're not using these bits, just subtract this value from 255, which will give us the mask value in this byte 255 – 15 = 240. I find it easier to add up the small values and subtract them from 255 than to add up the larger bit-decimal values. Eventually, you won't have to do this mathematical trick as you become accustomed to performing IP addressing and dealing with subnetting. Going back to our example, our subnet mask for network 192.168.1.0 is **255.255.255.240**, or 192.168.1.0/28.

Step 4: Figure Out the Network Addresses

In step 4, we need to figure out the networks that we created with our new subnet mask. Since IP addressing is done in binary, network addresses will always increment in a multiple of something. We'll use this to our advantage when figuring out what our network numbers are for our Class C network. Remember that the network number has all of the host bits set to 0's.

Actually, we already know what this multiplier is: we figured this out in the second part of step 2, using the $2^4 - 2 = 14$ formula. The 14 value is the number of valid host values for a subnet; however, this is *not* the total number of addresses for the subnet. The subnet also has a network and broadcast address, which is the reason the formula subtracts 2 since you can't use these addresses for host devices. Therefore, in our example, each network has a total of 16 addresses, and is incremented by 16 from subnet-to-subnet.

There is another method of verifying your multiplying value. In a byte, you can have numbers ranging from 0–255, resulting in a total of 256 numbers. For this verification, take the subnet mask decimal value in the interesting octet and subtract it from 256. The interesting octet is the octet that contains the network and host boundary. In our case, this is the fourth octet. Therefore, using this trick, 256 – 240 = 16. When you compare this number to the number in the last paragraph, you can be assured that you have done your math correctly.

Now that you have figured out the multiplier, write the very first network down, and then start adding 16 to the interesting octet. Table 3-12 lists the subnet numbers for 192.168.1.0. In this table, notice something interesting concerning the last subnet: 192.168.1.240. The network number in the last octet matches the interesting octet in our subnet mask (240). This will *always* be true when you perform subnetting.

There is one important item to point out about subnetting. In the original RFC for subnetting, you were not allowed to use the first and last subnet. For instance, in our example, we would not be able to use 192.168.1.0/28 and 192.168.1.240/28. However, today, assuming that your TCP/IP protocol stack supports subnet 0 (this refers to these two subnets—first and last), you can. You need to make sure, though, that each device on the segment that will have one of these subnets supports this function. In today's age, this shouldn't be an issue. However, I typically use this subnet for addressing only networking devices, like management devices, which typically support subnet 0.

TABLE 3-12 Network numbers for 192.168.1.0.

192.168.1.0	192.168.1.64	192.168.1.128	192.168.1.192
192.168.1.16	192.168.1.80	192.168.1.144	192.168.1.208
192.168.1.32	192.168.1.96	192.168.1.160	192.168.1.224
192.168.1.48	192.168.1.112	192.168.1.176	192.168.1.240

Step 5: Figure Out the Directed Broadcast Addresses

After figuring out all of your subnets, you next need to figure out what the directed broadcast address is for each subnet. This is very simple. The directed broadcast of a subnet is *one number less* than the next network number. Also, the broadcast address has all of its hosts bits set to binary 1s. Table 3-13 shows our network numbers and directed broadcast addresses. For the last table entry, the directed broadcast address will be the highest possible value in a byte: 255.

As a shortcut, remember that the directed broadcast address is one number less than the network address of the next network number.

TABLE 3-13 Network and Directed Broadcast Addresses for 192.168.1.0/28

Network Addresses	Mathematics	Directed Broadcast Addresses
192.168.1.0	16 – 1	192.168.1.15
192.168.1.16	32 – 1	192.168.1.31
192.168.1.32	48 – 1	192.168.1.47
192.168.1.48	64 – 1	192.168.1.63
192.168.1.64	80 – 1	192.168.1.79
192.168.1.80	96 – 1	192.168.1.95
192.168.1.96	112 – 1	192.168.1.111
192.168.1.112	128 – 1	192.168.1.127
192.168.1.128	144 – 1	192.168.1.143
192.168.1.144	160 – 1	192.168.1.159
192.168.1.160	176 – 1	192.168.1.175
192.168.1.176	192 – 1	192.168.1.191
192.168.1.192	208 – 1	192.168.1.207
192.168.1.208	224 – 1	192.168.1.223
192.168.1.224	240 – 1	192.168.1.239
192.168.1.240		192.168.1.255

Step 6: Figure Out the Host Addresses

Step 6 is the easiest step. If you recall, any address between the network and directed broadcast address is a host address for a given network. We can then complete the rest of our addressing for 192.168.1.0, as is shown in Table 3-14. If you look at the very first subnet in this table, 192.168.1.0, you'll see that it has a total of 14 host addresses, which matches are formula: $2^Y - 2$, $2^4 - 2 = 14$ hosts.

For the CCNA Exam, you will need to understand how to do IP addressing. Of course, on the job, you can cheat and use an IP subnet calculator. One of my favorites is from a company called *Boson Software*. They offer a free download of their subnet calculator (http://www.boson.com), but it is also included on the CD that comes with this book. Boson's subnet calculator will even do route summarization, which is a topic extensively covered in Cisco's BSCI exam for the CCNP and CCDP certifications.

TABLE 3-14 Addressing for 192.168.1.0/28

Network Numbers	Host Addresses	Directed Broadcast Addresses
192.168.1.0	192.168.1.1 – 192.168.1.14	192.168.1.15
192.168.1.16	192.168.1.17 – 192.168.1.30	192.168.1.31
192.168.1.32	192.168.1.33 – 192.168.1.46	192.168.1.47
192.168.1.48	192.168.1.49 – 192.168.1.62	192.168.1.63
192.168.1.64	192.168.1.65 – 192.168.1.78	192.168.1.79
192.168.1.80	192.168.1.81 – 192.168.1.94	192.168.1.95
192.168.1.96	192.168.1.97 192.168.1.110	192.168.1.111
192.168.1.112	192.168.1.113 – 192.168.1.126	192.168.1.127
192.168.1.128	192.168.1.129 – 192.168.1.142	192.168.1.143
192.168.1.144	192.168.1.145 – 192.168.1.158	192.168.1.159
192.168.1.160	192.168.1.161 – 192.168.1.174	192.168.1.175
192.168.1.176	192.168.1.177 – 192.168.1.190	192.168.1.191
192.168.1.192	192.168.1.193 – 192.168.1.206	192.168.1.207
192.168.1.208	192.168.1.209 – 192.168.1.222	192.168.1.123
192.168.1.224	192.168.1.225 – 192.168.1.238	192.168.1.239
192.168.1.240	192.168.1.241 – 192.168.1.254	192.168.1.255

EXERCISE 3-1

Planning IP Addressing Exercise

These last few sections dealt with how to create an addressing scheme for a network. This exercise will help reinforce these concepts, including the six steps that you should use to come up with an appropriate subnet mask value and network, directed broadcast, and host addresses.

1. You are given a Class C network (192.168.1.0) and you have 4 segments in your network, where the largest segment has 50 hosts. What subnet mask should you use and what is the layout of your addresses?

   Performing the six steps, the subnet mask is 255.255.255.192 (/26), giving you four network numbers: 192.168.1.0, 192.168.1.64, 192.168.1.128, and 192.168.1.192. Each of these four networks has a total of 64 addresses, where 62 of these can be used for host devices.

2. You are given a Class B network (172.16.0.0) and you have 490 segments in your network, where the largest segment needs 112 host addresses. What subnet mask should you use and what is the layout of your addresses?

   Performing the six steps, the subnet mask is 255.255.255.128 (/25), giving you 512 network numbers: 172.16.0.0, 172.16.0.128, 172.16.1.0, 172.16.1.128, 172.16.2.0, 172.16.2.128, and so on and so forth. Each of these 512 subnets has 128 addresses, of which 126 of these can be used to assign addressing information to host devices.

3. You are given a Class A network (10.0.0.0) and you have 9,000 segments in your network, where the largest segment needs 560 host addresses. What subnet mask should you use and what is the layout of your addresses?

   Performing the six steps, the subnet mask is 255.255.252.0 (/22), giving you 16,384 network numbers: 10.0.0.0, 10.0.4.0, 10.0.8.0, 10.0.12.0, 10.0.16.0, 10.0.20.0, 10.0.24.0, and so on and so forth. Each of these 16,384 subnets has 1,024 addresses, of which 1,022 of these can be used to assign addressing information to host devices.

Now you should be more comfortable with planning IP addressing. In the next section, you will be presented with how to figure out whether an IP address is a network, directed broadcast, or host address.

exam watch

Make sure that you practice, practice, and do more practice on exercises like the preceding when preparing for your exam. I can't stress this enough. Use Boson's subnet calculator to check your results.

CERTIFICATION OBJECTIVE 3.05

Figuring Out IP Address Components

For purposes of the CCNA exam, you might not be given an assignment like the one I described in the last section. However, you will have to know how to figure out how many host addresses are in a particular subnet, how many subnets you can create with a particular mask, and, given a specific IP address, is it a network, host, or directed broadcast address. The last section described how to plan IP addressing. This section, however, will teach you the tools that you will need to figure these out…more specifically, given a certain address, what type of address it is.

If you recall from the last section, there are three types of addresses for each network: a network, a directed broadcast, and host addresses. The trick to figuring this out goes back to step 4 of the last section. You need to figure out the number that networks are incrementing by. For exam purposes, you may be given an IP address and a subnet mask. Covert the decimal subnet mask to the number of bits in the mask. In our previous example, for instance 255.255.255.240 is a 28-bit mask. Take this number and subtract it from 32. In our example, this gives us 4 bits. Since the first 28 bits are network numbers, the last 4 bits are host addresses.

If you recall, every subnet has the same number of addresses. So all you need to do is raise this value to the power of 2 to figure out how many addresses are in a network, and therefore you know by how much each network number is incrementing. In our example, 2^4 gives you a total of 16 addresses in the subnet, including the network, host, and directed broadcast addresses. Based on this information, it is easy to figure out what type of address the exam is asking about.

As you will learn, subnetting is not a difficult task, but it does take **a lot of practice**. I've developed six steps to help you out. The following sections cover these six steps.

Six Step Approach For Figuring Out IP Address Components

When you are given a particular address and subnet mask, and asked whether the address is a network, host, or directed broadcast address, you should use the following six steps:

1. You need an IP address and a subnet mask (this is the easy part).
2. Examine the subnet mask and find the interesting octet. The interesting octet in the mask is the one where the network and host boundary is found. This includes the following mask values in an octet: 0, 128, 192, 224, 240, 248, 252, and 254. It does *not* include 255—an octet with a mask value of 255 (all 8 bits are 1s) indicates that this octet is part of the network number. Only when an octet contains binary 0's does it have a host component.
3. Subtract the interesting octet in the subnet mask from 256. This will give you the increment by which network numbers are increasing in the interesting octet.
4. On a piece of paper, start writing down the network numbers, starting at with the first subnet (0), and work your way up to a network number that is higher than the address in question.
5. After you have written down the network numbers, beside each of these, write down their corresponding broadcast addresses. Remember that the broadcast address is one number less than the *next* network number. You don't have to do this with every network number…just the networks near the network number in question.
6. Between the network and broadcast addresses, right down the host addresses. Host addresses are any number between the network and directed broadcast address.

Remember the preceding six steps when trying to determine if an IP address is a network, host, or directed broadcast number.

Based on these six steps, you should then be able to figure out if your address is a host, network, or broadcast address. Note that these six steps are somewhat similar to the six steps used in the *Planning IP Addressing* section. However, the steps in this section are for test purposes and the steps in the previous section are for design purposes.

Example #1 For Figuring Out IP Address Components

In order to help you out with the six steps, let's take a look at an example as an illustration. In step 1, you have an IP address and subnet mask. Let's assume that this is **192.168.1.37 255.255.255.224** (or 192.168.1.37/27). This is a Class C network.

In step 2, you need to find the interesting octet in the subnet mask. This is the octet where the boundary exists between network and host bits. In this example, this is the fourth octet: **224**. In step 3, you need to find the increment by which network numbers are increasing. To perform this step, subtract the interesting octet from 256: **256 – 224 = 32**. Therefore, there are 32 addresses in each network, and each network is incrementing by 32 in the interesting octet (fourth octet).

exam watch

Remember the shortcut of figuring out the multiples that network numbers are incrementing by in the interesting octet: 256 – subnet mask value = increment value.

In step 4, write down the network numbers starting with first subnet and work your way up. Here is the list of network numbers for our example: 192.168.1.0, 192.168.1.32, 192.168.1.64, 192.168.1.96, 192.168.1.128, 192.168.1.160, 192.168.1.192, and 192.168.1.224. In this example, there are eight subnets. Mathematically, this makes sense. There are 32 addresses per subnet, with a total of 256 addresses (0 – 255) in a Class C network. **256 ÷ 32 = 8**! Remember that the interesting octet in the subnet mask will be the subnet number in the last subnet of the IP class address.

In step five, list the directed broadcast address beside each network number. And in step 6, list the host addresses for each network. Remember that the broadcast address for a network is one number less than the next network number and that the host addresses are any IP addresses between the network and directed broadcast addresses. Table 3-15 shows the completion of steps 5 and 6.

Given Table 3-15, the host address of 192.168.1.37 is a ***host*** address, since it falls in the rage of host addresses for subnet 192.168.1.32/27. When you are taking the CCNA exam, I wouldn't build the entire table. Instead, I would list the network numbers until you had a network number greater than the address in the question. Once this was

TABLE 3-15 Network, Directed Broadcast, and Host Addresses of 192.168.1.0/27

Network Addresses	Host Addresses	Directed Broadcast Addresses
192.168.1.0	192.168.1.1 – 192.168.1.30	192.168.1.31
192.168.1.32	192.168.1.33 – 192.168.1.62	192.168.1.63
192.168.1.64	192.168.1.65 – 192.168.1.94	192.168.1.95
192.168.1.96	192.168.1.97 – 192.168.1.126	192.168.1.127
192.168.1.128	192.168.1.129 – 192.168.1.158	192.168.1.159
192.168.1.160	192.168.1.161 – 192.168.1.190	192.168.1.191
192.168.1.192	192.168.1.193 – 192.168.1.222	192.168.1.223
192.168.1.224	192.168.1.225 – 192.168.1.254	192.168.1.255

done, for the last three network numbers, I would list the directed broadcast and host addresses, and then I would know the answer to the exam question. In the above example, these networks would be 192.168.1.0, 192.168.1.32, and 192.168.1.64.

Example #2 For Figuring Out IP Address Components

Let's look at another example to help clarify the six steps. For step 1, you are given the following address and subnet mask: 192.168.1.132 255.255.255.192 (/26), which is a Class C address.

In the second step, you need to find the interesting octet in the subnet mask. This is the last octet. For a Class C network, this will *always* be the last octet. The value in this mask is **192**, indicating that the first two high-order bits in the octet are part of the network component and the last 6 low-order bits are the host component. In step 3, you need to find out by what number the network addresses are increasing by. To do this step, subtract the value in the subnet mask's interesting octet from 256: **256 – 192 = 64**. Therefore, network addresses are incrementing by 64 numbers and each network contains 64 addresses: a network address, a directed broadcast address, and 62 host addresses. Remember that since the interesting octet is in the fourth octet, the network addresses are increasing by 64 in the *interesting* (fourth) octet.

In step 4, write down the network numbers. In our example, this gives us 4 networks: 192.168.1.0, 192.168.1.64, 192.168.1.128, and 192.168.1.192. In the interesting octet, two bits are used for networking and 6 bits for host addresses. With 2 bits of networking, this gives you 4 networks: $2^2 = 4$ and with 6 bits of host addresses and 64 addresses in a network: $2^6 = 64$.

The address in question, 192.168.1.132 is between two networks: 192.168.1.128 and 192.168.1.192. This means that you should only have to perform steps 5 and 6 on these two networks, and possibly the network before it. However, let's go ahead and complete steps 5 and 6 for all of the networks since this is good practice. Remember that the directed broadcast address for a network is one number less than the next network number and that the addresses between the network and directed broadcast addresses are host addresses. Table 3-16 shows the addressing for the Class C address.

TABLE 3-16 Network, Directed Broadcast, and Host Addresses of 192.168.1.0/26

Network Addresses	Host Addresses	Directed Broadcast Addresses
192.168.1. 0	192.168.1.1 – 192.168.1.62	192.168.1.63
192.168.1.64	192.168.1.65 – 192.168.1.126	192.168.1.127
192.168.1.128	192.168.1.129 – 192.168.1.190	192.168.1.191
192.168.1.192	192.168.1.193 – 192.168.1.253	192.168.1.254

Our address, 192.168.1.132 is a ***host*** address based on this table, where its network number is 192.168.1.128 and its directed broadcast is 192.168.1.191.

Example #3 For Figuring Out IP Address Components

The first two examples were fairly simple, since the addresses were from a Class C network. In this third example, I'll complicate matters by using a Class B network. In step 1, the address assigned is 172.16.5.0 255.255.254.0, which can also be represented as 172.16.5.0/23. This is an excellent example of an address that most test takers would incorrectly identify on a test. Right now, I want you to guess what type of address this is (network, directed broadcast, or host) and then we'll work it through step-by-step to come up with an answer.

In step 2, you need to find the interesting octet—where the network and host boundary resides. In our case, this happens to be the *third* octet (**254**) of the subnet mask. It is important to point out that *all* of the *fourth* octet are host addresses. In step 3, you need to find the increment by which network numbers are increasing: **256 – 254 = 2**. Network numbers are incrementing by 2 in the *third* octet. This last sentence is very important. Remember that the entire fourth octet is the host component, since the subnet mask value in this position is set to 0 (all 8 bits are 0).

In step 4, you need to write down your network numbers, starting with the first subnet and work your way up until you go past the IP address in question: 172.16.0.0, 172.16.2.0, 172.16.4.0, 172.16.6.0, 172.16.8.0, and so on and so forth. Remember that with a Class B address, there are 16 bits in the host component. With our subnet mask, we're using 7 bits for subnets and 9 bits for hosts. Therefore, with 7 bits for subnets, we have a total of 128 subnets, where each subnet has 512 total addresses. Each network really has 510 *host* addresses, where the first and last addresses are used for the network and directed broadcast address respectively. Looking at our address, 172.16.5.0, we can tell that it at least is *not* a network address.

Let's go ahead and do steps 5 and 6, listing the directed broadcast addresses and host addresses for these subnets, as is shown in Table 3-17. Looking at this table, you

TABLE 3-17 Network, Directed Broadcast, and Host Addresses of 172.16.0.0/23

Network Addresses	Host Addresses	Directed Broadcast Addresses
172.16.0.0	172.16.0.1 – 172.16.1.254	172.16.1.255
172.16.2.0	172.16.2.1 – 172.16.3.254	172.16.3.255
172.16.4.0	172.16.4.1 – 172.16.5.254	172.16.5.255
172.16.6.0	172.16.6.1 – 172.16.7.254	172.16.7.255
172.16.8.0	172.16.8.1 – 172.16.9.254	172.16.9.255

can see that 172.16.5.0 is a ***host*** address! Even 172.16.0.255 is a host address! This example illustrates that you should *never* make assumptions about what type an address is without considering the subnet mask. Always remember that the subnet mask puts a context on the IP address and determines its type: network, directed broadcast, or host address.

For the CCNA exam, I would expect a trick question like this. In real life, I would typically not use addresses like 172.16.5.0 or 172.16.0.255 because this would *confuse* many network administrators. I've actually had to argue with people over the validity of these kinds of addresses as host addresses in network planning sessions. I've learned, though, it's pretty hard to teach an old dog new tricks, so instead of wasting my time arguing or explaining the address validity, I just don't use them. For test purposes, though, they *are* valid host addresses.

EXERCISE 3-2

Determining Network, Directed Broadcast, and Host Components

These last few sections dealt with how to differentiate what type an address is: network, directed broadcast, or host address. The following exercises will help you practice your IP addressing skills.

1. You are given the following address: 192.168.1.63/255.255.255.248. What type of address is this—network, directed broadcast, or host?

   The interesting octet is the *fourth*: 248. Subtract 256 from this: 256 – 248 = 8. Network numbers are incrementing by 8: 192.168.1.0, 192.168.1.8, 192.168.1.16, 192.168.1.24, 192.168.1.32, 192.168.1.40, 192.168.1.48, 192.168.1.56, 192.168.1.64, and so on and so forth. After writing down the directed broadcast addresses, you'll see that the network 192.168.1.56 has a directed broadcast address of 192.168.1.63 and host address of 57–62. Therefore, this is a broadcast address.

2. You are given the following address: 172.16.4.255/255.255.252.0. What type of address is this—network, directed broadcast, or host?

   The interesting octet is the *third*: 252. Subtract 256 from this: 256 – 252 = 4. Network numbers are incrementing by 4 in the third octet: 172.16.0.0, 172.16.4.0, 172.16.8.0, 172.16.12.0, and so on and so forth. After writing down the directed broadcast addresses, you'll see that the network 172.16.4.0 has a directed broadcast address of 172.16.7.255 and host addresses of 172.16.4.1-172.16.7.254. Therefore, this is a host address.

CERTIFICATION SUMMARY

TCP/IP has five layers: application, transport, internet, data link, and physical. At the transport layer, TCP provides a reliable connection through the use of sequence numbers and acknowledgments. TCP uses a three-way handshake when establishing a connection: SYN, SYN/ACK, and ACK. TCP uses PAR to recover lost segments, resending segments with a delay between transmissions, until an acknowledgment is received. Applications that use TCP include FTP (21), HTTP (80), SMTP (25), and telnet (23). UDP provides unreliable connections and is more efficient that TCP. Examples of applications that use UDP include DNS (53), RIP (520), SNMP (161) and TFTP (69).

IP functions at the internet layer and includes protocols like ICMP, ARP, RARP, OSPF, and others. ICMP is used to test connections. Ping uses ICMP echo messages to test layer-3 connectivity. ARP resolves an IP address to a MAC address. RARP, used by BOOTP and DHCP, resolve a MAC address to an IP address (used to acquire IP addressing information on a device). IP addresses are 32-bits in length and are broken up into 4 bytes, with a period between the bytes. This format is referred to as dotted decimal.

There are five classes of IP addresses: A (1–126), B (128–191), C (192–223), D (224–239), and E (240–254). Class A addresses have one network byte and three host bytes. Class B addresses have two network and two host bytes. Class C addresses have three network bytes and one host byte. Private IP addresses include networks 10.0.0.0/8, 172.16.0.0/16-172.31.0.0/16, and 192.168.0.0/24-192.168.255.0/24.IP addresses have three components: network, host, and broadcast. The very first number in a network is the network, or wire number. The very last address is the broadcast address of the network. Any addresses between the network and broadcast addresses are host addresses. What differentiates a network, host, and broadcast address is the context the subnet mask places on the address. The subnet mask is used to mark the boundary between the network and host bits.

TWO-MINUTE DRILL

TCP/IP Protocol Stack

- The TCP/IP protocol stack has the following layers: Physical, Data Link, Internet, Transport, and Application. Remember that the physical and data link layers are logically represented as a single layer, resulting in four layers for the TCP/IP protocol stack.
- The transport layer provides flow control (through the use of windowing), reliable connections, (through the use of sequence numbers and acknowledgments), and multiplexing (allowing multiples applications to simultaneously send and receive data). TCP provides reliable connections and goes through a 3-way handshake to establish a connection whereas UDP provides unreliable connections.
- The Internet layer corresponds to the Network layer of the OSI Reference Model. Many protocols function at this layer, like ARP, RARP, and ICMP. ARP resolves IP to MAC addresses, RARP is used by BOOTP and DHCP to help a device acquire an IP address, and ICMP is used to send error and control information. The ping utility uses ICMP.

IP Addressing Introduction

- IP addresses are 32 bits in length, and are broken into four bytes (8 bits) with a period between the bytes. This format is called dotted decimal.
- Hexadecimal digits are represented in 4 bit values, ranging from 0–F.
- IP addresses are broken into five classes: A (1–126), B (128–191), C (192–223), D (224–239) and E (240–254). IP addresses are broken into two components: network and host. With Class A addresses, the first byte is a network number, Class B, the first two bytes, and Class C, the first three bytes.
- The first few bits in the first octet identity the class of address. Class A addresses begin with "0," Class B with "10," Class C with "110," Class D with "1110," and Class E with "11110."
- Each network has three components to its address: network, directed broadcast, and host. The first number in the network is the network address, the last is the directed broadcast address, and any addresses between these two are host addresses.

Subnetting

- ❑ Subnetting allows you to break up and use your addressing space more efficiently. Basically, subnetting steals the higher-order bit or bits from the host component and uses these bits to create more subnets, with a smaller number of host addresses.
- ❑ Subnet masks are 32 bits long and are typically represented in dotted decimal, like 255.255.255.0 or the number of networking bits, like "/24". The networking bits in a mask must be contiguous and the host bits in the subnet mask must be contiguous. 255.0.255.0 is an invalid mask.

Planning IP Addressing

- ❑ There are six steps to design a network with IP addresses: 1) figure out your network and host requirements; 2) satisfy host and network requirements; 3) figure out the subnet mask; 4) figure out the network addresses; 5) figure out the directed broadcast addresses; 6) figure out the host addresses.
- ❑ When satisfying your host and networking requirements, you need to figure out how many bits you need to in order to meet your network segment requirements and how many bits you need in order to satisfy the maximum number of hosts on the largest segment in your network. When you add these two values together, they shouldn't exceed the original number of host bits in the host component of the address.

Figuring Out IP Address Components

- ❑ Use six steps in order to figure out the type of address: 1) List the IP address and mask; 2) find the interesting octet in the subnet mask; 3) Subtract the interesting octet from 256, which gives you the increment that network addresses are increasing by in the interesting octet; 4) Write down the network addresses; 5) Beside each network address, write down its directed broadcast address; 6) Host addresses are addresses between the network and directed broadcast addresses.
- ❑ When figuring out directed broadcast addresses, they will be one number less than the next network address.
- ❑ Subnet masks determine the context of IP addresses…whether an address is a network, broadcast, or host address.

SELF TEST

The following Self Test questions will help you measure your understanding of the material presented in this chapter. Read all the choices carefully, as there may be more than one correct answer. Choose all correct answers for each question.

TCP/IP Protocol Stack

1. The TCP/IP protocol stack has ________ layers.

   A. 4

   B. 5

   C. 6

   D. 7

2. Which of the following is not true concerning TCP?

   A. Provides for reliable connections

   B. Uses windowing for flow control

   C. Multiplexes applications

   D. Is more efficient than UDP

3. Which of the following is a Network layer protocol for the TCP/IP protocol stack?

   A. TCP

   B. UDP

   C. ICMP

   D. None of these

IP Addressing Introduction

4. You have this binary value: 11000001. This equates to _________ in decimal.

5. A Class A address has _________ host bits.

   A. 8

   B. 16

   C. 20

   D. 24

6. 191.75.39.24 is a Class __________ address.

A. A
B. B
C. C
D. None of the above

7. 172.16.240.256 is a Class __________ address.

A. A
B. B
C. C
D. None of the above

Subnetting

8. Which of the following is a valid subnet mask value?

A. 255.0.255.255
B. 0.0.0.255
C. 255.255.254.0
D. 255.255.255.256

9. The function of a _________ is to differentiate between the network address, the host addresses, and the directed broadcast address.

Planning IP Addressing

10. You are given a Class C network with 25 bits of networking. How many subnets do you have?

A. 1
B. 2
C. 3
D. 4

11. You are given a Class C network with a subnet mask of 255.255.255.248. How many host addresses are there on each subnet?

A. 4
B. 6
C. 8
D. 14

12. You are given a Class B network with a subnet mask of 255.255.255.192. How many host addresses are there on each subnet?

    A. 30
    B. 62
    C. 126
    D. 254

Figure Out IP Address Components

13. You are given the following addressing information: 192.168.37.192/25. What type of address is this?

    A. Network
    B. Directed broadcast
    C. Host

14. You are given the following addressing information: 172.17.16.255/23. What type of address is this?

    A. Network
    B. Directed broadcast
    C. Host

15. You are given the following addressing information: 10.0.8.0/22. What type of address is this?

    A. Network
    B. Directed broadcast
    C. Host

16. You are given a MAC address of 01A2.0482.FE12. What is the OUI value in binary?

    A. 00011011.10100010.00000100
    B. 00000000.00000001.00000100
    C. 00000001.10100010.00000100
    D. 00000001.10100001.00000010

SELF TEST ANSWERS

TCP/IP Protocol Stack

1. ☑ **B.** The TCP/IP protocol stack has 4 layers: Physical/Data Link, Internet, Transport, and Application.
☒ **A**, **C**, and **D** are incorrect.

2. ☑ **D.** UDP is more efficient than TCP since it doesn't have the overhead associated with it that TCP has. For instance, UDP doesn't go through a 3-way handshake to set up a connection and doesn't use sequence and acknowledgment numbers to implement flow control.
☒ **A**, **B**, and **C** are all true concerning TCP: it provides reliable connections, windowing for flow control, and multiplexing for applications.

3. ☑ **D.** The TCP/IP protocol stack doesn't have a Network layer…it has an Internet layer.
☒ **A** and **B** are transport layer protocols. **C** is an Internet layer protocol.

IP Addressing Introduction

4. ☑ 193.

5. ☑ **D.** Class A addresses have 24 host bits and 8 networking bits.
☒ **A** is true for Class C networks. **B** is true for Class B networks. **C** can only be true for subnetted Class A and B networks.

6. ☑ **B.** 191.75.39.24 is a Class B network. Class B networks range from 128–191.
☒ **A** addresses range from 1–126. **C** addresses range from 192–223. Since there is an answer, **D** is incorrect.

7. ☑ **D.** It's impossible to represent 256 in a byte—the values range from 0–255.
☒ **A**, **B**, and **C** are incorrect.

Subnetting

8. ☑ **C.** 255.255.254.0 is a valid subnet mask—the 1s and 0s must be contiguous.
☒ **A** has noncontiguous 1's. **B** is an inverted mask, with the network and host bits reversed. **D** has an invalid mask value in the fourth octet: 256.

9. ☑ **Subnet mask**. The function of a subnet mask is to differentiate between the network address, the host addresses, and the directed broadcast address.

Planning IP Addressing

10. ☑ **B.** Class C networks have 24 bits—this example steals one bit. 2 raised to the power of 1 equals 2 subnets.
☒ **A**, **C**, and **D** are incorrect.

11. ☑ **B.** There are 3 host bits, with 2 raised to the power of 3 resulting in 8 addresses in a network, but you lose 2 for the network and directed broadcast address, resulting in 6 host addresses. You could also subtract 248 from 256, resulting in a total of 8 addresses per network, of which the first and last are reserved.
☒ **A**, **C**, and **D** are incorrect.

12. ☑ **B.** There are 6 host bits, with 2 raised to the power of 6 resulting in 64 addresses in a network, but you lose 2 for the network and directed broadcast address, resulting in 62 host addresses. You could also subtract 192 from 256, resulting in a total of 64 addresses in a network…but you can't use the first and the last.
☒ **A**, **C**, and **D** are incorrect.

Figure Out IP Address Components

13. ☑ **C.** There is 1 subnet bit for this Class C network, resulting in two networks: 192.168.37.0 and 192.168.37.128, making 192.168.37.192 a host address. Host addresses for this subnet range from 192.168.37.129-192.168.37.254.
☒ **A** is true for 192.168.37.0 and 192.168.37.128. **B** is true for 192.168.37.127 and 192.168.37.255.

14. ☑ **C.** Network addresses are incrementing by 2 in the *third* octet. Where 172.17.16.255 is a host address. Host addresses range from 172.17.16.1–172.17.17.254.
☒ **A** is true for 172.17.16.0. **B** is true for 172.17.17.255.

15. ☑ **A.** Network addresses are incrementing by 4 in the third octet. Where 10.0.8.0 is a network address. Other network addresses include 10.0.0.0, 10.0.4.0, 10.0.8.0, 10.0.12.0, and so on and so forth.
☒ **B** is true for 10.0.3.255, 10.0.7.255, 10.0.11.255, 10.0.15.255, and so on and so forth. **C** is true for 10.0.8.1–10.0.11.255, as well as other host addresses in other subnets.

16. ☑ **C.** Remember that the OUI portion is the first six hexadecimal characters in a MAC address (Chapter 2). Hex characters are represented in 4 bits in binary. 0=0000, 1=0001, A=1010, 2=0010, 0=0000, and 4=0100. When you concatenate these together, the result is 00000001.01000010.0100 (the first six hexadecimal digits).
☒ **A** converts to 0B for the first byte, making it incorrect. **B** converts to 00 for the first byte, making it incorrect. D's first byte is correct, but the second byte converts to A1 and third byte to 02, making it incorrect

4

Preparing Network Connections

CHAPTER OBJECTIVES

- 4.01 Cisco's Networking Products
- 4.02 Chassis Information
- 4.03 Connections
- 4.04 Cabling
- ✓ Two-Minute Drill
- Q&A Self Test

The first three chapters of this book dealt with an introduction to networking, networking concepts, and IP addressing—basically theory and concept information. In this chapter, I'll begin discussing the applied side of networking. This chapter focuses on installing your networking devices (switches and routers), cabling up your LAN and WAN connections, and establishing a console connection so that you can put a configuration on these devices. Once you have established a console connection in this chapter, Chapter 5 will begin the basics of using the router's or switch's command-line interface (CLI) to put a basic configuration on these devices.

CERTIFICATION OBJECTIVE 4.01

Cisco's Networking Products

The last part of Chapter 2 discussed Cisco's three-layer hierarchical model for network design: core, distribution, and access. Once you have designed your network and have decided on the types of devices you'll be using at each of the three layers, you must then pick a specific product for each of these devices. When choosing a networking product, consider the following:

- Is the product easy to install and support?
- Does the product provide the necessary features/functions to meet your networking requirements?
- Does the product support enough ports and offer enough backplane capacity to meet your network's growth and bandwidth requirements?
- Is the product reliable, and can it provide redundancy?
- If it is a layer-3 device, does the product provide support for both mobile users and branch office connections?
- Can the product be easily upgraded, protecting your investment in the product?

When you have answered these questions, you are ready to pick the appropriate products for your networking design. The products discussed later in this chapter do not represent all of Cisco's products, nor do they include all of the products for a specific category. When choosing a product, you'll need to log on to Cisco's web site (http://www.cisco.com) and look up the specifications of the products that you are interested in before making a choice.

If you are implementing a WAN solution, you should consider the following when making a choice:

- Make sure the solution is cost-effective.
- Make sure the service you want to use is available in the location where you will be installing it. Some services, such as ATM, DSL, and ISDN, are not available in all areas.
- Make sure the solution you choose provides the necessary amount of bandwidth for your users' needs.

Remember that modem connections support up to only 53Kbps and therefore are best for telnet, e-mail, small file transfers, and limited web browsing traffic. ISDN and Frame Relay connections up to speeds of 128Kbps are more suitable for file transfers, Internet access, and voice traffic. Leased lines, DSL, ATM, and Frame Relay are best suited for multimedia applications, including voice and video, as well as for high-bandwidth needs (greater than 128Kbps).

Hubs

As was mentioned in Chapter 2, hubs function at the physical layer and provide a logical bus structure for Ethernet; devices connected to the hub have the illusion that they are all connected to the same physical piece of wire. Devices connected to a hub are in the same collision domain, since hubs are repeaters and they repeat any physical layer signal that they receive. Cisco has many hub products, including the following: 1500 Micro Hub; 1528 10/100 Micro Hub; 100, 200, 300, and 400 Fast Hubs.

exam watch

Hubs and repeaters are used to connect devices together in the same collision domain. These devices repeat any signal sent to them, including collisions. All devices connected via layer-1 are in the same collision domain, sometimes referred to as a bandwidth domain.

Switches

As discussed in Chapter 2, switches function at the data link layer. They are normally used to solve bandwidth and collision problems. If you experience a heavy amount of collisions or a lot of contention for bandwidth, in today's world, you would use a switch to solve your problem. Cisco supports different switching products, including the following: 1548 Micro Switch 10/100, Catalyst 1900 and 2800, Catalyst 2950, Catalyst 3550, Catalyst 4000, Catalyst 6x00, and Catalyst 8500 switches. Most of these switches support only a layer-2 functionality, like the Catalyst 1900, while others, such as the Catalyst 3550 switch, support both layer-2 and layer-3.

One of the things to keep in the back of your mind when choosing switches is that many of Cisco's switches use different command-line interfaces (CLIs). As you will see starting in Chapter 5, even the 1900 and 2950 use, for the most part, different commands to configure their settings. This can become confusing for someone new to switching and Cisco's products in general.

exam watch

Switches and bridges are used to solve collision and bandwidth problems. Each port connected to a bridge or switch is a separate collision or bandwidth domain.** Microsegmentation **is a term used with switches when each networking device has its own dedicated port on a switch.

Routers

As I mentioned in Chapter 2, routers are used to solve many problems, including the containment of broadcasts. Cisco has a wide range of routing products, including layer-3 switches that they support. Cisco groups these routing products into different categories, including home office, small office, branch office, and central site solutions, to better help you choose the appropriate product for your network.

Routers are used to connect broadcast domains together. In this sense, routers contain broadcast problems: routers, by default, do not propagate broadcast traffic.

For home office solutions, Cisco recommends the following products: 800, 900, 1600, and 1700 series routers. For small office solutions, Cisco recommends the 1600, 1700, and 2500 series of routers. For branch office solutions, Cisco recommends the 2600, 3600, and 3700 series routers. For central site solutions, Cisco recommends the 3600, 3700, 7x00, and 12000

GSR routers, as well as the 5x00 access server products. Of all of the router products that I mentioned, only the 700 series does not use the same CLI when performing configuration tasks. Therefore, if you know how to configure a 2500 router, configuring the 3600 router (or any other router, for that matter) is basically the same.

CERTIFICATION OBJECTIVE 4.02

Chassis Information

Before you begin connecting any cables to your Cisco products, you should first become familiar with their chassis and interfaces. First, you should understand how to turn on your Cisco device, what interfaces it has, and the meanings of the various LEDs (light-emitting diodes) on the chassis. The next few sections will cover this in more depth.

Catalyst 1900 Switch

The Catalyst 1900 and 2820 switches are basically the same product. Both switches support an optional external redundant power supply (RPS). The main difference is that the 1900 comes in a fixed chassis format, whereas the 2820 supports two modular slots. Otherwise, they both run the same software and have the same internal hardware infrastructure. There are two basic chassis formats for the 1900: the 1912 and the 1924. Table 4-1 shows the differences. The 1912 has a total of 15 ports, while the 1924 has 27 ports. As you can see from this table, the 1912 has 12 fixed 10BaseT ports, while the 1924 has 24.

The 2820 Catalyst switch comes in two varieties: 2822 and 2828. Both support 1 fixed AUI 10Base5 port on the rear of the chassis, 24 10BaseT ports on the front of

TABLE 4-1 1900 Ports

Port	Location	Number—1912	Number—1924
AUI 10Base5 port	Rear	1	1
100BaseTX/FX uplink ports	Front right	2	2
10BaseT ports	Front middle	12	24

the chassis, and two modular slots on the front of the chassis. The cards that fit into these slots support Ethernet, Fast Ethernet, ATM, and FDDI interfaces. The main difference between these two switches is the number of MAC addresses that they can put in their port address tables. The 2822 supports up to 2,048 MAC addresses while the 2828 supports up to 8,192 addresses (the 1900 supports 1,024 MAC addresses). Other than this difference, the two 2800 series switches are identical. One important item to point out is that you cannot upgrade a 2822 to a 2828—the number of MAC addresses is physically tied to the switch you bought.

1900 Chassis

Figure 4-1 shows a picture of the front and rear of a 1924 switch. The top part shows the front while the bottom part shows the rear. For the top part of the picture, there is a cut-out of the LEDs on the left-hand side of the switch. The front of the chassis contains the MODE button as well as the LEDs and all but one of the Ethernet ports.

The rear of the chassis has the management connections. You'll notice that there is no toggle switch to turn the switch on or off. To turn the switch on, plug one end of the power cable into the back of the switch and the other into a power outlet. To turn the switch off, unplug the power cable from either end. Also notice the 10Base5 Ethernet port, which uses a DB-15 AUI interface.

FIGURE 4-1 A 1924 switch

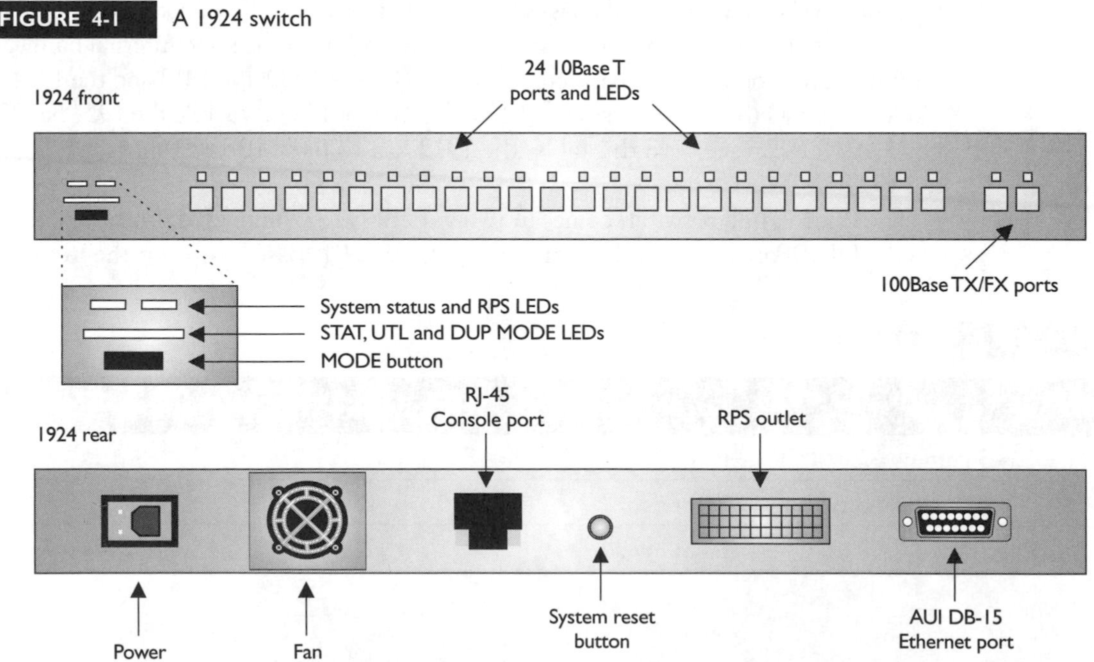

Depending on how old your switch is, you'll have either an RJ-45 (newer) or DB-9 (older) console interface. The DB-9 interface uses a null modem cable for connectivity to a terminal or terminal emulation device for console access. The RJ-45 interface uses a rollover cable, discussed later in this chapter. You can also see a very, very small reset button on the rear of the chassis. You need to use the tip of a pencil or paper clip in order to press this button. Pressing this button causes the switch to reboot, which is basically the same as pulling the power cord out of the chassis and putting it back in.

LEDs

The 1900 has four sets of LEDs on the front of its chassis: SYSTEM, RPS (redundant power supply), port, and mode LEDs. Table 4-2 shows the status of the SYSTEM and RPS LEDs. Note that for LEDs that say amber, this is a light orange color. The next section will cover the rest of the LEDs.

MODE Button

There is an LED above each port on the front of the 1900's chassis. The meaning of this LED is dependent upon what mode the LED is set to. You can change the mode by pressing the MODE button on the bottom-left side of the front of the chassis, below the SYSTEM and RPS LEDs. Right above the MODE button are three port-mode LEDs: STAT, UTL, and FDUP. By default, the STAT LED is lit: this indicates that the LEDs above the Ethernet ports refer to the status of the port. Table 4-3 shows the possible LED colors and descriptions for the various port statuses.

If you push the MODE button once, the mode LED will change from STAT to UTIL. The UTIL LED, when lit, indicates that the LEDs above the Ethernet ports are

TABLE 4-2 1900 SYSTEM and RPS LEDs

LED	Color	Description
SYSTEM	Green	The system is up and operational.
	Amber	The system experienced a malfunction.
	Off	The system is powered down.
RPS	Green	The RPS is attached and operational.
	Amber	The RPS is installed, but is not operational. Check the RPS to make sure that it hasn't failed.
	Flashing amber	Both the internal power supply and the external RPS are installed, but the RPS is providing power.
	Off	The RPS is not installed.

TABLE 4-3 Status Mode and Port LEDs

LED Color	LED Meaning
Green	There is a powered-up physical layer connection to the device attached to the port.
Flashing green	There is traffic entering and/or leaving the port.
Flashing green and amber	There is an operational problem with the port—perhaps excessive errors or a connection problem.
Amber	The port has been disabled manually (shut down) or because of a security issue.
Off	There is no powered-up physical layer connection on the port.

functioning as a utilization meter bar. This meter bar reflects the amount of bandwidth that the switch is currently using on its backplane. The meter readings are different for a 24-port switch than for a 12-port switch, as is shown in Table 4-4 and Table 4-5.

If you push the MODE button again, the LED will change from UTL to FDUP. When in FDUP mode, the LEDs about the ports represent the duplexing of the ports. If the LED is green, the port is set to full-duplex. If the port LED is off, the port is set to half-duplex. If you hit the MODE button again, the mode LED will change back to STAT. As you can see, the MODE button allows you to cycle through the different mode settings. If the mode LED is either UTL or FDUP, it will automatically change back to STAT after one minute.

Boot-Up Process and LEDs

Whenever you boot up any of Cisco's networking products, they will run through hardware diagnostics called the power-on self test (POST). This is also true with the 1900 switches. When you power up your 1900, initially, all of the port LEDs will be green. As each self-test in POST is running, a specific LED above an Ethernet port will turn off (while the others remain green). As the test completes, the LED turns back to green

TABLE 4-4 Utilization Mode and Port LEDs for a 1924

Port LEDs Lit Up	Backplane Bandwidth
1–8	< 6Mbps
9–16	< 120Mbps
17–24	< 280Mbps

TABLE 4-5 Utilization Mode and Port LEDs for a 1912

Port LEDs Lit Up	Backplane Bandwidth
1–4	< 1.5Mbps
5–8	< 20Mbps
9–12	< 120Mbps

and another, lower-numbered port LED will go off, signifying that the next POST test is being performed. Table 4-6 shows the various POST tests that are performed on the 1900.

If a particular self-test fails, then the LED above the port will turn from off to amber and remain in this state. Normally, if a self-test fails, this is fatal to the switch and the switch will not boot. If all of the self-tests have been successful, all of the LEDs should flash green and then turn off. In this state, the MODE LED will default to STAT.

TABLE 4-6 POST Tests Performed

Port LED	Test Performed	If the Test Fails
16	ECU DRAM	Switch will not boot
15	No self-tests performed	
14	No self-tests performed	
13	No self-tests performed	
12	Forwarding Engine ASIC	Switch will not boot
11	Forwarding Engine memory	Switch will not boot
10	RAM	Switch will not boot
09	ISL ASIC	Switch will not boot
08	Port control and status	Switch will not boot
07	System timer interrupt	Switch will not boot
06	Port address table RAM	Switch will not boot
05	Real-time clock	Switch will boot
04	Console port	Switch will boot
03	Port address table	Switch will not boot
02	Switch's MAC address	Switch will not boot
01	Port loopback test	A port might not function correctly

Catalyst 2950 Switch

The 2950 series of switches are Cisco's current desktop and workgroup switching solution, replacing the 1900 and 2820 switches. The 2950 series of switches come with two different versions of software: standard and enhanced. This book focuses on the standard version of software. The enhanced version handles advanced Quality of Service, telephony, and other features. The other major difference between the different types of 2950 switch models is the number and types of ports. Table 4-7 compares the 2950 switches and their port types and capacities. The 2950, like the 1900 series, supports an optional external RPS.

2950 Chassis

Figure 4-2 shows a picture of the front and rear of a 2950-24 switch. The top part shows the front, while the bottom part shows the rear. For the top part of the picture, there is a cut-out of the LEDs on the left-hand side of the switch. The front of the chassis contains the MODE button as well as the LEDs and all of the Ethernet ports.

The rear of the chassis has the management connections. You'll notice that there is no toggle switch to turn the switch on or off. To turn the switch on, plug one end of the power cable into the back of the switch and the other into a power outlet. To turn the switch off, unplug the power cable from either end.

Unlike the 1900 series, the 2950 doesn't have a 10Base5 Ethernet port. Also, the 2950 supports only an RJ-45 console interface, which uses a rollover cable for connectivity to a terminal or terminal emulation device for console access. The 2950 also doesn't have a reset button—if you want to reboot the switch, you need to either

TABLE 4-7 2950 Models

Switch	10/100BaseTX	100BaseFX	Gigabit
2950-12	12	0	0
2950-24	24	0	0
2950C-24	24	2	0
2950G-12-EI	12	0	2
2950G-24-EI	24	0	2
2950G-48-EI	48	0	2
2950SX-24	24	0	2
2950T-24	24	0	2

FIGURE 4-2 A 2950 switch

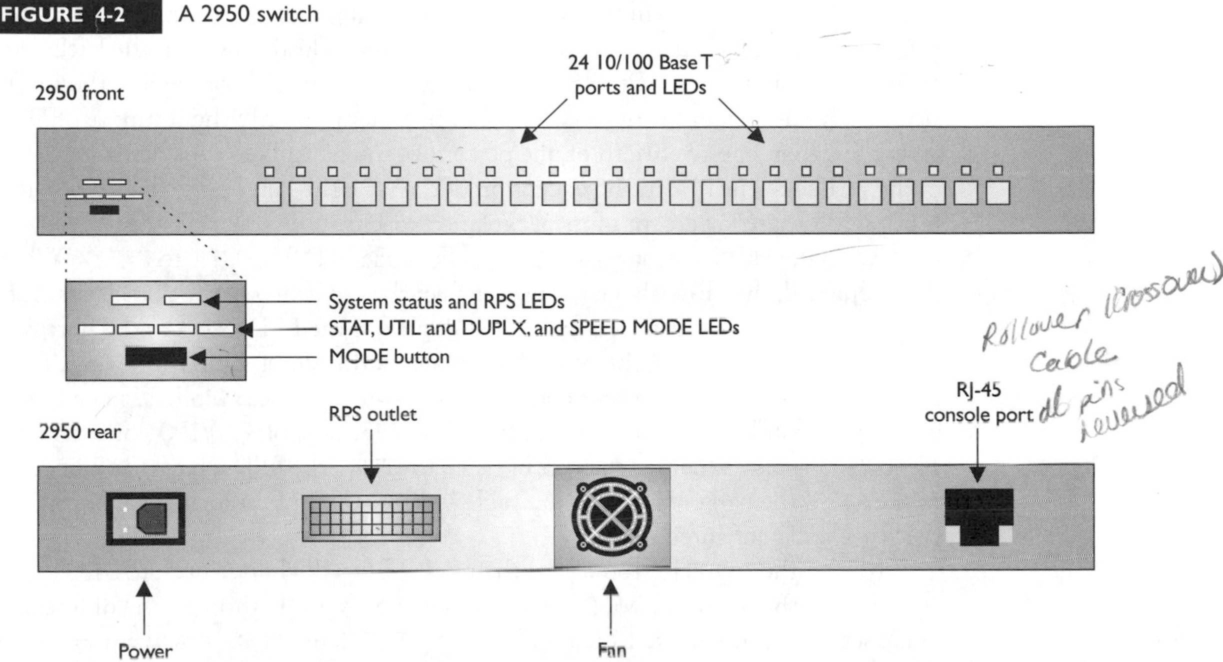

execute the **`reload`** command from the CLI or unplug the power connector from the switch and then reinsert it.

2950 LEDs and MODE Button

Like the 1900, the 2950 has many LEDs on the front of the chassis that you can use to monitor the switch's activity and performance. In the top left-hand corner of the front of the 2950's chassis are the SYSTEM and RPS LEDs. The colors of these LEDs and their meanings are the same as those for the 1900, which were shown in Table 2-2.

Below these two LEDs are four LEDs: STAT, UTIL, DUPLX, and SPEED. These LEDs function similar to the corresponding LEDs on the 1900—they are controlled by the MODE button below them. The default mode is STAT, which causes the LEDs above each port to reflect the status of the port. These were explained in Table 2-3.

Pressing the MODE button once changes the mode LED from STAT to UTIL. The LEDs above each of the ports in this mode reflect the bandwidth utilization of the backplane of the switch. The LEDs will turn green, acting like a meter bar. If an LED is amber, this indicates the maximum amount of bandwidth the switch has used since the switch was booted. This means that the port LEDs to the right of this will be off and the ones to the left will be green or off, indicating the current utilization. When you are reading the meter bar to measure the actual bandwidth used on the backplane of the switch, note each switch has a slightly different process for reading the LEDs, since each has a different number of ports. In general, if only the leftmost LED is green, less than one-twentieth of one percent of the backplane capacity is used. If all of the LEDs are green with the exception of the far right-hand port, then the switch is using less than 50 percent of its backplane capacity.

Pressing the MODE button again changes the mode LED from UTIL to DUPLX. When this is enabled, the LEDs above the ports reflect the duplexing of the port. If the LED above the port is off, the port is set to half-duplex; if the LED is green, the port is set to full-duplex. By pressing the mode button again, the MODE LED will change from DUPLX to SPEED. This LED isn't contained on the 1900 series switches, since their ports operate only at 10Mbps or 100Mbps. The 2950 supports 10/100 ports, and even 10/100/1000 ports. When the mode LED is set to SPEED, the LEDs above the port refer to the speed the port is operating at. Table 4-8 lists the LED colors of the ports by port type and configured speed.

If you hit the MODE button again, the mode LED will change back to STAT. As you can see, the use of the MODE button allows you to cycle through the different mode settings. If the mode LED is either UTL, DUPLX, or SPEED, it will automatically change back to STAT after one minute.

Boot-Up Process and LEDs

When power is applied to the 2950, the switch will begin its POST process. POST is used to verify that the different components of the switch are operational. When POST begins, the SYSTEM LED is off. Once POST completes all testing, and all tests have passed, the SYSTEM LED should turn green. If it is amber, then at least one test has failed during POST, which is usually catastrophic for the switch: in other words, the switch won't boot up.

TABLE 4-8 Port LED Colors for Speed Indication

Port Type	Off	Green	Flashing Green
10/100	10Mbps	100Mbps	Not used
10/100/1000	10Mbps	100Mbps	1Gbps
1000Base-X	Port disabled	1Gbps	Not used

Routers

Each Cisco router has its own unique chassis and, depending on the model, unique components. Cisco has attempted to modularize many of the components so that they can be used in related models. For instance, many of the cards for the 2600 and 3600 series routers are interchangeable. However, this is not the case for all of Cisco's routers. Therefore, there is typically no standardization as to what the router looks like and what LEDs it contains. This is also true of management ports. Most routers Cisco sells today have an RJ-45 console port. But many of Cisco's older routers, the 4000 and 7500 series, for example, use a DB-25 console port. The larger routers have both a console and an auxiliary port, while the smaller routers, like the 800, have only a console port.

Since each router is different from an external viewpoint, as well as its internal architecture, this book will not cover any of the chassis of the router models. If you are tested on any LEDs on the CCNA exam, it will be on the 1900 and 2950 switches. You might be tested on console connections, but I will cover this in more depth in the next section.

CERTIFICATION OBJECTIVE 4.03

Connections

Cisco's networking products support two types of external connections: ports (referred to as lines) and interfaces. Physical ports are used for management purposes and provide an out-of-band method for managing your Cisco product. Out-of-band means that your management tasks do not affect traffic that is flowing through your Cisco product. Interfaces are used to connect different networking devices together, such as a switch to router or a hub to a PC. Interfaces are connected to the backplane of the switch. You can also use interfaces for management purposes, but doing so can affect the performance of your network device. These types of connections are called in-band connections. The following sections will cover the console port as well as interfaces on your Cisco devices.

Out-of-band management does not affect the bandwidth flowing through your network, while in-band management does.

Console Port

Almost every Cisco product has a console port. This port is used to establish an out-of-band connection in order to access the CLI to manage your Cisco device. Once you have placed a basic configuration on your Cisco device, assigning it IP addressing information, for instance, you can then come in via one of its interfaces in order to manage your product in-band. Some methods of in-band management include telnet, a web browser, SNMP, and CiscoWorks 2000.

Assuming that your Cisco device has an RJ-45 console port, you will need two components in order to manage your Cisco device from your PC:

- An RJ-45 rollover cable
- An RJ-45-to-DB-9 or RJ-45-to-DB-25 terminal adapter: determined by the number of pins that your COM port has on your PC

If your router has a DB-25 console port, you'll also need a DB-25-to-RJ-45 modem adapter, which is plugged into the console port of the router.

exam watch ***Most console connections to Cisco devices require an RJ-45 rollover cable and an RJ-45-to-DB9 terminal adapter. The rollover cable pins are reversed on the two sides.***

The rollover cable used for the console connection looks like an Ethernet CAT-5 cable; however, this cable is proprietary to Cisco and will not work for other types of connections, such as Ethernet connections. The rollover cable has eight wires inside its plastic shielding and two RJ-45 connectors at each end. Each side of the rollover cable reverses the pins compared to the other side: pin 1 on one side is mapped to pin 8 on the other side; pin 2 is mapped to pin 7, pin 3 is mapped to pin 6, pin 4 is mapped to pin 5, pin 5 is mapped to pin 4, pin 6 is mapped to pin 3, pin 7 is mapped to pin 2, and pin 8 is mapped to pin 1.

exam watch ***Remember the terminal parameters in Table 4-9 to establish a console connection to a Cisco device.***

Once you have connected one end of the rollover cable to the console port of your Cisco product and the other end into the terminal adapter and into the COM port of your PC (or terminal), you are ready to configure your PC to access your Cisco product. You will need a terminal emulation package to do this. There are many available products that you can use, including HyperTerminal, which comes standard with Microsoft Windows operating systems. However, one of my personal favorites is TeraTerm. Within your terminal emulation software, you will need to set the parameters in Table 4-9 to the specified values. Once you have configured these

TABLE 4-9

COM Port Settings

COM Component	Setting
Speed	9,600bps
Data bits	8
Stop bits	1
Parity	None
Flow control	None

settings, you should be able to press the ENTER key a few times to gain access to the CLI. At this point, you are accessing the Cisco product out-of-band.

Hardware Interfaces

This section will cover the nomenclature that Cisco uses for both their switch and router interfaces. This is important when it comes to configuring the components of a specific interface, such as its duplexing, or connecting a cable to it. As you will see under the following two headings, there are some minor differences between these two types of products.

Switch Interface Nomenclature

The Catalyst 1900 and 2950 switches support only fixed interfaces, while the 2800 supports fixed and modular interfaces. Like their modular router counterparts, the nomenclature of an interface is: `type slot_#/port_#` The type of interface is the media type, like `ethernet`, `fastethernet`, or `gigabit`. Following this is the slot number. For all fixed interfaces on the 1900 and 2950 switches, the slot number is always `0`. For the 2820 switches, the fixed interfaces are referred to be in slot `0`, while the two modular slots are `1` and `2`.

The port number is the number of the port in the specified slot. Unlike in Cisco routers, port numbers start at `1` and work their way up. For instance, on a 1900, the very first port is `ethernet 0/1`, the second port is `ethernet 0/2`, and so on. For either the 1912 or 1924 switches, the AUI port on the back of the switch is

exam watch

The nomenclature of a switch interface is: `type slot_#/port_#`. The type of interface is the media type, like `ethernet`, `fastethernet`, or `gigabit`. Following this is the slot number. For all fixed interfaces on the 1900 and 2950 switches, the slot number is always 0. All port numbers start at `1` and work their way up.

ethernet 0/25 and the two Fast Ethernet uplink ports are fastethernet 0/26 and fastethernet 0/27. Another difference between Cisco routers and switches is that with Cisco routers, each port type's numbering begins with 0: ethernet 0, ethernet 1, . . ., and fastethernet 0, fastethernet 1, . . ., but the Catalyst switches use a different scheme: the numbers start with 1 with the first port and work their way up, even if the port type changes.

Router Interface Nomenclature

Depending on the Cisco router product, the interfaces are either fixed, modular, or a combination of the two. When referring to fixed interfaces on a Cisco product, the interface numbers *always* begin with 0 (not 1, like the switches) and work their way up within a particular interface type. Unlike switches, routers support many different data link layer media types, depending on their model. These types can include the following: atm, asynch, bri, ethernet, fddi, serial, tokenring, as well as many others.

For routers that have only fixed interfaces, the interface nomenclature is *type port_#*. For example, if a router has two fixed Ethernet interfaces and two fixed serial interfaces, they would be called ethernet 0 and ethernet 1 and serial 0 and serial 1. As you can see in this example, the port numbers begin at 0 within *each* interface type. Through use of an interface type and a number, each of the interfaces can be uniquely identified.

However, if a router has modular slots, where you can insert interface cards into these slots, the interface nomenclature is like the Catalyst switches: *type slot_#/port_#*. Each slot has a unique slot number beginning with 0, and within each slot, the ports begin at 0 and work their way up. For example, if you had a modular router with two slots, the first slot would be 0 and the second 1. If the first

exam watch

The nomenclature of a router interface is either type slot_#/port_# or type port_#. The type of interface is the media type, like atm, asynch, bri, ethernet, fddi, serial, tokenring, as well as many others. Following this is the slot number for modular routers. The slot numbers start at 0 and work their way up. All port numbers within a slot and type start at 0 and work their way up, which differs from the Catalyst switches.

slot had four Ethernet interfaces, the interface numbers would be `0-3` and if the second slot had two Ethernet interfaces, the interface numbers would be `0` and `1`.

Here's an example of a four-port serial module in the third slot of a 3640 router: `serial 2/0`, `serial 2/1`, `serial 2/2`, and `serial 2/3`. Here are some examples of routers with modular interfaces: 2600, 3600, 3700, 7000, 7200, and 7500. The exception to this is the 1600 and 1700 routers; even though they are modular, you don't configure any slot number when specifying a particular interface.

CERTIFICATION OBJECTIVE 4.04

Cabling

The last section of this chapter will deal with cabling. The CCNA focuses on Ethernet as a LAN technology and multiple types of WAN technologies. Therefore, this part of the chapter will focus on cables used for Ethernet and various WAN connections.

Ethernet Cabling

Ethernet has become the de facto standard for LAN implementations. At one time, there were three competing technologies: Ethernet, Token Ring, and FDDI. Because of the cost of FDDI, it was never really implemented on a wide scale but used only for backbone connections. Token Ring, however, was designed and heavily promoted by IBM. When Cisco purchased IBM's networking division, this stopped any further development on Token Ring technology. Therefore, most companies that used other LAN media types have converted to Ethernet. This section will provide a review from Chapter 2 on Ethernet, as well as the types of connections and cables you'll use to attach Ethernet devices together.

Cabling Specifications

IEEE 802.3 specifies the following standards for 10Mbps Ethernet: 10Base2, 10Base5, 10BaseT, and 10BaseFL. IEEE 802.3r specifies the following standards for 100Mbps Ethernet, called Fast Ethernet: 100BaseFX and 100BaseTX. At one time, there was another competing Fast Ethernet standard, 100BaseT4, but it has been supplanted by the two previous standards. When you look at Cisco's three-layer hierarchical model (core, distribution, and access), Cisco recommends that you use Ethernet only at the access layer, but you can use Fast Ethernet at any of the three layers.

Cabling Devices

With today's implementation of Ethernet over copper, two components make up the connection: an RJ-45 connector and a Category-5 UTP cable. The cable has eight wires in it (4-pair of wires). There are two types of implementations for the pinouts of the two sides of the cable: straight-through and crossover.

A straight-through cable has pin 1 on one side connected to pin 1 on the other side, pin 2 to pin 2, and so on. A straight-through cable is used for DTE-to-DCE connections. The terms DTE and DCE are typically used in WAN connections, where the DCE provides clocking. These terms will be discussed in more depth in Chapter 15. However, in LAN terms, a DTE is a router, PC, or file server and a DCE is a hub or a switch. Here is when you should use a straight-through cable:

- A hub to a router, PC, or file server
- A switch to a router, PC, or file server

A crossover cable crosses over two sets of wires: pin 1 on one side is connected to pin 3 on the other and pin 2 is connected to pin 6. Crossover cables should by used when you connect a DTE to another DTE or a DCE to another DCE. Use a crossover cable for the following:

- A hub to another hub
- A switch to another switch
- A hub to a switch
- A PC, router, or file server to another PC, router, or file server

Sometimes the Ethernet interface will give you a clue as to the type of cable to use. If there is an X on the port and the other port doesn't have an X labeled on it, then use a straight-through cable. If neither device has an X or both do have an X, then use a crossover cable. In some instances, this setting can be changed in software with

exam watch

For Ethernet, use a crossover cable for DTE-to-DTE and DCE-to-DCE devices and a straight cable for DTE-to-DCE connections. A DTE device is a PC, file server, or router. A DCE device is a hub or a switch. An Ethernet crossover cable crosses over pins 1 ⟷ 3 and 2 ⟷ 6.

a command or in hardware through the use of a DIP switch, which allows you to use the cable type that you currently have available.

WAN Cabling

In WAN connections, your router is the DTE and the equipment it attaches to, such as a modem, CSU/DSU, or an NT1, is a DCE. The DCE is responsible for providing the clocking and synchronization of the physical layer connection. The cabling discussed in this section applies only to DTE-to-DCE connections. The cabling used for WAN connection is dependent on the technology and speed of access that you are using. Table 4-10 lists the cables and when they are used.

exam watch

Most Cisco synchronous serial interfaces have either a DB-60 or DB-26 connector.

Each cable has two ends: one connects to the DCE and the other to the DTE. The DCE end point is defined in the Cable Standards column in Table 4-10. However, the DTE end is proprietary to Cisco. With the exception of RJ-45, most of the WAN DTE end points either use a Cisco proprietary DB-60 connector or the smaller Cisco proprietary DB-26 connector, which looks like a flat USB connector. An ISDN BRI connection uses an RJ-45 connector.

on the job

It is extremely important that you plug your ISDN BRI connection from the router into the appropriate ISDN outlet. The ISDN connection has a voltage that runs through it, and if you connect the cable from the ISDN outlet to another router port, such as the console port or an Ethernet interface, you will probably damage your non-ISDN interface.

TABLE 4-10 WAN Cable Types

Cable Standards	ISDN BRI	HDLC	PPP	Frame Relay	HSSI
EIA/TIA-232	No	Yes	Yes	Yes	No
EIA/TIA-449	No	Yes	Yes	Yes	No
EIA/TIA-612/613	No	No	No	No	Yes
X.21	No	Yes	Yes	Yes	No
V.24	No	Yes	Yes	Yes	No
V.35	No	Yes	Yes	Yes	No
RJ-45	Yes	No	No	No	No

CERTIFICATION SUMMARY

When choosing a networking product, you should consider ease-of-use, features and functions, capacity, reliability, and management. When choosing a WAN solution, consider cost, availability, and bandwidth requirements.

Hubs and repeaters are used to connect devices in the same bandwidth or collision domain. Switches are used to break up collision and bandwidth domains into smaller, more manageable segments through a process called microsegmentation. Routers are used to route between different broadcast domains.

The 1912 has 12 10BaseT interfaces and the 1924 has 24 10BaseT interfaces. Both have one 10Base5 AUI port and two 100BaseTX or FX uplink ports. The 2950 switches come in many varieties(hardware and software). Most interfaces support multiple auto-sensing speeds. The switch also supports two versions of software: standard and enhanced. On both switches, the RJ-45 console port is on the rear of the switch. When either switch boots up, it runs POST, which performs internal hardware diagnostics. Most test failures will cause the switch not to boot. To turn the switch off or on, remove or insert the power cord into the switch.

If the SYSTEM LED is amber, the switch experienced a malfunction. The MODE button is used to change the meanings of the LEDs for the Ethernet ports. mode LEDs include STAT, UTIL, FDUP/DUPLX, and SPEED (only the 2950). In STAT MODE, if the port LED is flashing green, the interface is passing traffic; if it is flashing green and amber, there is an operational problem with the port, like excessive collisions; if it is amber, the port has been disabled by a security violation or manually by an administrator. The UTIL MODE displays the current bandwidth usage of the backplane of the switch.

The console port requires an RJ-45 rollover cable and an RJ-45 to DB-9 terminal adapter. The rollover cable pins are reversed on the two sides. Your terminal emulator on your PC will need to be configured for 9,600bps, 8 data bits, 1 stop bit, no parity, and no flow control for a console connection.

The nomenclature of a switch interface is: `type slot_#/port_#`. The type of interface is the media type, like `ethernet`, `fastethernet`, or `gigabit`. Following this is the slot number. For all fixed interfaces on the 1900 and 2950 switches, the slot number is always `0`. All port numbers start at `1` and work their way up. The nomenclature of a router interface is either `type slot_#/port_#` or `type port_#`. The type of interface is the media type, like `atm`, `asynch`, `bri`, `ethernet`, `fddi`, `serial`, `tokenring`, as well as many others. Following this is the slot number for modular routers. The slot numbers start at `0` and work their way up. All port numbers within a slot and type start at 0 and work their way up, which is different from the Catalyst switches.

For Ethernet, use a crossover cable for DTE-to-DTE and DCE-to-DCE devices and a straight cable for DTE-to-DCE connections. A DTE device is a PC, file server, or router. A DCE device is a hub or a switch. Most Cisco synchronous serial interfaces use either a DB-60 or DB-26 connector.

TWO-MINUTE DRILL

Cisco's Networking Products

- When choosing a network product, consider: is it easy to install/support, does it support your requirements, does it have enough capacity, does it support redundancy, does it support mobile users, is it easily upgraded?
- For WAN solutions, ensure the following: that it is cost-effective, that the service is available, that you choose a solution with enough bandwidth.

Chassis Information

- The 1900 supports 1,024 MAC addresses. The 2800 supports two modular slots. All these switches have an AUI port on the rear and two 100Base uplink ports. The 1900 supports 10BaseT and 100Base fixed ports.
- The 1900 has a system LED: green is operational and amber is a malfunction. The MODE button is used to switch between the three mode LEDs: STAT (status of the port), UTL (backplane utilization), and FDUP (port duplexing). For port status, here are the LED colors: green, physical layer signal; flashing green, traffic entering the port; flashing green/amber, connection problem; amber, disabled. The default mode is port status.
- The 2950 supports fixed 10/100, 10/100/1000, and Gigabit ports. The 2950 has four port modes: STAT, UTIL, DUPLX, and SPEED. The colors of these LEDs are the same as on the 1900.
- Most failures during POST will cause the 1900 and 2950 switches to fail.

Connections

- Out-of-band management is done through the console or auxiliary ports; in-band is done through an interface.
- Console port connections require an RJ-45 rollover cable and an RJ-45–to–DB-9 terminal adapter. In your terminal emulation package, set the following: speed to 9600bps, data bits to 8, stop bits to 1, parity to none, and flow control to none.
- The slot number of the 1900 and 2950 is `0`; port numbers start at `1`. Router slot numbers begin with `0`; port numbers start at `0` and restart with each type within each slot.

Cabling

- ❑ Ethernet straight-through cables are used to connect a DTE to a DCE: hub or switch to a router, PC, or file server.
- ❑ Ethernet crossover cables cross over pins 1 ←→ 3 and pins 2 ←→ 6. These connections are used for DTE-to-DTE and DCE-to-DCE connections, such as a hub or switch to another hub or switch; or a router, PC, or file server to another router, PC, or file server. If a networking device has an *X* over it, its port is set to DCE.

SELF TEST

The following Self Test questions will help you measure your understanding of the material presented in this chapter. Read all the choices carefully, as there may be more than one correct answer. Choose all correct answers for each question.

Cisco's Networking Products

1. When choosing a networking product, you should consider all of the following except _______.
   A. Ease of installation and support
   B. Product features and functions
   C. Backplane capacity
   D. Amount of memory
2. When choosing a WAN solution, consider all of the following except __________.
   A. Number of devices
   B. Cost-effectiveness
   C. Availability
   D. Amount of bandwidth

Chassis Information

3. A 1924 has _________ Ethernet interfaces.
   A. 24
   B. 26
   C. 27
   D. 28
4. The function of the MODE button is to __________.
   A. Change the status of the ports
   B. Affect what the SYSTEM and RPS LEDs represent
   C. Affect what the port LEDs represent
   D. Change the status of all the LEDs

5. If the 1900 SYSTEM LED is __________, a system POST test has failed.
   A. Green
   B. Amber
   C. Flashing amber
   D. Flashing green and amber

6. If the port status LED on a 2950 is _________, there is a physical layer connection problem.
   A. Flashing green and amber
   B. Flashing green
   C. Amber
   D. Flashing amber

7. If the 1900's mode is FDUP, and the LED is __________, the port speed is set to autodetect.
   A. Green
   B. Off
   C. Amber
   D. None of these

8. If the 2950's RPS LED is _________, the external power supply is supplying power.
   A. Off
   B. Amber
   C. Flashing amber
   D. Green

Connections

9. When setting up an RJ-45 console connection, you need a RJ-45–to–DB-9 __________ adapter to attach to the COM port of your PC.
   A. Auxiliary
   B. Console
   C. Connection
   D. Terminal

10. With a rollover cable, pin 7 on one end is mapped to pin __________ on the other end.

11. The slot number of a 1900's Fast Ethernet uplink ports is ________.
    A. 0
    B. 1
    C. 2
    D. No slot number is used

12. When configuring your terminal emulation software for a console connection, set the flow control to __________.
    A. Hardware
    B. Software
    C. None

Cabling

13. When connecting a router to a PC, use a __________ cable.
    A. Crossover
    B. Straight-through
    C. Rollover

14. When connecting a switch to a router, use a ___________ cable.
    A. Crossover
    B. Straight-through
    C. Rollover

15. With a crossover cable, which pins are crossed over?
    A. 1 and 2, 3 and 6
    B. 1 and 3, 2 and 6
    C. 1 and 4, 2 and 6
    D. 1 and 3, 4 and 6

SELF TEST ANSWERS

Cisco's Networking Products

1. ☑ **D.** The amount of memory is not, typically, an important item when choosing between different networking products.
☒ **A**, **B**, and **C** should be considered when choosing between network products.

2. ☑ **A.** The number of devices is typically not as important as the cost-effectiveness, availability of the service, and amount of needed bandwidth when choosing a WAN solution.
☒ **B**, **C**, and **D** should all be considered when choosing a WAN solution.

Chassis Information

3. ☑ **C.** A 1924 has 27 Ethernet interfaces: 24 10BaseT, 1 AUI, and 2 100Base uplink interfaces.
☒ **A** is the number of 10BaseT interfaces. **B** is the number of interfaces on the front of the chassis. **D** specifies too many interfaces.

4. ☑ **C.** The function of the MODE button is to affect what the port LEDs represent.
☒ **A** is true of a physical problem or software configuration. **B** has nothing to do with these two LEDs. And **D** is partially true: it affects the port LEDs, but not the SYSTEM and RPS LEDs.

5. ☑ **B.** If the 1900 system LED is amber, a SYSTEM POST test has failed.
☒ **A** indicates that all POST tests passed. **C** and **D** aren't supported with this LED.

6. ☑ **A.** If the port status LED on a 2950 is flashing green and amber, there is a physical layer problem.
☒ **B** indicates traffic passing through the port. **C** indicates the interface is disabled. **D** is not an LED status.

7. ☑ **D.** The 1900 doesn't support different speeds on the same interface: they're 10BaseT, 10Base5, or 100BaseTX/FX. The 2950, however, supports this function.
☒ **A**, **B**, and **C** are thus incorrect.

8. ☑ **C.** If the 2950's RPS is flashing amber, the external power supply is supplying power.
☒ **A** indicates that the external RPS is not installed. **B** indicates that the external RPS has failed or has a problem. **D** indicates that the RPS is installed but the internal power supply is supplying power.

Connections

9. ☑ D. When setting up an RJ-45 console connection, you need a RJ-45–to–DB-9 terminal adapter to attach to the COM port of your PC.
☒ **A**, **B**, and **C** are incorrect adapters.

10. ☑ With a rollover cable, pin 7 on one end is mapped to pin **2** on the other end.

11. ☑ **A.** The slot number of a 1900's Fast Ethernet uplink ports is **0**.
☒ **B** is the first slot in a 2800. **C** is the second slot in a 2800. The 1900 has at least one, logical, slot, making **D** incorrect.

12. ☑ **C.** When configuring your terminal emulation software for a console connection, set the flow control to *none*.
☒ **A** and **B** are incorrect.

Cabling

13. ☑ **A.** When connecting a router to a PC, use a crossover cable.
☒ **B** is used for DTE-to-DCE connections. **C** is used for console connections.

14. ☑ **B.** When connecting a switch to a router, use a straight-through cable.
☒ **A** is true for DTE-to-DTE and DCE-to-DCE connections. **C** is for console connections.

15. ☑ **B.** For a crossover cable, pins 1 and 3 and 2 and 6 are crossed over.
☒ **A**, **C**, and **D** have the wrong pinouts crossed.

5

Basic Switch and Router Configuration

CERTIFICATION OBJECTIVES

5.01 IOS Introduction

5.02 IOS Basics

5.03 Basic Switch Configuration

5.04 Basic Router Configuration

 Two-Minute Drill

Q&A Self Test

This chapter presents the basics of configuring the 1900 and 2950 Catalyst switches as well as Cisco routers. As you continue throughout this book, you will build upon these fundamental and important concepts for accessing, configuring, and managing your Cisco devices. I am making the assumption that you have never configured a Cisco device before and therefore will begin with the very basics by explaining the operating system that these devices use, the advantages that Cisco's operating system provides, and how to use some basic operating system commands to configure your Cisco device.

CERTIFICATION OBJECTIVE 5.01

IOS Introduction

One of the main reasons that Cisco is number one in the enterprise networking market place is their *Internetwork Operating System (IOS)*. The IOS provides a similar function to Microsoft Windows XP or Linux: it controls and manages the hardware it is running on. Basically, the IOS provides the interface between you and the hardware, enabling you to execute commands to configure and manage your Cisco device. Originally, the IOS was developed for Cisco routers, but over the last few years, Cisco has been porting the IOS to its other platforms, including the Catalyst switches.

Cisco has spent many years tweaking and tuning the IOS, as well as adding features as new technologies are introduced to the marketplace. Advantages of the IOS include:

- **Features** The IOS includes a wide array of features for protocols and functions that provide connectivity, scalability, reliability, and security solutions for networks of any size.
- **Connectivity** The IOS supports a variety of data link layer technologies for the LAN and WAN environments, including copper and fiber wiring as well as wireless.
- **Scalability** The IOS supports both fixed and modular chassis platforms, enabling you to purchase the appropriate hardware for your needs, yet still allowing you to leverage the same IOS CLI to reduce your management costs.
- **Reliability** To ensure that your critical resources are always reachable, Cisco has developed many products and IOS features to provide network redundancy.
- **Security** With the IOS, you can strictly control access to your network and networking devices in accordance with your internal security policies.

IOS stands for Internetwork Operating System. **Its advantages include features, connectivity, scalability, reliability, and security.**

Because of the success of their IOS software, Cisco has grown from a garage-based router company to one of the largest companies in the world in a little over a decade. Most enterprise networks, as well as ISPs, use Cisco products in one form or another. Actually, a large portion of the Internet backbone is composed of Cisco products. With the IOS coupled with a first-class service and support team, few companies can compare to Cisco when it comes to customer satisfaction.

Device Startup

There are actually many ways of accessing a Cisco device, including the following: console, auxiliary (only certain Cisco routers), telnet, web browser, and an SNMP management station. A console interface provides serial connection access to a router—with console access, you can enter commands in a text-based mode. In order to access your Cisco device from a remote station, however, you first need to create a basic configuration, including IP addressing. Therefore, to perform your initial configurations, you need access to the console port of your Cisco device.

Before you can actually begin configuring your Cisco device, you first have to connect it to your network and set up a terminal connection to its console interface, as described in the Chapter 4. Here are the three steps your Cisco device goes through when booting up:

1. Perform hardware tests.
2. Locate and load the IOS.
3. Locate and execute the device's configuration file.

Once you power on your Cisco device, hardware tests are performed to ensure that it is operating correctly. These tests, *power-on self tests (POST)*, are discussed in Chapter 4. After these tests have completed, the Cisco device finds and locates the IOS and then proceeds to load it. Once the IOS is loaded, the IOS then searches for the device's configuration and executes it. With steps 2 and 3, there are typically fallback measures that the Cisco device goes through if it cannot find an IOS or locate a configuration file.

As you will see in this chapter, and as you work with Cisco devices in a production environment, each Cisco product is unique and may have its own methods for finding and loading its IOS and configuration file. As an example, a Catalyst 1900 switch, direct from Cisco, comes with a default configuration already on it. This configuration is enough to allow the switch to perform basic switching functions right out of the box. A Cisco router, by contrast, requires some basic configuration in order to route traffic between interfaces.

> **exam watch**
> ***When an IOS device boots up, it runs POST, finds and loads the IOS, and then finds and loads the device's configuration file.***

Accessing the Command-Line Interface (CLI)

How you access the IOS CLI on a Cisco device for the first time depends on the kind of device that you are configuring. In almost every case, you will use the console interface to initially interact with the device; however, gaining access to the CLI from the console port can be different from one device to another. On a Cisco router, for instance, you are taken directly to the IOS CLI when you log in from the console port. If the IOS cannot find a configuration file for the router, the IOS takes you through *Setup* mode, which is a basic configuration script that prompts you for information on how you want to configure your router. However, on a Catalyst 1900 switch, you are first taken to a menu-based interface where you must choose the option of configuring the switch from the CLI. And a 1900 never takes you through *Setup* mode unless you physically execute the command from the CLI to begin the script.

> **exam watch**
> ***Be familiar with the various types of access to the IOS CLI: console and auxiliary ports for local access and VTYs (telnet), TFTP, SNMP, and web browsers.***

Once you have configured your Cisco device via the console port, you can then use other methods of accessing and changing its configuration, such as telnet—Cisco calls this *virtual terminal (VTY)*—TFTP, SNMP, or a web browser. Cisco has a variety of management products to configure and manage your Cisco device, such as CiscoWorks 2000; however, the focus of this book is strictly on the IOS CLI.

IOS Differences

What you will see in this and consequent chapters is that even though both Cisco routers and switches run the IOS, the commands used by these products are frequently different! In other words, how you configure a feature on a Cisco router might be, and probably is, different than configuring the same feature on a Catalyst switch. This is even true among Cisco's Catalyst switches: how you configure a certain feature on a 1900 may be different from configuring the same feature on the 2950!

However, you access the IOS and maneuver around the IOS access levels, as well as using many of the management commands, the same way on *all* IOS products. This can become confusing to a Cisco novice, where one command for a particular feature is the same on all Cisco products, but configuring another feature might be different on a Cisco router than on a Catalyst switch.

Besides command differences between different products, such as routers and switches, there may be command differences within a product line, Cisco routers, for instance. As an example, Cisco sells different flavors of its IOS software for routers, depending on the features that you need. Or because of hardware differences, some commands work on some routers but not on others.

Interacting with the IOS

The CLI is a character- or text-based interface. To interact with the CLI, you only need to type in commands, just as you would do when typing an essay in a text editor or a message in an e-mail program. You can even use functions like cut-and-paste with the IOS CLI: you can copy the complete configuration of a router using a terminal emulator's copy function, paste this into a text editor, make changes to the configuration, select and copy the new configuration, and paste all of these commands back into the CLI.

The CLI supports a command parser. Whenever you press the ENTER key, the IOS parses the command and parameters that you entered and checks for correct syntax and options. When you paste multiple commands into the CLI, the IOS still performs this process for each command that is included in the paste function. If you made a mistake with one command, the CLI parser will display an error message, but continue with the next command in the pasted list.

EXEC Modes

Each Cisco device supports different access modes. For CLI interaction, there are actually three modes:

- *User EXEC* Provides basic access to the IOS, with limited command availability (basically simple monitoring and troubleshooting commands)
- *Privilege EXEC* Provides high-level management access to the IOS, including all commands available at *User EXEC* mode
- *Configuration* Allows configuration changes to be made to the device

Both *EXEC* modes can be password-protected, allowing you to limit the people who can access your device to perform management, configuration, and troubleshooting tasks. The next two sections cover the two *EXEC* modes.

User EXEC Mode

Your initial access to the CLI is via *User EXEC* mode, which has only a limited number of commands that you can execute. Depending on the Cisco device's configuration, you might be prompted for a password to access this mode. This mode is typically used for basic troubleshooting of networking problems. You can tell that you are in *User EXEC* mode by examining the prompt on the left-hand side of the screen:

```
Router>
```

If you see a ">" character at the end of the information, then you know that you are in *User EXEC* mode. The information preceding the ">" is the name of the Cisco device. For instance, the default name of all Cisco routers is "Router," whereas on the 1900 switch, there is no name by default, and you see only the ">" sign at the beginning of the line, like this:

```
>
```

The 2950 switch's *User EXEC* prompt looks like this: `Switch>`. These device names can be changed with the **`hostname`** command, which is discussed later in this chapter.

Privilege EXEC Mode

Once you have gained access to *User EXEC* mode, you can use the **`enable`** command to access *Privilege EXEC* mode:

```
Router> enable
Router#
```

Once you enter the **`enable`** command, if a *Privilege EXEC* password has been configured on the Cisco device, you will be prompted for it. Upon successfully authenticating, you will be in *Privilege EXEC* mode. You can tell that you are in this mode by examining the CLI prompt. In the preceding code example, notice that the ">" changed to a "#."

When you are in *Privilege EXEC* mode, you have access to all of the *User EXEC* commands as well as many more advanced management and troubleshooting commands. These commands include extended ping and trace abilities, managing configuration files and IOS images, and detailed troubleshooting using **debug** commands. About the only thing that you can't do from this mode is to change the configuration of the Cisco device—this can only be done from *Configuration* mode.

If you wish to return to *User EXEC* mode, from *Privilege EXEC* mode, use the **disable** command:

```
Router# disable
Router>
```

Again, by examining the prompt, you can tell that you are now in *User EXEC* mode.

Logging Out of Your Device

You can log out of your Cisco device from either *User* or *Privilege EXEC* mode by using the **logout** or **exit** command:

```
Router# logout
-or-
Router# exit
```

The Catalyst IOS-based switches do not support the logout command, but they do support the exit command.

5.01. The CD includes a multimedia demonstration of logging in and out of a Cisco router.

exam watch

Know the three different modes in the IOS—User EXEC, Privilege EXEC, and Configuration modes—and what you can do in each mode. Use the enable command to go from User EXEC mode to Privilege EXEC mode. Use the disable command to go from Privilege EXEC to User EXEC modes and use the exit command to log out of the IOS device from either of these two modes.

CERTIFICATION OBJECTIVE 5.02

IOS Basics

Now that you know how to log in to and out of a Cisco device, the next few sections describe some of the features built into the CLI that will make your configuration and management tasks easier. These features include how to abbreviate commands, how to bring up detailed help on commands and their specific parameters, the output of commands, recalling commands, and editing commands.

Command Abbreviation and Completion

The CLI of the IOS allows you to abbreviate commands and parameters to their most unique characters. This feature is very useful for those of us that are physically challenged at typing. As an example, you could type **en** instead of **enable** when you want to go from *User EXEC* to *Privilege EXEC* mode, like this:

```
Router> en
Router#
```

The Cisco device, internally, completes the command for you. However, the characters that you enter must make the command unique. As an example, you couldn't type just the letter *e*, since there are other commands that begin with the letter *e*, such as **exit**.

Context-Sensitive Help

One of the more powerful features of the IOS is the support of context-sensitive help. Context-sensitive help is supported at all modes within the IOS, including *User EXEC*, *Privilege EXEC*, and *Configuration* modes. There are a variety ways to use this feature. If you are not sure what command you need to execute, at the prompt, type either **help** or **?**. The Cisco device then displays a list of commands that can be executed at the level in which you are currently located, along with a brief description of each command. Here is an example from a router's CLI at *User EXEC* mode:

```
Router> ?
Exec commands:
  access-enable     Create a temporary Access-List entry
  cd                Change current device
  clear             Reset functions
  connect           Open a terminal connection
```

```
  dir               List files on given device
  disable           Turn off privileged commands
  disconnect        Disconnect an existing network connection
  enable            Turn on privileged commands
<--output omitted-->
-- More -
```

exam watch

Use the `help` command or the `?` to pull up context-sensitive help. Also, you can abbreviate commands to their most unique characters.

If you see "`-- More --`" at the bottom of the screen, this indicates that there is more help information than can fit on the current screen. On a Cisco device, if you press the SPACEBAR, the IOS pages down to the next screen of help information. On Cisco routers, if you press the ENTER key, the help scrolls down one line at a time. Any other keystroke breaks out of the help text. Please note that on the Catalyst switches, the ENTER key is considered a break and terminates the help.

For more detailed help, you can follow a command or parameter with a space and a **?**. This causes the CLI to list the available options or parameters that are included for the command. For instance, you could type **erase** followed by **?** to see all of the parameters available for the erase command:

```
Router# erase ?
/all              Erase all files(in NVRAM)
  flash:            Filesystem to be erased
  nvram:            Filesystem to be erased
  pram:             Filesystem to be erased
  slot0:            Filesystem to be erased
  slot1:            Filesystem to be erased
  startup-config    Erase contents of configuration memory
Router# erase
```

In this example, you can see at least the first parameter necessary after the **erase** command. Please note that there may be additional parameters, depending on the next parameter that you type.

Or if you're not sure how to spell a command, you can enter the first few characters and immediately follow these characters with "**?**"; **e?**, for instance, lists all of the commands that begin with **e** at the current mode:

```
Router# e?
enable  erase  exit
Router# e
```

In this example, there are three commands that being with the letter **e** at *Privilege EXEC* mode.

5.02. The CD includes a multimedia demonstration of using context-sensitive help on a Cisco router.

Command Output

Whenever you enter a command, there is chance that you have entered it incorrectly. If this is the case, the IOS tells you that there is a problem with the previously executed command. For instance, this message indicates a CLI input error:

```
% Invalid input detected at '^'.
```

What is important is to examine the line between the command that you typed in and the error message. Somewhere in this line, you'll see an "^" sign. This is used by the IOS to indicate that an error exists in the command line at that spot.

Here is another CLI error message:

```
% Incomplete command.
```

This error indicates that you have not entered all of the necessary parameters for the command: The syntax of the command is correct, but more parameters are necessary. You can use the context-sensitive help feature discussed earlier in this chapter to help you figure out what parameter or parameters you forgot.

You get the following error message if you do not type enough characters to make a command or parameter unique. Here is an example:

```
% Ambiguous command: "show i"
```

In this example, apparently, more than one parameter for the **show** command begins with the letter **i**. Again, you can use context-sensitive help to figure out what parameter to use:

```
Router# show i?
idb  interfaces  ip  ipv6
Router# show i
```

If you enter a command that the IOS does not understand, you'll see this error message:

```
% Unknown command or computer name, or unable to find computer address
```

If you see this, use the context-sensitive help in order to figure out the correct command to enter.

I cannot begin to stress how important the context-sensitive help is. I constantly use it to enter commands. As of the writing of this book, this feature is available in the router and switch simulation questions of the exam. Don't be afraid to take advantage of this feature during the simulation questions on the exam.

Entering Commands

Four key IOS features relate to entering commands:

- Symbolic translation
- Command prompting
- Syntax checking
- Command recall

Whenever you enter a command in the CLI, the command-line parser dissects the command, making sure that it is a valid command with valid parameters. In the case of Cisco routers only, if the CLI parser cannot find the actual command, the IOS assumes that you are trying to telnet to a machine by that name and attempts a DNS resolution of the name to an IP address. This process, called *symbolic translation*, can be annoying at times. But it does make telnetting to a remote machine much easier, since you only have to type the name or IP address of the machine instead of using the **telnet** command, discussed in the next chapter.

You have already been presented with the *command prompting* feature—this is most commonly seen when using the context-sensitive help, like the following:

```
Router# show ?
aaa                        Show AAA values
  aal2                       Show commands for AAL2
  access-expression          List access expression
  access-lists               List access lists
  accounting                 Accounting data for active sessions
  adjacency                  Adjacent nodes
  alarm-interface            Display information about a specific Alarm
                             Interface Card
  aliases                    Display alias commands
  alps                       Alps information
  arp                        ARP table
<--output omitted-->
Router# show
```

In this example, after you use the context-sensitive help with the **show** command, the command **show** is left on the command line after the displayed output. The IOS is assuming that you are entering one of the parameters of this command and thus reenters the command in the CLI. This can be annoying if you, like myself, forget that the router is performing this function and reenter the command again, like this:

```
Router# show show
```

The CLI always parses your commands and checks their validity by using the *syntax checking* feature. Any nonexisting commands or improperly entered commands cause the IOS to generate an error message with an appropriate error description.

on the Job

Whenever you enter a command correctly, very rarely will you see any output from the IOS, unless the command you typed in somehow changes the state of the router or one of its components, like an interface coming up or going down. Therefore, you should worry only when you enter a command and the IOS displays a message afterward—then you should assume that there might be a problem.

Of course, when you are configuring a Cisco router or Catalyst switch, you will typically make typing mistakes or enter invalid commands. If you typed in a 20-parameter command and made a mistake with the very last character, it would be sadistic on Cisco's part to have you type the complete command again. The *command recall* feature is an extremely useful one that allows you to recall and edit previously executed commands. The next two sections discuss how to recall and edit previous (or current) commands.

Command-Line History

On any IOS device, use the **show history** command to see your previous commands:

```
Router# show history
  enable
  show interface
  show version
  show history
Router#
```

By default, an IOS device stores the last ten commands that you executed. You can recall these commands by pressing either CTRL-P or the UP ARROW key. If you accidentally go past the command that you want to edit or reexecute, use CTRL-N or the DOWN ARROW key.

On IOS routers, you can increase the size of the history buffer from 10 commands up to 256 by using **terminal history size** command:

```
Router# terminal history size #_of_commands
```

Unfortunately, this command is not supported on the 1900 and 2950 Catalyst switches.

5.03. The CD includes a multimedia demonstration of using the history function on a Cisco router.

Editing the Command Line

The CLI editing features of the IOS are enabled by default. On the 1900 and 2950, you cannot disable the editing features; however, you can disable them on a Cisco router by using this command:

```
Router# terminal no editing
```

Remember the basic editing control sequences for editing commands in the CLI. By default, the IOS stores the last ten executed commands.

To reenable the editing features, remove the **no** parameter from the preceding command (**terminal editing**).

Table 5-1 shows the control or command sequences that you can use to edit information in the CLI.

5.04. The CD includes a multimedia demonstration of using the command-line editing features on a Cisco router.

TABLE 5-1 Editing Control Sequences for IOS Devices

Control Sequence	Description
CTRL-A	Moves the cursor to the beginning of the line
CTRL-E	Moves the cursor to the end of the line
ESC-B	Moves the cursor back one word at a time
ESC-F	Moves the cursor forward one word at a time
CTRL-B	Moves the cursor back one character at a time
<LEFT ARROW>	Moves the cursor back one character at a time
CTRL-F	Moves the cursor forward one character at a time

TABLE 5-1 Editing Control Sequences for IOS Devices *(continued)*

Control Sequence	Description
RIGHT ARROW	Moves the cursor forward one character at a time
CTRL-P	Recalls the last command
<UP ARROW>	Recalls the last command
CTRL-N	Recalls the most previously executed command
DOWN ARROW	Recalls the most previously executed command
CTRL-D	Deletes the character the cursor is under
<BACKSPACE>	Deletes the character preceding the cursor
CTRL-R	Redisplays the current line
CTRL-U	Erases the line completely
CTRL-W	Erases the word the cursor is under
CTRL-Z	Takes you from *Configuration* mode back to *Privilege EXEC* mode
<TAB>	Once you enter a few characters and hit the TAB key, the IOS device completes the word, assuming that you typed in enough characters to make the command or parameter unique
$	When this appears at the beginning of a command line, it indicates that there are more characters to the right of the $.

IOS Feature Example

Let's use the **clock** command to illustrate the helpfulness of some of the IOS's command-line features. This command is used on a router to set the current date and time. As an example, let's assume that English isn't your native language and that you are not sure how to spell "clock," but you do know that it begins with the letters "cl." Here's an example:

```
Router# cl?
clear    clock
Router# cl
```

Notice two things about the output in this example. First, two commands begin with **cl**: **clear** and **clock**. Second, notice the CLI after the help output—the IOS kept the **cl** on the command line. Some administrators like this feature and some hate it. I'm in the latter camp, since I commonly forget that the IOS device is doing this and I start typing from the beginning, like this:

```
Router# clclock
Translating "clclock"
% Unknown command or computer name, or unable to find computer address
Router#
```

If you haven't guessed, this is an invalid command. Now that we know how to spell "clock," if you don't know what parameter(s) to type after the **clock** command, use the context-sensitive help:

```
Router# clock ?
set  Set the time and date
Router# clock
```

The first column is the name of the parameter, and the second column is description. In this case, the IOS wants the word **set**:

```
Router# clock set ?
hh:mm:ss  Current Time
Router# clock set
```

The next parameter wants the current time. This is based on UTC and is in a 24-hour format. For example, 3 P.M. would be 15:00:00. Again, use the context-sensitive help to figure out if there are more parameters:

```
Router# clock set 15:00:00 ?
  <1-31>  Day of the month
  MONTH   Month of the year
Router# clock set 15:00:00
```

Whenever you see a range of numbers in angle brackets, you must choose a value in this range. If you see a parameter in all caps, like MONTH, you must supply a *name*. In our clocking example, the IOS wants the name of the month, such as "May". Again, using the context-sensitive help, the IOS wants the number of the year following the name of the month:

```
Router# clock set 15:00:00 23 May ?
  <1993-2035>  Year
Router# clock set 15:00:00 23 May
```

Again, use the context-sensitive help to see what's next:

```
Router# clock set 15:00:00 23 May 2004 ?
<cr>
Router# clock set 15:00:00 23 May 2004
Router#
```

If you see "<cr>," this means that you can hit the ENTER key and the IOS device will accept the command. On an IOS router, use the **show clock** command to see your current time and date:

```
Router# show clock
15:00:02.187 UTC Fri May 23 2003
Router#
```

5.05. The CD includes a multimedia demonstration of using a combination of the command-line editing features on a Cisco router.

EXERCISE 5-1

Using IOS Features

These last few sections have covered how you use the IOS features on your Cisco devices. Here are some exercises that you can perform on a Cisco router to enforce these skills. Use either the 2600 or 2500 router on the router simulator included on the CD-ROM, or you can use a real Cisco router. You can find a picture of the network diagram for the simulator in the Introduction to this book. Access the simulator and click the *Lab Navigator* button. Double-click *Exercise 5-1*, click the *Load Lab* button, and then the *OK* button. Click the *eRouters* button and choose *2600*.

1. Access *User EXEC* mode on your router.

   Hit the ENTER key. You should see the *EXEC* prompt: `Router>`.
2. Pull up the list of commands available at this mode.

   Use the **?**.
3. Go to *Privilege EXEC* mode.

   Use the **enable** command and your prompt should look like this: `Router#`.
4. Type the **show interfaces** and **show running-config** commands on two separate command lines.

   On one command line, type: **show interfaces**. Hit the ENTER key. On the next command-line type: **show running-config**.
5. Use the CLI editing features of your router by changing the **show running-config** command to **show startup-config** and execute this.

   Use the command recall (UP ARROW) to recall the **show running-config** command. Edit this command and replace "running" with "startup." You need to LEFT ARROW over to the "-" and BACKSPACE to delete the word "running." Then type **startup**. Use CTRL-E to go to the end of the line and hit the ENTER key to execute the command.

6. Log out of the router.

   Use the **exit** command.

Now you should be more comfortable with the CLI of the IOS. The next section shows you how to create a basic configuration on your 1900 and 2950 switch.

CERTIFICATION OBJECTIVE 5.03

Basic Switch Configuration

This section covers the basics of accessing the 1900 and 2950 Catalyst switches, creating a simple configuration on them, and using simple **show** commands.

Accessing the CLI

Accessing the CLI on the 1900 is different from accessing the CLI on the 2950. With the 1900, once the switch runs its hardware tests and loads the IOS, the IOS displays this menu:

```
------------------------------------------------
Catalyst 1900 Management Console
Copyright (c) Cisco Systems, Inc.  1993-1998
All rights reserved.
Enterprise Edition Software
Ethernet address:         00-C0-1D-81-A3-65

PCA Number:               73-3121-02
PCA Serial Number:        FAA0252A7RT
Model Number:             WS-C1924-EN
System Serial Number:     FAA0304S0T5
Power Supple S/N:         PHI025178F2
------------------------------------------------
1 user(s) now active on Management Console.
```

```
            User Interface Menu
      [M] Menus
      [K] Command Line
      [I] IP Configuration
      [P] Console Password

Enter Selection:
```

If there is a password configured on the switch, you will be prompted for it before this menu is displayed. To choose an option, just type the letter. There are four options from this menu:

- **M** Use the menus to configure the switch.
- **K** Use the IOS CLI to configure the switch, which takes you to *User EXEC* mode.
- **I** Use a menu to create a basic IP configuration on the switch (this appears only if the switch has no IP addressing configured on it).
- **P** Assign a password to the console (this appears only if there is no console password configured).

For exam purposes, you only have to know how to use the IOS CLI (not the menu structure) on the 1900. Type** K **from the 1900's main menu to access the IOS CLI.

5.06. The CD includes a multimedia demonstration of accessing the User EXEC CLI of the 1900.

EXEC Modes

On a 1900, once you type **K** from the main menu, you are taken into *User EXEC* mode. On the 2950, there is no menu system. When you boot up the 2950 switch, you are taken directly into *User EXEC* mode. Once there, use the **enable** command to go to *Privilege EXEC* mode:

```
> enable
#
```

Remember that the switches support context-sensitive help, so don't hesitate to take advantage of this powerful feature.

Accessing Configuration Mode

All changes on the 1900 and 2950 must occur within *Configuration* mode. To access this mode, you must first be at *Privilege EXEC* mode and use this command:

```
# configure terminal
(config)#
```

Use the `configure terminal` command to access Configuration mode. Use the `hostname` command to change the name of the device—this name has local significance only.

Notice that the prompt changed from "#" to "`(config)#`," indicating the change in modes. You can abbreviate **`configure terminal`** to **`conf t`**. *Configuration* mode allows you to execute commands that change your switch's configuration; however, you cannot actually view the changes from within this mode. To manage your switch, you'll have to go back to *Privilege EXEC* mode by either typing **`end`** or pressing the control sequence CTRL-Z.

Assigning a Hostname

One of your first tasks is to change the name of your switch. This has only local significance and is used for management purposes. For instance, the Cisco Discovery Protocol (CDP) uses the hostname. CDP is discussed in Chapter 6. On both models of switches, the **`hostname`** command is used to change the name. Here is a simple example of changing the name on a 1900:

```
(config)# hostname 1900
1900(config)#
```

First, notice that you place the name of the switch after the command. Second, as soon as you hit ENTER, the new CLI prompt is different—it contains the switch's new name.

5.07. The CD includes a multimedia demonstration of changing a 1900's hostname.

In order to undo changes or negate a command on a switch, typically you precede the command with the **`no`** parameter. As an example, to change the 1900's hostname back to the factory default, use this command:

```
1900(config)# no hostname 1900
(config)#
```

In certain cases, you don't have to include the parameters of the command. In the preceding example, you could easily have typed in **no hostname** to accomplish the same thing.

Assigning Passwords

Both the 1900 and the 2950 allow you to set up passwords to restrict access to both *User* and *Privilege EXEC* modes. However, the commands to configure these passwords are *different* on each switch. The following two sections show you how to configure the *EXEC* passwords on your switches.

1900 Password Configuration The 1900 uses the same command to set both the *User* and *Privilege EXEC* passwords: **enable password level**. Here is the format of this command:

```
(config)# enable password level level_# password
```

The level number is either **1** for *User EXEC* or **15** for *Privilege EXEC*. This is followed by the password. Please note that on the 1900 switch, the password is case-*insensitive*. To check your password configuration, log out of the switch and log back in: you should be prompted for your newly assigned passwords.

Use the enable password level 1/15 command to configure the EXEC passwords on the 1900.

5.08. The CD includes a multimedia demonstration of configuring passwords on a 1900 switch.

2950 Password Configuration Configuring passwords on a 2950 switch is the same as configuring passwords on an IOS router (which is discussed later in this chapter). Unlike the 1900, which has one command to create your passwords, on the 2950, there are two commands.

The first major difference between the 1900 and 2950 *User EXEC* password configurations is that on the 1900, you used a single command to configure your *User EXEC* password, and this password is used to secure access to *only* the IOS CLI (not the console port of the switch and not telnet access). On the 2950, you can secure both console and telnet access. In order to do this, you must first go into the console interface or the telnet interface on your 2950. On the 2950, the **line console 0** command is used to do this:

```
Switch(config)# line console 0
Switch(config-line)#  password console_password
```

The **0** in the first command specifies the console port. Lines and interfaces are numbered from 0 upward. Even though the 2950 has only a single console port, it is designated as 0. Next, notice that the prompt on the second line changed. *Configuration* mode actually has two different levels: *Global Configuration* and *Subconfiguration*. Certain commands on IOS devices take you into a specific *Subconfiguration* mode. Table 5-2 shows some configuration modes that you might see on IOS devices.

Please note that not all *Subconfiguration* modes are supported on all IOS devices. When you are in a *Subconfiguration* mode, the commands that you enter affect only that specific component of the router or switch. To leave a *Subconfiguration* mode and return to *Global Configuration* mode, use the **exit** command. Using the **end** command or CTRL-Z will always take you back to *Privilege EXEC* mode no matter what *Configuration* mode you are currently in. Here is an example:

```
Switch(config)# line console 0
Switch(config-line)# exit
Switch(config)#
```

5.09. The CD includes a multimedia demonstration of using* Configuration *and* Subconfiguration *modes on a 2950 switch.

In many cases, when you are in a *Subconfiguration* mode and type in a *Global Configuration* mode command, the IOS executes it and places you in *Global Configuration* mode, like this:

```
Switch(config)# line console 0
Switch(config-line)# hostname 2950
2950(config)#
```

Notice that when the **hostname** command was executed in *Line Subconfiguration* mode, the switch changed its name as well as the mode.

TABLE 5-2 Subconfiguration Modes on IOS Devices

IOS Prompt	Subconfiguration mode
(config-if)#	*Interface Subconfiguration* mode
(config-subif)#	*Subinterface Subconfiguration* mode
(config-line)#	*Line Subconfiguration* mode
(config-controller)#	*Controller Subconfiguration* mode
(config-router)#	*IP Routing Protocol Subconfiguration* mode

exam watch

Remember that *Global Configuration* ***mode commands can typically be executed at any*** *Configuration* ***level. These commands affect the IOS device as a whole, like the* `hostname` *command.*** *Subconfiguration* ***mode commands only affect one specific component of an IOS device. Use the exit command to go back one*** *Configuration* ***level. Use the*** *end* ***or*** *CTRL-Z* ***control sequence to exit*** *Configuration* ***mode.***

Once you are in *Line Subconfiguration* mode, you can use the **password** command to assign the console password. Unlike the 1900, the password on the 2950 *is* case-sensitive. Remember that the **password** command, when executed under **line console 0**, sets the *User EXEC* password only for someone trying to access the 2950 from the console port only. Someone telnetting into the 2950 would not be prompted for a password. To set up a telnet password, use this configuration:

```
Switch(config)# line vty 0 15
Switch(config-line)# password telnet_password
Switch(config-line)# login
```

The **vty** parameter in the preceding command refers to *virtual terminal*, a fancy name for telnet. The 2950 supports up to 16 simultaneous telnet connections, where each connection is internally tracked by a number: 0–15. You could assign a different password to each VTY, but then you really wouldn't know which password to use when telnetting into the switch. However, the IOS allows you to specify all 16 VTYs with the **line** command, simplifying your configuration.

5.10. The CD includes a multimedia demonstration of configuring passwords on a 2950 switch.

Once you are in *Line Subconfiguration* mode, use the **password** command to set your password. You also need to enter the **login** command to allow telnet access to the switch—this tells the IOS to use the password configured with the **password** command. There are other ways of checking access, such as a local username database or through an authentication server, but these concepts are beyond the scope of this book.

The second major difference between setting up passwords on the 1900 and the 2950 relates to configuring the *Privilege EXEC* password. Actually, the configuration is very similar between the two switches; however, the 2950 supports two commands for configuring this password:

```
Switch(config)# enable password Privilege_EXEC_password
-and/or-
Switch(config)# enable secret Privilege_EXEC_password
```

Both of these commands configure the *Privilege EXEC* password. The main difference is that using the **secret** parameter tells the 2950 to encrypt the password when it is saved, and using the **password** parameter doesn't. This is also true of the *Line Subconfiguration* mode **password** command. Passwords that are not encrypted can be encrypted by using the **service password-encryption** *Global Configuration* mode command. However, the **enable secret** command's encryption is much stronger than using the **service password-encryption** command. If you configure both the **enable password** and **enable secret** commands, the 2950 uses the password configured by the **enable secret** command to verify access to *Privilege EXEC* mode.

on the job

I recommend** against **using the enable password command along with service password-encryption, since there are utilities on the Internet, including Cisco's site, that can easily break this encryption. To my knowledge, there has been no report of anyone decrypting the password set with the enable secret command.

exam watch

You configure passwords on the 2950 as you do on the routers. Use the password command to secure line access and the enable password or enable secret command to secure Privilege EXEC access. Remember that the enable secret command encrypts the password. With VTY access, you must also specify the login command within Line Subconfiguration mode.

Accessing and Configuring Interfaces

To configure an interface, you must first enter *Interface Subconfiguration* mode:

```
Switch(config)# interface ethernet|fastethernet|gigabitethernet
                                          slot_#/port_#
Switch(config-if)#
```

You must specify two components to the **interface** command: the type and the location. On the 1900 switches, only Ethernet and Faster Ethernet interfaces are supported. On the 2950, the interfaces are Fast Ethernet and Gigabit Ethernet. Notice that the prompt changes, signifying that you are in *Interface Subconfiguration* mode.

You can't tell what interface that you are actually in by examining the prompt. If you aren't sure, use the history recall feature to recall the interface command and reexecute it.

Following the type is the location, which is specified by the slot number, a slash (/), and the port. On the 1900, there are no modular slots; therefore, all fixed ports are considered to be in slot 0. Port numbers begin with 1 and work there way up to 27. Numbers 1–24 are the Ethernet ports, 25 is the AUI port, and 26 and 27 are the Fast Ethernet uplink ports. The 2950 fixed ports are considered to be in slot 0. The port numbers on the 2950 start at 1: 1–24 for a 2950-24 switch.

When specifying the interface, you can use any of the following:

```
(config)# interface ethernet 0/1
(config)# interface ethernet0/1
(config)# int e 0/1
(config)# int e0/1
```

Remember how to enable and disable an interface on an IOS device: no shutdown and shutdown, respectively.

You can separate the type and location with a space, or concatenate the two together. Likewise, you can abbreviate the commands and parameters.

On the Catalyst switches, the interfaces are *enabled* by default. You can disable interfaces, though, with the **shutdown** *Interface Subconfiguration* mode command:

```
Switch(config)# interface type slot_#/port_#
Switch(config-if)# shutdown
```

To reenable the interface, use the **no shutdown** command.

Assigning IP Addressing Information

If you want to manage your 1900 or 2950 switch remotely, you need to assign it IP addressing information. For example, if you want to telnet to the switch, remotely manage it from a web browser or SNMP management station, or back up and restore configuration files or upgrade the switch, you'll need to set up IP addressing information on it. Each of the switches has different commands to assign this information. The next two sections cover the assignment of addressing information.

1900 IP Addressing One of the hardest concepts to grasp as a novice networker is IP addressing and how you perform subnetting. However, once you understand how IP addressing works, assigning IP addresses to your switches and routers is a simple process. Even though the 1900 has many interfaces, you can assign only a *single* IP address to the 1900 switch. This IP address is used only for management purposes and has nothing to do with how the 1900 switches frames between its interfaces.

Use the two following commands to set up basic IP connectivity:

```
(config)# ip address IP_address subnet_mask
(config)# ip default-gateway router's_IP_address
```

The **ip address** command assigns an IP address to the switch. Note that you must give both the IP address and the subnet mask in a dotted decimal format, like 192.168.1.5 255.255.255.0. By default, the IP address is placed in VLAN 1. (VLANs are covered in Chapter 8.) The **ip default-gateway** command tells the switch which router to use when the switch needs to reach a destination that is not in its configured subnet.

5.11. The CD includes a multimedia demonstration of configuring IP addressing information on a 1900 switch.

2950 IP Addressing On the 2950, IP addresses are configured differently than on the 1900:

```
Switch(config)# interface vlan1
Switch(config-vlan)# ip address IP_address subnet_mask
Switch(config-vlan)# exit
Switch(config)# ip default-gateway router's_IP_address
```

Unlike when working with the 1900, you must go into the VLAN interface that you want the IP address to be associated with. In most cases, this will be VLAN 1.

The same commands are used to configure IP addresses on the switches: *ip address* and *ip default-gateway*. The difference is that on the 2950, the address is configured under the VLAN interface.

(VLANs are covered in Chapter 8.) Once in the VLAN interface, use the **ip address** command to assign the address and mask. The 1900 and the 2950 use the same command to assign the default gateway: **ip default-gateway**.

5.12. The CD includes a multimedia demonstration of configuring IP addressing information on a 2950 switch.

Configuration Files

Configuration files can reside in many locations, including RAM, NVRAM, or a TFTP server, among other places. Whenever you make changes to a switch's configuration, these changes are made in RAM. These changes can then be saved to NVRAM (nonvolatile RAM), which is a static form of memory where, when the Cisco device is turned off, the contents are not erased and are available upon a power-up. The 1900 *automatically* copies any changes you make to NVRAM; the 2950, however, requires you to do this *manually*. Configuration changes can also be saved to a TFTP server—this, however, requires that you configure IP on your switch.

Viewing Your Configuration

To examine the active configuration on a 1900 or 2950 switch, use the **show running-config** command. You must be at *Privilege EXEC* mode to execute this command. Here is an example of this command from a 1900 switch:

```
# show running-config

Building configuration...
Current configuration:
!
interface Ethernet 0/1
!
interface Ethernet 0/2
!
<--output omitted-->
!
```

```
interface FastEthernet 0/27
!
line console
end
#
```

Saving Your Configuration

Configuration files are stored in NVRAM on both switches. When a switch boots up, the IOS then loads this configuration from NVRAM and places it in RAM. On the 1900 switch, you do *not* have to do anything to save the active, or running, configuration—within 30 seconds of executing a command, the 1900 automatically saves the configuration to NVRAM (therefore, wait at least this length of time before turning off the 1900).

This is *not* true on the 2950 switch or IOS routers. Instead, you must execute the **copy running-config startup-config** *Privilege EXEC* mode command to save your changes. Upon executing this command, the 2950 or router takes the active configuration in RAM and saves it to NVRAM. In this process, the old configuration file in NVRAM is overwritten. Here is an example of using this command:

```
Switch# copy running-config startup-config
Destination filename [startup-config]?
Building configuration...
[OK]
Switch#
```

When executing this command, you are asked for a filename for the configuration file—the default is "startup-config." This is the filename the IOS looks for when booting up. You can change the name for backup revisioning purposes (different versions of the backed-up configuration), but make sure that your most current configuration is saved as "startup-config." On the 2950, you can view the saved configuration in NVRAM with the **show startup-config** *Privilege EXEC* mode command.

5.13. The CD includes a multimedia demonstration of configuring and manipulating configuration files on a 2950 switch.

exam watch

The 1900's configuration is automatically saved. On the 2950, use the `copy running-config startup-config` command to save the configuration. The `show running-config` command displays the switch's currently running configuration in RAM.

Verifying Switch Operation

Besides using the **show running-config** command to verify your switch's configuration, you can use many other commands. This section covers the **show interfaces**, **show ip**, and **show version** commands. All of these commands can be executed at either *User* or *Privilege EXEC* mode.

The show interfaces Command

To view the interfaces, status, and statistics for an interface, use the **show interfaces** command:

```
> show interfaces [type slot_#/port_#]
```

If you don't list a specific interface, all of the interfaces on the switch are listed. Here is an example of this command on a 1900 switch:

```
> show interfaces ethernet 0/1
Ethernet 0/1 is Suspended-no-linkbeat
Hardware is Built-in 10Base-T
Address is 00E0.1EA1.a123
MTU 1500 bytes, BW 10000 Kbits
802.1d STP State:  Blocking     Forward Transitions:  2
Port monitoring: Disabled
Unknown unicast flooding: Disabled
Unregistered multicast flooding: Disabled
Description:
Duplex setting: Full duplex
Back pressure: Disabled

    Receive Statistics                          Transmit Statistics
-------------------------------   -------------------------------
Total good frames               0  Total frames                    0
Total octets                    0  Total octets                    0
Broadcast/multicast frames      0  Broadcast/multicast frames      0
Broadcast/multicast octets      0  Broadcast/multicast octets      0
Good frames forwarded           0  Deferrals                       0
Frames filtered                 0  Single collisions               0
Runt frames                     0  Multiple collisions             0
No buffer discards              0  Excessive collisions            0
                                   Queue full discards             0
Errors:                            Errors:
  FCS errors                    0    Late collisions               0
  Alignment errors              0    Excessive deferrals           0
```

```
  Giant frames                 0   Jabber errors              0
  Address violations           0   Other transmit errors      0
```

Table 5-3 explains the status of the interface. Table 5-4 explains some of the error fields shown in the preceding 1900 code listing.

5.14. The CD includes a multimedia demonstration of displaying interface statistics on a 1900 switch.

Here is an example of the **show interfaces** command on a 2950 switch:

```
Switch# show interfaces fastethernet 0/1
FastEthernet0/1 is up, line protocol is up
  Hardware is Fast Ethernet, address is 0005.7428.1234
                                      (bia 0005.7428.1234)
  MTU 1500 bytes, BW 10000 Kbit, DLY 1000 usec,
     reliability 255/255, txload 1/255, rxload 1/255
  Encapsulation ARPA, loopback not set
  Keepalive set (10 sec)
  Auto-duplex, Auto-speed
  input flow-control is off, output flow-control is off
  Last input never, output 4d21h, output hang never
  Last clearing of "show interface" counters never
  Input queue:0/75/0/0 (size/max/drops/flushes);
                                      Total output drops:0
  Queueing strategy:fifo
  Output queue :0/40 (size/max)
  5 minute input rate 0 bits/sec, 0 packets/sec
  5 minute output rate 0 bits/sec, 0 packets/sec
     1 packets input, 64 bytes, 0 no buffer
     Received 0 broadcasts, 0 runts, 0 giants, 0 throttles
<--output omitted-->
```

One of the first things that you want to examine in this display is the status of the interface: `FastEthernet0/1 is up, line protocol is up`. The first "up" refers to the status of the physical layer, and the second "up" refers to the status of the data link layer. Here are the possible values for the physical layer status:

- **Up** The switch is sensing a physical layer signal on the interface.
- **Down** The switch is not sensing a physical layer signal on the interface, a condition that can arise if the attached device is turned off, there is no cable attached, or you are using the wrong type of cable.
- **Administratively down** You used the **shutdown** command to disable the interface.

TABLE 5-3

Possible Statuses for a 1900 Interface

Interface Status	Description
Enabled	The interface is functioning and can send and receive.
Disabled-mgmt	The interface has been disabled with the **`shutdown`** command.
Suspended-no-linkbeat	The switch cannot detect a physical layer signal on the interface.
Suspended-jabber	The attached device is causing excessive jabbering.
Suspended-violation	The interface is suspended because an address violation occurred.
Suspended-Spanning-Tree Protocol	Spanning Tree is currently running on the port and the port is not forwarding traffic.
Disabled-self-test	The interface has failed a hardware test.
Disabled-violation	The interface has been disabled because of an address violation and must be reenabled with the **`no shutdown`** command.
Reset	The interface is being reinitialized.

TABLE 5-4

Error Fields in the 1900 **`show interfaces`** Command

Field Name	Description
FCS	Frame has the correct number of bytes, but an invalid FCS (frame check sequence—checksum).
Alignment	The frame has an incorrect number of bytes and an invalid FCS.
Giant Frames	The frame exceeds the maximum valid size.
Address Violations	The number of times an address violation occurred on the interface.
Late Collisions	The number of times a collision occurred after reading the first 512 bytes of a frame.
Excessive Deferrals	The number of times excessive collisions occurred, possibly causing frames to be dropped.
Jabber Errors	The number of times a frame was received on the interface that exceed a certain time period.

Here are the possible values for the data link layer status:

- **Up** The data link layer is operational.
- **Down** The data link layer is not operational, a condition that can be caused by missed keepalives on a serial link, no clocking, or an incorrect encapsulation type.

exam Watch

If the interface status is up and up, the interface is operational; if it is up and down, there is a problem with the data link layer; if it is down and down, there is a physical layer problem; if it is administratively down and down, the interface was disabled with the `shutdown` command.

5.15. The CD includes a multimedia demonstration of displaying interface statistics on a 2950 switch.

The show ip Command

The **show ip** command is available only on the 1900 switch. This command displays the IP configuration of the switch:

```
> show ip
IP Address:192.168.1.12
Subnet Mask:255.255.255.0
Default Gateway:192.168.1.1
Management VLAN: 1
Domain name: dealgroup.com
Name server 1:192.168.1.3
Name server 2:192.168.1.3
HTTP server :Disabled
HTTP port : 80
RIP :Enabled
```

5.16. The CD includes a multimedia demonstration of displaying the IP configuration on a 1900 switch.

The show version Command

All IOS devices support the **show version** command. This command allows you to see what the model of the device is, the software running on it, how long it has been up, and its hardware characteristics, including the number and types of interfaces. Here is an example of this command on a 1900 switch:

```
> show version
Cisco Catalyst 1900/2820 Enterprise Edition Software
Version V9.00.00(12) written from 172.16.1.1
Copyright (c) Cisco Systems, Inc.  1993-1999
DS2820-1 uptime is 0day(s) 0hour(s) 8minute(s) 27second(s)
cisco Catalyst 1924 (486sxl) processor with 2048K/1024K bytes of memory
Hardware board revision is 5
Upgrade Status: No upgrade currently in progress.
Config File Status: No configuration upload/download is in progress
27 Fixed Ethernet/IEEE 802.3 interface(s)
Base Ethernet Address: 00-C0-1D-81-A3-65
```

In this example, you can see that this switch is running software version 9.00.00(12) and that it has 27 Ethernet interfaces.

5.17. The CD includes a multimedia demonstration of displaying software and hardware information on a 1900 switch.

EXERCISE 5-2

Configuring the 1900 Switch

These last few sections have covered how you create a basic configuration for a 1900 switch. Here are some exercises that you can perform on a 1900 switch to enforce these skills. If you are using the Boson's NetSim simulator on the CD-ROM, use the 1900-1 switch, which is a 1912. Otherwise, you can use a real 1900-series switch with the Enterprise Edition software. You can find a picture of the network diagram for the simulator in the Introduction to this book.

1. Access *User EXEC* mode on your 1900.

   If you are using a real 1900-series switch, access the menus and type **K** to gain access to *User EXEC* mode; if you are using the simulator, start up the simulator. Click the *LabNavigator* button. Next, double-click *Exercise 5-2* and click the *Load Lab* button. At the top of the application in the menu bar, click the *eSwitches* icon, and choose *1900-1*. Next, hit ENTER to access *User EXEC* mode. You should see the *EXEC* prompt: >.

2. Access *Privilege EXEC* mode and then *Configuration* mode.

   Use **enable** to go to *Privilege EXEC* mode and then **configure terminal** to access *Configuration* mode. Your prompt should look like this: `(config)#`.

3. Assign a hostname of *1900-1* to the 1900 switch.

   Use the **hostname 1900-1** command and examine the prompt. Your prompt should look like this: `1900-1(config)#`.

4. Assign an IP address of 192.168.1.5/24 to the 1900, with a default gateway of 192.168.1.1.

   Enter **ip address 192.168.1.5 255.255.255.0** and **ip default-gateway 192.168.1.1**.

5. Examine your active configuration.

   Return to *Privilege EXEC* mode with the **end** command. Use the **show running-config** command.

6. Access Host1 and change its address to 192.168.1.10/24. Also set the default gateway to 192.168.1.1. Test the connection by pinging the 1900-1 switch.

   Click the *eStations* icon in the toolbar of the simulator and select *Host1*. On the CLI, type **ipconfig /ip 192.168.1.10 255.255.255.0**. Then, type **ipconfig /dg 192.168.1.1**. Test the connection: **ping 192.168.1.5**.

7. Go back to *Privilege EXEC* mode on the 1900-1 switch. Ping Host1. Disable interface `ethernet 0/1`. Trying pinging again. What happens? Enable interface `e0/1`. Ping Host1 again.

   Click the *eSwitches* icon in the toolbar of the simulator and select *1900-1*. Ping Host1: **ping 192.168.1.10**. Go into *Configuration* mode: **configure terminal**. Disable interface `e0/1`: **interface ethernet 0/1**, **shutdown**, **end**. Ping again: **ping 192.168.1.10**. The ping should fail. Reenable interface `e0/1`: **configure terminal**, **interface ethernet 0/1**, **no shutdown**, **end**. Ping again: **ping 192.168.1.10**. The ping test should be successful.

Now you should be more comfortable with the basic configuration of the 1900 switch. You'll build upon this configuration throughout the rest of this chapter.

EXERCISE 5-3

Configuring the 2950 Switches

In the last exercise, you created a basic configuration on a 1900 switch. In this exercise, you will create a basic configuration on a 2950 switch. If you are using Boson's NetSim simulator on the CD-ROM, use the 2950-1 switch. If you have closed the simulator since the last lab, the simulator will automatically load *Exercise 5-2*'s completed configuration. Start up the simulator. Click the *Lab Navigator* button. Next, double-click *Exercise 5-3* and click the *Load Lab* button. At the top of the application in the menu bar, click the *eSwitches* icon and choose *2950-1*. You can find a picture of the network diagram for the simulator in the Introduction to this book.

1. Go to *Configuration* mode on your 2950-1 switch.

   Access *User EXEC* mode. Use **enable** to go to *Privilege EXEC* mode and then **configure terminal** to access *Configuration* mode. Your prompt should look like this: `Switch(config)#`.

2. Assign a hostname of *2950-1* to the 2950-1 switch.

   Use the **hostname 2950-1** command and examine the prompt.

3. Assign an encrypted *Privilege EXEC* password of *cisco*.

   Enter **enable secret cisco**.

4. Assign an IP address of 192.168.1.4/24 to the 2950 in VLAN 1, with a default gateway of 192.168.1.1.

   Enter the VLAN interface with **interface vlan1**. Next, enter the addressing information: **ip address 192.168.1.4 255.255.255.0**. Enable the interface: **no shutdown**. Exit the interface with the **exit** command and configure the default gateway: **ip default-gateway 192.168.1.1**.

5. Save your configuration to NVRAM and view the configuration in NVRAM. Test connectivity by pinging the 1900-1 switch.

   Return to *Privilege EXEC* mode with the **end** command. Save it with **copy running-config startup-config** and view it with **show startup-config**. Test connectivity: **ping 192.168.1.5.** The ping should be successful.

6. Configure an IP address of 192.168.1.11 on *Host4* and a default gateway of 192.168.1.1. Test this by pinging Host1 and 1900-1.

   Click the *eStations* icon in the tool bar and select *Host4*. On the CLI, type **ipconfig /ip 192.168.1.11 255.255.255.0**. Then, type **ipconfig**

/dg 192.168.1.1. Test the connection: **ping 192.168.1.10** and **ping 192.168.1.5**.

7. Configure the 2950-2 switch. The commands are the same, just use the appropriate configuration information: the hostname is *2950-2* and the IP address is 192.168.1.3/24. Test connectivity to the 1900-1 and 2950-1 switches.

   Click the *eSwitches* icon in the tool bar and select *2950-2*. On the 2950-2 switch, access *User EXEC* mode, then enter: **enable, configure terminal**, **hostname 2950-2**, **enable secret cisco**, **interface vlan1**, **ip address 192.168.1.3 255.255.255.0**, **no shutdown**, **exit**, **ip default-gateway 192.168.1.1**, **end**, **copy running-config startup-config**, and **show startup-config**. Make sure you configured the right hostname and IP address. Test connectivity by pinging the 1900-1 and 2950-1 switches: **ping 192.168.1.5** and **ping 192.168.1.4**. The pings should be successful.

Now you should be more comfortable with the basic configuration of the 2950 switch. In the next section, you will be shown how to create a basic configuration on your Cisco router.

CERTIFICATION OBJECTIVE 5.04

Basic Router Configuration

This section covers some of the basic commands that you can use to access and configure a Cisco IOS router, which are, as you will see, much like those on the 2950 Catalyst switch. The advantage this provides is that the you don't have to learn a complete new CLI. The first thing that is covered is the *System Configuration Dialog* script, which prompts you for information about how you want to configure your router. I'll then cover the commands used to create a very basic configuration on your IOS router.

Setup Mode

When a router boots up, runs its hardware diagnostics, and loads the IOS software, the IOS then attempts to find a configuration file in NVRAM. If it can't find a configuration file to load, the IOS then runs the *System Configuration Dialog*, commonly referred to as *Setup* mode, which is a script that prompts you for configuration information. The purpose of this script is to ask you questions that will allow you to set up a basic configuration on your router: It is not intended as a full-functioning configuration tool. In other words, the script doesn't have the ability to perform all the router's configuration tasks. Instead, it is used by novices who are not that comfortable with the IOS CLI. Once you become familiar with the CLI and many of the commands on the router, you'll probably never use this script again in your life.

Running the *System Configuration Dialog*

As was mentioned in the last paragraph, one way to access the *System Configuration Dialog* is to boot up a router without a configuration in NVRAM. The second way is to use the **setup** *Privilege EXEC* mode command, shown here:

```
Router# setup

--- System Configuration Dialog ---

Continue with configuration dialog? [yes/no]: y
At any point you may enter a question mark '?' for help.
Use ctrl-c to abort configuration dialog at any prompt.
Default settings are in square brackets '[]'.

Basic management setup configures only enough connectivity
for management of the system, extended setup will ask you
to configure each interface on the system

First, would you like to see the current interface summary? [yes]:

Interface IP-Address  OK? Method Status                    Protocol
BRI0      unassigned  YES unset  administratively down down
BRI0:1    unassigned  YES unset  administratively down down
BRI0:2    unassigned  YES unset  administratively down down
Ethernet0 unassigned  YES unset  administratively down down
Serial0   unassigned  YES unset  administratively down down

Would you like to enter basic management setup? [yes/no]: n
Configuring global parameters:
  Enter hostname [Router]:
  The enable secret is a password used to protect access to
  privileged EXEC and configuration modes. This password, after
  entered, becomes encrypted in the configuration.
  Enter enable secret: dealgroup1
The enable password is used when you do not specify an
  enable secret password, with some older software versions,
  and some boot images.
  Enter enable password: dealgroup2
The virtual terminal password is used to protect
  access to the router over a network interface.
```

```
  Enter virtual terminal password: cisco
Configure SNMP Network Management? [no]:
  Configure LAT? [yes]: n
Configure AppleTalk? [no]:
  Configure DECnet? [no]:
  Configure IP? [yes]:
    Configure IGRP routing? [yes]: n
Configure RIP routing? [no]:
<--output omitted-->
BRI interface needs isdn switch-type to be configured
  Valid switch types are :
               [0]  none..........Only if you don't want to
                                  configure BRI.
               [1]  basic-1tr6....1TR6 switch type for Germany
               [2]  basic-5ess....AT&T 5ESS switch type for the
                                  US/Canada
               [3]  basic-dms100..Northern DMS-100 switch type
<--output omitted-->
  Choose ISDN BRI Switch Type [2]:

Configuring interface parameters:
Do you want to configure BRI0 (BRI d-channel) interface? [no]:
Do you want to configure Ethernet0  interface? [no]: y
Configure IP on this interface? [no]: y
IP address for this interface: 172.16.1.1
Subnet mask for this interface [255.255.0.0] : 255.255.255.0
Class B network is 172.16.0.0, 24 subnet bits; mask is /24
Do you want to configure Serial0  interface? [no]:
Do you want to configure BRI0 interface? [no]:

The following configuration command script was created:
hostname Router
enable secret 5 $1$/CCk$4r7zDwDNeqkxFO kJxC3G0
enable password dealgroup2
line vty 0 4
 password cisco
no snmp-server
!
no appletalk routing
no decnet routing
ip routing
 <--output omitted-->
end

[0] Go to the IOS command prompt without saving this config.
[1] Return back to the setup without saving this config.
[2] Save this configuration to nvram and exit.
Enter your selection [2]:
```

Information included in brackets ([]) are default values—if you just hit ENTER, the value in the brackets is used. One problem with the script is that if you make a mistake, there is no method of going back to the preceding question. Instead, you can use the CTRL-C break sequence to abort the script. The following sections break down the different components of the script.

The questions that the script asks you might be different from router to router, depending on the hardware model and the software running on it.

Status and Global Configuration Information

At the beginning of the script, you are asked whether or not you want to continue. If you answer "yes" or "y," the script will continue; otherwise, if you answer "no" or "n," the script is aborted and you are returned to *Privilege EXEC* mode. The second thing that you are asked is if you want to see the status of the router's interfaces. If you answer "y," then you'll see all of the interfaces on the router, the interfaces' IP addresses, and the status of the interfaces.

After the status information, you are taken into the actual configuration. The first part of the configuration deals with all configuration information for the router except for the interfaces, which is the second part. In this part of the configuration, you are asked for things like the *Privilege EXEC* password, VTY (telnet) password, which network protocols you want to activate, and other information.

Note that you are prompted for two* Privilege EXEC *passwords in the script: `enable secret` and `enable password`. These passwords are the same as discussed earlier in the 2950 configuration section. Even though you would normally configure only one, the script requires you to enter both; it also requires that both passwords be different. Just as with the 2950 configuration, the `enable secret` password takes precedence over the `enable password`.

Protocol and Interface Configuration Information

After configuring the global information for the router, you are then lead through questions about which interfaces you want to use and how they should be configured. The script is smart enough to ask only configuration questions based on how you answered the global questions. As an example, if you activate IP, the script asks you for each activated interface, if you want the interface to process IP, and if yes, the IP addressing information for the interface. If you have an ISDN interface in your router, as in the preceding example, you will be prompted for the ISDN type of the switch to which you are connecting your router. ISDN is covered in Chapter 17.

Exiting Setup Mode

After you answer all of the script's configuration questions, you are then shown the router configuration the script created using the answers to the script's questions. Please note that the IOS hasn't yet activated the configuration file. Examine the configuration closely and then make one of the three choices shown in Table 5-5. Also, if you enter **1** as your option, when the script starts over again, the information that you previously entered appears in brackets and will be the default values when you hit the ENTER key on an empty line. Older versions of the IOS asked a simple yes/no question at the end as to whether or not you wanted to use the configuration you just created with the script utility.

The 2950 switch also supports a *System Configuration Dialog;* ***however, as it is a layer-2 device, the number of questions asked is much smaller during the configuration and is typically used only to configure passwords and an IP address on it.***

5.18. The CD includes a multimedia demonstration of using the *System Configuration Dialog* ***on a Cisco router.***

Remember that this script is started when the router boots up and there is no configuration in NVRAM or you use the `setup` command from *Privilege EXEC* ***mode. Also, know the three options at the end of the Setup dialog script. You can use the CTRL-C break sequence to abort the script.***

TABLE 5-5 Options at the End of the ***System Configuration Dialog***

Option	Description
0	Discard the script's configuration and return to *Privilege EXEC* mode.
1	Return to the beginning of the script.
2	Activate the script's configuration, save the configuration to NVRAM, and return to *Privilege EXEC* mode.

Configuration Mode

In most situations, you'll enter *Configuration* mode on the router and manually enter the commands. One of the advantages of this approach is that you have full access to every command that the router supports, whereas the *System Configuration Dialog* supports only a small subset of commands. Accessing *Configuration* mode on the router is the same as accessing it on a 1900 or 2950 switch:

```
Router# configure terminal
Router(config)#
```

Moving around *Configuration* mode is also the same, as well as exiting *Configuration* mode with the **end** command or the CTRL-Z control sequence. And like the switches, the router supports both *Global Configuration* and *Subconfiguration* modes. The following sections cover some of the basic commands for configuring an IOS-based router.

Assigning a Hostname

When you get a router from Cisco, the default name of the router is "Router." To change your router's name, use the **hostname** command. Here is an example of its use:

```
Router(config)# hostname bullmastiff
bullmastiff(config)#
```

As you can see, this is the same command used on both of the Catalyst switches. Again, notice that the prompt changed: It now includes the name of the router.

Configuring Passwords

Cisco routers support two levels of passwords: *User EXEC* and *Privilege EXEC*. Configuring these passwords is exactly the same as configuring them on the 2950 switch. The following sections cover the configuration of these passwords on a Cisco router.

***User EXEC* Passwords** Configuring the router's *User EXEC* passwords is straightforward. For each type of access—console, telnet, or the auxiliary port—you can have the same or different passwords, since these passwords are configured under the appropriate line type. Here is the configuration for setting up *User EXEC* passwords:

```
Router(config)# line console 0
Router(config-line)# password console_password
Router(config-line)# exit
Router(config)# line vty 0 4
Router(config-line)# login
Router(config-line)# password telnet_password
```

Remember how to configure passwords on routers, especially how to type them in.

As you can see, this is no different from configuring the *User EXEC* passwords on a 2950 switch. The only difference between the switch and the router is the number of VTYs supported for telnet access. Depending on the router model and IOS software version, this number might range from 5 (0–4) on up to almost 1000.

About the only other minor difference is that some routers have an auxiliary port. This is typically used as a backup console port, or a remote access port with a modem attached to it. The following code shows the syntax for setting up password authentication on it:

```
Router(config)# line aux 0
Router(config-line)# login
Router(config-line)# password aux_password
Router(config-line)# exit
```

***Privilege EXEC* Passwords** Configuring the *Privilege EXEC* password on the router is the same as on a 2950 switch:

```
Router(config)# enable password Privileged_EXEC_password
                      -and/or-
Router(config)# enable secret Privileged_EXEC_password
```

Remember that the **enable secret** command encrypts the password, while the **enable password** command doesn't.

5.19. The CD includes a multimedia demonstration of setting up passwords on a Cisco router.

Setting Up a Login Banner

You can set up a login banner on your router that will display a message to every user attempting to access *User EXEC* mode. The **banner motd** command is used to create the login banner:

```
Router(config)# banner motd start_and_delimiting_character
enter_your_banner_here
enter_the_delimiting_character_to_end_the_banner
Router(config)#
```

"MOTD" is a carryover from the Unix world that stands for "message of the day." After the **banner motd** command, you must enter the starting character. This is the character that is used to signify the beginning and ending of the banner. Once you enter the starting character, when the IOS CLI parser sees this character later in your text, the IOS terminates the banner and returns you to the CLI prompt. One nice feature of the banner is that the ENTER key doesn't terminate the banner, and so you can have banners that span multiple lines. Whenever you have completed your banner, type the ending character (the one that you began the banner with).

Here is an example of setting up a login banner:

```
Router(config)# banner motd $
This is a private system and only authorized individuals
         are allowed!
All others will be prosecuted to the fullest extent of the law!
$
Router(config)#
```

In this example, the banner spans multiple lines and the delimiting character is the dollar sign ($).

A banner doesn't have to span multiple lines, though, but can be placed on a single line, as in this example:

```
Router(config)# banner motd 'Keep Out!'
Router(config)#
```

In this example, the single quote (') is the delimiting character. Once you have created a login banner, test it by logging out of the router and logging back in. You should see your banner appear before the *User EXEC* password prompt.

5.20. The CD includes a multimedia demonstration of setting up a login banner on a Cisco router.

Changing the Inactivity Timeout

By default, the router automatically logs you off after ten minutes of inactivity. You can change this with the **exec-timeout** *Line Subconfiguration* mode command:

```
Router(config)# line line_type line_#
Router(config-line)# exec-timeout minutes seconds
```

Use the banner motd command to set up a login banner. Use the exec-timeout command to set up the EXEC timeout.

If you don't want a particular line to ever time out, you can set the minutes and seconds values to zero, like this:

```
Router(config)# line console 0
Router(config-line)# exec-timeout 0 0
```

Disabling the timeout for a line is not recommended in a production environment, since it creates security issues. However, for training purposes, such as studying for the CCNA exam, this is okay.

To verify your line configuration, use the **show line** command:

```
Router# show line con 0
Tty Typ  Tx/Rx A Modem Roty AccO AccI Uses Noise Overruns
* 0 CTY          -    -    -    -    -    0     0      0/0

Line 0, Location: "", Type: ""
Length: 24 lines, Width: 80 columns
Status: Ready, Active
Capabilities: none
Modem state: Ready
Special Chars: Escape Hold Stop Start Disconnect Activation
                ^^x   none  -     -       none
Timeouts: Idle EXEC  Idle Session  Modem Answer  Session  Dispatch
          never      never                       none     not set
Session limit is not set.
Time since activation: 0:04:10
Editing is enabled.
History is enabled, history size is 10.
Full user help is disabled
Allowed transports are pad telnet mop.  Preferred is telnet.
No output characters are padded
No special data dispatching characters
```

In this example, notice that the timeout value is now set to "never."

5.21. The CD includes a multimedia demonstration of changing the idle timeout on a Cisco router.

CLI Output

One nice feature of an IOS device is that when certain types of events occur, such as an interface going down or up, an administrator making a configuration change, or output of **debug** commands, the router, by default, prints an informational message on the console port. It won't, however, display the same messages if you happen to have telnetted into the router or accessed it via the auxiliary port.

If this is the case, you can have the router display these messages on your screen by executing the *Privilege EXEC* **terminal monitor** command, as shown here:

```
Router# terminal monitor
```

You must execute this command once you have logged into the router from the VTY or auxiliary lines. This command is *not* saved to NVRAM when you execute the **copy running-config startup-config** command—it is used only during the active management session. Once you execute this command, the router displays the information messages on screen. Once you log out, however, this command does not apply to anyone else telnetting into the router. Each individual telnetting into the router must reexecute this command.

One annoying problem with the information messages, however, is that if you are typing in a router command, when the router displays the message, it starts printing it right where the cursor is, making it hard for you to figure out where you left off typing. If you remember, just keep typing your command; or hit CTRL-C to abort the command. A better approach, though, is to set up the router so that after the message prints on your screen, the router redisplays what you have already typed in on a new prompt. The **logging synchronous** command accomplishes this:

```
Router(config)# line line_type line_#
Router(config-line)# logging synchronous
```

Use the terminal monitor command to view console output on nonconsole lines.

First, notice that this command is executed under the *Line Subconfiguration* mode. Next, if you want to implement this feature, you'll need to set it up under all the lines from which you'll be accessing your router, including your VTYs and console port. Note that you can also use the CTRL-R control sequence to refresh the screen.

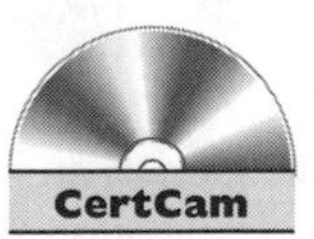

5.22. The CD includes a multimedia demonstration of using logging synchronous on a Cisco router.

Configuring Router Interfaces

Accessing interfaces on IOS routers is the same as accessing interfaces on the 1900 and 2950 Catalyst switches. To access an interface and enter *Interface Subconfiguration* mode, use the **interface** command:

```
Router(config)# interface type [slot_#/]port_#
Router(config-if)#
```

Unlike the Catalyst switches, which support only Ethernet-type interfaces, Cisco routers support a wide variety of interfaces, including synchronous **serial** and **async** serial, ISDN **bri** and **pri**, **atm**, **fddi**, **tokenring**, **ethernet**, **fastethernet**, and **gigabitethernet**, as well as others. Of course, not every Cisco router supports all types of interfaces. As an example, routers in the 800 series support only serial, ISDN, and Ethernet.

After the type comes the location of the interface. Slot numbers begin with 0 and port numbers begin with 0. Therefore, if you had an interface like **ethernet 0/0**, this would be the first slot in the router, and the very first port; whereas, **ethernet 1/1** would be in the second slot, and the port would be the second port.

Some routers do not support slots or modules, and therefore this is omitted—instead you just list the port number. Examples of routers that do not have slots or slot numbers are the 800, 1600, 1700, and 2500 routers. Here are some examples of interface names where the router lacks slots:

- **ethernet 0** or **e0**
- **serial 0** or **s0**
- **bri 0**

For those routers that support slots, the 3600 and 7200 routers, for example, you must specify the slot number, followed by a slash, and then the port number. Here are some examples:

- **ethernet 0/0** or **e0/0**
- **serial 1/0** or **s1/0**

Remember that when listing the type and slot and port numbers, you *can* concatenate these values as shown in these examples.

Including an Interface Description You can add a description to any interface on a router, or for that matter a switch, by using the **description** command:

```
Router(config)# interface type [slot_#/]port_#
Router(config-if)# description interface_description
```

The description is a one-line description describing the device that the interface is connected to, or whatever description you want to assign. This description appears in the output of the **show interfaces** command.

Enabling and Disabling Interfaces Unlike Catalyst switches, Cisco router interfaces are *disabled* by default. For each interface that you want to use, you must go into the interface with the **interface** command and activate it with the **no shutdown** command:

```
Router(config)# interface type [slot_#/]port_#
Router(config-if)# no shutdown
```

Whenever the interface changes status, the router prints an information message on the screen. Here is an example of where an interface on a router is being activated:

```
Router(config)# interface fastethernet0
Router(config-if)# no shutdown
1w0d: %LINK-3-UPDOWN: Interface FastEthernet0, changed state to up
1w0d: %LINEPROTO-5-UPDOWN: Line protocol on Interface
      FastEthernet0, changed state to up
Router(config-if)#
```

In this example, the first information line indicates that the physical layer is activated. The second line indicates that the data link layer is enabled. If you want to disable a router's interface, enter *Interface Subconfiguration* mode for that particular interface and execute the **shutdown** command.

5.23. The CD includes a multimedia demonstration of enabling and disabling interfaces on a Cisco router.

exam watch

When copying and pasting a configuration file into the router, and the router interface is disabled with the shutdown command, your pasted configuration file must contain the no shutdown command in order to active the interface. This is a common problem when copying and pasting a configuration file from an old router to a new router, where the interfaces on the new router are disabled by default.

Configuring LAN Interfaces Some routers, like the 4000 series, support dual Ethernet connectors for a single interface. With some of these routers, the IOS is intelligent enough to figure out which connector is being used and handles the configuration automatically. In other cases, though, you must tell the router which connector the interface should use by configuring the **media-type** command on the interface:

```
Router(config)# interface ethernet [slot_#/]port_#
Router(config-if)# media-type media_type
Router(config-if)# speed 10|100|auto
Router(config-if)# [no] half-duplex
```

Here are the media types that you can specify: **aui**, **10baset**, **100baset**, and **mii**.

For 10/100 Ethernet ports that support auto-sensing, it is recommended that you hard-code the speed and duplexing with the **speed** and **half-duplex** commands. Setting the **speed** to **auto** has the interface autosense both the speed and the duplexing. In order to hard-code the duplexing, you must first hard-code the speed to 10 or 100. To set the port to full-duplex, use the **no half-duplex** command.

Configuring Serial Interfaces When connecting a serial cable to the serial interface of the router, typically clocking is provided by an external device, such as a modem or a CSU/DSU. The router is the DTE and the external device is the DCE, where the DCE provides the clocking. This type of WAN connection is discussed further in Chapter 15.

In some cases, however, you might connect two routers back-to-back using the routers' serial interfaces. For instance, if you are building your own lab to practice CCNA commands, you'll more than likely connect the routers back-to-back to reduce equipment costs. In this situation, each router, by default, is a DTE. Since clocking is required in order for the interface to be enabled, one of the two routers will have to perform the function of an external DCE. This is accomplished by using the **clock rate** *Interface Subconfiguration* mode command on the a serial interface:

```
Router(config)# interface serial [slot_#/]port_#
Router(config-if)# clock rate rate_in_bits_per_second
```

When entering the clock rate, you can't just choose any arbitrary value. Use the context-sensitive help to find out which clock rates your serial interface supports. Here are some possible values: **1200**, **2400**, **4800**, **9600**, **19200**, **38400**, **56000**, **64000**, **72000**, **125000**, **148000**, **500000**, **800000**, **1000000**, **1300000**, **2000000**, and **4000000**.

exam watch

Use the show controller command to determine DTE and DCE connections. Use the clock rate command to configure the speed for DCE connections.

Please note that you can't choose an arbitrary router in the back-to-back connection to be DCE—this is based on how the two routers are cabled. One end of the cable is physically the DTE, and the other is the DCE. Some cables are marked and some are not, depending on where you purchased them from. If you are not sure which router has the DTE end of the cable and which one has the DCE end, you can determine this with the **show controller** command:

```
Router> show controller serial [slot_#/]port_#
```

This is one of the few commands where you *cannot* concatenate the type and the port number—you must separate them by a space. Here is an example of the use of this command:

```
Router> show controller serial 0
HD unit 0, idb = 0x121C04, driver structure at 0x127078
buffer size 1524 HD unit 0, DTE V.35 serial cable attached
<--output omitted-->
```

Notice that the second line of this example holds two important pieces of information: the connection type (DTE) and the type of cable (V.35). Here is an example of an interface connected to the end of a DCE cable:

```
Router> show controller serial 0
HD unit 0, idb = 0x1BA16C, driver structure at 0x1C04E0
buffer size 1524  HD unit 0, V.35 DCE cable, clockrate 64000
<--output truncated-->
```

In this example, the clocking has already been configured: 64,000 bps (bits per second).

5.24. The CD includes a multimedia demonstration of setting the clocking on a serial interface on a Cisco router.

Configuring the Bandwidth Parameter All interfaces have a bandwidth value assigned to them. This is used by certain routing protocols, such as IGRP, OSPF, and EIGRP, when making routing decisions. (Routing protocols are covered in Chapters 9, 10, and 11.) For LAN-based interfaces, the speed of the interface becomes the bandwidth value, where the bandwidth is measured in kilobits per second (Kbps). However, on synchronous serial interfaces, the bandwidth defaults to 1,554Kbps, or the speed of a T1 link. This is true no matter what the physical clock rate is on the interface (discussed in the preceding section). To change the bandwidth value for an interface, use the **bandwidth** *Interface Subconfiguration* mode command:

```
Router(config)# interface serial [slot_#/]port_#
Router(config-if)# bandwidth rate_in_Kbps
```

As an example, a serial interface clocked at 56,000 bps should have its bandwidth value changed to 56Kbps, like this:

```
Router(config)# interface serial 0
Router(config-if)# bandwidth 56
```

Please note that the `bandwidth` command does not change the clock rate on an interface: the `clock rate` command does this. The `bandwidth` command affects only routing protocols that use bandwidth as a metric.

Configuring IP Addressing Information

You can use many commands on the router to set up your IP addressing information. One of the most common is to assign an IP address to an interface; however, there are many more commands, including the setup of DNS, determining how subnet masks appear in the output of **show** commands, restricting directed broadcasts, and others. The following sections cover these configurations.

Assigning IP Addresses Unlike the 1900 and 2950, which only need a single IP address, routers need a unique IP address on each interface that will route IP traffic. Actually, each interface on a router is a separate network or subnet, and therefore you need to plan your IP addressing appropriately and assign a network number to each router segment and then take an unused host address from the segment and configure it on the interface of the router. IP addressing and its components is discussed in Chapter 3.

Let's look at a couple of examples of incorrectly and correctly assigning IP addresses to a router's interfaces. Figure 5-1 shows an invalid configuration example.

FIGURE 5-1

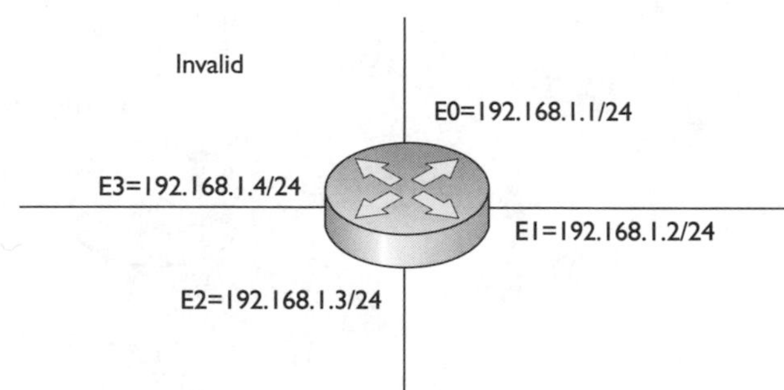

Invalid addressing configuration for a router

In this example, there is only one network number: 192.168.1.0/24. Notice that *each* interface on the router has an address from this network number. Actually, if you would try to configure this addressing scheme on a router, you would get an overlapping address error and be prevented from completing the addressing configuration.

Each interface needs a unique host address, as is shown in Figure 5-2. Notice that in this example, each interface has an address from a *different* network number when compared to the other interfaces on the router. As to which host address you choose for the router interface, this is up to personal preference. Many administrators either use the first or last host address in the network number for the router's interface, but any valid, unused host address from that network number can be used.

As you have probably already guessed, configuring an IP address on a router requires you to be in *Interface Subconfiguration* mode. Here is the syntax of this command:

```
Router(config)# interface type [slot_#/]port_#
Router(config-if)# ip address IP_address subnet_mask
```

This syntax, as you can see, is the same as configuring an IP address on the 2950 switch. You can verify your IP addressing configuration with the **show interfaces** or **show ip interfaces** command, discussed later, in the section "Verifying a Router's Operation."

Using the example in Figure 5-2, here would be the router's IP addressing configuration:

```
Router(config)# interface ethernet 0
Router(config-if)# ip address 192.168.1.1 255.255.255.0
Router(config-if)# no shutdown
Router(config-if)# exit
Router(config)# interface ethernet 1
Router(config-if)# ip address 192.168.2.1 255.255.255.0
Router(config-if)# no shutdown
<--output omitted-->
```

FIGURE 5-2

Correct addressing configuration for a router

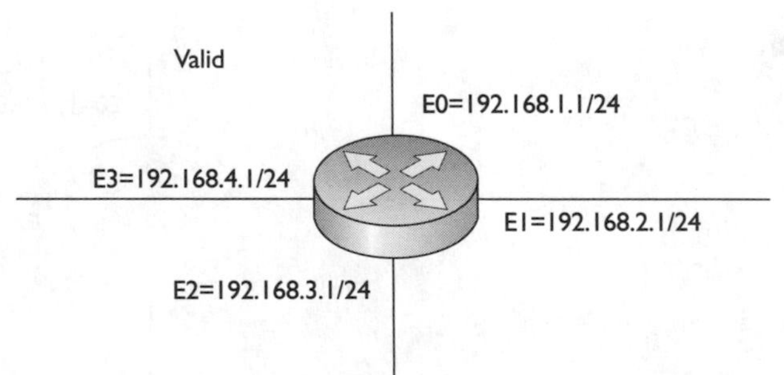

If you misconfigured an IP address on a router's interface, use the `no ip address` command to remove it. Optionally, you can use the `ip address` command with the correct IP address and subnet mask to overwrite the existing configuration. Remember how to configure IP addressing on a router!

5.25. The CD includes a multimedia demonstration of configuring an IP address on an interface of a Cisco router.

Subnet Zero Configuration Starting with IOS 12.0, Cisco automatically allows you to use IP subnet zero networks—the first network number in a subnetted network. Prior to IOS 12.0, you were not, by default, allowed to use these subnets. However, you could enable their use if you needed extra networks by configuring the **ip subnet-zero** command:

```
Router(config)# ip subnet-zero
```

Directed Broadcast Configuration In version 11.x and earlier of the IOS, the router would automatically forward directed broadcasts. As you may recall from Chapter 3, each network number has its own broadcast address. You can send packets with this address as a destination, which a router can forward to this destination segment so that all hosts on that segment receive it. However, many unscrupulous individuals have taken advantage of this process to flood a network segment with these broadcasts. Therefore, in IOS 12.0 and later, directed broadcasts are disabled on a router's interfaces, causing the router to drop any received directed broadcast packets. If you want to reenable this function, use the following *Interface Subconfiguration* mode command:

```
Router(config)# interface type [slot_#/]port_#
Router(config-if)# ip directed-broadcast
```

If you want to disable directed broadcasts again, just preface the preceding command with the **no** parameter. You can verify your directed broadcast configuration with the **show ip interfaces** command, discussed later, in the section "Verifying a Router's Operation."

IP Subnet Mask Display Configuration Whenever you use many **show** commands on your router and IP addresses are displayed, the default display format for subnet masks is dotted-decimal. You can change the display format of subnet masks with the following command:

```
Router# term ip netmask-format bit-count|decimal|hexadecimal
```

To begin with, execution of this command is *not* done from *Configuration* mode. Therefore, this change takes effect only for your current login session—as soon as you log out and log back in again, the default is to display the masking information in the dotted-decimal format. Here are your display options:

- **bit-count** Example: 192.168.1.0/24
- **decimal** Example: 192.168.1.0 255.255.255.0 (default format)
- **hexadecimal** Example: 192.168.1.0 0xFFFFFF00

Of course, you might get tired of continually retyping this command every time you log in. Therefore, you can configure a default behavior that can be saved by the router and will be the same every time that you log into the router. This is done from *Line Subconfiguration* mode:

```
Router(config)# line line_type line_#
Router(config-line)# ip netmask-format bit-count|decimal|hexadecimal
```

Note that you will need to execute this command on each line from which you access your router, as the following configuration shows:

```
Router(config)# line console 0
Router(config-line)# ip netmask-format bit-count
Router(config-line)# exit
Router(config)# line vty 0 4
Router(config-line)# ip netmask-format bit-count
```

To verify your configuration, use the **show interfaces** or **show ip interfaces** command to verify that the subnet mask is displaying correctly. These commands are discussed later, in the section "Verifying a Router's Operation."

5.26. The CD includes a multimedia demonstration of changing the subnet mask display on a Cisco router.

Static Host Configuration As you are well aware, in the IP world, we typically don't type in the IP address to reach a destination. For example, if you want to reach

Cisco's site, in your web browser address bar, you type **www.cisco.com** or **http://www.cisco.com**. Your web browser then resolves the host and domain names to an IP address. The router also supports hostnames for certain operations, such as ping and telnet, as is discussed in Chapter 6.

There are two basic ways to have your router resolve hostnames to IP addresses: static and dynamic (using DNS). You can create a static resolution table by using this command:

```
Router(config)# ip host name_of_host [TCP_port_#]
                        IP_address_of_host [2nd_IP_address...]
```

You must first specify the name of the remote host. Optionally, you can specify a port number for the host—this defaults to 23 for telnet if you omit it. After this, you can list up to eight IP addresses for this host. The router will try to reach the host with the first address, and if that fails, try the second address, and so on and so forth. Use the **show hosts** command to examine your static entries. This command is covered later, in the section "Verifying a Router's Operation."

DNS Resolution Configuration If you have access to a DNS server or servers, you can have your router use these to resolve names to IP addresses. This is configured with the **ip name-server** command:

```
Router(config)# ip name-server IP_address_of_DNS_server
                        [2nd_server's_IP_address ...]
```

You can list up to six DNS servers for the router to use with this command. Use the **show hosts** command to examine your static and dynamic entries. This command is covered later, in the section "Verifying a Router's Operation."

Many administrators don't like using DNS to resolve names to addresses on routers, because of one nuisance feature on the router: Whenever you type a nonexistent command on the router, the router assumes you are trying to telnet to a device by that *name* and tries to resolve it to an IP address. This is annoying because either you have to wait for the DNS query to time out or you must execute the break sequence (CTRL-SHIFT-6). You have another option, though, and that is to disable DNS lookups on the router with the following command:

```
Router(config)# no ip domain-lookup
```

5.27. The CD includes a multimedia demonstration of using and disabling name resolution on a Cisco router.

Verifying a Router's Operation

Once you have configured your router, there are many, many commands that you have available to use to examine and troubleshoot your configuration. This chapter covers some of the basic **show** commands that you have at your disposal. Chapter 6 covers some more commands, including **ping**, **telnet**, **show cdp**, and **debug**.

The show interfaces Command

One of the most common commands that you will use on a router is the **show interfaces** command. This command allows you to see the status and configuration of your interfaces, as well as some statistical information. Here is the syntax of this command:

```
Router> show interfaces [type [slot_#/]port_#]
```

If you don't specify a specific interface, the router displays all of its interfaces—those enabled as well as those disabled. Here is an example of the output of this command:

```
Router# show interfaces ethernet 0
Ethernet 0 is up, line protocol is up
  Hardware is MCI Ethernet, address is 0000.0c00.1234
                                  (bia 0000.0c00.1234)
  Internet address is 172.16.16.2, subnet mask is 255.255.255.252
  MTU 1500 bytes, BW 10000 Kbit, DLY 100000 usec, rely 255/255,
                       load 1/255
  Encapsulation ARPA, loopback not set, keepalive set (10 sec)
  ARP type: ARPA, ARP Timeout 4:00:00
  Last input 0:00:00, output 0:00:00, output hang never
  Last clearing of "show interface" counters 0:00:00
  Output queue 0/40, 0 drops; input queue 0/75, 0 drops
  Five minute input rate 0 bits/sec, 0 packets/sec
  Five minute output rate 4000 bits/sec, 8 packets/sec
     2240375 packets input, 887359872 bytes, 0 no buffer
     Received 722137 broadcasts, 0 runts, 0 giants
     0 input errors, 0 CRC, 0 frame, 0 overrun, 0 ignored, 0 abort
     10137586 packets output, 897215078 bytes, 0 underruns
     4 output errors, 1037 collisions, 3 interface resets,
                      0 restarts
```

The first line of output shows the status of the interface. This status was described previously, in the section "Verifying Switch Operation." The second line is the MAC address of the Ethernet interface. The third line has the IP address and subnet mask configured on the interface.

Make sure you understand the output of the *show interfaces* command, since this is a powerful layer-2 troubleshooting tool.

The fourth line has the MTU Ethernet frame size as well as the routing protocol metrics. (These metrics are discussed in more depth in Chapters 9, 10, and 11, which discuss routing protocols.) Notice the "BW" parameter in this line. Referred to as the bandwidth of the link, this is used by some routing protocols, such as IGRP, OSPF, and EIGRP, when making routing decisions. For Ethernet, this is always 10,000Kbps. You can change this value with the **bandwidth** command, discussed previously, in the section "Configuring the Bandwidth Parameter." Table 5-6 explains some of the elements that you may see with the **show interfaces** command. Please note that depending on the type of interface, the information displayed in the **show interfaces** command may be slightly different.

5.28. The CD includes a multimedia demonstration of using the show interfaces command on a Cisco router.

The show ip interface Command

Another common command that you will use on a router is the **show ip interface** command. This command enables you to see the IP configuration of your router's interfaces:

```
Router> show ip interface [type [slot_#/]port_#]
```

Here is an abbreviated output of the **show ip interface** command:

```
Router# show ip interface
Ethernet1 is up, line protocol is up
  Internet address is 192.168.1.1/24
  Broadcast address is 255.255.255.255
  Address determined by setup command
  MTU is 1500 bytes
  Helper address is not set
  Directed broadcast forwarding is disabled
  Outgoing access list is not set
  Inbound  access list is 100
<--output omitted-->
```

TABLE 5-6 Explanation of the Elements in the **show interfaces** Command

Element	Description
Address	The MAC address of the interface; BIA (burnt-in address) is the MAC address burnt into the Ethernet controller—this can be overridden with the **mac-address** command
Last input/output	The last time a packet was received on or sent out of the interface—can be used to determine if the interface is operating or not
Last clearing	Indicates the last time the **clear counters** command was executed on the interface
Output queue	Indicates the number of packets waiting to be sent out the interface—the number after the "/" is the maximum size of the queue and then the number of packets dropped because the queue was full
Input queue	Indicates the number of packets received on the interface and waiting to be processed—the number after the "/" is the maximum size of the queue and then the number of packets dropped because the queue was full
No buffers (input)	Number of received packets dropped because the input buffer was filled up
Runts (input)	Number of packets received that were less than 64 bytes in length
Giants (input)	Number of packets received that were greater than the maximum allowed size—1518 bytes for Ethernet
Input errors	The total number of input errors received on the interface
CRC (input)	Indicates packets received that had checksum errors
Frame (input)	Indicates the number of packets received that had both CRC errors and cases where the length of the frame was not on a byte boundary
Overruns (input)	Number of times the inbound packet rate exceeded the capabilities of the interface to process the traffic
Ignored (input)	Number of inbound packets that were dropped because of the lack of input buffer space
Aborts (input)	Number of received packets that were aborted
Collisions (output)	Number of times the interface tried transmitting a packet, but a collision occurred—this should be less than 0.1% of total traffic leaving the interface
Interface resets (output)	Number of times the interface changed state by going down and then coming back up
Restarts (output)	Number of times the controller was reset because of errors—use the **show controllers** command to troubleshoot this problem

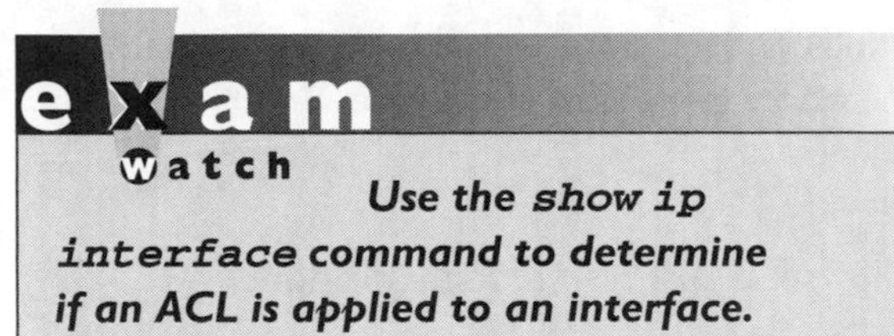

Use the *show ip interface* command to determine if an ACL is applied to an interface.

As you can see from this command, the IP address and mask are displayed, as well as the status of direct broadcast forwarding. Any access list applied to the interface is also displayed. Access lists are explained in Chapter 13.

An additional parameter to the preceding command, **brief**, will display a single-line description for each interface, as shown here:

```
Router# show ip interface brief
Interface   IP-Address   OK? Method Status                Protocol
Ethernet0   192.168.1.1 YES NVRAM  up                    up
Ethernet1   192.168.2.1 YES NVRAM  administratively down down
```

This is an extremely useful command when you want to see a quick overview of all of the interfaces on the router, their IP addresses, and their statuses.

5.29. The CD includes a multimedia demonstration of using the show ip interface command on a Cisco router.

The show hosts Command

To view the static and dynamic DNS entries in your router's resolution table, use this command:

```
Router# show hosts
Default domain is CHECK.COM
Name/address lookup uses domain service
Name servers are 255.255.255.255
Host           Flag         Age  Type  Address(es)
a.check.com    (temp, OK)  1     IP    172.16.9.9
b.check.com    (temp, OK)  8     IP    172.16.1.1
f.check.com    (perm, OK)  0     IP    172.16.1.2
```

The first two entries in the table were learned via a DNS server (*temp* flag), whereas the last entry was configured statically on the router with the **ip host** command (*perm* flag).

The show version Command

If you want to see general information about your router—its model number, the types of interfaces, the different kinds and amounts of memory, its software version, where the router located and loaded its IOS and configuration, as well as the configuration settings—then you will want to use the **show version** command:

```
Router> show version
Cisco Internetwork Operating System Software
IOS (tm) 3600 Software (C3640-JS-M), Version 12.0(3c), RELEASE SOFTWARE (fc1)
Copyright (c) 1986-1999 by cisco Systems, Inc.
Compiled Tue 13-Apr-99 07:39 by phanguye
Image text-base: 0x60008918, data-base: 0x60BDC000

ROM: System Bootstrap, Version 11.1(20)AA2, EARLY DEPLOYMENT
RELEASE SOFTWARE (fc1)

Router uptime is 2 days, 11 hours, 40 minutes
System restarted by power-on
System image file is "flash:c3640-js-mz.120-3c.bin"

cisco 3640 (R4700) processor (revision 0x00) with 49152K/16384K
bytes of memory.
<--output omitted-->
1 FastEthernet/IEEE 802.3 interface(s)
8 Low-speed serial(sync/async) network interface(s)
1 Channelized T1/PRI port(s)
DRAM configuration is 64 bits wide with parity disabled.
125K bytes of non-volatile configuration memory.
32768K bytes of processor board System flash (Read/Write)

Configuration register is 0x2102
```

At the very bottom of this output is the configuration register value. This value determines how the router will boot up, including how it will find its IOS and its configuration file. The bootup process of the router is discussed in much more depth in Chapter 6.

5.30. The CD includes a multimedia demonstration of using the show version command on a Cisco router.

exam watch

Be familiar with the output of the show version command, including what is displayed, like the IOS version, the uptime, the amount of RAM, NVRAM, and flash, the type and number of interfaces, and the configuration register value.

Router Configuration Files

Working with configuration files on a router is exactly the same as working on a 2950 switch. To view your running (active) configuration file, use the **show running-config** command:

```
Router# show running-config
Building configuration...
Current configuration:
!
version 12.0
no service udp-small-servers
no service tcp-small-servers
!
hostname Router
<--output omitted-->
```

Notice the references to "Building configuration. . ." and "Current configuration" in this example. Both of these refer to the configuration in RAM.

To save your configuration file from RAM to NVRAM, use the **copy running-config startup-config** command:

```
Router# copy running-config startup-config
Destination filename [startup-config]?
Building configuration..
Router#
```

To see the configuration file stored in NVRAM, use this command:

```
Router# show startup-config
Using 4224 out of 65536 bytes
!
version 11.3
no service udp-small-servers
no service tcp-small-servers
!
hostname Router
<--output omitted-->
```

One difference between this output and that from the **show running-config** command is the first line of output: `Using 4224 out of 65536 bytes`. This refers to the amount of NVRAM currently used by the saved configuration file. As you can see from these commands, the syntax and operation are the same on the 2950.

Unlike the 1900 switch, the router does not **automatically save configuration changes. You must manually enter the `copy running-config startup-config` command from** Privileged EXEC **mode. This command backs up your configuration to NVRAM. Also, anytime you want to examine or manipulate a configuration, you must be in Privilege EXEC mode.**

EXERCISE 5-4

Using the CLI to Set Up a Basic Router Configuration

In this exercise, you will use the CLI to create a basic configuration on your router. You'll perform these steps on the 2600 and 2500 routers using Boson's NetSim simulator. You can find a picture of the network diagram for the simulator in the Introduction to this book. After starting up the simulator, click the *LabNavigator* button. Next, double-click *Exercise 5-4* and click the *Load Lab* button. This will load the lab configuration based on *Exercises 5-2* and *5-3*. At the top of the simulator in the menu bar, click the *eRouters* icon and choose *2600*.

1. Starting with the 2600 router, go to *Privilege EXEC* mode and then enter *Configuration* mode.

   At the top of the simulator's tool bar, click the *eRouters* icon and select *2600*. One the 2600 router, access *User EXEC* mode and use **`enable`** to go to *Privilege EXEC* mode and then **`configure terminal`** to access *Configuration* mode.

2. Assign a hostname of *2600*.

   Use the **`hostname 2600`** command and examine the prompt.

3. Set a *User EXEC* password of *cisco* for telnet access.

   Enter the **`line vty 0 4`** command and follow it with the **`login`** and **`password cisco`** commands.

4. Assign an encrypted *Privilege EXEC* password of *cisco*.

   Enter **`enable secret cisco`**.

5. Assign an IP address of 192.168.1.1/24 to **`fastethernet 0/0`**. Enable the interface. Test connectivity by pinging the 2950-1 switch.

   Enter the interface with **`interface fastethernet 0/0`**. Next, enter the addressing information: **`ip address 192.168.1.1 255.255.255.0`**. Use the **`no shutdown`** command to enable the interface. Return to *Privilege EXEC* mode: **`end`**. Test connectivity: **`ping 192.168.1.4`**.

6. Check whether or not the serial 0 interface is DTE or DCE. If it is DCE, assign a clock rate of 64,000. Assign an IP address of 192.168.2.1/24 to `serial 0`. Enable the interface.

   Check the controller: **`show controller serial 0`**. Enter the interface with **`configure terminal`** and **`interface serial 0`**. Configure the clock rate: **`clock rate 64000`**. Next, enter the addressing information: **`ip address 192.168.2.1 255.255.255.0`**. Use the **`no shutdown`** command to enable the interface. Exit to *Privilege EXEC* mode: **`end`**.

7. Use a command to display all of the interfaces, their IP addresses, and their statuses on one screen and then show the details of `fastethernet0` and `serial0` separately.

   Use the **`show interfaces`** command followed by **`show interface fa0/0`** and **`show interface s0`**.

8. Save your configuration to NVRAM and view the active configuration.

   Save it with **`copy running-config startup-config`** and view it with **`show running-config`**.

9. Configure Host3's IP address (192.168.3.2/24) and default gateway (192.168.3.1). Configure Host2's IP address (192.168.3.3/24) and default gateway (192.168.3.1). Test connectivity between the two PCs.

   Configure Host3: Click the *eStation's* icon in the toolbar and select *Host3* within the simulator. On the CL1, type **`ipconfig`** `/ip 192.168.3.2 255.255.255.0`. Then, type **`ipconfig`** `/dg 192.168.3.1`. Configure Host2: Click the *eStation*'s icon within the simulator and select *Host2*. On the CL1, type **`ipconfig`** `/ip 192.168.3.3 255.255.255.0`. Then, type **`ipconfig`** `/dg 192.168.3.1`. Test the connection from Host2 by pinging Host3: **`ping 192.168.3.2`**.

10. Configure the 2500 router. Set the hostname (*2500*) as well as the telnet (*cisco*) and enable secret passwords (*cisco*); for the interfaces, enable `ethernet0` and `serial0` and assign the appropriate IP addresses to them. Test connectivity to the 2600 and Host-3 and Host-2.

At the top of the simulator's tool bar, click the *eRouters* icon and select *2500*. On the 2500 router, access *User EXEC* mode and use **enable** to go to *Privilege EXEC* mode and then **configure terminal** to access *Configuration* mode. Use the **hostname 2500** command and examine the prompt. Enter the **line vty 0 4** command and follow it with the **login** and **password cisco** commands. Enter **enable secret cisco**. Enter the interface with **interface ethernet 0**. Next, enter the addressing information: **ip address 192.168.3.1 255.255.255.0**. Use the **no shutdown** command to enable the interface. Exit Configuration mode (**end**) and check the serial0 controller: **show controller serial 0**. Enter the interface with **configure terminal** and **interface serial 0**. It's a DTE, so you don't have to configure the clock rate. Next, enter the addressing information: **ip address 192.168.2.2 255.255.255.0**. Use the **no shutdown** command to enable the interface. Exit *Configuration* mode: **end**. Test connectivity to the 2600: **ping 192.168.2.1**. Test connectivity to the two hosts connected to ethernet0: **ping 192.168.3.2** and **ping 192.168.3.3**. Save the configuration: **copy running-config startup-config**.

You should now be more comfortable with creating a basic configuration on a router from the CLI.

CERTIFICATION SUMMARY

The IOS provides a CLI with many features, including context-sensitive help with **help** or **?**, command history, and advanced editing features, which are available at all modes, including the *User* and *Privilege EXEC* and *Configuration* modes. Within *Configuration* mode, there are *Subconfiguration* modes. To access *Privilege EXEC* mode, use the **enable** command, and to access *Configuration* mode, use **configure terminal**.

You can protect access to your Cisco device by assigning *User EXEC* and *Privilege EXEC* passwords. On the 1900, use the **enable password level** command. The router and 2950 use the *Line Subconfiguration* mode **password** command and the **enable secret** or **enable password** command for the two respective levels.

The 1900 has a global IP address, whereas the 2950 has its IP address associated with a VLAN interface. The router needs an IP address on each interface where it will be processing IP traffic. All of these devices use the **ip address** command. For DCE serial interfaces, routers need a clock rate applied with the **clock rate** command. Use the **show interfaces** command to view the status and configuration of your interfaces.

To view the active configuration, use the **show running-config** command. On the 2950 and router, you must manually save your configuration to NVRAM with the **copy running-config startup-config** command.

TWO-MINUTE DRILL

CLI

- There are three basic CLI modes for IOS devices: *User EXEC* (">"), *Privilege EXEC* ("#"), and *Configuration* ("(config)#") modes.
- On the 1900, you must enter **K** from the main menu to access *User EXEC* mode.
- Use the **enable** command to access *Privilege EXEC* mode and **configure terminal** to access *Configuration* mode. Use **end** to exit this mode and return to *Privilege EXEC* mode and either **exit** or **logout** to log out of the IOS device.
- Access context-sensitive help with the **help** or **?**.

Switch Basics

- The **hostname** command assigns a name to any IOS device.
- Use the **enable password level** command to assign passwords to the 1900.
- The **shutdown** command disables an interface and **no shutdown** enables it; switch interfaces are enabled by default and router interfaces are disabled by default.
- On the 2950, you must be in a VLAN interface in order to assign an IP address. Use the **ip address** command to assign an IP address to either switch.
- Use the **ip default-gateway** command to assign an exit point to the subnet.
- Use the **show running-config** to view your switch's configuration.
- The 1900 automatically saves its configuration to NVRAM. The 2950 requires the **copy running-config startup-config** command in order to save its configuration.

Router Basics

- The *System Configuration Dialog* is presented automatically if a router boots up without a configuration file in NVRAM or if you execute the **setup** *Privilege EXEC* mode command.

- You can assign *User EXEC* passwords to restrict line access (console and VTY) with the **password** command. Use the **enable secret** command to encrypt the *Privilege EXEC* password. The **enable password** command doesn't encrypt it.
- DCE interfaces require a clock rate, assigned with the **clock rate** command. Use the **show controller** command to verify the interface type. The **bandwidth** command is used only for routing metrics, not clocking.
- Use the **show interfaces** command to see the physical and data link layer statuses.

SELF TEST

The following Self Test questions will help you measure your understanding of the material presented in this chapter. Read all the choices carefully, as there may be more than one correct answer. Choose all correct answers for each question.

IOS Introduction

1. Which command takes you from *Privilege EXEC* mode to *User EXEC* mode?

   A. `enable`

   B. `disable`

   C. `exit`

   D. `logout`

2. Which prompt indicates that you are at *User EXEC* mode?

   A. `>`

   B. `#`

   C. `%`

   D. `@`

3. The ________ command takes you from *User EXEC* mode to *Privilege EXEC* mode.

IOS Basics

4. If you wanted a list of parameters for the **show** command, you would type ________.

5. To recall a previous command, which of the following would you use?

   A. CTRL-P

   B. CTRL-N

   C. CTRL-R

   D. down arrow

6. Which control sequence moves the cursor to the end of the line?

   A. CTRL-A

   B. CTRL-P

   C. CTRL-E

   D. CTRL-Z

7. What would you enter to see the last few commands you entered?

   A. `show version`

   B. `show commands`

   C. `show previous`

   D. `show history`

8. Which would you use to move your cursor back one word?

   A. ESC-B

   B. ESC-P

   C. CTRL-B

   D. CTRL-P

9. If you enter a command in either *User EXEC* mode or *Privilege EXEC* mode that the IOS does not recognize, the switch or router

   A. Logs you out

   B. Tries to resolve the command to an IP address

   C. Executes the closest command that it can find in its command set

   D. Makes a "beep" sound

10. You are at *User EXEC* mode and type the letter *e*. What message appears?

    A. `% Incomplete command.`

    B. `% Ambiguous command:`

    C. `% Unknown command or computer name`

    D. `% Invalid input detected at '^'.`

Basic Switch Configuration

11. On the 1900 switch, how do you enter *User EXEC* mode?

    A. It comes up by default.

    B. Enter the letter **U** in the menu.

    C. Enter the letter **K** in the menu.

    D. Enter the letter **C** in the menu.

12. Enter the command to access *Configuration* mode: __________.

13. Enter the command to assign a name to a 1900 switch of *switch1*: ___________.

14. What command assigns a *User EXEC* password to a 2950 switch?

A. `password`

B. `login`

C. `enable password`

D. `enable password level`

15. Which command assigns a default gateway to the 2950 switch?

A. `(config)# default-gateway`

B. `(config-if)# default-gateway`

C. `(config-if)# ip default-gateway`

D. `(config)# ip default-gateway`

Basic Router Configuration

16. The router automatically saves its configuration.

A. True

B. False

17. You examine your interfaces, and the `Ethernet 0` interface status says: `Ethernet 0 is up, line protocol is down`. What does this indicate?

A. There is a physical layer problem.

B. There is a data link layer problem.

C. There is a network layer problem.

D. There is no problem.

18. You execute the **`line console 0`** command from *Configuration* mode. What will the router's prompt be?

A. `Router(config)#`

B. `Router(config-line)#`

C. `Router(config-interface)#`

D. `Router#(config-if)`

19. You are in *Interface Subconfiguration* mode and want to completely return to *Privilege EXEC* mode. What would you enter? (Choose all correct answers.)

A. CTRL-Z

B. `end`

C. `exit`

D. `logout`

20. What router command saves the active configuration to NVRAM?

A. `copy nvram startup-config`

B. `copy startup-config running-config`

C. `copy running-config nvram`

D. `copy running-config startup-config`

SELF TEST ANSWERS

IOS Introduction

1. ☑ **B.** The **`disable`** command takes you from *Privilege EXEC* mode to *User EXEC* mode.
   ☒ **A** does the reverse and therefore is incorrect, and **C** and **D** log you out of the router.

2. ☑ **A.** The ">" indicates *User EXEC* mode.
   ☒ **B** is incorrect because it indicates *Privilege EXEC* mode. **C** and **D** are incorrect because these are invalid prompts.

3. ☑ The **`enable`** command takes you from *User EXEC* mode to *Privilege EXEC* mode.

IOS Basics

4. ☑ To view all of the parameters for the **`show`** command, enter **`show ?`**.

5. ☑ **A.** CTRL-P recalls a previous command.
   ☒ **B** and **D** recall the next command, and **C** redisplays the current line.

6. ☑ **C.** CTRL-E takes you to the end of the CLI.
   ☒ **A** takes you to the beginning, **B** takes you to the previous line, and **D** takes you from *Configuration* to *Privilege EXEC* mode.

7. ☑ **D.** The **`show history`** command displays the last few commands that you entered.
   ☒ **A** displays software and hardware information. **B** and **D** are nonexistent commands.

8. ☑ **A.** The ESC-B control sequence takes you back one word on the CLI.
   ☒ **B** is incorrect because it is an invalid control sequence. **C** is incorrect because it takes you back one character. **D** is also incorrect, because it takes you back one line.

9. ☑ **B.** Whenever you enter an invalid command, the device attempts to first resolve the command to an IP address and telnet to this machine.
   ☒ **A** is incorrect because this requires you to execute the **`logout`** command. **C** is incorrect because the IOS doesn't know what command to execute. **D** is incorrect because sounds aren't supported with the CLI.

10. ☑ **B.** If you don't type enough characters for a command or parameter, you'll get an "ambiguous command" message.
    ☒ **A** is incorrect because you didn't type enough parameters for the command. **C** is incorrect because this message is shown when you enter an invalid command, and **D** is incorrect because you entered incorrect or invalid information for a valid command.

Basic Switch Configuration

11. ☑ **C.** Enter **K** to access *User EXEC* mode on a 1900 switch.
☒ **A** is true for the 2950 and the routers, not the 1900. **B** and **D** are incorrect because these are nonexistent options.

12. ☑ The **`configure terminal`** command takes you from *Privilege EXEC* mode to *Configuration* mode.

13. ☑ The **`hostname switch1`** command changes the name of the 1900 switch to "switch1."

14. ☑ **A.** The *Line Subconfiguration* mode **`password`** command assigns a console or telnet *User EXEC* mode password.
☒ **B** is incorrect because this specifies authentication with the **`password`** command. **C** is incorrect because this assigns a *Privilege EXEC* password. **D** is incorrect because this assigns passwords on a 1900 switch.

15. ☑ **D.** The **`ip default-gateway`** *Global Configuration* mode command assigns a default gateway to either a 1900 or 2950 switch.
☒ **C** is incorrect because it is in the wrong mode. **B** and **D** are incorrect because they are invalid commands.

Basic Router Configuration

16. ☑ **B.** The router does not automatically save its configuration; you need to use the **`copy running-config startup-config`** to save it to NVRAM.

17. ☑ **B.** The "line protocol is down" refers to the data link layer.
☒ **A** is incorrect because the physical layer is "up." **C** is incorrect because the status refers only to the physical and data link layers. Since there is a correct answer, **D** is incorrect.

18. ☑ **B.** When you execute the **`line console 0`** command, your prompt changes to "Router(config-line)#."
☒ **A** is incorrect because this is *Global Configuration* mode. **D** represents *Interface Subconfiguration* mode, and **C** is a nonexistent prompt.

19. ☑ **A** and **B.** The CTRL-Z control sequence and the **`end`** command take you from any *Configuration* mode back to *Privilege EXEC* mode.
☒ **C** only takes you back one level, while **D** is a *User* and *Privilege EXEC* mode command.

20. ☑ **D.** Use the **`copy running-config startup-config`** to back up your configuration from RAM to NVRAM.
☒ **B** is incorrect because this restores your configuration to RAM. **A** and **C** are incorrect because these commands use nonexistent parameters.

6

Managing Your Network Device

CERTIFICATION OBJECTIVES

- 6.01 Router Hardware Components
- 6.02 Router Bootup Process
- 6.03 Router Configuration Files
- 6.04 Changes in Your Network
- 6.05 Router IOS Image Files
- 6.06 IOS Troubleshooting
- ✓ Two-Minute Drill
- Q&A Self Test

This chapter covers important IOS features that you can use to manage your IOS device. Many of these features are supported across all IOS devices, but some of them are supported on only certain devices. This chapter focuses on these features as they relate to Cisco routers, beginning with how the router boots up, finds its operating system, and loads its configuration file, as well as how to back up and restore your IOS image. There are many tools that you can use on your router for troubleshooting connection problems, including the Cisco Discovery Protocol (CDP), ping, traceroute, telnet, and debug. These tools are discussed at the end of the chapter.

CERTIFICATION OBJECTIVE 6.01

Router Hardware Components

Each IOS device has two main components: hardware and software. Almost every IOS-based router uses the same hardware and firmware components to assist during the bootup process, including the following: ROM (read-only memory), RAM (random access memory), flash, NVRAM (nonvolatile RAM), a configuration register, and physical interfaces. All of these components can affect how the router boots up, finds its operating system and loads it, and finds its configuration file and loads it. The following sections cover these components in more depth.

Read-Only Memory (ROM)

The software in ROM cannot be changed unless you actually swap out the ROM chip on your router. ROM is nonvolatile—when you turn off your device, the contents of ROM are not erased. ROM contains the necessary firmware to boot up your router and typically has the following four components:

- **POST (power-on self-test)** Performs tests on the router's hardware components.
- **Bootstrap program** Brings the router up and determines how the IOS image and configuration files will be found and loaded.
- **ROM Monitor (ROMMON mode)** A mini–operating system that allows you to perform low-level testing and troubleshooting, the password recovery procedure, for instance. To abort the router's normal bootup procedure of loading the IOS, use the CTRL-BREAK control sequence to enter *ROMMON* mode. The

prompt in *ROMMON* mode is either ">" or "`rommon>`," depending on the router model.

- **Mini-IOS** A stripped-down version of the IOS that contains only IP code. This should be used in emergency situations where the IOS image in flash can't be found and you want to boot up your router and load in another IOS image. This stripped-down IOS is referred to as *RXBOOT* mode. If you see "`Router(rxboot)#`" in your prompt, then your router has booted up with the ROM IOS image. Not every router has a Mini-IOS image; on the other hand, some routers, such as the 7200, can store a full-blown IOS image here.

POST performs self-tests on the hardware. The bootstrap program brings the router up and finds the IOS image. ROMMON contains a mini-operating system used for low-level testing and debugging. The Mini-IOS is a stripped-down version of the IOS used for emergency booting of a router and is referred to as RXBOOT mode. All of these components are stored in ROM.

Other Components

Your router contains other components that are used during the bootup process, including RAM, flash, NVRAM, the configuration register, and the physical interfaces. The following paragraphs explain these components.

RAM is like the memory in your PC. On a router, it (in most cases) contains the running IOS image; the active configuration file; any tables (including routing, ARP, CDP neighbor, and other tables); and internal buffers for temporarily storing information, such as interface input and output buffers. The IOS is responsible for managing memory. When you turn off your router, everything in RAM is erased.

Flash is a form of nonvolatile memory in that when you turn the router off, the information stored in flash is not lost. Routers store their IOS image in flash, but other information can also be stored here. Note that some lower-end Cisco routers actually run the IOS directly from flash (not RAM). Flash is slower than RAM, a fact that can create performance issues.

NVRAM is like flash in that its contents are not erased when you turn off your router. It is slightly different, though, in that it uses a battery to maintain the information when the Cisco device is turned off. Routers use NVRAM to store their configuration files. In newer versions of the IOS, you can store more than one configuration file here.

The *configuration register* is a special register in the router that determines many of its bootup and running options, including how the router finds the IOS image and its configuration file. As you will see later in this chapter, you can manipulate this register to affect how your router boots up.

exam watch ***Flash is used to store the operating system, and NVRAM is used to store the configuration file. The configuration register is used to determine how the router will boot up.***

Every router has at least one port and one physical interface. *Ports* are typically used for management access; the console and auxiliary ports are examples. *Interfaces* are used to move traffic through the router; they can include media types such as Ethernet, Fast Ethernet, Token Ring, FDDI, serial, and others. These interfaces can be used during the bootup process—you can have the bootstrap program load the IOS from a remote TFTP server (instead of flash), assuming that you have a sufficient IP configuration on your router.

CERTIFICATION OBJECTIVE 6.02

Router Bootup Process

A router typically goes through five steps when booting up:

1. The router loads and runs POST (located in ROM), testing its hardware components, including memory and interfaces.
2. The bootstrap program is loaded and executed.
3. The bootstrap program finds and loads an IOS image: Possible locations of the IOS image include flash, a TFTP server, or the Mini-IOS in ROM.
4. Once the IOS is loaded, the IOS attempts to find and load a configuration file, which is normally stored in NVRAM—if the IOS cannot find a configuration file, it starts up the *System Configuration Dialog* discussed in Chapter 5.
5. After the configuration is loaded, you are presented with the CLI interface (remember that the first mode you are placed into is *User EXEC* mode).

If you are connected to the console port, you'll see the following output as your router boots up:

```
System Bootstrap, Version 11.0(10c), SOFTWARE
Copyright (c) 1986-1996 by cisco Systems
```

```
2500 processor with 6144 Kbytes of main memory

F3: 5593060+79544+421160 at 0x3000060

Cisco Internetwork Operating System Software
IOS (tm) 2500 Software (C2500-I-L), Version 12.0(5)
Copyright (c) 1986-1999 by cisco Systems, Inc.
Compiled Tue 15 Jun-99 19:49 by phanguye
Image text-base: 0x0302EC70, data-base: 0x00001000

<--output omitted-->

cisco 2501 (68030) processor (revision N) with
6144K/2048K bytes
of memory.
Processor board ID 18086269, with hardware revision
00000003
Bridging software.
X.25 software, Version 3.0.0.
Basic Rate ISDN software, Version 1.1.
1 Ethernet/IEEE 802.3 interface(s)
2 Serial network interface(s)
32K bytes of non-volatile configuration memory.
16384K bytes of processor board System flash (Read ONLY)

00:00:22: %LINK-3-UPDOWN: Interface Ethernet0, changed
state to up
00:00:22: %LINK-3-UPDOWN: Interface Serial0, changed
state to up
00:00:22: %LINK-3-UPDOWN: Interface Serial1, changed
state to up
00:00:23: %LINEPROTO-5-UPDOWN: Line protocol on Interface
Ethernet0, changed state to up
00:03:13: %LINK-5-CHANGED: Interface Serial0, changed
state to administratively down
00:03:13: %LINK-5-CHANGED: Interface Serial1, changed
state to administratively down

Cisco Internetwork Operating System Software
IOS (tm) 2500 Software (C2500-I-L), Version 12.0(5)
Copyright (c) 1986-1999 by cisco Systems, Inc.
Compiled Tue 15-Jun-99 19:49 by phanguye

Press RETURN to get started!
```

There are a few things to point out here. First, notice that the router is loading the bootstrap program (“`System Bootstrap, Version 11.0(10c)`”) and then the IOS image ("`IOS (tm) 2500 Software (C2500-I-L), Version 12.0(5)`"). During the bootup process, you cannot see the actual POST process. However, you will see information about the interfaces going up and/or down—this is where the IOS is loading the configuration and bringing up those interfaces that you previously activated. Sometimes, if the router has a lot of interfaces, the "`Press RETURN to get started!`" message is mixed in with the interface messages. Once the display stops, just hit ENTER to access *User EXEC* mode. This completes the bootup process of the router.

When a router boots up, it runs POST, loads the bootstrap program, finds and loads the IOS, and loads its configuration file . . . in that order.

6.01. The CD contains a multimedia demonstration of booting up a Cisco router.

Bootstrap Program

As you saw in the bootup code example, the bootstrap program went out and found the IOS and loaded it. The bootstrap program goes through the following steps when trying to locate and load the IOS image:

1. Examine the configuration register value. This value is a set of four hexadecimal digits. The last digit affects the bootup process. If the last digit is between 0x2 and 0xF, then the router proceeds to the next step. Otherwise, the router uses the values shown in Table 6-1 to determine how it should proceed next.
2. Examine the configuration file in NVRAM for **`boot system`** commands, which tell the bootstrap program where to find the IOS. These commands are shown in the following paragraph.
3. If no **`boot system`** commands are found in the configuration file in NVRAM, use the first valid IOS image found in flash.
4. If there are no valid IOS images in flash, generate a TFTP local broadcast to locate a TFTP server (this is called a *netboot* and is not recommended because it is very slow and not very reliable for large IOS images).
5. If no TFTP server is found, load the Mini-IOS in ROM (*RXBOOT* mode).
6. If there is a Mini-IOS in ROM, then the Mini-IOS is loaded and you are taken into *RXBOOT* mode; otherwise, the router either retries finding the IOS image or loads ROMMON and goes into *ROM Monitor* mode.

Table 6-1 contains the three common configuration register values in the fourth hex character of the configuration register that are used to influence the bootup process. The values in the configuration register are represented in *hexadecimal*, the register being 16 bits long.

The configuration register is used to influence how the IOS boots up.

For step 2 of the bootup process described in the last paragraph, here are the **boot system** commands that you can use to influence the order that the bootstrap program should use when trying to locate the IOS image:

```
Router(config)# boot system flash name_of_IOS_file_in_flash
Router(config)# boot system tftp IOS_image_name
                         IP_address_of_server
Router(config)# boot system rom
```

The **boot system flash** command tells the bootstrap program to load the specified IOS file in flash when booting up. Note that, by default, the bootstrap program loads the *first* valid IOS image in flash. This command tells the bootstrap program to load a different image. You might need this if you perform an upgrade and you have two IOS images in flash—the old one and new one. By default, the old one still loads first unless you override this behavior with the **boot system flash** command or delete the old IOS flash image.

You can also have the bootstrap program load the IOS from a TFTP server—this is not recommended for large images, since the image is downloaded via the UDP protocol, which is slow. And last, you can tell the bootstrap program to load the Mini-IOS in ROM with the **boot system rom** command. To remove any of these commands, just preface them with the **no** parameter.

The order that you enter the boot system commands is important, since the bootstrap program processes them in the order that you specify—once the program finds an IOS, it does not process any more boot system commands.

6.02. The CD contains a multimedia demonstration of using boot system commands on a router.

TABLE 6-1 Fourth Hex Character Configuration Register Values

Value in Last Digit	Bootup Process
0x0	Boot the router into *ROMMON* mode
0x1	Boot the router into *RXBOOT* mode using the Mini-IOS
0x2–0xF	Boot the router using the default boot sequence

exam watch

The* `boot system` *commands can be used to modify the default behavior of where the bootstrap program should load the IOS. When the bootstrap program loads, it examines the configuration file stored in NVRAM for* `boot system` *commands. If found, the IOS uses these commands to find the IOS. If no* `boot system` *commands are found, the router uses the default behavior in finding and loading the IOS image.

Configuration Register

As I mentioned in the last section, the configuration register is used by the bootstrap program to determine where the IOS image and configuration file should be loaded from. Once the router is booted up, you can view the configuration register value with the **show version** command:

```
Router> show version
Cisco Internetwork Operating System Software
IOS (tm) 3600 Software (C3640-JS-M), Version 12.0(3c),
RELEASE SOFTWARE (fc1)
Copyright (c) 1986-1999 by cisco Systems, Inc.
Compiled Tue 13-Apr-99 07:39 by phanguye
Image text-base: 0x60008918, data-base: 0x60BDC000

ROM: System Bootstrap, Version 11.1(20)AA2,
EARLY DEPLOYMENT RELEASE SOFTWARE (fc1)

Router uptime is 2 days, 11 hours, 40 minutes
System restarted by power-on
System image file is "flash:c3640-js-mz.120-3c.bin"

cisco 3640 (R4700) processor (revision 0x00) with 49152K/16384K
bytes of memory
<-- output omitted -->
125K bytes of non-volatile configuration memory.
32768K bytes of processor board System flash (Read/Write)

Configuration register is 0x2102
```

You need to go to the very bottom of the display in order to view the register value.

6.03. The CD contains a multimedia demonstration of using the `show version` command on a router.

Changing the Configuration Register from *Configuration* Mode

There are two ways of changing the configuration register value: from *Configuration* mode or from *ROMMON* mode. If you already have *Privilege EXEC* access to the router and want to change the register value, use this command:

```
Router(config)# config-register 0xhexadecimal_value
```

The register value is four hexadecimal digits, or 16 bits, in length. Each bit position in the register, though, indicates a function that the bootstrap program should take. Therefore, you should be very careful when configuring this value on your router.

The CD included with this book has a configuration register utility. Please take a look at this handy GUI-based tool from Boson--by selecting or deselecting specific boot options, the utility will *automatically* generate the correct register value for you.

When entering the register value, you must always precede it with "0x," indicating that this is a hexadecimal value. If you don't, the router assumes the value is decimal and converts it to hexadecimal. On a 2500 series router, the default configuration register value is 0x2102, which causes the router to use the default bootup process in finding and locating IOS images and configuration files. If you change this to 0x2142, this tells the bootstrap program that, upon the next reboot, it should locate the IOS using the default behavior, but *not* to load the configuration file in NVRAM; instead, you are taken directly into the *System Configuration Dialog*. This is the value that you will use to perform the password recovery procedure.

exam watch

The default configuration register value is 0x2102, which causes a router to boot up using its default bootup process. You can see the configuration register value with the `show version` command. If you've changed this value, you will see the existing value and the value the router will use upon rebooting.

Changing the Configuration Register from ROM Monitor

Of course, one problem with the *Configuration* mode method of changing the register value is that you must gain access to *Privilege EXEC* mode first. This can be a problem if you don't know what the passwords on the router are. There is a second method, though, that allows you to change the register value without having to log in to the router. To perform this method, you'll need console access to the router—you can't do this from the auxiliary port nor from a telnet session. Next, you'll turn the router off and then back on. As the router starts booting, you'll break into *ROMMON* mode with the router's break sequence. To break into the router, once you see the boot strap program has loaded, you can, in most cases, use the CTRL-BREAK control sequence to break into *ROMMON* mode. Please note that this control sequence may be different, depending on the terminal program and operating system you are using on your PC.

Once in *ROMMON* mode, you can begin the process of changing the register value. There are two methods to do this, depending on the router that you have. Some of Cisco's routers, such as the 2600 and 3600, use the **confreg** script. This script asks you basic questions about the function and bootup process of the router. What's nice about the script is that you don't need to know the hexadecimal values for the configuration register, since the router will create it for you as you answer these questions. Here is an example of using this script:

```
rommon 5 > confreg
Configuration Summary
enabled are:
load rom after netboot fails
console baud: 9600
boot: image specified by the boot system commands
or default to: cisco2-C3600

do you wish to change the configuration? y/n  [n]:  y
enable  "diagnostic mode"? y/n  [n]:
enable  "use net in IP bcast address"? y/n  [n]:
disable "load rom after netboot fails"? y/n  [n]:
enable  "use all zero broadcast"? y/n  [n]:
enable  "break/abort has effect"? y/n  [n]:
enable  "ignore system config info"? y/n  [n]:
change console baud rate? y/n  [n]:
change the boot characteristics? y/n  [n]:

Configuration Summary
enabled are:
load rom after netboot fails
console baud: 9600
boot: image specified by the boot system commands
or default to: cisco2-C3600
do you wish to change the configuration? y/n  [n]:  n
rommon 6 >
```

Just as in the *System Configuration Dialog,* any information in brackets ("[]") represents default values. The first question that it asks is if you want to "change the configuration," which means change the register: answer "y" to continue. If you answer "y" to "ignore system config info," the third hexadecimal digit becomes 4, making a 2500's register value appear as 0x2142. This option is used when you want to perform the password recovery procedure. The next-to-last question is "change the boot characteristics"—this question, if you answer "y," will repeat the questions again. Answer "n" to exit the script. If you make any changes, you are asked to save them ("do you wish to change the configuration?")—answer "y" to save your new register value.

on the job

As a shortcut, you could also execute the following command from *ROMMON* ***mode: confreg 0x2142.***

Other routers, such as those in the 2500 series, do not support the **confreg** command. Instead, you'll need to use the following command to change the register value:

```
> o/r 0x4-digit_hexadecimal_value
```

In this situation, you must know the actual hexadecimal value that you will use in order to change the register value. You can use the **o** command to list the value in the register. Once you are done with either method, reboot the router. On many routers, just type in the letter "**i**" or "**b**" in *ROMMON* mode to boot it up.

6.04. The CD contains a multimedia demonstration of changing the configuration register in ROMMON mode and using the config-register command on a router.

exam watch

When performing the password recovery procedure, break into ROMMON mode and change the configuration register value to 0x2142 and boot up the router. Once booted up, the router will ignore the configuration in NVRAM and take you into the System Configuration Dialog. Using CTRL-C will break you out of this utility and take you to User EXEC mode. Enter Privilege EXEC mode and restore your configuration with the copy startup-config running-config command. The no shutdown command is not listed in the router's NVRAM configuration, so you will have to manually enable the interfaces. This is also true if you copy and paste a configuration into a router with its interfaces disabled, like a newly booted router.

CERTIFICATION OBJECTIVE 6.03

Router Configuration Files

You've already had a basic introduction to configuration files in the last chapter. Remember that a configuration file contains the commands used to configure the router. Configuration files are typically located in one of three places: RAM, NVRAM, and/or a TFTP server. The configuration that the router is currently using is in RAM. You can back up, or save, this configuration to either NVRAM or a TFTP server.

As you may recall from the last chapter, the commands *related* to configuration files, even **show** commands, require you to be at *Privilege EXEC* mode. Also, only the 1900 switch automatically saves configuration files to NVRAM—you must manually do this on a router or 2950 switch. The following sections show you how to manipulate your configuration files on a router.

Saving Configuration Files

Chapter 5 explained how to save your configuration from RAM to NVRAM with the **copy running-config startup-config** command. When you execute this command, whatever filename (the default is "startup-config") you are copying to in NVRAM is completely overwritten. If you want to keep an old copy and a newer one in NVRAM, you'll need to specify a different name than "startup-config." Note that the **copy** command has two parameters. The first parameter refers to where the source information is (what you want to copy from), and the second parameter refers to where the destination is (what you want to copy to).

You can also back up your configuration to a TFTP server. This requires you to have TFTP server software on a server or PC and IP configured correctly on your router in order to access the server. The router command that you'll use is the **copy** command:

```
Router# copy running-config tftp
Address or name of remote host []? 192.168.1.11
Destination filename [Router-confg]?
!!
781 bytes copied in 5.8 secs (156 bytes/sec)
Router#
```

The syntax of the command for the 2950 switch is the same. You need to specify the IP address of the TFTP server as well as the filename that you want to save your configuration as. If the filename already exists on the server, the server *overwrites* the old file. After entering this information, you should see bang symbols ("!") indicating the successful transfer of UDP segments to the TFTP server. If you see periods ("."), this indicates an unsuccessful transfer. Plus, upon a successful transfer, you should also see how many bytes were copied to the server.

You can also back up configuration files to an FTP or RCP server. However, this is beyond the scope of this book.

The 1900 switch uses a different configuration file nomenclature for the **copy** commands. This is discussed in the section "Configuration File Nomenclature" later in this chapter.

You can also back up your saved configuration on your router or 2950 switch by replacing **running-config** in the preceding command with **startup-config**:

```
Router# copy startup-config tftp
```

This command backs up the configuration file in NVRAM to a TFTP server. As with the command before it, you will be prompted for the IP address of the TFTP server as well as the filename of the configuration file. Please note that if the file already exists on the TFTP server, the server will completely replace the old file with the new one.

6.05. The CD contains a multimedia demonstration of backing up the configuration file of a router.

Restoring Configuration Files

There may be situations when you have misconfigured your router or switch and wish to take a backed-up configuration file and load it back on to your Cisco device. You can do this by reversing the source and destination information in the **copy** command. There are actually three variations of the **copy** command that can accomplish this. Here is the first one:

```
Router# copy tftp startup-config
Address or name of remote host []? 192.168.101.1
Source filename []? router-confg
Destination filename [startup-config]?
Accessing tftp://192.168.101.1/p1r1-confg...
Loading Router-confg from 192.168.101.1 (via Ethernet0): !
[OK - 781/1024 bytes]
[OK]
781 bytes copied in 11.216 secs (71 bytes/sec)
Router#
```

In this example, the configuration file is copied from a TFTP server to NVRAM; if the file already exists there, it will be overwritten. Just as when backing up to a TFTP server, you must specify the server's IP address and the filename on the server.

You can also restore your configuration from a TFTP server to active memory:

```
Router# copy tftp running-config
```

There is one main difference between moving the configuration from TFTP to NVRAM and moving it from TFTP to RAM. With the former method, the file in NVRAM is replaced with the one being copied; with the latter method, a *merge* process is used. During a merge process, the IOS updates commands that are common to both places—the new file and in RAM. The IOS also executes any new commands it finds in the uploaded configuration file. However, the IOS does not delete any commands in RAM that it does not find in the uploaded configuration file. In other words, this is *not* a replacement process. As an example, assume that you have a configuration file on a TFTP server that has IPX and IP information in it, but your RAM configuration has IP and AppleTalk. In this example, the router updates the IP configuration, adds the IPX commands, but leaves the AppleTalk commands as they are.

This process is also true if you want to restore your configuration from NVRAM to RAM with this command:

```
Router# copy startup-config running-config
```

6.06. The CD contains a multimedia demonstration of restoring the configuration file on a router.

Creating and Deleting Configuration Files

Besides backing up and restoring configuration files, you also need to know how to create and delete them. Actually, you already know how to create a basic configuration file by going into *Configuration* mode with the *Privilege EXEC* **configure terminal** command. When you are executing commands within this mode (whether by typing or pasting them in), the IOS is using a merge process (unless you use the **no** parameter for a command to delete or negate it).

You can also delete your configuration file in NVRAM by using the following command:

```
Router# erase startup-config
```

To verify the erasure, use the **show startup-config** command:

```
Router# show startup-config
%% Non-volatile configuration memory is not present
Router#
```

The 1900 switch is slightly different. The command to erase your configuration file is **delete nvram**. To view the configuration file, there is only one command: **show running-config**. Remember that the 1900 automatically saves its configuration to NVRAM. When you execute the **show running-config** command, you are actually looking at the active configuration, which *is* stored in NVRAM.

The copy command backs up and restores configuration files: copy running-config startup-config and copy running-config tftp back up the configuration file. copy startup-config running-config and copy tftp running-config or copy tftp startup-config restores the configuration file. The erase startup-config deletes the config file on a 2950 or a router, while the delete nvram deletes the config on a 1900.

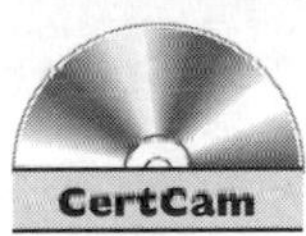

6.07. The CD contains a multimedia demonstration of deleting the NVRAM configuration file of a router.

Configuration File Nomenclature

Starting with IOS 12.0 and later, Cisco introduced command and naming nomenclatures that follow IFS guidelines (what you are used to when you are entering a URL in a web browser address text box). Therefore, instead of entering a command and having a router prompt you for such additional information as the IP address of a TFTP server as well as the filename, you can now put all of this information on a single command line. Commands that reference configuration files and IOS images contain prefixes in front of the file type, which include the following:

- **bootflash** bootflash memory
- **flash** flash memory
- **flh** flash load helper log files

- **ftp** FTP server
- **nvram** NVRAM
- **rcp** Remote Copy Protocol (RCP) server
- **slot0** PCMCIA slot 0
- **slot1** PCMCIA slot 1
- **system** RAM
- **tftp** TFTP server

Let's take a look at an example. For instance, say that you want to back up your router's configuration from RAM to NVRAM. With the new syntax, you could type in the following:

```
Router# copy system:running-config nvram:startup-config
```

You don't always have to put in the type; for instance, in the preceding example, you could easily have entered this:

```
Router# copy running-config nvram:startup-config
```

To view the active configuration, you can use this command:

```
Router# more system:running-config
```

To delete all files in NVRAM, you can use this command:

```
Router# erase nvram:
```

To delete a specific file in NVRAM, you can use this form of the command:

```
Router# erase nvram:file_name
```

The older style of entering configuration and IOS commands is still supported along with the new one.

The 1900, for the most part, uses the newer style of commands when dealing with the manipulation of configuration files. For instance, if you want to back up your configuration to a TFTP server, use the following syntax:

```
# copy nvram tftp://192.168.101.1/1900-config
```

In this example, the latter part of the command, referring to the TFTP server, follows the new nomenclature.

6.08. The CD contains a multimedia demonstration of using the new nomenclature for manipulating configuration files on a router.

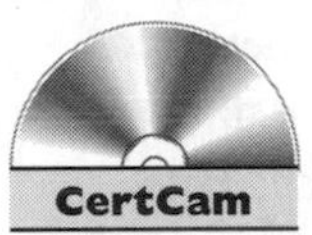

6.09. The CD contains a multimedia demonstration of backing up and restoring configuration files on a 1900 switch.

Review of Configuration Files

It is important that you understand what action the IOS will take when it is either backing up or restoring a configuration file to a particular location. Table 6-2 summarizes this information for the routers.

Here is a quick way of remembering whether the IOS is using a merge or overwrite process. Anything copied into RAM uses a merge process, whereas any other copy operation is an overwrite process.

TABLE 6-2 Overview of IOS Process When Dealing with Configuration Files

Location (From)	Location (To)	Command	IOS Process
RAM	NVRAM	**copy running-config startup-config**	Overwrite
RAM	TFTP	**copy running-config tftp**	Overwrite
NVRAM	RAM	**copy startup-config running-config**	Merge
NVRAM	TFTP	**copy startup-config tftp**	Overwrite
TFTP	RAM	**copy tftp running-config**	Merge
TFTP	NVRAM	**copy tftp startup-config**	Overwrite
CLI	RAM	**configure terminal**	Merge

EXERCISE 6-1

Manipulating Your Router's Configuration Files

These last few sections dealt with the router's configuration files and how you manipulate them. This exercise will help you reinforce this material. You'll perform these steps on the 2600 router using Boson's NetSim simulator. You can find a picture of the network diagram for the simulator in the Introduction of this book. After starting up the simulator, click the *LabNavigator* button. Next, double-click *Exercise 6-1* and click the *Load Lab* button. This will load the lab configuration based on Chapter 5's exercises. At the top of the simulator in the menu bar, click the *eRouters* icon and choose *2600*.

1. Access the 2600 router's *Privilege EXEC* mode and save your router's active configuration to NVRAM. Verify the copy.

   Access *Privilege EXEC* mode: **enable**. Use the **copy running-config startup-config** command. Verify the copy: **show startup-config**.
2. Change the hostname on the router to *different* and then reload the saved configuration from the NVRAM into RAM. What is the hostname?

   Access *Configuration* mode (**configure terminal**) and use the **hostname different** command to change the router's name to *different*. Exit *Configuration* mode: **end**. Restore your configuration with **copy startup-config running-config**. Your prompt should change back to the previous name of the router (you might have to wait a few seconds for this to complete).
3. Erase your router's configuration in NVRAM. Examine the configuration file in NVRAM. Save the active configuration file to NVRAM. Examine the configuration file in NVRAM.

   Use the **erase startup-config** command to erase your configuration in NVRAM. Use the **show startup-config** command to verify the configuration file was deleted. Use the **copy running-config startup-config** command to save your configuration to NVRAM. Use the **show startup-config** command to verify that your router's configuration was backed up from RAM to NVRAM.

Now you should be more comfortable with the manipulating a router's configuration files. In the next section, you will learn how you should deal with changes in your network.

CERTIFICATION OBJECTIVE 6.04

Changes in Your Network

When you decide to make any changes to your network, including the addition or deletion of devices, you should always do some preparation work *before* you make the change. Making changes can cause things to not function correctly, or not function at all, so you should always prepare beforehand. The following two sections cover the basics of handling changes.

Adding Devices

Before you add a device to your network, you should gather the following information and perform the following tasks:

1. Decide which IP address you'll assign to the device for management purposes.
2. Configure the ports of the device, including the console and VTY ports.
3. Set up your passwords for *User* and *Privilege EXEC* access.
4. Assign the appropriate IP addresses to the device's interface(s).
5. Create a basic configuration on the device so that it can perform its job.

Changing Devices

You will constantly be making configuration changes to your network to enhance performance and security. Before you make any changes to your network, you should *always* back up your configuration files. Likewise, before you perform a software upgrade on your Cisco device, you should always back up the old IOS image.

You should check a few things before loading the new image on your IOS device. First, does the new image contain all of the features that your previous image had? Or at least the features that you need? Also, does your router have enough flash *and* RAM to store and load the IOS image? You need to check these items out before proceeding to load the new image.

At times, you may need to upgrade the hardware or add a new module to your Cisco device. Some devices require you to turn them off to do the upgrade, while other devices do not. It is extremely important that you read the installation manual that comes with the hardware before performing the installation. If you install a hardware component into a device that requires the device to be turned off, and the device is running, you could damage your new component, or, worse, electrocute yourself.

Just remember that it is much easier to restore a backup copy than it is to recreate something from scratch. Whenever you make changes, always test the change to ensure that your Cisco device is performing as expected.

CERTIFICATION OBJECTIVE 6.05

Router IOS Image Files

The default location of IOS images is in flash. Some routers have flash built into the motherboard, some use PCMCIA cards for storage, and some use a combination of both. At times, you will have to deal with the router's flash when you want to do a router upgrade, for instance. To view your files in flash, use the **show flash** command:

```
Router# show flash
System flash directory:
File   Length    Name/status
1   10084696  c2500-js_l_120-3.bin
[10084696 bytes used, 6692456 available, 16777216 total]
16384K bytes of processor board System flash (Read ONLY)
```

Use the show flash command or show version command to see how much flash memory is installed on your router.

In this example, you can see that flash holds one file 10,084,696 bytes in length that is called *c2500-js_l_120-3.bin*. Below this, you can see how much flash is used (about 10 MB), how much is available (about 6 MB), and the total amount of flash on the router (16 MB). You can also see how much flash you have installed on your router with the **show version** command.

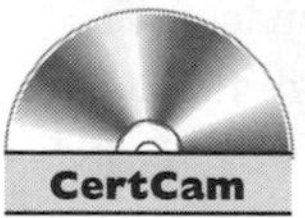

6.10. The CD contains a multimedia demonstration of viewing flash on a router.

Naming Conventions for IOS Images

Cisco has implemented a naming convention for its IOS images, allowing you to tell the platform, software version, and features included in the image . . . just by looking at the name of the image file. As example, I'll use the image name from the previous **show flash** command: "c2500-js_l-120-3.bin."

The "c2500" refers to the name of the platform that the image will run on. This is important because different router models have different processors; and an image compiled for one processor or router model will typically *not* run on a different model. Therefore, it is very important that you load the appropriate image on your router.

The "js" refers to the features included in this IOS version, commonly referred to as the *feature set*. In this example, "j" refers to the enterprise edition, while "s" means that the IOS image has enhanced features.

The "l" (the letter "l," not the number "1") indicates where the IOS image is run from. The "l" indicates relocatable and that the image can be run from RAM. Remember that some images can run directly from flash, depending on the router model. If you see "mz" or "z," this means that the image is compressed and must be uncompressed before running.

The "120-3" indicates the software version number of the IOS. In this instance, the version is 12.0(3). And the ".bin" at the end indicates that this is a binary image.

on the Job

The naming nomenclature discussed here applies to IOS images that are either included on your IOS device when you buy it from Cisco or applied when you download them from Cisco's web site. However, the name, in and of itself, has no bearing on the actual operation of the IOS when it is loaded on your IOS device. For instance, you can download an image from Cisco and rename it to "poorperformance.bin," and this will have no impact on the IOS device's performance.

exam Watch

Cisco uses a specialized naming convention when naming their IOS images. This convention contains the platform image, the feature set, whether or not the image is relocatable or is compressed, and the IOS version and revision numbers.

Before Upgrading the IOS Image

This section and the next section discuss how to upgrade and back up the IOS software on your router. Before you upgrade the IOS on your router, you should first back up the existing image to a TFTP server. There are two reasons that you might want to do this. First, your flash might not be large enough to support two images—the old one and the new. If you load the new one and you experience problems with it, you'll probably want to load the old image back onto your router. Second, Cisco doesn't keep every software version available on their web site. Older versions of the IOS are hard to locate, so if you are upgrading from an old version of the IOS, I would highly recommend backing it up first.

Before you back up your IOS image to a TFTP server, you should also perform the following checks:

- Is the TFTP server reachable (test with the **ping** command)?
- Is there enough disk space on the TFTP server to hold the IOS image?
- Does the TFTP server support the file nomenclature that you want to use?
- Does the file have to exist on the TFTP server before you can perform the copy? (This is true with certain TFTP servers in the Unix world.)

Once you have performed these checks, you are ready to continue with the backup process.

Backing Up an IOS Image

To back up your IOS image, you'll use the **copy flash tftp** command. When you execute this command, you'll be prompted for the following information:

- The name of the IOS image in flash to back up—use the **show flash** command to get this name
- The TFTP server's IP address
- The name that you want to call the image when it is copied to the TFTP server

Here is an example of the use of this command:

```
Router# copy flash tftp
Source filename []? c3640-js-mz.120-11
Address or name of remote host []? 192.168.1.1
Destination filename [c3640-js-mz.120-11]?
!!!!!!!!!!!!!!!!!!!!!!!!!!!!!!!!!!!!!!!!!!!!!!!!!!!!!!!!!!!!
!!!!!!!!!!!!!!!!!!!!!!!!!!!!!!!!!!!!!!!!!!!!!!!!!!!!!!!!!!!!
<--output omitted-->
6754416 bytes copied in 64.452 secs (105537 bytes/sec)
Router#
```

As the image is backed up, you should see a bunch of exclamation points ("!") filling up your screen—this indicates the successful copy of a UDP segment. If you see periods (".") instead, this indicates a failure. After a successful copy operation, you should see the number of bytes copied as well as how long it took. Compare the number of bytes copied to the file length in flash to verify that the copy was really successful.

6.11. The CD contains a multimedia demonstration of backing up the IOS flash image on a router.

Loading an IOS Image

If you want to upgrade your IOS or load a previously saved IOS image, you'll need to place the IOS image on a TFTP server and use the **`copy tftp flash`** command. You'll be prompted for the same information as you were when you used the **`copy flash tftp`** command; however, the process that takes place after you enter your information is different.

After your enter your information, the IOS first verifies that the image exists on the TFTP server. If the file exists on the server, the IOS then prompts you if you want to erase flash. Answer "y" if you don't have enough space in flash for the older image(s) as well as the new one. If you answer "y," flash is erased and reprogrammed; as this step proceeds, you will see a list of "**e**"s appear on the screen.

After flash is initialized, your router pulls the IOS image from the TFTP server. Just as in the copy operations with configuration files, a bunch of " ! "s indicate successful copies, while " . "s indicate unsuccessful copies.

Not every IOS version has the same upgrade process, so what you see on your router may be different from this book, especially if you are running IOS versions 11.x or earlier.

Here is an example of loading an IOS image into your router:

```
Router# copy tftp flash
Address or name of remote host []? 192.168.1.1
Source filename []? c3640-js-mz.120-7
Destination filename [c3640-js-mz.120-7]?
%Warning: There is a file already existing with this name
Do you want to over write? [confirm] y
Accessing tftp://192.168.1.1/c3640-js-mz.120-7...
Erase flash: before copying? [confirm] y
Erasing the flash filesystem will remove all files! Continue? [confirm] y
Erasing device... eeeeeeeeeeeeeeeeeeeeeeeeeeeeeeee ...erased
Erase of flash: complete
Loading c3640-js-mz.120-7 from 192.168.1.1 (via FastEthernet0/0):
!!!!!!!!!!!!!!!!!!!!!!!!!!!!!!!!!!!!!!!!!!!!!!!!!!!!!!!!!!!!
!!!!!!!!!!!!!!!!!!!!!!!!!!!!!!!!!!!!!!!!!!!!!!!!!!!!!!!!!!!!
<--output omitted-->
[OK - 6754416/13508608 bytes]

Verifying checksum...  OK (0xCAF2)
6754416 bytes copied in 66.968 secs (102339 bytes/sec)
Router#
```

Use the *copy flash tftp* command to back up the IOS image and the *copy tftp flash* command to restore or upgrade the IOS. The *reload* command reboots the router.

In this example, the router noticed that the name of the image that exists on the TFTP server is the same one that is in flash and verifies that you want to overwrite it. After the router copies the IOS image to flash, you must reboot your router in order for it to use the new image. There are two ways you can reboot your router: turn it off and back on or use the *Privilege EXEC* **reload** command. The first method is a hard reboot, and the second one is a soft reboot.

If you place an incorrect image on your router, for instance, a 3600 series image on a 2500 series router, the router will not reboot. You'll need to break into *ROMMON* mode and either do a TFTP boot or boot from the Mini-IOS in ROM.

The 2950 uses the same process as a Cisco router for backing up and loading IOS images. The 1900 switch doesn't support backing up of images; however, you can load an IOS image with this command: copy tftp://IP_address/IOS_image opcode.

6.12. The CD contains a multimedia demonstration of loading an IOS flash image on a router.

CERTIFICATION OBJECTIVE 6.06

IOS Troubleshooting

The remainder of this chapter focuses on troubleshooting tools that you can use on your routers and switches. One of your first troubleshooting tasks is to figure out in which layer of the OSI Reference Model things are not working. By narrowing the problem down to a specific layer, you've greatly reduced the amount of time that you'll need in order to fix it. Cisco has a wide variety of tools that you can use. Here is a list of the more common tools and what layer of the OSI Reference Model that they can be used for in troubleshooting:

- **show interfaces** command Layer-2 (covered in Chapter 5)
- Cisco Discovery Protocol (CDP) Layer-2
- **ping** command Layer-3
- **traceroute** command Layer-3

- **telnet** command Layer-7
- **debug** commands Layers-2–7

The following sections covers these tools in more depth.

Cisco Discovery Protocol (CDP)

CDP is a Cisco proprietary data link layer protocol that was made available in version 10.3 of the router IOS. Almost every Cisco device supports CDP, including Cisco routers and Catalyst switches. For those devices that support CDP, CDP is *enabled* by default. CDP messages received from one Cisco device, by default, are not forwarded to any other devices behind it. In other words, you can see CDP information only about other Cisco devices *directly* connected to you.

The important point to make about CDP is that if you are receiving CDP frames from a Cisco neighbor, then at least the data link layer is functioning correctly.

CDP Information

CDP, as mentioned in the last paragraph, works at the data link layer. However, since CDP uses a SNAP frame type, not every data link layer media type is supported. The media types that are supported are Ethernet, Token Ring, FDDI, PPP, HDLC, ATM, and Frame Relay.

The information shared in a CDP packet about a Cisco device includes the following:

- Name of the device configured with the **hostname** command
- IOS software version
- Hardware capabilities, such as routing, switching, and/or bridging
- Hardware platform, such as 2600, 2950, or 1900
- The layer-3 address(es) of the device
- The interface the CDP update was generated on

exam watch

CDP messages are generated every 60 seconds as multicast messages on each of its active interfaces. Interfaces supported include ATM, Ethernet, FDDI, Frame Relay, HDLC, and PPP. CDP information is not propagated to other Cisco devices behind your directly connected neighboring Cisco devices.

CDP Configuration

As I mentioned in the last section, CDP is enabled on all Cisco CDP-capable devices when you receive your product from Cisco. On Cisco routers and the 2950 switch, you can globally disable or enable it with this command:

```
Router(config)# [no] cdp run
```

There is no command on the 1900 switch to globally disable it. However, on Cisco routers, the 2950, and the 1900, you can enable or disable CDP on an interface-by-interface basis:

```
Router(config)# interface type [slot_#/]port_#
Router(config-if)# [no] cdp enable
```

Since CDP doesn't use up much resources (a small frame is generated once a minute), it is recommended to keep it enabled unless your router is connected to the Internet; and then you should at least disable CDP on the external, or public, interface. At a minimum, the information is only 80 bytes in length. There are other, optional commands related to CDP, such as changing the update and hold down timers, but these commands are beyond the scope of this book.

6.13. The CD contains a multimedia demonstration of disabling and enabling CDP on a router.

CDP Verification

To see the status of CDP on your Cisco device, use this command:

```
Router# show cdp
Global CDP information:
Sending CDP packets every 60 seconds
Sending a holdtime value of 180 seconds
Sending CDPv2 advertisements is  enabled
```

As you can see from this output, CDP is enabled and generating updates every 60 seconds. The hold down timer is 180 seconds. This timer determines how long a CDP neighbor's information is kept in the local CDP table without seeing a CDP update from that neighbor.

You can also see the CDP configuration on an interface-by-interface basis by adding the **interface** parameter to the **show cdp** command:

```
Router# show cdp interface
Serial0 is up, line protocol is up, encapsulation is HDLC
Sending CDP packets every 60 seconds
```

```
Holdtime is 180 seconds
Ethernet0 is up, line protocol is up, encapsulation is ARPA
Sending CDP packets every 60 seconds
Holdtime is 180 seconds
```

To see a summarized list of the CDP neighbors that your Cisco device is connected to, use the **show cdp neighbors** command:

```
Router# show cdp neighbors
Capability Codes: R - Router, T - Trans Bridge,
B - Source Route Bridge
S - Switch, H - Host, I - IGMP, r - Repeater

Device ID    Local Intrfce Holdtme Capability Platform Port ID
0090AB56EEC0 Fas 0/1         170      T S       1900     B
```

In this example, there is one device connected to a router with a device ID of "0090AB56EEC0," which is a 1900 switch without a hostname. In this situation, the MAC address of the switch is used as the ID. This update was received on `fastethernet 0/1` on this device 10 seconds ago (hold-down timer of 170 seconds). The `Port ID` refers to the port at the remote side—`B` is `fastethernet 0/27` on a 1900 switch—that the device advertised the CDP message from.

You can add the optional **detail** parameter to the preceding command to see the details concerning the connected Cisco device. On Cisco routers and the 2950, you can also use the **show cdp entry *** command. Here is an example of a CDP detailed listing:

```
Router# show cdp neighbor detail
-------------------------
Device ID: RouterA
Entry address(es):
IP address: 172.16.1.1
IPX address: 10.0000.0000.1111
Platform: cisco 4500,  Capabilities: Router
Interface: Ethernet0/0,  Port ID (outgoing port): Ethernet0/1
Holdtime : 137 sec

Version :
Cisco Internetwork Operating System Software
IOS (tm) 4500 Software (C4500-J-M), Version 11.1.10,
MAINTENANCE INTERIM SOFTWARE
Copyright (c) 1986-1997 by cisco Systems, Inc.
Compiled Mon 07-Apr-97 19:51 by dschwart

<-- output truncated -->
```

In this example, you can see that the connected device is a 4500 series router running IOS 11.1(10) and has IP and IPX addresses configured on the connected interface.

For the router and 2950, you can list the details of a specific neighbor with this command:

```
Router# show cdp entry neighbor's_name
```

The advantage of this approach over that in the preceding example is that this command lists only the specified neighbor. This command is not supported on the 1900.

The 2950 and router support one additional command, which allows you to view CDP traffic statistics:

```
Router# show cdp traffic
Total packets output: 350, Input: 223
Hdr syntax: 0, Chksum error: 0, Encaps failed: 0
No memory: 0, Invalid: 0, Fragmented: 0
```

If you are receiving CDP traffic, then the data link layer is functioning correctly.

6.14. The CD contains a multimedia demonstration of viewing CDP information on a router.

exam watch

CDP is enabled, by default, on all Cisco devices. CDP updates are generated as multicasts every 60 seconds with a hold-down period of 180 seconds for a missing neighbor. The `no cdp run` command globally disables CDP, while the `no cdp enable` command disables CDP on an interface. Use `show cdp neighbors` to list out your directly connected Cisco neighboring devices. Adding the `detail` parameter will display the layer-3 addressing configured on the neighbor.

Layer-3 Connectivity Testing

As you saw in the preceding section, CDP can be very useful in determining if the data link layer is working correctly. You can even see the layer-3 address(es) configured on your neighboring device and use this for testing layer-3 connectivity. Besides using CDP, you could also use the **show interfaces** command for data link layer testing.

However, the main limitation of these two tools is that they don't test layer-3 problems. Cisco, nevertheless, has tools for testing layer-3 connectivity. This chapter

The simple `ping` and `traceroute` commands can be executed from either** User **or** Privilege EXEC **modes. However, the extended `ping` and `traceroute` commands can only be executed from** Privilege EXEC **mode.

focuses on two of these commands: **`ping`** and **`traceroute`**. Both of these commands come in two versions: one for *User EXEC* mode and one for *Privilege EXEC*. The *Privilege EXEC* version provides additional options and parameters that can assist you in your troubleshooting process. Both of these tools are supported on Cisco routers and the 2950 switches; however, only the *User EXEC* mode of **`ping`** is supported on the 1900 switches. The following sections cover these tools in more depth.

Using Ping

Ping (Packet Internet Groper) was originally developed for the IP protocol stack to test layer-3 connectivity. With IP, the ICMP protocol is used to implement ping. However, Cisco's IOS has expanded the **`ping`** command to support other protocols, including Apollo, Appletalk, CLNS, DECnet, IP, IPX, Vines, and XNS. Cisco uses ping to test layer-3 connectivity with other protocols in a (typically) proprietary fashion.

When troubleshooting PC problems, first determine if the user can ping their loopback address: `ping 127.0.0.1`. If this fails, then there is something wrong with the TCP/IP protocol stack installation on the PC. Next, have the user try to ping their configured IP address. If this fails, there is something wrong with their IP address configuration. Next, have the user ping the default gateway. If this fails, then there is either something wrong with the configured default gateway address, the default gateway itself, or the subnet mask value configured on the user's PC.

Ping uses ICMP echo messages to initiate the test. If the destination is reachable, the destination responds back with an echo reply message for each echo sent by the source. Both the `ping` and `traceroute` commands test layer-3 connectivity.

Simple ping Command To execute a simple ping from either *User* mode or *Privilege EXEC* mode, enter the **ping** command on the CLI and follow it with the IP address or hostname of the destination:

```
Router> ping destination_IP_address_or_host_name
```

Here is a simple example of using this command:

```
Router> ping 192.168.101.1
Type escape sequence to abort.
Sending 5, 100-byte ICMP Echos to 192.168.1.1,
timeout is 2 seconds:
!!!!!
Success rate is 100 percent (5/5),
round-trip min/avg/max = 2/4/6 ms.
Router>
```

In this example, five test packets were sent to the destination and the destination responded back to all five, as is shown by the exclamation marks ("**!**"). The default timeout to receive a response from the destination is two seconds—if a response is not received from the destination for a packet within this time period, a period ("**.**") is displayed.

There are basically two reasons you might see a "**.**" in the output—a response was received, but after the timeout period, or no response was seen at all. If a response was received, but after the timeout problem, this might be because an ARP had to take place to learn the MAC address of a connected device or because of congestion. Here are two examples: "**.!!!!**" and "**!!..!**". If devices have to perform ARPs to get the MAC address of the next device, then you'll typically see the first example in your output. However, if your output looks like the second example, you're probably experiencing congestion or performance problems. Table 6-3 shows examples of ping messages that you might see in your output. The bottom of the output shows the success rate—how many replies were received and the minimum, average, and maximum round-trip times for the ping packets sent (in milliseconds). This information can be used to detect if there is a delay between you and the destination.

Extended ping Command The IOS routers and 2950 switches support an extended **ping** command, which can only be executed at *Privilege EXEC* mode. To execute this command, just type **ping** by itself on the command line:

```
Router# ping
Protocol [ip]:
Target IP address: 192.168.1.1
Repeat count [5]:
Datagram size [100]:
Timeout in seconds [2]
Extended commands [n]: y
Source address:
Type of service [0]:
Set DF bit in IP header? [no]:
Data pattern [0xABCD]:
Loose, Strict, Record, Timestamp, Verbose[none]:
Number of hops [9]:
Loose, Strict, Record, Timestamp, Verbose[RV]:
Sweep range of sizes [n]:
Type escape sequence to abort.
Sending 5, 100-byte ICMP Echos to 192.168.1.1,
timeout is 2 seconds:
<-- output truncated -->
```

TABLE 6-3 Output Codes for the **ping** Commands

Ping Output	Explanation
.	A response was not received before the timeout period expired.
!	A response was received within the timeout period.
U	A remote router responded that the destination is unreachable—the segment is reachable, but not the host.
N	A remote router responded that the network is unreachable—the network cannot be found in the routing table.
P	A remote device responded that the protocol is not supported.
Q	Source quench, telling the source to slow its output.
M	The ping packet needed to be fragmented, but a remote router couldn't perform fragmentation.
A	The ping packet was filtered by a device (administratively prohibited).
?	The ping packet type is not understood by a remote device.
&	The ping exceeded the maximum number of hops supported by the routing protocol.

Here is an explanation of the parameters that might be asked of you when you execute this command:

- **Protocol** The protocol to use for the ping (defaults to IP)
- **Target IP address** The IP address or hostname of the destination to test
- **Repeat count** How many echo requests should be generated for the test (defaults to 5)
- **Datagram size** The size, in bytes, of the ping packet (defaults to 100)
- **Timeout in seconds** The amount of time to wait before indicating a timeout for the echo (defaults to two seconds)
- **Extended commands** Whether or not the remaining questions should also be asked (this defaults to "`no`")
- **Source address** The IP address that should appear as the source address in the IP header (this defaults to the IP address of the interface the ping will use to exit the IOS device)
- **Type of service** The IP level for QoS (defaults to `0`)
- **Set DF bit in the IP header?** Whether or not the ping can be fragmented when it reaches a segment that supports a smaller MTU size (the default is no—don't set this bit). Sometimes a misconfigured MTU can cause performance problems. You can use this parameter to pinpoint the problem, since a device with a smaller MTU size will not be able to handle the large packet.
- **Data pattern** The data pattern that is placed in the ping. It is a hexadecimal four-digit (16-bit) number (defaults to 0xABCD) and is used to solve cable problems and crosstalk on cables.
- **Loose, Strict, Record, Timestamp, Verbose** IP header options (defaults to "`none`" of these). The *record* parameter records the route that the ping took—this is somewhat similar to traceroute. If you choose *record*, you will be asked for the maximum number of hops that are allowed to be recorded by the ping (defaults to 9, and can range 1–9).
- **Sweep range of sizes** Send pings that vary in size. This is helpful when trying to troubleshoot a problem related to a segment that has a small MTU size (and you don't know what that number is). This defaults to *n* for no.

To break out of a `ping` or `traceroute` command, use the* CTRL-SHIFT-6 *break sequence.

6.15. The CD contains a multimedia demonstration of using the simple and extended `ping` commands on a router.

Using Traceroute

One limitation of ping is that this command will not tell you where, between you and the destination, layer-3 connectivity is broken. Traceroute, on the other hand, will list each router along the way, including the final destination. Therefore, if there is a layer-3 connection problem, with traceroute, you'll know at least where the problem begins. Like the **`ping`** command, **`traceroute`** has two versions: one for *User EXEC* mode and one for *Privilege EXEC*. The following two sections cover the two different versions.

Simple `traceroute` Command The simple **`traceroute`** command, which works at both *User* and *Privilege EXEC* modes, has the following syntax:

```
Router> trace destination_IP_address_or_host_name
```

Here is an example of this command:

```
Router> traceroute www.trace.com
Type escape sequence to abort.
Tracing the route to www.trace.com (200.1.90.6)
1 router.dealgroup.com (192.168.1.1) 732 msec 8 msec 7 msec
2 router11.myisp.COM (200.1.89.1) 9 msec 8 msec 8 msec
3 www.trace.com (200.1.90.6) 10 msec 11 msec 11 msec
```

In this example, the destination was three hops away—each hop is listed on a separate line. For each destination, three tests are performed, where the round-trip time is displayed for each test. If you don't see round-trip time, this indicates a possible problem. Table 6-4 shows other values that you might see instead of the round-trip time.

In certain cases, for a specific destination, you might see three asterisks ("*") in the output—you shouldn't be alarmed if you see this, since a variety of things can cause it; for instance, there may be an inconsistency in how the source and destination devices have implemented traceroute, or the destination may be configured not to reply to these messages. However, if you continually find the same destination repeated in the output with these reply messages, this indicates a layer-3 problem starting with either this device or the device before it.

TABLE 6-4 Traceroute Messages

TracerouteOutput	Explanation
`*`	Either the wait timer expired while waiting for a response or the device did not respond at all.
`A`	The trace packet was filtered by a remote device (administratively prohibited).
`U`	The port of the device is unreachable (the destination received the trace packet but discarded it).
`H`	The destination is unreachable (the destination segment was reachable, but not the host).
`I`	The user interrupted the traceroute process.
`N`	The network is unreachable (the destination segment was not reachable).
`P`	The protocol is unreachable (the device doesn't support traceroute).
`Q`	Source quench.
`T`	The trace packet exceeded the configured timeout value.
`?`	The device couldn't identity the specific trace type in the trace packet.

If you have DNS lookups enabled on your Cisco device (on routers, this is the `ip domain-lookup` command), the IOS will attempt to resolve the IP address to a domain name before printing the output line for that device. If your traces seem to take a long time, this is usually the culprit. You can disable DNS lookups on your router with the `no ip domain-lookup` command.

Extended `traceroute` Command The extended **`traceroute`** command is similar to the extended **`ping`** command and requires *Privilege EXEC* mode access to execute it:

```
Router# trace
Protocol [ip]:
Target IP address: "IP_address_of_the_destination"
Source address:
Numeric display [n]:
Timeout in seconds [3]:
Probe count [3]:
Minimum Time to Live [1]:
Maximum Time to Live [30]:
```

```
Port number [33434]:
Loose, Strict, Record, Timestamp, Verbose [none]:
<-- output truncated -->
```

Some of these options are the same used by ping. Here is an explanation of the other options. The "Numeric Display" option turns off a DNS lookup for the names of the routers and the destination. The "Time to Live" options specify how many hops the trace is allowed to take. The "Loose" option tells the router that the hops you specify must appear in the trace path, but other routers can appear as well. The "Strict" option restricts the trace path to only those routers that you specify. The "Record" option specifies the number of hops to leave room for in the trace packet, and the "Timestamp" option allows you to specify the amount of space to leave room for in the trace packet for timing information. The "Verbose" option is automatically selected whenever you choose any of the options from this question; it prints the entire contents of the trace packet.

The* `ping` *command uses ICMP to test layer-3 connectivity to a device. The* `traceroute` *command lists each router along the way to the destination and is typically used to troubleshoot routing problems.

One important item to point out about this command is that if there is more than one path to reach the destination, the **`traceroute`** command will test *each* path.

6.16. The CD contains a multimedia demonstration of using the simple and extended* `traceroute` *commands on a router.

Layer-7 Connectivity Testing

The **`ping`** and **`traceroute`** commands can test only layer-3 connectivity. If you can reach a destination with either of these two commands, this indicates that layer-3 and below are functioning correctly. You can use other tools, such as telnet, to test the application layer. If you can telnet to a destination, then all seven layers of the OSI Reference model are functioning correctly. As an example, if you can telnet to a machine but can't send an e-mail to it, then the problem is *not* a networking problem, but an application problem (with the e-mail program).

The telnet application is used to test layer-7 (application layer) connectivity.

Using Telnet

If you've configured your Cisco devices correctly (with IP addressing and routing information), you should be able to successfully telnet to them. Cisco routers and 2950 switches support both incoming and outgoing telnet, whereas the 1900 supports only incoming telnet. This section, and the following sections on telnet, are applicable only to Cisco routers and the 2950 Catalyst switches.

To open up a telnet session from a router or 2950 switch, you can use any of the following three methods:

```
Router# name_of_the_destination | destination_IP_address
-or-
Router# telnet name_of_the_destination | destination_IP_address
-or-
Router# connect name_of_the_destination | destination_IP_address
```

All three of these methods perform in the same manner: they all have the IOS attempt to telnet the specified destination.

Suspending Telnet Sessions

If you are on a switch or router and telnet to a remote destination, you might want to go back to the original switch or router. One way of doing this is to exit the remote device; however, you might just want to go back to your source Cisco device, do something real quick, and then return to the remote device. Logging out of and back into the remote device is a hassle, in this instance.

Cisco, however, has solved this problem by allowing you to *suspend* a telnet connection, return to your original router or switch, do what you need to do, and then jump right back into your remote device . . . all without having you to log out of and back into the remote device. To suspend a telnet session, use the CTRL-SHIFT-6 X or CTRL-^ control sequence, depending on your keyboard. You must hold down the CTRL, SHIFT, and 6 keys simultaneously, let go, and then hit the X key.

On your source router or switch, if you want to see the open telnet sessions that you have currently suspended, use the **show sessions** command:

```
Router# show sessions
Conn Host        Address     Byte   Idle    Conn Name
   1 10.1.1.1    10.1.1.1       0      1    10.1.1.1
*  2 10.1.1.2    10.1.1.2       0      2    10.1.1.2
```

This example shows two open telnet connections. The one with the "*" preceding it is the default (last) session. To resume the last session, all you have to do is hit ENTER on an empty command line.

To resume a specific session, use this command:

```
Router# resume connection_#
```

The connection number to enter is the number in the "Conn" column of the **show sessions** command. If you are on the source router or switch and wish to terminate a suspended telnet session without having to resume the telnet session and then log out it, you can use this command:

```
Router# disconnect connection_#
```

Verifying and Clearing Connections

This section also deals with the router and 2950 switches. If you are logged into one of these devices, you can view the other users that are also logged in with this command:

```
Router# show users
    Line          User      Host(s)    Idle     Location
    0     con 0                        idle
    2     vty 0             idle          0     10.1.1.1
*   3     vty 1             idle          0     10.1.1.2
```

If you see a "*" in the first column, this indicates your current session. If you want to terminate someone's session, use the *Privilege* EXEC **clear line** command:

```
Router# clear line line_#
```

The line number that you enter can be found in the "Line" column of the output of the **show users** command.

6.17. The CD contains a multimedia demonstration of using telnet on a router.

exam watch

The telnet command is not supported on the 1900 switch. Use the CTRL-SHIFT-6 X ***control sequence to suspend a telnet session. Hitting*** ENTER ***on a blank line resumes the last suspended telnet session. Use the resume command to resume a suspended telnet connection. Use the show sessions command to see your suspended telnet sessions. Use the disconnect command to disconnect a suspended telnet session.***

Debug Overview

One of the most powerful troubleshooting tools of the IOS is the **debug** command, which enables you to view events and problems, in real time, on your Cisco device. One problem of using **show** commands is that they display only what is currently stored somewhere in the router's RAM, and this display is *static*. You have to reexecute the command to get a refreshed update. And **show** commands, unfortunately, do not always display detailed troubleshooting information. For instance, maybe you want the router to tell you when a particular event occurs and display some of the packet contents of that event. The **show** commands cannot do this; however, **debug** commands can.

debug commands, however, do have a drawback: since the router has to examine and display many different things when this feature is enabled, the performance of the IOS will suffer. As an example, if you want to see every IP packet that travels through a router, the router has to examine each packet, determine if it is an IP packet, and then display the packet or partial packet contents on the screen. On a very busy router, this debug process can cause serious performance degradation. Therefore, you should be very careful about enabling a debug process on your router; you might want to wait till after hours or periods of inactivity before using these commands.

on the Job

Also, you should never use the `debug all` command—this enables debugging for every process related to IOS features enabled on your router. In this situation, you'll just see pages and pages of output messages on all kinds of things and, on a busy router, probably crash it.

Typically, you will use **debug** commands for detailed troubleshooting. For instance, you may have tried using **show** commands to discover the cause of a particular problem, but without any success. You should then turn to using a particular **debug** command to uncover the cause of the problem. This command has many, many options and parameters—use the context-sensitive help to view them. Many of the remaining chapters in this book will cover specific **debug** commands and their uses. To enable debug, you must be at *Privilege EXEC* mode.

Once you've fixed your problem or no longer need to see the debug output, you should always disable the debug process. You can disable it by either prefacing the **debug** command with the **no** parameter or executing one of the following two commands:

```
Router# no debug all
Router# undebug all
```

These two commands disable all running **debug** commands on your router. You can first use the **show debug** command to see which events or processes you have enabled.

If you want to see timestamps displayed in your debug output, enter the following command:

```
Router(config)# service timestamps debug datetime msec
```

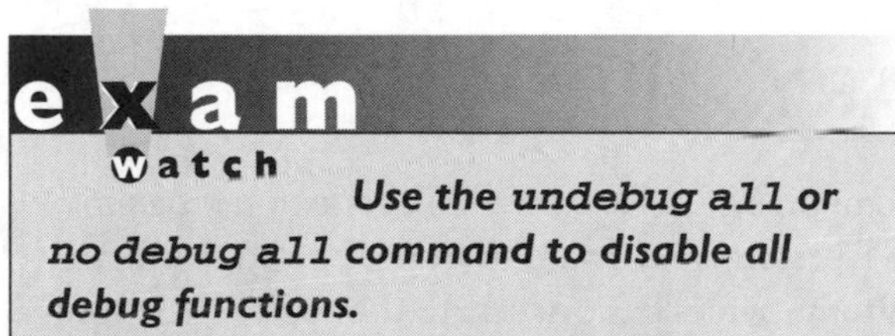

Use the undebug all or no debug all command to disable all debug functions.

The **datetime** parameter displays the current date and time, while the **msec** parameter displays an additional timing parameter: milliseconds.

If you think your **debug** commands are causing performance problems, use the **show processes** command to check your CPU utilization for the device's various processes, including debug.

6.18. The CD contains a multimedia demonstration of using debug on a router.

EXERCISE 6-2

Using the Router's Troubleshooting Tools

These last few sections dealt with the router's troubleshooting tools. This exercise will help you reinforce this material. You'll perform these steps using Boson's NetSim simulator. You can find a picture of the network diagram in the Introduction of this book. After starting up the simulator, click the *LabNavigator* button. Next, double-click *Exercise 6-2* and click the *Load Lab* button. This will load the lab configuration based on Chapter 5's exercises.

1. Access the 2600 router in the simulator on the CD. See what neighbors are directly connected to the router. What is the IP address of the 2500 router?

   At the top of the simulator in the menu bar, click the *eRouters* icon and choose *2600*. Use the **show cdp neighbors** command to view the 2600's neighbors—you may have to wait 60 seconds to see neighbors from this interface. You should see one of the 2950 switches and the 2500 router. Use the **show cdp neighbors detail** command to view the 2500's address: it is 192.168.2.2.

2. Access the 1900-1 switch in the simulator on the CD. See what neighbors are directly connected to the router. Which neighbors do you see? What are their IP addresses?

   At the top of the simulator in the menu bar, click the *eSwitches* icon and choose *1900-1*. Use the **show cdp neighbors** command to view your neighbors. You should see the 2950-1 and 2950-2 switches. Add the **detail** parameter to the preceding command to see their IP addresses.

CERTIFICATION SUMMARY

The router contains the following components in ROM: POST, bootstrap program, ROM Monitor, and Mini-IOS. POST performs hardware tests; the bootstrap program finds and loads the IOS. ROM Monitor provides basic access to the router to perform testing and troubleshooting. The Mini-IOS is used in emergency situations when an IOS image cannot be located: it contains a stripped-down version of the IOS.

The configuration register affects how the router boots up. By default, POST is run, the bootstrap program is loaded, the IOS image is located, and the configuration file is executed. You can change this by using **boot system** commands or by changing the configuration register value. The **show version** command displays the current register value and what it will be upon a reload. The default register value is typically 0x2102. For the password recovery, use 0x2142.

Use the **copy** commands to manipulate files, including the configuration file and IOS images. Anytime you copy something into RAM, the IOS uses a merge process. For any other location, the IOS uses an overwrite process. On a 1900 switch, use the **delete nvram** command to delete the configuration file in NVRAM. On the 2950s and routers, its **erase startup-config**.

CDP is a Cisco-proprietary protocol that functions at the data link layer. Every 60 seconds, Cisco devices generate a multicast on each of their interfaces containing basic information about themselves, including the device type, the version of software they're running, and their IP address. To disable CDP globally, use the **no cdp run** command. To see a list of your neighbors, use the **show cdp neighbors** command.

The **ping** and **traceroute** commands support an extended version at *Privilege EXEC* mode. The 1900 doesn't support telnet, but almost all other IOS devices do. If you want to suspend an active telnet session, use the CTRL-SHIFT-6 X control sequence. Hitting ENTER on a blank line resumes the last suspended telnet session. Use the **resume** command to resume a telnet connection. Use the **show sessions** command to see your open telnet session. Use the **disconnect** command to disconnect a suspended telnet session. To disable debug on your IOS device, use **undebug all** or **no debug all**. Debug functions only at *Privilege EXEC* mode.

TWO-MINUTE DRILL

Router Hardware Components and Bootup Process

- ROM stores the Mini-IOS, the bootstrap program, ROMMON, and POST. Flash stores the IOS images. NVRAM stores the configuration files. RAM stores the active configuration, including tables and buffers.
- When booting up, the router loads and runs POST from ROM. It then loads the bootstrap program from ROM, which, in turn, finds and loads the IOS. The IOS can be found in flash, TFTP, or ROM. The IOS then loads the configuration file, found in NVRAM.
- The configuration register and **boot system** commands can be used to override the default router bootup behavior. Use the **show version** command to see the register value. If the fourth hexadecimal character is 0x0, the router boots into *ROMMON* mode; if 0x1, the router boots the Mini-IOS; if 0x2—0xF, the router uses the default boot sequence. The default configuration register value is 0x2102. For the password recovery, it's 0x2142.
- Here is the default bootup process: the bootstrap program examines the configuration register to determine how to boot up. If it is the default, the bootstrap program looks for **boot system** commands in the configuration file in NVRAM. If none are found, it looks for the IOS in flash. If no files are found in flash, then the bootstrap program generates a TFTP local broadcast to locate the IOS. If no TFTP server is found, the bootstrap program loads the Mini-IOS in ROM. If there is no Mini-IOS in ROM, the bootstrap program loads ROMMON.

Router Configuration Files and Flash

- These commands perform a merge process: **copy startup-config running-config**, **copy tftp running-config**, and **configure terminal**. These commands perform an overwrite process: **copy running-config startup-config** and **copy running-config tftp**.
- The 1900 automatically saves its active configuration to NVRAM, while the router and the 2950 switch require you to execute the **copy running-config startup-config** command.

- When upgrading your IOS, make sure you download the version of IOS from Cisco that contains the features that you purchased and verify that your router has enough flash and RAM for the new image. Use the **copy tftp flash** command to perform an IOS upgrade.
- Use the **reload** command to reboot your router.

IOS Troubleshooting

- For layer-2 troubleshooting, use the **show interfaces** command and CDP. For layer-3 troubleshooting, use **ping** and **traceroute**. For layer-7 troubleshooting, use telnet. For detailed troubleshooting, use **debug**.
- CDP is used to learn basic information about directly connected Cisco devices. It uses a SNAP frame format and generates a multicast every 60 seconds. It is enabled, by default, on a Cisco device.
- To execute an extended **ping** or **traceroute**, you must be at *Privilege EXEC* mode. Ping tests only if the destination is reachable, while **traceroute** lists each layer-3 device along the way to the destination.
- To suspend a telnet session, use the CTRL-SHIFT-6 X or CTRL-^ X control sequence.
- The **debug** commands require *Privilege EXEC* access. To disable all **debug** commands, use **no debug all** or **undebug all**.

SELF TEST

The following Self Test questions will help you measure your understanding of the material presented in this chapter. Read all the choices carefully, as there may be more than one correct answer. Choose all correct answers for each question.

Router Hardware Components

1. Which of the following is stored in ROM?
   A. POST
   B. ROMMON
   C. Configuration file
   D. System recovery file
2. Which types of memory do not maintain their contents during a power-off state?
   A. NVRAM
   B. ROM
   C. RAM
   D. Flash

Router Bootup Process

3. The _______ program goes out and finds the IOS and loads it.
   A. ROMMON
   B. Bootstrap
   C. Mini-IOS
   D. Loader
4. Enter the router *Configuration* command to have it boot up from the Mini-IOS in ROM: __________
5. Which router command would you use to view the configuration register value?
   A. `show register`
   B. `show interfaces`
   C. `show configuration`
   D. `show version`
6. Enter the router *Configuration* mode command to change the configuration register to 0x2142: __________.

Router Configuration Files

7. Which router command performs an overwrite process?
   - A. `copy running-config startup-config`
   - B. `copy startup-config running-config`
   - C. `copy tftp running-config`
   - D. `copy running-config tftp`
8. Enter the router command to delete your configuration file in NVRAM: __________.

Router IOS Image Files

9. IOS images can be loaded from all the following except:
   - A. ROM
   - B. Flash
   - C. NVRAM
   - D. TFTP
10. When backing up your IOS image from flash, which of the following will the **`copy flash tftp`** command prompt you for? (Choose all correct answers.)
    - A. TFTP server IP address
    - B. Verification to copy
    - C. Source filename
    - D. Destination filename

IOS Troubleshooting

11. Which router command would you use to test only layer-3 connectivity?
    - A. `telnet`
    - B. `show cdp traffic`
    - C. `show interfaces`
    - D. `traceroute`
12. Extended **`traceroute`** works from which mode?
    - A. *User EXEC*
    - B. *Privilege EXEC*
    - C. *Configuration*
    - D. *User* and *Privilege EXEC*

13. How would you suspend a telnet session?

A. CTRL-SHIFT-X 6

B. CTRL-SHIFT-6 X

C. CTRL-6 X

D. CTRL-C

14. Which router command would take you back to a suspended telnet session?

A. `reconnect`

B. `connect`

C. `resume`

D. `toggle`

15. Enter the router command to disable all debug processing: __________.

SELF TEST ANSWERS

Router Hardware Components

1. ☑ **A** and **B.** POST, ROMMON, the Mini-IOS, and the bootstrap program are in ROM.
   ☒ **C** is stored in NVRAM, and **D** is nonexistent.

2. ☑ **C.** RAM contents are erased when you turn your device off.
   ☒ **A, B,** and **D** are incorrect; ROM, NVRAM, and flash maintain their contents when the device is turned off.

Router Bootup Process

3. ☑ **B.** The bootstrap program goes out and finds the IOS and loads it.
   ☒ **A** is incorrect because it applies to *Monitor* mode. **C** is incorrect because that is the IOS, though it may be a stripped-down one with only IP included. **D** is a nonexistent process.

4. ☑ Use the **`boot system rom`** or **`config-register 0x2401`** command to boot the Mini-IOS in ROM.

5. ☑ **D.** Use the **`show version`** command to view your configuration register value.
   ☒ **B** shows only interface statistics, and **A** is a nonexistent command. **C** is the old command version for **`show startup-config`**.

6. ☑ Enter the **`config-register 0x2142`** command in *Configuration* mode. This will cause the router to boot up and not load the configuration file in NVRAM.

Router Configuration Files

7. ☑ **A** and **D.** Copying to any other place besides RAM causes an overwrite.
   ☒ **B** and **C** are wrong because copying to RAM is a merge process, not an overwrite process.

8. ☑ Use the **`erase startup-config`** command to erase your configuration file in NVRAM.

Router IOS Image Files

9. ☑ **C.** NVRAM stores configuration files, not IOS images.
   ☒ **A, B,** and **D** are incorrect because IOS images can be loaded from ROM (the Mini-IOS, flash (the default), or a TFTP server.

10. ☑ **A**, **C**, and **D**. When you use the **copy flash tftp** command, you are prompted for the TFTP server's IP address, the source filename of the IOS in flash, and the name you want to call the IOS image on the TFTP server.
☒ **B** is incorrect because you are not prompted for a verification before the command is executed.

IOS Troubleshooting

11. ☑ **D**. The **traceroute** command tests layer-3.
☒ **A** is incorrect because it tests layer-7. **B** and **C** are incorrect because they test layer-2.

12. ☑ **B**. You need to be at *Privilege EXEC* mode to use extended **ping** and **traceroute**.
☒ **C** is incorrect because you can only make configuration changes here. **A** and **D** are incorrect because they include *User EXEC* mode.

13. ☑ **B**. Use CTRL-SHIFT-6 X to suspend a telnet session.
☒ **D** is incorrect because this break sequence is used to break out of the *System Configuration Dialog*. **A** and **C** are incorrect because these are nonexistent break sequences.

14. ☑ **C**. Use the **resume** command to reconnect to a suspended telnet session. You can also hit the ENTER key on a blank line to return to the last suspended telnet session.
☒ **B** is incorrect because this performs a telnet. **A** and **D** are incorrect because these are nonexistent commands.

15. ☑ Use **no debug all** or **undebug all** from *Privilege EXEC* mode to disable all debug processing.

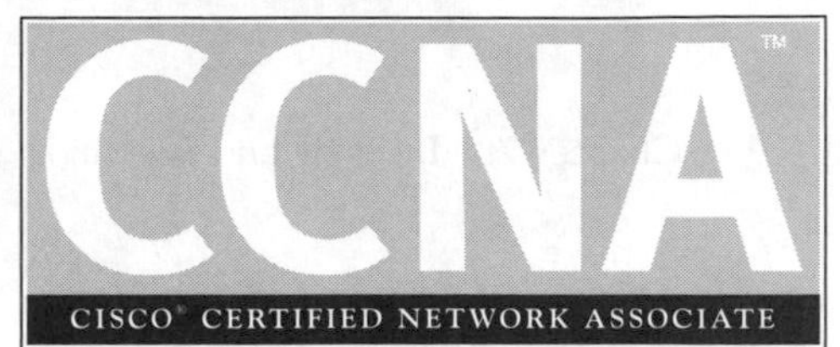

7

Bridging and Switching

CERTIFICATION OBJECTIVES

- 7.01 Bridges and Switches
- 7.02 Functions of Bridging and Switching
- 7.03 The Spanning Tree Protocol
- 7.04 1900 and 2950 Configuration
- ✓ Two-Minute Drill
- Q&A Self Test

Bridges and switches are both layer-2 devices, functioning at the data link layer of the OSI Reference Model. Even though they are both layer-2 devices and have many similarities between them, they also have many differences. With advancements in hardware and technology, switches perform faster and have many more features. However, the basic functions of these two devices are the same. This chapter covers the functions of bridges and switches, the Spanning Tree Protocol (STP), and basic switch configuration tasks on Cisco's Catalyst 1900 and 2950 switches.

CERTIFICATION OBJECTIVE 7.01

Bridges and Switches

The main function of bridges and switches is to solve bandwidth, or collision, problems. Remember that in Ethernet, multiple devices can share the same segment, so there is a chance that more than one device might try to transmit at the same time, creating a collision and a retransmission. The more devices you have in a shared medium, the more likely collisions will occur. This doesn't mean that Ethernet is a bad data link layer topology; it's just the way it functions.

In the old days of networking you used hubs to connect devices together, or used 10Base5 or 10Base2 cabling (where you would have many devices on one wire). If you experienced constant or excessive amounts of collisions, you could use bridges (and later on, switches) to break up the user devices to multiple segments, where each segment would have fewer users, and thus fewer collisions. You could also use a router to perform this function; however, the disadvantage of a router is that it costs a lot more than a bridge or switch. This section provides a brief overview of bridges and switches.

Bridging vs. Switching

Even though bridges and switches both operate at layer-2, there are many differences between them, as Table 7-1 shows.

Perhaps the biggest difference between the bridges and switches is performance. Bridges switch in software, providing a frame rate of about 50,000 frames per second (fps). Switches, on the other hand, perform their switching in hardware, using ASICs (application-specific integrated circuits). ASICs are specialized processors, and in the switching world, they are built to do one thing: switch frames very fast. As an example,

TABLE 7-1 Bridge and Switch Comparison

Functions	Bridges	Switches
Form of switching	Software	Hardware (in ASICs)
Method of switching	Store and forward	Store and forward, cut-through, fragment-free
Ports	2–16	Possibly hundreds
Duplexing	Half	Half and full
Collision/bandwidth domains	1 per port	1 per port
Broadcast domains	1	1 per VLAN
STP instances	1	1 per VLAN

the 1900 switch has a frame rate of 500,000 fps and can handle all ports at their maximum speed. Please note that the 1900 is a low-end switch. On Cisco's higher-end switches, the frame rate is in the millions of frames per second.

Methods of Switching

Another difference between bridges and switches is how they switch frames. The switching method affects how a layer-2 device receives, processes, and forwards a frame. Bridges support only one switching method, store-and-forward, while switches might support one, two, or three different switching methods. The three switching methods supported by layer-2 devices include the following:

- Store-and-forward
- Cut-through
- Fragment-free

The following sections cover these three switching methods.

Store-and-Forward

Store-and-forward switching is the most basic form of switching. With store-and-forward switching, the layer-2 device must pull the entire frame into the buffer of the port and check the CRC (checksum) of the frame before the layer-2 device will perform any additional processing of the frame. When checking the CRC, the layer-2 device will calculate a CRC value just as the source device did, and compare this value to what was included in the frame. If they are the same, then the frame is good and the layer-2 device can start processing the frame, including forwarding the frame out the correct destination port. If they are different, the layer-2 device will drop the frame.

Bridges support only a store-and-forward switching method. All switches support store-and-forward. However, some switches, like the 1900 series, may support an additional switching method(s), but this is dependent on the actual switch model.

Cut-Through

Some switches, like the 1900, support cut-through switching. With *cut-through* switching, the switch reads only the very first part of the frame before making a switching decision. Once the switch device reads the destination MAC address (eight-byte preamble and six-byte MAC address), it begins forwarding the frame (even though the frame may still be coming into the interface). One advantage of cut-through switching over store-and-forward is that it is much faster. Its biggest problem, though, is that the switch may be switching bad frames.

Most vendors solve this problem by supporting a dynamic switching method. When performing cut-through switching, the switch will still examine the CRC of the frame as it is being switched, looking for bad frames. Even though the frame may be bad, it is still switched. However, the switch keeps a count of these bad frames. If over a certain period of time the switch reaches a certain threshold of switching bad frames, the switch will dynamically switch its method from cut-through to store-and-forward. This function, though, is entirely dependent on whether or not the vendor included this function in its switching model. The 1900 supports this function.

Fragment-Free

The default switching method of the 1900 is fragment-free switching. *Fragment-free* switching is a modified form of cut-through switching. Whereas cut-through switching reads up to the destination MAC address field in the frame before making a switching decision, fragment-free switching makes sure that the frame is at least 64 bytes before switching it (64 bytes is the minimum legal size of an Ethernet frame). The goal of fragment-free switching is to reduce the number of Ethernet runt frames (frames smaller than 64 bytes) that are being switched. Sometimes fragment-free switching is also called *modified cut-through* or *runtless* switching.

Even with fragment-free switching, a switch could still be switching corrupt frames (frames with a bad CRC), since the switch is checking only the first 64 bytes, and the CRC is at the end of the frame. To overcome this problem, many vendors implement dynamic switching methods, as discussed in the last section. At least with fragment-free switching, most collisions typically create runts, and this switching method would prevent the forwarding of these frames, unlike cut-through switching.

Even though the 2950 doesn't support cut-through and fragment-free switching, like the 1900, it still switches frames faster. This is because the 2950 has much faster ASICs than the 1900 switch. Therefore, you shouldn't judge a switch by its switching method, but by a combination of factors, such as price, performance, and features.

exam watch

Store-and-forward switching pulls in the whole frame, checks the CRC, and then switches the frame. Bridges support only this mode, as does the 2950 switch. Cut-through switching switches a frame as soon as it sees the destination MAC address in the frame (first 14 bytes). Fragment-free switching will switch a frame after the switch sees at least 64 bytes, which prevents the switching of runt frames. This is the default switching method for the 1900 series.

Switch Connections

Duplexing affects how a device can send and receive frames. There are two modes to duplexing: half and full. With half-duplex, the device can either send or receive—it cannot do both simultaneously. Half-duplex connections are used in shared-medium, like 10Base2, 10Base5, and Ethernet hubs. In this environment, one device sends while all other devices in the collision domain listen for and receive the frame. In a shared environment like this, you can typically get 40–60 percent utilization out of your Ethernet segment. Please note, however, that every situation is different and these numbers are under normal, or average, conditions.

If your utilization in a half-duplex environment starts eclipsing the 40–60 percent utilization range, or your collisions exceed 2 percent of total traffic, you should consider either using full-duplex, increasing the speed of the link (like using Fast or Gigabit Ethernet), or breaking up the collision domain with switches.

Full-duplex, unlike half-duplex, allows a device to send and receive frames simultaneously. However, this will work only if there are two devices on the connection, like a PC connected to a switch, or a switch connected to a router. This is called a point-to-point connection. You cannot use a hub in a full-duplex connection. In order to set up a full-duplex connection, both devices need to support full-duplexing. Table 7-2 compares half- and full-duplex connections.

TABLE 7-2 Half-Duplex and Full-Duplex Comparison

	Half-Duplex	Full-Duplex
Send and/or receive	Send or receive	Send and receive
Connection type	Hub, 10Base2, 10Base5	Point-to-point
Collisions	Yes	No

As Table 7-2 points out, one main advantage that full-duplex connections have over half-duplex ones is that full-duplex connections do not experience collisions. Basically, the transmit circuit on one side is wired to the receive circuit on the other side, and vice versa. In this situation, the NIC (network interface card), or Ethernet card, disables the collision detection mechanism, since it isn't needed. Full-duplex connections are supported with the following media types: 10BaseT, 100BaseTX, 100BaseFX, and Gigabit Ethernet. Connections using 10Base5, 10BaseFL, and 10Base2 support only half-duplexing. Please note that some older 10BaseT NICs may not support full-duplex. An example of this is the 10BaseT interfaces on Cisco 2500 series routers.

When dealing with bridges and switches, bridges support only half-duplex connections, while most switches support both. For instance, the 1900 and 2950 switches support both connection types. Most switches will autosense the duplexing and appropriately configure it.

CERTIFICATION OBJECTIVE 7.02

Functions of Bridging and Switching

With all of these differences between bridges and switches, they are still, at heart, both layer-2 devices and perform the same three basic network functions:

- **Learning** They learn what device is connected to which port.
- **Forwarding** They intelligently switch frames to the port or ports where the destination is located.
- **Removing layer-2 loops** They remove loops with the Spanning Tree Protocol (STP), so that frames don't continually circle around the network.

These functions are functions of *transparent* bridges. There are other types of bridging, including source route bridging, source route transparent bridging, and source route translational bridging, that appear in mixed media networks, such as Ethernet, Token Ring, and FDDI. However, since the CCNA exam focuses on transparent bridging, and Token Ring and FDDI are, for the most part, dead technologies, this book focuses on transparent bridging.

The term *transparent* appropriately describes a transparently bridged network: the devices connected to the network are unaware that the bridge, or switch, is a part of the network and is forwarding frames to destinations. Basically, transparent-bridge networks physically look like a bunch of stars connected together. However, transparent bridges give the appearance to connected devices that every device in the broadcast domain is on the same logical segment, as shown in Figure 7-1.

The three main functions of a bridge/switch are learn, forward, and remove loops.

The following sections cover the three main functions of transparent bridges and switches in more depth. As you go through these sections, I'll be using the term switch to describe the layer-2 device; however, the terms *bridge* and *switch* are interchangeable when it comes to the three main functions.

Learning Function

One of the three main functions of a transparent switch is to learn which device is connected to each of the active ports of the switch. As a frame comes into the port of a switch, the switch examines the source MAC address of the frame and compares it to its switch table, commonly referred to as a CAM (content addressable memory) table or *port address* table. In the old days of bridging, CAM was a special form of high-speed

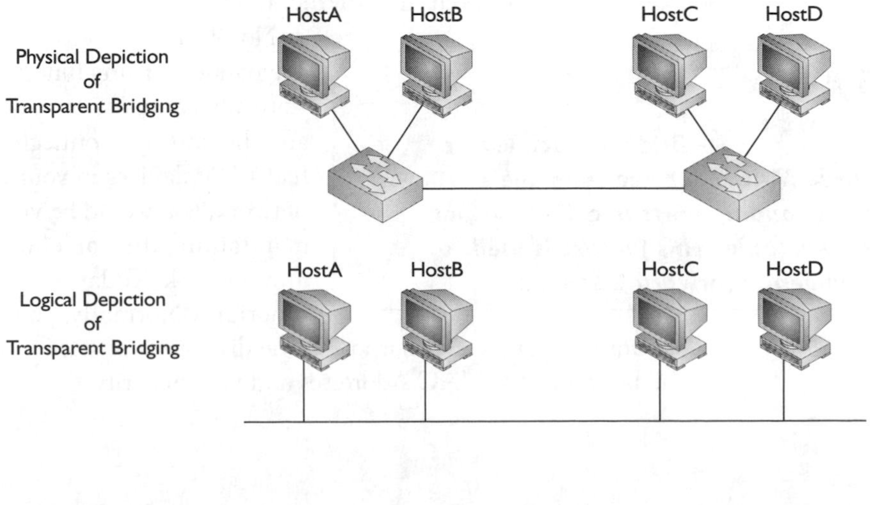

FIGURE 7-1 Physical and logical descriptions of a transparently bridged network

memory to facilitate the switching function in a bridge when it had to forward a frame out the correct destination port. Today, switches use RAM to store the MAC addresses, but the term CAM is still commonly used.

When the switch receives a frame on a port, and as it examines the source MAC address in the frame and doesn't see a corresponding entry in the CAM table, the switch will add the address to the table, including the source port number. If the address is already in the CAM table, the switch compares the incoming port with the port already in the table. If they are different, the switch updates the CAM table with the new port information. This is important because you might have moved the device from one port to another port, and you want the switch to learn where the new location is and have the switch forward frames to the device correctly (not to the old port).

Anytime the switch updates an entry in the CAM table, the switch also resets the timer for the specific entry. Switches use timers to age out old information in the CAM table, allowing room for new addresses. Each switch has different default timers for the aging process. Aging is important because once a CAM table is full, the switch will not be able to learn any new addresses. A switch will also reset the timer for an entry in the CAM table if it sees traffic from a source MAC address that is in the CAM table. In this manner, devices that are constantly sending information will always remain in the CAM table and devices that are not sending traffic will eventually be aged out of the table (removed from the table).

The CAM table can be built statically or dynamically. By default, when you turn on a switch, the CAM table is empty unless you have configured a static entry in it. As traffic flows through the switch, the switch will begin building its CAM table. This dynamic building process is a very nice feature. In the old days of bridging, there used to be two kinds of bridges: learning and non-learning. Learning bridges function as I have just described—they dynamically learn addressing locations by examining the source MAC addresses in the Ethernet frames.

exam watch

Bridges place learned source MAC addresses and their corresponding ports in a CAM or port address table. This feature is used to intelligently forward frames.

Non-learning bridges, by contrast, do not have a dynamic learning function. Instead, you must statically configure each device's MAC address and the port it is connected to. Of course, if you had 1,000 devices in your non-learning bridged network, you would be very busy building and maintaining this table, which would be an arduous task. Today, switches support both functions. Normally, you would use static configurations for security purposes. The discussion of static configurations is done in the later section "MAC Addresses and Port Security."

Forwarding Function

The second major function of a switch is to forward traffic intelligently. Whenever a frame comes into a port on the switch, the switch not only examines the source MAC address so that it can perform its learning function, it also examines the destination MAC address to perform its forwarding function. It examines the destination MAC address and compares this address to the addresses in its CAM table to determine which interface it should use when forwarding the frame to the destination.

If the destination address is found in the CAM table, the forwarding process is easy: the switch forwards the frame out the port for the corresponding CAM entry. If the switch examines the destination address and finds that the destination is associated with the same port as the source of the frame, the switch will drop the frame. In this situation, you might have a hub connected to this port of the switch, and both the source and destination are connected to this hub. Given this, the switch shouldn't forward any frames between these two machines to other switch segments, since this would be wasting bandwidth in your network. As you can see, the switch is *intelligently* forwarding traffic.

Frame Types

There are three different destination types: *unicast*, *broadcast*, and *multicast*. Depending on the type of destination address, there are certain situations where the switch will have to flood the frame out all of its ports (with the exception of the port the frame was received on). Here are the three frame types that are always flooded:

- **Broadcast address** Destination MAC address of FFFF.FFFF.FFFF
- **Multicast address** Destination MAC addresses between 0100.5E00.0000 and 0100.5E7F.FFFF
- **Unknown unicast destination MAC addresses** The MAC address is not found in the CAM table

With a unicast, the source device sends a separate copy of each frame to each destination. So, as an example, if a device needs to send the same information to 50 different destinations, the device would have to create 50 frames, with 50 different destination MAC addresses. When a switch receives a frame with a unicast address as the destination, the switch looks for the address in its CAM table in order to make a switching decision. If the switch doesn't have the address in its CAM table, the switch will flood the frame out all of its other ports.

It's important to remember that you are working with a *transparent* switch when dealing with the forwarding process. Therefore, if the switch doesn't know where the destination is, and obviously the source is assuming that the device is on same the "logical" segment, the switch will have to flood the frame to ensure that the destination, if it is somewhere in the broadcast domain, will receive the source's frame. This process, hopefully, won't happen every time. When the destination receives the frame, the destination will probably send a response frame to the source. Through the switch's learning process, it now knows where the destination is located, and any further frames sent from the source to the destination can be intelligently forwarded instead of flooded.

One issue with this process, however, is that if your CAM table is filled to capacity and your switch can't add new entries to the table, the switch will *always* flood traffic to these destinations that it couldn't fit into the CAM table. Therefore, it is very important that when you buy a switch, you buy one that will be able to handle the number of devices that you'll have in your switched network. You'll be creating problems if you have 2,000 devices in your switched network but your CAM table on each switch can hold only 1,000 entries. In this situation, the switches will be flooding traffic for half of the destinations, creating serious bandwidth and performance problems in your network.

A *broadcast* is a frame that is sent to all devices in a broadcast domain. As an example, if a source device needed to send the same information to 50 destinations, the source would create only one frame, and every destination would process this frame using the destination MAC address of FFFF.FFFF.FFFF. Remember to think of the switched network as a logical bus, where it appears that everyone is on the same piece of wire. Therefore, when a switch receives a broadcast, it needs to ensure that all machines will receive it, and thus the switch will flood this frame to make sure all devices receive the broadcast.

A *multicast* is a frame sent to a group of devices, where the group consists of devices interested in receiving the multicast stream. This group can contain no devices, all devices, or some devices in the broadcast domain. The problem of using unicast frames to disseminate certain types of information is that it can negatively impact the performance of your network. For instance, imagine that you have a network where ten devices wish to receive a specific multicast stream, like a real-time video presentation. One solution would be to have the multicast server use unicasts and send ten copies of the same information to each destination. Of course, if the multimedia stream is running at 5Mbps, then this would require the server to generate 50Mbps worth of traffic.

Another solution would be to use a broadcast. In this situation, the multicast server generates only one stream of information. The problem with this is that the switched infrastructure would flood this traffic to every destination, including the ten devices that are interested in seeing it. This solution wastes a lot of bandwidth.

watch ***The three types of frames that are always flooded by bridges and switches are multicasts, broadcasts, and unknown destination unicasts.***

The third solution is to use multicast frames. With multicasting, switches can learn which devices want to receive multicast traffic, and therefore forward the multicast frames to only those devices that want to see the multicast traffic. This topic is beyond the scope of this book, but it is covered in Cisco's Switching exam for the CCNP and CCDP certifications.

on the job ***If you have a large multicast solution deployment, you will definitely want to make sure that your switches supported advanced multicast features that allow them to intelligently forward multicast traffic instead of having to flood it. You want to have the switch forward multicast frames to end-stations that are running a multicast application that need to see them—you don't want your switch to flood multicasts to all end-stations.***

Example

To better understand what happens when a switch forwards rather than floods, take a look at an example shown in Figure 7-2. This example shows a hub and a switch, with various PCs connected to these two devices.

Let's assume that the switch was just turned on, which means that its CAM table is empty. PC-A generates a frame destined for PC-C. When the switch receives the frame, it looks in its CAM table and does not see the source MAC address (0000.0A01.AAAA), so it adds it along with port 1. It also examines the destination MAC address (0000.0A01.CCCC) and does not see this address in its CAM table, so the switch floods the frame out all of its remaining ports: 2, 3, and 4.

In this example, the switch did not need to do this because PC-C is connected to the same hub as PC-A; however, the switch doesn't know this yet. This is an example of flooding an unknown destination unicast address. Figure 7-3 shows an example of the switch adding the entry to its CAM table and flooding the frame. You can see from this figure that the switch now has one entry in its CAM table (PC-A's) as well as the flooding process performed. Since the destination, PC-C, is connected to the same hub as PC-A, it obviously receives the frame.

PC-C now responds back to PC-A with a unicast frame: the source MAC address is 0000.0A01.CCCC and the destination MAC address is 0000.0A01.AAAA. The switch performs its learning process, and since PC-C's MAC address is not in its CAM table, it adds it, as shown in Figure 7-4. Now the switch has two entries in its CAM table: PC-A's and PC-C's. To perform the forwarding process, the switch examines the destination MAC address, 0000.0A01.AAAA. It finds a match in its

FIGURE 7-2 Transparent switch forwarding example

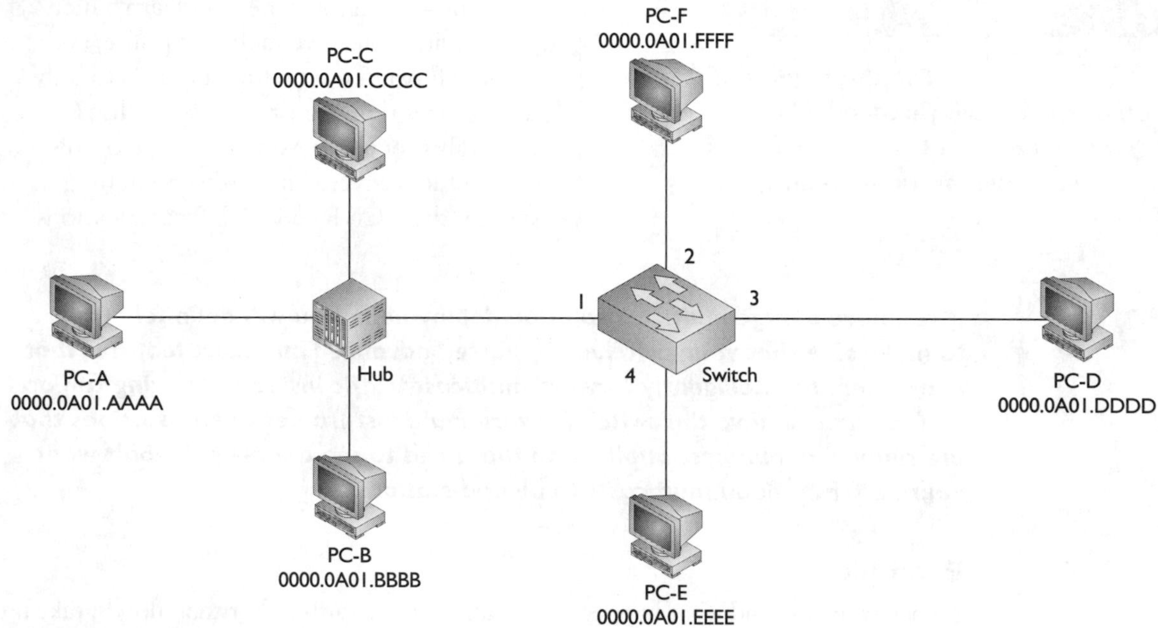

FIGURE 7-3 Adding PC-A's MAC address to the CAM table

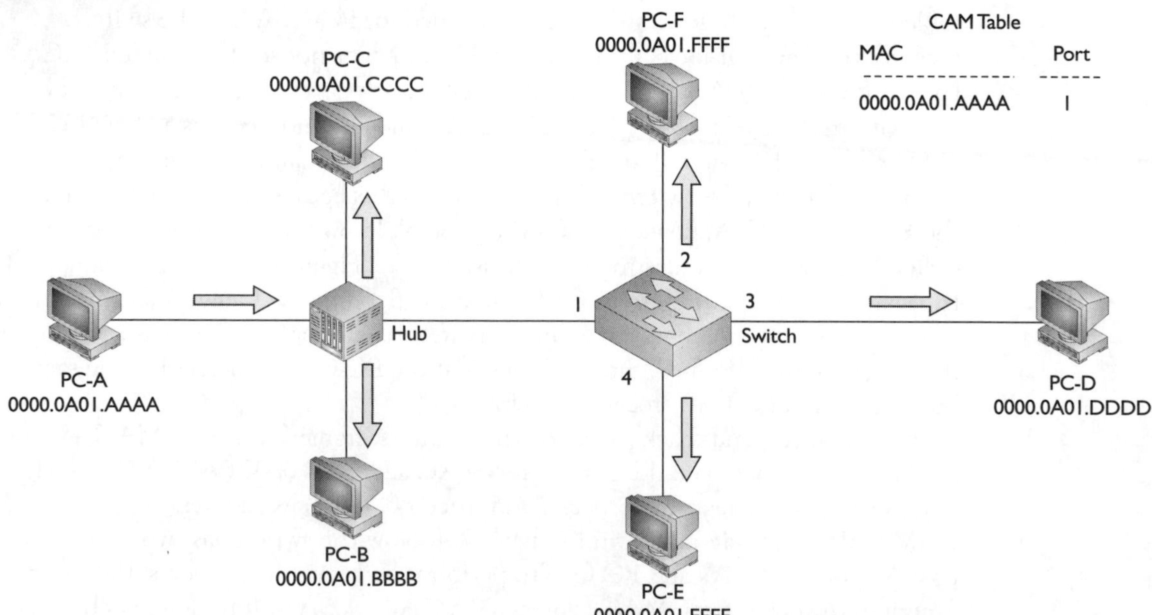

FIGURE 7-4 Adding PC-C's MAC address to the CAM table

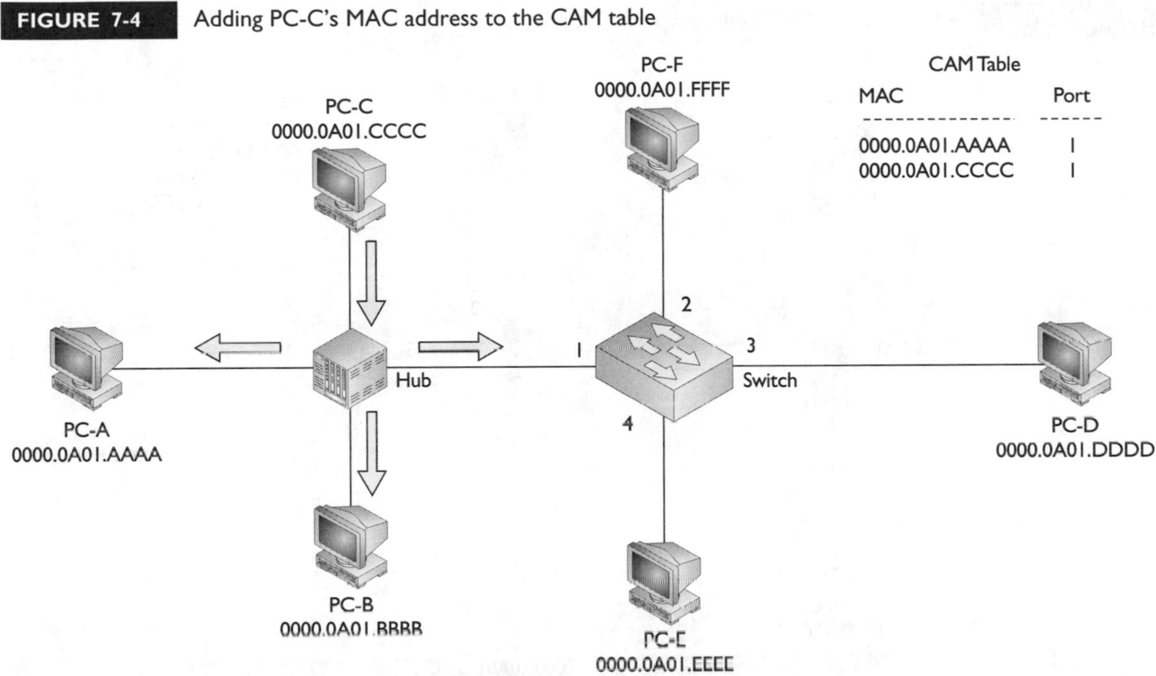

CAM table and discovers that the destination MAC address is associated with the same port as the source MAC address. Therefore, the switch drops the frame: It does not forward it out of any of its ports, as can be seen in Figure 7-4.

PC-B now sends a unicast frame to PC-F: These PCs are connected to different ports of the switch. When the switch receives the frame from PC-B, it again performs its learning process. Since PC-B is not in its CAM table, the Switch adds 0000.0A01.BBBB along with port 1 to its table. Now the switch performs its forwarding function: Since the destination MAC address 0000.0A01.FFFF is not in the CAM table, the switch floods the frame. This process can be seen in Figure 7-5.

The switch now has three MAC addresses in its CAM table. PC-F receives the frame and responds with an answer to PC-B. The switch again performs its learning function: since 0000.0A01.FFFF is not in its CAM table, it adds it. Now the switch performs its forwarding function. It sees 0000.0A01.BBBB in its CAM table with the port number of 1 and therefore forwards the frame out of port 1 *only*. This process can be seen in Figure 7-6.

In this last example, PC-E generates a broadcast (FFFF.FFFF.FFFF). When the switch receives the broadcast frame, it performs its learning function by adding 0000.0A01.EEEE to its CAM table. The switch then floods the frame, since it is a broadcast. This process can be seen in Figure 7-7.

FIGURE 7-5 Adding PC-B's MAC address to the CAM table

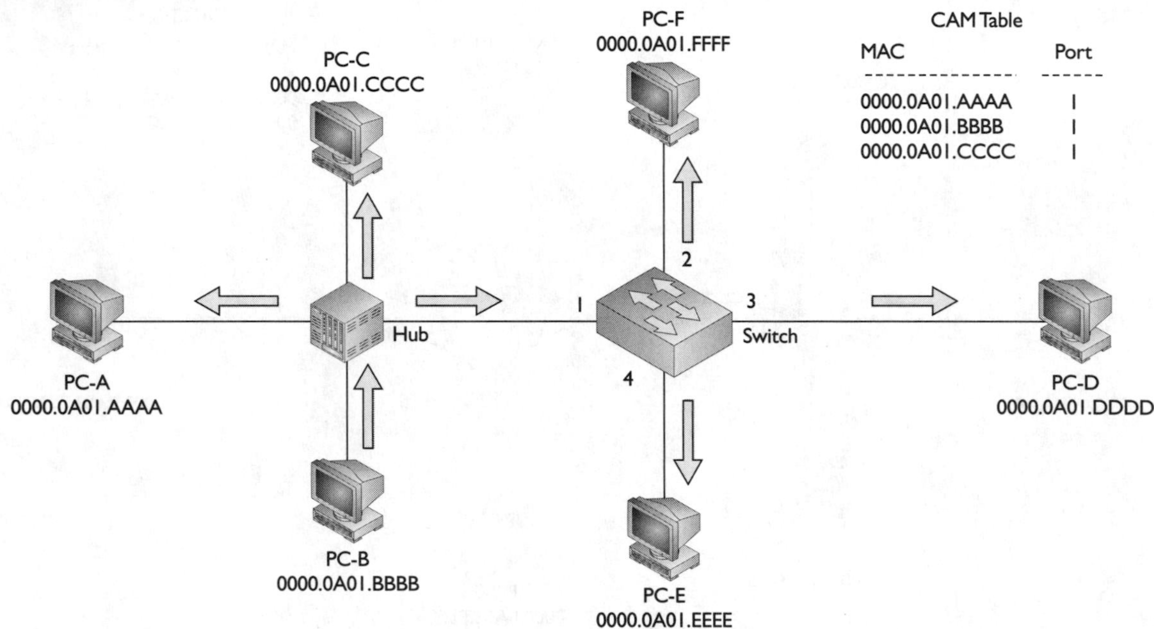

FIGURE 7-6 Forwarding PC-F's traffic out of Port 1 only

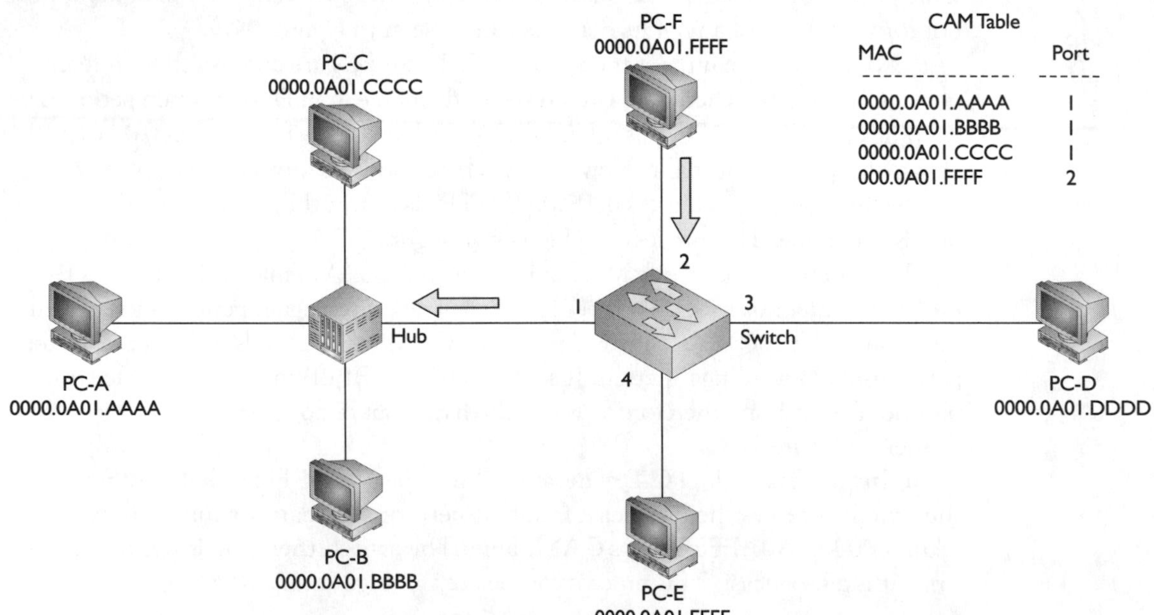

FIGURE 7-7 PC-E generates a broadcast

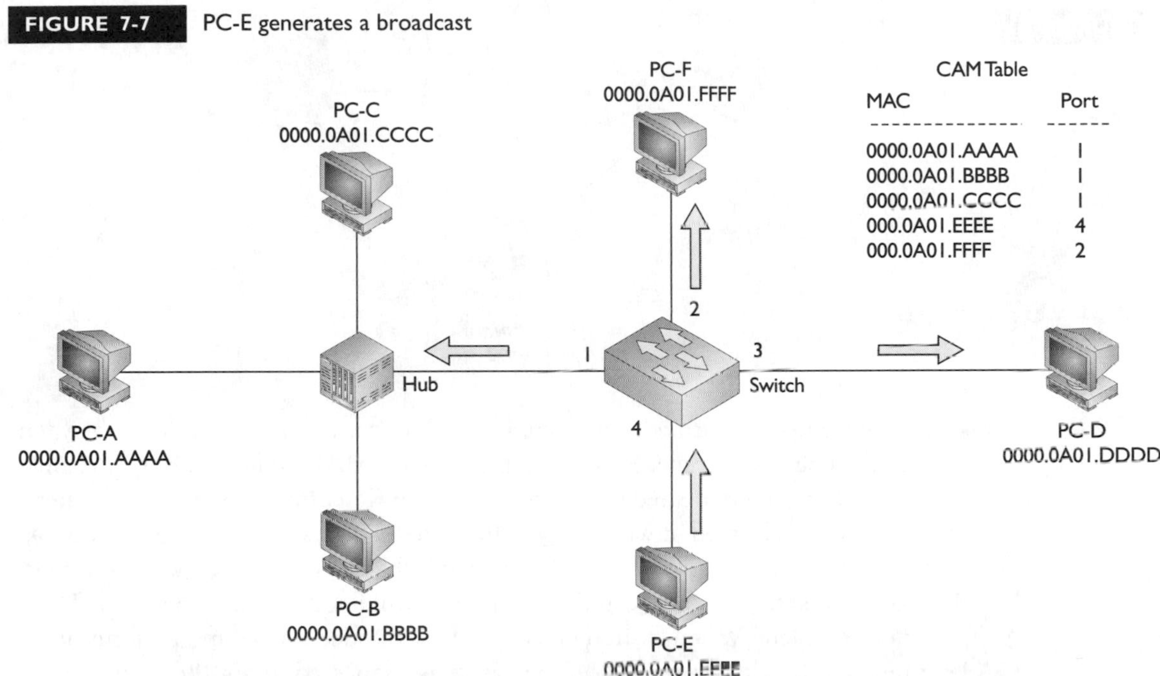

From this simple example, you can see the role of the switch is not a complicated one. First, the switch examines the source MAC address in the frame and updates the CAM table if necessary. Second, the switch examines the destination MAC address in the frame and makes a forwarding decision. As you will see in the next section, the switch's function becomes more complicated when there is more than one switch in the network, and there are layer-2 loops between the switches.

Loops

At the backbone of your network, or at least where you have critical resources, you'll probably incorporate some type of redundancy in your design. This might include redundancy with your switches at layer-2, creating layer-2 loops in your network as is shown in Figure 7-8. The problem with loops in your network is that when the switch floods certain types of traffic, such as broadcasts or multicasts, you don't want this traffic going around and around the loop forever, creating high utilization problems.

Plus, for unknown destinations, as the frame is going around the loop, the switches update their CAM tables with the source address, which eventually shows up as connected to another connected switch, creating confusion about where the

FIGURE 7-8

Looped layer-2 topology

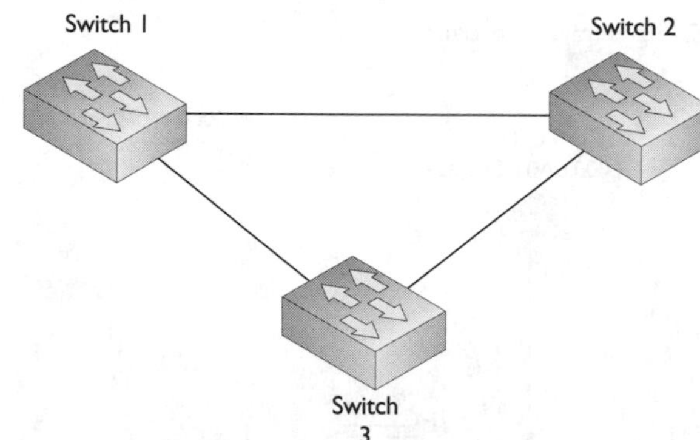

source device really is located. For example, if a device is connected to Switch3, when the device generates a frame, Switch3 adds the source MAC address to its CAM table and notes that it is connected to the incoming port. If Switch3 doesn't know where the destination is located, it will flood the frame to Switches1 and 2 on its two uplink ports. If both Switches1 and 2 don't know where the destination is, they also flood the frame across the link between them, and then will flood it back to Switch3. This presents a problem: When Switch3 receives these flooded frames and performs its learning function, it now looks as if the device is connected to not the original port, but one of the two uplink ports to Switch1 or 2.

The Spanning Tree Protocol (STP) is used to prevent these problems from occurring. STP removes loops in your network but still allows for redundancy. Actually, the loop removal process is done in software—you don't have to physically disconnect wires between your switches to remove the loops. The following section covers the basics of STP.

CERTIFICATION OBJECTIVE 7.03

The Spanning Tree Protocol

The main function of the Spanning Tree Protocol (STP) is to remove layer-2 loops from your topology. DEC, now a part of Compaq/HP, originally developed STP. IEEE enhanced the initial implementation of STP, giving us the 802.1d standard. The two different implementations of STP, DEC and 802.1d, are not compatible with each other—you need to make sure that all of your devices either support one or the other. All of Cisco's switches use IEEE's 802.1d protocol, which is enabled, by default, on the switches. If you have a mixed-vendor environment where some devices are running 802.1d and others are running DEC's STP, then you may run into layer-2 looping problems.

Bridge Protocol Data Units

For STP to function, the switches need to share information. What they share are *bridge protocol data units (BPDUs)*, which are sent out as multicast information that only other layer-2 devices are listening to. Switches will use BPDUs to learn the topology of the network: what device is connected to other devices, and if there are any layer-2 loops based on this topology.

If any loops are found, the switches will disable a port or ports in the topology to ensure that there are no loops. In other words, from one device to any other device in the switched network, only one path can be taken. If there are any changes in the layer-2 network, such as when a link goes down, a new link is added, a new switch is added, or a switch fails, the switches will share this information, causing the STP algorithm to be re-executed and a new loop-free topology to be created.

BPDUs are sent out every two seconds. This helps speed up convergence. *Convergence* is a term used in networking to describe the amount of time it takes to deal with changes and have the network back up and running. The shorter the time period to find and fix problems, the quicker your network is back on line. Setting the BPDU advertisement time to two seconds allows changes to be very quickly shared with all the other switches in the network, reducing the amount of time any disruption would create.

BPDUs contain a lot of information to help the switches determine the topology and any loops that result from that topology. For instance, each bridge has a unique identifier, called a *bridge* or *switch ID*. This is typically the priority of the switch and the MAC address of the switch itself. When switches advertise a BPDU, they place their switch ID in the BPDU so that a receiving switch can tell which switches it is receiving topology information from. The following sections cover the steps that occur while STP is being executed in a layer-2 network.

exam watch

Most bridges and switches use IEEE's 802.1d protocol to remove loops. BPDUs are used to share information, and these are sent out as multicasts every two seconds. The BPDU contains the bridge's or switch's ID, made up of a priority value and a MAC address.

Root Bridge

The term Spanning Tree Protocol describes the process that is used. The STP algorithm is similar to how link state routing protocols, such as OSPF, ensure that no layer-3 loops are created. (Link state routing protocols are discussed in Chapters 9 and 11.) A spanning tree is first created. Basically, a spanning tree is an inverted tree. At the top of the tree is the root, or what is referred to in STP as the *root bridge* or *switch*. From the root switch, there are branches (physical Ethernet connections) connecting to other switches, and branches from these switches to other switches, and so on.

Take a look at a physical topology of a network to demonstrate a spanning tree, shown in Figure 7-9. When STP is run, a logical tree structure is built, like that shown in Figure 7-10. As you can see from Figure 7-10, SwitchA is the root switch and is at the top of the tree. Underneath it are two branches connecting to SwitchB and SwitchC. These two switches are connected to SwitchE, creating a loop. SwitchB is also connected to SwitchD. At this point, STP is still running, and a loop still exists. As STP runs, the switches will determine, out of the four switches, SwitchA, SwitchB, SwitchC, and SwitchE, which port on these switches will be disabled in the software in order to remove the loop.

Actually, the very first step in STP is to elect the root switch. BPDUs are used for the election process. As was mentioned earlier, when a device advertises a BPDU, it puts its switch ID in the BPDU. The switch ID is used to elect the root switch. The

FIGURE 7-9

Physical layer-2 looped topology

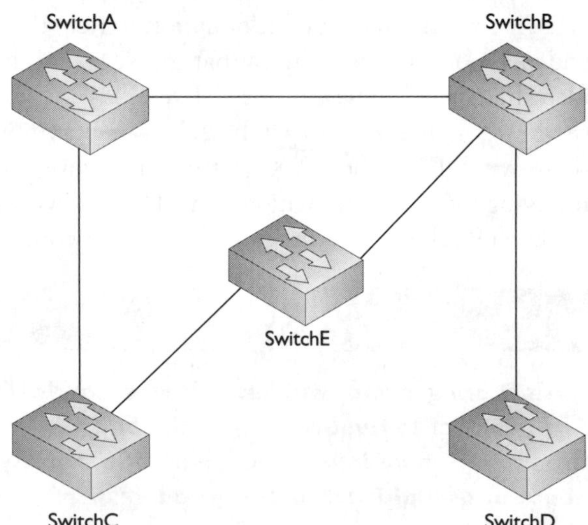

FIGURE 7-10 Logical layer-2 STP topology

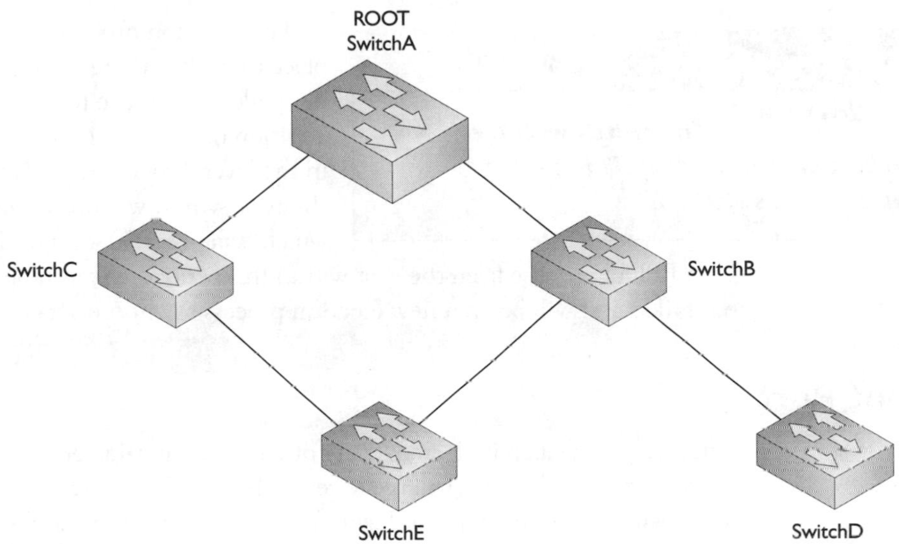

switch with the lowest switch ID is chosen as root. The switch ID is made up of two components:

- The switch's priority, which defaults to 32,768 on Cisco switches (two bytes in length)
- The switch's MAC address (six bytes in length)

With Cisco's switches, the default priority is 32,768, which is defined by IEEE 802.1d. Assuming that all your switches are Cisco switches, the switch with the *lowest* MAC address will be chosen as the root switch. You can override the election process by changing the priority value assigned to a switch. If you want one switch to be the root, assign it a priority value that is lower than 32,768. Through the sharing of the BPDUs, the switches will figure out which switch has the lowest switch ID, and that switch is chosen as the root switch. Please note that this election process is taking place almost simultaneously on each switch, where each switch will come up with the same result.

For Catalyst switches that implement VLANs (which are discussed in Chapter 8), the switches will have a different switch ID per VLAN, and a separate instance of STP per VLAN. Each VLAN has its own root switch (which can be the same switch for all VLANs, or different switches for each VLAN). And within each VLAN, STP will run and remove loops in that particular VLAN. Cisco calls this concept per-VLAN STP (PVST). This topic is beyond the scope of this chapter but is covered in Cisco's Switching exam for the CCNP and CCDP certifications.

The switch with the lowest switch (bridge) ID is chosen as the root switch.

This election process of the root switch takes place each time there is a topology change in the network, such as the root switch failing, or the addition of a new switch. All the other switches in the layer-2 topology expect to see BPDUs from the root switch within the *maximum age time*, which defaults to 20 seconds. If the switches don't see a BPDU message from the root within this period, they assume that the root switch has failed and will begin a new election process to choose a new root switch.

Root Port

After the root switch is elected, every other switch in the network needs to choose a single port on itself that it will use to reach the root. This port is called the *root port*. For some switches, like SwitchD in Figure 7-10, this is very easy—it has only one port it can use to access the switched topology. However, other switches, like SwitchB, SwitchC, and SwitchE in Figure 7-10, might have two or more ports that they can use to reach the root switch. If there are multiple ports to choose from, an intelligent method needs to be used to choose the best port. With STP, there are a few factors that are taken into consideration when choosing a root port. It is important to point out that the root switch itself will never have a root port—it's the root, so it doesn't need a port to reach itself.

First, each port is assigned a cost, called a *port cost*. The lower the cost, the more preferable the port is. The cost is an inverse reflection of the bandwidth of the port. There are actually two sets of costs for 802.1d's implementation of STP—one for the old method of calculation and one for the new, as is shown in Table 7-3. Cisco's 1900 switch uses the old 802.1d port cost values, while Cisco's other switches, including the 2950, 3500, 3550, 4000, 5500, 6000, and 6500 switches, use the newer cost values. Switches always prefer lower-cost ports over higher-cost ones. Each port also has a priority assigned to it, called a *port priority* value, which defaults to 32. Again, switches will prefer a lower priority value over a higher one.

TABLE 7-3 Port Costs for STP

Connection Type	New Cost Value	Old Cost Value
10Gb	2	1
1Gb	4	1
100Mb	19	10
10Mb	100	100

One of the main reasons for replacing the old cost method with a newer one is the inherent weakness in the algorithm used to calculate the port cost: 1,000 divided by the port speed. The assumption was that no port would have a speed greater than 1Gbps (1,000Mbps). As you can see from today's Ethernet standards, 10Gbps is slowly making its way into corporate networks. With the old port cost method, 1Gbps and 10Gbps links are treated as having the same speed.

Path costs are calculated from the root switch. A path cost is basically the accumulated port costs from a switch to the root switch. When the root advertises BPDUs out of its interfaces, the default path cost value in the BPDU is 0. When a connected switch receives this BPDU, it increments the path cost by the cost of the incoming port. If the port was a Fast Ethernet port, then the path cost would be: 0 (the root's path cost) + 19 (the switch's port cost) = 19. This switch, when it advertises BPDUs to switches behind it, will include the updated path cost. As the BPDUs propagate further and further from the root switch, the path costs become higher and higher.

Remember that path costs are incremented as a BPDU comes into a port, not when a BPDU is advertised out of a port.

If a switch has two or more choices of paths to reach the root, it needs to choose one path and thus have one root port. Here are the STP steps a switch will go through when choosing a root port:

1. Choose the path with the *lowest* accumulated path cost to the root if there is a choice between two or more paths to reach the root.
2. Choose the neighboring switch (that your switch would go through to reach the root) with the *lowest* switch ID value.
3. If you have multiple paths, and they all go through the same neighboring switch, choose the port with the lowest priority value.
4. If the priority values are the same between the ports, choose the physically lowest-numbered port on the switch (on a 1900, that would be Ethernet 0/1).

After going through this selection process, the switch will have one, and only one, port that will be its root port.

Designated Port

The last section discussed how each switch has a single root port that it uses to reach the root switch. Besides each switch having a root port, each segment also has a single port that is uses to reach the root. This port is called a *designated port*. For instance, imagine that there is a segment with two switches connected to it. Either one or the other switch will forward traffic from this segment (a LAN connection) to the rest of the network.

The third step in running STP is to elect a designated port on a single switch for each segment in the network. The switch (and its port) that is chosen should have the best path to the root switch. Here are the steps that are taken by switches in determining which port on which switch will be chosen as the designated port.

1. The connected switch on the segment with the lowest accumulated path cost to the root bridge will be used.
2. If there is a tie in accumulated path costs between two switches, then the switch with the lowest switch ID will be chosen.
3. If it happens that it is the same switch, but with two separate connections to the LAN segment, the switch port with the lowest priority is chosen.
4. If there is still a tie (the priorities of the ports on this switch are the same), then the physically lowest-numbered port on the switch is chosen.

After going through these steps for each segment, each segment will have a single designated port that it will use to reach the root switch. Sometimes the switch that contains the designated port is called a *designated switch*. This term is misleading, since it is a port on the switch that is responsible for forwarding traffic. There may be two segments a switch is connected to, but it may be the designated switch for only one of those segments; another switch may provide the designated port for the second segment.

Interestingly enough, *every* active port on the root switch is a designated port. This makes sense because the cost of the attached network segments to reach the root is 0, the lowest accumulated cost value. In other words, each of these LAN segments is directly attached to the root switch, so in reality, it costs nothing for the segment to reach the root switch itself.

Port States

There are five different states that a port can be in when it is participating in STP:

- Blocked
- Listening
- Learning

- Forwarding
- Disabled

Of the five states, only the first four are used when the algorithm is running. The following sections cover the different port states for STP.

Blocking

Ports will go into a *blocking* state under one of three conditions:

- Election of a root switch (for instance, when you turn on all the switches in a network)
- When a switch receives a BPDU on a port that indicates a better path to the root switch than the port the switch is currently using to reach the root
- If a port is not a root port or a designated port

A port in a blocked state will remain there for 20 seconds by default (the maximum age timer). During this state, the port is only listening to and processing BPDUs on its interfaces. Any other frames that the switch receives on a blocked port are dropped. In a blocking state, the switch is attempting to figure out which port is going to be the root port, which ports on the switch need to be designated ports, and which ports will remain in a blocked state to break up any loops. After the 20 seconds have expired, the port will then move to the listening state.

Listening

After the 20-second timer expires, a root port or a designated port will move to a *listening* state. Any other port will remain in a blocked state. During the listening state, the port is still listening for BPDUs and double-checking the layer-2 topology. Again, the only traffic that is being processed in this state consists of BPDUs; all other traffic is dropped. A port will stay in this state for the length of the *forward delay timer*. The default for this value is 15 seconds.

Learning

From a listening state, a port moves into a learning state. During the learning state, the port is still listening for and processing BPDUs on the port; however, unlike while in the listening state, the port begins to process user frames. When processing user frames, the switch is examining the source addresses in the frames and updating its CAM table, but the switch is still not forwarding these frames out destination ports. Ports stay in this state for the length of the forward delay time (which defaults to 15 seconds).

Forwarding

Finally, after the forward delay timer expires, ports that were in a learning state are placed in a forwarding state. In a forwarding state, the port will process BPDUs, update its CAM table with frames that it receives, *and* forward user traffic through the port.

Disabled

The disabled state is a special port state. A port in a disabled state is not participating in STP. This could be because the port has been manually shut down by an administrator, manually removed from STP, disabled because of security issues, or rendered nonfunctional because of a lack of a physical-layer signal (such as the patch cable being unplugged).

exam watch

There are four major port states in STP: blocking (20 seconds), listening (15 seconds), learning (15 seconds), and forwarding. It can take 30–50 seconds for STP convergence to take place. In blocking and listening states, only BPDUs are processed. In a learning state, the CAM table is being built. In a forwarding state, user frames are moved between ports.

Layer-2 Convergence

As noted in the last section, STP goes through a staged process, which slows down convergence. For switches, convergence occurs once STP has completed: a root switch is elected, root and designated ports have been chosen, the root and designated ports have been placed in a forwarding state, and all other ports have been placed in a blocked state.

If a port has to go through all four states, convergence takes 50 seconds: 20 seconds in blocking, 15 seconds in listening, and 15 seconds in learning. If a port doesn't have to go through the blocking state but starts at a listening state, convergence takes only 30 seconds. This typically occurs when the root port is still valid, but another topology change has occurred. Remember that during this time period (until the port reaches a forwarding state), no user traffic is forwarded through the port. So, if a user was performing a Telnet session, and STP was being recalculated, the Telnet session, from the user's perspective, would appear stalled, or the connection would appear lost. Obviously, a user will notice this type of disruption.

Therefore, the faster that convergence takes place, the less disruption this will cause for your users. You can reduce the two timers to lessen your convergence time, but this can create more problems if you aren't aware of what you are doing when you change them. For user ports, you can use the *PortFast* feature to speed up convergence. PortFast should be used only on ports that will not create layer-2 loops, such as ports connected to PCs, servers, and routers (sometimes referred to as a user, or edge, ports).

A port with PortFast enabled is always placed in a forwarding state—this is even true whenever STP is running and the root and designated ports are going through their different states. So, when STP is running, PortFast ports on the same switch can still forward traffic among themselves, limiting your STP disruption somewhat. However, if these devices wanted to talk to devices connected to other switches, they would have to wait until STP completed and the root and designated ports had moved into a forwarding state.

exam watch ***STP convergence has occurred when all root and designated ports are in a forwarding state and all other ports are in a blocking state.***

Rapid Spanning Tree Protocol

The 802.1d standard was designed back when waiting for 30–50 seconds for convergence wasn't a problem. However, in today's networks, this can cause serious performance problems for networks that use real-time applications, like Voice over IP (VoIP). To overcome these issues, Cisco developed proprietary bridging features called PortFast (discussed in the last section), UplinkFast, and BackboneFast. The problem with these features is that they are proprietary to Cisco.

The Rapid Spanning Tree Protocol (RSTP) is an IEEE standard, 802.1w, that is interoperable with 802.1d and an extension to it. With RSTP, there are only three port states: discarding, learning, and forwarding. A port in a discarding state is basically the grouping of 802.1d's blocking, listening, and disabled states. The following sections cover some of the enhancements included in RSTP.

Additional Port Roles

With RSTP, there are still root and designated ports, performing the same roles as those in 802.1d. However, RSTP adds two additional port types: *alternate* ports and *backup* ports. These two ports are similar to the ports in a blocking state in 802.1d. An alternate port is a port that has an alternative path or paths to the root but is currently in a discarding state. A backup port is a port on a segment that could be used to reach the root switch, but there is already an active designated port for the segment. The best way to look at this is that an alternate port is a secondary, unused root port, and a backup port is a secondary, unused designated port.

Given these new port roles, RSTP calculates the final spanning tree topology the same way as 802.1d. Some of the nomenclature was changed and extended, and this is used to enhance convergence times, as you will see later on in the "Convergence Features" section.

BPDUs

The 802.1w standard has introduced a change with BPDUs. Some additional flags were added to the BPDUs, so that switches could share information about the role of the port the BPDU is exiting. This can help a neighboring switch converge faster when changes occur in the network.

In 802.1d, if a switch didn't see a root BPDU within the maximum age time (20 seconds), STP would run, a new root switch would be elected, and a new loop-free topology would be created. This is a time-consuming process. With 802.1w, if a hello is not received in three expected hello periods (six seconds), STP information can be aged out instantly and the switch considers that its neighbor is lost and actions should be taken. This is different from 802.1d, where the switch had to miss the BPDUs from the root—here, if the switch misses three consecutive hellos from a neighbor, actions are immediately taken.

Convergence Features

The 802.1w standard includes new convergence features that are very similar to Cisco's proprietary UplinkFast and BackboneFast features. The first feature, which is like Cisco's BackboneFast feature, allows a switch to accept *inferior BPDUs*.

Look at Figure 7-11 to understand the inferior BPDU feature. In this example, the root bridge is SwitchA. Both of the ports on SwitchB and SwitchC directly connected to the root are root ports. For the segment between SwitchB and SwitchC, SwitchB provides the designated port and SwitchC provides a backup port (a secondary way of reaching the root for the segment). SwitchB also knows that its designated port is also an alternative port (a secondary way for the switch to reach the root), via SwitchC from SwitchC's BPDUs.

Following the example in Figure 7-11, the link between the root and SwitchB fails. SwitchB can detect this by either missing three hellos from the root port or detecting a physical layer failure. If you were running 802.1d, SwitchB would see an inferior root BPDU (worse cost value) coming via SwitchC, and therefore all ports would have to go through a blocking, listening, and learning state, which would take 50 seconds to converge. With the inferior BPDU feature, assuming that SwitchB knows that SwitchC has an alternative port for their directly connected segment, then SwitchB can notify SwitchC to take its alternative port and change it to a designated port, and SwitchB will change its designated port to a root port. This process takes only a few seconds, if even that.

FIGURE 7-11

Accepting inferior BPDUs

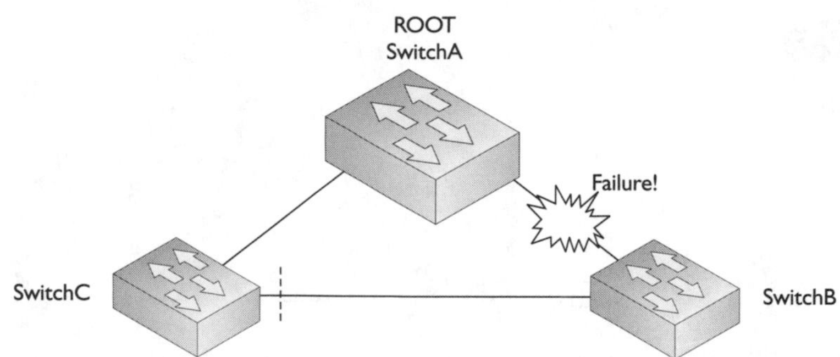

The second convergence feature introduced in 802.1w is rapid transition. Rapid transition includes two new components: edge ports and link types. An edge port is a port connected to a non-layer-2 device, such as a PC, server, or router. RSTP with rapid transition of edge ports to a forwarding state is the same as Cisco's proprietary PortFast. Changes in the state of these ports does not affect RSTP in order to cause a recalculation, and changes in other port types will keep these ports in a forwarding state.

Rapid transition can only take place in RSTP for edge ports and links that are point-to-point. The link type is automatically determined in terms of the duplexing of the connection. Switches make the assumption that if the port is configured for full-duplex between the two switches, the port can rapidly transition to a different state without having to wait for any timers to expire. If they are half-duplex, then this feature won't work by default, but you can manually enable it for point-to-point half-duplex switch links.

For the CCNA exam, you should be aware of the concepts of RSTP. The actual configuration and tuning of it is beyond the scope of this book and is covered in Cisco's Switching exam.

Let's take a look at an example of rapid transition of point-to-point links by using the topology in Figure 7-12. The topology in Figure 7-12 is the same as 7-11. In this example, however, the link between SwitchA (the root) and SwitchC fails. When this happens, SwitchC can no longer reach SwitchA on its root port. However, looking at the BPDUs it has been receiving from SwitchA and SwitchB, SwitchC knows that the root is reachable via SwitchB and that SwitchB provides the designated port (which is in a forwarding state) for the segment between SwitchB and SwitchC. SwitchC, knowing this, changes the state of the backup port to a root port and places it immediately into a forwarding state, notifying SwitchB of the change. This update typically takes less than a second, assuming that the failure of the segment between the root and SwitchC is a physical link failure, instead of three missed consecutive hello BPDUs.

FIGURE 7-12

Rapid transition example

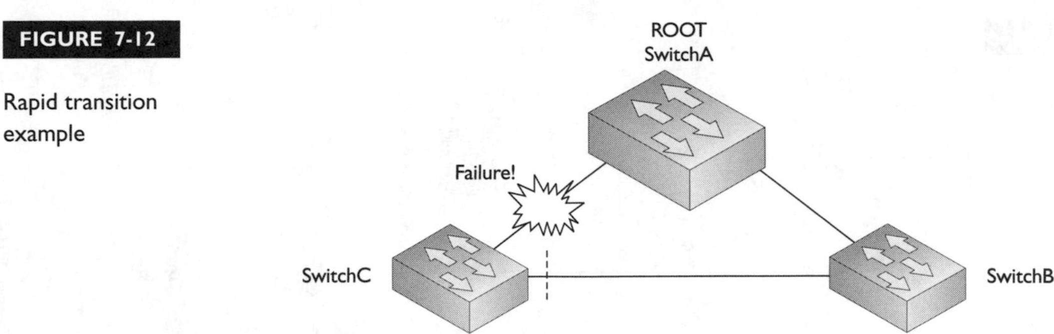

Simple STP Example

To grow more familiar with the workings of 802.1d STP, let's look at an example of STP in action. I'll use the network shown in Figure 7-13 as a starting point and make the assumption that these switches do not support RSTP, but only 802.1d STP. The ports on each switch are labeled with a letter and a number. The letter is the port designator, and the number is the cost of the port as a BPDU enters the port.

FIGURE 7-13 STP example network

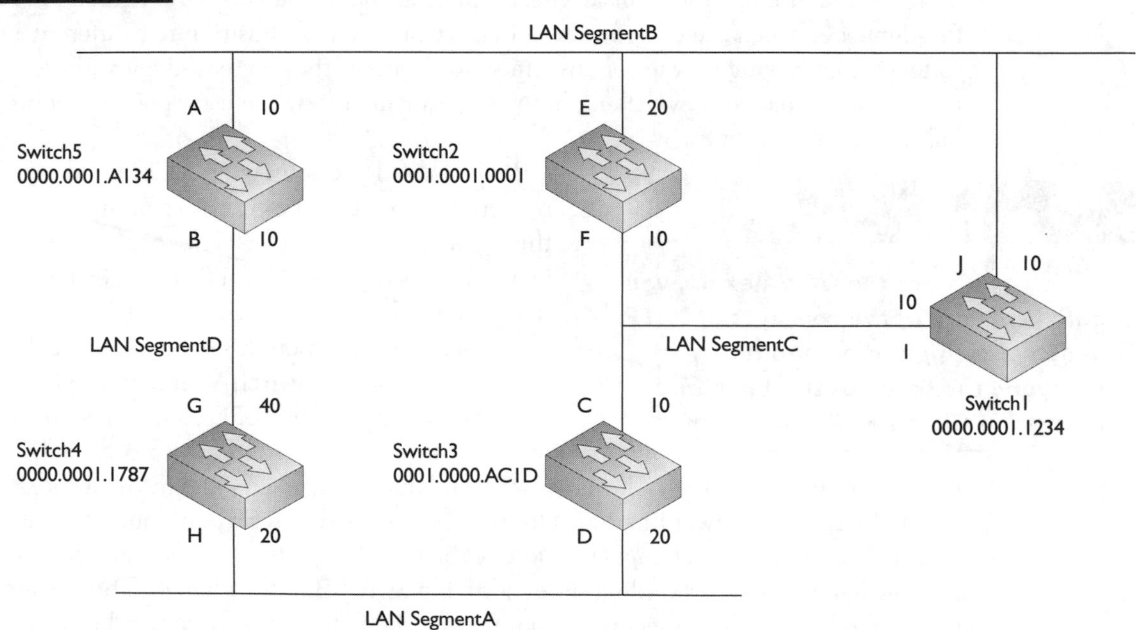

Electing the Root Switch

The first thing that occurs once all these switches are booted up is the election of the root switch. The switches share BPDUs with each other to elect the root. In this example, all of the switches are using the default priority (32,768). Remember that the switch with the lowest switch ID is elected as root. Since all of the switches have the same priority, the switch with the lowest MAC address, which is Switch1, is chosen as the root switch. Based on the election process, the new network topology looks like that shown in Figure 7-14.

Choosing Root Ports for Each Switch

After the root switch is elected, each non-root switch must choose one of its ports that it will use to reach the root, called the root port. Let's take this one switch at a time so that you can see the decision process in detail. With Switch1, which is the root switch, there are no root ports—if you recall, all ports on the root are designated ports.

Switch2 has two ports to use to reach the root: E and F. When Switch1 generates its BPDUs on ports I and J, the original path cost is set to 0. As these BPDUs are received by other switches, the receiving switch increments the path cost by the cost of the port that the BPDU was received on. As the BPDU comes into port E, Switch2 increments the path cost to 20 and for port F, 10. The first check that Switch2 makes

FIGURE 7-14 Root switch election

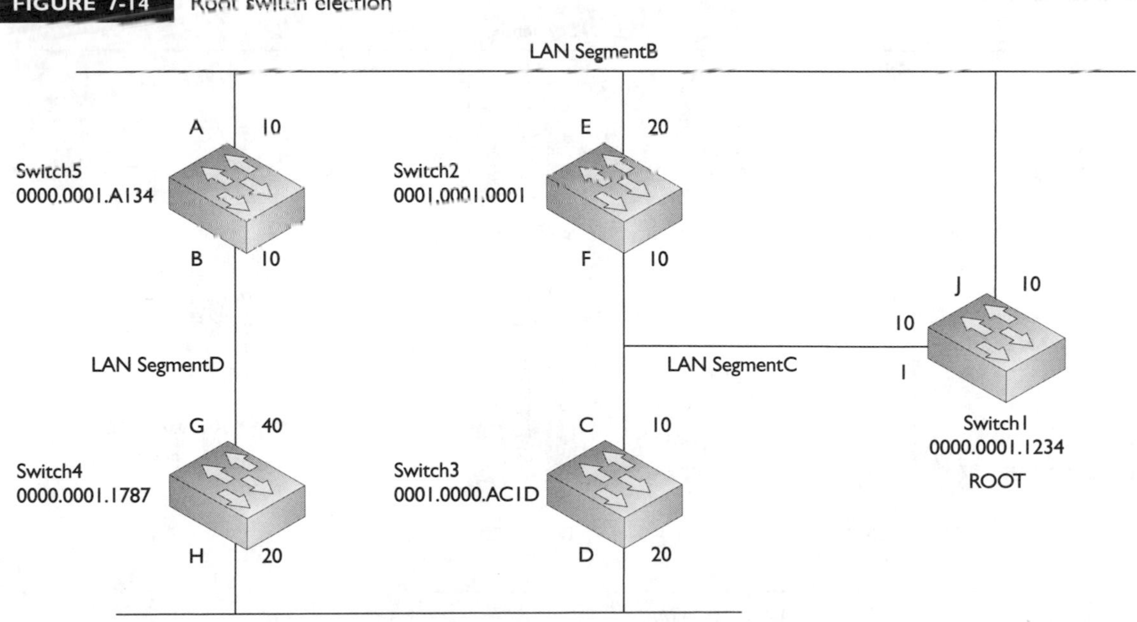

is to compare the path costs. Port F has the best path cost and therefore is chosen as the root port, which is shown as "RP" in Figure 7-15.

Switch3 also has two paths to reach the root: via ports C and D. Port C's accumulated path cost is 10, while D's cost is 70. Therefore, port C is chosen as the root port. Switch4 also has two ports to use to access the root: H and G. Port H has an accumulated path cost of 30, while G has a cost of 50, causing Switch4 to choose port H as the root port. Switch5's two ports, A and B, have accumulated path costs of 10 and 40, respectively, causing Switch5 to choose Port A as the root port.

Note that all the switches in the network are simultaneously running STP and figuring out for themselves who the root switch is and which port on themselves should be the root port. This is also true for choosing a designated port on a segment, which is discussed in the next section.

Choosing Designated Ports for Each Segment

After the root ports are chosen, each switch will figure out, on a segment-by-segment basis, if its connected port to the segment should be a designated port. Remember that the designated port on a segment is responsible for moving traffic back and forth between the segment and the switch. The segments themselves, of course, are completely unaware of this process of choosing a designated port—the switches are figuring this out.

FIGURE 7-15 Root ports

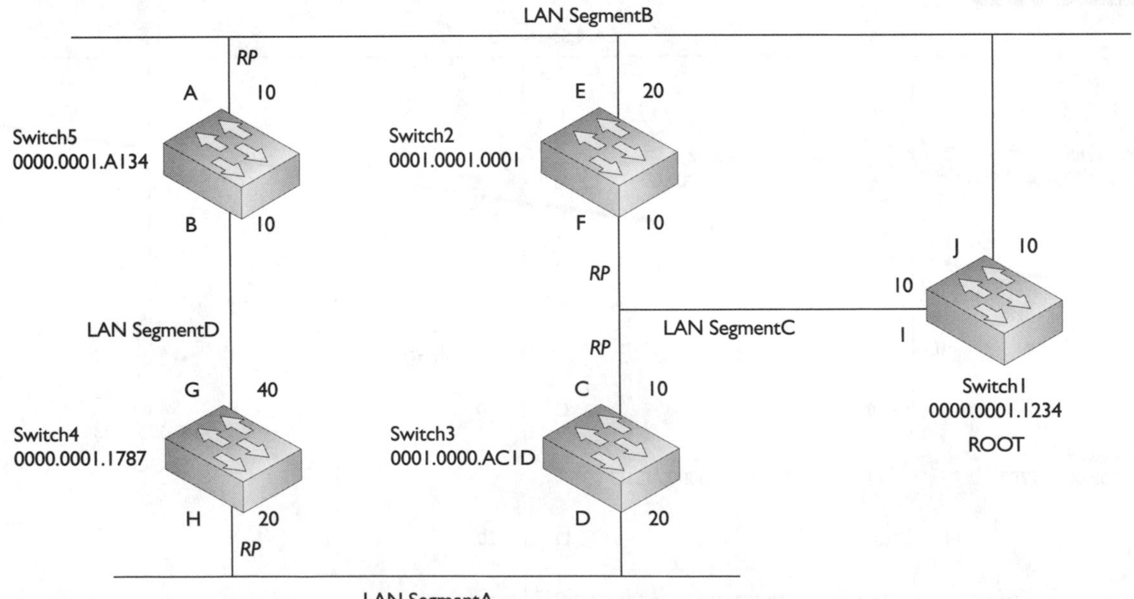

When choosing a designated port, the first thing that is examined is the accumulated path cost for the switch (connected to the segment) to reach the root. For two switches connected to the same segment, the switch with the lowest accumulated path cost will be the designated switch for that segment and its port connected to that segment becomes a designated port.

Going back to our network example, let's start with the easiest segments: B and C. For Switch1, the accumulated path cost for LAN SegmentB is 0, Switch2 is 20, and Switch5 is 10. Since the root switch (Switch1) has the lowest accumulated path cost, its local port (J) becomes the designated port for LAN SegmentB. This process is also true for LAN SegmentC—the root switch has the lowest accumulated path cost (0), making port I on Switch1 the designated port for LAN SegmentC.

LAN SegmentA has two choices: Switch3's D port and Switch4's H port. Switch3 has the lower accumulated path cost: 10 versus Switch4's 30. Therefore, Switch3's D port becomes the designated port for LAN SegmentA.

LAN SegmentD also has two choices for a designated port: Switch5's B port and Switch4's G port. Switch5 has an accumulated path cost of 10, and Switch4 has a cost of 30. Therefore Switch5's B port becomes the designated port for LAN SegmentD.

Figure 7-16 shows the updated STP topology for our network, where "DP" represents the designated ports for the LAN segments.

FIGURE 7-16 Root and designated ports

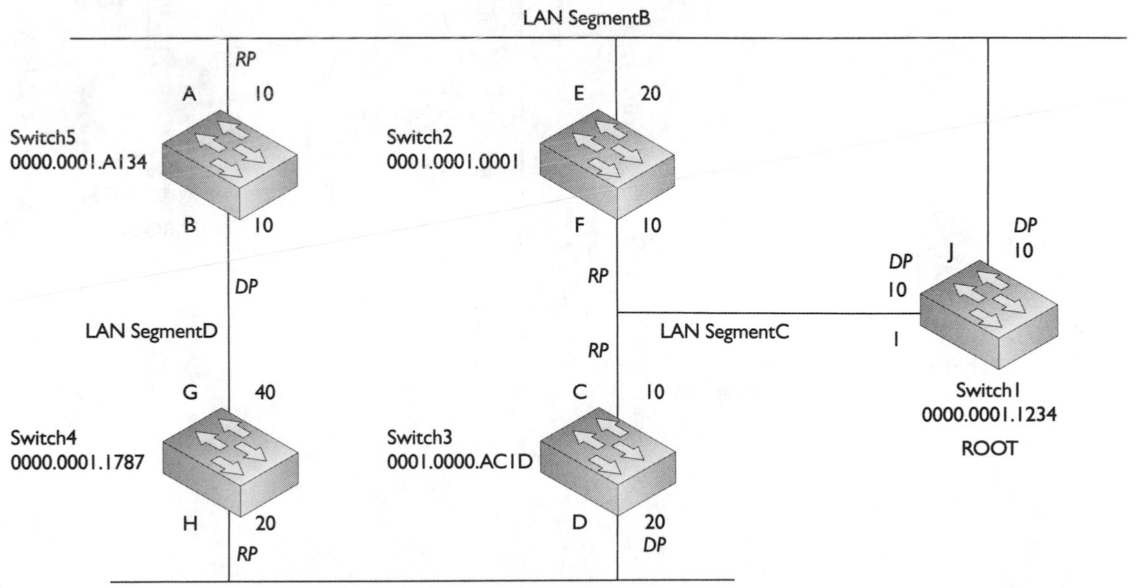

Changing Port States

After the designated ports are chosen, the switches will move their root and designated ports through the various states: blocking, listening, learning, and forwarding, whereas any other ports will remain in a blocked state. Figure 7-17 shows the ports in a blocked state, designated by an "X". Remember that on Switch2, only Port F (the root port) is in a forwarding state: Port E will remain in a blocked state. In this example, two ports are left in a blocked state: Switch2's E port and Switch4's G port.

STP guarantees only a layer-2 loop-free topology—it does* not *guarantee an optimal topology! For example, in the network shown in Figure 7-17, networking devices on LAN SegmentA would have to go through Switches3, 1, and 5 in order to reach LAN SegmentD, since Switch4's G port is in a blocked state.

FIGURE 7-17 Ports in a blocked state

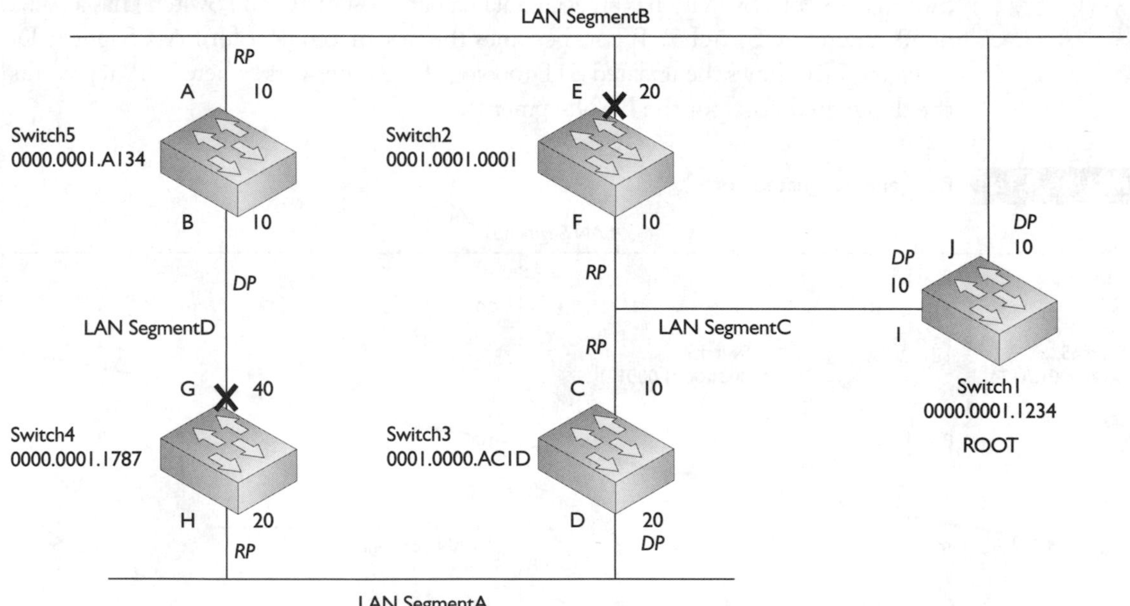

CERTIFICATION OBJECTIVE 7.04

1900 and 2950 Configuration

Chapter 5 covered some of the basics on configuring your 1900 and 2950 switches. This chapter expands upon these commands, including a quick overview of the 1900 and 2950 basic configuration process, configuring their interfaces, and manipulating configuration files. STP is discussed in Chapter 8.

Default Configuration

If you recall from Chapter 5, the 1900 switch requires the Enterprise Edition software in order to access the IOS CLI; otherwise, you are restricted to the menu-based interface for configuring the switch. This shouldn't be an issue unless you have a very old 1900, which might or might not be able to be upgraded, depending on the model number of the 1900. The 2950 switch, however, comes only with an IOS CLI. Both switches, nevertheless, share the same default configuration when you receive a brand new switch directly from Cisco. Here is the default configuration of the switches:

- All ports are enabled.
- The 10BaseT ports on the 1900 are set to half-duplex; the two 100 Mb ports are set for autonegotiating of the duplexing.
- All ports on the 2950 are set to autosensing for duplexing and speed.
- The 1900 default switching method is fragment free (the 2950 supports only store-and-forward switching).
- CDP is enabled on all ports.
- STP is enabled on all ports.
- The switches are not password protected.
- No IP addressing information is configured on the switches.

Remember the default configurations of the switches.

As you can see from this list, there are certain things that you will want to configure in order to manage your switch, as well as to optimize its configuration.

Quick Review

When you log into the 1900 switch, you are taken into the menu system. Type in "**K**" to access *User EXEC* mode. On the 2950, you are immediately taken to this mode. If you are not sure which switch model you are logged into, you can use the **show version** command. Here is the output of this command for the 1900 switch:

```
> show version
Cisco Catalyst 1900/2820 Enterprise Edition Software
Version V9.00.00(12) written from 172.16.1.11
Copyright (c) Cisco Systems, Inc.  1993-1999
Switch uptime is 0day(s) 0hour(s) 15minute(s) 59second(s)
cisco Catalyst 1900 (486sxl) processor with 2048K/1024K bytes
    of memory
Hardware board revision is 1
Upgrade Status: No upgrade currently in progress.
Config File Status: No configuration upload/download is
    in progress
27 Fixed Ethernet/IEEE 802.3 interface(s)
Base Ethernet Address: 00-E0-1E-86-37-AD
```

This contains the version of software running, the amount of RAM/flash, the types of interfaces, and the MAC address of the switch.

In this example, the switch is a 1924, based on the number of Ethernet interfaces ("27 Fixed Ethernet/IEEE 802.3 interface(s)"), and is running the Enterprise Edition software. Here is an example of this command on a 2950:

```
Switch# show version
Cisco Internetwork Operating System Software
IOS (tm) C2950 Software (C2950-I6Q4L2-M), Version 12.1(9)EA1,
     RELEASE SOFTWARE (fc1)
Copyright (c) 1986-2002 by cisco Systems, Inc.
Compiled Wed 24-Apr-02 06:57 by antonino
Image text-base: 0x80010000, data-base: 0x804E8000

ROM: Bootstrap program is CALHOUN boot loader
Switch uptime is 19 minutes
System returned to ROM by power-on
System image file is "flash:c2950-i6q4l2-mz.121-9.EA1.bin"

cisco WS-C2950-24 (RC32300) processor (revision E0) with
     20815K bytes of memory.
```

```
Processor board ID FHK0629Y004
Last reset from system-reset
Running Standard Image
24 FastEthernet/IEEE 802.3 interface(s)
32K bytes of flash-simulated non-volatile configuration memory.
Base ethernet MAC Address: 00:0A:41:BF:0A:40
Motherboard assembly number: 73-5781-10
Power supply part number: 34-0965-01
Motherboard serial number: FOC06270NZL
Power supply serial number: PHI062504VD
Model revision number: E0
Motherboard revision number: B0
Model number: WS-C2950-24
System serial number: FHK0629Y004
Configuration register is 0xF
```

This switch is a 2950 with 24 interfaces: "`24 FastEthernet/IEEE 802.3 interface(s)`".

Entering Configuration Mode

Remember that both of these switches support three basic modes: *User EXEC*, *Privilege EXEC*, and *Configuration* modes. To make configurations on your switch, you need to be in *Configuration* mode:

```
> enable
# configure terminal
(config)#
```

As you can see, this is just like the IOS-based routers. In this code example, the switch happened to be a 1900. The 2950 and routers put the device name in their prompts, which default to *Switch* and *Router* respectively. The 1900 has no default name. To assign a name on any IOS device, use the **`hostname`** *Configuration* mode command.

IP Configuration

As was mentioned in the introduction of this section, the switches have no IP configuration on them. Configuring IP addressing on your switches was covered in Chapter 5. Here is a quick code example of configuring IP on these two devices:

```
1900(config)# ip address IP_address subnet_mask
1900(config)# ip default-gateway router's_IP_address
```

```
2950(config)# interface vlan1
2950(config-vlan)# ip address IP_address subnet_mask
2950(config-vlan)# exit
2950(config)# ip default-gateway router's_IP_address
```

To verify your IP configuration on a 1900, use the **show ip** command:

```
1900# show ip
IP Address:192.168.1.12
Subnet Mask:255.255.255.0
Default Gateway:192.168.1.1
Management VLAN: 1
Domain name: dealgroup.com
Name server 1:192.168.1.77
Name server 2:
HTTP server :Disabled
HTTP port : 80
RIP :Enabled
```

On the 2950, use the **show ip interface brief** command to verify your IP configuration:

```
Switch# show ip interface brief

Interface          IP-Address     OK? Method Status Protocol
Vlan1              192.168.1.13   YES manual up     up
FastEthernet0/1    unassigned     YES unset  down   down
<--output omitted-->
```

7.01. The CD contains a multimedia demonstration overview of the 1900.

Basic Interface Configuration

The 1900 and the 2950 use the same nomenclature to identity interfaces:

```
(config)# interface type 0/port_number
```

The 1900 has two types of interfaces: **ethernet** and **fastethernet**. The 2950 also has two types: **fastethernet** and **gigabitethernet**.

For the 1912, there are 12 10BaseT ports (e0/1-e0/12) on the front of the switch, 1 AUI (e0/25) port on the rear, and 2 100BaseTX/FX ports on the front (fa0/26-fa0/27). For the 1924, there are 24 10BaseT ports (e0/1-e0/24), 1AUI port (e0/25), and 2 100BaseTX/FX ports (fa0/26-fa0/27).

7.02. The CD contains a multimedia demonstration overview of the 2950.

The 2950 comes in many models. The most popular is the 2950T-24 model, which comes with 24 10/100BaseTX interfaces (`fa0/1-fa0/24`) on the front of the switch. Unlike on routers, interface numbers on the switches begin with 1. Even though you must specify a module number of "0" for the switches, the two switches I mentioned are not modular. The 2820, a sister switch of the 1900, is modular, with slots 0, 1, and 2.

Accessing an Interface

To enter an interface, you use the same **interface** *Global Configuration* mode command as you would use on a Cisco router:

```
(config)# interface ethernet|fastethernet|gigabit 0/port_#
(config-if)#
```

Notice that this command took you into *Interface Subconfiguration* mode. In this mode, any changes made on an interface affect *only* that particular interface. Plus, if you enter a *Global Configuration* mode command, the switch will typically execute at the *Global* mode and return you here after executing the command.

Configuring Interface Duplexing

You can manually configure the duplexing on a switch's interface with the **duplex** *Interface Subconfiguration* mode command. On the 1900, use the following syntax:

```
1900(config)# interface ethernet|fastethernet 0/port_number
1900(config-if)# duplex auto|full|half|full-flow-control
```

Remember the default duplex settings on the 1900. One unique duplex setting is **full-flow-control**. This allows the interface and the connected device to share congestion information to implement flow control. Even though IEEE includes this for full-duplexing in its standard, not every vendor has implemented it, and for those vendors that have implemented it, the implementation might be slightly different from vendor to vendor.

To set the duplexing on the 2950 switch, use the following syntax:

```
2950(config)# interface fastethernet|gigabit 0/port_#
2950(config-if)# duplex auto|full|half
```

The 2950 doesn't support the flow control configuration that the 1900 does.

Unlike the 1900, the 2950 switches can autosense the speed of the connection (for the 10/100 ports). For these ports, you can hard-code the speed with the following syntax:

```
2950(config)# interface fastethernet|gigabit 0/port_#
2950(config-if)# speed 10|100|auto
```

on the job

Along with every network vendor, I recommend that you not use autosensing for an interface. The problem with autosensing is that the IEEE standard for this function isn't very specific and leaves some wiggle room for the vendors when implementing it. Of course, this can create conflicts between vendors when autosensing is trying to negotiate the duplexing and/or speed of the connection. Sometimes, one side might end up 100 half-duplex and the other side 100 full-duplex, creating massive number of collisions. You can use the `show interfaces` command to help troubleshoot this problem. Therefore, always manually configure the duplexing and speed of your autosensing interfaces.

Verifying Interface Configuration

Once you have configured the duplexing and/or speed of your interface, you can verify its configuration with this command:

```
> show interface [ethernet|fastethernet|gigabit 0/port_#]
```

The output of the 1900 command is different from the IOS router's output:

```
1900> show interface ethernet 0/1
Ethernet 0/1 is Suspended-no-linkbeat
Hardware is Built-in 10Base-T
Address is 00E0.1EA3.BC12
MTU 1500 bytes, BW 10000 Kbits
802.1d STP State:  Blocking     Forward Transitions:  3
Port monitoring: Disabled
Unknown unicast flooding: Disabled
Unregistered multicast flooding: Disabled
Description:
Duplex setting: Half duplex
Back pressure: Disabled
    Receive Statistics                  Transmit Statistics
-------------------------------   -------------------------------
Total good frames                0  Total frames                    0
Total octets                     0  Total octets                    0
```

```
Broadcast/multicast frames    0  Broadcast/multicast frames    0
Broadcast/multicast octets    0  Broadcast/multicast octets    0
Good frames forwarded         0  Deferrals                     0
Frames filtered               0  Single collisions             0
Runt frames                   0  Multiple collisions           0
No buffer discards            0  Excessive collisions          0
                                 Queue full discards           0
Errors:                          Errors:
  FCS errors                  0    Late collisions             0
  Alignment errors            0    Excessive deferrals         0
  Giant frames                0    Jabber errors               0
  Address violations          0    Other transmit errors       0
```

With this command, you can see the duplex configuration (half), STP mode (blocking), and statistics and error information about the interface. If you have a duplex-mismatch between your switch interface and a connected device, you will probably see an excessive number of collisions, especially late collisions, as well as an excessive number of FCS (frame checksum) errors. Remember my warning about autosensing an interface's configuration.

The output of this command looks like the following on a 2950 switch:

```
Switch# show interface fastethernet 0/2
FastEthernet0/2 is up, line protocol is up
  Hardware is Fast Ethernet, address is 000a.41bf.0a42
     (bia 000a.41bf.0a42)
  MTU 1500 bytes, BW 10000 Kbit, DLY 1000 usec,
     reliability 255/255, txload 1/255, rxload 1/255
  Encapsulation ARPA, loopback not set
  Keepalive set (10 sec)
  Half-duplex, 10Mb/s
  input flow-control is off, output flow-control is off
  ARP type: ARPA, ARP Timeout 04:00:00
  Last input never, output 00:00:01, output hang never
  Last clearing of "show interface" counters never
  Input queue: 0/75/0/0 (size/max/drops/flushes); Total output drops: 0
  Queueing strategy: fifo
  Output queue :0/40 (size/max)
  5 minute input rate 0 bits/sec, 0 packets/sec
  5 minute output rate 2000 bits/sec, 1 packets/sec
     530 packets input, 42856 bytes, 0 no buffer
     Received 187 broadcasts, 0 runts, 0 giants, 0 throttles
     0 input errors, 0 CRC, 0 frame, 0 overrun, 0 ignored
     0 watchdog, 57 multicast, 0 pause input
     0 input packets with dribble condition detected
     3653 packets output, 276663 bytes, 0 underruns
```

```
0 output errors, 0 collisions, 2 interface resets
0 babbles, 0 late collision, 0 deferred
0 lost carrier, 0 no carrier, 0 PAUSE output
0 output buffer failures, 0 output buffers swapped out
```

As you can see from the preceding output, it is similar to the output of a Cisco router. In this example, you can see that the duplexing is half and the speed of the interface is 10Mbps.

7.03. The CD contains a multimedia demonstration of configuring interfaces on the 1900.

Use the `duplex` command to configure the duplexing on both switches and the `speed` command on the 2950 to set the speed. Also, know how to look at the output of the `show interfaces` command to do basic troubleshooting.

7.04. The CD contains a multimedia demonstration of configuring interfaces on the 2950.

EXERCISE 7-1

Basic Interface Configuration

These last few sections dealt with interface configurations. This exercise will help you reinforce this material for the 1900 and 2950 switches. You'll perform this lab using Boson's NetSim simulator. You can find a picture of the network diagram for the simulator in the Introduction of this book. After starting up the simulator, click the *LabNavigator* button. Next, double-click *Exercise 7-1* and click the *Load Lab* button. This will load the lab configuration based on Chapter 5's exercises.

1. On the 1900-1 switch, set the inter-switch connections to full-duplex.

   At the top of the simulator in the menu bar, click the *eSwitches* icon and choose *1900-1*. Access configuration mode: **`enable`** and **`configure terminal`**. Enter the first uplink interface: **`interface fa0/26`**. Set the duplexing: **`duplex full`**. Exit the interface: **`exit`**. Enter the second uplink interface: **`interface fa0/27`**. Set the duplexing: **`duplex full`**. Exit configuration mode: **end**. Verify the configuration: **show interface fa0/26**. Make sure the duplexing is set correctly and the status of the interface is okay. Do the same with **fa0/27**.

2. On *both* the 2950 (2950-1 and 2950-2) switches, set the 1900 switch connection to 100Mbps and full-duplex.

   At the top of the simulator in the menu bar, click the *eSwitches* icon and choose *2950-1*. Use the **configure terminal interface fa0/1** command to enter the 1900 interface connection. Assign the speed with this command: **speed 100**. Set the duplexing: **duplex full**. Exit configuration mode: **end**. Verify the configuration: **show interface fa0/1**. Make sure the duplexing and speed are set correctly and the status of the interface is okay. Save the configuration: **copy running-config startup-config**. At the top of the simulator in the menu bar, click the *eSwitches* icon and choose *2950-2*. Use the **configure terminal interface fa0/1** command to enter the 1900 interface connection. Assign the speed with this command: **speed 100**. Set the duplexing: **duplex full**. Exit configuration mode: **end**. Verify the configuration: **show interface fa0/1**. Make sure the duplexing and speed are set correctly and the status of the interface is okay. Save the configuration: **copy running-config startup-config**.

3. Test connectivity with the **ping** command.

   From the 1900-1, use **ping 192.168.1.4** and **ping 192.168.1.3**. From the 2950-1 *and* 2950-2 switches, use **ping 192.168.1.5**. The ping should be successful.

Now you should be more comfortable with configuring switch interfaces. In the next section, you will be presented with examining and manipulating the CAM table, as well as setting up port security.

MAC Addresses and Port Security

If you recall, one of the three main functions of a switch is to learn which devices are associated with which interfaces. This information is stored in a port address, or CAM, table. On both switches, you can view the CAM table with the **show mac-address-table** command. Here is an example of the use of this command on a 1900 switch:

```
1900> show mac-address-table
Number of permanent addresses :1
```

```
Number of restricted static addresses :0
Number of dynamic addresses :4
Address         Dest Interface   Type       Source Interface List
-----------------------------------------------------------------
0000.0C7A.1210  FastEthernet0/26 Dynamic    All
0000.0C7A.341A  FastEthernet0/26 Dynamic    All
0000.0C7A.17AB  Ethernet0/1      Dynamic    All
0000.0C7A.E139  Ethernet0/2      Dynamic    All
0000.0C7A.BCE1  Ethernet0/3      Permanent  All
```

In this example, there are five entries in the CAM table. One is a statically configured entry, and the other four are dynamically learned entries. As an example, 0000.0C7A.1210 is connected to `fa0/26` and was dynamically learned. The 1900 can store up to 1,024 MAC addresses in its CAM table. An important thing to remember when designing your switched network is the number of devices that will be in the layer-2 network—you want to ensure that the switches you purchase support a CAM size to accommodate all of your devices. You definitely don't want your switches to be flooding traffic because your CAM tables are too small and can't learn additional entries.

Here is an example of the same command on a 2950 switch:

```
2950> show mac-address-table
Mac Address Table
------------------------------------------

Vlan    Mac Address       Type        Ports
----    -----------       ----        -----
   1    0008.7422.6d4a    DYNAMIC     Fa0/2
   1    0040.3399.b033    DYNAMIC     Fa0/2

Total Mac Addresses for this criterion: 2
```

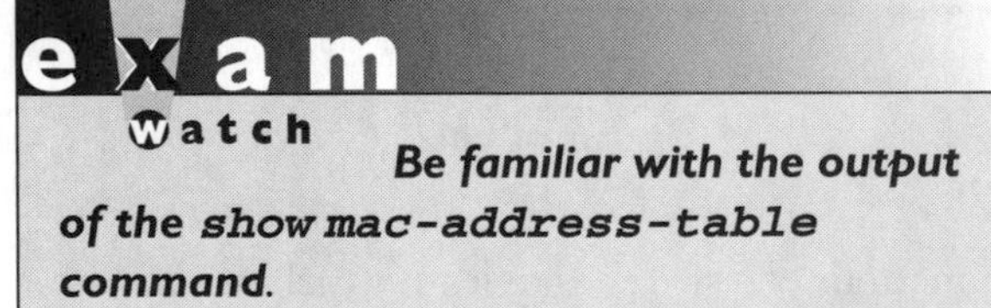

Be familiar with the output of the show ***`mac-address-table`*** ***command.***

In this example, there are two entries in the CAM table, both of which were learned dynamically and are connected to `fa0/2`. The 2950 switches can hold up to 8,192 entries in their CAM tables.

To clear dynamically learned entries from the CAM table, use the **`clear mac-address-table`** command from *Privilege EXEC* mode.

Static MAC Addresses

Besides having the switches learn MAC addresses dynamically, you can create static entries also. You may want to do this for security reasons. If a user moves their connection from one switch port to another, their traffic won't be forwarded correctly if you had statically configured their address to the old port. For traffic to flow correctly again, you would have to change the old entry to reflect the user's new interface. You may want to do this to ensure that the user doesn't unplug their connection from one port and connect it to another port, where the user might have access to more networking resources.

Unlike dynamic entries in a CAM table, static entries do not age out. This is true even if you reboot the switch (assuming your configuration has been saved). Also, if you have a static entry for a device and you move that device to a different port, even though the switch will see the change, the static entry will always override the learning function of the switch.

On a 1900 switch, use the following command to create a static entry in the CAM table:

```
1900(config)# mac-address-table permanent MAC_address interface
```

This command is straightforward. You need to specify the MAC address of the device in question, along with the interface associated with the device.

The 2950 command is slightly different:

```
2950(config)# mac-address-table static MAC_address vlan VLAN_#
                        interface type module/port_#
```

Besides specifying the MAC address of the device, and the interface where the device is located, you must also specify the VLAN that the device is located in. (VLANs are discussed in Chapter 8.) With either of the two switches, use the **show mac-address-table** to view your new entries.

7.05. The CD contains a multimedia demonstration of configuring static CAM entries on the 1900.

7.06. The CD contains a multimedia demonstration of configuring static CAM entries on the 2950.

Port Security on the 1900

The 1900 supports both static and dynamic port security. This allows you to restrict access to or from a particular MAC address. Use this command to set up static port security on a 1900 switch:

```
1900(config)# mac-address-table restricted static MAC_address
                        source_port list_of_allowed_interfaces
```

Here is a simple example of this command:

```
1900(config)# mac-address-table restricted static 0000.0C7A.4444
                ethernet0/1 ethernet0/2
```

In this example, any devices connected to `ethernet0/2` can access the device 0000.0C7A.4444, which is connected to `ethernet0/1`—any other traffic is prohibited from reaching this device. Use the **show mac-address-table** command to view your new restricted entries.

The problem of using the preceding configuration is that you must manually secure each MAC address that requires security. A better approach is to use dynamic port security, also called sticky learning. With sticky learning, the switch can learn up to a maximum of 132 MAC addresses associated with each port. It then converts these entries into static entries with the **mac-address-table permanent** command. If you reboot your switch, the static entries are still used. Note that sticky learning is really used to initially create the static entries and then is no longer used. For example, assume you have 30 PCs attached to a hub, which, in turn, is connected to a switch port with sticky learning. In this situation, the maximum number of allowable learned addresses is 132 (the default). As your PCs send traffic through the switch, the switch dynamically learns these addresses (one of its learning functions) and, using sticky learning, creates a secure static entry in the CAM table for them.

To enable this feature, use the following configuration:

```
1900(config)# interface ethernet|fastethernet 0/port_#
1900(config-if)# port secure
1900(config-if)# port secure max-mac-count value
```

The first command on the interface enables the feature. The second command restricts the number of addresses that the sticky feature can learn. The default is 132; but you can change it to anything in the range 1–132.

After you have enabled port security, you may want to change your security options:

```
1900(config)# address-violation suspend|ignore|disable
```

Notice that this command is executed from *Global Configuration* mode. Here are your three options:

- **suspend** Suspend the port until the violation is fixed, then automatically reenable the port (the default value)
- **disable** Shut down the port; the port can be reenabled only with the **no shutdown** command
- **ignore** Generate a security violation alert

To remove sticky learning from an interface, perform the following:

```
1900(config)# interface ethernet|fastethernet 0/port_#
1900(config-if)# port secure max-mac-count 132
1900(config-if)# no port secure
```

Make sure you are familiar with the basic configuration of port security on the 1900, as well as its removal.

First, you must reset the maximum number of secure addresses back to 132. Second, you need to disable port security. One often forgotten item is to remove the sticky learned addresses that the switch converted to **mac-address-table permanent** entries in the CAM table. To do this, view your configuration with the **show running-config** command and for each one of these commands, negate the command by preceding it with the **no** parameter.

Once you have enabled port security, you can verify it with this command:

```
1900> show mac-address-table security
Action upon address violation : Suspend
               Addressing  Address Table
Interface      Security        Size       Clear Address
-------------------------------------------------------
Ethernet 0/1   Enabled          1              Yes
Ethernet 0/2   Disabled        N/A             No
Ethernet 0/3   Disabled        N/A             No
```

In this example, the security violation, when it occurs, causes the interface to be suspended. Only one interface has port security enabled: e0/1, and sticky learning is allowed to learn a maximum of one address associated with this interface before disabling this feature on the interface.

7.07. The CD contains a multimedia demonstration of configuring port security on a 1900.

Port Security on the 2950

The 2950 formerly used the **mac-address-table secure** and **port-security** commands to set up port security, but this was replaced in IOS 12.1(6)EA2 with the **switchport port-security** command. This book will focus on the new syntax:

```
2950(config)# interface fastethernet|gigabit 0/port_#
2950(config-if)# switchport mode access
2950(config-if)# switchport port-security
2950(config-if)# switchport port-security maximum value
2950(config-if)# switchport port-security violation
                 protect|restrict|shutdown
2950(config-if)# switchport port-security mac-address MAC_address
2950(config-if)# switchport port-security mac-address sticky
```

As you can see, it is a little more complicated than the old method. First, you must enter the appropriate interface where you want to set up restricted security. The first command, **switchport mode access**, defines the interface as a host port instead of a trunk port (trunking is explained in Chapter 8). The second command on the interface, **switchport port-security**, enables port security. The third command, **switchport port-security maximum**, specifies the maximum number of devices that can be associated with the interface. This defaults to 1 and can range 1–132. The third command on the interface specifies what should occur if there is a security violation—the MAC address is seen connected to a different port. There are three options:

- **protect** When the number of secure addresses reaches the maximum number allowed, any additionally learned addresses will be dropped. This really applies only if you have enabled the sticky option, discussed in the next paragraph.
- **restrict** Causes the switch to generate a security violation alert.
- **shutdown** Causes the switch to generate an alert and to disable the interface. The only way to reenable the interface is to use the **no shutdown** command.

The last two commands in the preceding code listing affect how the switch learns the secure MAC addresses on the interface. The first one has you specify the exact MAC address that is allowed to be associated with this interface. The second one uses the sticky feature, which allows the switch to dynamically learn the MAC address(es) associated with the interface and convert these dynamic entries to static entries. The interface will learn MAC addresses only up to the maximum configured value for that interface. After you save your configuration, and when you reboot your switch, the sticky-learned addresses appear as statically secure addresses. Basically, sticky learning lets you avoid having to configure the MAC addresses associated with the interface.

To verify your configuration, use the **show port interface** command:

```
2950# show port interface fa0/2
Port Security : Enabled
Port status : SecureUp
Violation mode : Restrict
Maximum MAC Addresses : 132
Total MAC Addresses : 1
Configured MAC Addresses : 1
Aging time : 0 mins
Aging type : Absolute
SecureStatic address aging : Disabled
Security Violation count : 0
```

In this example, you can see that port security is disabled. However, if it were enabled, the violation mode would be *restrict* and there would be one statically configured MAC address.

7.08. The CD contains a multimedia demonstration of configuring port security on a 2950.

EXERCISE 7-2

CAM Tables

These last few sections deal with the CAM table and port security. This exercise will help you become more familiar with the CAM table on the 1900-1 switch. You'll perform this lab using Boson's NetSim simulator. You can find a picture of the network diagram for the simulator in the Introduction of this book. After starting up the simulator, click the *LabNavigator* button. Next, double-click *Exercise 7-2* and click the *Load Lab* button. This will load the lab configuration based on Exercise 7-1.

1. On the 1900-1 switch, access *Privilege EXEC* mode and examine the CAM table. If there are any entries, clear them.

   At the top of the simulator in the menu bar, click the *eSwitches* icon and choose *1900-1*. Enter *Privilege EXEC* mode: **`enable`**. View the CAM table: **`show mac-address-table`**. Clear the CAM table: **`clear mac-address-table`**.
2. On the 1900-1, ping Host1. Examine the CAM table. What is the MAC address of Host1? What interface is it associated with?

   Use the **`ping 192.168.1.10`** command. View the CAM table: **`show mac-address-table`**. The MAC address is __________ (this will be different for each PC NetSim is installed on). The interface is `ethernet0/1`.

Backing Up and Restoring Your 1900's Configuration

The 2950 uses the same commands as IOS routers to back up and restore configuration files. (For more information on these commands, see Chapters 5 and 6.) The 1900, however, uses a slightly different syntax. First, the 1900 automatically saves its configuration from RAM to NVRAM within 30 seconds of your executing a command. Normally, this takes only one or two seconds; however, if you have made any changes on your switch, wait at least 30 seconds before powering it off.

The 1900 does support additional commands to manipulate its configuration file. If you want to back up your configuration file to a TFTP server, use this command:

```
1900# copy nvram tftp://IP_address_of_TFTP_server/file_name
```

To restore your configuration, just reverse the two parameters in the preceding **copy** command:

```
1900# copy tftp://IP_address_of_TFTP_server/file_name nvram
```

Here's a quick example of backing up and restoring the 1900's configuration file:

```
1900# copy nvram tftp://172.16.1.128/switch.cfg
Configuration upload is successfully completed
1900#
1900# copy tftp://172.16.1.128/switch.cfg nvram
TFTP successfully downloaded configuration file
1900#
```

To set your 1900 back to its factory defaults, erase its configuration file by using the **delete nvram** command. On a Cisco router or the 2950 switch, the corresponding command is **erase startup-config**.

Remember how to back up (copy nvram tftp:), restore (copy tftp: nvram), and delete (delete nvram) the configuration file on the 1900.

7.09. The CD contains a multimedia demonstration about manipulating configuration files on the 1900.

CERTIFICATION SUMMARY

Switches switch in hardware using ASICs and support both full- and half-duplex. Full-duplex allows you to send and receive simultaneously but requires a point-to-point connection. There are three switching modes: store-and-forward (reads whole frame), cut-through (reads up to the destination MAC address), fragment-free (reads the first 64 bytes).

Bridges have three main functions: learn, forward, and remove loops. They learn by placing source MAC addresses and associated bridge ports in a port address or CAM table. They will flood traffic if the destination address is a multicast, broadcast, or unknown destination. IEEE's 802.1d STP is used to remove loops.

BPDUs are used by STP to learn about other neighboring switches. These are generated every two seconds as multicasts. When building the STP, a root switch is elected—the one with the lowest switch or bridge ID. The switch ID is composed of a priority and the switch's MAC address. Each switch chooses a root port to reach the root switch—the one with the lowest accumulated path cost. Each segment has one port on one switch that becomes a designated port, which is used to forward traffic to and from the segment. This is typically the port on the switch with the lowest accumulated path cost. There are five port states: blocking (20 seconds), listening (15 seconds), learning (15 seconds), forwarding, and disabled. PortFast puts a port immediately into forwarding mode and should be used only on non-switch-to-switch ports.

All ports are enabled on Cisco's switches by default. CDP and STP is enabled. Use the **ip address** and **ip default-gateway** commands to configure IP addressing information. Use the **duplex** command to change the duplexing of an interface. Use the **show mac-address-table** command to examine the CAM table. With port security, you can dynamically learn up to 132 addresses per port. On the 1900, use the **port secure** *Interface* command to enable this feature. On the 1900, use the **delete nvram** command to erase its configuration.

TWO-MINUTE DRILL

Bridges and Switches

- With store-and-forward switching, the layer-2 device must pull the entire frame into port and check the CRC before any additional processing of the frame is done. With cut-through switching, the switch reads up to and including the destination MAC address in the frame before switching the frame. Fragment-free switching makes sure that the frame is at least 64 bytes before switching it. The default switching method on the 1900 is fragment-free; on the 2950, it's store-and-forward.
- In half-duplex connections, a device can either send or receive. In full-duplex connections, a device can simultaneously send and receive. Full-duplex connections don't experience collisions and therefore have the collision detection mechanism in the NIC disabled.
- Bridges switch frames in software, use store-and-forward switching, use half-duplex connections and support 2–16 ports. Switches switch frames in hardware (ASICs), use multiple switching methods, support both half- and full-duplex connections, and can support hundreds of ports.

Functions of Bridging and Switching

- The three main functions of layer-2 devices are: learning, forwarding, and removing loops.
- During the learning process, layer-2 devices add the source MAC address of the frame and the incoming port number to the port address, or CAM, table.
- Three types of frames are flooded: broadcast (all devices), multicast (a group of devices), and unknown (one device) destination.

The Spanning Tree Protocol

- STP is defined in 802.1d. It removes loops from your network. The switch with the lowest switch ID (priority + MAC address) is elected as root. Each switch chooses the best path to the root, and this port is called a root port. Each segment needs a switch port to access the rest of the network—this port is called a designated port.

- BPDUs are used to elect root switches and to share topology information. BPDUs are multicasts that are advertised every two seconds.
- There are five STP port states: blocking (only processing BPDUs—20 seconds), listening (only processing BPDUs—15 seconds), learning (processing BPDUs and building the CAM table—15 seconds), forwarding (processing BPDUs, building the CAM table, and forwarding user traffic), disabled (the port is not enabled). Root and designated ports will eventually move into a forwarding state, which can take between 30 and 50 seconds.
- RSTP supports two additional port types: alternate (secondary to a root port) and backup (secondary to a designated port).

1900 and 2950 Configuration

- Default configuration: all ports enabled, 1900 10BaseT ports are half-duplex and all other ports on the 1900 and 2950 are autosensing, STP is enabled, CDP is enabled, and there is no IP addressing configured.
- Assign duplexing and speed: **duplex** and **speed**. Use the **show interfaces** command to verify.
- To view the CAM table: **show mac-address-table**.
- Configuring port security on the 1900's interfaces: **port secure**, **port secure max-mac-count**. The default maximum for addresses associated with an interface is 132. There are three options for address violations: suspend (default), disable, and ignore.
- Configuring port security on the 2950's interfaces: **switchport port-security**, **switchport port-security maximum**, and **switchport port-security violation**.

SELF TEST

The following Self Test questions will help you measure your understanding of the material presented in this chapter. Read all the choices carefully, as there may be more than one correct answer. Choose all correct answers for each question.

Bridges and Switches

1. Which of the following is true concerning bridges?
   A. They switch frames in hardware.
   B. They support half- and full-duplexing.
   C. They support one collision domain for the entire bridge.
   D. They do only store-and-forward switching.

2. With _________ switching, the switch reads the destination MAC address of the frame and immediately starts forwarding the frame.
   A. Store-and-forward
   B. Cut-through
   C. Fragment-free
   D. Runtless

3. Which of the following is true concerning full-duplexing?
   A. It can either send or receive frames, but not both simultaneously.
   B. It can be used with hubs.
   C. It can be used with 10Base5 cabling.
   D. It uses point-to-point connections.

Functions of Bridging and Switching

4. Which is not one of the three main functions of a layer-2 device?
   A. Learning
   B. Forwarding
   C. Listening
   D. Removing loops

5. During the learning function, the switch places addresses and ports in a(n) ________ table.
   A. IP address
   B. learning
   C. CAM
   D. memory
6. Which type of traffic is sent to a group of devices?
   A. Multicast
   B. Unicast
   C. Broadcast
   D. Groupcast
7. Which type of traffic is not flooded?
   A. Multicast
   B. Known unicast
   C. Broadcast
   D. Unknown unicast

The Spanning Tree Protocol

8. BPDU stands for ____________.
   A. Bridge Protocol Description Unicast
   B. Bridge Protocol Data Unit
   C. Bridge Protocol Description Unit
   D. Bridge Protocol Data Unicast
9. BPDUs are generated every __________ seconds.
10. The root switch is the one elected with the ____________________.
   A. Lowest MAC address
   B. Highest MAC address
   C. Lowest switch ID
   D. Highest switch ID

11. The switch port that is chosen to forward traffic for a segment is called a __________.
    A. Root port
    B. Alternate port
    C. Backup port
    D. Designated port

12. Which is true concerning a port in a listening state? (Choose all correct answers.)
    A. It remains there for 15 seconds.
    B. It forwards BPDUs and builds the CAM table.
    C. It remains there for 20 seconds.
    D. It forwards BPDUs.

1900 and 2950 Configuration

13. Enter the 1900 switch command to set an interface to autosense the duplexing: __________.

14. Enter the switch command to view the CAM table: __________.

15. Which 1900 command enables port security?
    A. **`port security`**
    B. **`switchport security`**
    C. **`port secure`**
    D. **`switchport port-security`**

SELF TEST ANSWERS

Bridges and Switches

1. ☑ **D.** Bridges support only the store-and-forward switching method.
☒ **A** and **B** are done by switches, not bridges. **C** is incorrect because each port on a bridge or switch is a separate collision domain.

2. ☑ **B.** With cut-through switching, the switch reads the destination MAC address of the frame and immediately starts forwarding the frame.
☒ With **A**, the entire frame is read and the CRC is checked before further processing. **C** and **D** are the same thing—once the first 64 bytes of the frame are read, the switch begins to forward it.

3. ☑ **D.** Full duplex connections require point-to-point connections and cannot involve hubs.
☒ **A**, **B**, and **C** are true of half-duplex connections.

Functions of Bridging and Switching

4. ☑ **C.** Listening is a port state, not one of the three main functions of a layer-2 device.
☒ **A**, **B**, and **D** are the three main functions of a layer-2 device.

5. ☑ **C.** During the learning function, the switch places addresses and ports in a CAM table—another term is port address table.
☒ **A**, **B**, and **D** are not terms used to describe this table.

6. ☑ **A.** Multicast traffic is sent to a group of devices.
☒ **B** is sent to a single device, and **C** is sent to all devices. **D** is a nonexistent traffic type.

7. ☑ **B.** Unicast traffic is not flooded if the destination MAC address is in the CAM table.
☒ **A**, **C**, and **D** traffic is always flooded, to maintain the transparency of the layer-2 device.

The Spanning Tree Protocol

8. ☑ **B.** BPDU stands for Bridge Protocol Data Unit.
☒ **A** and **C** are incorrect because of the word *description*, and the fact that BPDUs use multicasts, which also makes **D** incorrect.

9. ☑ BPDUs are generated every two seconds.

10. ☑ **C.** The switch with the lowest switch ID is elected as the root switch.
☒ **A** and **B** are incorrect because the decision is based on the switch ID, which includes the switch's priority and MAC address. **D** is incorrect because it is the lowest, not the highest.

11. ☑ **D.** The switch port that is chosen to forward traffic for a segment is called a designated port.
☒ **A** is the port that the switch uses to reach the root. **B** is used in RSTP and is a secondary root port, and **C** is used in RSTP and is a secondary designated port.

12. ☑ **A** and **D.** In a listening state, the port processes and forwards BPDUs. A port stays in the listening state for 15 seconds.
☒ **B** occurs in the learning state. **C** is the time period for the blocking state.

1900 and 2950 Configuration

13. ☑ Use the **`duplex auto`** command on the interface to set duplexing to autosensing.

14. ☑ Use the **`show mac-address-table`** command to view the CAM table on either switch.

15. ☑ **C.** The **`port secure`** command enables port security on a 1900 switch.
☒ **D** is used on the 2950 switch. **A** and **B** are nonexistent commands.

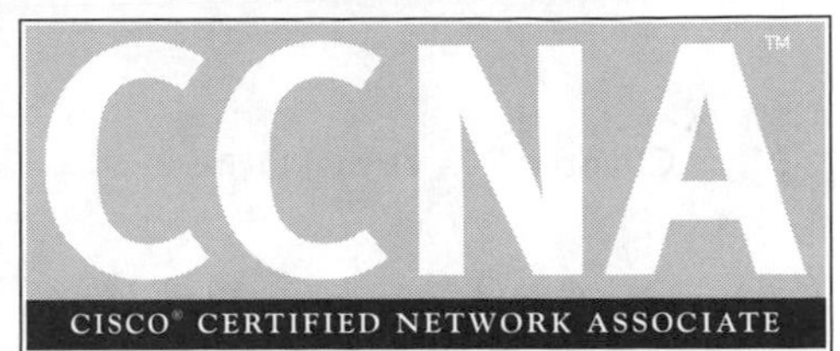

8

Virtual LANs

CERTIFICATION OBJECTIVES

8.01	Virtual LAN Overview	8.04	1900 and 2950 VLAN Configuration
8.02	VLAN Connections	✓	Two Minute Drill
8.03	VLAN Trunk Protocol	Q&A	Self Test

As was mentioned in Chapters 2 and 7, layer-2 devices, including bridges and switches, always propagate certain kinds of traffic in the broadcast domain: broadcasts, multicasts, and unknown destination traffic. This process impacts every machine in the broadcast domain (layer-2 network). It impacts the bandwidth of these devices' connections as well as their local processing. If you were using bridges, the only solution available to solve this problem would be to break up the broadcast domain into multiple broadcast domains and interconnect these domains with a router. With this approach, each new broadcast domain would be a new logical segment and would need a unique network number to differentiate it from the other layer-3 logical segments. Unfortunately, this is a costly solution, since each broadcast domain, each logical segment, needs its own port on a router. The more domains that you have, the bigger the router that you have to purchase. As you will see in this chapter, switches also have the same problem with traffic that must be flooded. You will see, however, that switches have a unique solution to reduce the number of router ports required, and thus the cost of the layer-3 device that you need to obtain: virtual LANs and trunking.

CERTIFICATION OBJECTIVE 8.01

Virtual LAN Overview

A *virtual LAN (VLAN)* is a group of networking devices in the same broadcast domain. The top part of Figure 8-1 shows an example of a simple VLAN, where every device is in both the same collision and broadcast domains. In this example, a hub is providing the connectivity, which represents, to the devices connected to it, that the segment is a logical segment.

The bottom part of Figure 8-1 shows an example of a switch with four PCs connected to it. One major difference between the switch and the hub is that all devices connected to the hub are in the same collision domain whereas in the switch example, each port of the switch is a separate collision domain. By default, all ports on a switch are in the same broadcast domain. In this example, however, the configuration of the switch places PC-E and PC-F in one broadcast domain (VLAN) and PC-G and PC-H in another broadcast domain.

Switches are used to create VLANs, or separate broadcast domains. VLANs are not restricted to any physical boundary in the switched network, assuming that all

FIGURE 8-1 VLAN examples

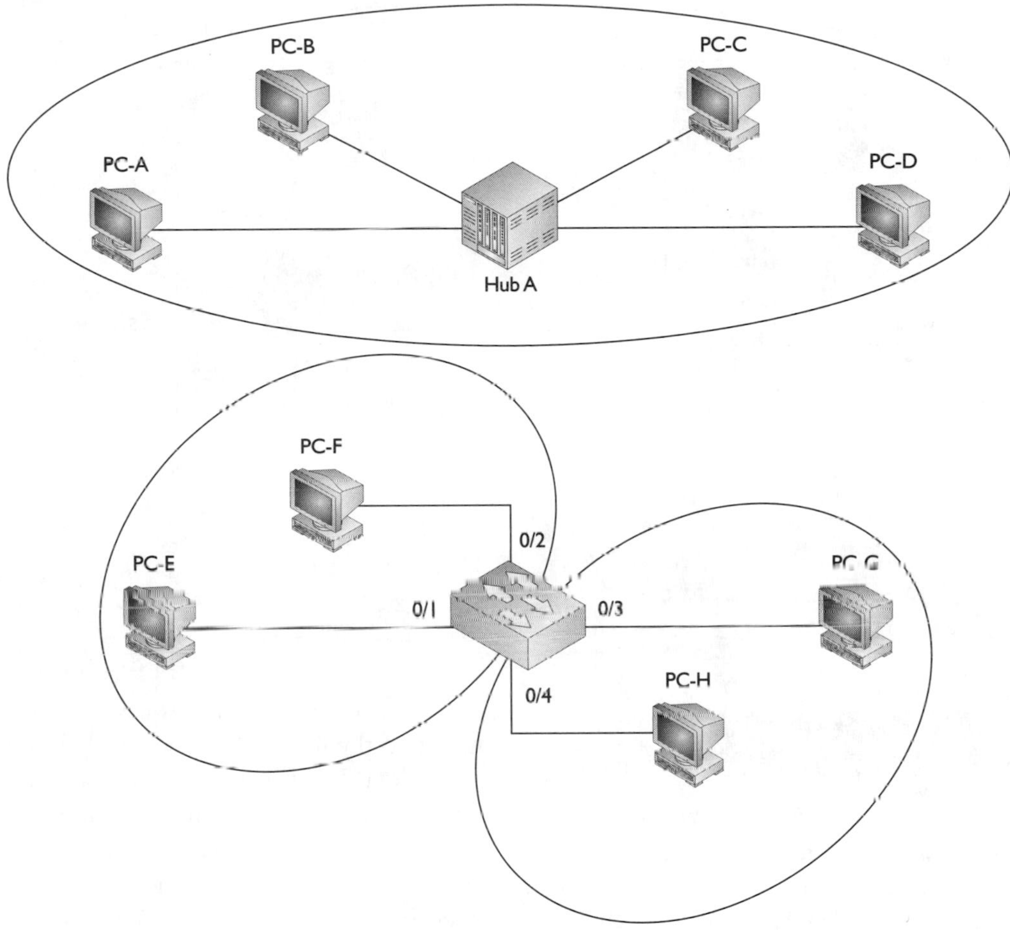

the devices are interconnected via switches and that there are no intervening layer-3 devices. For example, a VLAN could be spread across multiple switches, or be contained in the same switch, as is shown in Figure 8-2. In this example, there are three VLANs. Notice that VLANs are not tied to any physical location: PC-A, PC-B, PC-E, and PC-F are in the same VLAN, but are connected to different ports of different switches. However, a VLAN could be contained to one switch, as PC-C and PC-D are connected to SwitchA.

FIGURE 8-2 Physical switched topology using VLANs

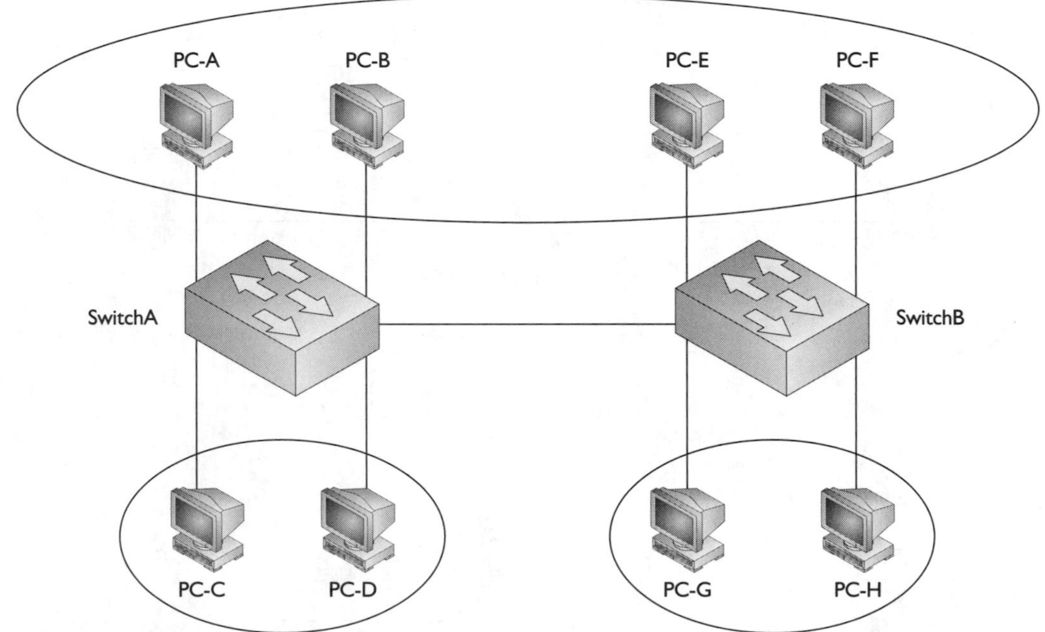

exam watch

A VLAN is a group of devices in the same broadcast domain or subnet. You need a router to move traffic between VLANs. The 1900 and the 2950 SI support 64 VLANs.

The switches in your network are what maintain the integrity of your VLANs. For example, if PC-A generates a broadcast, SwitchA and SwitchB will make sure that only other devices in that VLAN (PC-B, PC-E, and PC-F) will see the broadcast, and that other devices will not, and that holds true even across switches, as is the case in Figure 8-2.

Subnets and VLANs

Logically speaking, VLANs are also subnets. A subnet, or a network, is a contained broadcast domain. A broadcast that occurs in one subnet will not be forwarded, by default, to another subnet. Routers, or layer-3 devices, provide this boundary function. Each of these subnets requires a unique network number. And to move from one network number to another, you need a router. In this case of broadcast domains and switches, each of these separate broadcast domains is a separate VLAN; and therefore, you still need a routing function.

From the user's perspective, the physical topology shown in Figure 8-2 would actually look like Figure 8-3. And from the user's perspective, the devices know that to reach another VLAN, they must forward their traffic to the default gateway address in their VLAN—the IP address on the router's interface.

One advantage that switches have over bridges, though, is that in a switched VLAN network, assuming your routing function supports VLANs, the switch can handle multiple VLANs on a single port and a router can route between these VLANs on the same single port. With a bridge, each VLAN must be placed on a separate port of a router, increasing the cost of your routing solution.

Cisco has recommendations as to the number of devices in a VLAN, which are shown in Table 8-1. Remember that these numbers are recommendations from Cisco, recommendations backed by many years of designing and implementing networks. Each network has its own, unique, characteristics. I once saw a broadcast domain that had almost 1,500 devices in it; it worked, but not very well.

FIGURE 8-3 Logical topology using VLANs

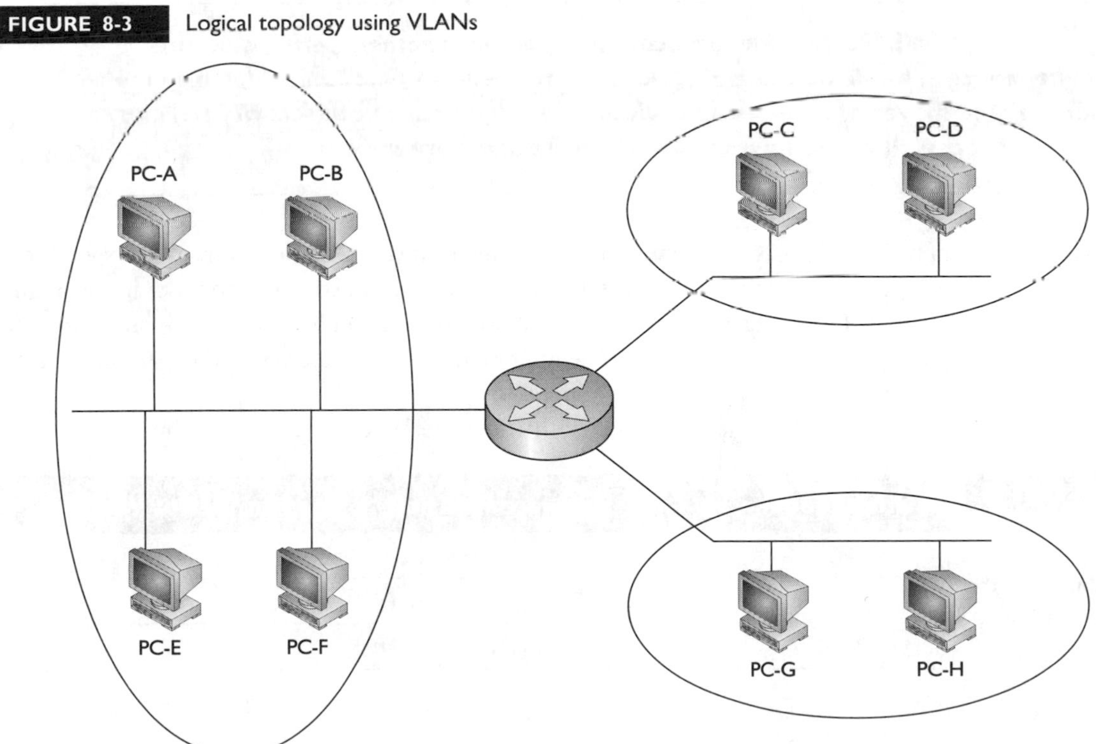

TABLE 8-1

Recommendations for Number of Devices in a VLAN

Protocol	Number of Devices
IP	500
IPX	300
NetBIOS	200
AppleTalk	200
Mixed protocols	200

Scalability

Through segmentation of broadcast domains, VLANs increase your scalability. Since VLANs are a logical construct, a user can be located anywhere in the switched network and still belong to the same broadcast domain. If you move a user from one switch to another switch in the same switched network, you can still keep the user in his original VLAN. This includes a move from one floor of a building to another floor, or from one part of the campus to another. The limitation is that the user, when moved, must still be connected to the same layer-2 network.

exam watch

VLANs provide for location independence. This flexibility makes adds, changes, and moves of networking devices a simple process. It also allows you to group people together, perhaps according to their job function, which also makes implementing your security policies straightforward.

Table 8-2 lists the VLAN capabilities of the 1900 and 2950 switches.

TABLE 8-2

VLAN Capabilities of the Cisco Switches

Switch Model	Software Revision	Number of VLANs
1900	Enterprise IOS	64
2950	IOS Standard Image (SI)	64
2950	IOS Enhanced Image (EI)	250

VLAN Membership

A device's membership in a VLAN can be determined by one of two methods: static or dynamic. These methods affect how a switch will associate a port in its chassis with a particular VLAN. When you are dealing with static VLANs, you must manually assign a port on a switch to a VLAN using an *Interface Subconfiguration* mode command. VLANs configured in this way are typically called *port-based* VLANs.

With dynamic VLANs, the switch automatically assigns the port to a VLAN using information from the user device, such as its MAC address, IP address, or even directory information (a user or group name, for instance). The switch then consults a policy server, called a *VLAN membership policy server (VMPS)*, which contains a mapping of device information to VLANs. One of the switches in your network must be configured as this server. The 1900 and 2950 switches cannot serve as a VMPS server switch, but other switches, such as the Catalyst 6500, can. In this situation, the 1900 and 2950 switches act as clients and use the 6500 to store the dynamic VLAN membership information.

Dynamic VLANs have one main advantage over static VLANs: they support plug-and-play movability. For instance, if you move a PC from a port on one switch to a port on another switch and you are using dynamic VLANs, the new switch port will automatically be configured for the VLAN the user belongs to. About the only time that you have to configure information with dynamic VLANs is if you hire an employee, an employee leaves the company, or the employee changes job functions.

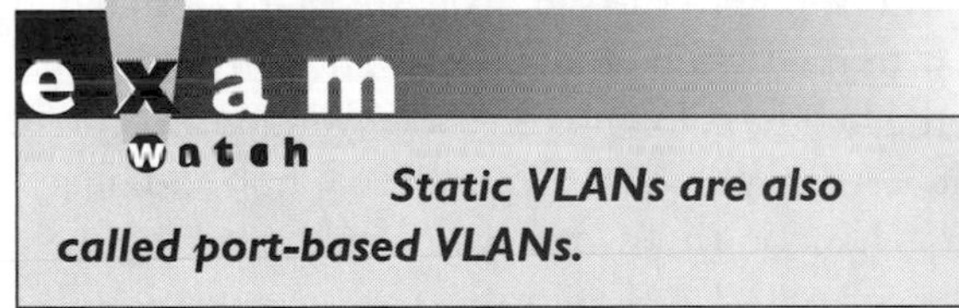

Static VLANs are also called port-based VLANs.

If you are using static VLANs, not only will you have to manually configure the switch port with this updated information, but if you move the user from one switch to another, you will also have to perform this manual configuration to reflect the user's new VLAN membership. One advantage, though, that static VLANs have over dynamic VLANs is that, since they have been around much longer than dynamic VLANs, the configuration process is easy and straightforward. With dynamic VLANs, a lot of initial preparation must be made involving matching users to VLANs. This book focuses exclusively on static VLANs. Dynamic VLANs are beyond the scope of this book, though they are covered in Cisco's CCNP and CCDP Switching exam.

CERTIFICATION OBJECTIVE 8.02

VLAN Connections

When dealing with VLANs, switches support two types of connections: access links and trunks. When setting up your switches, you will need to know what type of connection an interface is and configure it appropriately. As you will see, the configuration process for each is different. The remainder of this section discusses the two types of connections.

Access-Link Connections

An *access-link* connection is a connection to a device that has a standardized Ethernet NIC that understands only standardized Ethernet frames—in other words, a normal NIC card that understands IEEE 802.3 and/or Ethernet II frames. Access-link connections can only be associated with a single VLAN. This means that any device or devices connected to this port will be in the same broadcast domain.

An access-link connection is a connection between a switch and a device with a normal Ethernet NIC, where the Ethernet frames are transmitted unaltered.

For example, if you have ten users connected to a hub, and you plug the hub into an access-link interface on a switch, then all of these users will belong to the same VLAN that is associated with the switch port. If you wanted five users on the hub to belong to one VLAN and the other five to a different VLAN, you would need to purchase an additional hub and plug each hub into a different switch port. Then, on the switch, you would need to configure each of these ports with the correct VLAN identifier.

Trunk Connections

Unlike access-link connections, *trunk* connections are capable of carrying traffic for multiple VLANs. In order to support trunking, the original Ethernet frame must be modified to carry VLAN information. This is to ensure that the broadcast integrity is maintained. For instance, if a device from VLAN 1 has generated a broadcast and the connected switch has received it, when this switch forwards it to other switches, these switches need to know the VLAN origin so that they forward this frame only out of VLAN 1 ports and not other VLAN ports.

Cisco supports four trunk methods to maintain VLAN integrity:

- Cisco's proprietary InterSwitch Link (ISL) protocol for Ethernet
- IEEE's 802.1Q, commonly referred to as *dot1q* for Ethernet
- LANE for ATM
- 802.10 for FDDI (proprietary Cisco implementation)

A trunk modifies the original frame to carry VLAN information. Remember the four trunking methods.

These trunking methods create the illusion that instead of a single physical connection between the two trunking devices, there is a separate logical connection for each VLAN between them. When trunking, the switch adds the source port's VLAN identifier to the frame so that the device at the other end of the trunk understands what VLAN originated this frame and can make intelligent forwarding decisions on not just the destination MAC address, but also the source VLAN identifier.

Since information is added to the original Ethernet frame, normal NICs will not understand this information and will typically drop the frame. Therefore, you need to ensure that when you set up a trunk connection on a switch's interface, the device at the other end also has trunking configured. If the device at the other end doesn't understand these modified frames or is not set up for trunking, it will drop the frames.

The modification of these frames, commonly called *tagging,* is done in hardware by application-specific integrated circuits (ASICs). ASICs are specialized processors. Since the tagging is done in hardware at faster than wire speeds, no latency is involved in the actual tagging process. And to ensure compatibility with access-link devices, switches will strip off the tagging information and forward the original Ethernet frame to the device connected to the access-link connection. From the user's perspective, the source generates a normal Ethernet frame and the destination receives this frame, which is an Ethernet 802.3 or II frame coming in and the same going out. In reality, this frame is tagged as it enters the switched infrastructure and sheds the tag as it exits the infrastructure: the process of tagging and untagging the frame is hidden from the users on access-link connections.

Trunk links are common between certain types of devices, including switch-to-switch, switch-to-router, and switch-to-file server connections. Using a trunk link on a router is a great way of reducing your layer-3 infrastructure costs. For instance, in the old days of bridging, in order to route between different broadcast domains, you needed a *separate* physical router interface for each broadcast domain. If you had two broadcast domains, you needed two router ports; if you had 20 broadcast domains, you needed 20 router ports. As you can see, the more broadcast domains you had, the more expensive the router would become.

Today, with the advent of VLANs and trunk connections, you can use a single port on a router to route between your multiple broadcast domains. If you had 2 or 20 broadcast domains, you could use just one port on the router to accomplish the routing between these different subnets. Of course, you would need a router and an interface that supported trunking. (Not every Cisco router supports trunking; you would need at least a 1751 or 2600 series router.) If you had a router that didn't support trunking, you would have to have a separate router interface for each VLAN you had created in order to route between the VLANs. Therefore, if you have a lot of VLANs, it makes sense to economize and buy a router that supports trunking.

You can also buy specialized NICs for PCs or file servers that support trunking. For instance, you might have a file server that you want multiple VLANs to access. One solution would be to use a normal NIC and set this up with an access-link connection to a switch. Since this is an access-link connection, the server could belong to only one VLAN. The users in the same VLAN, when accessing the server, would have all their traffic switched via layer-2 devices to reach it. Users in other VLANs, however, would have to have their traffic routed to this server via a router, since the file server is in a different broadcast domain.

If throughput is a big concern, you might want to buy a trunk NIC for the file server. Configuring this NIC is different from configuring a normal NIC on a file server. For each VLAN that you want the file server to participate in, you would create a virtual NIC, assign your VLAN identifier and layer-3 addressing to the virtual NIC for the specific VLAN, and then associate it with the physical NIC. Once you have created all of these logical NICs on your file server, you need to set up a trunk connection on the switch to the server. Once you have done this, members of VLANs that you have configured on the file server will be able to directly access the file server without going through a router. Since these cards can be expensive, many administrators will purchase these devices only for critical services.

Trunking Example

Figure 8-4 shows an example of a trunk connection between SwitchA and SwitchB in a network that has 3 VLANs. In this example, PC-A, PC-F, and PC-H belong to one VLAN, PC-B and PC-G belong to a second VLAN, and PC-C, PC-D, and PC-E belong to a third VLAN. The trunk between the two switches is also tagging VLAN information so that the remote switch understands the source VLAN of the originator.

FIGURE 8-4 Trunking example

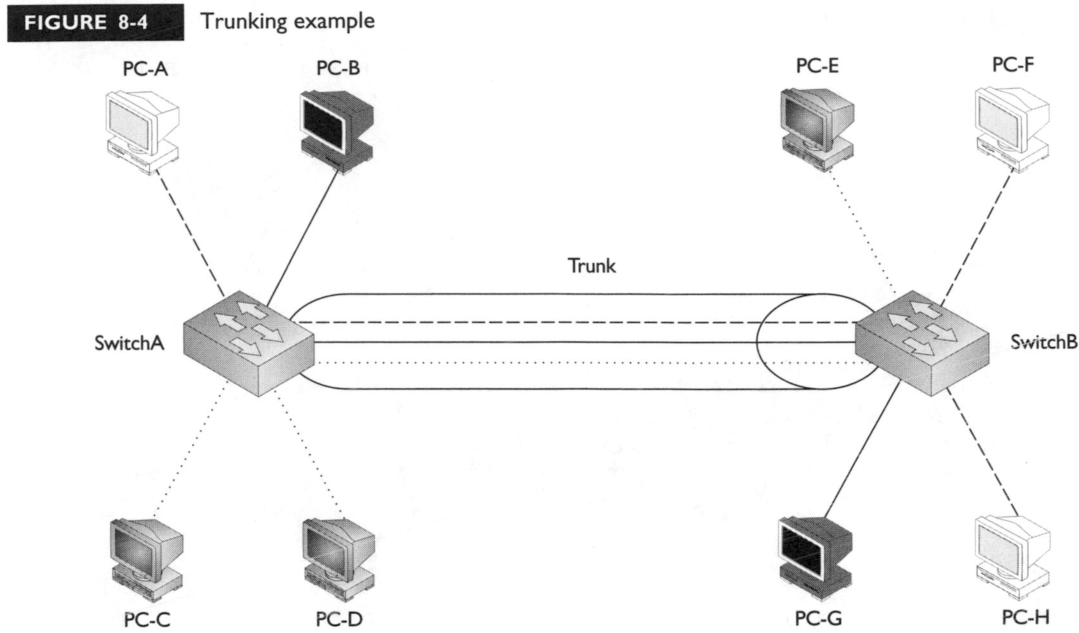

Let's take a look at an example of the use of VLANs and the two different types of connections by using the network shown in Figure 8-5. In this example, PC-C generates a local broadcast. When SwitchA receives the broadcast, it examines the incoming port and knows that the source device is from the gray VLAN (the access-link connections are marked with dots). Seeing this, the switch knows to forward this frame only out of ports that belong to the same VLAN: this includes access-link connections with the same VLAN identifier and trunk connections. On this switch, one access-link connection belongs to the same VLAN, PC-D, so the switch forwards the frame directly out this interface.

The trunk connection between SwitchA and SwitchB handles traffic for multiple VLANs. A VLAN tagging mechanism is required in order to differentiate the source of traffic when moving it between the switches. For instance, let's assume that there was no tagging mechanism taking place between the switches. PC-C generates a broadcast frame, and SwitchA forwards it, unaltered, to PC-D and SwitchB across the trunk. The problem with this process is that when SwitchB receives the original Ethernet frame, it has no idea what port or ports to forward the broadcast to, since it doesn't know the origin VLAN.

FIGURE 8-5 Broadcast traffic

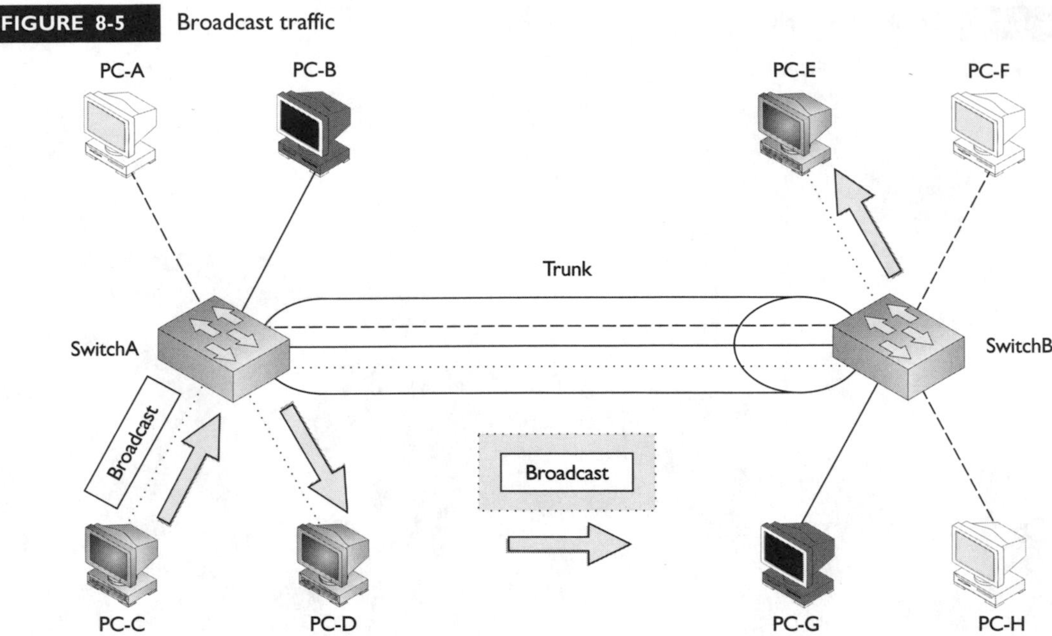

As shown in Figure 8-5, SwitchA tags the broadcast frame, adding the source VLAN to the original Ethernet frame (the broadcast frame is encapsulated). When SwitchB receives the frame, it examines the tag and knows that this is meant only for the VLAN that PC-E belongs to. Of course, since PC-E is connected via an access-link connection, SwitchB first strips off the tagging and then forwards the original Ethernet frame to PC-E. This is necessary because PC-E has a standard NIC and doesn't understand VLAN tagging.

Through this process, both switches maintained the integrity of the broadcast domain. The following two sections cover in more depth two different trunking methods: Cisco's ISL and IEEE's 802.1Q. Other trunking methods are beyond the scope of this book.

ISL

ISL is a proprietary tagging method that Cisco developed to use for Ethernet and Token Ring trunk connections. Cisco no longer sells Token Ring products today, so ISL is used only on Ethernet connections. Most of Cisco's switches and routers that support trunking also support ISL; however, there are some exceptions. For instance, some of the older Cisco Catalyst 4000 switches did not support ISL; they supported only 802.1Q.

For those Cisco devices that do support ISL, the interface must support at least 100Mbps speeds, which includes Fast Ethernet, 10/100 auto-sensing Fast Ethernet, and Gigabit Ethernet. And even though an interface might fit one of these three types, it still must have the appropriate ASIC in the interface to perform tagging. Some interfaces on Cisco switches, even though they might support Fast Ethernet, do not support ISL.

on the job

You need to be careful when ordering your switches and routers: make sure the switch supports the appropriate trunking method with the interfaces that you plan on purchasing.

The top part of Figure 8-6 shows a simple ISL frame. ISL encapsulates the original frame by adding a 26-byte header and a 4-byte CRC trailer. The original Ethernet frame is placed between the header and trailer. Given that a normal Ethernet frame can have a maximum size of 1,518 bytes, adding the header and trailer size gives an ISL frame a maximum size of 1,548 bytes. You can understand, now, why a switch needs to strip off the header and trailer of the ISL frame before forwarding it out an access-link connection. If the switch didn't strip this information off, the standardized Ethernet NIC connected to the access-link connection would assume that this frame was a giant (larger than the allowed maximum frame size) and drop it. On top of this, even if the frame was a valid size, a normal Ethernet NIC wouldn't know how to interpret the header and trailer information.

ISL is a Cisco-proprietary trunking method that adds a 26-byte header and a 4-byte trailer to the original Ethernet frame. Cisco's 1900 switch supports only ISL, while the 2950 supports only 802.1Q.

The 26-byte ISL header contains the fields found in Table 8-3.

FIGURE 8-6 ISL frame examples

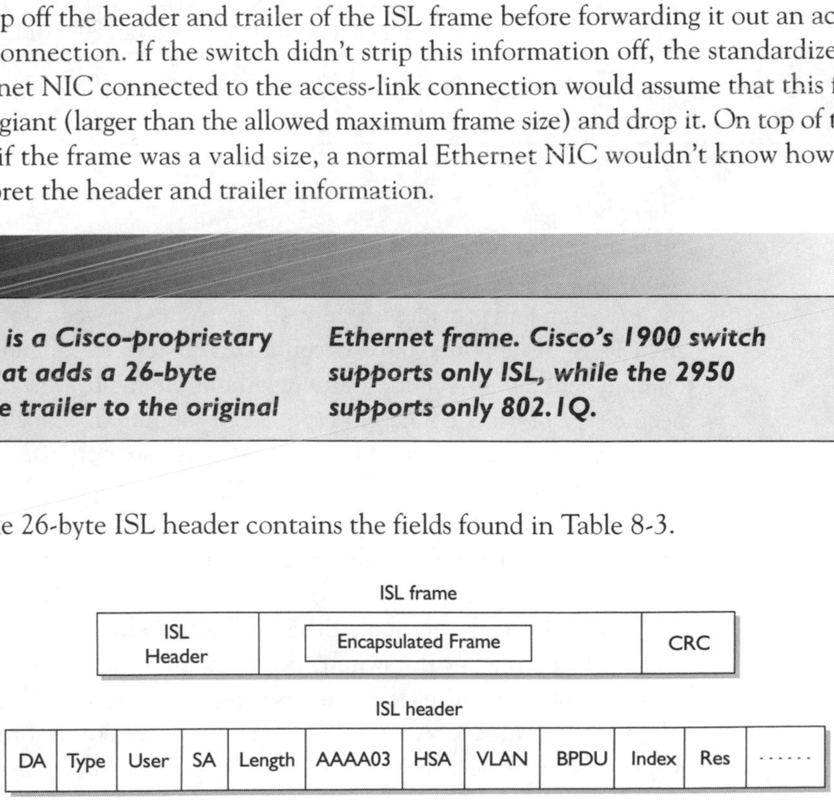

ISL frame

ISL Header	Encapsulated Frame	CRC

ISL header

DA	Type	User	SA	Length	AAAA03	HSA	VLAN	BPDU	Index	Res	......

TABLE 8-3 ISL Header Information

ISL Field	Description
Destination MAC Address	This MAC address is duplicated from the encapsulated frame's destination address.
Type	This is the type of frame that is encapsulated: ATM, Ethernet, FDDI, or Token Ring.
User	This indicates the priority of the frame.
Source MAC address	This MAC address is duplicated from the encapsulated frame's source address.
Length	This indicates the total length of the ISL frame, including the lengths of the ISL header, the trailer, and the encapsulated frame.
AAAA03	This indicates that this is an IEEE 802.2 LLC SNAP header.
VLAN Identifier	This is a 15-bit field, of which only 10 bits are used, allowing for a maximum of 1,024 VLAN numbers to identify VLANs (0–1,023).
BPDU	This indicates whether the encapsulated frame is an STP BPDU or a CDP frame.
Index	This indicates the port number from which the switch is sending the frame.
Reserved	This is a reserved field and is currently not used.

802.1Q

ISL is slowly being replaced in Cisco's products with IEEE's 802.1Q trunking standard. This standard was introduced in the early summer of 1998. One of the advantages that the IEEE standard provides is that it allows trunks between different vendors' devices, whereas ISL is supported only on certain Cisco devices. Therefore, you should be able to implement a multivendor solution without having to worry about whether or not a specific type of trunk connection is or is not supported. The 2950 switches, as well as Cisco's higher-end switches, like the 6000 series, support 802.1Q. Actually, the 2950 switches *only* support 802.1Q trunking—they don't support ISL.

Unlike ISL trunks, where every frame traversing the trunk is tagged, or encapsulated, with an ISL header and a trailer, 802.1Q trunks support two types of frames: tagged and untagged. An untagged frame does not carry any VLAN identification information in it—basically, this is a simple Ethernet frame. The VLAN membership for the frame is determined by the switch's port configuration: if the port is configured in VLAN 1, then the untagged frame belongs to VLAN 1. This VLAN is commonly called a *native* VLAN. A tagged frame contains VLAN information, and only other 802.1Q-aware devices on the trunk will be able to process this frame.

One of the unique aspects of 802.1Q trunking is that you can have *both* tagged and untagged frames on a trunk connection, like that shown in Figure 8-7. In this example, the white VLAN (PC-A, PC-B, PC-E, and PC-F) uses tagged frames on the trunk between SwitchA and SwitchB. Any other device that is connected on this trunk line would have to have 802.1Q trunking enabled to see the tag inside the frame in order to determine the source VLAN of the frame. In this network, a third device is connected to the trunk connection: PC-G. I'm assuming that a hub connects the two switches and the PC together.

PC-G has a normal Ethernet NIC and obviously wouldn't understand the tagging and would drop these frames. However, this presents a problem: PC-G belongs to the dark VLAN, where PC-C and PC-D are also members. Therefore, in order for frames to be forwarded between these three members, the trunk must also support untagged frames, so that PC-G can process them. To set this up, you would configure the switch-to-switch connection as an 802.1Q trunk but set the native VLAN as the dark one, so that frames from this VLAN would go untagged across it and allow PC-G to process them.

One restriction placed on an 802.1Q trunk configuration is that it must be the *same* on both sides. In other words, if the dark VLAN is the native VLAN on one switch, the switch at the other end must have the native VLAN set to the dark VLAN.

FIGURE 8-7 802.1Q trunk and native VLAN

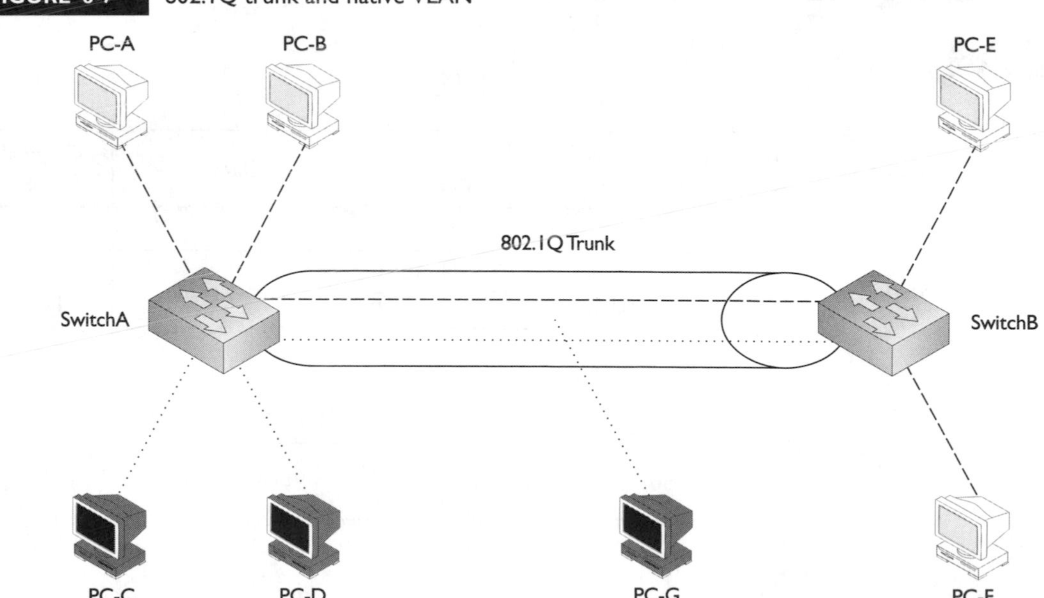

Likewise, if the white VLAN is having its frames tagged on one switch, the other switch must also be tagging the white VLAN frames with 802.1Q information.

Both ISL and 802.1Q tag trunk frames; however, the tagging processes that they use are different. ISL adds a 26-byte header at the beginning of the frame and a 4-byte trailer at the end, with the original, unaltered, frame inserted between these two. The 802.1Q method, however, modifies the original frame. A 4-byte field, called a *tag* field, is *inserted* into the middle of the original Ethernet frame, and the original frame's FCS (checksum) is recomputed on the basis of this change. The first two bytes of the tag are the protocol identifier. For instance, an Ethernet type frame has an identifier value of 0x8100. The next three bits are used to prioritize the frame. The fourth bit indicates if this is an encapsulated Token Ring frame, and the last 12 bits are used for the VLAN identifier.

exam watch

802.1Q is a standardized trunking method that inserts a four-byte field into the original Ethernet frame and recomputes the FCS. The 2950 only supports 802.1Q.

Figure 8-8 shows the process that occurs when converting an Ethernet frame to an 802.1Q tagged frame. As you can see in this figure, step 1 is the normal Ethernet frame. Step 2 inserts the tag and recomputes a new FCS value. Below step 2 is a blow-up of the actual tag field. As you can see in this figure, the tag is inserted after the source and destination addresses.

FIGURE 8-8

802.1Q framing process

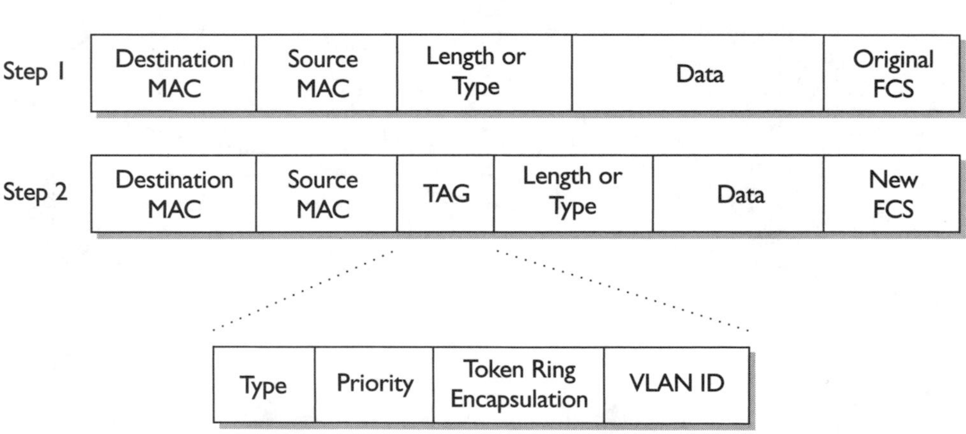

One advantage of using this tagging mechanism is that since you are adding only four bytes, in most instances, your frame size will not exceed 1,518 bytes, and thus you could actually forward 802.1Q frames through the access-link connections of switches, since these switches forward the frame as a normal Ethernet frame.

Per-VLAN STP

One of the issues of STP, as was discussed in the last chapter, is that STP doesn't guarantee an optimized loop-free network. For instance, let's look at the network shown in Figure 8-9. In this example, the network has two VLANs, and the root switch is Switch8. The Xs are ports placed in a blocked state to remove any loops. If you look at this configuration for VLAN 2, it definitely isn't optimized. For instance, VLAN 2 devices on Switch1, if they want to access VLAN 2 devices on Switch4, have to go to Switches2, 3, 6, 9, 8, and then 4. Likewise, VLAN 1 devices on either Switch5 or Switch7 that want to access VLAN 1 devices on Switch4 must forward their traffic first to Switch8 and then to Switch4.

FIGURE 8-9 STP and VLANs

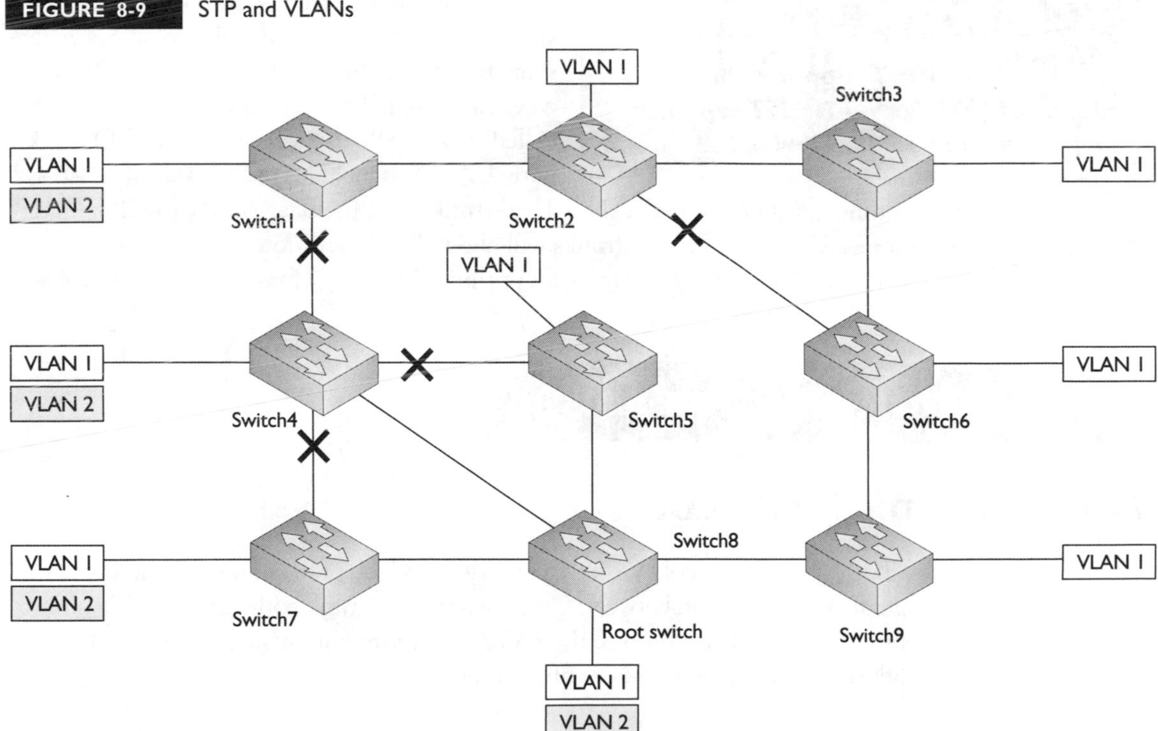

When one instance of STP is running, this is referred to as *Common Spanning Tree (CST)*. Cisco also supports a process called *Per-VLAN Spanning Tree (PVST)*. With PVST, each VLAN has its own instance of STP, with its own root switch, its own set of priorities, and its own set of BPDUs. Given this information, each VLAN will develop its own loop-free topology. Of course, PVST, just like CST, doesn't create an optimized loop-free network; however, you can make STP changes in *each* VLAN to optimize traffic patterns for each separate VLAN. It is highly recommended that you tune STP for each VLAN to optimize it. Another advantage that PVST has is that if STP changes are occurring in one VLAN, they do not affect other instances of STP for other VLANs, making a more stable topology. Given this, it is highly recommended that you implement VTP pruning to prune off VLANs from trunks of switches that are not using those VLANs. Pruning is discussed later in this chapter.

The downside of PVST is that each VLAN has its own instance of STP. There is more overhead involved: more BPDUs and larger STP tables on each switch. Plus, it makes no sense to use PVST unless you tune it for your network, which requires a lot of work and monitoring on your part.

PVST supports one instance of STP per VLAN. CST supports one instance of STP for all VLANs.

CST is supported on 802.1Q trunks, and PVST is supported on ISL trunks. So what happens if you have a network with mixed trunk types, where some trunks are ISL and some are 802.1Q? In this case, Cisco supports an enhanced version of PVST called PVST+. With PVST+, the 802.1Q trunk's native VLAN is included in PVST for that VLAN. For instance, if the native VLAN is 1, all trunks that include VLAN 1 will be in one instance of STP. All other ISL trunks will allow PVST. The downside of this approach is that it becomes difficult to create an optimized topology for the native VLAN.

CERTIFICATION OBJECTIVE 8.03

VLAN Trunk Protocol

The VLAN Trunk Protocol (VTP) is a proprietary Cisco protocol used to share VLAN configuration information between Cisco switches on trunk connections. VTP allows switches to share and synchronize their VLAN information, which ensures that your network has a consistent VLAN configuration.

For instance, let's assume that you have a network with two switches and you need to add a new VLAN. This could easily be accomplished by adding the VLAN manually on both switches. However, this process becomes more difficult and tedious if you have 30 switches. In this situation, you might make a mistake in configuring the new VLAN on one of the switches, giving it the wrong VLAN identifier, or you might forget to add the new VLAN to one of the 30 switches. VTP can take care of this issue. With VTP, you can add the VLAN on one switch and have this switch propagate this information via VTP messages to all of the other switches in your layer-2 network, causing them to add the new VLAN also.

This is also true if you modify a VLAN's configuration or delete a VLAN—VTP can verify that your VLAN configuration is consistent across all of your switches. VTP can even perform consistency checks with your VLANs, to make sure that all of the VLANs are configured identically. For instance, some of these components include the VLAN number, name, and type. So if you have a VLAN number of 1 and a name of "admin" on one switch, but a name of "administrator" on a second switch for this VLAN, VTP can check for and fix these kinds of configuration mismatches.

VTP messages will propagate *only* across *trunk* connections. Therefore, you will need to set up trunking between your switches in order to share VLAN information via VTP. VTP messages are propagated as layer-2 multicast frames. Therefore, if a router separates two of your switches, the router will *not* forward the VTP messages from one of its interfaces to another.

In order for VTP to function correctly, you must associate your switch with a VTP domain. A *domain* is a group of switches that have the same VLAN information applied to them. Basically, a VTP domain is similar to an autonomous system, which some routing protocols use (autonomous systems and routing protocols are discussed in Chapters 9, 10, and 11). A switch can belong to only a single domain. Domains are given names, and when they generate VTP messages, they include the domain in the message. An incoming switch will not incorporate the VLAN changes in this message if the domain name in the message doesn't match the domain name configured on the switch.

exam watch

VTP is a Cisco-proprietary protocol that traverses trunks. It is used to create a consistent VLAN configuration across all switches in the same domain.

In other words, a switch in one domain will ignore VTP messages from switches in other domains. This is almost like how VLANs contain broadcasts—a broadcast in one domain isn't propagated to other broadcast domains. The following sections cover the components and messages that VTP uses, as well as some of the advantages that it provides, such as pruning.

VTP Modes

When you are setting up VTP, you have three different modes to choose from for your switch's configuration:

- Client
- Server
- Transparent

Table 8-4 shows the differences between these VTP modes. A switch configured in either VTP server or transparent mode can add, modify, and delete VLANs. The main difference between these modes is that the configuration changes made to a transparent switch affect only *that* switch, and no other switch in the network. A VTP server switch, however, will make the change and then propagate a VTP message concerning the change on all of its trunk ports. If a server switch receives a VTP message, it will incorporate the update and forward the message out its remaining trunk ports. A transparent switch, on the other hand, ignores VTP messages—it will accept them on trunk ports and forward them out its remaining trunk ports, but it will not incorporate the changes in the VTP message in its local configuration. In this sense, transparent switches are like little islands, where changes on a transparent switch affect no one else but the transparent switch, and changes on other switches do not affect other transparent switches.

A VTP client switch cannot make changes to its VLAN configuration itself—it requires a server switch to tell it about the VLAN changes. When a client switch receives a VTP message from a server switch, it incorporates the changes and then floods the VTP message out its remaining trunk ports. An important point to make is that a client switch does not store its VLAN configuration information in NVRAM. Instead, it learns this from a server switch every time it boots up.

TABLE 8-4 Description of VTP Modes

	Server	Client	Transparent
Can add, modify, and delete VLANs	Yes	No	Yes
Can generate VTP messages	Yes	No	No
Can propagate VTP messages	Yes	Yes	Yes
Can accept changes in a VTP message	Yes	Yes	No
Default VTP mode	Yes	No	No

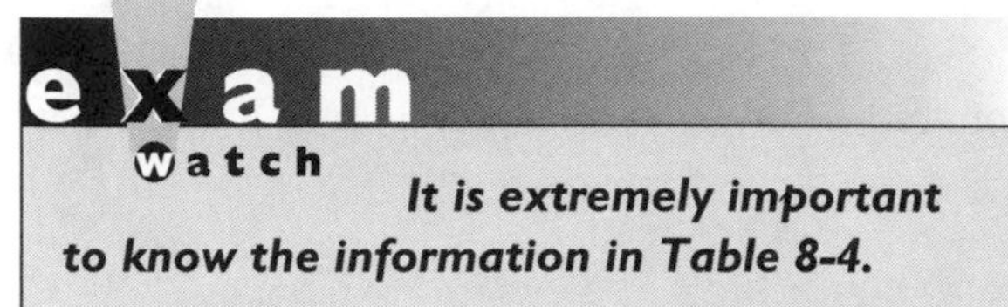

It is extremely important to know the information in Table 8-4.

Normally, you would set up one switch in server mode, and all other switches in client mode. Then, you could control who could make changes on the server switch. However, one thing you need to be aware of is that if you make a VLAN configuration mistake on the server switch, this mistake is *automatically propagated* to all the client switches in your network. Imagine that you accidentally deleted a VLAN on your server switch, and this VLAN had 500 devices in it. When this occurs, all the switches remove the VLAN from their configuration. For those devices that used to belong to that VLAN, assuming that you used static VLANs, these devices are placed into VLAN 1.

You would think that to fix this problem, you would just have to add the VLAN back on the server switch, which would then cause all of the client switches to put everything back the way it was. Unfortunately, VTP does not tell switches which VLAN a particular device resides in; it only tells switches what VLANs are out there, providing, for instance, their names, numbers, and types. So in this example, you would have to go around and reconfigure your ports to put them back into the correct VLAN. In this instance, if you were using dynamic VLANs, you would only have to add the VLAN back on the server switch; for static VLANs, you would have your work cut out for you.

Given this problem, some administrators don't like to use VTP server and client modes; instead, they prefer to configure all of their switches in transparent mode. The problem with transparent mode is that it isn't very scalable; if you need to add a VLAN to your network and your network has 20 switches, you would have to manually add the VLAN to each individual switch, which is a time-consuming process. Of course, the advantage of this approach is that if you make a mistake on a transparent switch, the problem is *not* propagated to other switches.

You could also set up all of your switches in server mode. Actually, some features, such as VTP pruning, require all your switches to be configured in VTP server mode. As you can see, you have a wide range of VTP configuration options. You could even mix and match these options. Set up a couple of server switches, and have the remaining switches as clients, or set your switches initially as servers and clients, add all your VLANs on the server switch, allow the clients to acquire this information, and then change all the switches to transparent mode. This process allows you to easily populate your switches' configurations with a consistent VLAN configuration during the setup process. An important item to point out is that if you don't specify the VTP mode for your switch, it will default to *server*.

VTP Messages

If you use a client/server configuration for VTP, there are three types of VTP messages that these switches can generate:

- Advertisement request
- Subset advertisement
- Summary advertisement

An *advertisement request* message is a VTP message a client generates. If you recall, clients don't store VLAN configuration information in NVRAM—instead, they learn this every time that they are booted up. In this instance, when the switch boots up, it generates an advertisement request VTP message, which a server will respond to.

When the server responds to a client's request, it generates a *subset advertisement*. A subset advertisement contains detailed VLAN configuration information, including the VLAN numbers, names, types, and other information. The client will then configure itself appropriately.

A *summary advertisement* is also generated by a switch in VTP server mode. Summary advertisements are generated every five minutes by default (300 seconds), or when a configuration change takes place on the server switch. Unlike a subset advertisement, a summary advertisement contains only summarized VLAN information.

When a server switch generates a VTP advertisement, it can include the following information:

- The number and name of the VLAN
- The MTU size used by the VLAN
- The frame format used by the VLAN
- The SAID value for the VLAN (needed if it is an 802.10 VLAN)
- The configuration revision number
- The name of the VTP domain

The preceding list includes a couple of important items that I want to spend more time discussing. Switches in either server or client mode will process VTP messages if they are in the same VTP domain; however, there are some restrictions placed on whether the switch should incorporate the changes or not. For instance, one function of the VTP summary advertisements is to ensure that all of the switches have the most current changes. If you didn't make a change on a server switch in the five-minute update interval, when the countdown timer expires, the server switch still sends out a summary advertisement, with the same exact summary information. It makes no sense to have other switches, which have the most up-to-date information, incorporate the same information in their configuration.

To make this process more efficient, the *configuration revision number* is used to keep track of what server switch has the most recent changes. Initially this number is set to 0. If you make a change on a server switch, it increments its revision number and advertises this to the other switches across its trunk links. When a client or server switch receives this information, it compares the revision number in the message to the last message it had received (this is stored in its RAM). If the newly arrived message has a higher number, then this server switch must have made changes. If the necessary information isn't in the VTP summary advertisement, all client and server switches will generate an advertisement request and the server will respond with the details in a subset advertisement.

If a server switch receives a VTP message from another server, and the advertising server has a lower revision number, the receiving server switch will respond to the advertising server with a VTP message with its current configuration revision number. This will tell the advertising server switch that it doesn't have the most up-to-date VLAN information and should request it from the server that does. In this sense, the revision number used in a VTP message is somewhat similar to the sequence number used in TCP. Also, remember that transparent switches are not processing these VTP advertisements—they only passively forward these messages to other switches.

exam watch

VTP servers generate VTP multicasts every five minutes. There are three types of VTP messages. Clients generate advertisement requests, and servers generate subset and summary advertisements. The configuration version number is used to determine which server has the most up-to-date VLAN information: the highest number is the most current.

VTP Pruning

VTP pruning is a Cisco VTP feature that allows your switches to dynamically delete or add VLANs to a trunk, creating a more efficient switching network. By default, all VLANs are associated with a trunk connection. This means that if a device in *any* VLAN generates a broadcast or multicast, or an unknown unicast, the switch will flood this frame out all ports associated with the source VLAN port, including trunks. In many situations, this flooding is necessary, especially if the VLAN spans multiple switches. However, it doesn't make sense to flood a frame to a neighboring switch if that switch doesn't have any active ports in the source VLAN.

Let's take a look at a simple example by examining Figure 8-10. In this example, VTP pruning is not enabled. PC-A, PC-B, PC-E, and PC-F are in the same VLAN. If PC-A generates a broadcast, SwitchA will forward this to the access link that PC-B is connected to as well as the trunk (since a trunk is a member of all VLANs, by default). This makes sense, since PC-E and PC-F, connected to SwitchB, are in the same VLAN.

Figure 8-10 shows a second VLAN with two members: PC-C and PC-D. If PC-C generates a local broadcast, SwitchA will obviously send to this to PC-D's port. What doesn't make sense is that SwitchA will flood this broadcast out its trunk port to SwitchB, considering that there are no devices on SwitchB that are in this VLAN. This is an example of wasting bandwidth and resources. A single broadcast isn't a big problem; however, imagine this were a video multicast stream at 10Mbps coming from PC-A. This network might experience serious throughput problems on the trunk, since a switch treats a multicast just like a broadcast—it floods it out all ports associated with the source port's VLAN.

FIGURE 8-10 Without VTP pruning

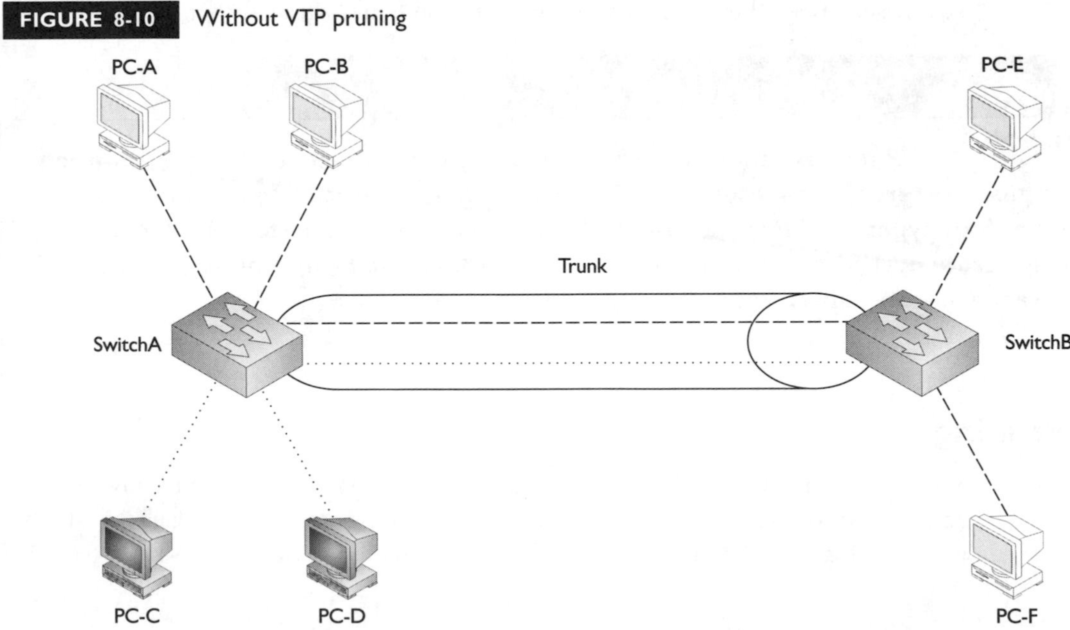

There are actually two methods you could use to fix this problem: static and dynamic VLAN pruning. With a static configuration, you would manually prune the inactive VLAN off of the trunk on both switches, as shown in Figure 8-11. Notice that in this figure, the dark VLAN has been pruned from the trunk. The problem with manual pruning is that if you add a dark VLAN member to SwitchB, you will have to log into both switches and manually add the pruned VLAN to the trunk. This can become very confusing in a multiswitched network with multiple VLANs, where every VLAN is not necessarily active on every switch. You could easily accidentally prune a VLAN from a trunk that shouldn't have been pruned, thus creating connectivity problems.

VTP pruning is a feature that allows the switches to share additional VLAN information and that allows them to dynamically prune inactive VLANs from trunk connections. In this instance, the switches share what VLANs are active. For example, SwitchA tells SwitchB that it has two active VLANs (the white one and the dark one). SwitchB, on the other hand, has only one active VLAN, and it shares this fact with SwitchA. Given the shared information, both SwitchA and SwitchB realize that the dark VLAN is inactive across their trunk connection and therefore should be dynamically removed from the trunk's configuration.

The nice thing about this feature is that if you happen to activate the dark VLAN on SwitchB by connecting a device to a port on the switch and assigning that port

FIGURE 8-11 VLAN pruning

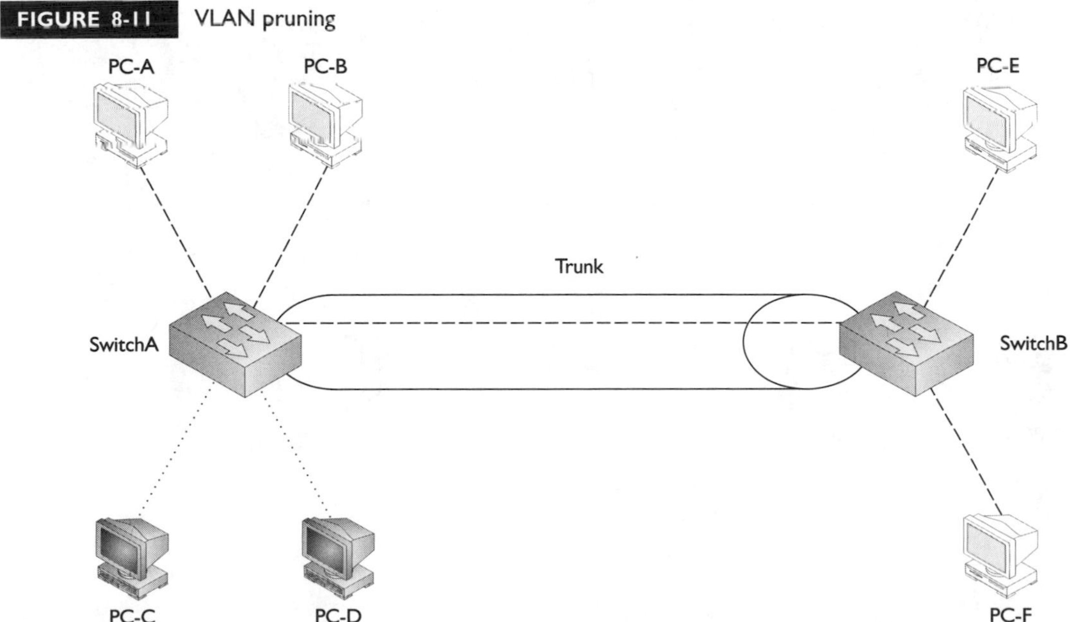

to the dark VLAN, SwitchB will notify SwitchA about the newly active VLAN and both switches will dynamically add the VLAN back to the trunk's configuration. This will allow PC-C, PC-D, and the new device to send frames to each other, as is shown in Figure 8-12.

exam watch

VTP pruning is used on trunk connections to dynamically remove VLANs not active between the two switches. It requires all of the switches to be in server mode.

About the only drawback of VTP pruning is that it requires all switches in the VTP domain to be configured in *server* mode. Remember that switches in server mode can make VLAN changes as well as accept VLAN changes, which can create havoc if multiple administrators are making VLAN changes simultaneously on multiple server switches.

FIGURE 8-12 VTP pruning activating a VLAN on a trunk

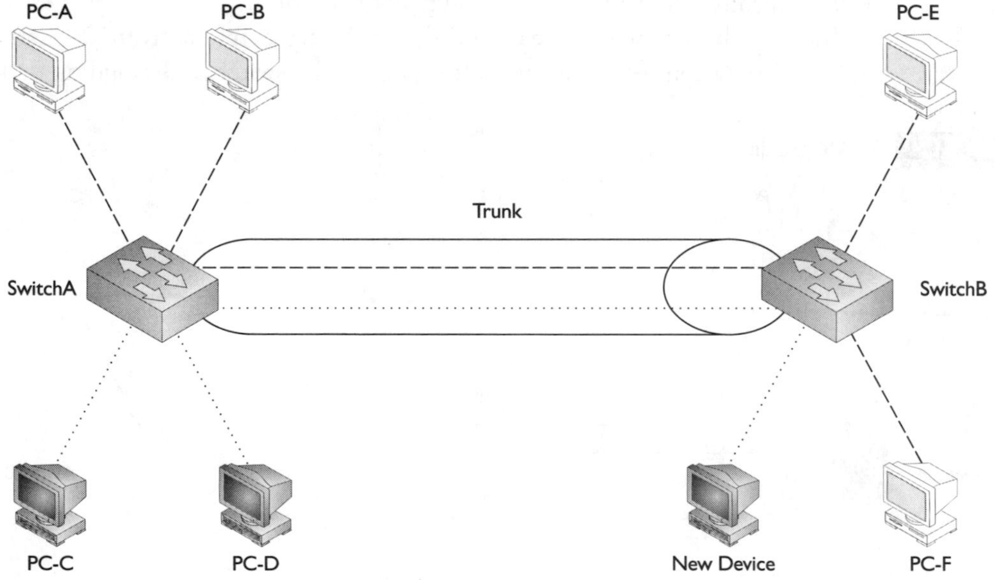

CERTIFICATION OBJECTIVE 8.04

1900 and 2950 VLAN Configuration

Unlike Cisco routers, every switch that Cisco sells comes with a default configuration. For instance, there are already some preconfigured VLANs on the switch, including VLAN 1. During the configuration, all VLAN commands refer to the VLAN number, even though you can configure an optional name for the VLAN. Every port on your switch will be associated with VLAN 1. And all communications from the switch itself—VTP messages, CDP multicasts, and other traffic the switch originates—occur in VLAN 1. With the 1900, this is even true of its IP traffic. If you recall from Chapter 5, the 2950's IP configuration is based on the VLAN interface for which you configure your IP address.

VLAN 1 is sometimes called the *management VLAN*, even though you can use a different VLAN. It is a common practice to put all of your management devices—switches, manageable hubs, and management stations—in their own VLAN. If you decide to put your switch in a different VLAN, it is recommended to change this configuration on all your management devices so that you can more easily secure them, since other VLANs would have to go through a layer-3 device to access them; and on this layer-3 device, you can set up access control lists to filter unwanted traffic.

It's important that all your switches are in the same VLAN, since many of the switches' management protocols, such as CDP, VTP, and the Dynamic Trunk Protocol (DTP), which is discussed later in this chapter, occur within the switch's management VLAN. If one switch had its management VLAN set to 1 and another connected switch had it set to 2, the two switches would lose a lot of functionality.

Configuring VTP

One of the very first VLAN configuration tasks you'll perform on your switch is to set up VTP. Table 8-5 shows the default VTP configuration of the 1900 and 2950 switches. The following sections cover the configuration of VTP on the two switches.

exam watch

Memorize the VTP defaults listed in Table 8-5.

TABLE 8-5 VTP Default Configuration Values

VTP Component	1900	2950
Domain name	None	None
Mode	Server	Server
Password	None	None
Traps	Enabled	Disabled
Pruning	Enabled	Disabled

1900 VTP Configuration

The VTP configuration on your 1900 switch is done from *Global Configuration* mode. Here are the commands to use in order to set up VTP:

```
1900(config)# vtp domain VTP_domain_name
1900(config)# vtp server|client|transparent
1900(config)# vtp password VTP_password
1900(config)# vtp pruning enable|disable
1900(config)# vtp trap enable
```

The first **vtp** command defines the domain name for your switch. Remember that in order for switches to share VTP information, they must be in the same domain. Messages received from other domains are ignored.

The rest of the commands in the configuration are optional. The second **vtp** command defines the VTP mode of the switch. If you don't configure this command, the default mode is **server**. You can configure a VTP MD5 password for your switches, which must match the password configured on every switch in the domain. Switches will use this password to verify VTP messages from other switches; if the hashed values don't match, the switches ignore the VTP messages.

Remember the basic configuration commands for configuring VTP on a 1900.

On the 1900, pruning is enabled by default, but you can disable, or enable, it with the **vtp pruning** command. It is important to point out that if pruning is enabled on a server switch, the server switch will propagate this to all other switches in the domain. The VTP SNMP traps feature is also enabled by default and can be toggled off or on with the **vtp trap** command.

Once you have configured VTP, you can verify your configuration with the **show vtp** command. Here's an example:

```
1900# show vtp
VTP version: 1
```

```
Configuration revision: 1
Maximum VLANs supported locally: 1005
Number of existing VLANs: 5
VTP domain name          : dealgroup
VTP password             : BullMastiff
VTP operating mode       : Server
VTP pruning mode         : Enabled
VTP traps generation     : Enabled
Configuration last modified by: 0.0.0.0 at 00-00-0000 00:00:00
```

In this example, you can see that the domain name is *dealgroup* and the VTP password is *BullMastiff*. Remember that all the switches in the same domain need these two things to be configured identically.

8.01. The CD contains a multimedia demonstration of configuring VTP on the 1900.

2950 VTP Configuration

Depending on your IOS version, the 2950 can be configured in one of two ways. Interestingly enough, the old way is *not* done from *Global Configuration* mode. Instead, it is done from *Privilege EXEC* mode. This is one of the few instances that a configuration command is performed at this mode. To configure VTP on your 2950 configuration with the old method, use the following commands:

```
2950# vlan database
2950(vlan)# vtp domain VTP_domain_name
2950(vlan)# vtp server|client|transparent
2950(vlan)# vtp password VTP_password
2950(vlan)# vtp pruning
2950(vlan)# abort
-or-
2950(vlan)# exit
2950# configure terminal
2950(config}# snmp-server enable traps vtp
```

At *Privilege EXEC* mode, use the **vlan database** command to access your VLAN and VTP configuration. Within this mode, the **vtp** commands are basically

Remember that you must perform the 2950 configuration from** Privilege EXEC **mode with the** `vlan database` **command. The rest of the commands are almost the same as the 1900.

the same as on the 1900. The exception is the configuration of SNMP VTP traps, which is done from *Global Configuration* mode with the **snmp-server** command. There are two commands that affect whether or not your changes are saved while in the VLAN database. If you enter the **abort** command, you are returned to *Privilege EXEC* mode and your changes are *not* saved; if you use **exit**, your changes are saved.

If you are running IOS 12.1(11)EA1 or later, you can perform your entire configuration from *Global Configuration* mode:

```
2950(config)# vtp domain VTP_domain_name
2950(config)# vtp mode server|client|transparent
2950(config)# vtp password VTP_password
2950(config)# vtp pruning
```

Once you are done configuring VTP (old or new), use this command to check your configuration:

```
2950# show vtp status
VTP Version : 1
Configuration Revision : 17
Maximum VLANs supported locally : 250
Number of existing VLANs : 7
VTP Operating Mode : Server
VTP Domain Name : dealgroup
VTP Pruning Mode : Enabled
VTP V2 Mode : Disabled
VTP Traps Generation : Disabled
MD5 digest : 0x95 0xAB 0x29 0x44 0x32 0xA1 0x2C 0x31
Configuration last modified by 0.0.0.0 at 3-1-03 15:18:37
Local updater ID is 192.168.1.4 on interface Vl1
   (lowest numbered VLAN interface found)
```

In this example, there have been 17 configuration changes (examine the "`Configuration Revision`" field). The switch is operating in server mode in the *dealgroup* domain. The following command displays VTP statistics concerning VTP messages sent and received:

```
2950 # show vtp counters
VTP statistics:
  Summary advertisements received : 12
  Subset advertisements received : 0
  Request advertisements received : 0
  Summary advertisements transmitted : 7
```

```
  Subset advertisements transmitted : 0
  Request advertisements transmitted : 0
  Number of config revision errors : 0
  Number of config digest errors : 0
  Number of V1 summary errors : 0
<--output omitted-->
```

In this example, you can see that the switch has sent and received VTP summary advertisements.

8.02. The CD contains a multimedia demonstration of configuring VTP on the 2950.

Configuring Trunks

This section covers the setup of trunk connections on your switches. There are four types of trunk connections (ISL, 802.1Q, LANE, and 802.10); however, the 1900 switch supports only ISL, and the 2950 supports only 802.1Q. Therefore, you cannot set up a trunk connection between a 1900 and 2950.

Dynamic Trunk Protocol (DTP)

Before I begin discussing how to configure an interface to be a trunk, you first need to be aware of a Cisco proprietary trunking protocol that is used on trunk connections. The Dynamic Trunk Protocol (DTP) is used to dynamically form and verify a trunk connection between two Cisco switches. DTP is the enhanced version of Dynamic ISL (DISL). DISL was used when 802.1Q wasn't available on Cisco switches. With the incorporation of 802.1Q in Cisco's switches, DTP was enhanced to include 802.1Q in its trunking negotiation.

DTP supports five trunking modes, shown in Table 8-6.

TABLE 8-6 DTP Modes and Operation

DTP Mode	Generate DTP Messages	Frame Tagging
On or Trunk	Yes	Yes
Desirable	Yes	No
Auto-Negotiate	No	No
Off	No	No
No-Negotiate	No	Yes

If the trunk mode is set to *on* or *trunk* (2950) for an interface, this causes the interface to generate DTP messages on the interface as well as to tag frames on the interface, based on the trunk type (802.1Q or ISL). When set to on, the trunk interface always assumes the connection is a trunk, even if the remote end does not support trunking.

If the trunk mode is set to *desirable*, the interface will generate DTP messages on the interface, but it makes the assumption that the other side is not trunk-capable and will wait for a DTP message from the remote side. In this state, the interface starts as an access-link connection. If the remote side sends a DTP message, and this message indicates that trunking is compatible between the two switches, a trunk will be formed, and the switch will start tagging frames on the interface. If the other side does not support trunking, the interface will remain as an access-link connection.

If the trunk mode is set to *auto-negotiate*, the interface passively listens for DTP messages from the remote side and leaves the interface as an access-link connection. If the interface receives a DTP message, and the message matches trunking capabilities of the interface, then the interface will change from an access-link connection to a trunk connection and start tagging frames. This is the default DTP mode for an interface that is trunk-capable.

If an interface is set to no-negotiate, the interface is set as a trunk connection and will automatically tag frames with VLAN information; however, the interface will not generate DTP messages: DTP is disabled. This mode is typically used when connecting trunk connections to non-Cisco devices that don't understand Cisco's proprietary trunking protocol and thus won't understand the contents of these messages.

If an interface is set to *off*, the interface is configured as an access link. No DTP messages are generated in this mode, nor are frames tagged.

Table 8-7 shows when switch connections will form a trunk. In this table, one side needs to be configured as either on or desirable and the other side as on, desirable, or auto, or both switches need to be configured as no-negotiate. Note that if you use the no-negotiate mode, trunking is formed, but DTP is not used, whereas if you use on,

TABLE 8-7 Forming Trunks

Your Switch	Remote Switch
On	On, Desirable, Auto
Desirable	On, Desirable, Auto
Auto	On, Desirable
No-Negotiate	No-Negotiate

Know the material in Tables 8-6 and 8-7 for the exam.

desirable, or auto, DTP is used. One advantage that DTP has over no-negotiate is that DTP checks for the trunk's characteristics: if they don't match on the two sides (for instance, as to the type of trunk), then the trunk will not come up and the interfaces will remain as an access-link connection. With no-negotiate, if the trunking characteristics don't match on the two sides, there is a possibility that the trunk connection will fail.

1900 Trunk Configuration

Setting up a trunk connection on a 1900 switch is very easy, where the trunking configuration is done within an interface. Only the two 100BaseTX/FX interfaces (`fa0/26` or `fa0/27`) support trunking—all of the 10BaseT and AUI ports can only be access-link connections. Use this configuration to set up trunking:

```
1900(config)# interface fastethernet 0/port_#
1900(config-if)# trunk on|off|desirable|auto
```

Remember that the 1900 supports only ISL trunking. Once you are in the interface, you need to specify your trunking type.

To verify that your interface is trunking, use the **`show trunk A|B`** command: Interface `A` is `fastethernet 0/26` and `B` is `fastethernet 0/27`. Here's an example of this command:

```
1900# show trunk A
DISL state: autoTrunking    status: On
Encapsulation type: ISL
```

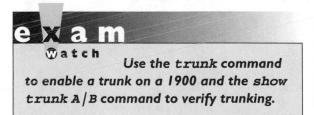

Use the `trunk` command to enable a trunk on a 1900 and the `show trunk A|B` command to verify trunking.

In this example, `fa 0/26`'s DTP state is set to *auto*, and the interface is trunking (`status` is on). The default mode is auto. Because the 1900 supports only ISL, the output from the preceding command says *DISL* instead of *DTP*. DTP-capable switches understand DISL messages.

8.03. The CD contains a multimedia demonstration of configuring trunking on the 1900.

2950 Trunk Configuration

Setting up a trunk on a 2950 is similar to doing so on a 1900 switch, though the command is different:

```
2950(config)# interface type 0/port_#
2950(config-if)# switchport mode trunk|dynamic desirable|
                       dynamic auto|nonegotiate
2950(config-if)# switchport trunk native vlan VLAN_#
```

exam watch *Use the* ***switchport mode*** *command to enable trunking on the 2950 and the* ***show interfaces switchport | trunk*** *command to verify trunking.*

Unlike on a 1900 switch, all ports on a 2950 switch support trunking. Remember that the 2950 supports only 802.1Q trunking. If you want a trunk to be in an *on* state, use the **trunk** parameter. For a desirable DTP state, use **dynamic desirable**, and for an auto-negotiate state, use **dynamic auto**. The default mode is auto-negotiate. If you don't want to use DTP but still want to perform trunking, use the **nonegotiate** parameter. For 802.1Q trunks, the native VLAN is VLAN 1. You can change this with the **switchport trunk native vlan** command.

After you have configured your trunk connection, you can use this command to verify it:

```
2950# show interfaces type 0/port_# switchport|trunk
```

Here's an example using the **switchport** parameter:

```
2950# show interface fastEthernet0/1 switchport
Name: Fa0/1
Switchport: Enabled
Administrative mode: trunk
Operational Mode: trunk
Administrative Trunking Encapsulation: dot1q
Operational Trunking Encapsulation: dot1q
Negotiation of Trunking: Disabled
Access Mode VLAN: 0 ((Inactive))
Trunking Native Mode VLAN: 1 (default)
Trunking VLANs Enabled: ALL
Trunking VLANs Active: 1,2
Pruning VLANs Enabled: 2-1001
Priority for untagged frames: 0
```

```
Override vlan tag priority: FALSE
Voice VLAN: none
```

In this example, `FA0/1`'s trunking mode is set to trunk (on), with the native VLAN set to 1. Here's an example of using the **`trunk`** parameter:

```
2950# show interfaces trunk
Port Mode Encapsulation Status Native vlan
Fa0/1 on 802.1q trunking 1
Port Vlans allowed on trunk
Fa0/1 1-4094
Port Vlans allowed and active in management domain
Fa0/1 1-2
Port Vlans in spanning tree forwarding state and not pruned
Fa0/1 1-2
```

In this example, there is one interface that is trunking, `fa0/1`, with a native VLAN of 1.

8.04. The CD contains a multimedia demonstration of configuring trunking on the 2950.

EXERCISE 8-1

Configuring Trunks on Your Switches

These last few sections dealt with the setting up trunks on the 1900 and 2950 switches. You'll perform this lab using Boson's NetSim simulator. This exercise has you set up a trunk link between the two 2950 switches (2950-1 and 2950-2). You can find a picture of the network diagram for Boson's NetSim simulator in the Introduction of this book. After starting up the simulator, click the *LabNavigator* button. Next, double-click *Exercise 8-1* and click the *Load Lab* button. This will load the lab configuration based on Chapter 5's and 7's exercises.

1. On the 2950-1 switch, set the trunk mode to *on* for the connection between the two 2950 switches and examine the status. Does the trunk come up?

   At the top of the simulator in the menu bar, click the *eSwitches* icon and choose *2950-1*. Access *Configuration* mode: **`enable`** and **`configure terminal`**. Go into the interface: **`interface fa0/2`**. Set the trunk mode to *trunk*: **`switchport mode trunk`**. Exit *Configuration* mode: **`end`**. Use the **`show interfaces trunk`** command to verify the status. You might have to wait a few seconds, but the trunk should come up. If one side is set to on, or desirable, and the other is set to on, desirable, or auto (default), then the trunk should come up.

2. On the 2950-2 switch, set the trunk mode to *on* for the connection between the two 2950 switches and verify the trunking status of the interface.

   At the top of the simulator in the menu bar, click the *eSwitches* icon and choose *2950-2*. Access *Configuration* mode: **`enable`** and **`configure terminal`**. Go into the interface: **`interface fa0/2.`** Set the trunk mode to trunk: **`switchport mode trunk`**. Exit *Configuration* mode: **`end`**. Use the **`show interfaces trunk`** command to verify the status.

Now you should be more comfortable with setting up trunks on your switches. In the next section, you will be presented with setting up VLANs and associating interfaces to your VLANs.

Creating VLANs

This section covers how you can create VLANs on your switches and then assign access-link connections (interfaces) to your newly created VLANs. As you will see, the configurations on the 1900 and 2950 are slightly different.

Here are some guidelines to remember when creating VLANs:

- The number of VLANs you can create is dependent on the switch model and IOS software.
- There are some preconfigured VLANs on every switch, including VLAN 1 and 1,002–1,005.
- To add or delete VLANs, your switch must be in either VTP server or transparent mode.
- VLAN names can be changed—VLAN numbers can't: you must delete a VLAN and re-add in order to renumber it.
- All interfaces, by default, belong to VLAN 1.
- CDP, DTP, and VTP advertisements are sent in VLAN 1, by default.
- Cisco supports Per-VLAN STP for its VLANs across ISL trunks.
- Before deleting VLANs, reassign any ports from the current VLAN to another; if you don't, any ports from the deleted VLAN will be placed in VLAN 1.

The following two sections cover the configuration of the 1900 and 2950 switches.

1900 VLAN Configuration

The first VLAN configuration task on a 1900 switch is to create your VLANs:

```
1900(config)# vlan VLAN_# [name VLAN_name]
```

VLAN numbers can range 1–1000; however, only 64 VLANs can be active on the 1900 at a time. When creating your VLANs, you can give them an optional name. If you omit this, it defaults to the name "vlan" with the VLAN number concatenated to it. All VLAN configuration tasks refer to the VLAN by its number, not its name—the name is used more for descriptive purposes. Remember that if you are using VTP servers and clients, you only need to create the VLAN on a server switch, which will propagate this to all other server and client switches in the VTP domain.

Once you have created your VLANs, you need to assign your interfaces to your VLANs:

```
1900(config)# interface type 0/port_#
1900(config-if)# vlan-membership static VLAN_#
```

The preceding command shows you how to statically assign an interface to a VLAN. (The configuration of dynamic VLANs is beyond the scope of this book.) Once you have configured your VLANs and assigned interfaces to them, you can use the **show vlan** and **show vlan-membership** commands to verify your configuration. Here's an example of the first command:

```
1900# show vlan
VLAN Name                             Status    Ports
---- --------------------------------- --------- -----------------------
1    default                          active    1-13,21-27
2    VLAN0002                         active    14-17
3    VLAN0003                         active    18-20
<--output omitted-->
VLAN Type SAID   MTU  Parent RingNo BridgeNo Stp  Tran1 Tran2
---- ---- ------ ---- ------ ------ -------- ---- ----- -----
1    enet 100001 1500 0       0      0        IEEE 0     0
2    enet 100002 1500 0       0      0        IEEE 0     0
<--output omitted-->
```

In the preceding output, there are three VLANS—1, 2, and 3—with e0/1-13, e0/21-25, and fa0/26-27 belonging to VLAN 1, e0/14-17 belonging to

VLAN 2, and e0/18-20 belonging to VLAN 3. With the preceding command, you are shown more details concerning each VLAN at the bottom of the display, including its type and frame size ("MTU"). The default type for a VLAN when you create it is Ethernet ("enet"), and the default MTU size for frames is 1,500 bytes. You can shorten the preceding display by including the VLAN number after the command.

Here's an example of the **show vlan-membership** command:

```
1900#  show vlan-membership
Port  VLAN  Membership Type     Port  VLAN  Membership Type

----------------------------------------------------------------
  1     1        Static           14      2         Static
  2     1        Static           15      2         Static
  3     1        Static           16      2         Static
  4     1        Static           17      2         Static
  5     1        Static           18      3         Static
  6     1        Static           19      3         Static
  7     1        Static           20      3         Static
  8     1        Static           21      1         Static
  9     1        Static           22      1         Static
  10    1        Static           23      1         Static
  11    1        Static           24      1         Static
  12    1        Static           AUI     1         Static
  13    1        Static
  A     1        Static
  B     1        Static
```

In this example, you can see each port, the VLAN assigned to the port, and how it was assigned ("Static").

To examine STP information for a VLAN, use this command:

```
1900# show spantree [VLAN_#]
```

Here's an example of the output of this command:

```
1900# show spantree 1
VLAN1 is executing the IEEE compatible Spanning Tree protocol
  Bridge Identifier priority 32768, address 00e0.1e22.1111
  Configured hello time 2, max age 20, forward delay 15
  Current root priority 32768, address 00e0.4522.aaaa
  Root port is Ethernet 0/4, cost of root path is 130
  Topology change flag not set, detected flag not set
Topology changes 12, last topology change occurred
      0d00h04m17s ago
```

```
  Times:  hold 1, topology change 35
          hello 2, max age 20, forward delay 15
  Timers: hello 0, topology change 0, notification 0
Port Ethernet 0/1 of VLAN1 is down
   Port path cost 10, Port priority 128
   Designated root priority 32768, address 00e0.4522.aaaa
   Designated bridge priority 32768, address 00e0.1e22.1111
   Designated port is Ethernet 0/1, path cost 130
   Timers: message age 0, forward delay 14, hold 0
<--output omitted-->
```

In this example, this switch (00e0.1e22.1111) is not the root (00e0.4522.aaaa). Since the switch has booted, it has seen 12 STP topology changes. You will want to keep track of the number of topology changes to ensure that you don't have any STP problems. There is at least one port in the VLAN—`e0/1`—that is a member of VLAN 1.

8.05. The CD contains a multimedia demonstration of configuring VLANs on the 1900.

Use the `vlan` command to create VLANs. Use the `vlan-membership static` command to assign a VLAN to an interface. The `show vlan` and `show vlan-membership` commands display VLAN information. The `show spantree` command displays STP information.

2950 VLAN Configuration

Just as when configuring the 1900 switch, the first thing you'll want to do on your 2950 switch is to create your VLANs. There are actually two methods—old and new—that you can use in order to do this. The old method requires you to go into the VLAN database and create the VLAN, like this:

```
2950# vlan database
2950(vlan)# vlan VLAN_# [name VLAN_name]
```

Actually, the same command is used here as is with the 1900 switch; the only difference is where the command is executed.

Starting in IOS 12.1(9)EA1 and later, you can use this configuration:

```
2950(config)# vlan VLAN_#
2950(config-vlan)# name VLAN_name
```

When you execute the **vlan** command, you are taken into *VLAN Subconfiguration* mode, where you can enter your configuration parameters for the VLAN, such as its name.

Once you have created your VLANs, you need to assign your VLANs to your 2950's interfaces using the following configuration:

```
2950(config)# interface type 0/port_#
2950(config-if)# switchport mode access
2950(config-if)# switchport access vlan VLAN_#
```

The first thing you must do is specify that the connection is an access-link connection with the **switchport mode access** command. The **switchport access vlan** command assigns a VLAN to the access-link connection.

Once you have created and assigned your VLANs, you can use various **show** commands to review and verify your configuration. The **show vlan** command displays the same output as the same command on the 1900 switch—the list of VLANs and which ports are assigned to them. You can add the **brief** parameter to this command and it will not display the details for each VLAN at the bottom of the display. You can also use the **show interface switchport** command to see a specific interface's VLAN membership information. This command was shown in the trunking section of the 2950, *2950 Trunk Configuration*.

To examine STP information for a VLAN, use this command: **show spanning-tree vlan** *VLAN_#*. The output of this command is similar to the output of the 1900 series command.

8.06. The CD contains a multimedia demonstration of configuring VLANs on the 2950.

exam watch

Use the vlan database or vlan commands to create VLANs. Use the switchport mode access and switchport access vlan commands to assign a VLAN to an interface. The show vlan command displays VLAN information. The show spanning-tree command displays STP information.

Basic Troubleshooting of VLANs and Trunks

Now that you know how to set up a VLAN-based network, you will eventually run into a problem that is related to your VLAN configuration. Basically, you should check the following, in order, to determine the cause of the problem:

1. Check the status of your interface to determine if it is a physical layer problem.
2. Check your switch's and router's configuration to make sure nothing was added or changed.
3. Verify that your trunks are operational.
4. Verify that your VLANs are configured correctly and that STP is functioning correctly.

The following sections cover some of the basic things that you should check whenever you experience switching problems.

Performance Problems

If you are experiencing slow performance, or intermittent connection problems, you should first check the statistics on the interfaces of your switch with the **`show interfaces`** command. Are you seeing a high number of errors, such as collisions?

There are a few things that can cause these problems. The most common is a mismatch in either the duplexing or the speed on a connection. Examine the settings on both sides of the connection. Also make sure that you are using the correct cabling type: straight for a DTE-to-DCE connection and a crossover for a DTE-to-DTE or DCE-to-DCE connection (this was covered in Chapter 4). And make sure that the cable does not exceed the maximum legal limit. Also, make sure that the connected NIC is not experiencing a hardware problem or failure.

Local Connection Problems

If you are attempting to access the console port of a switch or router, and all you see is garbage in your terminal session, this could indicate an incorrect terminal setting. Usually the culprit is an incorrect baud rate. Some devices allow you to perform an operating system upgrade via the console port, and an administrator might change it to the highest possible value but forgot to change it back to 9,600 bps. If you suspect this, keep on changing your baud rate to find the right speed.

If you are having problems accessing devices in the switched network, there are a few things you should look at. First, is the device you are trying to reach in the same VLAN? If so, make sure that you are using the correct IP addressing scheme in the VLAN and that the two devices trying to share information have their ports in the same VLAN. If the two devices are Cisco devices, you can use CDP to elicit some of this information, for instance the IP address, by using the **show cdp** commands. Is the switch learning about the devices in your network? You might want to examine your CAM tables and make sure that a security violation is not causing your connectivity problem.

For VLAN information, use the **show** commands on your switches to check your VLAN configuration. Also check the VLAN configuration on each switch and make sure the VLANs are configured with the same parameters by using the **show vlan** command. If you are using trunks between the switches, make sure that the trunks are configured correctly. Use the **show trunk** (1900) or **show interface** (2950) commands. Also check VTP if you are using it by executing the **show vtp** commands.

Also check the operation of STP for the VLAN. Is it recalculating fairly often? Are you using some of the advanced STP features, like RSTP, to reduce convergence times? Use the **show spantree** (1900) or **show spanning-tree vlan** (2950) command to verify STP.

Inter-VLAN Connection Problems

If you are having problems reaching devices in other VLANs, make sure that, first, you can ping the default gateway (router) that is your exit point from the VLAN. If you can't, then go back to the preceding section and check local VLAN connectivity issues. If you can, then check the router's configuration—make sure that it has a route to the destination VLAN (**show ip route**). This is covered in Chapters 9, 10, and 11. If you do have a route to the destination, make sure the destination VLAN is configured correctly and that the default gateway in that VLAN can reach the destination device.

Know the commands you should use to troubleshoot VLAN problems and trunk connection issues.

EXERCISE 8-2

Configuring VLANs on Your Switches

These last few sections dealt with the creation of VLANs and the assignment of interfaces to them. This lab builds upon this information and allows you to perform some of these configurations. You can find a picture of the network diagram for the simulator in the Introduction of this book. After starting up Boson's NetSim simulator, click the *LabNavigator* button. Next, double-click *Exercise 8-2* and click the *Load Lab* button. This will load the lab configuration based on Exercise 8-1.

1. From the 1900-1, verify that you can ping Host1 connected to `e0/1`. Also ping Host4 connected to 2950-2's `fa0/3` interface.

   At the top of the simulator in the menu bar, click the *eSwitches* icon and choose *1900-1*. Access the CLI of the 1900-1. Execute **`ping 192.168.1.10`** and **`ping 192.168.1.11`**. Both should be successful.

2. On the 1900-1, create VLAN 2. Then assign `ethernet0/1` to VLAN 2. Examine your VLANs.

   Access *Configuration* mode: **`enable`** and **`configure terminal`**. Use the **`vlan 2`** command to create your VLAN. Go into the interface: **`interface ethernet0/1`**. Assign the VLAN: **`vlan-membership static 2`**. Exit out of *Configuration* mode: **`exit`** and **`exit`**. View your VLANs: **`show vlan`**. Make sure that all interfaces are in VLAN 1 except for `e0/1`, which should be in VLAN 2.

3. On either of the 2950s, does the VLAN appear?

   At the top of the simulator in the menu bar, click the *eSwitches* icon and choose *2950-1*. Use the **`show vlan`** command on the 2950-1. This VLAN shouldn't appear, since you don't have any trunks to the 1900 (the 1900 supports ISL and the 2950 supports 802.1Q).

4. From Host1, ping Host4 (192.168.1.11) connected to the 2950-2 switch. Is the ping successful?

   At the top of the simulator in the menu bar, click the *eStations* icon and choose *Host1*. Execute **`ping 192.168.1.11`**. The ping should fail, since the two uplinks on the 1900 (`fa0/26` and `fa0/27`) are in VLAN 1 and Host4 is in VLAN 1, while Host1 is in VLAN 2.

5. On the 1900-1 switch, associate the uplink ports to the 2950-2 to VLAN 2 and verify your configuration.

   At the top of the simulator in the menu bar, click the *eSwitches* icon and choose *1900-1*. On the 1900-1, go into the uplink interface: **`configure terminal`** and **`interface fa0/27`**. Assign the VLAN: **`vlan-membership static 2`**. Exit out of *Configuration* mode: **`end`**. View your VLANs: **`show vlan`**. Use **`ping 192.168.1.11`**. The ping should fail, since the `fa0/3` interface on 2950-2 (Host4) is still in VLAN 1.

6. On the 2950-2 switch, create VLAN 2. Move the Host4 and 1900-1 uplink connections to VLAN2 and verify your configuration.

At the top of the simulator in the menu bar, click the *eSwitches* icon and choose *2950-2*. On the 2950-2, go into the vlan database: **enable** and **vlan database**. Create VLAN 2: **vlan 2** and **exit**. Go into the Host4 interface: **configure terminal** and **interface fa0/3**. Assign the VLAN: **switchport mode access**, **switchport access vlan 2**, and **exit**. Go into the 1900-1 uplink interface: **interface fa0/1**. Assign the VLAN: **switchport mode access** and **switchport access vlan 2**. Exit out of *Configuration* mode: **exit** and **exit**. View your VLANs: **show vlan**. Make sure that fa0/1 and fa0/3 are in VLAN 2.

7. From Host1, ping Host4 (192.168.1.11), which is connected to the 2950-2 switch. Is the ping successful? Can Host1 ping either the 1900-1 or the 2950-2 switch?

   At the top of the simulator in the menu bar, click the *eStations* icon and choose *Host1*. Execute **ping 192.168.1.11**. The ping should be successful, since all connections from Host1 to Host4 are in VLAN 2. Execute **ping 192.168.1.5** and **ping 192.168.1.3**. Both should fail, since both of these switches, by default, are in VLAN 1 and the hosts are in VLAN 2.

CERTIFICATION SUMMARY

A VLAN is a group of devices in the same broadcast domain (subnet). To go between VLANs, you need a router. The 1900 and 2950 support 64 VLANs. Static VLAN assignment to devices is also called port-based VLANs.

An access link is a connection to a device that processes normal frames. Trunk connections modify frames to carry VLAN information. Trunking methods include ISL, 802.1Q, LANE, and 802.10. ISL, which is proprietary to Cisco, adds a 26-byte header and a 4-byte trailer to Ethernet frames; it is supported on the 1900 switches. The 802.1Q method inserts a 4-byte field and recomputes the FCS for Ethernet frames; it is supported on the 2950 switches. PVST supports a separate instance of STP per VLAN, while CST supports one instance of STP for all VLANs.

VTP is a Cisco-proprietary protocol that transmits VLAN information across trunk ports. Switches must be in the same domain to share messages. There are three modes for VTP: client, server, and transparent. Server and transparent switches can add, change, and delete VLANs, but server switches advertise these changes. Clients can accept updates only from server switches. There are three VTP messages: advertisement request and subset and summary advertisement. Servers generate summary advertisements every five minutes on trunk connections. The configuration revision number is used to determine which server switch has the most current VLAN information. VTP pruning is used to prune off VLANs that are not active between two switches, but it requires switches to be in server mode.

On the 1900, use the **vtp domain** command and **vtp server|client|transparent** commands to configure VTP. The default mode is server. On the 2950, perform these commands in *Privilege EXEC* mode after entering the **vlan database**.

DTP is a Cisco-proprietary trunking protocol. There are five modes: on, off, desirable, auto, and no-negotiate. On and desirable actively generate DTP messages. Auto is the default. Use no-negotiate for non-Cisco switch connections. On the 1900, use the **trunk** command to enable trunking and the **show trunk A|B** command to verify it. On the 2950, use the **switchport mode** command to set trunking and the **show interfaces switchport|trunk** command to verify it.

By default, all interfaces are in VLAN 1. When you delete a VLAN, all interfaces that were in that VLAN are placed back into VLAN 1. On the 1900, use the **vlan** command to create VLANs. Assign an interface to a VLAN with the **vlan-membership static** command. To verify your configuration, use the **show vlan** and **show vlan-membership** commands. The **show spantree** command displays STP information for each VLAN. On the 2950, use the **vlan database** command at *Privilege EXEC* mode to create VLANs (the **vlan** command). Use the **switchport mode** access and **switchport access vlan** commands to associate an interface with a VLAN. The **show vlan** command displays your VLAN configuration and the **show spanning-tree** command displays your STP operation.

TWO-MINUTE DRILL

VLAN Overview

- A VLAN is a group of devices in the same broadcast domain, which have the same network number.
- The 1900 supports 64 VLANs and the 2950 supports either 64 (SI) or 250 (EI).
- VLANs are not restricted to physical locations: users can be located anywhere in the switched network.
- Static, or port-based, VLAN membership is manually assigned by the administrator. Dynamic VLAN membership is determined by information from the user device, such as its MAC address.

VLAN Connections

- An access link is a connection to another device that supports standard Ethernet frames and supports only a single VLAN. A trunk is a connection that tags frames and allows multiple VLANs. Trunking is supported only on ports that are trunk-capable: Not all Ethernet ports support trunking.
- ISL is a Cisco proprietary trunking method. The 1900 supports only this method. ISL adds a 26-byte header and 4-byte trailer to the original Ethernet frame.
- IEEE 802.1Q is a standardized trunking method. The 2950 supports only this method. The 802.1Q method inserts a VLAN tag in the middle of the frame and recomputes the frame's checksum. It supports a native VLAN—this is a VLAN that is not tagged on the trunk link. On Cisco switches, this defaults to VLAN 1.
- With ISL trunks, Cisco supports PVST, which has a separate instance of STP per VLAN. With 802.1Q trunks, CST is used—only one STP instance for the network. When a mixture of trunks are used, PVST+ incorporates PVST and CST.

VLAN Trunk Protocol

- VTP is used to share VLAN information to ensure that switches have a consistent VLAN configuration.
- VTP has three modes: server (allowed to make and accept changes, and propagates changes), transparent (allowed to make changes, ignores VTP

messages), and client accepts changes from servers and doesn't store this in NVRAM. The default mode is server.

- VTP messages are propagated only across trunks. For a switch to accept a VTP message, the domain name and optional password must match. There are three VTP messages: advertisement request (client or server request), subset advertisement (server response to an advertisement), and summary advertisement (server sends out every five minutes). The configuration revision number is used in the VTP message to determine if it should be processed or not.
- VTP pruning allows for the dynamic addition and removal of VLANs on a trunk based on whether or not there are any active VLANs on a switch. Requires switches to be in server mode.

1900 and 2950 VLAN Configuration

- On a 1900, to configure VTP, use the **vtp domain** command to assign the domain and the **vtp *mode*** command to assign the mode. Use the **show vtp** command to verify. On the 2950, first enter the VLAN database: **vlan database**. Then use the same two commands on the 1900. Use the **show vtp status** command to verify.
- DTP is a Cisco-proprietary protocol that determines if two interfaces on connected devices can become a trunk. There are five modes: on, desirable, auto-negotiate, off, and no-negotiate. If one side's mode is on, desirable, or auto, and the other is on or desirable, a trunk will form. No-negotiate mode enables trunking but disables DTP.
- To enable trunking on a 1900, use the **trunk on** command on the interface. To verify it, use **show trunk A|B**. To enable trunking on a 2950's interface, use **switchport mode trunk**. To verify trunking, use the **show interfaces switchport|trunk** command.
- All ports on a switch are automatically placed in VLAN 1. To add a VLAN on a 1900, use the **vlan** command; on the 2950, enter the **vlan database** command and then use this command. To assign an interface to a VLAN on a 1900, use **vlan-membership static**—on the 2950, use **switchport mode access** and **switchport access vlan**. To view your VLANs, use **show vlan**.
- To view STP information on the 1900, use **show spantree**; on the 2950, use **show spanning-tree vlan**.

SELF TEST

The following Self Test questions will help you measure your understanding of the material presented in this chapter. Read all the choices carefully, as there may be more than one correct answer. Choose all correct answers for each question.

VLAN Overview

1. Which of the following is false concerning VLANs?

   A. A VLAN is a broadcast domain.

   B. A VLAN is a logical group of users.

   C. A VLAN is location-dependent.

   D. A VLAN is a subnet.

2. The 1900 switch supports ________ VLANs.

   A. 10

   B. 32

   C. 64

   D. 250

VLAN Connections

3. A connection that supports multiple VLANs is called a __________.

4. Which of the following trunking methods is/are proprietary to Cisco? (Choose all correct answers.)

   A. 802.1Q

   B. 802.10

   C. LANE

   D. ISL

5. Which of the following is true concerning ISL?

   A. It is supported on both the 1900 and 2950 switches.

   B. It adds a 26-byte trailer and 4-byte header.

   C. Tagging is done in software.

   D. The original Ethernet frame is not modified.

6. Which of the following is true concerning 802.1Q?
   A. It supports hub connections.
   B. It is supported on both the 1900 and 2950 switches.
   C. The native VLAN is tagged.
   D. The original Ethernet frame is not modified.

VLAN Trunk Protocol

7. You have ISL trunks in your network and five VLANs configured. How many instances of STP are running?
   A. 1
   B. 5
8. The __________ is a proprietary Cisco protocol used to share VLAN configuration information between Cisco switches on trunk connections.
9. Which VTP mode(s) will propagate VTP messages?
   A. Client and server
   B. Server
   C. Client, server, and transparent
   D. Transparent
10. A VTP server switch generates a summary advertisement every __________ minutes.
   A. 1
   B. 2
   C. 3
   D. 5

1900 and 2950 VLAN Configuration

11. Enter the 1900 switch command to set the VTP domain to *dealgroup*: __________.
12. Enter the switch command to set the VTP mode to *server*: ___________.
13. Which 2950 command enables trunking?
   A. `switchport mode trunk`
   B. `trunking on`
   C. `trunking enable`
   D. `switchport trunk on`

14. Enter the 1900 command to view the status of trunking on **`fa0/26`**: ___________.

15. Enter the 1900 command to create VLAN 2 with a name of *test*: __________.

16. Which 2950 command assigns a VLAN to an interface?

A. `vlan-membership static`

B. `vlan`

C. `switchport access vlan`

D. `switchport mode access`

SELF TEST ANSWERS

VLAN Overview

1. ☑ **C.** VLANs are location-independent, assuming the devices are connected via layer-2.
   ☒ **A**, **B**, and **D** are true, and thus incorrect answers.

2. ☑ **C.** The 1900 supports 64 VLANs.
   ☒ **D** is true for the 2950 (EI). **A** and **B** are incorrect answers.

VLAN Connections

3. ☑ A connection that supports multiple VLANS is called a *trunk*.

4. ☑ **B** and **D.** ISL and 802.10 are Cisco-proprietary VLAN tagging methods.
   ☒ **A** and **C** are standard VLAN tagging methods.

5. ☑ **D.** With ISL, the original Ethernet frame is not modified; it is encapsulated in a 26-byte header and 4-byte.
   ☒ **A** is incorrect because the 2950 supports only 802.1Q. **B** is incorrect because the two numbers are reversed. **C** is incorrect because tagging is done in hardware, not software.

6. ☑ **A.** 802.1Q, because it supports a Native VLAN, can use point-to-point and multipoint (hub) connections.

   ☒ **B** is false, since the 1900 supports only ISL. **C** is incorrect because the native VLAN is not tagged. **D** is incorrect because the original Ethernet frame is modified—a VLAN field is inserted and a new FCS is computed.

VLAN Trunk Protocol

7. ☑ **B.** ISL trunks work with PVST, so if you have five VLANs, you have five instances of STP.
   ☒ **A** is true for CST, not PVST.

8. ☑ The *VLAN Trunk Protocol (VTP)* is a proprietary Cisco protocol used to share VLAN configuration information between Cisco switches on trunk connections.

9. ☑ **C.** Switches in all VTP modes will propagate VTP messages; however, only client and server switches will process these messages.
   ☒ **A** is incorrect because it doesn't include transparent. **B** is incorrect because it doesn't include client and transparent. **D** is incorrect because it doesn't include server and client.

10. ☑ **D.** A VTP server switch generates a summary advertisement every five minutes.
    ☒ **A**, **B**, and **C** are incorrect because they are the wrong interval.

1900 and 2950 VLAN Configuration

11. ☑ **`vtp domain dealgroup`**

12. ☑ **`vtp server`**

13. ☑ **A.** The **`switchport mode trunk`** command enables trunking on a 2950 switch.
☒ **B** enables trunking on a 1900 switch. **C** and **D** are nonexistent commands.

14. ☑ **`show trunk A`**

15. ☑ **`vlan 2 name test`**

16. ☑ **C.** The **`switchport access vlan`** command assigns a VLAN to an interface on a 2950 switch.
☒ **A** assigns a VLAN to an interface on a 1900. **B** creates a VLAN. **D** sets the interface connection as an access link.

9

Routing Introduction

CERTIFICATION OBJECTIVES

9.01 Types of Routes

9.02 Static Routes

9.03 Router-on-a-Stick

9.04 Dynamic Routing Protocols

9.05 Problems with Distance Vector Protocols

✓ Two-Minute Drill

Q&A Self Test

The last two chapters focused on products and protocols that function at layer-2. This chapter moves up one layer in the OSI Reference Model to discuss layer-3, the network layer. Layer-3 devices are generically called *routers*. Routers basically have two functions:

1. To find a layer-3 path to a destination network
2. To move packets from one interface to another to get a packet to its destination

In order to accomplish the first function, a router will need to:

- Learn about routers it is connected to in order to learn the networks that they know about
- Find locations of destination network numbers
- Choose a *best* path to each destination
- Maintain the most up-to-date routing information about how to reach destination networks

In order to accomplish its second function, the router will need to examine the destination IP address in an incoming IP packet, determine the network number of the destination, look in its routing table, and switch the packet to an outgoing interface. As you will see in this chapter, the routing table contains a list of destination network numbers, the status of these networks, which interface the router should use to reach the destination, and which neighboring router the router should use if the destination is more than one hop away.

This chapter covers an overview of routing, including how to set up static routes and how dynamic routing protocols—distance vector, link state, and hybrid protocols—function. Chapter 10 covers the configuration of two distance vector routing protocols, and Chapter 11 covers the configuration of a link state routing protocol and a hybrid routing protocol.

CERTIFICATION OBJECTIVE 9.01

Types of Routes

A router can learn a route via one of two methods: *static* and *dynamic*. A static route is a route that is manually configured on the router. There are actually two ways that a router can learn a static route. First, a router will look at its active interfaces, examine the addresses configured on the interfaces and determine the corresponding network numbers, and populate the routing table with this information. This is commonly called a *connected* route. The second way that a router can learn a static route is for you to manually configure it.

Remember the difference between a routed protocol and a routing protocol.

Dynamic routes are routes that a router learns by running a routing protocol. Routing protocols will learn about routes from other neighboring routers running the same routing protocol. Dynamic routing protocols share network numbers a router knows about and reachability information concerning these networks. Through this sharing process, eventually a router will learn about all of the reachable network numbers in the network. There is a difference between the terms *routed* protocol and *routing* protocol. A routing protocol learns about routes for a routed protocol. A routed protocol is a layer-3 protocol, like IP or IPX. A routed protocol carries user traffic such as e-mail, file transfers, and web downloads. Table 9-1 shows some common routed protocols and the routing protocols that they use.

This book only focuses on routing for IP traffic and covers the basics of the RIP, IGRP, OSPF, and EIGRP routing protocols.

Autonomous Systems

Some routing protocols understand the concept of an autonomous system, and some do not. An *autonomous system* (AS) is a group of networks under a single administrative control, which could be your company, a division within your company, or a group of companies. An *Interior Gateway Protocol* (IGP) refers to a routing protocol that handles routing within a single autonomous system. IGPs include RIP, IGRP, EIGRP, OSPF, and IS-IS. An *Exterior Gateway Protocol* (EGP) handles routing between different autonomous systems. Today, there is only one active EGP: the Border Gateway Protocol (BGP). BGP is used to route traffic across the Internet backbone between different autonomous systems.

Not every routing protocol understands the concept of an AS. An AS can provide distinct boundaries for a routing protocol, and thus provides some advantages. For instance, you can control how far a network can be propagated by routers. Plus, you

TABLE 9-1 Routed and Routing Protocols

Routed Protocols	Routing Protocols
IP	RIP, IGRP, OSPF, EIGRP, BGP, IS-IS
IPX	RIP, NLSP, EIGRP
AppleTalk	RMTP, AURP, EIGRP

can control what routes you will advertise to other autonomous systems and what routes you'll accept from these systems.

exam watch

An autonomous system (AS) is a group of networks under a single administrative control. Each AS is assigned a unique number in order to differentiate it from other autonomous systems.

To distinguish one autonomous system from another, an AS can be assigned a unique number from 1 to 65,535. The Internet Assigned Numbers Authority (IANA) is responsible for assigning these numbers. Just like the public and private IP addresses defined in RFC 1918, there are public and private AS numbers. If you will be connected to the Internet backbone, are running BGP, and want to accept BGP routes from the Internet, you will need a public AS number. However, if you only need to break up your internal network into different systems, you only need to use the private numbers. Routing protocols that understand the concept of an AS are IGRP, EIGRP, OSPF, IS-IS, and BGP. RIP doesn't understand autonomous systems, while OSPF does; but OSPF doesn't require you to configure the AS number, whereas other protocols, such as IGRP and EIGRP, do. Cisco's BSCI exam spends a lot of time discussing autonomous systems and routing between them. The CCNA exam focuses only on the basics of IGPs.

Administrative Distance

One of the items mentioned in the chapter introduction is that each router needs to choose a *best* path to a destination. This can become somewhat complicated if the router is receiving routing update information for a single network from multiple sources, such as connected, static, and IGP routing protocols, and must choose *one* of these sources as the best and place it in the router's routing table. As you will see in this section and the section "Dynamic Routing Protocol," there are two things a router looks at when choosing a *best* path.

The first thing a router looks at is the administrative distance for a route source. Administrative distance is a Cisco-proprietary mechanism used to rank the IP routing protocols. As an example, if a router were running two IGPs, RIP and IGRP, and were learning network 10.0.0.0/8 from both of these routing protocols, which one should the router pick and place in its routing table? Which one should the router *believe* more? Actually, the term *administrative distance* is somewhat misleading, since the term has nothing to do with measuring distance. The term *believability* better describes the process.

Administrative distance ranks the IP routing protocols, assigning a value, or weight, to each protocol. Distances can range from 0 to 255. A smaller distance is more believable by a router, with the best distance being 0 and the worst, 255. Table 9-2 displays some of the default administrative distances Cisco has assigned to its routing protocols:

TABLE 9-2

Administrative Distance Values

Administrative Distance	Route Type
0	Connected interface
0 or 1	Static route
90	Internal EIGRP route (within the same AS)
100	IGRP route
110	OSPF route
120	RIP route
170	External EIGRP (from another AS)
255	Unknown route (is considered an invalid route and will not be used)

Going back to our previous example of a router learning network 10.0.0.0/8 from RIP and IGRP, since RIP has a value of 120 and IGRP, 100, the router will use the IGRP route, since this protocol has a better (lower) administrative distance value.

CERTIFICATION OBJECTIVE 9.02

Static Routes

A *static route* is a manually configured route on your router. Static routes are typically used in smaller networks. With a network that has hundreds of routes, static routes are not scalable, since you would have to configure each route, and any redundant paths for that route, on each router. This section covers the configuration of static routes and some of the issues associated with them.

Static Route Configuration

To configure a static route for IP, use one of these two commands:

```
Router(config)# ip route destination_network_# [subnet_mask]
                    IP_address_of_next_hop_neighbor
                    [administrative_distance] [permanent]
   -or-
Router(config)# ip route destination_network_# [subnet_mask]
                    interface_to_exit
                    [administrative_distance] [permanent]
```

The first parameter that you must specify is the destination network number. If you omit the subnet mask for the network number, it defaults to the Class A (255.0.0.0), B (255.255.0.0), or C (255.255.255.0) default subnet mask, depending on the network number of the destination.

After the subnet mask parameter, you have two ways to specify how to reach the destination network: you can tell the router either the next hop neighbor's IP address or the interface the router should exit to reach the destination network. You should use the former method if the link is a multiaccess link (the link has more than two devices on it, three routers, for instance). You can use the latter method if it is a point-to-point link. In this instance, you must specify the *name* of the interface on the router, like **serial0**.

Optionally, you can change the administrative distance of a static route. If you omit this value, it will have one of two defaults, depending on the configuration of the previous parameter. If you specified the next hop neighbor's IP address, then the administrative distance defaults to 1. If you specified the interface on the router it should use to reach the destination, the router treats the route as a connected route and assigns an administrative distance of 0 to it. Please note that you can create multiple static routes to the *same* destination. For instance, you might have primary and backup paths to the destination. For the primary path, use the default administrative distance value. For the backup path, use a number higher than this, such as 2. Once you have configured a backup path, the router will use the primary path, and if the interface on the router fails for the primary path, the router will use the backup route.

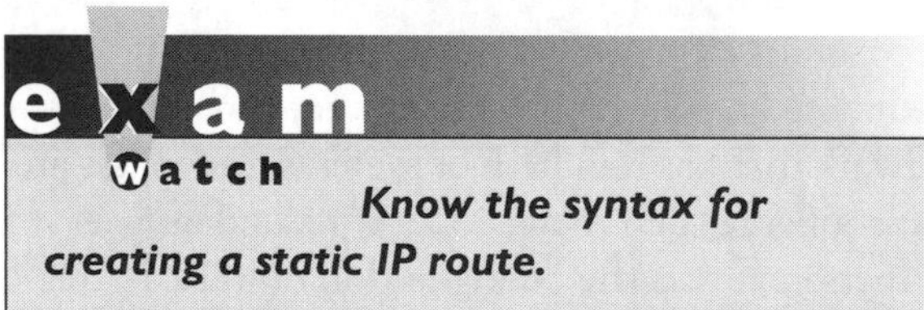

Know the syntax for creating a static IP route.

The **permanent** parameter will keep the static route in the routing table even when the interface the router uses for the static route fails. If you omit this parameter, and the interface fails that the static route uses, the router will remove this route from its routing table and attempt to find an alternative path to place in the routing table. You might want to use this parameter if you never want packets to use another path to a destination, perhaps because of security reasons.

Default Route Configuration

A *default route* is a special type of static route. Where a static route specifies a path a router should use to reach a *specific* destination, a default route specifies a path the router should use if it *doesn't* know how to reach the destination.

Note that if a router does not have any path in its routing table telling it how to reach a destination, and the router receives a packet destined for this network, the router will *drop* the packet. This is different from a switch, which will flood unknown destinations. Therefore, a default route can serve as a *catch-all*: if there is no specific path to the destination, the router will use the default route to reach it.

To set up a default route, use the following syntax for a static route:

```
Router(config)# ip route 0.0.0.0 0.0.0.0
                    IP_address_of_next_hop_neighbor
                    [administrative_distance] [permanent]
   -or-
Router(config)# ip route 0.0.0.0 0.0.0.0
                    interface_to_exit
                    [administrative_distance] [permanent]
```

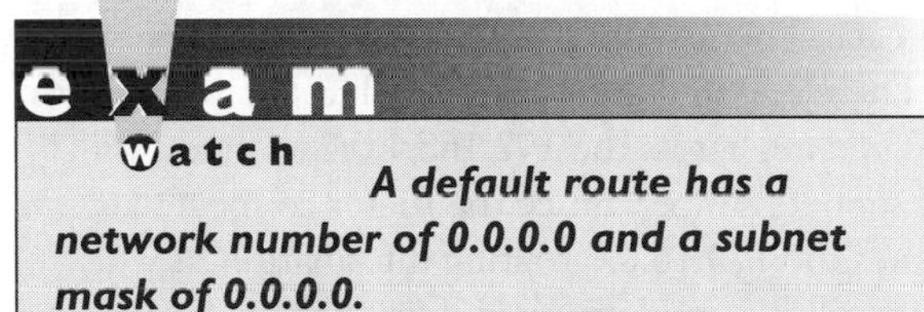

exam
watch
A default route has a network number of 0.0.0.0 and a subnet mask of 0.0.0.0.

The network number of 0.0.0.0/0 at first appears a bit strange. Recall from Chapter 3, however, that network 0.0.0.0 represents all networks, and a mask of all 0's in the bit position represents all hosts in the specified network.

Default Routes and Distance Vector Protocols

A default route sometimes causes problems for certain routing protocols. There are two additional categories that a routing protocol can fall under: classful and classless. Examples of classful protocols include RIPv1 and IGRP. Examples of classless protocols include RIPv2, OSPF, EIGRP, IS-IS, and BGP.

A *classful* routing protocol understands only class subnets. For instance, if you have 192.168.1.0/23 in a routing update, a classful routing protocol wouldn't understand it, since a Class C network requires 24 bits of network numbers. This creates a problem with a default route, which has a /0 mask.

Also, when a classful router advertises a route outside its interface, it does not include the subnet mask. For example, you might have 192.168.1.1/26 configured on your router's interface, and the router receives a routing updated with 192.168.1.0. With a classful routing protocol, the router will comprehend subnet masks only for network numbers configured on its interfaces. In this example, the router assumes that for 192.168.1.0, the only valid mask is /26. Therefore, if the router sees the 192.168.1.0/26 as the network number, but the network is really 192.168.1.0/27, this can create a lot of routing confusion.

Classless protocols, on the other hand, do not have any issues accepting routing updates with any bit value for a subnet mask. However, for classful protocols, you must configure the following command to accept nonconforming subnet masks, such as a default route:

```
Router(config)# ip classless
```

This command is also used to deal with *discontiguous* subnets in a network that is using a classful protocol: subnets separated by a different class network. For example, let's assume that you have networks 172.16.1.0/24, 172.16.2.0/24, and 172.16.3.0/24. However, a different class network, 192.168.1.0/24, sits between the first two Class B subnets and 172.16.3.0/24. In this situation, the router connected to 172.16.1.0/24 and 172.16.2.0/24, when it receives 172.16.0.0 from the side of the network connected to the discontiguous subnet, will *ignore* this routing entry.

Remember that when routes cross a class boundary in a classful protocol, the network number is sent as its classful number. Therefore, the router connected to 192.168.1.0/24 and 172.16.3.0/24, when it advertises updates across the 192.168.1.0/24 subnet, will advertise 172.16.0.0—not the actual subnet number. Since the router connected to 172.16.1.0/24 and 172.16.2.0/24 ignores the 172.16.0.0 routing information, it will not be able to reach 172.16.3.0. On top of this problem, even if you have a default route configured, since the router is connected to the 172.16.0.0 subnets, it assumes that 172.16.3.0 must also be connected; and if it isn't in the routing table, then the route cannot be reached.

By using the **ip classless** command, you are overriding this behavior; you're allowing your classful router to use a default route to reach discontiguous subnets. Not that this is a recommended design practice, but it does allow you to solve reachability problems for discontiguous subnets.

exam watch

Classful protocols, such as IP RIPv1 and IGRP, understand only class subnets—you can apply only one subnet mask to a class address. Classless protocols, such as RIPv2, EIGRP, OSPF, and IS-IS, do not have this restriction.

Verifying Static Route Configuration

To verify the configuration of static and default routes on your router, use the **show ip route** command:

```
Router# show ip route
Codes: C - connected, S - static, I - IGRP, R - RIP,
```

```
            M - mobile, B - BGP, D - EIGRP, EX - EIGRP external,
            O - OSPF, IA - OSPF inter area, N1 - OSPF NSSA
            external type 1, N2 - OSPF NSSA external type 2,
            E1 - OSPF external type 1, E2 - OSPF external type 2,
            E - EGP, i - IS-IS, L1 - IS-IS level-1, L2 - IS-IS level-2,
            * - candidate default, U - per-user static route, o - ODR,
            T - traffic engineered route

Gateway of last resort is not set
     172.16.0.0/24 is subnetted, 3 subnets
C       172.16.1.0 is directly connected, Ethernet0
C       172.16.2.0 is directly connected, Serial0
S       172.16.3.0 is directly connected, Serial0
```

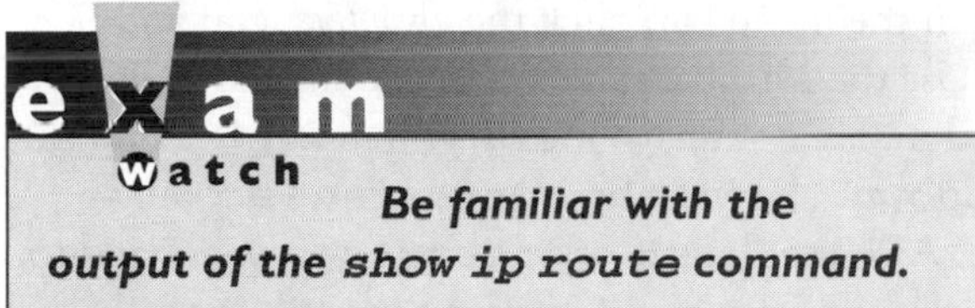

Be familiar with the output of the show ip route command.

The top portion of the display for this command has a table of codes. These codes, which describe a type of route that may appear in the routing table, are shown in the first column at the bottom part of the display. In this example, there are two connected routes, and one static route — the static route is treated as a directly connected route, since it was created by specifying the interface to exit the router. This command is discussed in depth in Chapters 10 and 11.

9.01. The CD contains a multimedia demonstration of setting up static routes on a router.

EXERCISE 9-1

Static Route Configuration

These last few sections dealt with static routes and their configuration. This exercise will help you reinforce this material for the configuration of static routes. You'll perform this lab using Boson's NetSim simulator. This exercise has you set static routes on the two routers (2600 and 2500). You can find a picture of the network diagram for Boson's NetSim simulator in the Introduction to this book. After starting up the simulator, click the *LabNavigator* button. Next, double-click *Exercise 9-1* and click the *Load Lab* button. This will load the lab configuration based on Chapter 5's and 7's exercises.

1. On the 2600, verify that the `fa0/0` and `s0` interfaces are up. If not, bring them up. Examine the IP addresses configured on the 2600 and look at its routing table.

At the top of the simulator in the menu bar, click the *eRouters* icon and choose *2600*. Use the **show interfaces** command to verify your configuration. If `fa0/0` and `s0` are not up, go into the interfaces (`fa0/0` and `s0`) and enable them: **no shutdown**. Use the **show interfaces** command to verify that the IP addresses you configured in Chapter 5 are still there. Use the **show ip route** command. You should have two connected networks: 192.168.1.0 connected to `fa0/0` and 192.168.2.0 connected to `s0`.

2. On the 2500, verify that the `e0` and `s0` interfaces are up. If not, bring them up. Examine the IP addresses configured on the 2500 and look at its routing table.

   At the top of the simulator in the menu bar, click the *eRouters* icon and choose *2500*. On the 2500, Use the **show interfaces** command to verify your configuration. If `e0` and `s0` are not up, go into the interfaces (`e0` and `s0`) and enable them: **no shutdown**. Use the **show interfaces** command to verify your configuration. Also use the **show interfaces** command to verify that the IP addresses you configured on Chapter 5 are still there. Use the **show ip route** command. You should have two connected networks: 192.168.3.0 connected to `e0` and 192.168.2.0 connected to `s0`.

3. Test connectivity between Host1 and the 2600. Test connectivity between Host3 and the 2500. Test connectivity between Host3 and Host1.

   At the top of the simulator in the menu bar, click the *eStations* icon and choose *Host1*. From Host1, ping the 2600: **ping 192.168.1.1**. The ping should be successful. If it is not, then you may have used the configuration from the VLAN lab in Chapter 8 and have a VLAN configuration problem. At the top of the simulator in the menu bar, click the *eStations* icon and choose *Host3*. From Host3, ping the 2500 router: **ping 192.168.3.1**. The ping should be successful. Also from Host3, ping Host1: **ping 192.168.1.10**. The ping should fail: there is no route from the 2500 to this destination. Look at the 2500's routing table: it doesn't list 192.168.1.0/24: **show ip route**.

4. On the 2500, configure a static route to 192.168.1.0/24, which is connected to the 2600. View the routing table.

   At the top of the simulator in the menu bar, click the *eRouters* icon and choose *2500*. Configure the static route: **configure terminal**, **ip route 192.168.1.0 255.255.255.0 192.168.2.1**, and **end**. View the static route: **show ip route**. Make sure that 192.168.1.0/24 shows up in the routing table as a static route (S).

5. On the 2600, configure a static route to 192.168.3.0/24, which is connected to the 2500. View the routing table.

At the top of the simulator in the menu bar, click the *eRouters* icon and choose *2600*. Configure the static route: **configure terminal**, **ip route 192.168.3.0 255.255.255.0 192.168.2.2**, and **end**. View the static route: **show ip route**. Make sure that 192.168.3.0/24 shows up in the routing table as a static route (S).

6. From Host3, ping the fa0/0 interface of the 2600. From Host3, ping Host1.

   At the top of the simulator in the menu bar, click the *eStations* icon and choose *Host3*. Access Host3 and ping the fa0/0 interface of the 2600 router: **ping 192.168.1.1**. The ping should be successful. Ping Host1 **ping 192.168.1.10**. The ping should be successful.

Now you should be more comfortable with configuring static routes. In the next section, you will grow acquainted with routing between VLANs by using a router-on-a-stick.

CERTIFICATION OBJECTIVE 9.03

Router-on-a-Stick

Typically, we think of routing as traffic coming in one interface and leaving another interface. As you learned in Chapter 8, however, trunks can be used to support multiple broadcast domains, where each broadcast domain has a unique layer-3 network or subnet number. Certain router models, like the 2600 series, support trunk connections. A *router-on-a-stick* is a router that has a single trunk connection to a switch and that routes between the VLANs on this trunk connection. You could easily do this without a trunk (access-link connections), but each VLAN would require a separate access-link (physical) connection on the router, and this would increase the price of the router solution.

A router-on-a-stick is a router that has a single trunk connection to a switch and that routes between different VLANs on this trunk.

For instance, if you had five VLANs, and your router didn't support trunking, you would need five physical LAN interfaces on your router in order to route between the five VLANs. However, with a trunk connection, you can route between all five VLANs on a *single* interface. Because of cost and scalability, most administrators prefer using a router-on-a-stick approach to solve their routing problems in switched networks.

Subinterface Configuration

In order to set up a router-on-a-stick, you need to break up your router's physical interface into multiple logical interfaces, called *subinterfaces*. Cisco supports up to 300 interfaces on a router, which includes both physical and logical interfaces. Once you create a subinterface, a router will treat this logical interface just like a physical interface: you can assign layer-3 addressing to it, enable, it, disable it, and many other things.

To create a subinterface, use the following command:

```
Router(config)# interface type port_#.subinterface_#
                         [point|multipoint]
Router(config-subif)#
```

After entering the physical interface type and port identifier, follow this with a "." and a subinterface number. This number can range from 0 to 4,294,967,295. The number that you use for the subinterface number is only for reference purposes within the IOS, and the only requirement is that when creating a subinterface, you use a unique number. Many administrators prefer to use the VLAN number that the subinterface will handle for the subinterface number; however, this is not a requirement.

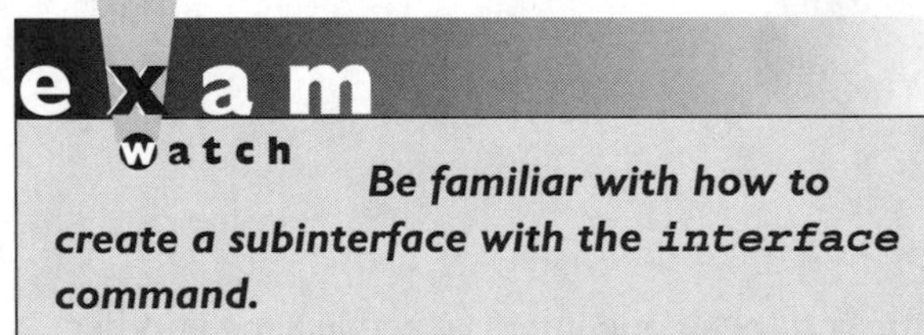

Be familiar with how to create a subinterface with the `interface` command.

At the end of the statement, you must specify the type of connection *if* the interface is of type `serial`; otherwise, you can omit it. The **`point`** parameter is used for point-to-point serial connections, and **`multipoint`** is used for multipoint connections. The **`multipoint`** parameter is used for connections that have more than one device connected to them (physically or logically). Prior to IOS 12.0, if you omitted the connection type, it defaulted to **`multipoint`**. In 12.0 and higher, however, you must specify the type—there is no default. (This point is covered in more depth in Chapter 16.) For a router-on-a-stick configuration, *omit* the connection type, since it isn't used.

Interface Encapsulation

Once you create a subinterface, you'll notice that your CLI prompt has changed and that you are now in *Subinterface Configuration* mode. If you are routing between VLANs, you'll need an interface that supports trunking. There are some things configured on the major interface and some things configured on the subinterface. Configurations like duplexing and speed are done on the major (or physical) interface. Most other tasks are done on the subinterface, including which VLAN the subinterface belongs to and its IP addressing information.

When setting up your subinterface for a router-on-a-stick, one thing that you must configure is the type of trunking—ISL or 802.1Q—and the VLAN the subinterface is associated with, like this:

```
Router(config)# interface type port_#.subinterface_#
Router(config-subif)# encapsulation isl|dot1q VLAN_#
```

Use the **encapsulation** command to specify the trunk type and the VLAN associated with the subinterface. The VLAN number you specify here *must* correspond to the correct VLAN number in your switched network. You must also set up a trunk connection on the switch for the port that the router is connected to. Once you do this, the switch will send tagged frames to the router, and the router, using your encapsulation, will understand how to read the tags. The router will be able to see which VLAN the frame came from and match it up with the appropriate subinterface that will process it.

Example Configuration

Let's look at an example to see how a router-on-a-stick is configured. I'll use Figure 9-1 for this configuration. I'll assume that this is a 3600 router, that the Fast Ethernet interface is the first interface in the first slot, and that the switch is using ISL trunking.

Here's the code example for this router:

```
Router(config)# interface fastethernet 0/0
Router(config-if)# no half-duplex
Router(config-if)# no shutdown
Router(config-if)# exit
Router(config)# interface fastethernet 0/0.10
Router(config-subif)# encapsulation isl 1
Router(config-subif)# ip address 172.16.1.1 255.255.255.0
Router(config-subif)# exit
Router(config)# interface fastethernet 0/0.20
Router(config-subif)# encapsulation isl 2
Router(config-subif)# ip address 172.16.2.1 255.255.255.0
Router(config-subif)# exit
```

Notice in this example that the subinterface numbers (10 and 20) do not match the VLAN numbers in the encapsulation (1 and 2)—remember that the subinterface numbers are used by the IOS only to reference the particular subinterface and do not have to match any configuration on the subinterface.

FIGURE 9-1

Router-on-a-stick example

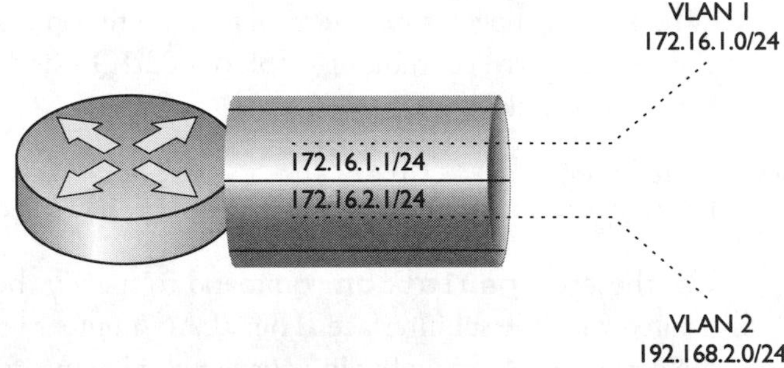

If you are configuring static routes and want to route traffic out of a particular subinterface, specify the major interface along with the subinterface number, like `fastethernet0/0.20`.

9.02. The CD contains a multimedia demonstration of setting up a router-on-a-stick.

CERTIFICATION OBJECTIVE 9.04

Dynamic Routing Protocols

Unlike static routes that require manual configuration to tell the router where destination networks are, *dynamic routing protocols* learn about destination networks from neighboring routers. Dynamic routing protocols fall under one of three categories: distance vector, link state, and hybrid. Each of these routing protocol types takes a different approach in sharing routing information with neighboring routers and choosing the best path to a destination.

Because of the differences between the various routing protocol types, each has advantages and disadvantages. One choice you'll have to make will be which routing protocol you'll run on the routers in your network. There are various factors that you'll have to examine when choosing a routing protocol:

- Routing metrics used to choose paths
- How routing information is shared
- Convergence speed of the routing protocol
- How routers process routing information
- Overhead of the routing protocol

Routing Metrics

As mentioned in the section "Administrative Distance" earlier in the chapter, if your router has two types of routes, such as RIP and IGRP, for the same network number, the router uses the administrative distance to choose the best one. However, a situation might arise where there are two paths to the destination network, and the same routing protocol, RIP, for instance, discovers these multiple paths to the destination network. If this is the case, a routing protocol will use a measurement called a *metric* to determine which path is the best path.

Table 9-3 lists some common metrics, the routing protocols that use them, and brief descriptions. As you can see from this table, some routing protocols use only a single metric. For instance, IP RIP uses hop count as a metric, and OSPF uses cost. Other routing protocols use multiple metric values to choose a best path to a destination. For instance, IP EIGRP and IGRP can use bandwidth, delay, reliability, load, and MTU when choosing a best path to a destination.

Distance Vector Protocols

Of the three types of routing protocols—distance vector, link state, and hybrid—distance vector protocols are the simplest. *Distance vector* routing protocols use the distance and direction (vector) to find paths to destinations. Most distance vector protocols use the Bellman-Ford algorithm for finding paths to networking destinations. Sometimes these protocols are referred to as *routing by rumor,* since the routers learn routing information from directly connected neighbors, and these

TABLE 9-3 Routing Protocol Metrics

Metric	Routing Protocols	Description
Bandwidth	IP EIGRP, IP IGRP	The capacity of the links in Kbps (T1=1,554)
Cost	IP OSPF, IPX NSLP	Measurement in the inverse of the bandwidth of the links
Delay	IP EIGRP, IP IGRP	Time it takes to reach the destination
Hop count	IP RIP, IPX RIP	How many routers away from the destination
Load	IP EIGRP, IP IGRP	The path with the least utilization
Maximum Transmission Unit (MTU)	IP EIGRP, IP IGRP	The path that supports the largest frame sizes
Reliability	IP EIGRP, IP IGRP	The path with the least amount of errors or downtime
Ticks	IPX RIP	Measurement in delay (55 milliseconds)

neighbors might have learned these networks from other neighboring routers. Some examples of IP routing protocols that are distance vector protocols are RIPv1 and IGRP. These protocols are discussed in depth in Chapter 10.

Advertising Updates

One of the mechanisms of a routing protocol is to share information with neighboring routers. Some protocols use local broadcasts to disseminate information, some use multicasts, and some use unicasts. Distance vector protocols periodically use local broadcasts with a destination IP address of 255.255.255.255 to share routing information. These protocols do this religiously, whether or not something has changed: once their periodic timer expires, they broadcast their routing information to any devices connected to their interfaces. Note that distance vector protocols really don't care who listens to these updates, nor do they verify if neighboring routers received the broadcast update.

Routers running distance vector protocols learn who their neighbors are by listening for routing broadcasts on their interfaces. There is no formal handshaking process or hello process to discover who the neighboring routers are. Distance vector protocols assume that through the broadcast process, neighbors will be learned, and if a neighbor fails, the missed broadcasts from these neighbors will eventually be detected. And even if changes occur and your router misses an update from a neighbor, it is assumed that your router will learn about the change in the next broadcast update.

Processing Updates

When a distance vector protocol receives a routing update, it performs these steps:

1. Increment the metrics of the incoming routes in the advertisement (for IP RIP, add 1 to the hop count).
2. Compare the network numbers in the routing update from the neighbor to what the router has in its routing table.
3. If the neighbor's information is better, place it in the routing table and remove the old entry.
4. If the neighbor's information is worse, ignore it.
5. If the neighbor's information is exactly the same as the entry already in the table, reset the timer for the entry in the routing table (in other words, the router already learned about this route from the same neighbor).
6. If the neighbor's information is a different path to a known destination network, but with the same metric as the existing network in the routing table, the router will add it to the routing table along with the old one. This

assumes you have not exceeded the maximum number of equal-cost paths for this destination network number. In this situation, your router is learning about the same network number from two different neighbors, and both neighbors are advertising the network number with the same metric.

Remember the advantages of distance vector protocols and how they process updates with the Bellman-Ford algorithm. Distance vector protocols use broadcasts to disseminate routing information and do not care if neighbors listen to their routing updates.

The six steps are generally referred to as the Bellman-Ford algorithm. As you can see from step 6, Cisco supports load balancing for equal-cost paths to a destination within a particular route type, such as IP RIP routes.

Since distance vector protocols are the simplest of the three, they are easy to set up and troubleshoot. They have very low overhead on the router, requiring few CPU cycles and memory to process updates: they receive an incoming update, increment the metrics, compare the results to the routes in the routing table, and update the routing table if necessary.

Link State Protocols

Link state protocols use an algorithm called the *Shortest Path First (SPF)* algorithm, invented by Dijkstra, to find the best path to a destination. Whereas distance vector protocols rely on *rumors* from other neighbors about remote routes, link state protocols will learn the complete topology of the network: which routers are connected to which networks. Because of the size of a network, this can create scalability problems. Therefore, link state protocols typically contain capabilities to limit the scope of their learning process, limiting a router's knowledge of the network topology to a smaller number of routers and routes.

Examples of link state protocols include IP's OSPF and IS-IS and IPX's NLSP. OSPF is covered in more depth in Chapter 11. IS-IS is an ISO link state protocol. It was originally developed by DEC as the DECnet Phase V routing protocol. It can route for both TCP/IP traffic and CLNP and CLNS traffic. IS-IS provides for more scalability than OSPF but is more complex to configure. Quite a few ISPs use IS-IS as the routing protocol for their own network. IS-IS is covered in Cisco's BSCI CCNP exam. IPX supports three routing protocols: RIP (IPX version), NSLP, and EIGRP. NSLP allows IPX networks to scale to very large sizes.

Advertising Updates

Whereas distance vector protocols use local broadcasts to disseminate routing information, link state protocols use multicasts. A distance protocol will send out its routing table religiously on its periodic interval whether there are changes or not. Link state protocols are smarter. They multicast what is called a Link State Advertisement (LSA), which is a piece of routing information that contains who originated the advertisement and what the network number is.

LSAs are typically generated only when there are changes in the network, which is more friendly to your networking resources. In other words, periodic updates are rare occurrences. Whereas distance vector protocols use local broadcasts, which are processed by every machine on the segment, link state protocols use multicasts, which are processed only by other devices running the link state protocol. Plus, link state protocols send their updates reliably. A destination router, when receiving an LSA update, will respond to the source router with an acknowledgment. This process is different from distance vector protocols, which don't verify that a routing update was received from neighboring routers.

As a router learns routes from the LSAs of routers in the network, it builds a complete topology of the network—what routers are connected to other routers, and what the network numbers are. Whereas distance vector protocols are referred to as *routing by rumor*, link state protocols are referred to as *routing by propaganda*, since link state routers are learning which routers are sourcing (connected to) a network number. The LSAs gathered by a link state router are then stored in a local database. Anytime there is a change in the database, the router runs the SPF algorithm. The SPF algorithm builds an inverted tree, with the router itself at the top, and other routers and network segments beneath it. This algorithm is somewhat similar to the STP algorithm that layer-2 devices use to remove loops. Depending on the tree structure and the metrics used, the link state router then populates the routing table with the best (shortest) paths to the networks in the SPF tree.

Advantages of Link State Protocols

One advantage link state protocols have is that they use a hierarchical structure that helps limit the distance that an LSA travels. This reduces the likelihood that a change in the network will impact every router. This process is different from distance vector protocols, which use a flat topology. With distance vector protocols, a change in one part of the network will eventually impact every router in the network. Depending on the configuration of routers in a link state protocol, this is not necessarily true. For instance, OSPF uses areas to help contain changes; therefore, a change in one area won't necessarily impact other areas.

A second advantage of link state protocols is that they use multicasts to share routing information. Multicasts are sent to a group of devices, whereas broadcasts are sent to everyone. Only other routers running the link state protocol will process these LSA packets. Plus, link state routers send out only *incremental* updates. Incremental updates are updates sent out when there is a change in the state of the network. This is much more advantageous than what distance vector protocols do: broadcast updates based on a periodic timer, which is typically either 30 or 60 seconds. Once all the link state routers are booted up and they learn the topology of the network, updates are sent out only when changes take place, which shouldn't be that often. The advantage of this process is that you are using your network's bandwidth and resources more efficiently than with distance vector protocols.

A third advantage that link state protocols have over distance vector protocols is that they support classless routing. Classless routing allows you to summarize a large group of contiguous routes into a smaller number of routes. This process is called variable-length subnet masking (VLSM) and classless inter-domain routing (CIDR). These concepts are discussed in depth in Chapter 12.

By summarizing routes, you are making the routing process more efficient. First, you are advertising a smaller number of routes. And second, in order for the summarized route to fail, all of the subnets or networks in the summarization must fail. As an example, you might have a WAN link that is *flapping*. A flapping route is going up and down, up and down, over and over again. This can create serious performance problems for link state protocols.

When you perform summarization, if the specific route within a summarized route is flapping, this will not affect the status of the summarized route, and thus won't impact many of the routers in your network. Third, by summarizing routes, you reduce the size of your router's routing link state database, which will reduce the number of CPU cycles required to run the SPF algorithm and update the routing table, as well as reduce your router's memory requirements.

A fourth advantage is that with the use of the SPF algorithm, routing loops will not be included in the population of the routing table. Routing loops can create problems with distance vector protocols; they are discussed in the section "Problems with Distance Vector Protocols" section later in this chapter.

Disadvantages of Link State Protocols

Given the advantages of link state protocols, they do have disadvantages. For instance, even though link state protocols can scale a network to a much larger size than distance vector protocols, they come with their own set of problems. First, link state protocols are more CPU- and memory-intensive. Link state protocols have to maintain more tables in memory: a neighbor table, a link state database, and a routing table. When changes take place in the network, the routers must update the link state database, run the SPF algorithm, build the SPF tree, and then rebuild the routing table, which requires a lot more CPU cycles than a distance vector protocol's approach: increment the metrics of incoming routes and compare this to the current routes in the routing table.

As an example, a flapping route in a link state network can kill the processing on many routers, especially if the change is occurring every 10–15 seconds. The advantage that distance vector protocols have is that the only time the routers have to perform a function is when they receive the periodic updates, and then processing these updates is router-friendly.

exam watch

Link state protocols use the SPF algorithm to choose the best path. They are more CPU- and memory-intensive than distance vector protocols. However, they are more network friendly in that they use multicasts to disseminate routing information and only advertise changes. Plus, with route summarization and hierarchical routing, link state protocols can scale to very large network sizes.

Hybrid Protocols

A *hybrid* protocol takes the advantages of both distance vector and link state protocols and merges them into a new protocol. Typically, hybrid protocols are based on a distance vector protocol but contain many of the features and advantages of link state protocols. Examples of hybrid protocols include RIPv2, EIGRP, and BGP. RIPv2 is covered in more depth in Chapter 10, and EIGRP is covered in Chapter 11. BGP is beyond the scope of this book but is heavily emphasized on the CCNP BSCI exam.

As an example, Cisco's EIGRP routing protocol reduces the CPU and memory overhead by acting like a distance vector protocol when it comes to process routing updates. Instead of sending out periodic updates like a distance vector protocol, EIGRP sends out incremental, reliable updates via multicast messages, providing a more network- and router-friendly network. EIGRP supports many other features of link state protocols, such as VLSM and route summarization.

BGP is also a hybrid protocol, drawing a lot of its functionality from distance vector protocols. It is based on a standard (RFC 1772) and is used as the de facto routing protocol to interconnect ISPs on the Internet. Unlike most of the other protocols that use multicasts or broadcasts for dissemination, BGP sets up a TCP connection (port 179) to a neighboring peer and uses TCP to get reliable share connection information. Like EIGRP and OSPF, BGP supports route summarization. Unlike these protocols, BGP was meant to route between autonomous systems.

The focus of the CCNA exam for routing configuration is primarily on RIPv1 and IGRP; however, you will need to be familiar with the basics of RIPv1 and v2, IGRP, EIGRP, and OSPF. The following chapters in this book spend more time on the operation of these protocols, as well as their configuration.

CERTIFICATION OBJECTIVE 9.05

Problems with Distance Vector Protocols

The remainder of this chapter focuses on the problems that pertain to distance vector routing protocols: they converge slowly, and they are prone to routing (layer-3) loops. The next few sections cover these problems, as well as present solutions implemented by distance vector protocols to solve these problems

Problem: Convergence

The term *convergence*, in routing terms, refers to the time it takes for all of the routers to understand the current topology of the network. Link state protocols tend to converge very quickly, while distance vector protocols tend to converge slowly.

Convergence Example

To understand the issue that distance vector protocols have with convergence, look at an example. Here, I'll assume that the periodic timer for the distance vector protocol is set to 60 seconds. I'll use the network shown in Figure 9-2. I'll also assume that the distance vector protocol is using hop count as a metric and that no special features are implemented in this example to solve convergence or routing loop problems.

This example has three routers: RouterA, RouterB, and RouterC, where these routers were just turned on. As you can see from the routers' routing tables, the only routes these routers initially know about are the directly connected routes, which they learn by examining the status of their interfaces, making sure that they are *up* and *up*; they then take the network numbers (learned from the IP address and subnet mask) and put this information in their routing tables. Currently, each router contains two routes in its routing table. Also notice the metric: these routes have a hop count of 0, since they are directly connected.

FIGURE 9-2 Convergence example after routers are turned on

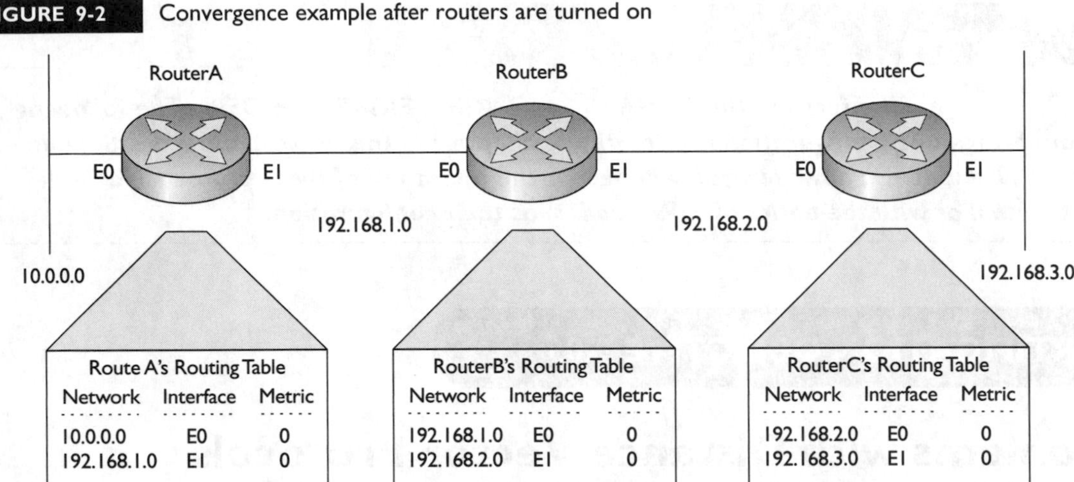

Now that their interfaces are active and the routers have an initial routing table, they'll send out their first routing broadcast on these interfaces (they don't wait for their periodic timer in this instance). This broadcast contains the entries that they have in their routing tables. Let's assume that all routers are synchronized when they advertise their routing broadcasts, even though this would be highly unlikely in a production environment. This list shows which routers are advertising which routes on their active interfaces:

- **RouterA** Networks 10.0.0.0 and 192.168.1.0
- **RouterB** Networks 192.168.1.0 and 192.168.2.0
- **RouterC** Networks 192.168.2.0 and 192.168.3.0

After this first exchange of routing tables, each router will process its neighbor's received update and incorporate these changes, if necessary. Figure 9-3 displays the contents of the routing tables on the routers after this first exchange.

Let's break this process down one router at a time, starting with RouterA:

1. Receives networks 192.168.1.0 and 192.168.2.0 from RouterB and increments the metric by one hop for each route
2. Compares the advertised routes from RouterB to what it has in its routing table
3. Adds 192.168.2.0 because it is not in the routing table
4. Ignores 192.168.1.0 from RouterB because RouterB has a hop count of 1, while the current routing table entry in the routing table has a hop count of 0

FIGURE 9-3 Convergence example after first routing update

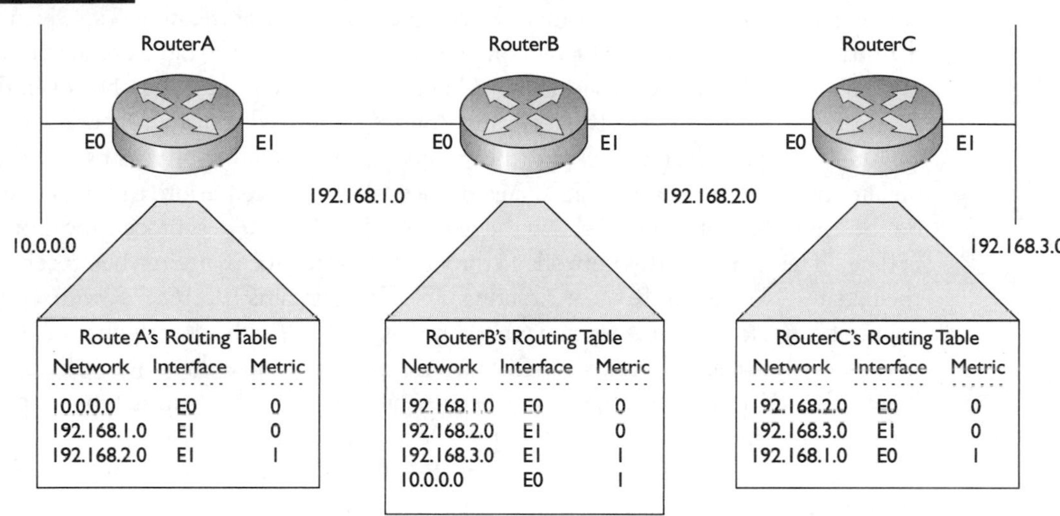

Let's look at RouterC next:

1. Receives networks 192.168.1.0 and 192.168.2.0 from RouterB and increments the metric by one hop
2. Compares the advertised routes from RouterB to what it has in its routing table
3. Adds 192.168.1.0 because it is not in the routing table
4. Ignores 192.168.2.0 from RouterB because RouterB has a hop count of 1 while the current routing table entry has a metric of 0

I've saved RouterB for last, since it presents a more complicated situation: it is receiving routes from both RouterA and RouterB. Here are the steps RouterB goes through:

1. Receives networks 10.0.0.0 and 192.168.1.0 from RouterA and 192.168.2.0 and 192.168.3.0 from RouterC and increments the metric by one hop
2. Compares the advertised routes from RouterA and RouterC to what it has in its routing table
3. Adds 10.0.0.0 and 192.168.3.0 because they are not currently in the routing table
4. Ignores 192.168.1.0 and 192.168.2.0 from RouterA and RouterC respectively because RouterA and RouterC have a metric of 1 for these routes, while the current routing table entries have a metric of 0

Looking at Figure 9-3, have the routers converged? Remember the definition of convergence: the routers understand the complete topology of the network. Given this definition, the routers have not yet converged. RouterA's routing table doesn't contain 192.168.3.0 and RouterC's routing table doesn't contain 10.0.0.0. Note, however, that RouterB has converged, but RouterA and RouterC still need additional routes.

After their periodic timers expire, the routers, again, generate local routing broadcast updates on each of their interfaces. Again, they broadcast their entire routing tables on these interfaces. Figure 9-4 shows the network after these routers process these new updates. The routers in this network go through the same process again when receiving the updates. Notice that RouterA's routing table now contains 192.168.3.0, with a hop count of 2, while RouterC's routing table contains 10.0.0.0, with a hop count of 2. Both of these routers learned these networks via RouterB. And since these networks have a hop count of 1 on RouterB, when the edge routers receive the routing table from RouterB, they increment the hop count to 2 for these network numbers.

Given the routing tables shown in Figure 9-4, the routers have fully converged. The problem, however, is that convergence took place only after two updates. The first update took place as soon as the interface was active, and the second took place 60 seconds later. So, in this example, it took over 60 seconds for convergence to take place. You can imagine that if you have a few hundred routers in your network, it might take many minutes before your network converges and each router knows about all of the destinations that are reachable.

Let's use the same network, but assume that RouterA's E0 interface has failed and that RouterA has lost its connection to network 10.0.0.0, as shown in Figure 9-5. As

FIGURE 9-4 Convergence example after second routing update

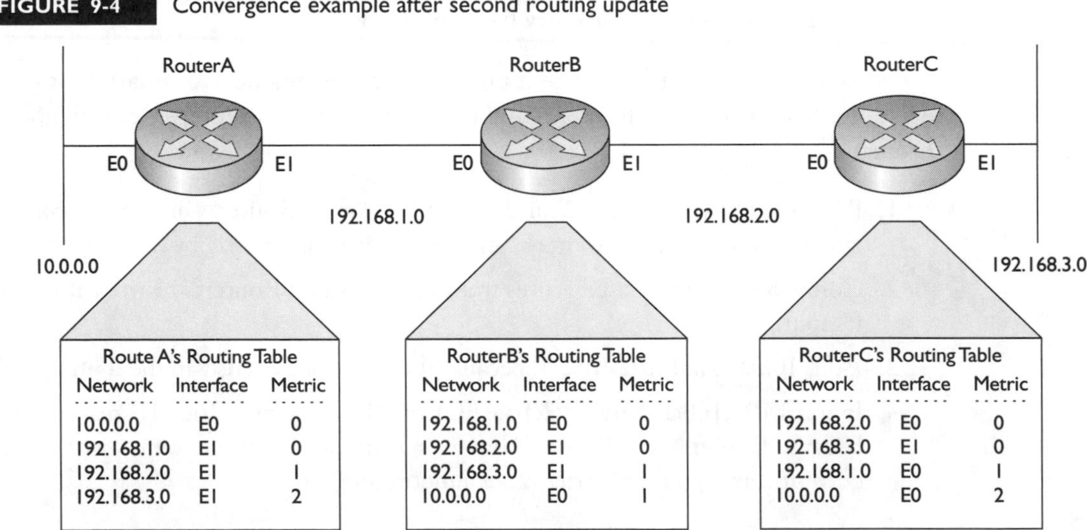

FIGURE 9-5 RouterA's **E0** interface has failed.

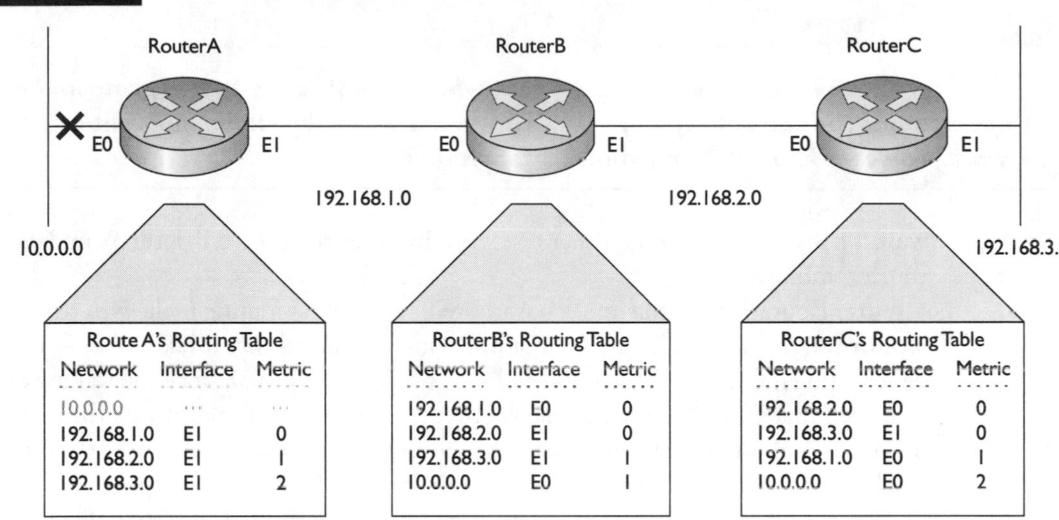

you can see in this example, RouterA's routing table lists the network as unreachable. Unfortunately, RouterA cannot tell the rest of the network about the downed route *until* its periodic timer expires.

After the timer expires, RouterA advertises its routing table to RouterB, which is shown in Figure 9-6. After RouterB receives its update, it has converged. However, RouterC is still lacking this information about the updated topology and must

FIGURE 9-6 RouterB receives the updated information.

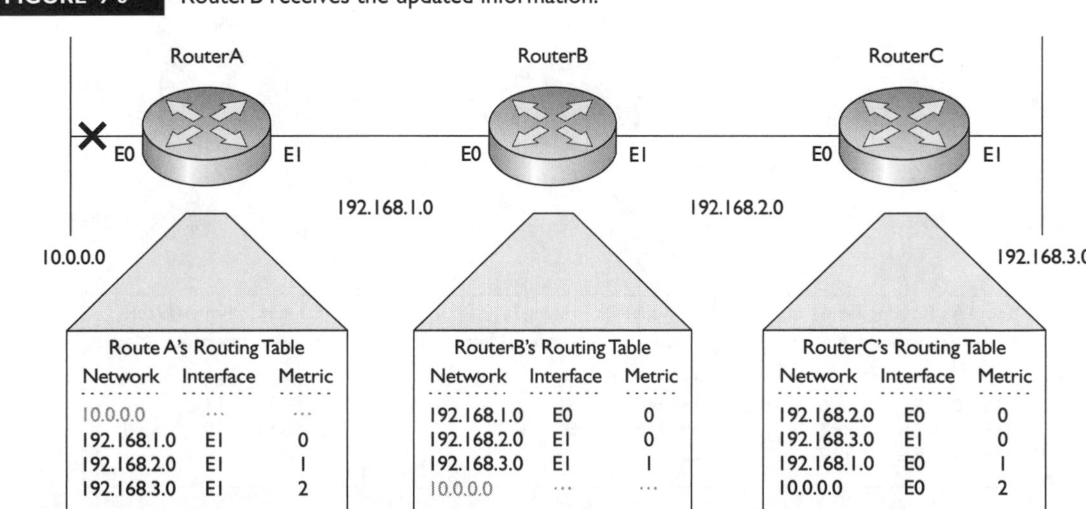

Convergence is when all router understands the current topology of the network. You should be able to figure out whether a distance vector protocol has converged or not by examining routing tables on routers.

wait for RouterB's periodic timer to expire in order to receive RouterB's updated routing table.

After RouterB's periodic timer has expired, it shares its routing table with RouterC, as shown in Figure 9-7. Up to this point, RouterC assumed that it had the most up-to-date routing information and would still send packets to 10.0.0.0, since the routing table indicated that 10.0.0.0 was reachable via RouterB. However, after receiving the routing update from RouterB, RouterC updates its routing table and knows that 10.0.0.0 is not reachable; it will now drop any packets being sent to 10.0.0.0.

Now all three routers have converged. Here are the three things that affected convergence in this example: the time it took for RouterA to discover that e0 failed (a few seconds); the periodic timer on RouterA to advertise this to RouterB (up to 60 seconds); and the periodic timer on RouterB to advertise this to RouterC (up to 60 seconds). Given these three items, it could take over two minutes to converge. As you can see from the past two examples, convergence, with distance vector protocols, is a slow process.

FIGURE 9-7 RouterC receives the updated information.

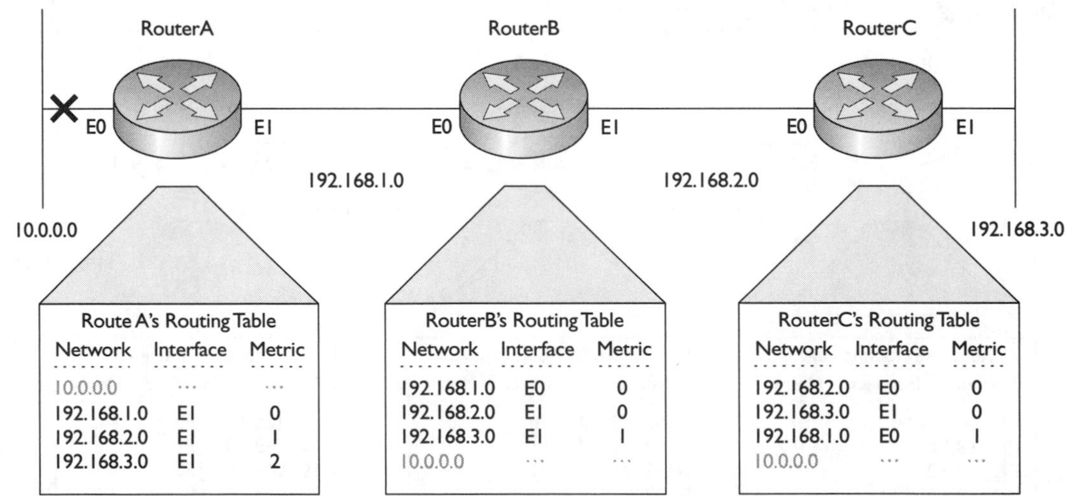

Solution: Triggered Updates

Now that you understand some of the problems associated with convergence in distance vector protocols, let's talk about a possible solution. Given the last three items I listed that affected convergence with the unreachable network (10.0.0.0), the two items that slowed down convergence were periodic timers. You actually have two solutions that you can use in order to speed convergence: change the periodic timer interval and/or use triggered updates.

One solution is to change the periodic timer interval. For instance, in our example the timer was set to 60 seconds. To speed up convergence, you might want to set the interval to 10 seconds. In our example, then, convergence would take only about 20 seconds. However, in today's networks, even waiting this amount of time still creates network disruptions. Also, by setting the timer to 10 seconds, you are creating six times the amount of routing broadcast traffic, which is not very efficient.

A second solution is to implement triggered updates. Triggered updates complement periodic updates. The distance vector routing protocol would still generate periodic updates; however, whenever a change takes place, the router will immediately generate an update without waiting for the periodic timer to expire. This can decrease convergence times, but it also creates a problem. If you have a flapping route, then an update will be triggered each time the route changes state, which creates a lot of unnecessary broadcast traffic in your network and could cause a broadcast storm. IGRP is an example of a distance vector protocol that implements triggered updates.

Problem: Routing Loops

The other main problem of distance vector protocols is that they are prone to routing loops. A *routing loop* is a layer-3 loop in the network. Basically, it is a disagreement about how to reach a destination network.

Routing Loop Example

Let's take a look at a simple example of what kind of problems routing loops can create. I'll use the network shown in Figure 9-8. In this example, I'll assume that RouterX was originally advertising 192.168.4.0 to RouterA, which passed this on to RouterB. RouterX, though, has failed and is no longer advertising 192.168.4.0. However, both RouterA and RouterB advertise 192.168.4.0 to each other, creating confusion about how to reach 192.168.4.0, if it can even be reached (which in this case, it can't). In this example, RouterA thinks that to reach 192.168.4.0, it should

FIGURE 9-8 Simple routing loop example

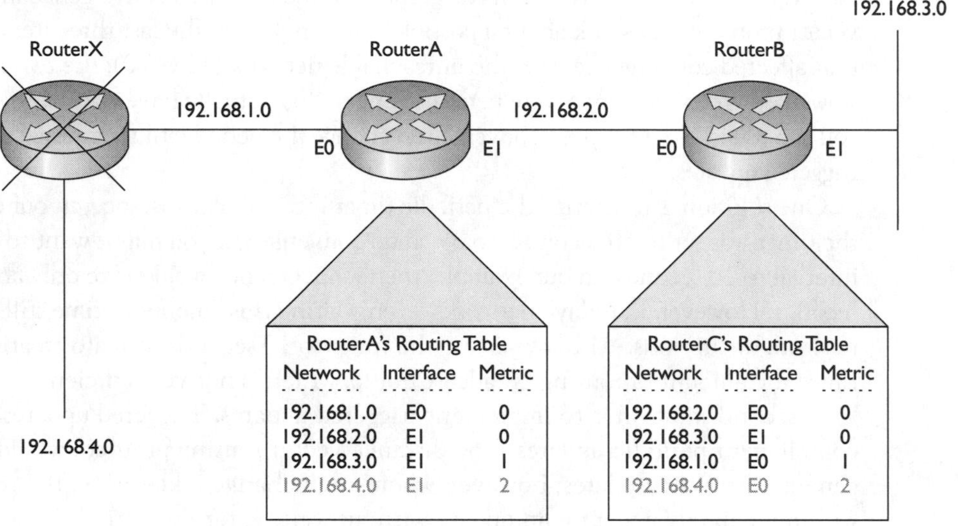

send these packets to RouterB. RouterB, on the other hand, thinks that to reach 192.168.4.0, it should use RouterA. This is a very simple example of a routing loop. Typically, routing loops are created because of confusion in the network related to the deficiencies of using periodic timers.

Distance vector protocols have mechanisms that they can use to deal with routing loop problems. However, these solutions slow down convergence. Link state and some hybrid protocols deal with routing loops with more intelligent methods that don't slow down convergence. The following sections cover the methods that a distance vector protocol might implement to solve routing loop problems.

Counting to Infinity Solution: Maximum Hop Count

One problem with a routing loop is the *counting to infinity* symptom. When a routing loop occurs and a packet or packets are caught in the loop, they continuously circle around the loop, wasting bandwidth on the segments and CPU cycles on the routers that are processing these packets.

To prevent packets from circling around the loop forever, distance vector protocols typically place a hop count limit as to how far a packet is legally allowed to travel. As a packet travels from router to router, a router keeps track of the hops in the TTL field in the IP datagram header: for each hop a packet goes through, the packet's TTL field is decremented by one. If this value reaches 0, the packet is dropped by the router that decremented the value from 1 to 0. The function of the TTL field was covered in Chapter 3.

Placing a maximum hop count limitation on packets, however, doesn't solve routing loop problems—the loop still exists. This solution only prevents packets from getting stuck in the loop. Another issue with placing a hop count limit on packets is that in some instances, the destination that the packet is trying to reach exceeds the maximum hop count allowed. A router doesn't distinguish between valid destinations and routing loop destinations when examining the TTL field; if the maximum is reached, then the packet is dropped.

IP RIP and IPX RIP set a hop count limit of 15, by default, and IGRP allows a hop count of 100. When a packet comes into an interface of a router, it decrements the TTL field, and if the hop count falls to 0, the router immediately drops the packet. If you have a destination that is beyond these limits, you can change the maximum hop count for your routing protocol; however, you should do this on every router in your network.

Routing loops are a misunderstanding about the reachability of a destination and are a common problem with distance vector protocols. Different solutions are used to deal with routing loops and their problems. Counting to infinity is dealt with by assigning a hop count limit to restrict how far a packet can travel.

Solution: Split Horizon

Distance vector protocols implement a few solutions to deal with routing loops. *Split horizon* is used with small routing loops. Split horizon states that if a neighboring router sends a route to a router, the receiving router will *not* propagate this route back to the advertising router on the same interface.

Consider Figure 9-9 to see how split horizon functions. RouterA advertises 192.168.1.0 to RouterB out its E1 interface. Without split horizon in effect, RouterB could advertise this network right back to RouterA. Obviously, RouterA would ignore this, since the directly connected path is better than RouterB's advertised path. However, what would happen if RouterA's E0 interface failed and it received an update from RouterB stating that it had an *alternative* path to 192.168.1.0?

FIGURE 9-9 Split horizon example

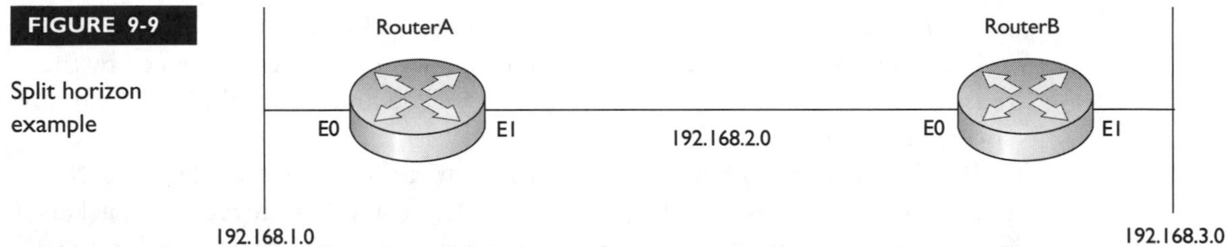

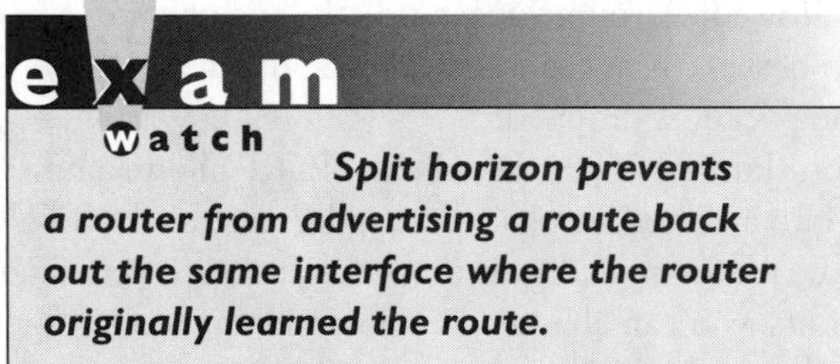

Split horizon prevents a router from advertising a route back out the same interface where the router originally learned the route.

In this situation, the network obviously has connectivity problems. With split horizon, though, RouterB would never advertise 192.168.1.0 back to RouterA. Therefore, if RouterA's E0 interface would fail, both RouterA and RouterB would realize that there is no alternative path to reach this network until RouterA's E0 connection is fixed.

Solution: Route Poisoning

Whereas split horizon is used to solve small routing loop problems, distance vector protocols use two mechanisms to deal with large routing loop problems: *route poisoning* and *hold down timers*. Route poisoning is a derivative of split horizon. When a router detects that one of its connected routes has failed, the router will *poison* the route by assigning an infinite metric to it. In IP RIP, the route is assigned a hop count of 16 (15 is the maximum), thus making it an *unreachable* network.

exam watch

A poisoned route has an infinite metric assigned to it. A poison reverse causes the router to break the split horizon rule and advertise the poisoned route out all interfaces.

When a router advertises a poisoned route to its neighbors, its neighbors break the rule of split horizon and send back to the originator the same poisoned route, called a *poison reverse*. This ensures that everyone received the original update of the poisoned route.

Hold-Down Timers

In order to give the routers enough time to propagate the poisoned route and to ensure that no routing loops occur while propagation is occurring, the routers implement a *hold-down* mechanism. During this period, the routers will freeze the poisoned route in their routing tables for the period of the hold-down timer, which is typically three times the interval of the routing broadcast update.

When hold-down timers are used, a poisoned route will remain in the routing table until the timer expires. However, if a router with a poisoned route receives a routing update from a neighboring router with a metric that is the same or better than the original route, the router will abort the hold-down period, remove the poisoned route, and put the new route in its table. However, if a router receives a worse route from a neighboring router, the router treats this as a suspect route and assumes that this route is probably part of a routing loop, ignoring the update. Of course, the worse-metric route really might be a valid alternative path to the network; however, the function of hold-down timers and poisoning routes prohibits the use of this route until the hold period expires. While in a hold-down state, a poisoned route in the routing table will appear as *possibly down*.

One of the problems of using hold-down timers is that they cause the distance vector routing protocol to converge slowly—if the hold-down period is 180 seconds, you can't use a valid alternative path with a worse metric until the hold-down period expires. Therefore, your users will lose their connections to this network for at least three minutes.

Hold-down timers are used to keep the poisoned route in the routing table long enough that the poisoned route has a chance to be propagated to all other routers in the network. One downside to hold-down timers is that they slow down convergence.

Example of Route Poisoning and Hold-Down Timers

Understanding how poisoned routes and hold-down timers work can become complex. Let's take a look at an example to see how these two mechanisms work hand-in-hand to solve large routing loop problems. I'll use the network shown in Figure 9-10. In this example, I'll assume the routers are running IP RIPv1.

In this example, RouterA's E0 interface fails, causing it to lose its connection to 192.168.1.0. Since RIPv1 doesn't use triggered updates, as IGRP does, the routing protocol must wait for its periodic timer to expire before broadcasting its routing information to RouterB and RouterC. In RIPv1, the periodic update timer is set to 30 seconds. RouterA will poison the route (assign an infinite metric of 16 to 192.168.1.0) and send this to the other two routers when the periodic update timer expires.

When RouterB and RouterC receive the routing update with the poisoned route from RouterA, they will send back a poison reverse to RouterA. All routers will freeze

FIGURE 9-10

Route poisoning and hold-down timer example

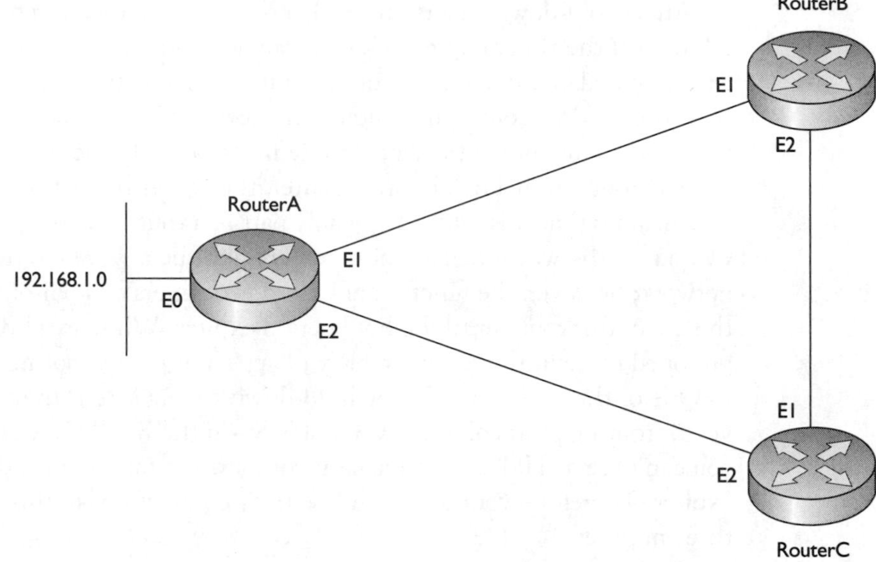

the poisoned route in their routing table for the period of the hold-down timer. In RIPv1, this defaults to 180 seconds. RouterB and RouterC also advertise the poisoned route in their routing updates out any other active interfaces (once their periodic timers expire). As the propagation of the poisoned route is occurring, the routers that have already received it are counting down from their hold-down timer value.

If another router in the network advertises a worse path to 192.168.1.0 (this has to be a worse hop count than the route originally advertised from RouterA), the three routers shown in the network diagram won't use it, since they have frozen the poisoned route in their routing tables. The reason for this hold-down period is that someone else might be advertising 192.168.1.0, but it might not be a valid path. In other words, another router might be advertising reachability to 192.168.1.0, but it is assuming that this network is reachable via RouterA. In this situation, this rogue router hasn't received the poisoned route—the hold-down timer for the other routers, however, ensures that these rogue routers don't corrupt the routing tables by introducing incorrect or bad routing information, causing a routing loop.

During this process, if RouterA is able to fix its connection to 192.168.1.0, it will start advertising the reachability of the network to RouterB and RouterC. Since the metric RouterA is advertising is the same as the metric it had previously announced for this route, RouterB and RouterC will cancel their hold-down times and replace the poisoned route with the new information.

EXERCISE 9-2

Basic IP and Routing Troubleshooting

This chapter dealt with the basics of routers and routing. This exercise is a troubleshooting exercise and is different from the other exercises you have performed so far. In previous exercises, you were given a configuration task. In this exercise, the network is already configured; however, there are three problems in this network you'll need to find and fix in order for it to operate correctly. All of these problems deal with IP (layer-3) connectivity. You'll perform this exercise using Boson's NetSim simulator. You can find a picture of the network diagram for Boson's NetSim simulator in the Introduction of this book. The addressing scheme is the same. After starting up the simulator, click the *LabNavigator* button. Next, double-click *Exercise 9-2* and click the *Load Lab* button. This will load the lab configuration based on Chapter 5's exercises.

Lets' start with your problem: Host1 cannot ping Host3. Your task is to figure out what the problems are and fix them: there are three problems. I would recommend that you try this troubleshooting process on your own first; and if you have problems, come back to the steps and solutions shown here.

1. Test connectivity from Host1 to Host3 with ping as well as from Host1 to its default gateway.

   At the top of the simulator in the menu bar, click the *eStations* icon and choose *Host1*. On Host1, ping Host3: **ping 192.168.3.2**. Note that the ping fails. Examine the IP configuration on Host1 by executing: **winipcfg**. Make sure the IP addressing information is correct: IP address of 192.168.1.10, subnet mask of 255.255.255.0, and default gateway address of 192.168.1.1. Click the *Cancel* button to close **winipcfg**. Ping the default gateway address: **ping 192.168.1.1**. The ping should be successful, indicating that at least layer-3 is functioning between Host1 and the 2600.

2. Test connectivity from Host3 to its default gateway.

   At the top of the simulator in the menu bar, click the *eStations* icon and choose *Host3*. Examine the IP configuration on Host3 by executing: **winipcfg**. Make sure the IP addressing information is correct: IP address of 192.168.3.2, subnet mask of 255.255.255.0, and default gateway address of 192.168.3.1. Click the *Cancel* button to close **winipcfg**. Ping the default gateway address: **ping 192.168.3.1**. The ping should fail, indicating that there is a problem between Host3 and the 2500. In this example, layer-2 is functioning correctly; therefore, the problem must lie with the 2500.

3. Check the 2500's IP configuration.

   At the top of the simulator in the menu bar, click the *eRouters* icon and choose *2500*. From the 2500, ping Host3: **ping 192.168.3.2**. The ping should fail. Examine the interface on the 2500: **show interface e0**. The interface is disabled, but has the correct IP address: 192.168.3.1. Enable the interface: **configure terminal**, **interface e0**, **no shutdown**, **end**. The interface should come up. Retry the ping test: **ping 192.168.3.2**. The ping should be successful.

4. Access Host1 and retry pinging Host3.

   At the top of the simulator in the menu bar, click the *eStations* icon and choose *Host1*. Test connectivity to Host3: **ping 192.168.3.2**. The ping should still fail. So far, at least there is connectivity within 192.168.1.0 and 192.168.3.0; but there is still a problem between these two networks.

5. Check the interface statuses on the 2600 and verify connectivity to the 2500.

   At the top of the simulator in the menu bar, click the *eRouters* icon and choose *2600*. Check the status of the interfaces: **show ip interface brief**. Notice that the `fa0/0` and `s0` are *up and up*. Try pinging the 2500's `serial0` interface: **ping 192.168.2.2**. The ping fails. Examine the CDP information that the 2600 has learned about the 2500: **show cdp entry 2500**. Notice that the 2500 has the wrong IP address (192.168.22.2).

6. Fix the IP addressing problem on the 2500 and retest connectivity across the serial connection.

   At the top of the simulator in the menu bar, click the *eRouters* icon and choose *2500*. Fix the IP address: **configure terminal**, **interface serial0**, **ip address 192.168.2.2 255.255.255.0**, **end**. Retest the connection to the 2600: **ping 192.168.2.1**. The ping should be successful.

7. Test connectivity from the 2500 to Host1. Examine the routing table.

   Test the connection to Host1: **ping 192.168.1.10**. The ping should be successful. This indicates that you have full layer-3 connectivity between the 2500 and Host1 and the 2500 and Host3; however, there is an issue getting traffic through the 2500. Examine the routing table: **show ip route**. As you can see, 192.168.1.0 shows up as a static route and points to 192.168.2.1.

8. Access Host3 and try connectivity between its default gateway and the 2600 router.

   At the top of the simulator in the menu bar, click the *eStations* icon and choose *Host3*. Test the connection to the 2500: **ping 192.168.3.1**. The ping should be successful, considering that we already tested it. Test connectivity to the 2600: **ping 192.168.2.1**. The ping should fail. This presents an interesting problem. The 2600 can ping the 2500. Host3 can ping the 2500. Therefore, on a hop-by-hop basis, we have IP connectivity. The 2500 can even ping Host1, indicating that some routing functioning is working.

9. Access the 2600 router and examine its routing table. Fix the problem.

   At the top of the simulator in the menu bar, click the *eRouters* icon and choose *2600*. Examine the routing table: **show ip route**. Does the 2600 know how to reach 192.168.3.0/24? It does not. The 2500 router could ping Host1 since the 2600 router is directly connected to these segments; but any traffic from the 2600 to 192.168.3.0/24 will fail since the router doesn't have a path. Add a static route to 192.168.3.0/24: **configure terminal**, **ip route 192.168.3.0 255.255.255.0 192.168.2.2** and **end**. Test connectivity to Host3: **ping 192.168.3.2**. The ping should be successful.

10. Now test connectivity between Host1 and Host3.

    At the top of the simulator in the menu bar, click the *eStations* icon and choose *Host1*. Test connectivity to Host3: **ping 192.168.3.2**. The ping should be successful.

CERTIFICATION SUMMARY

Routers find layer-3 paths to destination networks and switch packets from one interface to another to get the packets to their respective destinations. Routers learn about neighboring routers, find locations to destination locations, choose the best paths, and maintain up-to-date routing information. A routed protocol is a layer-3 protocol, like IP or IPX. A routing protocol defines how to find destinations for a routed protocol.

Some routing protocols, such as IGRP and EIGRP, use autonomous systems, which group networks under a single administrative control. Administrative distance is used by a Cisco router to choose among multiple routing protocols to put a destination in the routing table. The routing protocol with the lowest administrative distance with a path to the destination is placed in the routing table.

There are two types of routing protocols: static and dynamic. To create a static route, use the **ip route** command. For a default route, use `0.0.0.0/0` as the network number and subnet mask. To view your router's routing table, use the **show ip route** command.

A router-on-stick uses a single trunk connection from a router to a switch to route among multiple VLANs. You must create a subinterface on your router for each VLAN. Each subinterface requires the **`encapsulation isl|dot1q`** command and a layer-3 address or addresses.

When choosing a dynamic routing protocol, you should consider routing metrics, how routing information is shared, convergence time, how routing information is processed, and routing overhead. Routing metrics define the method used to calculate a cost to a destination. For instance, IP RIP uses hop count.

Distance vector protocols use broadcasts to share routing information and don't verify if neighbors receive routing updates. They use the Bellman-Ford algorithm to process updates, which requires very little CPU processing and memory: They receive an update, increment the metrics, compare the results to the routing table, and update the routing table if necessary.

Link state protocols use the SPF algorithm to build the routing table, providing a loop-free topology. They use multicasts to share routing information incrementally and verify that neighbors received this information. Link state protocols support classless routing and allow you to summarize networking information in your routing table. The main downside of these protocols is that they require more CPU cycles and memory to process and store routing information. They are also prone to flapping route problems.

Hybrid protocols are based on the simplicity of a distance vector protocol but borrow on many features of link state protocols to make them more efficient and scalable. RIPv2, EIGRP, and BGP are examples of hybrid protocols.

Distance vector protocols have problems with convergence and routing loops. Convergence is the amount of time it takes for all of the routers in the network to understand the current topology. Triggered updates can be used to speed up convergence. A routing loop is basically a disagreement about how to reach a particular network. Counting to infinity is resolved by placing a hop count limit to prevent packets from circling around the loop forever. Split horizon is used to prevent the creation of small routing loops: It prevents a router from advertising a route out the same interface from which the route was learned.

Route poisoning, poison reverse, and hold-down timers are used to prevent large routing loops. A route is poisoned if a network connected to a router goes down. Poison reverse has a router advertise a poisoned route out all interfaces, including the interface from which it was learned. Hold-down timers keep the poisoned route in the routing table to ensure the poisoned route is propagated to all routers before any (worse) alternative paths are chosen.

TWO-MINUTE DRILL

Types of Routes

- ❑ Routers learn about connected routers, find locations of destination networks, choose the best paths to each destination, and maintain their routing tables.
- ❑ A static route is a manually configured route. A connected route is a network that the router is directly connected to on an interface.
- ❑ An autonomous system (AS) is a group of networks under a single administrative control, which could be your company, a division within your company, or a group of companies.
- ❑ Administrative distance is a Cisco-proprietary mechanism used to rank IP routing protocols and helps the router populate the routing table. If you are running more than one routing protocol, this is used to determine which routing protocol to use when populating the routing table. The lower the administrative distance number, the more preferred it is.

Static Routes

- ❑ Use the **ip route** command to configure a static route.
- ❑ After the subnet mask parameter, you have two ways of specifying how to reach the destination network: you can tell the router either the next hop neighbor's IP address or the interface the router should exit to reach the destination network. The former has an administrative distance of 1 and the later, 0 (a directly connected route).
- ❑ Use the **ip classless** command to allow a routing protocol to accept a route with a nonconforming subnet mask value.

Router-on-a-Stick

- ❑ A *router-on-a-stick* is a router with a single trunk connection to a switch; it routes between the VLANs on this trunk connection.
- ❑ To route between VLANs with a router-on-a-stick, use subinterfaces and specify the VLAN with the **encapsulation isl|dot1q** command on the subinterface.

Dynamic Routing Protocols

- Internally, a routing protocol will use a metric to choose a best path to reach a destination.
- Distance vector protocols, such as RIPv1 and IGRP, use distance and direction to find paths to a destination and are referred to as routing by rumor. They generate periodic updates as broadcasts and build no formal relationship with other routers. They require little processing and memory, since they only need to increment metrics and compare these to routes in the routing table.
- Link state protocols, such as OSPF, use the SPF algorithm and understand the complete topology of the network (routing by propaganda). They multicast LSAs, which are specific routes, when changes occur in the network. The LSAs are stored in a link state database. These protocols converge fast, since they use incremental updates, but require more memory and processing power. They also support a hierarchical structure and route summarization.
- Hybrid protocols, such as RIPv2 and EIGRP, take the advantages of both distance vector and link state protocols and merge them together.

Problems with Distance Vector Protocols

- Distance vector protocols converge slowly because of periodic updates. IGRP overcomes this by using triggered updates.
- Distance vector protocols are prone to routing loops. To solve this, they use these mechanisms: hop count limits, split horizon, poisoned routes, and hold-down timers.
- To prevent packets from circling around the loop forever, distance vector protocols typically place a hop count limit as to how far a packet is legally allowed to travel, referred to as maximum hop count, or time-to-live (TTL).
- Split horizon states that if a neighboring router sends a route to a router, the receiving router will not propagate this route back to the advertising router on the same interface.
- With route poisoning, when a router detects that one of its connected routes has failed, the router will *poison* the route by assigning an infinite metric to it and advertising it to neighbors. When a router advertises a poisoned route to its neighbors, its neighbors break the rule of split horizon and send back to the originator the same poisoned route, called a *poison reverse*.
- In order to give the routers enough time to propagate the poisoned route and to ensure that no routing loops happen while propagation is occurring, the routers implement a hold-down mechanism.

SELF TEST

The following Self Test questions will help you measure your understanding of the material presented in this chapter. Read all the choices carefully, as there may be more than one correct answer. Choose all correct answers for each question.

Types of Routes

1. __________ is/are a routed protocol.

A. RIP

B. OSPF

C. Both RIP and OSPF

D. Neither RIP or OSPF

2. A __________ routes between different autonomous systems.

A. BPG

B. EGP

C. IFP

D. IGP

3. Your router is running RIP and OSPF, and both routing protocols are learning 192.168.1.0/24. Which routing protocol will your router use for this route?

A. RIP

B. OSPF

Static Routes

4. Enter the command to set up a static route to 192.168.1.0/24, where the next hop address is 192.168.2.2: __________.

5. What subnet mask would you use to set up a default route?

A. 0.0.0.0

B. 255.255.255.255

C. Depends on the type of network number

D. None of these answers

6. Enter the command to allow your routing protocol to accept nonconforming subnet masks, like a default route: __________.

Router-on-a-Stick

7. When configuring a router-on-a-stick, the configuration is done on __________.
   A. Physical interfaces
   B. Major subinterfaces
   C. Subinterfaces
8. Which router-on-a-stick command defines the VLAN for the interface?
   A. `vlan`
   B. `encapsulation`
   C. `trunk`
   D. `frame-type`

Dynamic Routing Protocols

9. When choosing a dynamic routing protocol, which of the following should not be considered?
   A. Metrics used
   B. How routing information is shared
   C. How routing information is processed
   D. Number of PCs in the network
10. A routing protocol will use a(n) _________ to determine which path is the best path.
    A. Administrative distance
    B. Metric
    C. Hop count
    D. Cost
11. Distance vector protocols use ___________ to disseminate routing information.
    A. Unicasts
    B. Multicasts
    C. Broadcasts
12. Which type of routing protocol uses the Shortest Path First algorithm?
    A. Distance vector
    B. Link state
    C. Hybrid

13. Which is an example of a hybrid protocol?

A. IGRP

B. EIGRP

C. RIPv1

D. OSPF

Problems with Distance Vector Protocols

14. What would you use to prevent a packet from traveling around a routing loop forever?

A. Split horizon

B. Poison reverse

C. Hold-down timer

D. TTL

15. __________ states that if a neighboring router sends a route to a router, the receiving router will not propagate this route back to the advertising router on the same interface.

A. Split horizon

B. Poison reverse

C. Hold-down timer

D. Hop count limit

SELF TEST ANSWERS

Types of Routes

1. ☑ **D.** RIP and OSPF are *routing* protocols. Routed protocols are IP, IPX, AppleTalk, and so on.
☒ **A**, **B**, and **C** are routing protocols.

2. ☑ **B.** An Exterior Gateway Protocol (EGP) routes between autonomous systems.
☒ **D** routes within an AS. **A** and **C** are nonexistent routing protocols.

3. ☑ **B.** OSPF has a lower administrative distance: 110. The lower one is given preference.
☒ **A** has a higher administrative distance: 120.

Static Routes

4. ☑ **`ip route 192.168.1.0 255.255.255.0 192.168.2.2`**

5. ☑ **A.** A default route is set up with an IP address and mask of 0.0.0.0 0.0.0.0.
☒ **B** indicates that the complete IP address is a network number. **C** is dependent on the mask, not the network number. And since there is a correct answer, **D** is incorrect.

6. ☑ **`ip classless`**

Router-on-a-Stick

7. ☑ **C.** When configuring a router-on-a-stick, the configuration is done on subinterfaces.
☒ **A** is used for access-link connections, not trunk connections. **B** is non-existent.

8. ☑ **B.** Use the **`encapsulation`** command to specify the trunking encapsulation and the VLAN number for the subinterface.
☒ **A**, **C**, and **D** are nonexistent router commands.

Dynamic Routing Protocols

9. ☑ **D.** It's not the number of devices, but the number of networks, that might affect the routing protocol that you choose.
☒ **A**, **B**, and **C** are incorrect because they are things you should consider when choosing a routing protocol.

10. ☑ **B.** A routing protocol will use a metric to determine which path is the best path.
☒ **A** is used to choose between different routing protocols, not within a routing protocol. **C** and **D** are types of metrics.

11. ☑ **C.** Distance vector protocols use broadcasts to share routing information.
☒ **A** is used by BGP, which is a hybrid protocol. **B** is used by link state and hybrid protocols.

12. ☑ **B.** Link state protocols use the SPF algorithm, developed by Dijkstra, in order to choose the best path to a destination.
☒ **A** uses distance and direction when choosing best paths. **C** protocols typically use methods based on distance vector protocols.

13. ☑ **B.** EIGRP is a hybrid protocol, along with RIPv2.
☒ **D** is a link state protocol. **A** and **C** are distance vector protocols.

Problems with Distance Vector Protocols

14. ☑ **D.** TTL, which implements a hop count limit, prevents an IP packet from traveling around a routing loop forever.
☒ **A** is used to prevent small routing loops, preventing the advertisement of a route out the same interface it was learned on. **B** and **C** are used to prevent large routing loops: they allow network stabilization by waiting until every router learns about the downed route before accepting an alternative path.

15. ☑ **A.** Split horizon is used to prevent small routing loops, preventing the advertisement of a route out the same interface it was learned on.
☒ **B** assigns an infinite metric to the route, sends it to a neighboring router, and has the neighbor advertise this back to you. **C** sets a timer that a poisoned route is held in the routing table. **D** is used to prevent a packet from traveling around a routing loop forever.

10

Configuring Distance Vector Protocols

CERTIFICATION OBJECTIVES

10.01 IP Routing Protocol Basics

10.02 IP RIP

10.03 IP IGRP

✓ Two-Minute Drill

Q&A Self Test

In the preceding chapter, you gained an overview of routing protocols, including the different types and their advantages and disadvantages. This chapter covers the basic configuration of distance vector protocols, specifically the IP Routing Information Protocol (RIP) and the Interior Gateway Routing Protocol (IGRP). It focuses on the basics of these protocols; advanced configuration of these protocols is beyond the scope of this book. However, by the end of the chapter, you'll be able to configure routers running RIP and IGRP that will route traffic in a network.

CERTIFICATION OBJECTIVE 10.01

IP Routing Protocol Basics

Before learning about how to configure RIP and IGRP, consider some basic configuration tasks that are required no matter what routing protocol you are running. You need to perform two basic steps when setting up IP routing on your router:

- Enable the routing protocol.
- Assign IP addresses to your router's interfaces.

Memorize the two basic steps for setting up IP routing.

Please note that the order of these tasks is not important. You already know how to configure an IP address on the router's interface: this was discussed in Chapter 5. The following sections cover the first bullet point in more depth.

The `router` Command

Enabling an IP routing protocol is a two-step process. First, you must go into *Router Subconfiguration* mode. This mode determines the routing protocol that you'll be running. Within this mode, you'll configure the characteristics of the routing protocol. To enter the routing protocol's configuration mode, use the following command:

```
Router(config)# router name_of_the_IP_routing_protocol
Router(config-router)#
```

The **router** command is used to access the routing protocol that you wish to configure; it doesn't enable it. If you are not sure of the name of the routing protocol that you wish to enable, use the context-sensitive help feature:

```
Router(config)# router ?
  bgp                    Border Gateway Protocol (BGP)
  egp                    Exterior Gateway Protocol (EGP)
  eigrp                  Enhanced Interior Gateway Routing
                              Protocol (EIGRP)
  igrp                   Interior Gateway Routing Protocol (IGRP)
  isis                   ISO IS-IS
  iso-igrp               IGRP for OSI networks
  mobile                 Mobile routes
  odr                    On Demand stub Routes
  ospf                   Open Shortest Path First (OSPF)
  rip                    Routing Information Protocol (RIP)
  static                 Static routes
  traffic-engineering    Traffic engineered routes
Router(config)#
```

As you can see from the context-sensitive help output, you have a lot of IP routing protocols at your disposal. One important item to point out is that the **router** command doesn't turn on the routing protocol. This process is done in the protocol's *Router Subconfiguration* mode, indicated by the (config-router) prompt.

The network Command

Once in the routing protocol, you need to specify what interfaces are to participate in the routing process. By default, no interfaces participate. To specify which interfaces will participate, use the **network** *Router Subconfiguration* mode command:

```
Router(config-router)# network IP_network_#
```

As soon as you enter a network number, the routing process is *active*. For distance vector protocols like RIP and IGRP, you need to enter only the Class A, B, or C network number or numbers that are associated with your interface. In other words, if you have subnetted 192.168.1.0 with a subnet mask of 255.255.255.192 (/26), and you have subnets 192.168.1.0/26, 192.168.1.64/26, 192.168.1.128/26, and 192.168.1.192/26, you don't need to enter each specific subnet. Instead, just enter 192.168.1.0, and this will accommodate all interfaces that are associated with this Class C network. If you specify a subnet, the router will *convert* it to the class address, because RIP and IGRP are classful protocols.

Let's take a look at a simple example to show the configuration, shown in Figure 10-1. In this example, I'll focus on the configuration of the **network** commands, assuming that the routing protocol is a classful protocol, such as RIP or IGRP. In this example, the router is connected to a Class B network (172.16.0.0) and a Class C network (192.168.1.0), both of which are subnetted.

FIGURE 10-1

Simple network example

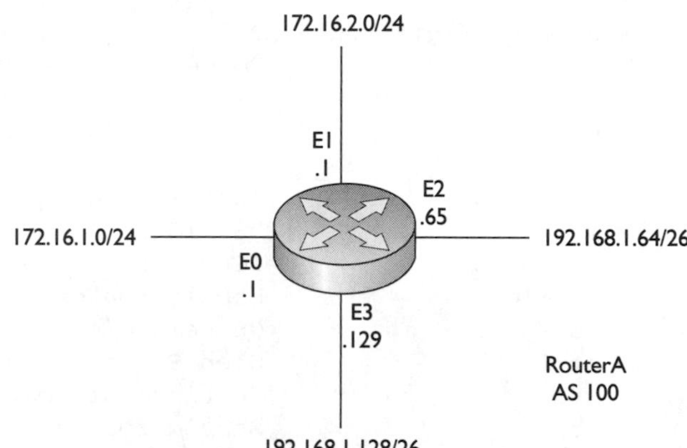

Let's assume that you forgot that you need to enter only the classful network numbers, and that you entered the subnetted values instead, like this:

```
Router(config-router)# network 172.16.1.0
Router(config-router)# network 172.16.2.0
Router(config-router)# network 192.168.1.64
Router(config-router)# network 192.168.1.128
```

When entering your **network** statements, you need to include any network that is associated with your router's interfaces; if you omit a network, then your router will not include the omitted interface in the routing process. As you can see from the preceding example, all of the subnets were included. Remember, however, that the router requires only that you enter the class addresses. If you were to execute a **show running-config** command, you would not see the four networks just listed, but just the Class B and C network numbers. You shouldn't worry about this; it's just that you entered more commands than were necessary. In reality, you needed to enter only two **network** commands:

```
Router(config-router)# network 172.16.0.0
Router(config-router)# network 192.168.1.0
```

exam watch

For exam purposes, I would recommend that you enter the class networks instead of the subnets on the simulator questions. Remember that the simulator is just that—a simulator. It's not a full-functioning IOS router. You'll need to be very familiar with the `router` and `network` commands.

Both ways of entering your statements is correct, but the latter is what the router will use if you type in all of the specific subnets.

10.01. The CD contains a multimedia demonstration of an introduction to basic IP routing protocol configuration.

CERTIFICATION OBJECTIVE 10.02

IP RIP

IP RIP (Routing Information Protocol) comes in two different versions: 1 and 2. Version 1 is a distance vector protocol and is defined in RFC 1058. Version 2 is a hybrid protocol and is defined in RFCs 1721 and 1722. The CCNA exam focuses on version 1. However, you still need to know a few things about RIPv2, specifically its characteristics. This section covers the basics of configuring and troubleshooting your network using IP RIP.

Characteristics of RIPv1 and RIPv2

As you recall from the last chapter, RIP is a distance vector protocol. RIP is a very old protocol and therefore is very stable; in other words, Cisco really doesn't do that much development on the protocol, unlike other, more advanced protocols. Therefore, you can feel very safe that when you upgrade your IOS to a newer version, RIP will function the same way that it did in the previous release. This section includes brief overviews of both versions of RIP.

RIPv1

RIPv1 uses local broadcasts to share routing information. These updates are periodic in nature, occurring, by default, every 30 seconds, with a hold-down period of 180 seconds. Both versions of RIP use *hop count* as a metric, which is not always the best metric to use. For instance, if you had two paths to reach a network, where one was a two-hop Ethernet connection, and the other was a one-hop 64Kbps WAN connection, RIP would use the slower 64Kbps connection because it has a lesser hop count value. You have to remember this little tidbit when looking at how RIP will populate your router's routing table. To prevent packets from circling around a loop forever, both versions of RIP solve counting to infinity by placing a hop count limit of *15* hops on packets. Any packet that reaches the sixteenth hop will be dropped.

And as I mentioned in the last section, RIPv1 is a *classful* protocol. This is important for configuring RIP and subnetting your IP addressing scheme: you can use only one subnet mask value for a given Class A, B, or C network. For instance, if you have a Class B network such as 172.16.0.0, you can subnet it with only one mask. As an example, you couldn't use 255.255.255.0 and 255.255.255.128 on 172.16.0.0—you can choose only one.

Another interesting feature is that RIP supports up to six equal-cost paths to a single destination, where all six paths can be placed in the routing table and the router can load-balance across them. The default is actually four paths, but this can be increased up to a maximum of six. Remember that an equal-cost path is where the hop count value is the same. RIP will not load-balance across *unequal*-cost paths.

IP RIPv1, a classful protocol, broadcasts updates every 30 seconds, and has a hold-down period of 180 seconds. Hop count is used as a metric.

Let's look at Figure 10-2 to illustrate equal-cost-path load balancing. In this example, RouterA has two equal-cost paths to 10.0.0.0 (with a hop count of 1) via RouterB and RouterC. There are actually two advantages of putting both of these paths in RouterA's routing table:

- First, the router can perform load balancing to 10.0.0.0, taking advantage of the bandwidth on both of these links.
- And second, convergence is sped up if one of the paths fails. For example, if the connection between RouterA and RouterB fails, RouterA can still access network 10.0.0.0 via RouterC and has this information in its routing table; therefore, convergence is instantaneous.

For these two reasons, many routing protocols support parallel paths to a single destination. Some protocols, such as IGRP and EIGRP, even support unequal-cost load balancing, which is discussed in the section "IGRP" of this chapter.

RIPv2

One thing you have to keep in the back of your mind when dealing with RIPv2 is that it is based on RIPv1 and is, at heart, a distance vector protocol with routing enhancements built into it. Therefore, it is commonly called a hybrid protocol. I pointed out some of the characteristics that both versions of RIP have in common in the preceding section. This section focuses on the characteristics unique to RIPv2.

One major enhancement to RIPv2 pertains to how it deals with routing updates. Instead of using broadcasts, RIPv2 uses *multicasts*. And to speed up convergence,

FIGURE 10-2

Equal-cost load balancing

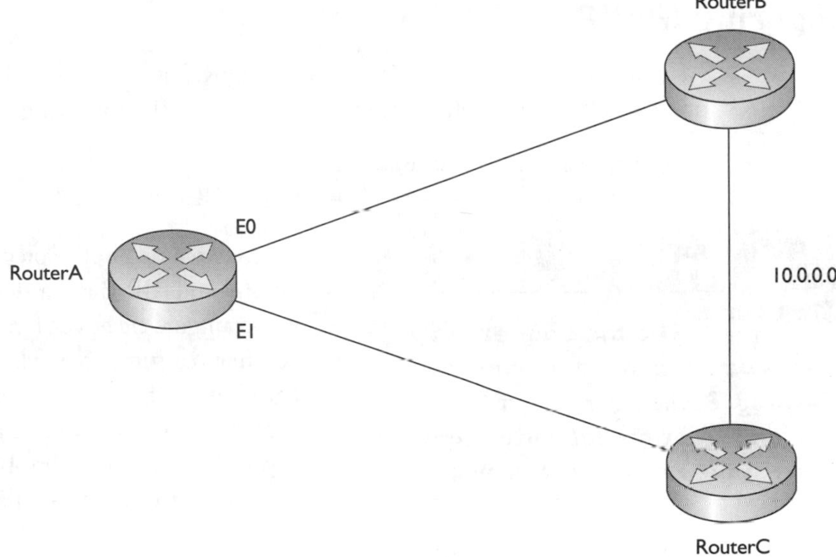

RIPv2 supports *triggered* updates—when a change occurs, a RIPv2 router will immediately propagate its routing information to its connected neighbors.

A second major enhancement that RIPv2 has is that it is a *classless* protocol. RIPv2 supports variable-length subnet masking (VLSM), which allows you to use more than one subnet mask for a given class network number. VLSM allows you to maximize the efficiency of your addressing design as well as to summarize routing information to create very large, scalable networks. VLSM is discussed in Chapter 12.

As a third enhancement, RIPv2 supports authentication. You can restrict what routers you want to participate in RIPv2. This is accomplished using a hashed password value.

Even with all of these advanced characteristics, RIPv2 is still, at heart, a distance vector protocol. It uses hop count as a metric, supports the same solutions to solve routing loop problems, has a 15-hop count limit, and shares other characteristics of RIPv1.

exam watch

RIPv2 is a hybrid protocol, based on RIPv1. It uses multicasts to disseminate routing information and supports triggered updates. Unlike RIPv1, RIPv2 supports VLSM, which allows you to summarize routing information. Otherwise, its characteristics are like RIPv1.

Configuring IP RIP

As you will see in this section, configuring RIP is a very easy and straightforward process. The basic configuration of RIP involves the following two commands:

```
Router(config)# router rip
Router(config-router)# network IP_network_#
```

Use the router rip and network commands to configure RIP routing. Remember to put in the class address (not the subnetted network number) in the network statement.

As explained in the preceding section, RIPv1 is classful and RIPv2 is classless. However, whenever you configure *either* version of RIP, the **network** command assumes *classful*: You need to enter only the Class A, B, or C network number, not the subnets, as was discussed earlier in this chapter. If you refer back to Figure 10-1, the router's RIPv1 configuration would look like this:

```
Router(config)# router rip
Router(config-router)# network 172.16.0.0
Router(config-router)# network 192.168.1.0
```

10.02. The CD contains a multimedia demonstration of a basic RIP configuration on a router.

Specifying RIP Version 1 and 2

By default, the IOS *accepts* both RIPv1 and RIPv2 routing updates; however, it *generates* only RIPv1 updates. You can configure your router to

- Accept and send RIPv1 only
- Accept and send RIPv2 only
- Use a combination of the two, depending on your interface configuration

To accomplish either of the first two items in the list, you need to set the version in your RIP configuration:

```
Router(config)# router rip
Router(config-router)# version 1|2
```

When you specify the appropriate version number, your RIP routing process will send and receive only the version packet type that you configured.

You can also control which version of RIP is running on an interface-by-interface basis. For instance, you might have a bunch of new routers at your site that support both versions and a remote office that understands only RIPv1. In this situation, you can configure your routers to generate RIPv2 updates on all their LAN interfaces, but for the remote access connection at the corporate site, you could set the interface to run only RIPv1.

To control which version of RIP should handle generating updates on an interface, use the following configuration:

```
Router(config)# interface type [slot_#/]port_#
Router(config-router)# ip rip send version 1 | version 2 |
                         version 1 2
```

A Cisco router running RIP, by default, generates only RIPv1 updates but processes received v1 and v2 updates. Use the `version` command to change the RIP version.

With the **`ip rip send`** command, you can control which version of RIP the router should use on the specified interface when *generating* RIP updates. You can be specific by specifying version 1 or 2, or you can specify both.

To control what version of RIP should be used when receiving RIP updates, use the following configuration:

```
Router(config)# interface type [slot_#/]port_#
Router(config-router)# ip rip receive version 1 | version 2 |
                         version 1 2
```

10.03. The CD contains a multimedia demonstration of RIPv2 configuration on a router.

Configuration Example

Let's use a simple network example, shown in Figure 10-3, to illustrate configuring RIPv1.Here's RouterA's configuration:

```
RouterA(config)# router rip
RouterA(config-router)# network 192.168.1.0
RouterA(config-router)# network 192.168.2.0
```

Here's RouterB's configuration:

```
RouterB(config)# router rip
RouterB(config-router)# network 192.168.2.0
RouterB(config-router)# network 192.168.3.0
```

As you can see, to configure RIP is very easy.

FIGURE 10-3 RIPv1 configuration example

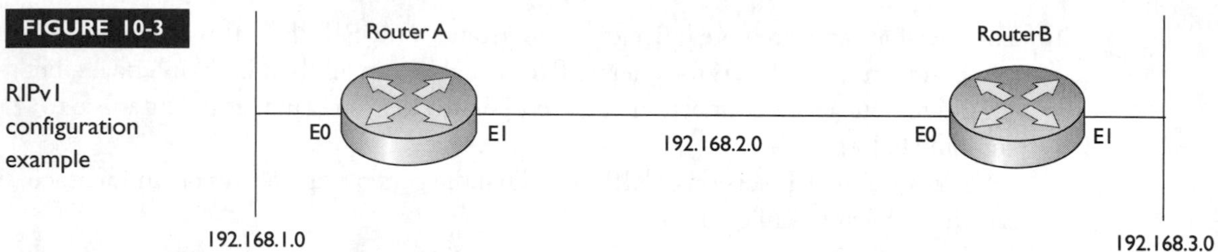

Troubleshooting IP RIP

Once you have configured IP RIP, you have a variety of commands available to view and troubleshoot your configuration and operation of RIP:

- **`show ip protocols`**
- **`show ip route`**
- **`debug ip rip`**

The following sections cover these commands in more depth.

One other important command to point out is the **`clear ip route *`** *Privilege EXEC* mode command. This command clears and rebuilds the IP routing table. Any time that you make a change to a routing protocol, you should clear and rebuild the routing table with this command. You can replace the "*" with a specific network number, if you choose to do so—this will only clear the specified route from the routing table. Please note that the **`clear`** command only clears dynamic routes; static and connected routes cannot be cleared from the routing table with this command.

The show ip protocols Command

The **`show ip protocols`** command displays all of the IP routing protocols that you have configured and are running on your router. Here's an example of this command:

```
Router# show ip protocols
Routing Protocol is "rip"
  Sending updates every 30 seconds, next due in 5 seconds
  Invalid after 180 seconds, hold down 180, flushed after 240
  Outgoing update filter list for all interfaces is not set
  Incoming update filter list for all interfaces is not set
  Redistributing: rip
  Default version control: send version 1, receive any version
Interface        Send  Recv   Key-chain
Ethernet0        1     1      2
Ethernet1        1     1      2
```

```
Routing for Networks:
  192.168.1.0
  192.168.2.0
Routing Information Sources:
  Gateway          Distance       Last Update
  192.168.2.2           120       00:00:22
Distance: (default is 120)
```

RIP advertises routes every 30 seconds. Its hold-down period is 180 seconds, and its flush period is 240 seconds. Know the output of the `show ip protocols` command.

In this example, RIP is running on the router. The routing update interval is 30 seconds, with the next update being sent in 5 seconds. You can see that two interfaces are participating: `ethernet0` and `ethernet1`. On these interfaces, RIPv1 is being used to generate updates and both versions are accepted if they are received on these two interfaces. You can see the two networks specified with the **`network`** commands: 192.168.1.0 and 192.168.2.0. In this example, this router received an update 22 seconds ago from a neighboring router: 192.168.2.2. And last, the default administrative distance of RIP is 120.

10.04. The CD contains a multimedia demonstration of the `show ip protocols` command for RIP on a router.

The show ip route Command

Your router keeps a list of the best paths to destinations in a routing table. There is a separate routing table for each routed protocol. For instance, if you are running IP and IPX, your router will have two routing tables: one for each. However, if you are running two *routing* protocols for a single routed protocol, such as IP RIPv1 and IGRP, your router will have only one routing table for IP.

To view the routing table, use the **`show ip route`** command:

```
Router# show ip route
Codes: C - connected, S - static, I - IGRP, R - RIP,
       M - mobile, B - BGP, D - EIGRP, EX - EIGRP external,
       O - OSPF, IA - OSPF inter area, N1 - OSPF NSSA
       external type 1, N2 - OSPF NSSA external type 2,
       E1 - OSPF external type 1, E2 - OSPF external type 2,
       E - EGP, i - IS-IS, L1 - IS-IS level-1,
       L2 - IS-IS level-2, * - candidate default,
       U - per-user static route, o - ODR,
       T - traffic engineered route
```

```
Gateway of last resort is not set
     172.16.0.0/24 is subnetted, 2 subnets
C       172.16.1.0 is directly connected, Ethernet0
R       172.16.2.0 [120/1] via 172.16.1.2, 00:00:21, Ethernet0
     192.168.1.0/24 is subnetted, 2 subnets
C       192.168.1.0 is directly connected, Serial0
R    192.168.2.0/24 [120/2] via 192.168.1.2, 00:00:02, Serial2
```

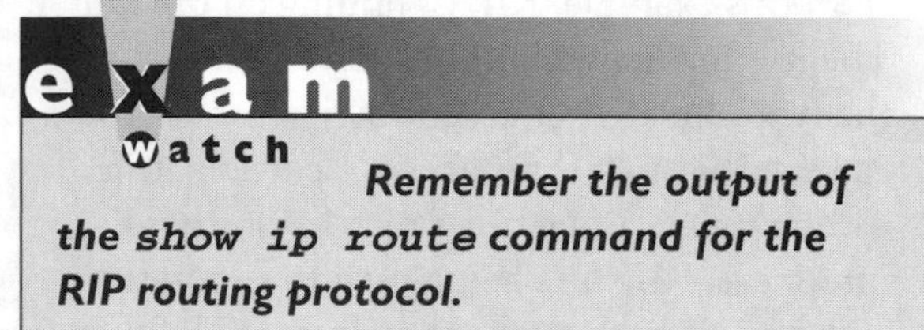

Remember the output of the show ip route command for the RIP routing protocol.

In this example, you can see that there are two types of routes in the routing table: *R* is for RIP, and C is for a directly connected network. For the RIP entries, you can see two numbers in brackets: the administrative distance of the route and the metric. For instance, 172.16.2.0 has an administrative distance of 120 and a hop count of 1. Following this is the neighboring RIP router that advertised the route (172.16.1.2), how long ago an update for this route was received from the neighbor (21 seconds), and on which interface this update was learned (`Ethernet0`).

10.05. The CD contains a multimedia demonstration of the `show ip route` command for RIP on a router.

The `debug ip rip` Command

Remember that the **show** commands show a static display of what the router knows and sometimes don't display enough information concerning a specific issue or problem. For instance, you might be looking at your routing table with the **show ip route** command and expect a certain RIP route to be appearing from a connected neighbor, but this network is not being shown. Unfortunately, the **show ip route** command won't tell you why a route is or isn't in the routing table. However, you can resort to **debug** commands to assist you in your troubleshooting.

For more detailed troubleshooting of IP RIP problems, you can use the **debug ip rip** command, shown here:

```
Router# debug ip rip
RIP protocol debugging is on
Router#
00:12:16: RIP: received v1 update from 192.168.1.2 on Serial0
00:12:16:      192.168.2.0 in 1 hops
00:12:25: RIP: sending v1 update to 255.255.255.255 via Ethernet0
172.16.1.1)
00:12:26:      network 192.168.1.0, metric 0
00:12:26:      network 192.168.2.0, metric 1
```

This command displays the routing updates sent and received on the router's interfaces. In this code example, the router received an update from 192.168.1.2 on `Serial0`. This update contained one network: 192.168.2.0. After this update, you can see that your router generated a RIP update (local broadcast—255.255.255.255) on its `Ethernet0` interface. This update contains two networks: 192.168.1.0 and 192.168.2.0. Also notice the metrics associated with these routes: 192.168.1.0 is connected to this router, while 192.168.2.0 is one hop away. When the neighboring router connected to `Ethernet0` receives this update, it will increment the hop count by 1 for each route in the update.

When using **debug** commands, you must be at *Privilege EXEC* mode. To disable a specific **debug** command, negate it with the **no** parameter. To turn off debugging for all **debug** commands, use either the **undebug all** or **no debug all** command.

10.06. The CD contains a multimedia demonstration of the debug ip rip command for RIP on a router.

Be familiar with the output of the debug ip rip command and how to disable debug: preface the debug command with the no parameter or use the undebug all or no debug all command.

EXERCISE 10-1

Configuring RIP

These last few sections dealt with configuring RIP on a router. This exercise will help you reinforce this material for setting up and troubleshooting RIP. You'll perform this lab using Boson's NetSim simulator. This exercise has you set IP RIP on the two routers (2600 and 2500). You can find a picture of the network diagram for Boson's NetSim simulator in the Introduction for this book. After starting the simulator, click the *LabNavigator* button. Next, double-click *Exercise 10-1* and click the *Load Lab* button. This will load the lab configuration based on Chapter 5's and 7's exercises.

1. On the 2600, verify that the `fa0/0` and `s0` interfaces are up. If not, bring them up. Examine the IP addresses configured on the 2600 and look at its routing table.

At the top of the simulator in the menu bar, click the *eRouters* icon and choose *2600*. On the 2600, use the **show interfaces** command to verify your configuration. If fa0/0 and s0 are not up, go into the interfaces (fa0/0 and s0) and enable them: **configure terminal**, **interface** *type [slot_#/]port_#*, **no shutdown**, and **end**. Use the **show interfaces** command to verify that the IP addresses you configured in Chapter 5 are still there. Use the **show ip route** command. You should have two connected networks: 192.168.1.0 connected to fa0/0 and 192.168.2.0 connected to s0.

2. On the 2500, verify that the e0 and s0 interfaces are up. If not, bring them up. Examine the IP addresses configured on the 2500 and look at its routing table.

   At the top of the simulator in the menu bar, click the *eRouters* icon and choose *2500*. On the 2500, Use the **show interfaces** command to verify your configuration. If e0 and s0 are not up, go into the interfaces (e0 and s0) and enable them: **configure terminal**, **interface** *type port_#*, **no shutdown**, and **end**. Use the **show interfaces** command to verify your configuration. Use the **show interfaces** command to verify that the IP addresses you configured in Chapter 5 are still there. Use the **show ip route** command. You should have two connected networks: 192.168.3.0 connected to e0 and 192.168.2.0 connected to s0.

3. Test connectivity between Host1 and the 2600. Test connectivity between Host3 and the 2500. Test connectivity between Host3 and Host1.

   At the top of the simulator in the menu bar, click the *eStations* icon and choose *Host1*. From Host1, ping the 2600 router (the default gateway): **ping 192.168.1.1**. The ping should be successful. At the top of the simulator in the menu bar, click the *eStations* icon and choose *Host3*. From the Host3, ping the 2500 router (the default gateway): **ping 192.168.3.1**. The ping should be successful. From the Host3, ping Host1: **ping 192.168.1.10**. The ping should fail. Why? there is no route from the 2500 to this destination. (Look at the 2500's routing table: it doesn't list 192.168.1.0/24.)

4. Access the 2500 and examine the routing table to see why the ping failed.

   At the top of the simulator in the menu bar, click the *eRouters* icon and choose *2500*. Examine the routing table: **show ip route**. Notice that it doesn't list 192.168.1.0/24, which explains why Host3 can't reach Host1.

5. Enable RIP on the 2600 and 2500 routers.

   At the top of the simulator in the menu bar, click the *eRouters* icon and choose *2600*. On the 2600, execute the following: **configure terminal**,

router rip, **network 192.168.1.0**, **network 192.168.2.0**, and **end**. At the top of the simulator in the menu bar, click the *eRouters* icon and choose *2500*. On the 2500, execute the following: **configure terminal**, **router rip**, **network 192.168.2.0**, **network 192.168.3.0**, and **end**.

6. On the 2600 and 2500, verify the operation of RIP.

   At the top of the simulator in the menu bar, click the *eRouters* icon and choose *2600*. Use the **show ip protocols** command to make sure that RIP is configured—check for the neighboring router's IP address. Use the **show ip route** command and look for the remote LAN network number as a RIP *(R)* entry in the routing table. On the 2600, you should see 192.168.3.0, which was learned from the 2500. At the top of the simulator in the menu bar, click the *eRouters* icon and choose *2500*. Use the **show ip protocols** command to make sure that RIP is configured—check for the neighboring router's IP address. Use the **show ip route** command and look for the remote LAN network number as a RIP *(R)* entry in the routing table. On the 2500, you should see 192.168.1.0, which was learned from the 2600.

7. On Host1, test connectivity to Host3.

   At the top of the simulator in the menu bar, click the *eStations* icon and choose *Host1*. On Host1, test connectivity: **ping 192.168.3.2**. The ping should be successful.

EXERCISE 10-2

Basic RIP Troubleshooting

This exercise is a troubleshooting exercise and is similar to Exercise 9-2. In the previous exercise (10-1), you were given a configuration task to set up RIP. In this exercise, the network is already configured; however, there are three problems that you'll need to find and fix in order for the network to operate correctly. All of these problems deal with IP (layer-3) connectivity. You'll perform this exercise using Boson's NetSim simulator. The addressing scheme is the same as that configured in Chapter 5. After starting up the simulator, click the *LabNavigator* button. Next, double-click *Exercise 10-2* and click the *Load Lab* button. This will load the lab configuration based on Chapter 5's exercises (with problems, of course).

Let's start with your problem: Host1 cannot ping Host3. Your task is to figure out what the problems are (there are three) and fix them. In this example, RIPv1 has been preconfigured on the routers. I recommend that you try this troubleshooting process on your own first; if you have trouble with it, come back to the steps and solutions provided here.

1. Test connectivity from Host1 to Host3 with ping as well as from Host1 to its default gateway.

   At the top of the simulator in the menu bar, click the *eStations* icon and choose *Host1*. On Host1, ping Host3: **`ping 192.168.3.2`**. Note that the ping fails. Examine the IP configuration on Host1 by executing: **`winipcfg`**. Make sure the IP addressing information is correct: IP address of 192.168.1.10, subnet mask of 255.255.255.0, and default gateway address of 192.168.1.1. Click the *Cancel* button to close **`winipcfg`**. Ping the default gateway address: **`ping 192.168.1.1`**. The ping should fail, indicating that at least layer-3 is functioning between Host1 and the 2600.

2. Check the 2600's IP configuration.

   At the top of the simulator in the menu bar, click the *eRouters* icon and choose *2600*. From the 2600, ping Host1: **`ping 192.168.1.10`**. The ping should fail. Examine the interface on the 2600: **`show interface fa0/0`**. The interface is enabled, but has an incorrect IP address: 192.168.1.254. Fix the IP address: **`configure terminal`**, **`interface fa0/0`**, **`ip address 192.168.1.1 255.255.255.0`**, **`end`**. Verify the IP address: **`show interface fa0/0`**. Retry the ping test: **`ping 192.168.1.10`**. The ping should be successful. Save the configuration on the router: **`copy running-config startup-config`**.

3. Test connectivity from Host1 to Host3 with ping.

   At the top of the simulator in the menu bar, click the *eStations* icon and choose *Host1*. On Host1, ping Host3: **`ping 192.168.3.2`**. Note that the ping still fails.

4. Test connectivity from Host3 to its default gateway.

   At the top of the simulator in the menu bar, click the *eStations* icon and choose *Host3*. Examine the IP configuration on Host3 by executing: **`winipcfg`**. Make sure the IP addressing information is correct: IP address of 192.168.3.2, subnet mask of 255.255.255.0, and default gateway address of 192.168.3.1. Click the *Cancel* button to close **`winipcfg`**. Ping the default gateway address: **`ping 192.168.3.1`**. The ping should be fail, indicating that there is a problem between Host3 and the 2500. In this example, layer-2 is functioning correctly; therefore, it must be a problem with the 2500.

5. Check the interface statuses and IP configuration on the 2500 and verify connectivity to the 2600. Also verify RIP's configuration.

   At the top of the simulator in the menu bar, click the *eRouters* icon and choose *2500*. Check the status of the interfaces: **`show interfaces`**. Notice that the `e0` is disabled, but `s0` is enabled (*up and up*). Go into `e0` and enable it: **`configure terminal`**, **`interface e0`**, **`no shutdown`**, **`end`**. Verify the status of the e0 interface: **`show interface e0`**. Try pinging Host3: **`ping 192.168.3.2`**. The ping should succeed. Try pinging the 2600's `serial0` interface: **`ping 192.168.2.1`**. The ping succeeds. Examine the 2500's RIP configuration: **`show ip protocol`**. You should see RIP as the routing protocol and networks 192.168.2.0 and 192.168.3.0 included. From this output, it looks like RIP is configured correctly on the 2500. Save the configuration on the router: **`copy running-config startup-config`**.

6. Test connectivity from the 2500 to Host1. Examine the routing table.

   Test the connection to Host1: **`ping 192.168.1.10`**. The ping should fail. This indicates a layer-3 problem between the 2500 and Host1. Examine the routing table: **`show ip route`**. Notice that there are only two connected routes (192.168.2.0/24 and 192.168.1.0/24), but no RIP routes.

7. Access the 2600 router and examine RIP's configuration. Fix the problem.

   At the top of the simulator in the menu bar, click the *eRouters* icon and choose *2600*. Examine the routing table: **`show ip protocol`**. What networks are advertised by the 2600? You should see 192.168.1.0 and 192.168.20.0. Obviously, serial0's interface isn't included since 192.168.2.0 is not configured. Fix this configuration problem: **`configure terminal`**, **`router rip`**, **`no network 192.168.20.0`**, **`network 192.168.2.0`**, **`end`**. Test connectivity to Host3: **`ping 192.168.3.2`**. The ping should be successful. Save the configuration on the router: **`copy running-config startup config`**.

8. Now test connectivity between Host1 and Host3.

   At the top of the simulator in the menu bar, click the *eStations* icon and choose *Host1*. Test connectivity to Host3: **`ping 192.168.3.2`**. The ping should be successful.

In the next section, you will be presented with IGRP and how to configure it.

CERTIFICATION OBJECTIVE 10.03

IP IGRP

The Interior Gateway Routing Protocol (IGRP) is a Cisco-proprietary routing protocol for IP. Like IP RIPv1, it is a distance vector protocol. However, it scales better than RIP because of these advantages:

- It uses a sophisticated metric based on bandwidth and delay.
- It uses triggered updates to speed-up convergence.
- It supports unequal-cost load balancing to a single destination.

IGRP uses a composite metric, which includes *bandwidth*, *delay*, *reliability*, *load*, and *MTU*, when choosing paths to a destination. By default, the algorithm uses only bandwidth and delay, but the other metric components can be enabled. Reliability and load are measured 1–255. A reliability of 1 is least reliable, while 255 is most reliable. A load of 1 is least utilized, while 255 is 100 percent utilized. The MTU refers to the size of the frame. Cisco refers to this component as MTU, but in reality, it really is just a constant value in the metric algorithm. These components are run through an algorithm and a *single* metric value is computed. The lower the metric value, the more preferred the route.

Based on the metric components used by IGRP, you can see that it will normally choose better paths than RIP, which uses hop count. For instance, if you have a 64Kbps WAN link to a destination and a two-hop Ethernet connection to the same destination, RIP would choose the slow WAN link, but IGRP would choose the two-hop Ethernet connection. IGRP routing updates are broadcasted every 90 seconds with a hold-down period of 280 seconds. To speed up convergence, triggered updates are used when network changes occur.

exam watch

IGRP, which is Cisco-proprietary, uses bandwidth, delay, reliability, load, and MTU as its metrics (bandwidth and delay be default). It broadcasts updates every 90 seconds with a hold-down period of 280 seconds. It also supports triggered updates and load balancing across unequal-cost paths.

One of the key components of the metric is *bandwidth*. A router will automatically compute this value for LAN links. For instance, a 10Mbps link will have a default bandwidth value of 10,000Kbps. This is *different* for serial connections, where no matter what the speed is, the bandwidth will default to 1,544Kbps (for synchronous serial interfaces). For serial interfaces, it is important that you configure the bandwidth metric correctly by using the **bandwidth** *Interface Subconfiguration* mode command. This command was discussed in Chapter 5.

Configuring IP IGRP

Setting up IGRP is almost as simple as configuring RIP:

```
Router(config)# router igrp autonomous_system_#
Router(config-router)# network IP_network_#
```

Unlike RIP, IGRP understands the concept of an autonomous system and requires you to configure the autonomous system number in the routing process. For routers to share routing information, they *must* be in the same AS. IGRP routing updates contain the AS number of the advertising router. When a receiving router examines the advertisement, it compares the AS in the update and its own AS number. If they don't match, the router discards the update.

The **network** command configuration is as the same as for RIP. To specify which interfaces are participating in the IGRP routing process, you use the **network** command. The syntax and configuration of this command are exactly like those for RIP. Since IGRP is a distance vector protocol, you need to specify only the class network number. Any interfaces that match this network number will send and receive IGRP routing updates.

10.07. The CD contains a multimedia demonstration of configuring IGRP on a router.

Remember that IGRP requires an AS number in its `router` command; plus, when entering network numbers for the `network` command, they are entered as the classful network number, as they are for RIP.

Load Balancing

With RIP, you don't need to configure anything to enable equal-cost load balancing; and RIP doesn't support unequal-cost load balancing. IGRP supports both equal- and unequal-cost paths for load balancing to a single destination. Equal-cost paths are enabled by default, where IGRP supports up to six equal-cost paths (four by default) to a single destination in the IP routing table. IGRP, however, also supports unequal-cost paths, but this feature is disabled by default. The variance feature allows you to include equal- and unequal-cost IGRP routes in the routing table.

To enable unequal-cost paths for IGRP, use the **variance** *Router Subconfiguration* mode command:

```
Router(config-router)# variance multiplier
```

The *multiplier* value is a positive integer. By default, it is equal to 1. To use an unequal-cost path (less preferred), you multiply the best metric path by the multiplier value; if the less preferred path's metric is less than this value, the router will include it in the routing table along with the best metric path.

The multiplier can range from 1 to 128. The default is 1, which means the IGRP router will use only the best metric path(s). If you increase the multiplier, the router will use any route that has a metric less than the best metric route multiplied by the variance value. Care must be taken, however, to ensure that you do not set a variance value too high, such that routing loops are not created.

When load balancing, the router will do the process intelligently. In other words, if you have two WAN links (64Kbps and 128Kbps) included in the routing table to reach a single destination, it makes no sense to send half of the traffic down the 64Kbps link and the other half down the 128Kbps link. In this situation, you would probably saturate your slower-speed 64Kbps link. IGRP, instead, will load-balance traffic in proportion to the inverse of the metric for the path. So given this example, about one-third of the traffic would be sent down the 64Kbps link and two-thirds down the 128Kbps link.

You can override this behavior with the **traffic-share** *Router Subconfiguration* mode command:

```
Router(config-router)# traffic-share balanced
-or-
Router(config-router)# traffic-share min across-interfaces
```

The first command provides the default behavior for load balancing, as was explained in the preceding paragraph. The **min** parameter has the router put the unequal-cost paths in the router's routing table; however, the router won't use these routes unless the

Use the `variance` *command to load-balance across unequal-cost paths. The default is to use only equal-cost paths.*

best metric route fails. This is used when you don't want to use the worse connections, which perhaps are dial-up connections, but still want to take advantage of fast convergence; when the primary path fails, the secondary path is already in the routing table.

Note that by using the variance feature, you can introduce additional paths to a destination in your IP routing table. By doing this, when one path fails, you already have a backup path in the routing table, so convergence is instantaneous. If you want your router to use only the best path, but you want to put the alternative paths in the routing table, use the **traffic-share min across-interfaces** command.

10.08. The CD contains a multimedia demonstration of the **`variance`** ***and*** **`traffic-share`** ***commands for IGRP on a router.***

Configuration Example

Let's return to the example shown in earlier Figure 10-1, to help illustrate how to configure IGRP on a router. Here's the complete configuration of the router:

```
Router(config)# router igrp 100
Router(config-router)# network 172.16.0.0
Router(config-router)# network 192.168.1.0
Router(config-router)# exit
Router(config)# interface ethernet 0
Router(config-if)# ip address 172.16.1.1 255.255.255.0
Router(config-if)# no shutdown
Router(config-if)# exit
Router(config)# interface ethernet 1
Router(config-if)# ip address 172.16.2.1 255.255.255.0
Router(config-if)# no shutdown
Router(config-if)# exit
Router(config)# interface ethernet 2
Router(config-if)# ip address 192.168.1.65 255.255.255.192
Router(config-if)# no shutdown
Router(config-if)# exit
Router(config)# interface ethernet 3
Router(config-if)# ip address 192.168.1.129 255.255.255.192
Router(config-if)# no shutdown
Router(config-if)# exit
```

Troubleshooting IP IGRP

You have the same tools available to you in IGRP as you did in RIP to help troubleshoot the routing protocol:

- **show ip protocols**
- **show ip route**
- **debug ip igrp events**
- **debug ip igrp transactions**

The following sections cover these commands.

The show ip protocols Command

You can use the **show ip protocols** command to display the IP routing protocols that have been configured and are running on your router. Here is an example of this command:

```
Router# show ip protocols
Routing Protocol is "igrp 100"
  Sending updates every 90 seconds, next due in 20 seconds
  Invalid after 270 seconds, hold down 280, flushed after 630
  Outgoing update filter list for all interfaces is not set
  Incoming update filter list for all interfaces is not set
  Default networks flagged in outgoing updates
  Default networks accepted from incoming updates
  IGRP metric weight K1=1, K2=0, K3=1, K4=0, K5=0
  IGRP maximum hopcount 100
  IGRP maximum metric variance 1
  Redistributing: igrp 100
  Routing for Networks:
    172.16.0.0
  Routing Information Sources:
    Gateway         Distance      Last Update
    172.16.1.2           100      0:00:21
    172.16.2.2           100      0:00:59
  Distance: (default is 100)
```

This screen holds a lot of important information. First, notice that only IGRP for AS 100 is running on the router. Next, notice that the periodic routing update timer is set to 90 seconds but also supports triggered updates. The next update will be in 20 seconds. The hold-down timer is set to 280 seconds and is used to hold a poisoned

IGRP's routing update period is every 90 seconds. Its hold-down period is 280 seconds, and its flush period is 630 seconds. Remember the output of the `show ip protocols` command for IGRP.

route in the routing table to prevent routing loops. The flush period, which is 630 seconds, has the router remove a route from its table if it doesn't see an update for the route within this time period. The K metric values affect which metric components are available: K1 and K3 refer to the bandwidth and delay metric components. The default hop count for IGRP is 100 (with a maximum of 255), and the default variance is 1 (load-balance only across equal-cost paths).

This IGRP process is in autonomous system 100 and is advertising 172.16.0.0. It knows about two neighboring IGRP routers in this AS: 172.16.1.2 and 172.16.2.2. The default administrative distance is 100.

10.09. The CD contains a multimedia demonstration of the `show ip protocols` command for IGRP on a router.

The show ip route Command

To view the IGRP routes in your router's routing table, use the **`show ip route`** command:

```
Router# show ip route
Codes: C - connected, S - static, I - IGRP, R - RIP,
       M - mobile, B - BGP, D - EIGRP, EX - EIGRP external,
       O - OSPF, IA - OSPF inter area, N1 - OSPF NSSA
       external type 1, N2 - OSPF NSSA external type 2,
       E1 - OSPF external type 1, E2 - OSPF external type 2,
       E - EGP, i - IS-IS, L1 - IS-IS level-1,
       L2 - IS-IS level-2, * - candidate default,
       U - per-user static route, o - ODR,
       T - traffic engineered route

Gateway of last resort is not set
     172.16.0.0/24 is subnetted, 2 subnets
C       172.16.1.0 is directly connected, Ethernet0
I       172.16.2.0 [100/11000] via 172.16.1.2, 00:00:21, Ethernet0
     192.168.1.0/24 is subnetted, 2 subnets
C       192.168.1.0 is directly connected, Serial0
I    192.168.2.0/24 [100/22000] via 192.168.1.2, 00:00:02, Serial2
```

Memorize the output of the *show ip route* command for IGRP.

At the bottom of the display, an *I* in the first column refers to an IGRP route. As you can see from this display, there are two IGRP routes. If you look at the last IGRP route, it has an administrative distance of 100 and a metric of 22,000 (first and second numbers in brackets). The metric is an algorithmic value based on the bandwidth and delay metric components. The rest of the information is the same as for an IP routing table and was discussed in the earlier section "IP RIP."

10.10. The CD contains a multimedia demonstration of the show ip route command for IGRP on a router.

The debug Commands

IGRP supports two **debug** commands for detailed troubleshooting. The **debug ip igrp transactions** command shows the actual IGRP routing updates that your router broadcasts out of its interfaces and receives from neighboring routers. Here is an example of this command:

```
Router# debug ip igrp transactions
IGRP protocol debugging is on
Router#
00:12:17: IGRP: sending update to 255.255.255.255 via Ethernet0 (172.16.1.1)
00:12:17:       network 192.168.1.0, metric=88956
00:12:18: IGRP: sending update to 255.255.255.255 via Serial0 (10.1.1.1)
00:12:18:       network 172.16.0.0, metric=1100
00:12:27: IGRP: received update from 192.168.1.2 on Serial0
00:12:27:       network 192.168.2.0, metric 90956 (neighbor 88956)
```

This output is similar to the output of the **debug ip rip** command. The first two lines show the router sending out a routing update on `Ethernet0`, which contains one route (192.168.1.0) with a metric of 88,956. The last two lines show the router receiving a routing update from 192.168.1.2 on its `Serial0` interface. This update contains one network: 192.168.2.0. The neighbor advertised a metric of 88,956 for this route, but as it came into the interface, this router incremented it, resulting in a metric of 90,956.

10.11. The CD contains a multimedia demonstration of the debug ip igrp transactions command for IGRP on a router.

The problem with the **debug ip igrp transactions** command is that it generates a lot of debug output. If you just want to see a summary of the routing updates that your router sends and receives, use the **debug ip igrp events** command:

```
Router# debug ip igrp events
IGRP event debugging is on
Router#
00:12:31: IGRP: sending update to 255.255.255.255 via Ethernet0
(172.16.1.1)
00:12:31: IGRP: Update contains 0 interior, 2 system, and 0
exterior routes.
00:12:31: IGRP: Total routes in update: 2
00:12:31: IGRP: sending update to 255.255.255.255 via Serial0
(192.168.1.1)
00:12:32: IGRP: Update contains 0 interior, 1 system, and 0
exterior routes.
00:12:32: IGRP: Total routes in update: 1
00:12:35: IGRP: received update from 192.168.1.1 on Serial0
00:12:35: IGRP: Update contains 1 interior, 1 system, and 0
exterior routes.
00:12:35: IGRP: Total routes in update: 2
```

Remember the differences between the debug ip igrp events and debug ip igrp transactions commands.

In this example, you can see from the first line that the router is generating an update on its Ethernet0 interface. Notice that you don't see the actual routes that are being sent (or received).

10.12. The CD contains a multimedia demonstration of the debug ip igrp events command for IGRP on a router.

CERTIFICATION SUMMARY

When setting up IP routing, you must enable the routing protocol and configure IP routing on your router's interfaces. The **router** command takes you into the routing process, while the **network** command specifies what interfaces will participate in the routing process. Use the **ip address** command to assign IP addresses to your router's interfaces.

RIPv1 generates local broadcasts every 30 seconds to share routing information, with a hold-down period of 180 seconds. Hop count is used as the metric for choosing paths. RIP will load-balance across six equal-cost paths to a single destination. RIPv2 uses multicasts instead of broadcasts and also supports VLSM for hierarchical routing and route summarization. RIPv2, to speed up convergence, uses triggered updates. Use the **`router rip`** command to go into the routing process and the **`network`** command to specify your connected networks. When specifying your connected networks, specify only the Class A, B, or C network number (not subnet numbers), since RIPv1 is classful: even though RIPv2 is classless, configure it as a classful protocol. The **`debug ip rip`** command will display the actual routing contents that your router advertises in its updates or receives in neighbors' updates.

IGRP is a Cisco-proprietary protocol. It uses bandwidth and delay as its default metrics, but it also supports load, reliability, and MTU. IGRP routers use broadcasts to share their routing information and generate updates every 90 seconds, with a hold-down period of 280 seconds. Unlike RIPv1, IGRP uses triggered updates to speed up convergence and also will load-balance across unequal-cost paths (requiring the configuration of the **`variance`** command). When configuring IGRP, you must specify the AS number. Otherwise, it is configured like RIPv1. The **`debug ip igrp transactions`** command shows the actual IGRP routing updates that your router broadcasts out of its interfaces and receives from neighboring routers. If you just want to see a summary of the routing updates that your router sends and receives, use the **`debug ip igrp events`** command.

The **`show ip protocols`** command displays information about the IP routing protocols currently configured and running on your router. It shows metric information, administrative distances, neighboring routers, and routes that are being advertised. The **`show ip route`** command displays the IP routing information currently being used by your router. An *R* in the left-hand column indicates a RIP route, while an *I* indicates an IGRP route.

TWO-MINUTE DRILL

IP Routing Protocol Basics

- To set up IP on your router, you need to enable the routing protocol and assign IP addresses to your router's interfaces.
- Use the **router** and **network** commands to enable routing. With classful protocols, use the class address in the **network** command.

IP RIP

- RIP uses hop count as a metric and has a hop count limit of 15. IP RIP supports up to six equal-cost paths to a single destination.
- RIPv1 sends out periodic routing updates as broadcasts every 30 seconds. The hold-down timer is 180 seconds. It is a classful protocol.
- RIPv2 uses triggered updates and sends its updates out as multicasts. It is a classless protocol and supports VLSM and route summarization.
- Use the **router rip** and **network** commands to set up RIP. Use the **version** command to hard-code the version. Use the following commands for troubleshooting: **show ip protocols**, **show ip route**, and **debug ip rip**.
- After making a change to an IP routing protocol, use the **clear ip route *** command to clear the IP routing table and rebuild it.

IP IGRP

- IGRP is a proprietary Cisco distance vector protocol. It uses a composite of metrics (bandwidth, delay, reliability, load, and MTU) and triggered updates. Its update interval is 90 seconds, and its hold-down time is 280 seconds. It supports both equal- and unequal-cost paths in the routing table. IGRP is a classful protocol.
- IGRP requires an AS number when configuring it. Use these commands to set it up: **router igrp** *AS_#* and **network**. Use the **variance** command to allow unequal-cost paths. Use the following commands for troubleshooting: **show ip protocols**, **show ip route**, **debug ip igrp events**, and **debug ip igrp transactions**.

SELF TEST

The following Self Test questions will help you measure your understanding of the material presented in this chapter. Read all the choices carefully, as there may be more than one correct answer. Choose all correct answers for each question.

IP Routing Protocol Basics

1. What must you do to enable IP routing on your router?

   A. Enable the routing protocol.

   B. Set clocking on all serial interfaces.

   C. Assign IP addresses to your router's interfaces.

   D. Assign the bandwidth parameter to your serial interfaces.

2. What command activates the IP routing process?

   A. `router`

   B. `enable`

   C. `network`

   D. `no shutdown`

3. You have a distance vector protocol such as RIP. On one of your router's interfaces, you have the following IP address: 192.168.1.65 255.255.255.192. Enter the command to allow IP routing for this network: ____________.

IP RIP

4. RIP generates routing updates every _________ seconds.

   A. 15

   B. 30

   C. 60

   D. 90

5. RIP has a hold-down period of ____________ seconds.

   A. 60

   B. 120

   C. 180

   D. 280

6. RIP has a maximum hop count of ___________ hops.
   A. 10
   B. 15
   C. 16
   D. 100

7. RIP supports load balancing for up to ____________________ paths.
   A. Six, unequal-cost
   B. Four, unequal-cost
   C. Four, equal-cost
   D. Six, equal-cost

8. Which of the following is true concerning RIPv2?
   A. It uses triggered updates.
   B. It uses broadcasts.
   C. It is classful.
   D. It doesn't support route summarization.

9. Enter the router command to access the RIP configuration: ________________.

10. Enter the router command to view which routing protocols are active on your router, as well as their characteristics and configuration: __________.

11. Enter the router command to clear the routing table: __________.

IP IGRP

12. IGRP generates an update every ___________ seconds.
    A. 30
    B. 60
    C. 90
    D. 120

13. Which metric components, by default, are used in IGRP?
    A. Delay
    B. Reliability
    C. Load
    D. Bandwidth

14. Your router is in autonomous system 150. Enter the IGRP command to go into the routing process: ___________.

15. Enter the router command to view the IP routing table: ___________.

16. Which IGRP command allows unequal-cost load balancing?

A. `variance`

B. `load`

C. `balance`

D. `network`

SELF TEST ANSWERS

IP Routing Protocol Basics

1. ☑ **A** and **C.** To enable IP routing on your router, you must enable your routing protocol and assign IP addresses to your router's interfaces.
   ☒ **B** is required only on DCE interfaces, not DTE interfaces. **D** is used to set the bandwidth metric for those routing protocols that use it, like IGRP.

2. ☑ **C.** The first **`network`** command that you enter activates an IP routing process.
   ☒ **A** takes you into the process; it doesn't activate it. **B** takes you into *Privilege EXEC* mode. **D** enables an interface.

3. ☑ **`network 192.168.1.0`**. Remember that RIPv1 and IGRP are classful.

IP RIP

4. ☑ **B.** RIP generates routing updates every 30 seconds.
   ☒ **A**, **C**, and **D** are invalid update intervals.

5. ☑ **C.** RIP has a hold-down period of 180 seconds.
   ☒ **A**, **B**, and **D** are invalid hold-down periods.

6. ☑ **B.** RIP has a maximum hop count of 15 hops.
   ☒ **A**, **C**, and **D** are invalid maximum hop count values.

7. ☑ **D.** RIP supports load-balancing for up to six equal-cost paths.
   ☒ **A** and **B** are invalid because RIP doesn't support unequal-cost paths. **C** is incorrect because four is the default, but six is the maximum.

8. ☑ **A.** RIPv2 supports triggered updates.
   ☒ **B** is incorrect because RIPv2 uses multicasts. **C** is incorrect because RIPv2 is classless. **D** is incorrect because RIPv2 supports VLSM and route summarization.

9. ☑ To access RIP, enter **`router rip`**.

10. ☑ To view the IP routing protocols running on your router, use **`show ip protocols`**.

11. ☑ Any time you make a change to an IP routing protocol, you should clear the routing table: **`clear ip route *`**.

IP IGRP

12. ☑ **C.** IGRP broadcasts routing updates every 90 seconds.
☒ **A**, **B**, and **D** are incorrect update intervals.

13. ☑ **A.** and **D.** The default metric values used in IGRP are bandwidth and delay. Reliability, load, and MTU are disabled by default.
☒ **B** and **C** are disabled by default.

14. ☑ Access your IGRP process using AS 150: **`router igrp 150`**.

15. ☑ Use this command to view your IP routing table: **`show ip route`**.

16. ☑ **A.** Use the **`variance`** command to allow for unequal-cost load balancing in IGRP.
☒ **B** and **C** are invalid commands. **D** specifies which interfaces will participate in the IGRP routing process.

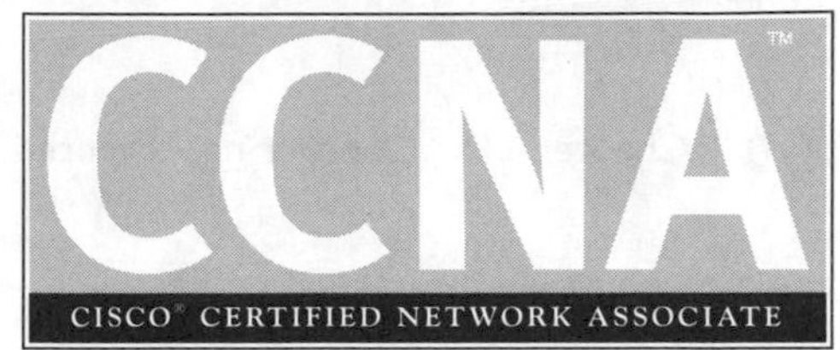

Configuring Advanced Routing Protocols

CERTIFICATION OBJECTIVES

11.01 OSPF

11.02 EIGRP

✓ Two-Minute Drill

Q&A Self Test

In Chapter 10, you were introduced to the configuration of two distance vector routing protocols: IP RIP and IGRP. This chapter focuses on two advanced routing protocols: OSPF and EIGRP. OSPF is a link state protocol, and EIGRP is a hybrid protocol. This chapter covers only basic operation and configuration of these protocols. A more thorough discussion is covered in Cisco's BSCI CCNP and CCDP exam.

CERTIFICATION OBJECTIVE 11.01

OSPF

The Open Shortest Path First (OSPF) protocol is a link state protocol that handles routing for IP traffic. Its newest implementation, version 2, which is explained in RFC 2328, is an open standard, like RIP. Chapter 9 offered a brief introduction to link state protocols. As you will see in this section, OSPF draws heavily on the concepts described in that chapter, but it also has some features of its own. Besides covering the characteristics of OSPF, you'll be presented with enough information to undertake a very basic routing configuration using OSPF.

Characteristics of OSPF

OSPF was created in the mid-1980s in order to overcome many of the deficiencies and scalability problems that RIP had in large enterprise networks. Because it is based on an open standard, OSPF is very popular in many corporate networks today and has many advantages, including these:

- It will run on most routers, since it is based on an open standard.
- It uses the SPF algorithm, developed by Dijkstra, to provide a loop-free topology.
- It provides fast convergence with triggered, incremental updates via Link State Advertisements (LSAs).
- It is a classless protocol and allows for a hierarchical design with VLSM and route summarization.

Given its advantages, OSPF does have its share of disadvantages:

- It requires more memory to hold the adjacency (list of OSPF neighbors), topology (a link state database containing all of the routers and their routes), and routing tables.

- It requires extra CPU processing to run the SPF algorithm, which is especially true when you first turn on your routers and they are initially building the adjacency and topology tables.
- For large networks, it requires careful design to break up the network into an appropriate hierarchical design by separating routers into different *areas*.
- It is complex to configure and more difficult to troubleshoot.

Knowing the advantages and disadvantages of any routing protocol is useful when it comes to picking a protocol. Typically, OSPF is used in large enterprise networks that have either a mixed routing vendor environment or a policy that requires an open standard for a routing protocol, which gives a company flexibility when it needs to replace any of its existing routers.

Remember the advantages and disadvantages of OSPF, listed in the preceding bullets. Also, classless protocols include the subnet mask value along with the route when advertising routing information: distance vector protocols do not include the subnet mask in their routing updates.

Hierarchical Design: Areas

To provide scalability to very large networks, OSPF supports two important concepts: autonomous systems and areas. Autonomous systems were discussed in Chapter 9. Within an AS, *areas* are used to provide hierarchical routing. Basically, areas are used to control when and how much routing information is shared across your network. In flat network designs, such as IP RIP, if a change occurs on one router, perhaps a flapping route problem, it affects *every* router in the entire network. With a correctly designed hierarchical network, these changes can be contained within a single area.

OSPF implements a two-layer hierarchy: the backbone (area 0) and areas off of the backbone (areas 1–65,535), as is shown in Figure 11-1. This network includes a backbone and three areas off of the backbone. Through a correct IP addressing design, you should be able to summarize routing information between areas. By summarizing your routing information, perhaps one summarized route for each area, you are reducing the amount of information that routers need to know about. For instance, each area in Figure 11-1 is assigned a separate Class B network number. Through summarization on the border routers between areas, other areas would not need to see all the Class B subnets—only the summarized network numbers.

FIGURE 11-1 OSPF hierarchical design

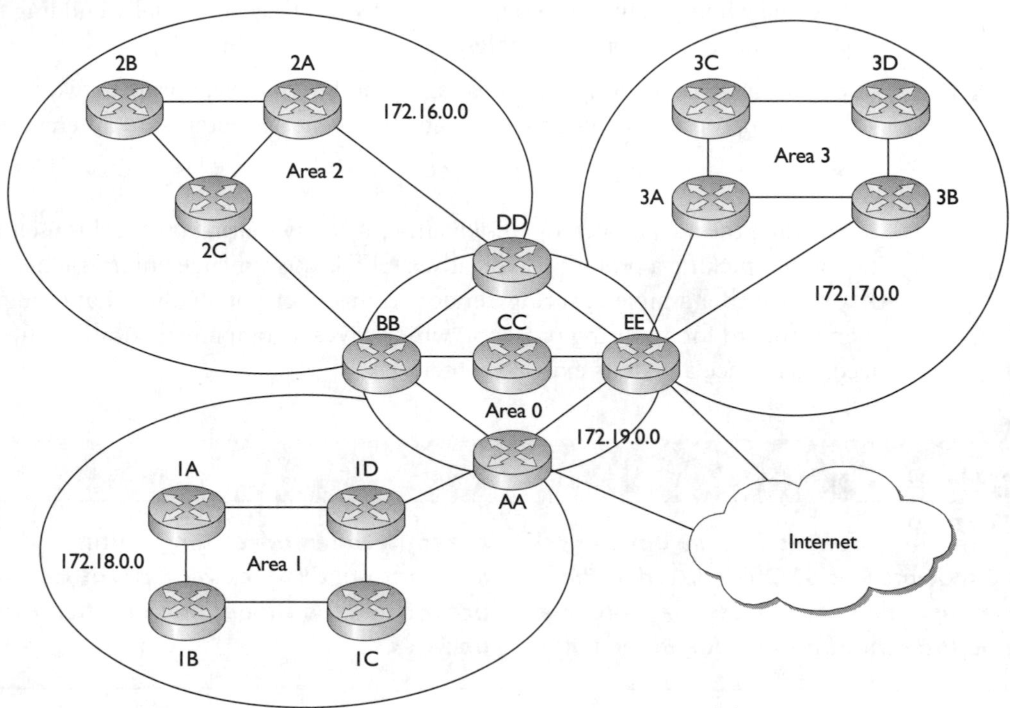

For instance, Area 2 doesn't need to see all of the subnets of Area 1's 172.18.0.0 network number, since there are only two paths out of Area 2 to the backbone. Area 2, however, needs to see all of its internal subnets to create optimized routing tables to reach internal networks. Therefore, each area should contain specific routes only for its own areas and summarized routes to reach other areas. By performing this summarization, the routers have a smaller topology database (they know only about links in their own area and the summarized routes) and their routing tables are smaller (they know only about their own area's routes and the summarized routes). Through a correct hierarchical design, you can scale OSPF to very large sizes.

> **exam watch**
> ***OSPF supports a two-layer hierarchy: the backbone (area 0) and areas connected to the backbone.***

Note that the CCNA exam focuses on single-area designs, and throughout the rest of the sections, the material covers only single-area concepts. The BSCI exam for the CCNP and CCDP certifications, however, spends a lot of time on both single- *and* multi-area designs. Designing a multi-area OSPF network can become very complicated and requires a lot of networking knowledge and skill.

Metric Structure

Unlike RIP, which uses hop count as a metric, OSPF uses cost. Cost is actually the inverse of the bandwidth of a link: the faster the speed of the connection, the lower the cost. The most preferred path is the one with the lowest cost. By using cost as a metric, OSPF will choose more intelligent paths than RIP.

Remember that on synchronous serial links, no matter what the clock rate of the physical link is, the bandwidth always defaults to 1544 Kbps. You'll want to code this correctly with the **`bandwidth`** *Interface Subconfiguration* mode command. This is important if you have multiple synchronous serial paths to a destination, especially if they have different clock rates. OSPF supports load balancing of up to six equal-cost paths to a single destination. However, if you don't configure the bandwidth metric correctly on your serial interfaces, your router might accidentally include paths with different clock rates, which can cause load-balancing issues.

For example, if you have one serial connection clocked at 1,544Kbps and another clocked at 256Kbps and you don't change the bandwidth values, OSPF will see *both* connections as 1,544Kbps and attempt to use both when reaching a single destination. This can create throughput problems when the router is performing load balancing—half of the traffic will go down one link and half down the other, creating congestion problems.

OSPF uses cost as a metric, which is the inverse of the bandwidth of a link.

Router Identities

Each router in an OSPF network needs a unique ID. The ID is used to provide a unique identity to the OSPF router. This is included in any OSPF messages the router generates. The router ID is chosen according to one of the two following criteria:

- The highest IP address on its loopback interfaces (this is a logical interface on a router)
- The highest IP address on its active interfaces

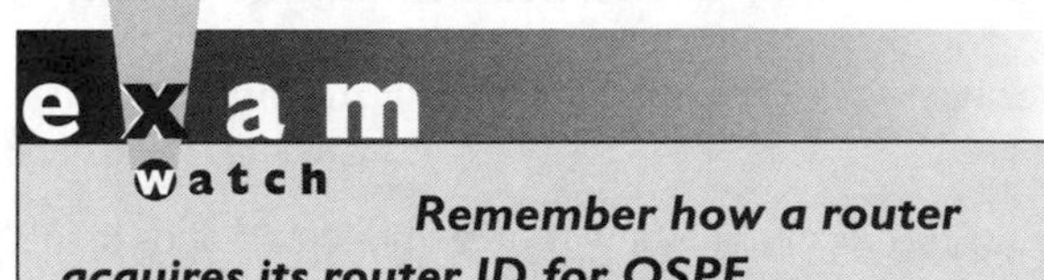

exam
watch
Remember how a router acquires its router ID for OSPF.

If you have an IP address on an active loopback interface, the router will use the highest IP address from the bunch for its router ID. The router ID is used by the router to announce itself to the other OSPF routers in the network. This ID must be unique. If you have no loopback interfaces configured, then the router will use the highest IP address from one of its physical interfaces. If there is no active interface, the OSPF process will not start and therefore you will not have any OSPF routes in your routing table. It is highly recommended that you use a loopback interface because it is always up and thus the router can obtain a router ID.

Finding Neighbors

OSPF learns about its neighbors and builds its adjacency and topology tables by sharing LSAs. There are different types of LSAs. When learning about the neighbors that a router is connected to, as well as keeping tabs on known neighbors, OSPF routers will generate hello LSAs every 10 seconds. When a neighbor is discovered and an adjacency is formed with the neighbor, a router expects to see hello messages from the neighbor. If a neighbor is not seen within the dead interval time, which defaults to 40 seconds, the neighbor is declared dead. When this occurs, the router will advertise this information, via an LSA message, to other neighboring OSPF routers.

Whereas RIP accepts routing updates from just about any other RIP router, OSPF has some rules concerning if and how routing information should be shared. First, before a router will accept any routing information from another OSPF router, they have to build an *adjacency* with each other on their connected interfaces. When this adjacency is built, the two routers (on the connected interfaces) are called *neighbors*, which indicates a special relationship between the two. In order for two routers to become neighbors, the following must match on each router:

- The area number and its type
- The hello and dead interval timers
- The OSPF password (optional), if it is configured
- The area stub flag (used to contain OSPF messages and routing information, this is beyond the scope of this book)

If these items do not match, then the routers will not form an adjacency and will ignore each other's routing information.

Let's assume that you turned on all your routers simultaneously on a segment. In this case, the OSPF routers will go through three states called the *exchange process*:

1. ***Down* state** The new router has not exchanged any OSPF information with any other router.
2. ***Init* state** A destination router has received a new router's hello and adds it to its neighbor list (assuming that certain values match). Note that communication is only unidirectional at this point.

3. ***Two-Way* state** The new router receives a unidirectional reply to its initial hello packet and adds the destination router to its neighbor database.

Once the routers have entered a *two-way* state, they are considered neighbors. At this point, an election process takes place to elect the designated router (DR) and the backup designated router (BDR).

Designated and Backup Designated Routers

An OSPF router will not form adjacencies to just any router. Instead, a client/server design is implemented in OSPF. For each network multi-access segment, there is a DR and a BDR as well as other routers. As an example, if you have ten VLANs in your switched area, you'll have ten DRs and ten BDRs. The one exception of a segment not having these two routers is on a WAN point-to-point link.

When an OSPF router comes up, it forms adjacencies with the DR and the BDR on each multi-access segment that it is connected to. Any exchange of routing information is between these DR/BDR routers and the other OSPF neighbors on a segment (and vice versa). An OSPF router talks to a DR using the IP multicast address of 224.0.0.6. The DR and the BDR talk to all routers using the 224.0.0.5 multicast IP address.

The OSPF router with the highest priority becomes the DR for the segment. If there is a tie, the router with the highest router ID will become the DR. By default, all routers have a priority of *1* (priorities can range 0–255). If the DR fails, the BDR is promoted to DR and another router is elected as the BDR. Figure 11-2 shows an example of the election process, where RouterE is elected as the DR and RouterB, the BDR.

exam watch

OSPF routers use Link State Advertisements (LSAs) to communicate with each other. One type of LSA is a hello, which is used to form neighbor relationships and as a keep-alive function. Hellos are generated every ten seconds. When sharing link information (directly connected routes), links are sent to the DR (224.0.0.6) and the DR disseminates this to everyone (224.0.0.5) else on the segment. The router with the highest priority (or highest router ID) becomes the DR. This process is true for multi-access segments, but not point-to-point links, where DRs are not necessary.

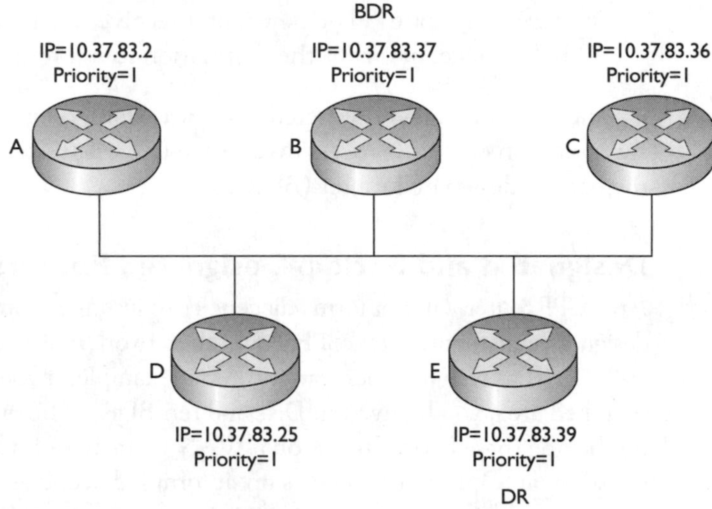

FIGURE 11-2 DR and BDR election process

Sharing Routing Information

After electing the DR/BDR pair, the routers continue to generate hellos to maintain communication. This is considered an *exstart* state, in which the OSPF routers are ready to share link state information. The process the routers go through is called an *exchange protocol*:

1. ***Exstart* state** The DR and BDR form adjacencies with the other OSPF routers on the segment, and then within each adjacency, the router with the highest router ID becomes the master and starts the exchange process first (shares its link state information)—note that the DR is not necessarily the master for the exchange process. The remaining router in the adjacency will be the slave.
2. ***Exchange* state** The master starts sharing link state information first, with the slave. These are called DBDs (database description packets), also referred to as DDPs. The DBDs contain the link-state type, the ID of the advertising router, the cost of the advertised link, and the sequence number of the link. The slave responds back with an LSACK—an acknowledgment to the DBD from the master. The slave then compares the DBD's information with its own.
3. ***Loading* state** If the master has more up-to-date information than the slave, the slave will respond to the master's original DBD with an LSR (Link State Request). The master will then send a LSU (Link State Update) with the detailed information of the links to the slave. The slave will then incorporate this into its local link state database. Again, the slave will generate an LSACK

to the master to acknowledge the fact that it received the LSU. If a slave has more up-to-date information, it will repeat the "exchange" and "loading" states.

4. ***Full* state** Once the master and the slave are synchronized, they are considered to be in a full state.

To summarize these four steps, OSPF routers share a type of LSA message in order to disclose information about available routes. Basically, an LSA update message contains a link and a state, as well as other information. A *link* is the router interface on which the update was generated (a connected route). The *state* is a description of this interface, including the IP address configured on it as well as the relationship this router has with its neighboring router. However, OSPF routers will not share this information with just any OSPF router.

OSPF uses incremental updates after entering a full state. This means that whenever changes take place, only the change is shared with the DR, which will then share this information with other routers on the segment. Figure 11-3 shows an example of this. In this example, Network Z, connected to RouterC, goes down. RouterC sends a multicast to the DR and the BDR (with a destination multicast address of 224.0.0.6), telling them about this change. Once the DR and the BDR incorporate the change internally, the DR then tells the other routes on the segment (via a multicast message sent to 224.0.0.5, which is all OSPF routers) about the change concerning Network Z. Any router receiving the update will then share this update to the DRs of other segments that they are connected to.

Note that the communications between OSPF routers are connection-oriented, even though multicasts are used. For example, if a router tells a DR about a change, the DR acknowledges this new piece of information. Likewise, when the DR shares this information with the other routers on the segment, the DR expects acknowledgments back from each of these neighbors. Remember that when an OSPF router exchanges

exam watch

OSPF routers share information about their connected routes with the DR, which includes the link-state type, the ID of the advertising router, the cost of the advertised link, and the sequence number of the link. This is different from distance vector protocols. Distance vector protocols share their entire routing table with their neighbors with the exception of routes learned from the same interface of the neighbor (split horizon) and the connected route of the interface where the neighbor resides.

FIGURE 11-3

LSA update process

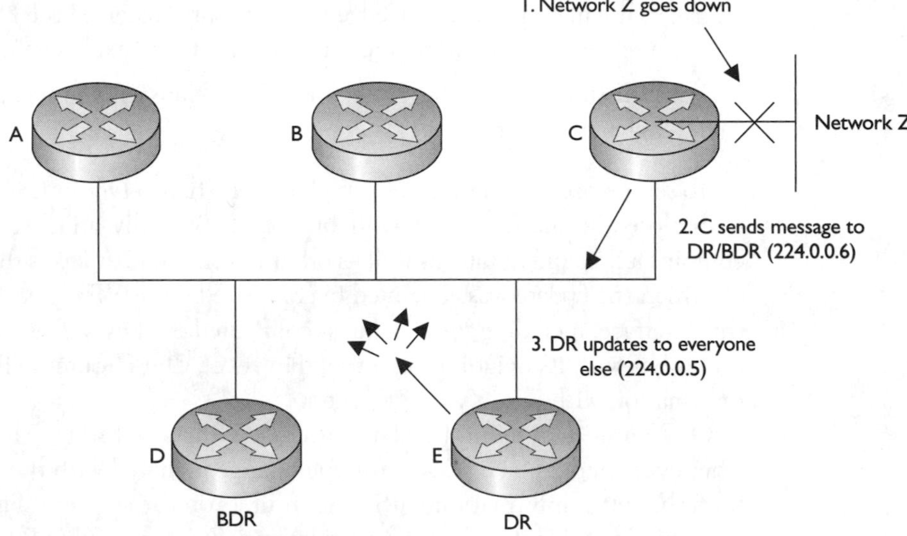

updates with another, the process requires an acknowledgment: this ensures that router or routers have received the update.

The exception to the incremental update process is that the DR floods its database every 30 minutes to ensure that all of the routers on the segment have the most up-to-date link state information. It does this with a destination address of 224.0.0.5 (all OSPF routers on the segment).

When building the routing table using link state information, an OSPF router can keep up to six paths to a destination in its routing table. The only restriction is that the paths must have the same cost.

A two-way state indicates that two OSPF routers are neighbors. A full state indicates the completion of sharing of links between routers.

Configuring OSPF

Configuring OSPF is slightly *different* from configuring RIP or IGRP. When configuring OSPF, use the following syntax:

```
Router(config)# router ospf process_ID
Router(config-router)# network IP_address wildcard_mask
                          area area_#
```

The *process_ID* is locally significant and is used to differentiate between different OSPF processes running on the router. Your router might be a boundary router between two OSPF autonomous systems, and to differentiate them on your router, you'll give them unique process IDs. Note that these numbers do *not* need to match between different routers and that they have nothing to do with autonomous system numbers.

When specifying what interfaces go into an area for OSPF, use the **network** command. As you can see in the preceding example, the syntax of this command is different than for RIP's and IGRP's configuration, where you specify only a class address. OSPF is classless. With this command, you can be very specific about what interface belongs to a particular area. The syntax of this command is to list an IP address followed by a *wildcard mask*. This is *different* from a subnet mask. A wildcard mask tells the router the interesting component of the address—in other words, what part of the address it should match on. This mask is also used with access lists, which are discussed in Chapter 13.

A wildcard mask is 32 bits in length. A 0 in a bit position means there must be a match, and a 1 in a bit position means the router doesn't care. Actually, a wildcard mask is an *inverted* subnet mask, with the 1's and 0's switched. Using a wildcard mask, you can be very specific about which interfaces belong to which areas. The last part of the command tells the router which area these addresses on the router belong to.

Let's look at some code examples to see how the wildcard mask works. I'll use the router shown in Figure 11-4 as an illustration.

```
Router(config)# router ospf 1
Router(config-router)# network 10.1.1.1  0.0.0.0  area 0
Router(config-router)# network 10.1.2.1  0.0.0.0  area 0
Router(config-router)# network 172.16.1.1  0.0.0.0  area 0
Router(config-router)# network 172.16.2.1  0.0.0.0  area 0
```

In this example, the interfaces with addresses of 10.1.1.1, 10.1.2.1, 172.16.1.1, and 172.16.1.1 all are associated with area 0. A wildcard mask of 0.0.0.0 says that there must be an exact match against the address in order to place it into area 0. Here's another example:

```
Router(config)# router ospf 1
Router(config-router)# network 10.0.0.0 0.255.255.255 area 0
Router(config-router)# network 172.16.0.0 0.0.255.255 area 0
```

In this example, interfaces beginning with 10 or 172.16 are to be associated with area 0. Or, if all the interfaces on your router belonged to the same area, you could use this configuration:

```
Router(config)# router ospf 1
Router(config-router)# network 0.0.0.0 255.255.255.255 area 0
```

FIGURE 11-4

OSPF network configuration example

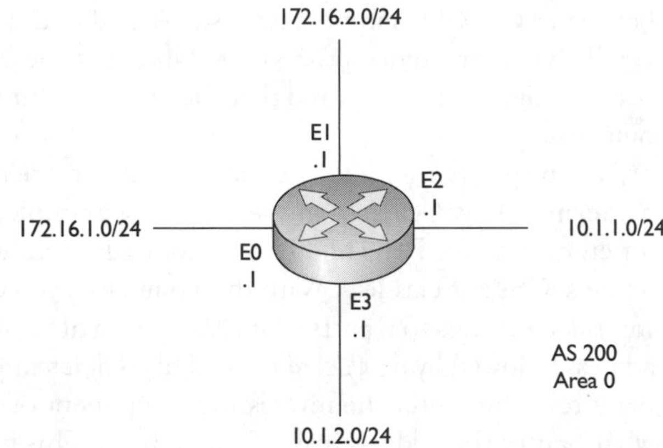

In this example, all interfaces are placed in area 0. As you can see, OSPF is very flexible in allowing you to specify which interface or interfaces will participate in OSPF and which area or areas they will belong to.

11.01. The CD contains a multimedia demonstration of configuring OSPF on a router.

When configuring the OSPF routing process, you must specify a process ID. Unlike in RIP or IGRP, the `network` statement allows you to specify an IP address and a wildcard mask, which is an inverted subnet mask. You must also specify the area that this address or addresses will belong to: `network network_# wildcard_mask area area_#`.

Loopback Interfaces

A *loopback interface* is a logical, virtual interface on a router. By default, the router doesn't have any loopback interfaces, but they can easily be created. All IOS platforms support loopback interfaces, and you can create as many of these interfaces as you need. These interfaces are treated as physical interfaces on a router: you can assign addressing information to them, include their network numbers in routing updates, and even terminate IP connections on them, like telnet. Here are some reasons you might want to create a loopback interface:

- To assign a router ID to an OSPF router
- To use for testing purposes, since this interface is always up
- To terminate special connections, such as GRE tunnels or IPSec connections, since this interface is always up

To create a loopback interface, use the following command:

```
Router(config)# interface loopback port_#
Router(config-if)# ip address IP_address subnet_mask
```

A loopback interface is a logical interface that always remains up. Use the `interface loopback` command to create it.

As you can see, creating a loopback interface is easy. You can specify port numbers from 0 to 2147483647. The number you use is only locally significant. Once you enter the loopback interface, you can execute almost any interface command on it; for instance, you can assign it an IP address with the **ip address** command.

11.02. The CD contains a multimedia demonstration of creating a loopback interface on a router.

Changing Metrics

You have two ways to affect the cost metric that OSPF uses in picking the best-cost routes for the routing table. First, remember that the cost metric is the inverse of the accumulated bandwidth values of routers' interfaces. The default measurement that Cisco uses in calculating the cost metric is: cost = 10^8/(interface bandwidth). You can also affect the value of the cost by changing the 10^8 value with the **auto-cost reference-bandwidth** command. Table 11-1 contains some costs for different interface types:

Remember the OSPF interface costs in Table 11-1; especially for serial connections.

To change the cost of an interface, use the following configuration:

```
Router(config)# interface type [slot_#/]port_#
Router(config-if)# ip ospf cost cost_value
```

Notice that the cost is assigned within an interface. This value can range from 1 to 65,535. Note that each vendor might use a different calculation to come up with a cost value. It is very important that the costs for a link match for every router on a

TABLE 11-1 OSPF Costs for Different Interfaces

Bandwidth Value	Interface Type
1785	56Kbps serial line
1562	64Kbps serial line
64	T1
25	4 Mb Token Ring
10	Ethernet
6	16 Mb Token Ring
1	Fast Ethernet and FDDI

given segment. Mismatched cost values on a segment can cause routers to continually run the SPF algorithm, greatly affecting the routers' performance.

Normally, you won't be changing the default cost values on an interface. However, since OSPF uses the inverse of bandwidth as a metric, and serial interfaces default to a bandwidth of 1,544Kbps, you will definitely want to match the bandwidth metric on the serial interface to its real clock rate. To configure the bandwidth on your router's interfaces, use the following command:

```
Router(config) interface type [slot_#/]port_#
Router(config-if)# bandwidth speed_in_Kbps
```

As an example, if the clock rate were 64,000, you would use the following command to correctly configure the bandwidth: **bandwidth 64**. Note that the speed is in Kbps. For example, let's assume you configured the bandwidth with this: **bandwidth 64000**. By doing this, the router would assume the bandwidth metric of the interface is 64Mbps, not Kbps.

11.03. The CD contains a multimedia demonstration of changing OSPF metrics on a router.

The `bandwidth` command should be used on synchronous serial interfaces to match the bandwidth metric to the clocked rate of the interface. Synchronous serial interfaces default to a bandwidth metric of 1,544Kbps.

Troubleshooting OSPF

Once you have configured OSPF, you have a variety of commands available to view and troubleshoot your configuration and operation of OSPF:

- **show ip protocols**
- **show ip route**
- **show ip ospf interface**
- **show ip ospf neighbor**
- **debug ip ospf adj**
- **debug ip ospf events**
- **debug ip ospf packet**

The following sections cover these commands.

The show ip protocols Command

The **show ip protocols** command displays all of the IP routing protocols that you have configured and are running on your router. Here's an example of this command with OSPF:

```
Router# show ip protocols
Routing Protocol is "ospf 1"
  Outgoing update filter list for all interfaces is not set
 Incoming update filter list for all interfaces is not set
  Router ID 192.168.100.1
  Number of areas in this router is 1. 1 normal 0 stub 0 nssa
  Maximum path: 4
  Routing for Networks:
    0.0.0.0 255.255.255.255 area 0
  Routing Information Sources:
    Gateway          Distance      Last Update
    192.168.1.100         110      00:00:24
    192.168.100.1         110      00:00:24
  Distance: (default is 110)
```

In this example, the router's ID is 192.168.100.1. All interfaces are participating in OSPF (0.0.0.0 255.255.255.255) and are in Area 0. There are two OSPF routers in this network: 192.168.1.100 (another router) and 192.168.100.1 (this router). Notice that the default administrative distance is 110.

11.04. The CD contains a multimedia demonstration of using the `show ip protocols` command on an OSPF router.

The `show ip route` Command

Your router keeps a list of the best paths to destinations in a routing table. To view the routing table, use the **`show ip route`** command:

```
Router# show ip route
Codes: C - connected, S - static, I - IGRP, R - RIP,
       M - mobile, B - BGP, D - EIGRP, EX - EIGRP external,
       O - OSPF, IA - OSPF inter area, N1 - OSPF NSSA
       external type 1, N2 - OSPF NSSA external type 2,
       E1 - OSPF external type 1, E2 - OSPF external type 2,
       E - EGP, i - IS-IS, L1 - IS-IS level-1,
       L2 - IS-IS level-2, * - candidate default,
       U - per-user static route, o - ODR,
       T - traffic engineered route

Gateway of last resort is not set
     10.0.0.0/24 is subnetted, 1 subnets
O       10.0.1.0 [110/65] via 192.168.1.100, 00:04:18, Serial0
C    192.168.1.0/24 is directly connected, Serial0
C    192.168.100.0/24 is directly connected, Ethernet0
```

OSPF routes show up as an O in the output of the `show ip route` command.

In this example, there is one OSPF route (O): 10.0.1.0. This route has an administrative distance of 110, has a cost of 65, and can be reached via neighbor 192.168.1.100.

11.05. The CD contains a multimedia demonstration of using the `show ip route` command on an OSPF router.

The `show ip ospf interface` Command

On an interface-by-interface basis, your OSPF router keeps track of what area an interface belongs to and what neighbors, if any, are connected to the interface. To view this, use the **`show ip ospf interface`** command:

```
Router# show ip ospf interface
Ethernet 1 is up, line protocol is up
Internet Address 172.16.255.1/24, Area 0
Process ID 100, Router ID 172.16.255.1, Network Type BROADCAST, Cost: 10
```

```
Transmit Delay is 1 sec, State DROTHER, Priority 1
Designated Router id 172.16.255.11, Interface address 172.16.255.11
Backup Designated router id 172.16.255.10, Interface addr 172.16.255.10
Timer intervals configured, Hello 10, Dead 40, Wait 40, Retransmit 5
Hello due in 0:00:03
Neighbor Count is 3, Adjacent neighbor count is 2
  Adjacent with neighbor 172.16.255.10  (Backup Designated Router)
  Adjacent with neighbor 172.16.255.11  (Designated Router)
```

In this example, the router ID is 172.16.255.1. Its state is DROTHER, which means that it is *not* the DR or BDR. Actually, the DR is 172.16.255.11 and the BDR is 172.16.255.10. There are a total of three neighbors, with two adjacencies—remember that adjacencies are built only between routers and the DR and BDR.

11.06. The CD contains a multimedia demonstration of using the `show ip ospf interface` command on an OSPF router.

exam watch

The `show ip ospf interface` command displays your router's ID, the ID of the DR and BDR, the hello timer (10 seconds), the dead interval (40 seconds), the number of neighbors, and the number of adjacencies.

The `show ip ospf neighbor` Command

To see all of your router's OSPF neighbors, use the **`show ip ospf neighbor`** command:

```
Router# show ip ospf neighbor
   ID            Pri   State          Dead Time     Address           Interface
172.16.255.11     1    FULL/DR         0:00:31    172.16.255.11      Ethernet0
172.16.255.10     1    FULL/BDR        0:00:33    172.16.255.10      Ethernet0
172.16.255.9      1    2WAY/DROTHER    0:00:35    172.16.255.9       Ethernet0
172.16.254.2      1    FULL/DR         0:00:39    172.16.254.2       Serial0.1
```

The `show ip ospf neighbor` command lists all of the router's OSPF neighbors, their OSPF states, their router IDs, and which interface the neighbors are connected to.

In this example, there are three routers connected to `Ethernet0`: 172.16.255.11 is a DR, 172.16.255.10 is a BDR, and 172.16.255.9 is another OSPF router (DROTHER). Notice that for the DR and the BDR, the state is *full*, which is to be expected, since this router and the DR/BDR share routing information with each other. The DROTHER router is in a *two-way* state, which indicates that the router is a neighbor, but this router and the DROTHER router will not share routing information directly with each other.

11.07. The CD contains a multimedia demonstration of using the `show ip ospf neighbor` command on an OSPF router.

The `debug ip ospf adj` Command

For more detailed troubleshooting, you can use **`debug`** commands. If you want to view the adjacency process that a router builds to other routers, use the **`debug ip ospf adj`** command:

```
Router# debug ip ospf adj
172.16.255.11 on Ethernet0, state 2WAY
OSPF: end of Wait on interface Ethernet0
OSPF: DR/BDR election on Ethernet0
OSPF: Elect BDR 172.16.255.10
OSPF: Elect DR 172.16.255.11
       DR: 172.16.255.11 (Id) BDR: 172.16.255.10 (Id)
OSPF: Send DBD to 172.16.255.11 on Ethernet0
       seq 0x10DB opt 0x2 flag 0x7 len 32
OSPF: Build router LSA for area 0, router ID 172.16.255.11
```

In this example, you can see the election process for the DR and BDR and the sharing of links (DBDs) with the DR.

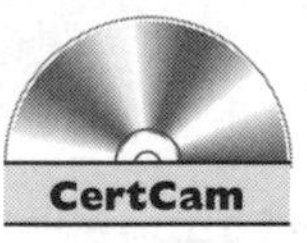

11.08. The CD contains a multimedia demonstration of using the `debug ip ospf adj` command on an OSPF router.

The `debug ip ospf events` Command

If you want to view OSPF events on your router, use the **`debug ip ospf events`** command:

```
Router# debug ip ospf events
4d02h: OSPF: Rcv hello from 192.168.1.100 area 0 from Serial0
192.168.1.100
4d02h: OSPF: End of hello processing
```

In this example, the router received a hello packet from 192.168.1.00, which is connected to `Serial0`. Other kinds of information that you might see are these:

- Hello intervals that do not match for routers on a segment

- Dead intervals that do not match for routers on a segment
- Mismatched subnet masks for OSPF routers on a segment

11.09. The CD contains a multimedia demonstration of using the `debug ip ospf events` command on an OSPF router.

The `debug ip ospf packet` Command

If you want to view OSPF packet contents of LSAs, use the **`debug ip ospf packet`** command:

```
Router# debug ip ospf packet
4d02h: OSPF: rcv. v:2 t:1 l:48 rid:192.168.1.100
      aid:0.0.0.0 chk:15E4 aut:0 auk: from Serial0
```

Be familiar with the terms in Table 11-2.

Table 11-2 explains the values shown in this command.

11.10. The CD contains a multimedia demonstration of using the `debug ip ospf packet` command on an OSPF router.

TABLE 11-2 Field Values of the **`debug ip ospf packet`** Command

Field Value	Explanation
`Aid:`	OSPF Area ID number
`Auk:`	OSPF authentication key used for neighbor authentication
`Aut:`	Type of OSPF authentication (0-none, 1-simple password, 2-MD5 hashing)
`Keyid:`	MD5 key value if this authentication mechanism is enabled
`L:`	Length of the packet
`Rid:`	OSPF router ID
`Seq:`	Sequence number
`T:`	OSPF packet type (1-hello, 2-data description, 3-link state request, 4-link state update, 5-link state acknowledgment
`V:`	OSPF version number

EXERCISE 11-1

Configuring OSPF

These last few sections dealt with the configuring of OSPF on a router. This exercise will help you reinforce this material for setting up and troubleshooting OSPF. You'll perform this lab using Boson's NetSim™ simulator. This exercise has you set OSPF on the two routers (2600 and 2500). You can find a picture of the network diagram for Boson's NetSim™ simulator in the Introduction of this book. After starting up the simulator, click the *LabNavigator* button. Next, double-click *Exercise 11-1* and click the *Load Lab* button. This will load the lab configuration based on Chapter 5's and 7's exercises.

1. On the 2600, verify that the `fa0/0` and `s0` interfaces are up. If not, bring them up. Examine the IP addresses configured on the 2600 and look at its routing table.

   At the top of the simulator in the menu bar, click the *eRouters* icon and choose *2600*. On the 2600, use the **`show interfaces`** command to verify your configuration. If `fa0/0` and `s0` are not up, go into the interfaces (`fa0/0` and `s0`) and enable them: **`configure terminal`**, **`interface`** *`type port`*, **`no shutdown`**, **`end`**, **`show interfaces`**. Use the **`show ip route`** command. You should have two connected networks: 192.168.1.0 connected to `fa0/0` and 192.168.2.0 connected to `s0`.

2. On the 2500, verify that the `e0` and `s0` interfaces are up. If not, bring them up. Examine the IP addresses configured on the 2500 and look at its routing table.

   At the top of the simulator in the menu bar, click the *eRouters* icon and choose *2500*. On the 2500, verify that the `e0` and `s0` interfaces are up. If not, bring them up: **`configure terminal`**, **`interface`** *`type port`*, **`no shutdown`**, **`end`**, **`show interfaces`**. Use the **`show interfaces`** command to verify that the IP addresses you configured on Chapter 5 are still there. Use the **`show ip route`** command. You should have two connected networks: 192.168.3.0 connected to e0 and 192.168.2.0 connected to s0.

3. Test connectivity between Host1 and the 2600. Test connectivity between Host3 and the 2500. Test connectivity between Host3 and Host1.

At the top of the simulator in the menu bar, click the *eStations* icon and choose *Host1*. From Host1, ping the 2600: **`ping 192.168.1.1`**. The ping should be successful. At the top of the simulator in the menu bar, click the *eStations* icon and choose *Host3*. From Host3, ping the 2500 router: **`ping 192.168.3.1`**. The ping should be successful. From Host3, ping Host 1: **`ping 192.168.1.10`**. The ping should fail: there is no route from the 2500 to this destination (look at the 2500's routing table: it doesn't list 192.168.1.0/24).

4. Enable OSPF on the 2600 and 2500 routers, using a process ID of 1, and put all interfaces in area 0.

   At the top of the simulator in the menu bar, click the *eRouters* icon and choose *2600*. On the 2600 router, configure the following: **`configure terminal`**, **`router ospf 1`**, **`network 0.0.0.0 255.255.255.255 area 0`**, **`end`**. At the top of the simulator in the menu bar, click the *eRouters* icon and choose *2500*. On the 2500 router, configure the following: **`configure terminal`**, **`router ospf 1`**, **`network 0.0.0.0 255.255.255.255 area 0`**, **`end`**.

5. On the 2600 and 2500, verify the operation of OSPF. Is either router a DR or BDR on the WAN link?

   At the top of the simulator in the menu bar, click the *eRouters* icon and choose *2600*. Use the **`show ip protocols`** command to make sure that OSPF is configured—check for the neighboring router's update. Use the **`show ip route`** command and look for the remote LAN network number as a RIP (O) entry in the routing table. Use the **`show ip ospf neighbor`** command to view your neighboring router. Neither should be a DR or BDR on the serial link, since point-to-point connections don't use DRs and BDRs. At the top of the simulator in the menu bar, click the *eRouters* icon and choose *2500*. Use the same above commands, **`show ip protocols`**, **`show ip route`**, and **`show ip ospf neighbor`**, to verify the operation of OSPF.

6. On Host1, test connectivity to Host3.

   At the top of the simulator in the menu bar, click the *eStations* icon and choose *Host1*. On Host1, execute this: **`ping 192.168.3.2`**. The ping should be successful.

EXERCISE 11-2

Troubleshooting OSPF

The last exercise dealt with configuring OSPF on the 2600 and 2500 routers. This exercise will help introduce you to an already configured network, but with some configuration issues which are preventing OSPF connectivity. You'll perform this lab using Boson's NetSim™ simulator. You can find a picture of the network diagram for Boson's NetSim™ simulator in the Introduction of this book. After starting up the simulator, click the *LabNavigator* button. Next, double-click *Exercise 11-2* and click the *Load Lab* button. This will load the lab configuration based on Chapter 5's and 7's exercises (with problems, of course).

Lets' start with your problem: Host1 cannot ping Host3. Your task is to figure out what the problems are and fix them: there are three problems. In this example, OSPF has been preconfigured on the routers. I would recommend that you try this troubleshooting process on your own first; and if you have problems, come back to the steps and solutions provided below.

1. Test connectivity from Host1 to Host3 with ping as well as from Host1 to its default gateway.

   At the top of the simulator in the menu bar, click the *eStations* icon and choose *Host1*. On Host1, ping Host3: **`ping 192.168.3.2`**. Note that the ping fails. Ping the default gateway address: **`ping 192.168.1.1`**. The ping should fail, indicating that at least layer-3 is not functioning between Host1 and the 2600. Examine the IP configuration on Host1 by executing: **`winipcfg`**. Make sure the IP addressing information is correct: IP address of 192.168.1.10, subnet mask of 255.255.255.0, and default gateway address of 192.168.1.1. Notice that the IP address is 192.168.100.10. Change this address to 192.168.1.10. Click the *OK* button to save your changes and close **`winipcfg`**. Try pinging the 2600 again: **`ping 192.168.1.1`**. The ping should succeed. On Host1, ping Host3: **`ping 192.168.3.2`**. Note that the ping still fails.

2. Test connectivity from Host3 to its default gateway.

   At the top of the simulator in the menu bar, click the *eStations* icon and choose *Host3*. Examine the IP configuration on Host3 by executing: **`winipcfg`**. Make sure the IP addressing information is correct: IP address of 192.168.3.2, subnet mask of 255.255.255.0, and default gateway address of 192.168.3.1. Click the *Cancel* button to close **`winipcfg`**. Ping the default gateway address: **`ping 192.168.3.1`**. The ping should be fail, indicating that there is a problem between Host3 and the 2500. In this example, layer-2 is functioning correctly; therefore, it must be a problem with the 2500.

3. Check the interface statuses and IP configuration on the 2500 and verify connectivity to the 2600. Also verify OSPF's configuration.

   At the top of the simulator in the menu bar, click the *eRouters* icon and choose *2500*. Check the status of the interfaces: **`show interfaces`**. Notice that the `e0` is has the wrong IP address (192.168.30.1) and is disabled. Go into `e0`, fix the IP address, and enable it: **`configure terminal`**, **`interface e0`**, **`ip address 192.168.3.1 255.255.255.0`**, **`no shutdown`**, **`end`**. Verify the status of the `e0 interface`: **`show interface e0`**. Try pinging Host3: **`ping 192.168.3.2`**. The ping should succeed. Try pinging the 2600's `serial0 interface`: **`ping 192.168.2.1`**. The ping succeeds. Examine the 2500's OSPF configuration: **`show ip protocol`**. You should see OSPF as the routing protocol and networks 192.168.2.0 and 192.168.3.0 included (0.0.0.0 255.255.255.255). From this output, it looks like OSPF is configured correctly on the 2500. Save the configuration on the router: **`copy running-config startup-config`**.

4. Test connectivity from the 2500 to Host1. Examine the routing table.

   From the 2500 router, test the connection to Host1: **`ping 192.168.1.10`**. The ping should fail. This indicates a layer-3 problem between the 2500 and Host1. Examine the routing table: **`show ip route`**. Notice that there are only two connected routes (192.168.2.0/24 and 192.168.3.0/24), but no OSPF routes.

5. Access the 2600 router and examine OSPF's configuration. Fix the problem.

   At the top of the simulator in the menu bar, click the *eRouters* icon and choose *2600*. Examine the routing table: **`show ip protocol`**. What networks are advertised by the 2600? You should see 192.168.100.0 and 192.168.2.0. Obviously, `fa0/0`'s interface isn't included since 192.168.1.0 is not configured. Fix this configuration problem: **`configure terminal`**, **`router ospf 1`**, **`no network 192.168.100.0 0.0.0.255 area 0`**, **`network 192.168.1.0 0.0.0.255 area 0`**, **`end`**. Test connectivity to Host3: **`ping 192.168.3.2`**. The ping should be successful. Save the configuration on the router: **`copy running-config startup-config`**.

6. Examine the routing table on the 2500. Test connectivity from the 2500 to Host1.

   At the top of the simulator in the menu bar, click the *eRouters* icon and choose *2500*. Examine the routing table: **`show ip route`**. Notice that there are only two connected routes (192.168.2.0/24 and 192.168.3.0/24) *and* one OSPF route (192.168.1.0/24). From the 2500 router, test the connection to Host1: **`ping 192.168.1.10`**. The ping should succeed.

7. Now test connectivity between Host1 and Host3.

   At the top of the simulator in the menu bar, click the *eStations* icon and choose *Host1*. Test connectivity to Host3: **`ping 192.168.3.2`**. The ping should be successful.

In the next section, you will learn about EIGRP and how to configure it.

CERTIFICATION OBJECTIVE 11.02

EIGRP

The Enhanced Interior Gateway Routing Protocol (EIGRP) is a Cisco-proprietary routing protocol for IP. It's actually based on IGRP, with many enhancements built into it. Because it has its roots in IGRP, the configuration is similar; however, it has many link state characteristics that were added to it to allow EIGRP to scale to enterprise network sizes. These characteristics include:

- Fast convergence
- Loop-free topology
- VLSM and route summarization
- Multicast and incremental updates
- Routes for multiple routed protocols

The following sections cover some of the characteristics of EIGRP, its operation, and its configuration.

Characteristics of EIGRP

Here is a brief comparison of EIGRP and IGRP:

- Both offer load balancing across six paths (equal or unequal).
- They have similar metric structures.

- EIGRP has faster convergence (triggered updates and saving a neighbor's routing table locally).
- EIGRP has less network overhead, since it uses incremental updates.

EIGRP and IGRP use the same metric structure. Both can use bandwidth, delay, reliability, load, and MTU when computing a best metric path to a destination. By default, only *bandwidth* and *delay* are used in the metric computation.

One interesting point about these protocols is that if you have some routers in your network running IGRP and others running EIGRP, and both sets have the same autonomous system number, routing information will *automatically* be shared between the two. The routers have to perform a conversion concerning the metrics. Even though both protocols use the same metric components, they store them in different size values: EIGRP uses a 32-bit metric, while IGRP uses a 24-bit metric. When integrating the two protocols together, EIGRP routes are divided by 256 to fit a 24-bit metric structure when passed to IGRP and IGRP routes are multiplied by 256 to fit a 32-bit metric structure when passed to EIGRP.

EIGRP uses the Diffusing Update Algorithm (DUAL) to update the routing table. This algorithm can enable very fast convergence by storing a neighbor's routing information in a local topology table. If a primary route in the routing table fails, DUAL can take a backup route from the topology table and place this into the routing table without necessarily having to talk to other EIGRP neighboring routers to find an alternative path to the destination.

Unlike IGRP, EIGRP supports both automatic and manual summarization. Remember that EIGRP is, at heart, a distance vector protocol, and therefore it will automatically summarize routes across Class A, B, and C network boundaries. You can also manually summarize within a class network, at your discretion. Configuration of summarization is beyond the scope of this book, but it is covered in depth on Cisco's BSCI CCNP and CCDP exams.

One really unique feature of EIGRP is that it supports three routed protocols: IP, IPX, and AppleTalk. In other words, EIGRP can route for all three of these protocols simultaneously. If you are running these routed protocols in your environment, EIGRP is a perfect fit. You only need to run one routing protocol for all three instead of a separate routing protocol for each, definitely reducing your routing overhead.

exam watch

The Cisco-proprietary EIGRP routing process uses the same metrics as IGRP. Unlike IGRP, EIGRP supports multicast and incremental updates, route summarization, and routing for IP, IPX, and AppleTalk. The DUAL algorithm is used to build a loop-free routing topology.

Interaction with Other EIGRP Routers

EIGRP uses hello packets to discover and maintain neighbor relationships, much as OSPF does. EIGRP generates hello packets every 5 seconds on LAN, point-to-point, and multipoint connections with speeds of at least T1/E1 speeds. Otherwise, hellos are generated every 60 seconds. The dead interval period is three times the hello interval. EIGRP uses the multicast address of 224.0.0.10 for the destination in the hello packets.

Hello packets are generated every five seconds on LAN interfaces as multicasts (224.0.0.10).

For EIGRP routers to become neighbors, the following information must match:

- The AS number
- The K-values (these enable/disable the different metric components)

Unlike OSPF, the hello and hold-down timers on two routers do not need to match in order for the routers to become neighbors. When two routers determine whether they will become neighbors, they go through the following process:

1. The first router generates a Hello with configuration information.
2. If the configuration information matches, the second router responds with an Update message with topology information.
3. The first router responds with an ACK message, acknowledging the receipt of the second's ACK.
4. The first router sends its topology to the second router via an Update message.
5. The second router responds back with an ACK.

At this point, the two routers have converged. This process is different from OSPF, where routing information is disseminated via a designated router. With EIGRP, any router can share routing information with any other router. As you can see from the preceding steps, EIGRP, like OSPF, is connection-oriented: certain EIGRP messages sent by a router will cause it to expect an acknowledgment (ACK) from the destination(s). Here are the message types for which an EIGRP router expects an ACK back:

- **Update** Contains a routing update
- **Query** Asks a neighboring router to validate routing information
- **Reply** Responds to a query message

Become familiar with the five EIGRP message types: hello, update, query, reply, and acknowledgment.

If an EIGRP router doesn't receive an ACK from these three packet types, the router will try a total of 16 times to resend the information. After this, the router declares the neighbor dead. When a router sends a hello packet, no corresponding ACK is expected.

Choosing Routes

EIGRP can use the following metric components when choosing a route: bandwidth, delay, reliability, load, and MTU. By default, however, only bandwidth and delay are activated. These are the K1 and K3 values. Table 11-3 explains important terms used by EIGRP.

EIGRP uses a less complicated approach than OSPF to choosing best-path routes to a destination and is less CPU intensive, but it requires more processing than IGRP or RIP. EIGRP routers keep topology information in a *topology table*, which contains the routes that neighbors are advertising, the advertised distances of the neighbor for these routers, and the feasible distances of this router to reach these destinations. A *successor*

TABLE 11-3 Important EIGRP Terms

Term	Definition
Neighbor table	This contains a list of the EIGRP neighbors and is similar to the adjacencies that are built in OSPF between the DR/BDR and the other routers on a segment. Each routed protocol for EIGRP has its own neighbor table.
Topology table	Similar to OSPF's database, this contains a list of all destinations and paths the EIGRP router learned—it is basically a compilation of the neighboring router's routing tables. There is a separate topology table for each routed protocol.
Successor	This is the best path to reach a destination within the topology table.
Feasible successor	This is the best backup path to reach a destination within the topology table—there can be multiple feasible successors for a particular destination.
Routing table	This is all of the successor routes from the topology table. There is a separate routing table for each routed protocol.
Advertised distance	This is the distance (metric) that a neighboring router is advertising for a specific route.
Feasible distance	This is the distance (metric) that your router will use to reach a specific route: the advertised distance plus the router's interface metric.

route is a path in the topology table that has the best metric compared to all the other alternative paths to the same destination. A *feasible successor* is a backup route to the successor route.

Not just any route can be chosen as a feasible successor. In order for a route to be considered as feasible successor in the topology table, the neighbor router's advertised distance must be *less than* that of the original route's feasible distance.

If a successor route in the routing table fails and a feasible successor exists in the topology table, the EIGRP router goes into a *passive* state—it immediately takes the feasible successor route from the topology table and puts it in the routing table, converging almost instantaneously. If the EIGRP router does not have a feasible successor in the topology table, it will go into an *active* state and generate a query packet for the route in question. This query is sent to the neighbor or neighbors that originally advertised this route.

The concern that EIGRP has with nonfeasible successor routes is that the path these routers are advertising might be part of a routing loop. EIGRP goes into an active state for these paths to verify this by double-checking with these neighbors. The neighbors will verify the information that they have in their topology table and reply to the requester with the appropriate information concerning these alternative paths. The terms *passive* and *active* can be misleading—passive means that a valid alternative route exists and can be used in the routing table, while active indicates that an alternative path exists but might or might not be valid.

Configuring EIGRP

Setting up EIGRP is almost as simple as configuring IGRP:

```
Router(config)# router eigrp autonomous_system_#
Router(config-router)# network IP_network_#
```

As you can see from these commands, EIGRP is configured the same as IGRP: you need to enter an autonomous system number and **network** statements for interfaces that will participate in EIGRP. Please note that the network numbers you specify are *classful* network numbers, even though EIGRP is *classless*.

You must specify the AS number when configure EIGRP. Even though EIGRP is classless, you must configure it as a classful protocol when specifying your network numbers with the `network` command.

Other Commands

This section briefly touches on two other commands you should be aware of when configuring EIGRP. Since EIGRP uses bandwidth as a metric, make sure that your serial interfaces have the correct bandwidth value configured. Use the **bandwidth** *Interface Subconfiguration* mode command to configure this value. Remember to put the bandwidth value in Kbps. This command was covered in the section "OSPF" earlier in this chapter.

Also, EIGRP, like IGRP, supports load balancing across six paths. By default, EIGRP will do only equal-cost load balancing, like IGRP. However, you can enable *unequal*-cost load balancing of EIGRP routes by using the **variance** and **traffic-share** *Router Subconfiguration* mode commands. These commands were discussed in Chapter 10.

Configuration Example

Let's look at an example, shown previously in Figure 11-4, to help illustrate how to configure EIGRP on a router. Here's the routing configuration of the router:

```
Router(config)# router eigrp 200
Router(config-router)# network 172.16.0.0
Router(config-router)# network 10.0.0.0
```

This router has four interfaces: 172.16.1.1/24, 172.16.2.1/24, 10.1.1.1/24, and 10.1.2.1/24. Remember, when configuring your **network** commands, to put in only the Class A, B, or C network numbers. In the preceding example, the Class B and A network numbers were entered, activating EIGRP routing on all four interfaces.

11.11. The CD contains a multimedia demonstration of configuring EIGRP on a router.

Troubleshooting EIGRP

Here are some of the main commands you'll use when viewing and troubleshooting EIGRP:

- **show ip protocols**
- **show ip route**
- **show ip eigrp neighbors**
- **show ip eigrp topology**
- **show ip eigrp traffic**
- **debug ip eigrp**

The following sections cover these commands.

The show ip protocols Command

You can use the **show ip protocols** command to display the IP routing protocols that have been configured and are running on your router. Here is an example of this command for EIGRP:

```
Router# show ip protocols
Routing Protocol is "eigrp 200"
  Outgoing update filter list for all interfaces is not set
  Incoming update filter list for all interfaces is not set
  Default networks flagged in outgoing updates
  Default networks accepted from incoming updates
  EIGRP metric weight K1=1, K2=0, K3=1, K4=0, K5=0
  EIGRP maximum hopcount 100
  EIGRP maximum metric variance 1
  Redistributing: eigrp 200
  Automatic network summarization is in effect
  Automatic address summarization:
    10.0.0.0/8 for Serial0
  Maximum path: 4
  Routing for Networks:
    10.0.0.0
    192.168.4.0
  Routing Information Sources:
    Gateway          Distance      Last Update
    (this router)          90      00:00:08
    192.168.4.101          90      00:00:06
  Distance: internal 90 external 170
```

In this command, you can see that the AS is 200 and the variance is 1 (only equal-cost load balancing). Two **network** statements were configured: 10.0.0.0 and 192.168.4.0. There is one neighboring router, 192.168.4.101. The administrative distance of internal EIGRP is 90.

11.12. The CD contains a multimedia demonstration of the show ip protocols command for EIGRP on a router.

The show ip route Command

To view the EIGRP routes in your router's routing table, use the **show ip route** command:

```
Router# show ip route
Codes: C - connected, S - static, I - IGRP, R - RIP,
```

```
       M - mobile, B - BGP, D - EIGRP, EX - EIGRP external,
       O - OSPF, IA - OSPF inter area, N1 - OSPF NSSA
       external type 1, N2 - OSPF NSSA external type 2,
       E1 - OSPF external type 1, E2 - OSPF external type 2,
       E - EGP, i - IS-IS, L1 - IS-IS level-1,
       L2 - IS-IS level-2, * - candidate default,
       U - per-user static route, o - ODR,
       T - traffic engineered route

Gateway of last resort is not set
     10.0.0.0/8 is variably subnetted, 2 subnets, 2 masks
C       10.0.4.0/24 is directly connected, FastEthernet0
D    192.168.100.0/24 [90/2195456] via 192.168.4.101, 00:00:08, Serial0
C    192.168.4.0/24 is directly connected, Serial0
```

EIGRP routes show up as D in the output of the* `show ip route` *command.

At the bottom of the display, a *D* in the first column refers to an EIGRP route. In this example, there is one EIGRP route that was learned from 192.168.4.101.

11.13 The CD contains a multimedia demonstration of the* `show ip route` *command for EIGRP on a router.

The `show ip eigrp neighbors` Command

To view the list of EIGRP neighbors that your router has, use the **`show ip eigrp neighbors`** command:

```
Router# show ip eigrp neighbors
IP-EIGRP neighbors for process 200
Address          Interface Hold  Uptime     SRTT  RTO   Q    Seq
                           (sec)            (ms)        Cnt  Num
192.168.4.101 Se0           13   00:02:10   610   3660  0     4
```

This example has one neighbor (192.168.4.101). Table 11-4 explains the output of this command.

11.14. The CD contains a multimedia demonstration of the* `show ip eigrp neighbors` *command for EIGRP on a router.

TABLE 11-4 Fields from the **show ip eigrp neighbors** Command

Field	Description
Process	AS number of the router
Address	IP address of the EIGRP neighbor
Interface	Your interface on which you are receiving the neighbor's hellos
Hold	The remaining time left before you declare your neighbor dead
Uptime	Length of time that you have known your neighbor
SRTT (smooth round-trip time)	The amount of time, in milliseconds, that it takes for your router to send EIGRP information to a neighbor and to get an ACK back
RTO	The amount of time, in milliseconds, that your router will wait before resending an EIGRP packet from the transmission queue to a neighbor
Q Cnt	The number of update/query/reply packets that you have queued up, ready to be sent
Seq Num	The sequence number of the last update/query/reply packet that your neighbor last sent

The show ip eigrp topology Command

To see the list of successor and feasible successors, as well as other types of routes, use the **show ip eigrp topology** command:

```
Router# show ip eigrp topology
IP-EIGRP Topology Table for AS(200)/ID(192.168.4.100)

Codes: P - Passive, A - Active, U - Update, Q - Query,
       R - Reply,r - Reply status
P 10.10.10.0 255.255.255.0, 2 successors, FD is 0
         via 10.10.1.1    (46251776/46226176), Ethernet0
         via 10.10.2.1    (46251776/46226176), Ethernet1
         via 10.10.1.3    (46277376/46251776), Ethernet0
```

Be able to pick out successor and feasible successor routes from the output of the show ip eigrp topology command.

In this example, there are two successor routes (the first two), but no feasible successor routes (FD = 0). Also notice that 10.10.10.0 is in a passive state, since it has two successor routes.

11.15. The CD contains a multimedia demonstration of the `show ip eigrp topology` command for EIGRP on a router.

The `show ip eigrp traffic` Command

To see information about traffic statistics for EIGRP, use the following command:

```
Router# show ip eigrp traffic
IP-EIGRP Traffic Statistics for process 200
  Hellos sent/received: 274/139
  Updates sent/received: 3/4
  Queries sent/received: 1/0
  Replies sent/received: 0/1
  Acks sent/received: 4/3
  Input queue high water mark 1, 0 drops
  SIA Queries sent/received: 0/0
  SIA-Replies sent/received: 0/0
```

As you can see from this output, the router is sending and receiving hellos and updates and is sharing information with neighboring EIGRP routers.

11.16. The CD contains a multimedia demonstration of the `show ip eigrp traffic` command for EIGRP on a router.

The `debug ip eigrp` Command

To troubleshoot EIGRP routing problems, you can use **debug** commands. The following command displays EIGRP events (there are other parameters available for this command):

```
Router# debug ip eigrp
1w0d: IP-EIGRP: 10.0.4.0/24 - don't advertise out Serial0
1w0d: IP-EIGRP: 192.168.4.0/24 - do advertise out Serial0
1w0d: IP-EIGRP: 10.0.0.0/8 - do advertise out Serial0
1w0d: IP-EIGRP: Int 10.0.0.0/8 metric 28160 - 25600 2560
1w0d: IP-EIGRP: Processing incoming UPDATE packet
1w0d: IP-EIGRP: Int 192.168.100.0/24 M 2195456 - 1657856
          537600 SM 281600 - 56000 25600
1w0d: IP-EIGRP: 192.168.100.0/24 routing table not updated
1w0d: IP-EIGRP: 10.0.4.0/24 - don't advertise out Serial0
1w0d: IP-EIGRP: 192.168.4.0/24 - do advertise out Serial0
1w0d: IP-EIGRP: 10.0.0.0/8 - do advertise out Serial0
1w0d: IP-EIGRP: Int 10.0.0.0/8 metric 28160 - 25600 2560
```

```
1w0d: IP-EIGRP: Processing incoming UPDATE packet
1w0d: IP-EIGRP: Int 10.0.0.0/8 M 4294967295 - 1657856
        4294967295 SM 4294967295 - 1657856 4294967295
```

Be familiar with the use of the debug ip eigrp command.

In this example, I disabled and reenabled `Serial0`. As you can see, it is advertising 192.168.4.0 to its neighbor connected to this interface.

11.17. The CD contains a multimedia demonstration of the debug ip eigrp command for EIGRP on a router.

CERTIFICATION SUMMARY

OSPF is an open-standard routing protocol for IP, which uses cost as a metric. It uses the Dijkstra algorithm (SPF) to provide a loop-free routing topology and uses incremental updates with route summarization support. OSPF is hierarchical, supporting two layers: backbone (Area 0) and areas connected to the backbone. Its downside is that OSPF requires more memory and CPU processes than distance vector protocols, as well as being difficult to configure and troubleshoot.

Each OSPF router has a router ID, which is either the highest IP address on a loopback interface or the highest IP address on an active interface. LSAs are used to develop neighbor relationships and are sent as multicasts every ten seconds. For LAN segments, a DR and a BDR are elected (highest router ID) to disseminate routing information. Routers use 224.0.0.6 to send information to the DR/BDR. OSPF is connection-oriented in that any routing information sent to another router requires a responding ACK. When DRs share routing information to their neighbors, the multicast it via 224.0.0.5.

Configuring OSPF requires you to specify a process ID, which is locally significant to the router. When configuring the **network** command, you specify an IP address or network number, a wildcard mask (inverted subnet mask), and a number for the area the address or network belongs to. The **show ip ospf interface** displays OSPF information about the router's ID, the DR and BDR, and timer information. The **show ip ospf neighbor** command displays your router's neighbors as well as their OSPF states.

EIGRP, a Cisco-proprietary protocol, is based on IGRP. Enhancements of EIGRP include fast convergence, a loop-free topology, route summarization, multicast and incremental updates, and routing for IP, IPX, and AppleTalk. Hellos are sent every five seconds as multicasts to develop and maintain a neighbor relationship. EIGRP's metrics are bandwidth, delay, reliability, load, and MTU.

The DUAL algorithm is used to provide a loop-free topology. This algorithm provides fast convergence by storing a neighbor's routing information locally in a topology table. The best path is called a successor route, and any valid alternative paths are called feasible successors. The advertised distance is a neighbor's metric to reach a destination, while the feasible distance is your router's metric to reach the same destination. There are five EIGRP messages: hello, update, query, reply, and acknowledgment.

Configuring EIGRP is the same as configuring IGRP: you must specify an AS number with the **router** command and you enter classful network numbers with the **network** command. The **show ip eigrp topology** command shows the topology table the DUAL algorithm uses to build the routing table. EIGRP routes show up as *D* in the IP routing table.

TWO-MINUTE DRILL

OSPF

- OSPF is an open-standard, link-state protocol. It's classless and supports hierarchical routing and route summarization. It uses cost as a metric, which is the inverse of the bandwidth of a link.
- OSPF requires more memory and faster processors to handle OSPF's additional information.
- Each OSPF router has an ID, which is either the highest IP address on a loopback interface, if one exists, or the highest IP address on an active interface.
- Routers use LSAs to learn the topology of the network. To share information with another router, they must be neighbors: their area numbers and types, timers, and passwords must match.
- DRs and BDRs assist in sharing topology information. Traffic sent to a DR/BDR pair is multicast to 224.0.0.6. Traffic sent to all routers on a segment has a destination address of 224.0.0.5. Hello messages are sent out every 10 seconds, with a dead interval timer of 40 seconds. The DR sends a periodic update every 30 minutes.
- You must give the OSPF routing process a process ID, which is locally significant to the router. You use a wildcard mask when specifying which interfaces are in which areas and are participating in OSPF: **`network`** *`IP_address wildcard_mask`* **`area`** *`area_#`*.
- Use the following commands to troubleshoot OSPF: **`show ip ospf interface`** and **`show ip ospf neighbor`**.

EIGRP

- EIGRP, which is based on IGRP, is a hybrid protocol with many distance vector protocol characteristics. It supports fast convergence, provides a loop-free topology, supports route summarization and VLSM, and uses multicasts and incremental updates.
- EIGRP sends hello multicasts (224.0.0.10) out every five seconds on its interfaces. To form a neighbor relationship, EIGRP routers must have matching AS numbers and K-values.

- EIGRP uses the DUAL algorithm to maintain the topology table and update the routing table. A successor route is the route with the best path to the destination. A feasible successor route is a valid backup route (not part of a routing loop). The advertised distance is the distance for a neighbor to reach a destination network, and the feasible distance is the distance for this router to reach the same network.
- EIGRP maintains separate neighbor, topology, and routing tables for each routed protocol: IP, IPX, and AppleTalk.
- Configuring EIGRP is just like configuring IGRP, and it requires an AS number. Remember to use classful network numbers in your **network** statements.
- To verify your EIGRP configuration, use the following commands: **show ip eigrp neighbors**, **show ip eigrp topology**, and **show ip eigrp traffic**.

SELF TEST

The following Self Test questions will help you measure your understanding of the material presented in this chapter. Read all the choices carefully, as there may be more than one correct answer. Choose all correct answers for each question.

OSPF

1. Which of the following is false concerning OSPF?
   A. It provides a loop-free topology.
   B. It is a classful protocol and allows for a hierarchical design.
   C. It requires more memory and processing cycles than distance vector protocols.
   D. It is complex to configure and difficult to troubleshoot.
2. The OSPF process ID is __________.
   A. Locally significant and is the router ID
   B. Globally significant and must be configured on every router
   C. Locally significant
   D. OSPF doesn't use a process ID, but an AS number
3. Enter the OSPF command to include all of its interfaces in area 0: __________.
4. OSPF uses __________ as a metric.
   A. Bandwidth
   B. Delay
   C. Cost
   D. Hop count
5. An OSPF's router ID is based on __________.
   A. The lowest IP address on its loopback interface, if configured, or the lowest IP address on its active interfaces
   B. The highest IP address on its loopback interface, if configured, or the highest IP address on its active interfaces
   C. The highest IP address on its active interfaces, if configured, or the highest IP address on its loopback interfaces
   D. The lowest IP address on its active interfaces, if configured, or the lowest IP address on its loopback interfaces
6. OSPF hellos are sent every __________ seconds on a multi-access medium.

A. 5
B. 10
C. 15
D. 40

7. Enter the OSPF command to view all of a router's neighbors: __________.

8. OSPF supports a ________-layer hierarchical design.

A. 1
B. 2
C. 3
D. Multi

EIGRP

9. When examining the IP routing table, an EIGRP route will be shown as what letter?

A. I
B. E
C. O
D. D

10. EIGRP uses the _________ algorithm to update its routing table.

A. Bellman-Ford
B. Dijkstra
C. DUAL
D. Integrated

11. EIGRP generates hellos every _________ seconds on LAN segments.

A. 5
B. 10
C. 15
D. 30

12. EIGRP will route for ___________.

A. IP
B. IP and IPX
C. IP and AppleTalk
D. IP, IPX, and AppleTalk

13. A __________ route is the best path to reach a destination within the topology table.

    A. Successor

    B. Feasible successor

    C. Advertised distance

    D. Feasible distance

14. Enter the EIGRP command or commands to include the interfaces with 192.168.1.1/26, 192.168.1.65/26, and 192.168.1.129/26 in the routing process: __________.

15. Enter the EIGRP command to view only the successor routes: __________.

16. Enter the EIGRP command to view both the successor and feasible successor routes: __________.

SELF TEST ANSWERS

OSPF

1. ☑ **B.** OSPF is a classless, not a classful protocol.
☒ **A**, **C**, and **D** are true concerning OSPF.

2. ☑ **C.** The OSPF process ID is locally significant.
☒ **A** is not true, because the router ID is based on the highest IP address of a loopback or active interface. **B** is not true, because it is locally significant. **D** is not true, because OSPF requires a process ID to be configured.

3. ☑ **`network 0.0.0.0 255.255.255.255 area 0`**.

4. ☑ **C.** OSPF uses bandwidth as a metric.
☒ **A** is used to compute the cost, which is the inverse of the bandwidth. **B** is used by IGRP and EIGRP. **D** is used by RIP.

5. ☑ **B.** An OSPF's router ID is based on the highest IP address on its loopback interface, if configured, or the highest IP address on its active interfaces.
☒ **A** is incorrect because specifies lowest. **C** is incorrect because the loopback is used first, if configured. **D** is incorrect because the loopback is checked first.

6. ☑ **B.** OSPF hellos are sent every ten seconds.
☒ **D** is the dead interval timer, and **A** and **C** are incorrect timers.

7. ☑ **`show ip ospf neighbor`**.

8. ☑ **B.** OSPF supports a two-layer hierarchical design: the backbone (area 0) and areas off of the backbone.
☒ **A** is incorrect because this is a flat design. **C** is incorrect because only two layers are supported. **D** is true, but **B** is more correct.

EIGRP

9. ☑ **D.** A `D` in the routing table indicates an EIGRP route.
☒ **A** indicates an IGRP route. **B** indicates an EGP route. **C** is an OSPF route.

10. ☑ **C.** EIGRP uses the DUAL algorithm to update its routing table.
☒ **A** is incorrect because this is what distance vector protocols use. **B** is incorrect because this is what link state protocols use. **D** is a nonexistent routing algorithm.

11. ☑ **A.** EIGRP generates hellos every five seconds.
☒ **B**, **C**, and **D** are incorrect hello periods.

12. ☑ **D.** EIGRP supports three routed protocols: IP, IPX, and AppleTalk.
☒ **A** is incorrect because it omits IPX and AppleTalk. **B** is incorrect because it omits AppleTalk. **C** is incorrect because it omits IPX.

13. ☑ **A.** A successor route is the best path to reach a destination within the topology table.
☒ **B** is incorrect because this is a valid backup route. **C** refers to a neighbor's distance to a route. **D** refers to a router's distance to a route.

14. ☑ **`network 192.168.1.0`**. Remember that this configuration is classful.

15. ☑ Use this command to view EIGRP's successor routes: **`show ip route`**.

16. ☑ Use this command to view both the successor and feasible successor routes: **`show ip eigrp topology`**.

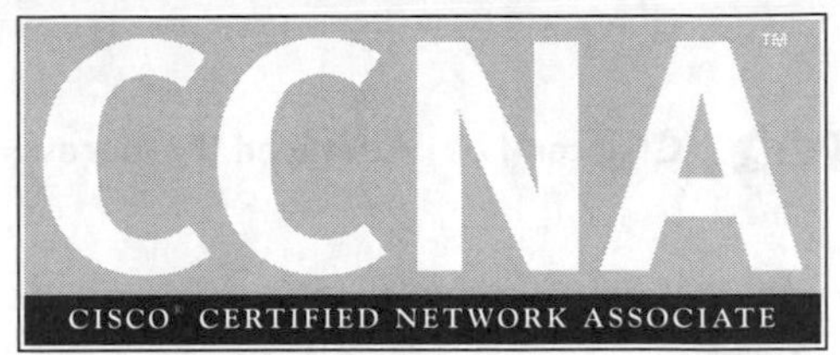

12

Advanced IP Addressing

CERTIFICATION OBJECTIVES

12.01	VLSM	✓	Two-Minute Drill
12.02	Route Summarization	Q&A	Self Test

In Chapter 11, you were introduced to two advanced routing protocols: OSPF and EIGRP. Both of these protocols are classless protocols that support advanced IP addressing concepts, including variable-length subnet masking (VLSM) and route summarization. This chapter focuses on these two advanced concepts.

CERTIFICATION OBJECTIVE 12.01

VLSM

VLSM, defined in RFC 1812, allows you to apply different subnet masks to the same class address. For instance, a good mask for point-to-point links is 255.255.255.252, which provides for two host addresses in each network. A good mask for a LAN connection might be 255.255.255.192, which provides for 62 host addresses for each network. Using a 255.255.255.252 mask for a LAN connection will not give you enough host address, and using a 255.255.255.192 mask on a point-to-point connection wastes addresses. One solution would be to divide the mask values in the middle to limit the waste of addresses, but this doesn't scale well. VLSM solves this problem by enabling you to use different subnet mask values on the same class address space. The following sections cover the advantages that VLSM provides as well as how to use VLSM in your own network.

Features of VLSM

VLSM enables you to have more than one mask for a given class of address, albeit a Class A, B, or C network number. Classful protocols, such as RIPv1 and IGRP, do not support VLSM. To deploy VLSM requires a routing protocol that is classless—BGP, EIGRP, IS-IS, OSPF, or RIPv2, for instance. VLSM provides two major advantages:

VLSM allows you to use more than one subnet mask for a given class address. Remember the two major advantages of VLSM.

- More efficient use of addressing
- Ability to perform route summarization

As these bullets suggest, one advantage of VLSM is that it allows you to make more efficient use of your IP addressing. Figure 12-1

FIGURE 12-1 Using VLSM

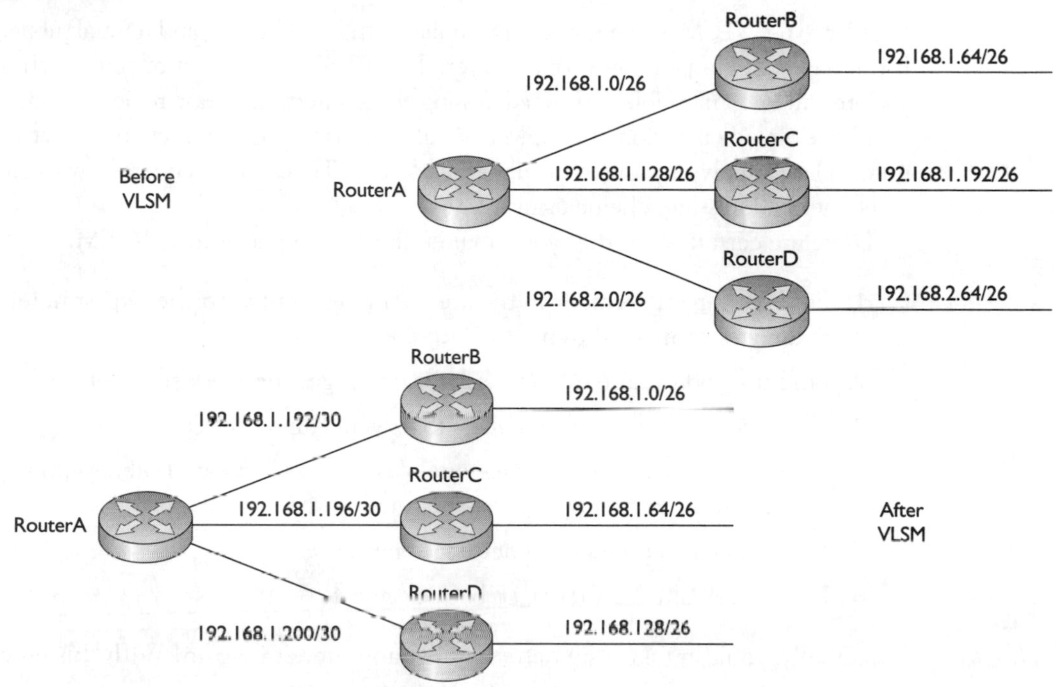

shows a simple before-and-after example of using VLSM. In this example, there is a router at the corporate site (RouterA) with point-to-point WAN connections to the remote office routers (RouterB, RouterC, and RouterD). The LAN segments at these remote sites have about 50 devices (thus the /26) mask. In the *before* design, a single subnet mask is chosen: 255.255.255.192, which allows 62 hosts per subnet. Because of the number of segments, two Class C networks were needed. On the WAN segments, this wastes a lot of addressing space.

The bottom part of Figure 12-1 shows a more efficient use of addressing, using VLSM. In this example, the three remote sites have a 255.255.255.192 mask, but the last subnet, 192.168.1.192/26 was assigned a *different* subnet mask. And these little subnetted subnets were then assigned to the point-to-point links of the WAN connections. Given the VLSM solution, only one Class C network was needed to assign addressing to this network. The second advantage of VLSM, route summarization, is discussed later in this chapter.

Addressing with VLSM

In order to use VLSM, you must be very familiar with IP addressing and normal subnetting. If you have not grasped these concepts yet, then VLSM will be out of your reach. If you are still uncomfortable with IP addressing and subnetting, please review Chapter 3. As I have already mentioned, VLSM basically means taking a subnet (not a network number) and applying a different subnet mask to it. This section covers how to create an efficient addressing scheme using VLSM.

There are certain steps that you should follow when performing VLSM:

1. Find the largest segment in the area—the segment with the largest number of devices connected to it.
2. Find the appropriate subnet mask for the largest network segment.
3. Write down your subnet numbers to fit your subnet mask.
4. For your smaller segments, take one of these newly created subnets and apply a different, more appropriate, subnet mask to it.
5. Write down your newly subnetted subnets.
6. For even smaller segments, go back to step 4.

Actually, you can take a subnetted subnet and subnet it again! With this process, you can come up with a very efficient addressing scheme.

For example, let's assume that you have a Class C network (192.168.1.0) and three LAN segments: one with 120 devices, one with 60 devices, and one with 30 devices. In steps 1 and 2, you find the largest segment and an appropriate subnet mask for it. This would be the segment with 120 devices. To accommodate the 120 devices, you would need a subnet mask of 192.168.1.0/25. In step 3, write down the newly created subnets: 192.168.1.0/25 and 192.168.1.128/25. We'll assign the first subnet to this LAN segment. We now have two segments left: 60 and 30 devices. Again, start with the larger segment first. Next we perform step 4. Which subnet mask is appropriate for 60 devices? If you guessed /26 (255.255.255.192), then you guessed correctly—this gives you 62 host addresses. In step 5, you write down your newly created subnetted subnets: 192.168.1.128/26 and 192.168.1.192/26. Let's assign 192.168.1.128/26 to the segment with 60 devices.

This leaves us with one extra subnet. You could easily assign it to the remaining segment, but this segment needs only 30 hosts and the mask has 62 hosts, which is not the most efficient mask. If you want, you can go back to step 4 and repeat the process for this subnet. The mask /27 (255.255.255.224) is a subnet mask that results in 30 host addresses, resulting in two more subnets: 192.168.1.192/27 and 192.168.1.224/27. In this example, you have one extra subnet that you could use for future growth!

> **exam watch**
> ***Remember how to perform VLSM. Therefore, know the six steps mentioned previously and also go over the next two VLSM examples thoroughly.***

As you can see, with VLSM, you can be very efficient in your IP addressing design. I do recommend that you leave room in each subnet for future growth. For instance, in the last example, using a mask of /27 on the 192.168.1.192 subnet creates two more subnets, each with 30 host addresses. If you use this address scheme and the 30-host segment grows, then you'll have to go back and readdress a portion of your network, which is not fun.

VLSM Example 1

Now that you have an understanding of the basics of performing VLSM, let's look at a more difficult example. I'll use the network shown in Figure 12-2. In this example, you are given a Class C network: 192.168.2.0/24. You are tasked to use VLSM to accommodate the following requirements: each remote site (total of 7) has no more than 30 devices. The links between the central and remote routers are point-to-point.

FIGURE 12-2

VLSM example 1

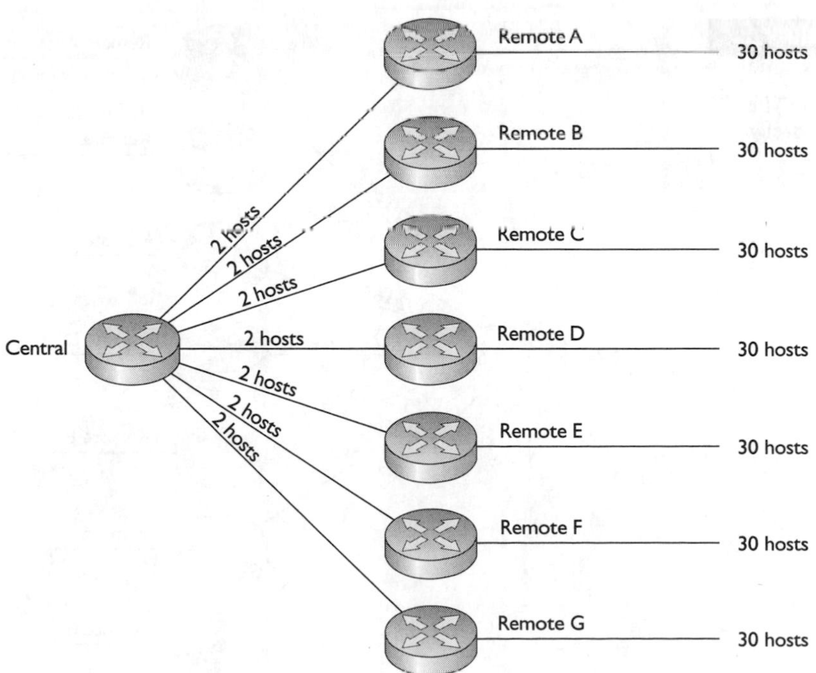

For this example, you first need to worry about handling the largest segments, which are the remote sites with 30 devices. To handle 30 devices, you need a 225.255.255.224 (/27) subnet mask. This mask results in the following subnets: 192.168.2.0/27, 192.168.2.32/27, 192.168.2.64/27, 192.168.2.96/27, 192.168.2.128/27, 192.168.2.160/27, 192.168.2.192/27, and 192.168.2.224/27.

With a /27 mask, you have actually created eight subnets; however, you need only seven for the remote offices. This leaves you one subnet mask, but seven point-to-point links between the central and remote routers. Let's assign the first seven subnets for the remote LAN segments and use the last subnet (192.168.2.224/27) for the point-to-point links. To accommodate the point-to-point links, use a 255.255.255.252 (/30) subnet mask. This results in the following subnetted subnets: 192.168.2.224/30, 192.168.2.228/30, 192.168.2.232/30, 192.168.2.236/30, 192.168.2.240/30, 192.168.2.244/30, 192.168.2.248/30, and 192.168.2.252/30.

With a /30 mask on the 192.168.2.224 subnet, you have created eight little subnets. You need only seven for the point-to-point links, which leaves one small subnet left over. Figure 12-3 shows the actual networking layout based on this example. Notice that this example used two subnet mask values: 255.255.255.224 and 255.255.255.252.

FIGURE 12-3

VLSM example 1 address design

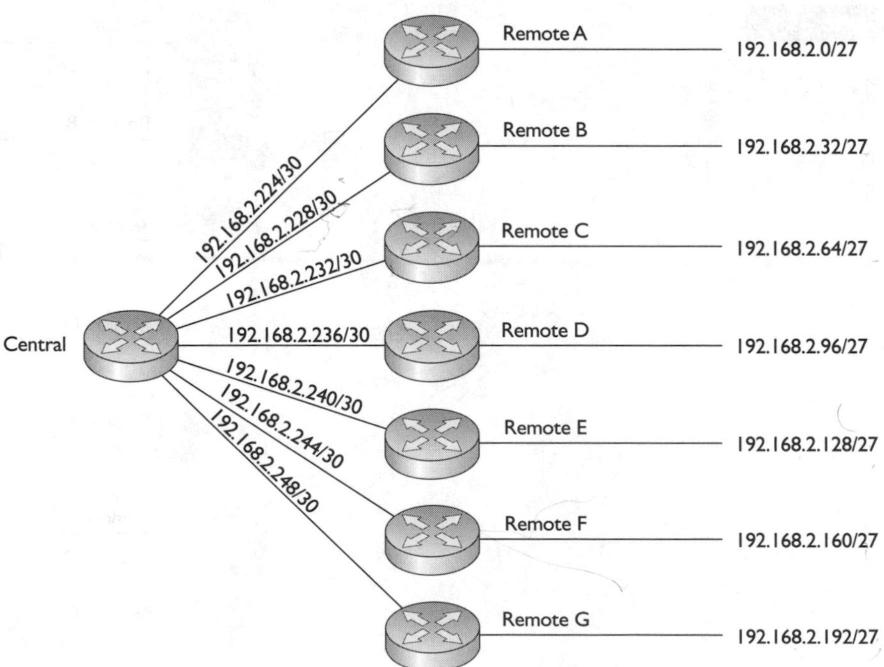

VLSM Example 2

Let's take a look at another example, shown in Figure 12-4. You have been given a Class C network: 192.168.3.0, with the addressing requirements shown in the figure. You need to come up with a VLSM solution to accommodate all of the network segments with the single Class C network.

For this example, the first network you should worry about is the backbone router segment, since it is the largest. It requires 126 host addresses. Therefore, you will need to use a subnet mask that accommodates 126 hosts: 255.255.255.128 (/25). This results in two subnets: 192.168.3.0/25 and 192.168.3.128/25. Let's assign the first subnet to the backbone router, leaving us the second subnet for further subnetting.

You next need to be concerned about the second largest subnet: the smaller router LAN segments. Each of these sites needs networks that will accommodate 30 host addresses. Take the remaining subnet (192.168.3.128/25) and apply a mask to it that will give you your remote site's addresses. The mask of 255.255.255.224 (/27) will do this for you. This results in the following subnets: 192.168.3.128/27, 192.168.3.160/27, 192.168.3.192/27, and 192.168.3.224/27.

You now have four subnets, with 30 host addresses each. Take the first three of these and assign them to your smaller router LAN segments. Use the last subnet for your router-to-router connections. These links need six host addresses each. A 255.255.255.248 (/29) subnet mask will accommodate your addressing needs. Applying this to the fourth subnet results in the following smaller subnets: 192.168.3.224/29, 192.168.3.232/29, 192.168.3.240/29, and 192.168.3.248/29. You need only three of these subnets, leaving one for future growth. In all, this network design, shown in Figure 12-5, used three different subnet masks: 255.255.255.128, 255.255.255.224, and 255.255.255.248.

FIGURE 12-4

VLSM example 2

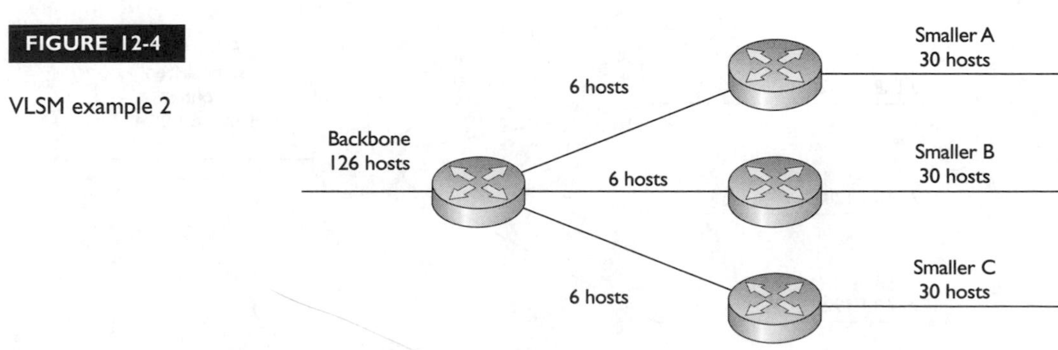

FIGURE 12-5

VLSM example 2 address design

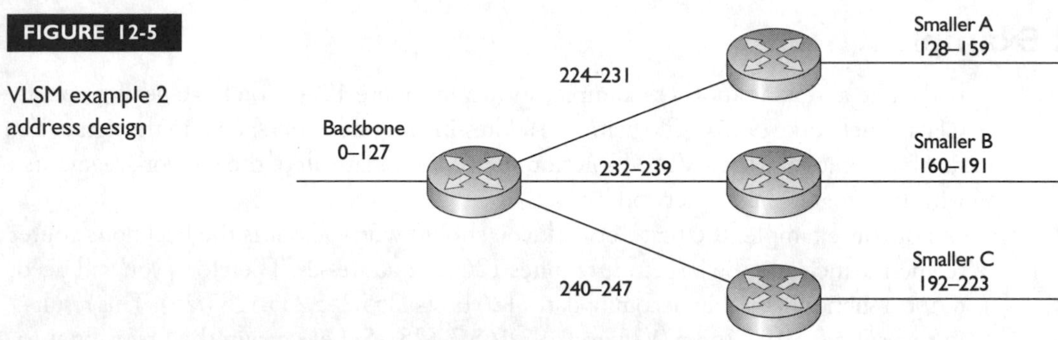

CERTIFICATION OBJECTIVE 12.02

Route Summarization

Route summarization is the ability to take a bunch of contiguous network numbers in your routing table and advertise these contiguous routes as a single summarized route. VLSM allows you to summarize subnetted routes back to the class boundary. For instance, if you have 192.168.1.0/24 and have subnetted it to 192.168.1.0/26, giving you four networks, you could summarize these subnets in your routing table and advertise them as the Class C network number 192.168.1.0/24, as is shown in Figure 12-6.

In this example, you have reduced your routing entries from 4 down to 1 in your routing updates. Summarization is a form of VLSM. Notice in the preceding

FIGURE 12-6

Simple route summarization example

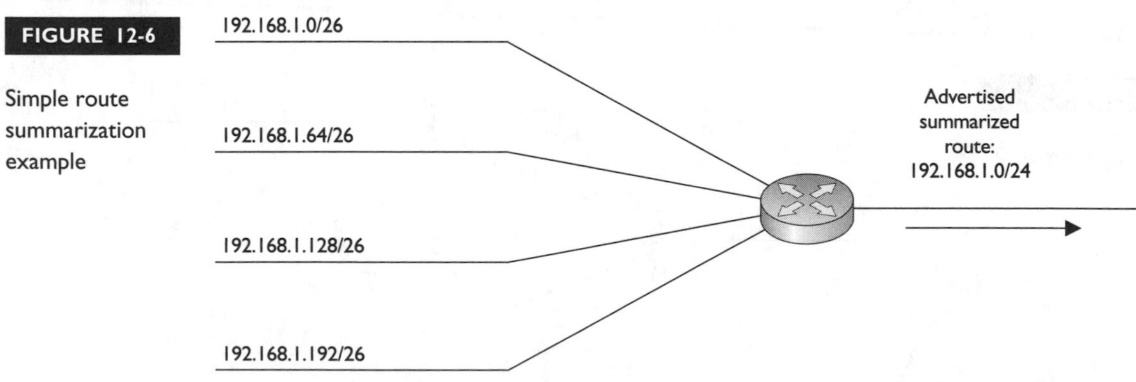

example that the same class network, 192.168.1.0, has two masks associated with it: 255.255.255.192 and 255.255.255.0.

Advantages of Summarization

Summarization allows you to create a more efficient routing environment by providing the following advantages:

- It reduces the size of routing tables, requiring less memory and processing.
- It reduces the size of updates, requiring less bandwidth.
- It contains network problems.

As you can see from the design shown in Figure 12-6, the size of the routing table update was reduced from four routes to one route, which requires less processing to any routers receiving this information. Thus, less bandwidth is required to advertise the update and less memory and processing are required on the receiving routers to process the update.

Another advantage of route summarization is that it helps contain certain kinds of network problems. For example, assume that 192.168.1.64/26 was going up and down, up and down (a flapping route). This condition obviously affects the connected router and any router that knows about this specific subnet. However, routers that only know the summarized route are not affected by the subnet that is flapping. In order for these routers to be affected, all four subnets would have to fail, causing the router performing the summarization to stop advertising the summarized route.

This, obviously, is an advantage, but it does have a down side. Route summarization hides the complete picture of the network. This can cause problems with routers making bad assumptions. For instance, assume that 192.168.1.64/26 really is down but that routers in another part of the network are still receiving updates

Route summarization is taking a bunch of contiguous network numbers in a routing table and reducing them to a smaller number of routes.

Route summarization benefits include smaller routing tables and updates and containment of networking problems.

concerning the summarized route (192.168.1.0/24). From their perspective, since the router summarizing the route is still advertising this route, all addresses from 192.168.1.0 through 192.168.1.255 must be available. Obviously, this is not true, and thus other routers will still send traffic to 192.168.1.64/26, since they still think it's reachable.

Classless Interdomain Routing

Classless Interdomain Routing (CIDR), specified in RFC 2050, is an extension to VLSM and route summarization. With VLSM, you can summarize subnets back to the Class A, B, or C network boundary. For example, if you have a Class C network 192.168.1.0/24 and subnet it with a 26-bit mask, you have created four subnets. Using VLSM and summarization, you can summarize these four subnets back to 192.168.1.0/24. CIDR takes this one step further and allows you to summarize a block of contiguous Class A, B, and C network numbers. This practice is commonly referred to as *supernetting*. Today's classless protocols support supernetting. However, it is most commonly configured by ISPs on the Internet using BGP.

> **exam watch**
>
> ***CIDR is similar to VLSM in that CIDR allows you to summarize multiple contiguous class networks together, like multiple Class C networks. This is also called supernetting.***

Figure 12-7 shows an example of CIDR. In this example, a router is connected to four networks: 192.168.0.0/24, 192.168.1.0/24, 192.168.2.0/24, and 192.168.3.0/24. The router is summarizing these routes into a single entry: 192.168.0.0/22. Notice the subnet mask for this summarization: 255.255.252.0. This mask, along with the beginning network, 192.168.0.0, includes addresses from 192.168.0.0 to 192.168.3.255, which are behind this router.

FIGURE 12-7

CIDR example

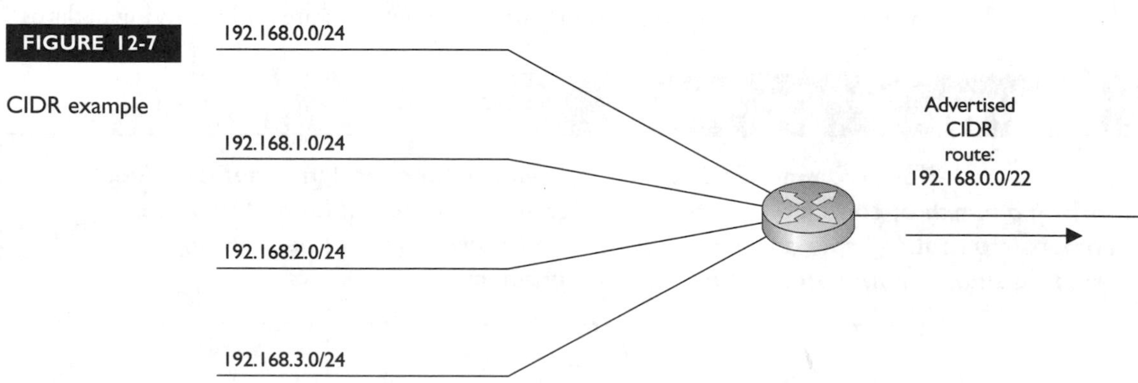

Hierarchical Addressing

In order to perform route summarization, you will need to set up your addressing in a hierarchical fashion. Hierarchical addressing provides the following benefits:

- It enables more efficient routing.
- It uses route summarization to decrease the size of routing tables.
- It decreases the amount of memory needed to store the smaller routing tables.
- It decreases the impact on the router when needing to rebuild the routing table.
- It provides a design to simplify your troubleshooting process.

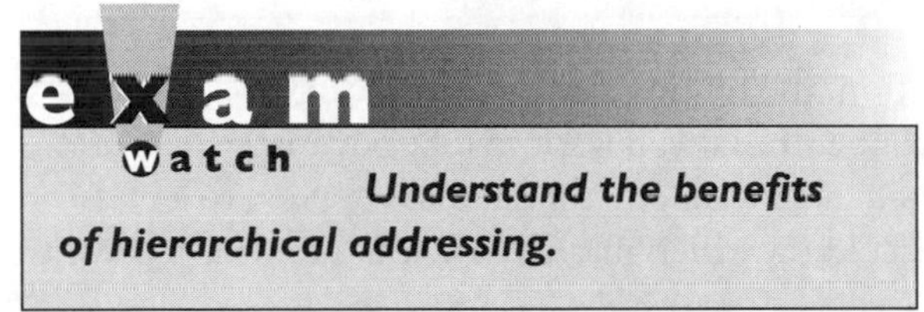

exam
watch
Understand the benefits of hierarchical addressing.

Figure 12-8 shows a simple example of hierarchical addressing. In this example, the network is using 10.0.0.0/8. This is summarized before being sent to another network. This addressing space is broken up into three campuses: 10.1.0.0/16, 10.2.0.0/16, and 10.3.0.0/16. Each of these sets of addresses is summarized when sharing routes between the campuses. Within each campus, the addressing is further broken up for the two buildings: 10.x.1.0/24 and 10.x.2.0/24.

To implement a hierarchical addressing design and to take advantage of route summarization, you'll need a routing protocol that supports VLSM: BGP, EIGRP,

FIGURE 12-8

Simple hierarchical addressing example

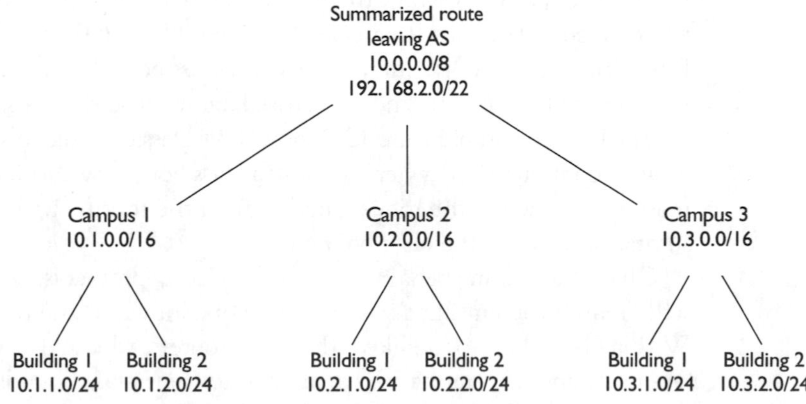

IS-IS, OSPF, or RIPv2. And when implementing route summarization, you'll need to consider the following items:

- The routing protocol must carry the subnet mask with the corresponding network entries.
- Routing decisions must be made on the entire destination IP address.
- In order to summarized routing entries, they must have the same highest-order matching bits.

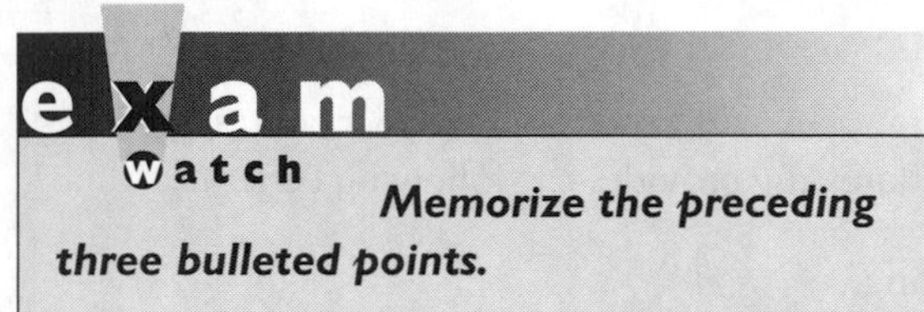

exam
watch
Memorize the preceding three bulleted points.

Routing and Subnet Masks

As mentioned in the preceding section, the routing protocol must carry the subnet mask with the corresponding network entries if you want to take advantage of route summarization. Otherwise, if you had more than one subnet mask applied to a class network number, the router wouldn't know which mask to use when routing a packet to a destination.

A good example of this problem is apparent in classful protocols, such as RIPv1 and IGRP, and how you lay out your IP addresses in your network. With classful protocols, routing updates are sent out with only network entries: no subnet masks are included. The assumption is that the routers on other segments are connected to the same class network and thus know about the subnet mask.

If a network number crosses boundaries from one class network to another, the classful protocol will *automatically* summarize it to the class address network number (A, B, or C), as is shown in the top part of Figure 12-9. As you can see, the classful protocol advertises just the network number (172.16.0.0) without any subnet mask. Plus, since the network number crosses a class boundary (172.16.0.0 to 192.168.1.0), the subnet (172.16.1.0) is not advertised, but instead the class address (172.16.0.0) is.

The bottom part of Figure 12-9 shows how classless protocols react (either by default or with configuration) when crossing a class boundary. Notice two things: the subnet mask is included in the routing update, and the routing update is *not* automatically summarized across the class boundary.

Given the routing behavior of classful routing protocols, certain addressing designs will create problems. Let's use the network shown in the top part of Figure 12-10. With a classful protocol, like RIPv1, the routers, when advertising networks across a class boundary, summarize them back to their class boundary. In this example, both RouterA and RouterB advertise 172.16.0.0—they don't advertise their specific subnets for 172.16.0.0. This creates a problem with RouterC, which receives two

FIGURE 12-9 Classful versus classless protocols and routing updates

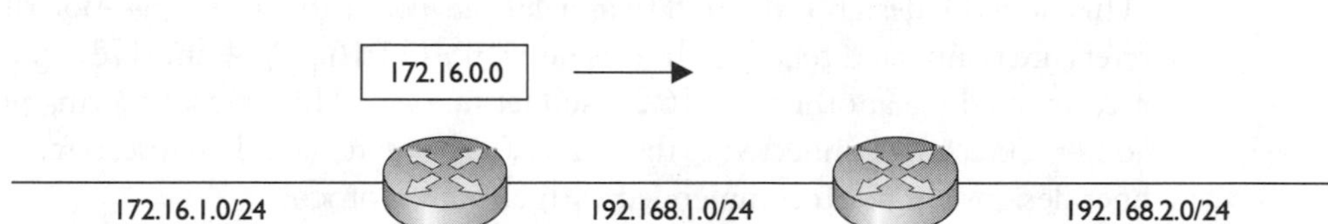

FIGURE 12-10 Discontiguous subnets

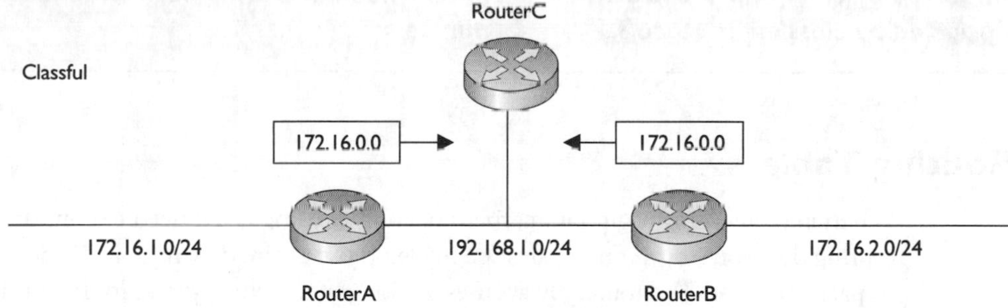

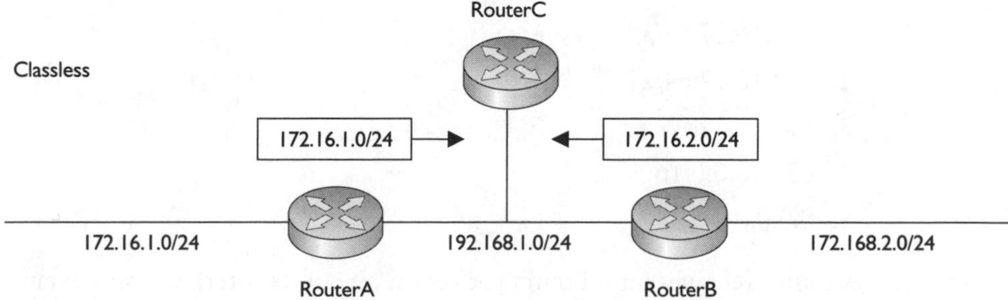

routes for 172.16.0.0. If RouterC wanted to reach 172.16.1.0/24, it really wouldn't know which router (RouterA or RouterB) to send its packets to.

This network design is referred to as a *discontiguous* subnet design—not all of the subnets are connected together. In this network, 172.16.1.0/24 and 172.16.2.0/24 are not connected via another 172.16.0.0 subnet number. This creates routing problems for other routers not connected to the 172.16.0.0 network, and therefore, discontiguous subnet designs are not recommended with classful protocols.

Discontiguous subnets *are*, however, supported by *classless* protocols. As is shown in the bottom part of Figure 12-10, classless protocols include the subnet mask in the routing update. In this example, RouterC knows exactly where 172.16.1.0/24 and 172.16.2.0/24 are located, since the mask is included in the routing updates. However, discontiguous subnets are not recommended even with classless protocols, since they limit your ability to summarize routing information in the most efficient fashion.

exam watch

Discontiguous subnets are not supported by classful protocols but are supported by classless protocols. Classful protocols do not include the subnet mask when advertising network and subnet numbers.

The Routing Table

When implementing route summarization, another thing you'll need to consider is that routing decisions, by a router, must be made on the entire destination IP address in the IP packet header. The router always uses the longest matching prefix in the routing table to perform its routing decision. Let's use the following simplified routing table to illustrate the router's decision-making process:

1. 172.16.17.66/32
2. 172.16.17.64/27
3. 172.16.17.0/24
4. 172.16.0.0/16
5. 0.0.0.0/0

A router receives an inbound packet on one of its interfaces and examines the destination IP address in the packet header: 172.16.17.65. The router then needs to examine its routing table and find the best match for this packet and then route the packet out the corresponding interface to reach the destination. The router will basically sort the entries in the routing table from the most bits in a mask to the least number of bits.

In the preceding routing table, entry 1 isn't a valid match, since the mask for the entry indicates a *host* address (32 bits). When comparing all 32 bits of 172.16.17.66 with 172.16.17.65, there isn't a match. Typically, host address routes are placed in the routing table whenever you have moved a host from its native network segment to another but, for logistical purposes, cannot change the address on the device to correspond to its new segment. In other words, you need this device to retain its old IP address.

When comparing entry 2 in the routing table, the router is comparing the first 27 bits of 172.16.17.64 with the first 27 bits of 172.16.17.65, which *do* match. When comparing entry 3, the router compares the first 24 bits of 172.16.17.0 with the first 24 bits of 172.16.17.64, which *also* match. When comparing entry 4, the router compares the first 16 bits of 172.16.0.0 with the first 16 bits of 172.16.17.65, which also match.

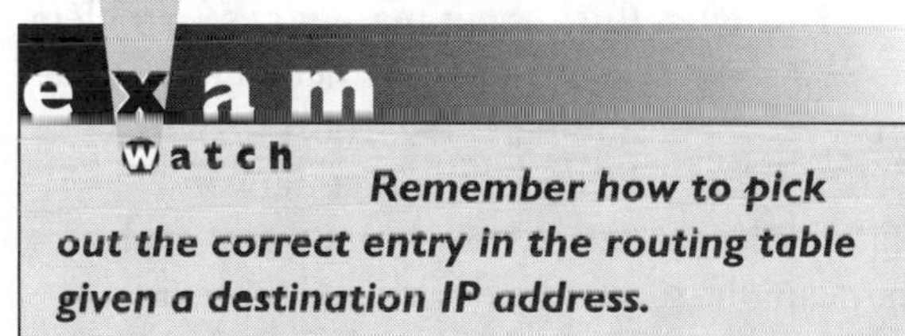

Remember how to pick out the correct entry in the routing table given a destination IP address.

When comparing entry 5, the router finds that the entry is a default route and matches any packet. Given this example, the first entry doesn't match, but the last four do match. The router needs to pick one entry and use it. When picking an entry, it uses the one that best matches—the one with the longest number of matching bits. Therefore, the router will use entry 2 to route this packet to the corresponding destination.

Performing Summarization

As was mentioned earlier, in order to summarize routing entries, they must have the same highest-order matching bits. In other words, you can perform summarization when the network numbers in question are a power of 2, like 2, 4, 8, 16, etcetera, or a multiple of a power of 2. For example, assume you are given 4, which is a power of 2. Valid multiples of this value would be 4, 8, 12, 16, etcetera. The network boundary is based on the subnet mask. If you have a subnet mask of 255.255.255.240, you cannot start the summarization on a network number that is not a multiple of 16 (the number of address accommodated by a mask of 240).

For instance, 192.168.1.16/28 is a valid summarization for this mask, while 192.168.1.8 is not (doesn't start on a multiple of 16). If the increment is not a power of 2 or a multiple of a power of 2, you can sometimes take the addresses and summarize them into a set of smaller summarized routes. Here is a list of power-of-2 numbers: 0, 2, 4, 8, 16, 32, 64, and 128. Also, when performing summarization, you want to make sure that *all* of the routes that are aggregated are associated with the router (or behind the router) that is advertising the summarized route. The rest of this section talks about the basics of summarizing routes.

When summarizing, remember that you can summarize routes only on a bit boundary (power of 2), or a multiple of a power-of-2 boundary. The trick to summarization is to look at your subnet mask options: 0, 128, 192, 224, 240, 248, 252, 254, and 255. Each of these masks cover a range of numbers, as is shown in Table 12-1. For instance, say you have a set of Class C subnets: 192.168.1.0/30 and 192.168.1.4/30. These networks contain a total of eight addresses and start on a power-of-2 boundary: 0. Therefore, you could summarize these as 192.168.1.0/29, which encompasses addresses from 192.168.1.0 through 192.168.1.7.

Let's take a look at another example. Say you have a set of Class C subnets: 192.168.1.64/26 and 192.168.1.128/26. Each of these networks has 64 addresses, totaling 128 addresses. A mask value that accommodates 128 addresses in a Class C network is 255.255.255.128 (25 bits). However, this subnet mask poses a problem, since the bit value must be a power of 2 *and* start on a power-of-2 network boundary. With a 25-bit mask, there are only two network numbers: 192.168.1.0/25 and 192.168.1.128/25. The address 192.168.1.64/26 falls under the first network number, and the 192.168.1.128/26 falls under the second one—so even though the two networks are contiguous, they can't be summarized with a 25-bit mask (255.255.255.128). You could use a 24-bit mask (255.255.255.0); however, this

TABLE 12-1 Summarizing Network Numbers

Mask Value	Range of Numbers	Number of Bits
0	256 numbers	0
128	128 numbers	1
192	64 numbers	2
224	32 numbers	3
240	16 numbers	4
248	8 numbers	5
252	4 numbers	6
254	2 numbers	7
255	1 number	8

includes a total of 256 addresses, not just the 128 addresses in question. And as was mentioned in the first paragraph, you should summarize only for addresses that are connected to or behind your router. If 192.168.1.0/26 and 192.168.1.192/26 were also behind your router, you could summarize all four of these as 192.168.1.0/24.

These first two summarization examples were pretty simple. Let's look at a more complicated example to illustrate how difficult summarization can be if you don't lay out your addressing correctly in your network. I'll use the network shown in Figure 12-11. In this network, RouterA needs to summarize routes that it and RoutersB, C, and D are connected to, realizing, though, that there are other networks to the left of RouterA. The goal is to have RouterA advertise the least number of routes to routers to the networking cloud to the left.

First, remember that RouterA should create summarizations only for the routes either that it is connected to or that are behind it (it is connected to RoutersB, C, and D). Second, these summarizations should either be a power of 2 or start on a power-of-2 networking boundary. In this example, the first thing you want to do is put the routes that RouterA knows about (to its right) in numerical order:

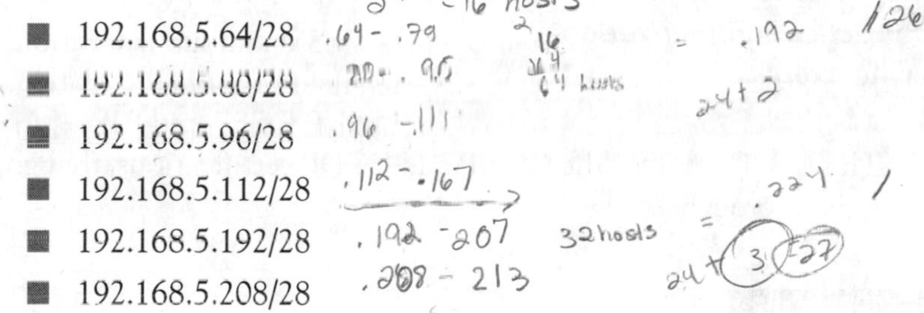

- 192.168.5.64/28
- 192.168.5.80/28
- 192.168.5.96/28
- 192.168.5.112/28
- 192.168.5.192/28
- 192.168.5.208/28

Note that there are other subnets of 192.168.5.0 to the *left* of RouterA that should not be included in the summarization. In this example, subnets 64, 80, 96,

FIGURE 12-11 Complex route summarization example

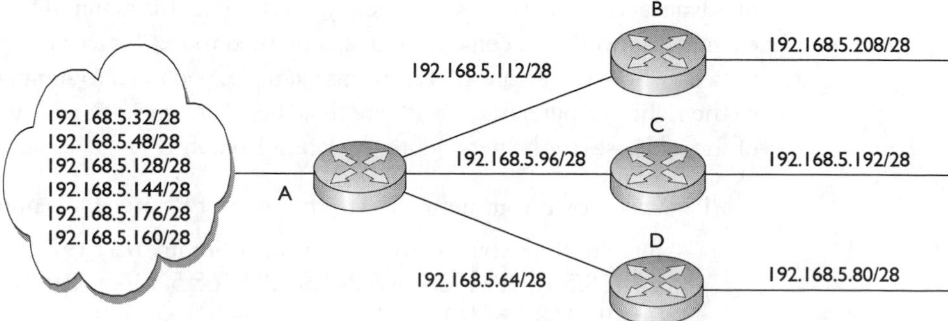

and 112 are contiguous, and if you use a 26-bit summarization mask, this would accommodate addresses from 64 through 127. These addresses are contiguous, and the summarization mask starts on a power-of-2 network boundary (address 64). In order to summarize subnets 192 and 208, you would need a 27-bit mask (255.255.255.224), which would include a block of 32 addresses: from 192 through 223.

RouterA can advertise the following summarized routes to the left network cloud:

- **192.168.5.64/26** This covers addresses 64–127, which are to the right of RouterA.
- **192.168.5.192/27** This covers addresses 192–223, which are also to the right of RouterA.

Understand the summarization examples in this section and practice summarization in the following exercise.

As you can see, the number of network entries RouterA originally advertised was six network numbers. Through summarization, this was reduced to two summarized routes.

The CCNA exam covers only the concepts of VLSM and summarization. You will not be required to configure routing protocols, such as EIGRP, OSPF, and RIPv2, to use summarization. The BSCI exam for the CCNP and CCDP certifications, though, does cover this topic thoroughly.

EXERCISE 12-1

Performing Route Summarization

The preceding few sections dealt with route summarization, its advantages and disadvantages. This exercise will help you reinforce this material by looking at an example network and come up with summarized routes for a router. You'll use the network shown in Figure 12-12. In this example, you need to summarize the routes to the right of RouterA, making sure that these summarizations don't overlap any of the addresses in the network to the left of RouterA.

1. Write down your networks (to the right of RouterA) in numerical order:

   Here are the networks that you want to summarize: 192.168.5.8/29, 192.168.5.16/29, 192.168.5.24/29, 192.168.5.32/29, 192.168.5.40/29, and 192.168.5.56/29.

FIGURE 12-12

Summarization exercise

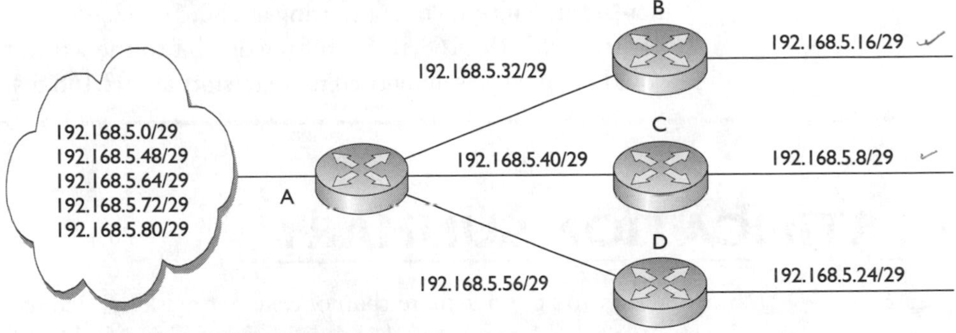

2. Break up the networks into contiguous blocks of addresses, starting on a power-of-2 network boundary

   Given that the subnet mask is 255.255.255.248 (29 bits), here are the blocks of addresses:

   - 192.168.5.8/29
   - 192.168.5.16/29, 192.168.5.24/29
   - 192.168.5.32/29, 192.168.5.40/29
   - 192.168.5.56/29

   Notice that even though subnets 8 and 16 are contiguous, a summarized mask would have to include subnet 0, which is to the left of RouterA. Remember that the summarization must begin on a power-of-2 boundary and must correspond to valid network numbers for this mask value.

3. Assign an appropriate *summarized* mask to each of these contiguous blocks:

   For the given subnets, here is a list of the ones that can and can't be summarized, as well as the summarized masks.

   - **192.168.5.8/29** Can't be summarized
   - **192.168.5.16/29, 192.168.5.24/29** Can be summarized: 192.168.5.16/28
   - **192.168.5.32/29, 192.168.5.40/29** Can be summarized: 192.168.5.32/28
   - **192.168.5.56/29** Can't be summarized

   The subnet 192.168.5.8/29 can't be summarized, since, when you shift one bit to the left in the subnet mask, this would include the network 192.168.5.0/29, which is to the left of RouterA. Remember that on a 28-bit mask, the networks increase in multiples of 16, starting at 0: 0, 16, 32, 48, 64, and so on. This is also true with 192.168.5.56. Shifting one bit to the left in the summarization would require the summarized route to start at 192.168.5.48.

CERTIFICATION SUMMARY

VLSM allows you to have more than one subnet mask applied to the same class address. VLSM's advantages include more efficient use of addressing and route summarization. Only classless protocols such as RIPv2, EIGRP, OSPF, IS-IS, and BGP support VLSM.

In order to perform VLSM, find the segment with the largest number of devices. Find an appropriate mask for the segment and write down all of your network numbers using this mask. Take one of these network numbers and apply a different mask to it to create more, yet smaller, subnets.

Route summarization is the ability to take a group of contiguous entries in your routing table and advertise these entries as a single summarized entry. Through proper configuration of summarization, your routing table sizes will decrease, the number of advertised network numbers will decrease, and you'll be able to contain certain networking problems, especially flapping routes. CIDR is a special type of route summarization. VLSM allows you to summarize back only to the class boundary of the network: the Class A, B, or C network number. CIDR allows you to summarize a group of contiguous class network numbers.

Summarization can be achieved only by laying out hierarchical addresses in your network. Used with a proper address design, hierarchical addressing allows for more efficient routing: it decreases routing table sizes, the amount of memory for routing, the number of processing cycles required, and difficulties with troubleshooting.

When implementing route summarization, note that the routing protocol must carry the subnet mask along with the routing entry: Only classless protocols allow this process. And since the mask is carried with the network number, discontiguous subnets are supported with classless protocols, but not classful ones. When the router makes routing decisions, it will use the entire destination IP address to make them.

When creating summarized entries, note that the network numbers being summarized must have the same highest-order matching bits. Remember that you can summarize routes only on a bit boundary, which is a power of 2, or a multiple of a power of 2. When summarizing, you need to know the ranges of addresses a mask value in an octet covers; for example, a subnet mask value of 192 covers 64 numbers.

TWO-MINUTE DRILL

Variable-Length Subnet Masking

- ❑ VLSM allows you to have different subnet masks applied to the same class address.
- ❑ Classless protocols, such as BGP, IS-IS, OSPF, and RIPv2, support VLSM.
- ❑ VLSM uses addressing more efficiently and allows you to configure route summarization.
- ❑ When setting up a network with VLSM, first find the largest segment. Then find an appropriate subnet mask for this network. Write down the subnet numbers according to this mask. For smaller segments, take one of the subnets and subnet it further, writing down your newly subnetted subnets.

Route Summarization

- ❑ Route summarization is the ability to take a bunch of contiguous network numbers in your routing table and advertise those contiguous routes as a single summarized route. The summarization must begin on a power-of-2 boundary based on the subnet mask value.
- ❑ Summarization reduces the routing table size, reduces the bandwidth required for routing updates, and contains network problems. Proper summarization requires a hierarchical addressing design in your network.
- ❑ CIDR, commonly called supernetting, allows you to summarize routes to the left of the class boundary, such as a group of Class C networks.
- ❑ Routing protocols must carry the subnet mask with the network entry to perform route summarization. Routing decisions must be made on the entire destination IP address. Summarization requires that the routing entries have the same highest-order matching bits.
- ❑ Classful protocols have problems with discontiguous subnet masks; classless protocols don't.

SELF TEST

The following Self Test questions will help you measure your understanding of the material presented in this chapter. Read all the choices carefully, as there may be more than one correct answer. Choose all correct answers for each question.

Variable-Length Subnet Masking

1. VLSM allows you to summarize 192.168.2.0/24 and 192.168.3.0/24 as 192.168.2.0/25.

A. True

B. False

2. VLSM allows a network segment to have more than one subnet mask.

A. True

B. False

3. Which protocol supports VLSM?

A. RIP

B. IGRP

C. RIP and IGRP

D. None of these

4. You are given a Class C network, 192.168.1.0/24. You need one network with 120 hosts and two networks with 60 hosts. How many subnet masks do you need?

A. 1

B. 2

C. 3

D. 4

5. You are given a Class C network, 192.168.1.0/24. You need one network with 120 hosts and three networks with 60 hosts. What subnet mask values would you use?

A. 255.255.255.128 and 255.255.255.192

B. 255.255.255.128

C. 255.255.255.192

D. None of these

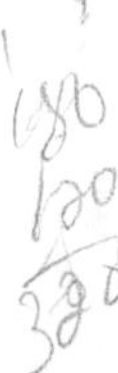

6. You are given a Class C network, 192.168.1.0/24. You need a total of three networks: one with 60 hosts and two with 30 hosts. What are the subnet mask values you could choose? (Choose all correct answers.)
   A. 255.255.255.128 and 255.255.255.192
   B. 255.255.255.224 and 255.255.255.240
   C. 255.255.255.192 and 255.255.255.224
   D. None of these

7. You are given this address space: 172.16.5.0/25. You need one network with 64 hosts and two with 30 hosts. What are the most specific subnet mask values to use?
   A. /25 and /26
   B. /26 and /27
   C. /27 and /28
   D. None of these

8. You are given a Class C network and you have four LAN segments with the following numbers of devices: 120, 60, and two with 30. What subnet mask values would you use to accommodate these segments?
   A. /24, /25, and /26
   B. /25, /26, and /27
   C. /26, /27, and /28
   D. None of these

Route Summarization

9. VLSM allows you to summarize __________ back to the class boundary.
   A. Subnets
   B. Networks

10. Which of the following is not an advantage of route summarization?
    A. It requires less memory and processing.
    B. It supports smaller routing update sizes.
    C. It contains network problems.
    D. It supports discontiguous subnets.

11. __________ allows you to create this summarization: 10.0.0.0/7.
   A. Subnetting
   B. CDR
   C. Supernetting
   D. VLSM

12. Which of the following are classless protocols?
   A. IGRP
   B. EIGRP
   C. IGRP and EIGRP
   D. Neither IGRP or EIGRP

13. A routing protocol that supports route summarization must perform all except which of the following?
   A. Carry the subnet mask with the network entry.
   B. Make routing decisions based on the entire destination IP address.
   C. Summarize entries so that the same lowest-order bits match.
   D. None of these.

14. You have the following two routes: 192.168.1.64/27 and 192.168.1.96/27. Enter the most specific summarized route for these two subnets: ___________.

15. You have the following four routes: 192.168.1.32/30, 192.168.1.36/30, 192.168.1.40/30, and 192.168.1.44/30. Enter the most specific summarized route for these four subnets: ___________.

SELF TEST ANSWERS

Variable-Length Subnet Masking

1. ☑ **B.** CIDR allows you to summarize class networks together; VLSM allows you to summarize subnets only back to the class network boundary.

2. ☑ **B.** Each segment has a single network number and mask. VLSM allows a class address, not a network segment, to have more than one subnet mask.

3. ☑ **A.** RIPv2 supports VLSM (RIPv1 doesn't).
   ☒ **B** is classful and doesn't support VLSM. **C** includes a classful protocol. There is a correct answer, so **D** is incorrect.

4. ☑ **B.** You need two subnet masks: 255.255.255.128 (/25) and 255.255.255.192 (/26). This creates three networks, for instance, 192.168.1.0/25, 192.168.128/26, and 192.168.1.192/26.

5. ☑ **D.** This is impossible with a single Class C network. One hundred twenty hosts require a 255.255.255.128 mask, which is half a Class C network. Sixty hosts require a 255.255.255.192 mask; however, you need three of these, which is 3/4 of a Class C network. Therefore it is impossible.
   ☒ **A** is incorrect because it accommodates only the 120-host and two 60-host segments. **B** is incorrect because it accommodates only two subnets. **C** is incorrect because it accommodates the three 60-host segments, but not the 120-host segment.

6. ☑ **A** and **C. A** creates one 126-host segment and two 62-host segments. **C** creates three 62-host segments and two 30-host segments.
   ☒ **B's** second mask supports only 14 hosts. **D** is incorrect because there is a correct answer.

7. ☑ **D.** Sixty-four hosts require a 25-bit mask, and you are only given this to begin with—62 hosts would work with a 26-bit mask.
   ☒ **A**, **B**, and **C** don't support enough addresses.

8. ☑ **B.** A bit mask of 25 creates two networks: 0 and 128. If you take one of these subnets and apply a 26-bit mask, you have two more networks, such as 128 and 192. Taking one of these two subnets, applying a 27-bit mask creates two more subnets, such as 192 and 224.
   ☒ **A**, **C**, and **D** don't support enough addresses to accommodate all four LAN segments.

Route Summarization

9. ☑ **A.** VLSM allows you to summarize subnets back to the Class A, B, or C network boundary.
☒ **B** is a non-subnetted address space and therefore is a Class A, B or C network number and can't be summarized with VLSM, but can be with CIDR.

10. ☑ **D.** Discontiguous subnets are supported by classless protocols, but they are not an advantage of summarization. Actually, summarization is more difficult if you have discontiguous subnets.
☒ **A**, **B**, and **C** are advantages of route summarization.

11. ☑ **C.** Supernetting, or CIDR, supports summarization of contiguous blocks of Class A, B, or C networks.
☒ **A** is the opposite of summarization. **B** should be CIDR, not CDR. **D** allows you to summarize subnets, not networks.

12. ☑ **B.** EIGRP, as well as IS-IS, BGP, OSPF, and RIPv2, is a classless protocol.
☒ **A** is not a classless protocol. **C** includes a classful protocol (IGRP). **D** is incorrect because there is a correct answer.

13. ☑ **C.** Summarized entries must have the same *highest*-order matching bits, not lowest.
☒ **A** and **B** are things a routing protocol supporting route summarization must perform. **D** is incorrect because there is a correct answer.

14. ☑ 192.168.1.64/26: this includes addresses from 192.168.1.64 through 192.168.1.127.

15. ☑ 192.168.1.32/28: this includes addresses from 192.168.1.32 through 192.168.1.47.

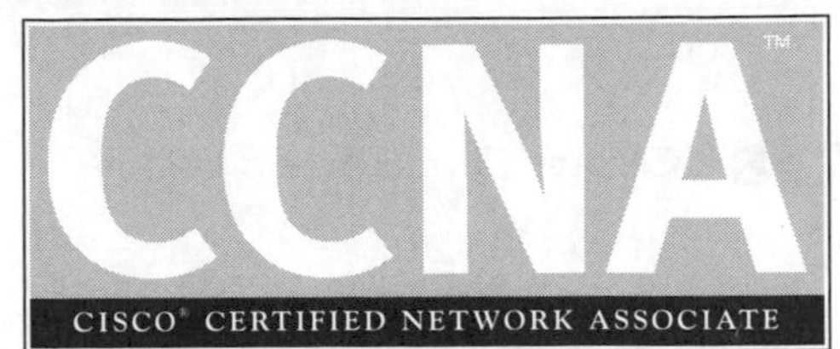

13

IP Access Lists

CERTIFICATION OBJECTIVES

- 13.01 ACL Overview
- 13.02 Basic ACL Configuration
- 13.03 Wildcard Masks
- 13.04 Types of ACLs
- 13.05 Placement of ACLs
-  Two-Minute Drill
- Q&A Self Test

The last few chapters introduced you to routing protocols and their basic configuration. By default, once you set up routing, your router will allow any packet to flow from one interface to another. You may want to implement policies to restrict the flow of traffic, for either security or traffic policy reasons. Cisco allows you affect the flow of traffic from one interface to another by using access control lists (ACLs). ACLs, pronounced *ackles,* are a very powerful feature of the IOS. Cisco actually supports ACLs for other protocols besides IP, including IPX, XNS, DECnet, AppleTalk, and others. The remainder of this chapter focuses on IP ACLs, which are also the focus of the CCNA exam.

CERTIFICATION OBJECTIVE 13.01

ACL Overview

ACLs, known for their ability to filter traffic as it either comes into or leaves an interface, can also by used for other purposes, including the following:

- Restricting telnet (VTY) access to a router
- Filtering routing information
- Prioritizing WAN traffic with queuing
- Triggering phone calls with dial-on-demand routing (DDR), discussed in Chapter 17
- Changing the administrative distance of routes

This list contains just a small subset of ways that ACLs can be used to implement other IOS features. This chapter focuses on restricting the flow of traffic to or through a router.

Definition

ACLs are basically a set of commands, grouped together by a number or name, that are used to filter traffic entering or leaving an interface. ACL commands define specifically which traffic is permitted and which is denied. ACLs are created in *Global Configuration* mode. Once you create your group of ACL statements, you must activate them. For filtering traffic between interfaces, the ACL is activated in *Interface Subconfiguration* mode. This can be a physical interface, like `ethernet0` or `serial0`, or a logical interface, like `ethernet0.1` or `serial0.1`. When activating an ACL on an interface, you must specify in which direction the traffic should be filtered:

- Inbound (as the traffic comes into an interface)
- Outbound (before the traffic exits an interface)

exam watch

For inbound ACLs, the ACL is processed before any further processing; with outbound ACLs, the packet is routed to the interface and then the outbound ACL is processed.

With inbound ACLs, the router compares the packet to the interface ACL before the router will forward it to another interface. With outbound ACLs, the packet is received on an interface and forwarded to the exit interface; the router then compares the packet to the ACL. One restriction that ACLs have is that they cannot filter traffic that the router originates itself. For example, if you execute a ping or traceroute from the router, or if you telnet from the router to another device, ACLs applied to the router's interfaces cannot filter these connections. However, if an external device tries to ping, traceroute, or telnet *to* the router or *through* the router to a remote destination, the router can filter these packets.

Types

ACLs come in two varieties:

- Numbered and named
- Standard and extended

watch

Remember the filtering abilities of standard and extended ACLs as described in Table 13-1.

Numbered and named ACLs define how the router will reference the ACL. You can view this as something similar to an index value. A numbered ACL is assigned a unique number among all ACLs, whereas a named ACL is assigned a unique name among all named ACLs. These are then used by the router to filter traffic.

Each of these references to ACLs supports two types of filtering: standard and extended. Standard IP ACLs can filter only on the source IP address inside a packet, whereas an extended IP ACLs can filter on the source and destination IP addresses in the packet, the IP protocol (TCP, UDP, ICMP, and so on), and protocol information (such as the TCP or UDP source and destination port numbers). With an extended ACL, you can be very precise in your filtering. For example, you can filter a specific

TABLE 13-1 Comparing Standard and Extended ACLs

Filtered Information	Standard IP ACL	Extended IP ACL
Source address	Yes	Yes
Destination address	No	Yes
IP protocol (i.e., TCP or UDP)	No	Yes
Protocol information (i.e., port number)	No	Yes

telnet session from one of your user's PCs to a remote telnet server. Standard ACLs do not support this form of granularity. With a standard ACL, you can either permit or deny all traffic from a specific source device. Table 13-1 compares the two types of filtering for IP traffic.

Processing

ACLs are basically statements that are grouped together by either a name or a number. Within this group of statements, when a packet is processed by an ACL on the router, the router will go through certain steps in finding a match against the ACL statements.

ACLs are processed top-down by the router. Using a top-down approach, a packet is compared to the first statement in the ACL, and if the router finds a match between the packet and the statement, the router will execute one of two actions included with the statement:

- Permit
- Deny

If the router doesn't find a match of packet contents to the first ACL statement, the router will proceed to the next statement in the list, again going through the same matching process. If the second statement matches, the router executes one of the two actions. If there isn't a match on this statement, the router will keep on going through the list until it finds a match. If the router goes through the entire list and doesn't find a match, the router will *drop* the packet.

The top-down processing of ACLs brings out the following very important points:

- Once a match is found, no further statements are processed in the list.
- The order of statements is important.
- If no match is found in the list, the packet is dropped.

If there is a match on a statement, no further statements are processed. Therefore, the order of the statements is *very* important in an ACL. If you have two statements, one denying a host and one permitting the same host, whichever one appears *first* in the list will be executed and the second one will be ignored. Because order of statements is important, you should always place the most specific ACL statements at the top of the list and the least specific at the bottom of the list.

Let's take a look at an example to illustrate this process. In this example, you have an ACL on your router with two statements in this order:

1. Permit traffic from subnet 172.16.0.0/16.
2. Deny traffic from host 172.16.1.1.

Remember that the router processes these statements *top-down*. Let's assume that a packet is received on the router with a source IP address of 172.16.1.1. Given the preceding ACL, the router compares the packet contents with the first statement. Does the packet have a source address from network 172.16.0.0/16? Yes. Therefore, the result indicates that the router should permit the packet. Notice that the second statement is never processed once the router finds a match on a statement. In this example, any traffic from the 172.16.0.0/16 subnet is permitted, even traffic from 172.16.1.1.

Let's reverse the order of the two statements and see how this reordered ACL will affect traffic flow:

1. Deny traffic from host 172.16.1.1.
2. Permit traffic from subnet 172.16.0.0/16.

If 172.16.1.1 sends traffic through the router, the router first compares these packets with the first ACL statement. Since the source address matches 172.16.1.1, the router drops the packet and stops processing statements in the ACL. In this example, it doesn't matter what traffic 172.16.1.1 is sending. If another device, say 172.16.1.2, sends traffic through the router, the router compares the packet contents to the first ACL statement. Since the source address in the packet doesn't match the source address in the ACL statement, the router proceeds to the next statement in the list. Comparing the packet contents to the statement, there is a match. Therefore, the router will execute the results, permitting the traffic from 172.16.1.2.

As you can see from both of these ACL examples, the order of statements in the ACL is very important and *definitely* impacts what traffic is permitted or denied.

Implicit Deny

Another important aspect of the top-down process is that if the router compares a packet to every statement in the list and does not find a match against the packet contents, the router will *drop* the packet. This process is referred to as *implicit deny*. At the end of every ACL is an invisible statement that drops all traffic that doesn't match any of the preceding statements in the ACL. Given this process, it makes no sense to have a list of only deny statements, since the implicit deny drops all traffic anyway. Therefore, every ACL should have at least *one permit* statement; otherwise, an ACL with only deny statements will drop all traffic, given the deny statements and the hidden implicit deny statement.

exam watch

There are two actions an ACL can take: permit or deny. Statements are processed top-down. Once a match is found, no further statements are processed—therefore, order is important. If no match is found, the invisible implicit deny statement at the end of the ACL drops the packet. An ACL should have at least one permit statement; otherwise, all traffic will be dropped because of the hidden implicit deny statement at the end of every ACL.

Important Configuration Guidelines

Configuring an ACL is not a simple process. To get the configuration process right, you should be guided by the following list:

- Order of statements is important: put the most restrictive statements at the top of the list and the least restrictive at the bottom.
- ACL statements are processed top-down until a match is found, and then no more statements in the list are processed.
- If no match is found in the ACL, the packet is dropped (implicit deny).
- Each ACL needs either a unique number or a unique name.
- The router cannot filter traffic that it, itself, originates.
- You can have only one IP ACL applied to an interface in each direction (inbound and outbound)—you can't have two or more inbound or outbound ACLs applied to the same interface. (Actually, you can have one ACL for each protocol, like IP and IPX, applied to an interface in each direction.)
- Applying an empty ACL to an interface permits all traffic by default: in order for an ACL to have an implicit deny statement, you need at least one actual permit or deny statement.

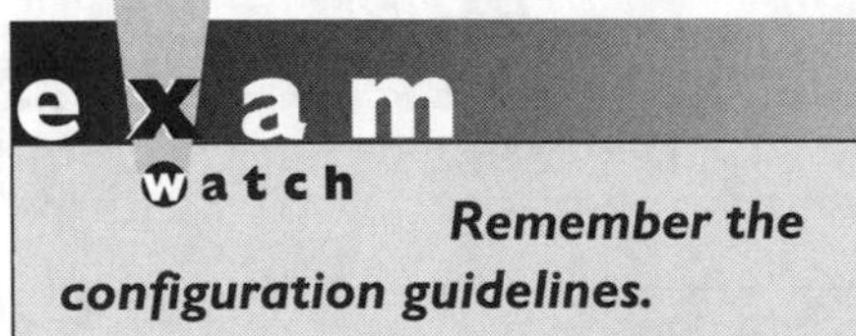

Remember the configuration guidelines.

As you can see from this list, ACLs are not a simple matter. ACLs are one of the IOS's more complex, yet powerful, features. The configuration, management, and troubleshooting of ACLs can become very complex and create many headaches for you. Therefore, it is important for you to understand the process the router uses when it compares packets to ACLs and how to create and maintain them. The following sections cover the basic configuration of ACLs on your router.

CERTIFICATION OBJECTIVE 13.02

Basic ACL Configuration

This section provides a brief introduction to the two basic commands you'll use to configure IP ACLs. The sections following this cover the actual details of configuring numbered versus named and standard versus extended ACLs.

To create an ACL, use the following command.

```
Router(config)# access-list ACL_# permit|deny conditions
```

Prior to IOS 11.2, you could give an ACL only a number as an identifier. Starting with IOS 11.2, an ACL can be referenced by a number or name. The purpose of the *ACL_#* is to group your statements together into a single list. You cannot choose just any number for an ACL. Each layer-3 protocol is assigned its own range or ranges of numbers.

Remember the numbers you can use for IP ACLs. Standard ACLs can use numbers ranging 1–99 and 1300–1999, and extended ACLs can use 100–199 and 2000–2699.

Table 13-2 shows the valid numbers and the protocols that can use them. As you can see from this table, one advantage that named ACLs have over numbered ACLs is that with numbered ACLs, you have a limited number of lists that you can create, which is based on the range of numbers assigned to a protocol type. However, named ACLs do not have this restriction. Basically, the number of named ACLs on a router is restricted only by the amount of RAM and NVRAM your router has.

The *condition* in an ACL statement tells the router what contents in the packet need to match in order for the router to execute the action (**permit** or **deny**). The

TABLE 13-2

ACL Types and Numbers

ACL Type	ACL Numbers
IP Standard	1–99, 1300–1999
Standard Vines	1–99
IP Extended	100–199, 2000–2699
Extended Vines	100–199
Bridging type code (layer-2)	200–299
DECnet	300–399
Standard XNS	400–499
Extended XNS	500–599
AppleTalk	600–699
Bridging MAC address and vendor code	700–799
IPX Standard	800–899
IPX Extended	900–999
IPX SAP filters	1000–1099
Extended transparent bridging	1100–1199
IPX NLSP	1200–1299

condition can include matching of IP addresses and protocol information. When the router compares a packet to the condition, if it finds a match, no more ACL statements are processed; otherwise, the router proceeds to compare the packet to the next ACL statement in the list. Remember that at the end of every ACL, unseen, is the implicit deny statement.

Activating an ACL

Once you have built your IP ACL, it will do nothing until you apply it to a process in the IOS. This chapter focuses on filtering traffic through interfaces. Therefore, to have your router filter traffic between interfaces, you must enter the appropriate interface or interfaces and activate your ACL. Here's the command to activate it on an interface:

```
Router(config)# interface type [slot_#]port_#
Router(config-if)# ip access-group ACL_# in|out
```

At the end of the **ip access-group** command, you must specify which ACL you are activating and in which direction:

- **in** As traffic comes into the interface
- **out** As traffic leaves the interface

In IOS 12.0 and later, you have to specify one of the two directions. In 11.3 and earlier, you did not have to enter the direction. If you omitted the direction, it defaulted to **out**.

Note that you can have the same ACL applied to multiple interfaces on a router, or the same ACL activated twice on the same interface: inbound and outbound. You can also apply a nonexistent ACL to an interface. This is an ACL that has no statements in it—an empty ACL will permit *all* traffic. For an ACL to have an implicit deny, it needs at least one **permit** or **deny** statement. It is highly recommended that you do *not* apply nonexistent ACLs to a router's interface. In this situation, when you create the very first statement in the list, the implicit deny is automatically placed at the bottom, which might create reachability issues for you.

exam watch

Use the ip access-group command to activate an ACL on an interface. You must specify the ACL number or name and the direction: either in or out.

Let's take a look at an example that has a nonexistent ACL and examine the kinds of problems that you might experience. Let's assume that you have applied an ACL (#10) to a router's `ethernet0` interface and this ACL currently doesn't have any **permit** or **deny** statements (it's empty). You are currently telnetted into the router via this interface, and your PC has an IP address of 192.168.1.1. You create an entry in ACL #10 that permits traffic from 172.16.0.0/16. As soon as you do this, you will lose your telnet connection. If you guessed that the implicit deny caused the router to drop your connection, you guessed correctly. As soon as the router has one statement in it, the implicit deny is added at the bottom. In our example, since your PC had a source address of 192.168.1.1, and this wasn't included in the first statement, the router dropped your connection because it couldn't find any matching statements in ACL #10.

Editing Entries

As you can see in the last section, creating and maintaining an ACL can be a complex process. This section covers some of the editing basics that you should know when adding, modifying, or deleting ACL statements.

First, you cannot delete a specific entry in an ACL—you can only delete the entire list. This statement is true with numbered ACLs, but not true with named ACL statements, as you will see later on in this chapter. To delete an ACL, use the **no access-list** command, followed by the number of the ACL. This deletes the entire list. If you try to delete a specific entry in the list, the router processes only the first three parameters of the command: **no access-list** *ACL_#*. Second, you cannot insert an entry at the beginning or middle of an access list. Whenever you enter an ACL command on the command line, the command is always added at the *end* of the list. And third, you cannot modify an existing entry in an ACL.

You will, at some point in time, need to either add, delete, or modify an entry in an ACL. Given the preceding issues, you will need to perform the following steps in order to easily manage the editing process of your list:

1. Execute the **show running-config** command and scroll down to your router's ACL entries.
2. Use your mouse to select and copy the ACL commands.
3. Paste the copied ACL commands into a text editor, such as Notepad.
4. Edit your ACL in the text editor, adding entries, deleting entries, and modifying entries.
5. Select and copy the ACL in your text editor.
6. On the router, remove the application of the ACL on the interface: **no ip access-group** *ACL_#* **in**|**out**.
7. Delete the old access list: **no access-list** *ACL_#*.
8. Paste the ACL from your text editor into *Configuration* mode. When you do this, the router accepts and processes each statement individually. If there is a syntax problem with an ACL command, the router will tell you. If this is the case, go back to step 4.
9. Reactivate the ACL on your router's interface with the **ip access-group** *Interface Subconfiguration* mode command.

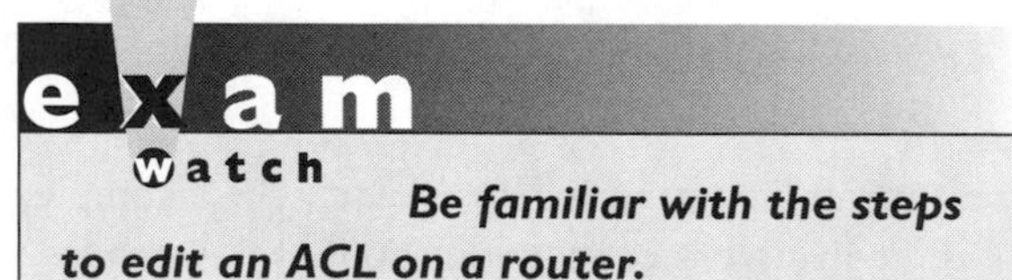

Be familiar with the steps to edit an ACL on a router.

I've used this procedure successfully for many years. If you attempt to fix ACL problems from the CLI, you are just opening yourself up to a lot of headaches. For instance, if you delete your ACL and reenter it manually, and you make a mistake on the very last command, you'll need to delete the whole ACL and start over again.

CERTIFICATION OBJECTIVE 13.03

Wildcard Masks

When dealing with IP addresses in ACL statements, you can use wildcard masks to match on a range of addresses instead of having to manually enter every IP address that you want to match on. Wildcard masks were briefly discussed under the heading "OSPF" in Chapter 11. This section goes into more depth about wildcard masks and how they are used in ACLs.

First, a wildcard mask is *not* a subnet mask. Like an IP address or a subnet mask, a wildcard mask is composed of 32 bits. Table 13-3 compares the bit values in a subnet mask and a wildcard mask. With a wildcard mask, a 0 in a bit position means that the corresponding bit position in the address of the ACL statement *must* match the bit position in the IP address in the examined packet. A 1 in a bit position means that the corresponding bit position in the address of the ACL statement does *not* have to match the bit position in the IP address in the examined packet. In other words, the wildcard mask and the address in the ACL statement work in tandem. The wildcard mask tells the router which addressing bits must match in the address of the ACL statement.

In reality, a wildcard mask is more like an *inverted* subnet mask. For instance, if you want to match on any address in a subnet or network, all you need to do is to take the subnet mask, invert its bit values (change the 1's to 0's and the 0's to 1's), and you have a corresponding wildcard mask. Let's look at a simple example of performing a binary conversion of a subnet mask to a wildcard mask. Let's assume that you have subnet mask of 255.255.0.0. Its binary representation is 11111111.11111111.0000000.00000000. When you convert this to a wildcard mask, invert the bits, like this: 00000000.00000000.11111111.11111111.

Then covert this to decimal: 0.0.255.255. This is the corresponding wildcard mask for the subnet mask of 255.255.0.0. In this example, the wildcard mask tells the router that the first 16 bits of the corresponding IP address in the ACL statement must match the contents in the IP address of the packet for the router to continue processing the statement; otherwise, the router will proceed to the next ACL statement. As you can see, this was an example that was easy to convert.

TABLE 13-3 Subnet Mask Versus Wildcard Mask

Bit Value	Subnet Mask	Wildcard Mask
0	Host component	Must match
1	Network component	Ignore

Let's look at a more difficult example. Let's assume that you want to match on a subnet that has a subnet mask of 255.255.240.0. Here's the entire subnet mask in binary: 11111111.11111111.11110000.00000000.

In this example, the first, second, and fourth octets are easy to convert: the difficult conversion is in the third octet. To convert the subnet mask to a wildcard mask, invert all of the bits, as is shown here: 00000000.00000000.00001111.11111111.

Next convert this back to decimal. This results in a wildcard mask of 0.0.15.255. As you can see from the last two examples, if a subnet mask has 0 in an octet, the wildcard mask has a value of 255; and if the subnet mask has 255 in an octet, the wildcard mask has a value of 0. However, the third octet in the last example makes this process more difficult.

In reality, I've developed a shortcut to alleviate the conversion of a subnet mask to a wildcard mask. When doing the conversion, subtract each byte in the subnet mask *from* 255. The result will be the corresponding byte value for the wildcard mask. Going back to the 255.255.240 example, here is the short cut:

- First byte: 255 – 255 (first subnet byte value) = 0 (wildcard mask value)
- Second byte: 255 – 255 (second subnet byte value) = 0 (wildcard mask value)
- Third byte: 255 – 240 (third subnet byte value) = 15 (wildcard mask value)
- Fourth byte: 255 – 0 (fourth subnet byte value) = 255 (wildcard mask value)

As you can see, this results in a wildcard mask of 0.0.15.240. This simple trick makes converting subnet masks to wildcard masks very easy.

exam watch

Wildcard masks are used to match against bits in a packet. A 0 in a bit position means match, and a 1 means ignore. If you want to match against a subnet, take the corresponding subnet mask and invert it. The trick is to subtract each octet in the mask from 255, resulting in the wildcard mask.

Special Wildcard Masks

There are two special types of wildcard masks:

- 0.0.0.0
- 255.255.255.255

A wildcard mask of 0.0.0.0 tells the router that all 32 bits of the address in the ACL statement must match those found in the IP packet in order for the router to execute the action for the statement. A 0.0.0.0 wildcard mask is called a *host mask*. Here's a simple example of this information in an ACL statement: 192.168.1.1 0.0.0.0. This statement tells the router to look for the exact same IP address (192.168.1.1) in the IP packet. If the router doesn't find a match, the router will go to the next ACL statement. If you configure 192.168.1.1 0.0.0.0 on your router, the router will covert this to the following: `host 192.168.1.1`. Note the keyword `host` that precedes the IP address.

Be familiar with how wildcard masks work, as well as the special notation Cisco uses for a match on all devices or a specific host, as shown in Table 13-4.

A wildcard mask of 255.255.255.255 tells the router the exact opposite of a 0.0.0.0 mask. In this mask, all of the bit values are 1's, which tells the router that it doesn't matter what is in the packet that it is comparing to the ACL statement—*any* address will match. Typically, you would record this as an IP address of 0.0.0.0 and a wildcard mask of 255.255.255.255, like this: 0.0.0.0 255.255.255.255. If you enter this, the router will cover the address and mask to the keyword `any`. Actually, the IP address that you enter with this mask doesn't matter. For instance, if you enter 192.168.1.1 255.255.255.255, this still matches any IP address. Remember that it's the wildcard mask that determines what bits in the IP address are *interesting* and should match.

Examples

Since the concept of a wildcard mask can be confusing, let's look at some examples. Table 13-4 shows some examples of addresses and wildcard masks.

TABLE 13-4 Wildcard Mask Examples

IP Address	Wildcard Mask	Matches
0.0.0.0	255.255.255.255	Match on any address (keyword `any`).
172.16.1.1	0.0.0.0	Match only if the address is 172.16.1.1 (preceded by the keyword `host`).
172.16.1.0	0.0.0.255	Match only on packets that are in 172.16.1.0/24 (172.16.1.0–172.16.1.255)
172.16.2.0	0.0.1.255	Match only on packets that are in 172.16.2.0/23 (172.16.2.0–172.16.3.255)
172.16.0.0	0.0.255.255	Match only on packets that are in 172.16.0.0/16 (172.16.0.0–172.16.255.255)

CERTIFICATION OBJECTIVE 13.04

Types of ACLs

The following sections cover the configuration of both numbered and named ACLs. The first two sections deal with configuring numbered standard and extended ACLs; they are followed by a section on configuring named ACLs and then a section on how to verify your ACL configuration.

Standard Numbered ACLs

Standard IP ACLs are simple and easy to configure. First, standard IP ACLs filter on only the *source IP address* in an IP packet. Use the following command to create an entry in a standard numbered IP ACL:

```
Router(config)# access-list 1-99|1300-1999 permit|deny
                    source_IP_address
                      [wildcard_mask] [log]
```

Be very familiar with the syntax of a standard ACL, as well as the fact that it can filter only on source addresses in a packet.

If you omit the wildcard mask in a standard ACL, it defaults to 0.0.0.0 (an exact match is required).

With a standard numbered IP ACL, you can use list numbers of 1–99 and 1300–1999. Following this is the action the router should take if there is a match on the condition. The condition is based solely on the source IP address. You enter this followed by an optional wildcard mask. If you omit the mask, it defaults to 0.0.0.0—an exact match is required in order to execute the action.

Following this is the optional `log` parameter, which is new to standard ACLs in IOS 12.0. This parameter will cause any match of this statement to be printed to the console port of the router. These messages, by default, will not appear on a telnet connection to the router unless you execute the following:

```
Router# terminal monitor
```

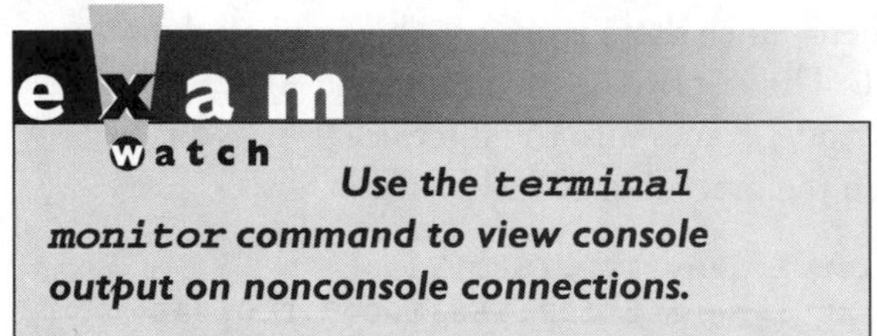

exam watch
Use the terminal monitor command to view console output on nonconsole connections.

You can also forward these messages to a syslog server. This setup is useful for debugging and security purposes.

Activating a Standard IP ACL

Once you have created your ACL, you can proceed to activate it on a router's interface with the following configuration:

```
Router(config)# interface type [slot_#]port_#
Router(config-if)# ip access-group ACL_# in|out
```

In IOS version 12.0 and later, you *must* specify either **in** or **out**. In previous versions, you could omit this and it would default to **out**.

Standard IP ACL Examples

Now that you have been introduced to the two basic commands to create and activate a standard numbered IP ACL, let's look at some examples to help you further your understanding. Here's the first example:

```
Router(config)# access-list 1 permit 192.168.1.1
Router(config)# access-list 1 deny 192.168.1.2
Router(config)# access-list 1 permit 192.168.1.0 0.0.0.255
Router(config)# access-list 1 deny any
Router(config)# interface serial 0
Router(config-if)# ip access-group 1 in
```

In this example, the first ACL statement in ACL #1 says that in order to execute the **permit** action, the IP packet must have a source address of 192.168.1.1—if it doesn't, the router proceeds to the second statement. Remember that if you omit the wildcard mask on a standard ACL, it defaults to 0.0.0.0—an exact match of the corresponding address in the ACL statement. The second ACL statement says that in order to execute the **deny** action, the IP packet must have a source address of 192.168.1.2; if it doesn't, the router proceeds to the third statement. The third ACL statement says that in order to execute the **permit** action, the IP packet must have a source address between 192.168.1.0 and 192.168.1.255—if it doesn't, the router proceeds to the fourth statement. The fourth statement is actually not necessary: it drops any packet. You don't need this statement, since there is an invisible implicit deny any statement at the end of every ACL. The last two commands in the ACL example activate ACL #1 on `serial0` as traffic comes into the interface.

Actually, you could have written the preceding ACL like this:

```
Router(config)# access-list 1 deny 192.168.1.2
Router(config)# access-list 1 permit 192.168.1.0 0.0.0.255
Router(config)# interface serial 0
Router(config-if)# ip access-group 1 in
```

This example reduces your configuration from four ACL statements in the list down to two, which increases the performance of your router.

Here's another example of a standard ACL:

```
Router(config)# access-list 2 deny 192.168.1.0
Router(config)# access-list 2 deny 172.16.0.0
Router(config)# access-list 2 permit 192.168.1.1
Router(config)# access-list 2 permit 0.0.0.0 255.255.255.255
Router(config)# interface ethernet 0
Router(config-if)# ip access-group 1 out
```

This ACL example has a few problems with it. Examine it and see if you can spot them.

The first ACL statement appears to deny all traffic from 192.168.1.0/24. In reality, it will accomplish nothing. Remember that if you omit the wildcard mask for the address, it defaults to 0.0.0.0—an exact match. The problem with this is that you'll never have a packet with a source address of 192.168.1.0, since this is a network number, and not a host address. The second statement has the same problem. The third and fourth statements are okay.

As you can see, configuring ACLs can be tricky. For the preceding example, here's the updated configuration:

```
Router(config)# access-list 2 deny 192.168.1.0 0.0.0.255
Router(config)# access-list 2 deny 172.16.0.0 0.0.255.255
Router(config)# access-list 2 permit 192.168.1.1
Router(config)# access-list 2 permit 0.0.0.0 255.255.255.255
Router(config)# interface ethernet 0
Router(config-if)# ip access-group 1 out
```

In this example, the first statement now says that any packet with a source address from network 192.168.1.0/24 should be dropped. The second statement will drop any traffic from the ClassB network 172.16.0.0/16. The third statement will permit traffic from 192.168.1.1. The fourth statement will permit traffic from anywhere. Actually, there is *still* a problem with this configuration—look at the first and third statements. Will the third statement ever be executed? If you answered *no*, then you would be correct. In this situation, you need to put the more specific entry before the less specific. Another minor point to make is that the fourth statement in the list could represent the address as the keyword **any**. Here's the updated configuration:

```
Router(config)# access-list 2 permit 192.168.1.1
Router(config)# access-list 2 deny 192.168.1.0 0.0.0.255
Router(config)# access-list 2 deny 172.16.0.0 0.0.255.255
Router(config)# access-list 2 permit any
Router(config)# interface ethernet 0
Router(config-if)# ip access-group 1 out
```

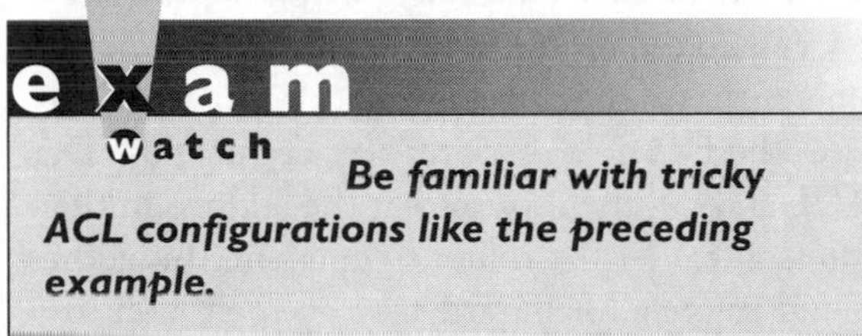

Be familiar with tricky ACL configurations like the preceding example.

There's actually one more problem with this ACL. If you guessed the ACL number used on the interface is not correct, then you guessed correctly. Notice that the ACL created has a number of 2, while the application of the ACL on the interface uses 1. To fix this, use the following configuration:

```
Router(config)# interface ethernet 0
Router(config-if)# no ip access-group 1 out
Router(config-if)# ip access-group 2 out
```

Note that you must first remove the old ACL from the interface before applying the new ACL.

13.01. The CD contains a multimedia demonstration of configuring a standard numbered ACL on a router.

Restricting Telnet Access to the Router

Besides using standard IP ACLs to filter traffic as it enters and/or leaves an interface, you can also use them to restrict telnet access *to* your router. You might want to do this to allow only network administrators to telnet into your router. Setting this up is almost the same as what you would do to restrict access on an interface.

First, you need to create a standard ACL that has a list of **permit** statements that allow your corresponding network administrators telnet access; include the IP addresses of their PCs in this list. Next, you need to activate your ACL. However, you will not do this on any of the router's interfaces. If you were to activate this ACL on an interface, it would allow any type of traffic from your administrators but drop *all* other traffic. As you may recall from Chapter 5, when someone telnets into your router, the router associates this connection with a virtual terminal (VTY) line. Therefore, you'll apply your standard ACL to the VTYs, like this:

```
Router(config)# line vty 0 4
Router(config-line)# access-class standard_ACL_# in|out
```

Remember that your router supports five telnets by default (0–4). You can configure all VTYs simultaneously by specifying the beginning and ending line numbers after the **vty** parameter. If you don't apply the restriction to all of your VTYs, then you are leaving a backdoor into your router, which might cause a security problem.

Also, notice the command used to apply the ACL to the line: **access-class**. This is different from activating an ACL on a router's interface. If you use the **in** parameter, you are restricting telnet access to the router itself. The **out** parameter is kind of unique. By using this parameter, you are restricting what destinations this router can telnet *to* when someone uses the **telnet** or **connect** commands. This creates an exception to a standard ACL and has the router treat the address in the ACL statements as a destination address; it causes the router to compare this address to the address in the **telnet** command before allowing the user on the router to telnet to the specified destination.

Here's a simple example of using a standard ACL to filter telnet traffic to a router:

```
Router(config)# access-list 99 permit 192.168.1.0 0.0.0.255
Router(config)# line vty 0 4
Router(config-line)# access-class 99 in
```

In this example, only traffic from 192.168.1.0/24 is allowed to telnet in this router. Because of the implicit deny at the end of **access-list 99**, all other telnets to this router will be dropped.

As you will see in the next section, you can also use extended ACLs to restrict access to the router; but this configuration is much more complex. Second, extended ACLs are applied to interfaces and thus won't be able to restrict telnet access *from* the router to a remote destination. And third, whenever you apply an ACL to an interface on the router, you'll affect the performance of the router on that interface. Depending on the router model, the IOS version, and the features you have enabled, the degradation in performance will vary. Therefore, if you only want to restrict telnet access to or from the router, using a standard ACL and the **access-class** statement on your VTYs is the best approach.

13.02. The CD contains a multimedia demonstration of configuring a standard numbered ACL to restrict telnet access on a router.

You can restrict telnets to your router by applying a standard ACL to the VTY lines on your router. You need to apply them with the `access-class` Line Subconfiguration mode command. Please note that you can also do this with an Extended ACL, but this requires more configuration on your part.

EXERCISE 13-1

Configuring Standard Numbered ACLs

These last few sections dealt with the configuration of standard numbered ACLs. This exercise will help you reinforce this material by configuring a standard numbered ACL on a router to restrict access through it. You'll perform this lab using Boson's NetSim simulator. This exercise has you first set up static routes on two routers (2600 and 2500) and verify network connectivity. Following this, you'll configure your ACL. You can find a picture of the network diagram for Boson's NetSim simulator in the Introduction of this book. After starting up the simulator, click the *LabNavigator* button. Next, double-click *Exercise 13-1* and click the *Load Lab* button. This will load the lab configuration based on Chapter 5's and 7's exercises.

1. On the 2500, configure a static route to 192.168.1.0/24, which is off of the 2600. View the routing table.

   At the top of the simulator in the menu bar, click the *eRouters* icon and choose *2500*. Configure the static route: **`configure terminal`**, **`ip route 192.168.1.0 255.255.255.0 192.168.2.1`**, and **`end`**. View the static route: **`show ip route`**. Make sure that 192.168.1.0/24 shows up in the routing table as a static route (`S`).

2. On the 2600, configure a static route to 192.168.3.0/24, which is off of the 2500. View the routing table.

   At the top of the simulator in the menu bar, click the *eRouters* icon and choose *2600*. Configure the static route: **`configure terminal`**, **`ip route 192.168.3.0 255.255.255.0 192.168.2.2`**, and **`end`**. View the static route: **`show ip route`**. Make sure that 192.168.3.0/24 shows up in the routing table as a static route (`S`).

3. From Host3, test connectivity to the 2600 and Host1.

   At the top of the simulator in the menu bar, click the *eStations* icon and choose *Host3*. Ping the `serial0` and `fa0/0` interface of the 2600 router: **`ping 192.168.2.1`** and **`ping 192.168.1.1`**. The pings should be successful. Ping Host1: **`ping 192.168.1.10`**. The ping should be successful.

4. Check network connectivity between the 2950-1 switch, the 2500 router, and the 2600 router.

   At the top of the simulator in the menu bar, click the *eSwitches* icon and choose *2950-1*. From the 2950-1 switch, ping the 2600 router: **`ping 192.168.1.1`**. At the top of the simulator in the menu bar, click the *eRouters* icon and choose *2500*. From the 2500 router, ping the 2600 router: **`ping 192.168.1.1`**. At the top of the simulator in the menu bar, click on the *eRouters* icon and choose *2600*. From the 2600 router, ping the 2950-1 switch: **`ping 192.168.1.4`**. From the 2600 router, ping the 2500 router: **`ping 192.168.2.2`**.

5. Configure a standard numbered ACL on the 2600 to allow traffic from the 2950-1 switch to the 2600, but to deny all other traffic. Enable logging of all traffic for the ACL statements.

   At the top of the simulator in the menu bar, click the *eRouters* icon and choose *2600*. On the 2600, create a standard ACL statement to permit access from the 2950-1 switch, logging matches: **`configure terminal`** and **`access-list 1 permit 192.168.1.4 0.0.0.0 log`**. Create a second ACL statement to deny all traffic, logging matches: **`access-list 1 deny any log`**. Exit configuration mode: **`end`**. Examine the ACL configuration: **`show access-lists`**.

6. Activate the ACL on the 2600 router on `fa0/0`.

   Activate the ACL on the 2600 router by applying the ACL to `fa0/0`: **`configure terminal`** and **`interface fa0/0`**. Apply the ACL: **`ip access-group 1 in`**.

7. Test the ACL from the 2950-1.

   At the top of the simulator in the menu bar, click the *eSwitches* icon and choose *2950-1*. From the 2950-1 switch, ping the 2600: **`ping 192.168.1.1`**. The ping should be successful. Examine the ACL matches on the 2600. At the top of the simulator in the menu bar, click the *eRouters* icon and choose *2600* and then **`show access-lists`**. There should be five matches on the **`permit`** statement.

8. Test the ACL from the 1900-1.

   At the top of the simulator in the menu bar, click the *eSwitches* icon and choose *1900-1*. From the 1900-1 switch, ping the 2600: **`ping 192.168.1.1`**. The ping should fail. Examine the ACL matches on the 2600: At the top of the simulator in the menu bar, click the *eRouters* icon and choose *2600* and **`show access-lists`**. There should be five matches on the **`deny`** statement.

9. Remove the ACL configuration from the router.

   At the top of the simulator in the menu bar, click the *eRouters* icon and choose *2600*. On the 2600 router, remove the application of the ACL. Go into the interface: **`configure terminal`** and **`interface fa0/0`**. Deactivate the ACL: **`no ip access-group 1 in`**. Go back to *Global Configuration* mode: **`exit`**. Delete the ACL statements: **`no access-list 1`**. Exit configuration mode: **`end`**. Use the **`show access-list`** command to verify the ACL no longer exists.

10. Test connectivity from both switches.

    At the top of the simulator in the menu bar, click the *eSwitches* icon and choose *2950-1*. From the 2950-1 switch, ping the 2600: **`ping 192.168.1.1`**. The ping should be successful. At the top of the simulator in the menu bar, click the *eSwitches* icon and choose *1900-1*. From the 1900-1 switch, ping the 2600: **`ping 192.168.1.1`**. The ping should also be successful.

Now you should be more comfortable with configuring standard numbered ACLs on a router.

Extended Numbered ACLs

Extended IP ACLs are much more flexible in what you can match on than standard ACLs. Extended ACLs can match on all of the following information:

- Source *and* destination IP addresses
- IP protocol—IP, TCP, UDP, ICMP, and so on
- Protocol information, such as port numbers for TCP and UDP, or message types for ICMP

The following sections cover the configuration and use of extended numbered IP ACLs.

Command Syntax

Here is the generic command to configure an extended numbered IP ACL:

```
Router(config)# access-list 100-199|2000-2699 permit|deny
                    IP_protocol
                    source_address source_wildcard_mask
                        [protocol_information]
                    destination_address destination_wildcard_mask
                        [protocol_information] [log]
```

As you can see from this command, the configuration of an extended ACL is more complicated than that of a standard one. Extended IP numbered ACLs can use list numbers in the ranges 100–199 and 2000–2699. After the action (**permit** or **deny**) comes the IP protocol that you want to match on. This is the first major difference between an extended ACL and a standard one. These IP protocols include the following: **ip**, **icmp**, **tcp**, **gre**, **udp**, **igrp**, **eigrp**, **igmp**, **ipinip**, **nos**, and **ospf**. If you want to match on any IP protocol—TCP, UDP, ICMP, and so on—use the **ip** keyword for the protocol. For the CCNA exam, you'll want to focus on the **ip**, **icmp**, **tcp**, and **udp** parameters.

Be very familiar with the general syntax of an extended ACL statement.

The second major difference is that you must specify both the source *and* destination addresses *and* wildcard masks. With a standard ACL, you can specify only the source address, and the wildcard mask is optional. Depending on the IP protocol, you might be able to add additional protocol information for the source and/or destination. For example, TCP and UDP allow you to specify both source and destination port numbers, and ICMP allows you to specify ICMP message types. As with standard ACLs, you can log messages to the console or a logging server with the **log** parameter.

TCP and UDP

Use the following syntax to configure an extended ACL for TCP or UDP.

```
Router(config)# access-list 100-199|2000-2699 permit|deny
                    tcp|udp
                    source_address source_wildcard_mask
                        [operator source_port_#]
                    destination_address destination_wildcard_mask
                        [operator destination_port_#]
                    [established] [log]
```

After specifying the action (**permit** or **deny**), you configure the IP protocol: **tcp** or **udp**.

Know the syntax of an extended ACL statement when filtering TCP or UDP traffic.

Operators With TCP and UDP, you can specify the source, destination, or both source and destination port numbers or names. To specify how to perform the match, you must configure an *operator*. The operator tells the router how to match on the port number or numbers. Table 13-5 lists the valid operators for TCP and UDP connections. Note that these operators apply only to TCP and UDP connections. Other IP protocols do not use them.

Ports Numbers *and Names* For TCP and UDP connections, you can list either the name of the port or the number of the port. For example, if you wanted to match on telnet traffic, you could use either the keyword **telnet** or the number **23**. Table 13-6 lists some of the most common port names and numbers for TCP connections.

Here is the complete list of TCP port names that you can use: **bgp**, **chargen**, **daytime**, **discard**, **domain**, **echo**, **finger**, **ftp**, **ftp-data**, **gopher**, **hostname**, **irc**, **klogin**, **kshell**, **lpd**, **nntp**, **pop2**, **pop3**, **smtp**, **sunrpc**, **syslog**, **tacacs-ds**, **talk**, **telnet**, **time**, **uucp**, **whois**, and **www**. The name **pop3** is commonly used by e-mail clients to access their e-mail from an e-mail server; **www** is a web connection to an HTTP web server. If you don't find the port name in this list, you can still specify the port by its number. If you omit the port number or name, then the ACL looks for a match on all TCP connections.

Table 13-7 shows some of the common UDP port names and numbers.

TABLE 13-5 TCP and UDP Operators

Operator	Explanation
lt	Less than
gt	Greater than
neq	Not equal to
eq	Equal to
range	Range of port numbers

TABLE 13-6 Common TCP Port Names and Numbers

Port Name	Command Parameter	Port Number
FTP Data	**ftp-data**	**20**
FTP Control	**ftp**	**21**
Telnet	**telnet**	**23**
SMTP	**smtp**	**25**
WWW	**www**	**80**

Here is the complete list of UDP port names that you can use: **biff**, **bootpc**, **bootps**, **discard**, **dns**, **dnsix**, **echo**, **mobile-ip**, **nameserver**, **netbios-dgm**, **netbios-ns**, **ntp**, **rip**, **snmp**, **snmptrap**, **sunrpc**, **syslog**, **tacacs-ds**, **talk**, **tftp**, **time**, **who**, and **xdmcp**. If you don't find the port name in this list, you can still specify the port by its number. If you omit the port number or name, then the ACL looks for a match on all UDP connections.

established Keyword The **established** keyword is used only for TCP connections. The assumption behind the use of this keyword is that you are originating TCP traffic on the inside of the network and filtering the returning traffic as it comes back into your network. In this situation, this keyword allows (or denies) any TCP traffic that has the RST or ACK bit set in the TCP segment header. Refer to Chapter 2 for an explanation of connection-oriented transport protocols and Chapter 3 for the mechanics of TCP.

Understand the use of the established keyword with TCP ACL statements.

13.03. The CD contains a multimedia demonstration of configuring an extended numbered ACL to allow telnet traffic through a router.

ICMP

The following command shows the syntax of filtering ICMP traffic:

```
Router(config)# access-list 100-199|2000-2699 permit|deny icmp
                    source_address source_wildcard_mask
                    destination_address destination_wildcard_mask
                        [icmp_message] [log]
```

Unlike TCP and UDP, ICMP doesn't use ports. Instead, ICMP uses message types. And where TCP and UDP extended ACLs allow you to specify both source and

TABLE 13-7 Common UDP Port Names and Numbers

Port Name	Command Parameter	Port Number
DNS Query	**dns**	**53**
TFTP	**tftp**	**69**
SNMP	**snmp**	**161**
IP RIP	**rip**	**520**

exam watch

Remember the information provided in Tables 13-6, 13-7, and 13-8: TCP application names and numbers, UDP application names and numbers, and ICMP message types.

destination ports, ICMP allows you to enter an ICMP message. Table 3-8 shows some of the common ICMP messages and a brief explanation.

You can enter the ICMP message by either its name or its number. Here is a list of message names: **administratively-prohibited**, **alternate-address**, **conversion-error**, **dod-host-prohibited**, **dod-net-prohibited**, **echo**, **echo-reply**, **general-parameter-problem**, **host-isolated**, **host-precedence-unreachable**, **host-redirect**, **host-tos-redirect**, **host-tos-unreachable**, **host-unknown**, **host-unreachable**, **information-reply**, **information-request**, **mask-reply**, **mask-request**, **mobile-redirect**, **net-redirect**, **net-tos-redirect**, **net-tos-unreachable**, **net-unreachable**, **network-unknown**, **no-room-for-option**, **option-missing**, **packet-too-big**, **parameter-problem**, **port-unreachable**, **precedence-unreachable**, **protocol-unreachable**, **reassembly-timeout**, **redirect**, **router-advertisement**, **router-solicitation**, **source-quench**, **source-route-failed**, **time-exceeded**, **timestamp-reply**, **timestamp-**

TABLE 13-8 Common ICMP Messages

Message Type	Message Description
administratively-prohibited	Message that says that someone filtered a packet
echo	Used by ping to check a destination
echo-reply	Is a response to an echo message created by ping
host-unreachable	The subnet is reachable, but the host is not responding
net-unreachable	The network/subnet is not reachable
traceroute	Filters on traceroute information

request, **traceroute**, **ttl-exceeded**, and **unreachable**. If you omit the ICMP message type, all message types are included.

13.04. The CD contains a multimedia demonstration of configuring an extended numbered ACL to permit ICMP traffic through a router.

Activating an Extended IP ACL

Once you have created your extended numbered IP ACL, you must activate it on your router's interface with the following configuration:

```
Router(config)# interface type [slot_#]port_#
Router(config-if)# ip access-group ACL_# in|out
```

Note that this is the *same* configuration used with a standard ACL. Once you activate the ACL, the router will begin filtering traffic on the interface.

Extended IP ACL Example 1

Now that you have seen the syntax for creating extended numbered IP ACLs, let's take a look at a couple of configuration examples. Here's the first example:

```
Router(config)# access-list 100 permit tcp
                    any 172.16.0.0 0.0.255.255
                    established log
Router(config)# access-list 100 permit udp
                    any host 172.16.1.1 eq dns log
Router(config)# access-list 100 permit tcp
                    172.17.0.0 0.0.255.255
                    host 172.16.1.2 eq telnet log
Router(config)# access-list 100 permit icmp
                    any 172.16.0.0 0.0.255.255
                    echo-reply log
Router(config)# access-list 100 deny ip any any log
Router(config)# interface ethernet 0
Router(config-if)# ip access-group 100 in
```

The assumption behind this example is that it is restricting what traffic can come into a network. The first statement says that if any TCP session has any source address and is destined to 172.16.0.0/16, it will be permitted if the RST/ACK bits are set (**established**) in the TCP segment header. Remember that the keyword **any** is the same as 0.0.0.0 255.255.255.255. Also, the **log** keyword will cause a match on this statement to be printed on the console. Since a TCP port isn't specified, all TCP connections will match on this statement.

The second line of this example allows a DNS query from any source device to be sent to an internal DNS server (172.16.1.1). Remember that the 0.0.0.0 wildcard mask is removed and the keyword **host** is inserted in the front of the IP address. A match on this statement is also logged.

The third line allows any telnet connection from devices in the 172.17.0.0/16 network if the destination device is 172.16.1.2. Remember that telnet uses TCP. A match on this statement is also logged.

The fourth line allows any replies to ping to come back to devices with an address of 172.16.0.0/16. Note that only the echo replies are allowed—echoes are not allowed. A match on this statement is also logged.

The fifth line isn't necessary because all traffic not matching on the previous **permit** statements will be dropped. However, if you want to log what is dropped, you'll need to configure this statement with the **log** parameter, as is shown in the example. The last part of the configuration shows the ACL applied inbound on `ethernet0`.

Extended IP ACL Example 2

Here's a second extended numbered IP ACL configuration:

```
Router(config)# access-list 101 permit tcp
                      host 199.199.199.1
                      host 200.200.200.1 eq dns
Router(config)# access-list 101 permit udp
                      any host 200.200.200.1 eq dns
Router(config)# access-list 101 permit tcp
                      any host 200.200.200.2 eq www
Router(config)# access-list 101 permit icmp
                      any 200.200.200.0 0.0.0.255
Router(config)# access-list 101 permit tcp
                      any host 200.200.200.3 eq smtp
Router(config)# access-list 101 permit udp
                      host 201.201.201.2
                      host 201.201.201.1 eq rip
Router(config)# interface ethernet 0
Router(config-if)# ip address 201.201.201.1 255.255.255.0
Router(config-if)# ip access-group 101 in
```

The assumption behind this example is that it is restricting traffic as it comes into the network. The first ACL statement allows DNS zone transfers (done via TCP) from 199.199.199.1 to 200.200.200.1; 200.200.200.1, which is on the inside of this network.

The second ACL statement allows DNS queries from anyone to the internal DNS server (200.200.200.1). The third statement allows web traffic from any source to the internal web server (200.200.200.2). The fourth statement allows any ICMP traffic to the 200.200.200.0/24 internal network. The fifth statement allows anyone to send e-mail to the internal email (SMTP) server at 200.200.200.3. The sixth line allows RIP updates to be received from 201.201.201.2, which is a neighboring router off of the `ethernet0` interface. The last part of the configuration activates the ACL on the `ethernet0` interface.

Go back and look at these examples again and make sure you understand how they function. Understanding the configuration, activation, verification, and operation of ACLs is very important.

Named ACLs

Starting with IOS 11.2, Cisco routers support both numbered and named ACLs. One of the original limitations of numbered ACLs was that you could create only so many of them. Originally, you could have only 99 standard IP ACLs and 100 extended IP ACLs. The additional numbers weren't added until recently. Starting with IOS 11.2, Cisco allowed you to use names to reference your ACLs instead of, or in combination with, numbered ACLs.

Named ACLs support both the IP and IPX protocols. Unlike in numbered ACLs, in named ACLs you *can* delete a single entry in the ACL. However, there is currently no ability to modify an existing entry or insert a new entry into the middle of an existing ACL. Therefore, you will still need to use the process described earlier in this chapter, in the section "Editing Entries."

Creating Named ACLs

To create a named IP ACL, use the following command:

```
Router(config)# ip access-list standard|extended ACL_name
```

The first thing you must specify is the type of ACL: standard or extended. Second, you must give the ACL a name that groups the ACL statements together. This name must be unique among all named ACLs. Once you enter this command, you are taken into the appropriate *ACL Subconfiguration* mode, as is shown here:

```
Router(config-std-acl)#
-or-
Router(config-ext-acl)#
```

Once you are in the *Subconfiguration* mode, you can enter your ACL commands. For a standard named ACL, use the following configuration:

```
Router(config)# ip access-list standard ACL_name
Router(config-std-acl)# permit|deny source_IP_address
                        [wildcard_mask]
```

For an extended named ACL, use the following configuration:

```
Router(config)# ip access-list extended ACL_name
Router(config-ext-acl)# permit|deny IP_protocol
                        source_IP_address wildcard_mask
                            [protocol_information]
                        destination_IP_address wildcard_mask
                            [protocol_information] [log]
```

As you can see, creating a standard or extended named IP ACL is similar to creating a numbered one.

Be familiar with how to create a named ACL and the two different Subconfiguration modes you are taken into depending on whether the ACL is standard or extended.

Activating a Named ACL

Once you have created your named ACL, you need to activate it on your router's interface with the following configuration:

```
Router(config)# interface type [slot_#]port_#
Router(config-if)# ip access-group ACL_name in|out
```

The only difference between activating a named versus a numbered ACL on an interface is that you specify the name of the ACL instead of the number.

Example of a Named Access List

In this example, I'll convert the extended IP numbered ACL from the section "Extended IP ACL Example 1" earlier in this chapter. Here's the named version of this ACL:

```
Router(config)# ip access-list extended do_not_enter
Router(config-ext-acl)# permit tcp
                          any 172.16.0.0 0.0.255.255
                          established log
Router(config-ext-acl)# permit udp
                          any host 172.16.1.1 eq dns log
Router(config-ext-acl)# permit tcp
                          172.17.0.0 0.0.255.255
                          host 176.16.1.2 eq telnet log
Router(config-ext-acl)# permit icmp
                          any 176.16.0.0 0.0.255.255
                          echo-reply log
Router(config-ext-acl)# deny ip any any log
Router(config)# interface ethernet 0
Router(config-if)# ip access-group do_not_enter in
```

Both this example and the numbered example do the *exact same thing*. Therefore, it is a matter of personal preference whether you use a named or numbered ACL. My preference is to use numbered ACLs, if only because I've been using them for ten years.

13.05. The CD contains a multimedia demonstration of configuring a named IP ACL on a router.

You should be very familiar with the syntax of all ACL statements, especially how to configure them and how to evaluate them. Therefore, make sure you really study your ACLs!

Access List Verification

Once you have created and activated your ACLs, you can verify their configuration and operation with various **show** commands. One common command that you can use is the *Privilege EXEC* **show running-config** command, which will display your ACL and which interface or interfaces it is activated on. However, there are many other commands you can also use.

If all you want to see is which ACLs are activated on your router's interfaces, you can use the **show ip interfaces** command:

```
Router# show ip interfaces
Ethernet0 is up, line protocol is up
  Internet address is 172.16.1.1/24
  Broadcast address is 255.255.255.255
  Address determined by setup command
  MTU is 1500 bytes
  Helper address is not set
  Directed broadcast forwarding is disabled
  Outgoing access list is not set
  Inbound  access list is 100
  Proxy ARP is enabled
  Security level is default
  Split horizon is enabled
  ICMP redirects are always sent
  ICMP unreachables are always sent
  ICMP mask replies are never sent
<-- output omitted -->
```

From the output of this command, you can see that ACL 100, an extended numbered IP ACL, is applied inbound on `ethernet0`.

13.06. The CD contains a multimedia demonstration of using the show ip interfaces command on a router to verify the activation of your ACLs.

To view the statements in your ACLs, use either of the following two commands:

```
Router# show access-lists [ACL_#_or_name]
Router# show ip access-list [ACL_#_or_name]
```

Here is an example of the **show access-lists** command:

```
Router# show access-lists
Extended IP access list 100
    permit tcp 172.16.0.0 0.0.255.255 any established
          (189 matches)
    permit udp host 172.16.1.39 any eq domain
          (32 matches)
    permit icmp host 199.199.199.1 any
IPX sap access list 1000
    deny FFFFFFFF 7
    permit FFFFFFFF 0
```

First, notice that the router keeps track of matches on each statement. The first statement in ACL 100 has had 189 matches against it. You can clear these counters with this command:

```
Router# clear access-list counters [ACL_#_or_name]
```

Also notice that using the **show access-lists** command displays all ACLs from all protocols on your router. From the preceding output, there are two ACLs: an extended numbered IP ACL and an IPX SAP ACL. If you want to view only ACLs for IP, use the following command:

```
Router# show ip access-list
Extended IP access list 100
    permit tcp 172.16.0.0 0.0.255.255 any established
         (189 matches)
    permit udp host 172.16.1.39 any eq domain
         (32 matches)
    permit icmp host 199.199.199.1 any
```

If you want to view only a particular ACL, use either of the following two commands:

```
Router# show access-lists 100
Extended IP access list 100
    permit tcp 172.16.0.0 0.0.255.255 any established
         (189 matches)
    permit udp host 172.16.1.39 any eq domain
         (32 matches)
    permit icmp host 199.199.199.1 any
-or-
Router# show ip access-list 100
Extended IP access list 100
    permit tcp 172.16.0.0 0.0.255.255 any established
         (189 matches)
    permit udp host 172.16.1.39 any eq domain
         (32 matches)
    permit icmp host 199.199.199.1 any
```

13.07. The CD contains a multimedia demonstration of using the show [ip] access-list command on a router to verify the activation of your ACLs.

exam watch

Use the show ip interfaces command to see whether or not an IP ACL is applied to your router's interfaces. Use the show access-lists command to view all of the ACLs on your router. The show ip access-list lists only the IP ACLs on your router. You can always qualify your output by specifying the ACL number in the show command.

CERTIFICATION OBJECTIVE 13.05

Placement of ACLs

This section covers design issues with ACLs: where you should place ACLs of a given type (standard or extended). In other words, given the source and destination that you are filtering, on what router and what interface on that router should you activate your ACL? This section covers some of the important points you should be aware of when determining where to put your ACLs.

First, don't go crazy with ACLs and create dozens and dozens of them across all of your routers. This makes testing and troubleshooting your filtering rules almost impossible. If you have followed Cisco's three-layer hierarchy—core, distribution, and access—you'll want to put your ACLs on your distribution layer routers.

The second point to make is that you will want to limit the number of statements in your ACL. An ACL with hundreds of statements is almost impossible to test and troubleshoot. As an example, I had a student in one of the router classes I taught who had a question on an ACL they used at their site—it was six pages long! After I sat with this student, we were able to reduce this to about a page and a half. The original ACL had a lot of unnecessary and overlapping commands that we removed or changed.

Remember the two rules as to where you should apply your ACLs.

As to where you should place your ACLs, the following two rules hold true in most situations:

- Standard ACLs should be placed as close to the *destination* devices as possible.
- Extended ACLs should be placed as close to the *source* devices as possible.

Standard ACLs

You want to place standard ACLs as close to the *destination* that you want to prevent the source from reaching, since they allow you to filter only on the source IP address in the packet headers. If you put the standard ACL too close to the source, then you could be preventing the source from accessing other valid services in your network. By putting the standard ACL as close to the destination as possible, you are still allowing the source to access other resources, while restricting it from accessing the remote destination device or devices.

Let's take a look at an example to illustrate the placement of standard ACLs. I'll use the network shown in Figure 13-1. In this example, the user (192.168.5.1) should be prevented from accessing the server (192.168.1.1). Here is the ACL configuration:

```
Router(config)# access-list 1 deny 192.168.5.1 0.0.0.0
Router(config)# access-list 1 permit any
```

As you can see from this example, the goal is to prevent 192.168.5.1 from accessing 192.168.1.1, but to allow everyone else to access it. Let's discuss the options as to where you can place this ACL. Your first choice is to place this ACL on RouterC. If you placed it here, 192.168.5.1 would not be able to reach 192.168.1.1, but the user wouldn't be able to access anything else either. If you placed the ACL on RouterB, the user would be able to access the 192.168.4.0 network, but nothing

FIGURE 13-1 Placement of ACLs

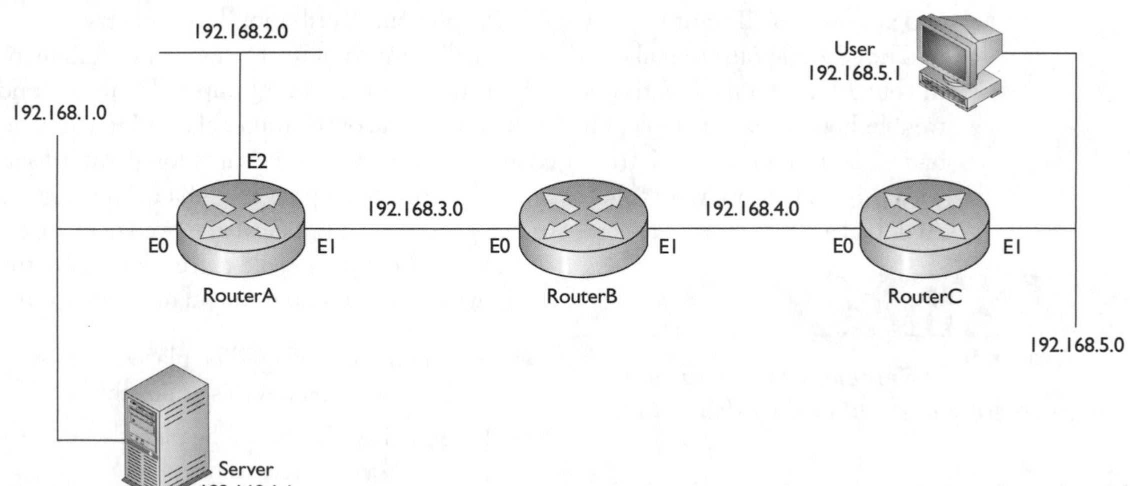

else. You actually have two choices for placing the ACL on RouterA: interfaces E0 and E1. If you placed it inbound on E1, then the user wouldn't be able to access network 192.168.2.0. Therefore, you would have to place it outbound on E0 of RouterA.

Note that there is still an issue with using standard ACLs—any traffic from 192.168.5.1 is dropped as it attempts to leave this interface. So, the user is prevented from reaching not only the server but anything else on this segment. Another issue with standard ACLs, since you typically place them as close to the destination as possible, is that they are not very network-friendly: packets travel almost all of the way to the destination and *then* they are dropped. This wastes bandwidth in your network, especially if the source is sending a lot of traffic to the destination.

Extended ACLs

Given the preceding example, it would be much better to place the standard ACL as close to the source as possible to prevent unwanted traffic from traversing almost the whole network before being dropped. With a standard ACL, though, you would be preventing the user from accessing most of the resources in the network.

Extended ACLs, however, don't have this limitation, since they can filter on *both* the source and destination addresses in the IP packet headers. Given this ability, it is recommended that you place extended ACLs as *close* to the source as possible, thus preventing unwanted traffic from traversing your network. With an extended ACL, since you can filter on both addresses, you can prevent a source from accessing a particular destination or destinations but still allow it to access others.

With our preceding example, your configuration would look like this when using an extended ACL:

```
Router(config)# access-list 100 deny ip host 192.168.5.1
                                        host 192.168.1.1
Router(config)# access-list 100 permit ip any any
```

This configuration example is preventing only traffic from 192.168.5.1 to 192.168.1.1. Now the question is, where you should place this ACL? Again, you want to put this ACL as close to the source as possible. This means that you should place it on RouterC. RouterC has two interfaces, though. Again, remember that it should be placed as close to the *source* as possible. This means that the ACL should be placed on RouterC's E1 interface. If you were to place it on E0, and the router had another interface that it could use to reach the destination, the source still might be able to get around the filter. If you place it on RouterC's E1 interface, 192.168.5.1 can access every location except 192.168.1.1. Likewise, any other traffic is permitted to go anywhere in the network.

You can be more specific with your filtering in this example. For example, if you want to restrict just telnet access, but allow other types of access from 192.168.5.1 to 192.168.1.1, then you should specify the IP protocol (**`tcp`**) and the destination port name or number (**`telnet`** or **`23`**).

CERTIFICATION SUMMARY

ACLs can be used to filter traffic and routing information, restrict telnets to your router, prioritize traffic, trigger DDR phone calls, and many other things. ACLs are statements grouped together by a number or name that defines traffic that should be permitted or denied. ACLs can be applied in either the inbound or outbound direction. With an inbound ACL, the ACL is processed first before any other processing is done on the packet. With an outbound ACL, the packet is routed to the outbound interface first and then the ACL is processed.

Standard IP ACLs allow you to filter on the source IP address, while extended IP ACLs allow you to filter on the source and destination IP addresses, the IP protocol, and protocol information (such as port numbers). ACLs are processed top-down until a match is found; at that point, no other statements are processed. Therefore, the order of the statements is important. If no match is found, the implicit deny rule takes place and the packet is dropped. You can have one ACL, per protocol, per interface, per direction on that interface. There are two special filtering rules for ACLs: you cannot filter traffic the router itself originates, and applying an empty ACL to an interface permits all traffic by default.

Standard ACLs can have numbers ranging 1–99 and 1300–1999, and extended ACLs can have numbers ranging 100–199 and 2000–2699. Standard ACLs should be placed as close to the destination as possible, while extended ACLs should be placed as close to the source as possible.

To create a numbered ACL, use the **`access-list`** command. Use the **`ip access-group`** command to activate your ACL on an interface. To filter telnet traffic to and from your router, activate the standard IP ACL on your VTY lines with the **`access-class`** command. When making changes to ACLs, paste the ACL configuration into a text editor, make your changes, remove the application of the ACL on the router's interface(s), delete the ACL, paste the text editor ACL into your router, and reactivate it. To create a named ACL, use the **`ip access-list standard|extended`** command. This will take you into the appropriate *Subconfiguration* mode.

Wildcard masks allow you to match a single address, a range of addresses, or all addresses. Basically, a wildcard mask is like an inverted subnet mask. A 0 in a bit position means match, and a 1 means ignore. To convert a subnet mask to a wildcard mask, subtract each octet in the subnet mask from 255, resulting in the corresponding octet value for the wildcard mask. With standard ACLs, if you omit the wildcard mask, it defaults to 0.0.0.0.

The **established** keyword in an extended ACL allows you to look at the TCP flags to determine whether or not to allow the packets. The **log** keyword will display matches of all matched packets.

The **show ip interfaces** command will display any ACLs that have been activated on your router's interfaces. The **show access-lists** command displays all ACLs configured on your router for all protocols. The **show ip access-list** command displays only IP ACLs.

TWO-MINUTE DRILL

ACL Overview

- ACLs allow you to filter traffic, restrict telnets to the router, filter routing information, prioritize WAN traffic, trigger dialup connections, change administrative distances of routes, and many other things.
- ACLs can be created using either numbers or names. There are two basic types: standard and extended. Standard ACLs allow you to filter only the source IP address, whereas extended IP ACLs allow you to filter on source and destination addresses, IP protocols, and protocol information.
- There are two actions the router can take when a match is found on an ACL: permit or deny. ACLs are processed top-down, where the order is important. Upon the first match, no other statements are processed. There is an implicit deny at the end of the list. You cannot filter traffic the router itself originates. When adding ACL statements, note that they are always added to the bottom. Only named ACLs allow you to delete a specific entry.

Basic ACL Configuration

- The **access-list** command creates an ACL, and the **ip access-group** command activates the ACL on an interface. You can filter traffic as it enters (**in**) or leaves (**out**) an interface. To delete a complete access control list, use the **no access-list** command, followed by its number.
- Standard IP ACLs use numbers in the ranges 1–99 and 1300–1999, and extended IP ACLs use list numbers 100–199 and 2000–2699.

Wildcard Masks

- A wildcard mask is like an inverted subnet mask. A 0 in a bit position of the wildcard mask means the corresponding bit position in the condition's address must match that in the IP packet. A 1 in a bit position of the wildcard mask means there doesn't have to be a match.
- A wildcard mask of 0.0.0.0 means that the entire address must match. Precede the word **host** before an address accomplishes the same thing. A wildcard mask of 255.255.255.255 indicates that any address matches: you can replace the address and wildcard mask with the keyword **any**.

- To invert a subnet mask into a wildcard mask, subtract each octet in the subnet mask from 255, which will result in the corresponding octet value for the wildcard mask.

Types of ACLs

- Standard ACLs can filter only on the source IP address. If you omit the wildcard mask, it defaults to 0.0.0.0. Use the **`access-class`** command to activate a standard ACL to restrict telnet access to a router.
- Use the **`terminal monitor`** command to view console output on nonconsole connections, such as VTYs.
- Extended IP ACLs allow you to filter on both the source and destination IP addresses (where you must specify the wildcard mask for both), the IP protocol (TCP, UDP, ICMP, and so on), and protocol information (such as ICMP message types or TCP and UDP source and destination port numbers). If you want to match on all IP traffic, use the keyword **`ip`** for the protocol parameter.
- Use the **`ip access-list standard|extended`** *`ACL_name`* command to create a named ACL. This takes you into the *ACL Subconfiguration* mode.
- The **`show running-config`** command will display your configured ACLs and the interfaces they are activated on. The **`show ip interfaces`** command shows the ACLs activated on a router's interfaces. The **`show [ip] access-lists`** command displays the statements in a router's ACLs.

Placement of ACLs

- Standard ACLs should be placed as close to the *destination* devices as possible.
- Extended ACLs should be placed as close to the *source* devices as possible.

SELF TEST

The following Self Test questions will help you measure your understanding of the material presented in this chapter. Read all the choices carefully, as there may be more than one correct answer. Choose all correct answers for each question.

ACL Overview

1. Which of the following are not features of ACLs?
   A. Restricting telnet access to a router
   B. Prioritizing WAN traffic
   C. Filtering traffic from the router
   D. Triggering dialup phone calls
2. Which of the following is true concerning ACLs?
   A. Order of the statements is automatic.
   B. All statements are processed.
   C. If no match is found, the packet is permitted.
   D. You can delete a specific statement in a named list.
3. The last statement in an ACL is called the __________ __________ statement.

Basic ACL Configuration

4. There are __________ actions a router can take when there is a match on an ACL statement (enter a number).
5. Which command activates an IP ACL on a router's interface?
   A. `access-list`
   B. `ip access-group`
   C. `access-class`
   D. `access-group`

Wildcard Masks

6. A __________ in a bit position of a wildcard mask means that the same bit position in the condition address must match the same bit position in the wildcard mask in order to execute the ACL's action.
   A. 0
   B. 1

7. Enter the wildcard mask value to match on every bit position in an address: __________.

8. Enter the wildcard mask value for the subnet mask of 255.255.248.0: ____________.

Types of ACLs

9. Choose the following that a standard IP ACL can match on.

   A. Destination address
   B. IP protocol
   C. IP protocol information
   D. None of the above

10. Enter the router command to view console output on a non-console line connection: __________.

11. Enter the standard IP ACL command to permit traffic from 192.168.1.0/24, using a list number of 10: ___________.

12. Enter the extended IP ACL command to permit all ICMP traffic from 172.16.0.0/16 to 172.17.0.0/17, using a list number of 101: ___________.

13. Which router command creates a standard named ACL called *test*?

   A. `ip access-list test`
   B. `access-list test`
   C. `ip access-list standard test`
   D. `access-list standard test`

14. Enter the router command to activate an ACL with a name of *test* inbound on an interface: ___________.

15. Enter the router command to delete all of the statements in access-list 100: __________.

Placement of ACLs

16. Extended IP ACLs should be placed as close to the ____________ device as possible.

   A. Source
   B. Destination

SELF TEST ANSWERS

ACL Overview

1. ☑ **C.** ACLs cannot filter traffic the router originates, such as pings or traceroutes.
   ☒ **A**, **B**, and **C** are ACL features.

2. ☑ **D.** You can delete a specific ACL statement in a named ACL, but not a numbered ACL.
   ☒ **A** is not true because all statements are always added at the bottom of the ACL. **B** is not true because as soon as there is a statement match, no more statements are processed. **C** is not true because the implicit deny at the end of every ACL drops a non-matching packet.

3. ☑ The last statement in an ACL is called an *implicit deny* statement: this statement, which cannot be seen with any **show** commands, causes the router to drop any packet that doesn't match any preceding ACL statements.

Basic ACL Configuration

4. ☑ There are 2 actions a router can take when there is a match on an ACL statement: **permit** or **deny**.

5. ☑ **B.** The **ip access-group** command activates an ACL on a router's interface.
   ☒ **A** is incorrect because it creates an ACL statement in a list. **C** is incorrect because it activates a standard ACL on a line, not an interface. **D** is a nonexistent command.

Wildcard Masks

6. ☑ **A.** A 0 in a bit position of a wildcard mask means that the same bit position in the condition address must match that bit position in the wildcard mask in order to execute the ACL's action.
   ☒ **B** means that the bit position doesn't have to match.

7. ☑ The value **0.0.0.0** is a wildcard mask that says to match on every bit position in an address.

8. ☑ The inverted subnet mask for 255.255.248.0 is **0.0.7.255**. The trick is to subtract the subnet mask octets from 255.

Types of ACLs

9. ☑ D. Standard IP ACLs can match only on source IP addresses.
   ☒ A, B, and C are things extended IP ACLs can match on.

10. ☑ Use the **terminal monitor** command to view console output on a nonconsole line connection, such as a VTY or an auxiliary line.

11. ☑ Enter the standard IP ACL command to permit traffic from 192.168.1.0/24, using a list number of 10: **access-list 10 permit 192.168.1.0 0.0.0.255**.

12. ☑ Enter the extended IP ACL command to permit all ICMP traffic from 172.16.0.0/16 to 172.17.0.0/17, using a list number of 101: **access-list 101 permit icmp 172.16.0.0 0.0.255.255 172.17.0.0 0.0.127.255**. Notice the subnet mask value for 172.17.0.0, which is 17 bits!

13. ☑ C. The **ip access-list standard test** command creates a standard ACL called *test*.
    ☒ A, B, and D are invalid commands.

14. ☑ Enter the router command to activate an access list with a name of *test* inbound on an interface: **ip access-group test in**.

15. ☑ Enter the router command to delete access-list 100: **no access-list 100**.

Placement of ACLs

16. ☑ A. Extended IP ACLs should be placed as close to the source device as possible.
    ☒ B is true for standard ACLs.

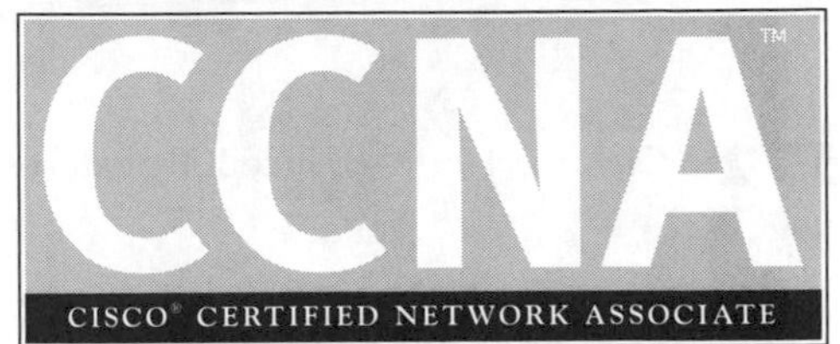

14

Advanced IP Features

CERTIFICATION OBJECTIVES

14.01 Address Translation Overview

14.02 Address Translation Configuration

14.03 Dynamic Host Configuration Protocol

✓ Two-Minute Drill

Q&A Self Test

The preceding chapter introduced you to ACLs, one of the advanced features of the router's IOS. This chapter covers two more advanced features: address translation and the Dynamic Host Configuration Protocol (DHCP). Address translation allows you to change the source or destination address inside the IP packet. This is typically done if you are using private IP addresses inside your network, or have overlapping addresses. The first half of this chapter provides an overview of address translation, including the many terms used and the different types of address translation and its configuration. The second half of this book has a brief overview of DHCP, which allows you to assign and acquire IP addressing information dynamically, and its configuration.

CERTIFICATION OBJECTIVE 14.01

Address Translation Overview

Address translation was originally developed to solve two problems: handling a shortage of IP addresses and hiding network addressing schemes. Most people think that address translation is used primarily to solve the first problem. However, as the first half of this chapter illustrates, address translation provides solutions for many problems and has many advantages.

Running Out of Addresses

Because of the huge Internet explosion during the early 1990s, it was foreseen that the current IP addressing scheme would not accommodate the number of devices that would need public addresses. A long-term solution was conceived to address this; it called for the enhancement of the TCP/IP protocol stack, including the addressing format. This new addressing format was called IPv6. Whereas the current IP addressing scheme (IPv4) uses 32 bits to represent addresses, IPv6 uses 128 bits for addressing, creating billions of extra addresses.

Private Addresses

It took a while for IPv6 to become a standard, and on top of this, not many companies have implemented it, even ISPs on the Internet backbone. The main reason that this standard hasn't been embraced is the success of the two short-term solutions to the address shortage problem: schemes to create additional addresses, called private addresses, and to translate these addresses to public addresses using address translation.

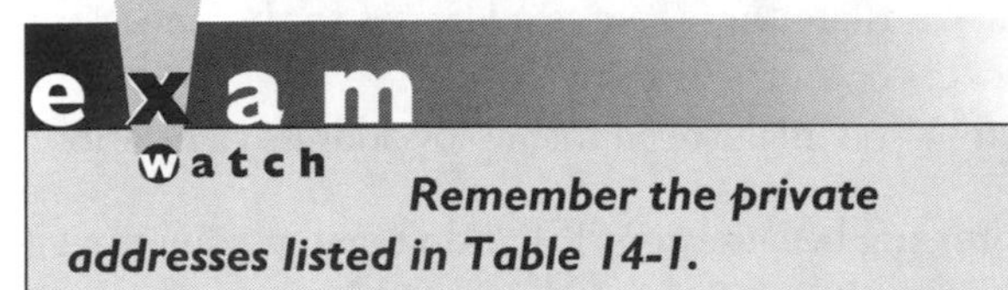

Remember the private addresses listed in Table 14-1.

RFC 1918, by the Internet Engineering Task Force (IETF), is a document that was created to address the shortage of addresses. When devices want to communicate, each device needs a unique IP address. RFC 1918 has created a private address space that any company can use internally. Table 14-1 shows the range of private addresses that RFC 1918 set aside. As you can see from this table, you have 1 ClassA, 16 ClassB, and 256 ClassC addresses at your disposal. Just the single ClassA address of 10.0.0.0 has over 17 million IP addresses, more than enough to accommodate your company's needs.

One of the main issues of RFC 1918 addresses is that they can be used only internally within a company and cannot be used to communicate to a public network, such as the Internet. For this reason, they are commonly referred to as *private addresses*. If you send packets with RFC 1918 addresses in them to your ISP, for instance, your ISP will either filter them or not be able to route this traffic back to your devices. Obviously, this creates a connectivity problem, since many of your devices with private addresses need to send and receive traffic from public networks.

Address Translation

A second standard, RFC 1631, was created to solve this problem. It defines a process called Network Address Translation (NAT), which allows you to change an IP address in a packet to a different address. When communicating to devices in a public network, your device needs to use a source address that is a public address. Address translation allows you to translate your internal private addresses to public addresses before these packets leave your network.

Remember the reasons you might want to use address translation in your network.

Actually, RFC 1631 doesn't specify that the address you are changing has to be a private address—it can be any address. This is useful if you randomly chose someone else's public address space but still want to connect to the Internet. Obviously, you don't own this address space, but address translation allows you to keep

TABLE 14-1 RFC 1918 Private Addresses

Class	Range of Addresses
A	10.0.0.0–10.255.255.255
B	172.16.0.0–172.31.255.255
C	192.168.0.0–192.168.255.255

your current addressing scheme and translate these source addresses to the ones your ISP assigned to you before your packets enter the Internet.

Here are some common reasons that you might need to employ address translation:

- You have to use private addressing because your ISP didn't assign you enough public addresses.
- You are using public addresses but have changed ISPs, and your new ISP won't support these public addresses.
- You are merging two companies together and they are using the same address space, for instance, 10.0.0.0, which creates routing and reachability issues.
- You want to assign the same IP address to multiple machines so that users on the Internet see this offered service as a single logical computer.

Types of Address Translation

Address translation comes in a variety of types, like Network Address Translation (NAT), Port Address Translation (PAT), dynamic address translation, and static address translation. Because of the many terms used, the concept of address translation can be confusing, especially since many people use the address translation terms incorrectly. The following sections cover the different types of address translation.

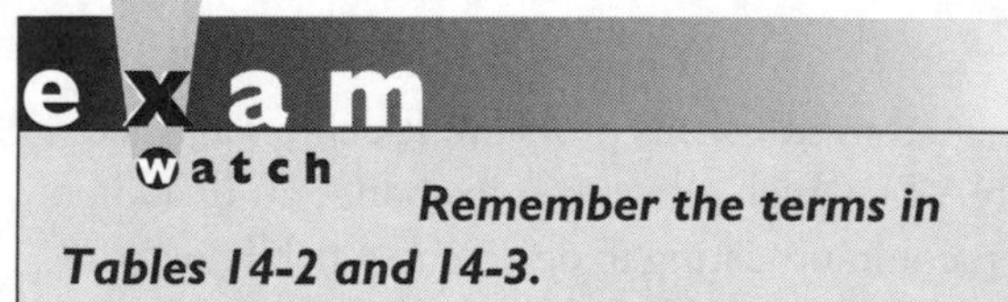

Remember the terms in Tables 14-2 and 14-3.

Terms and Definitions

Table 14-2 shows some common terms used in address translation, and Table 14-3 shows some terms used for types of address translation.

Network Address Translation

Network Address Translation (NAT) translates one IP address to another. This can be a source address or a destination address. There are two basic implementations of NAT: static and dynamic. The following two sections cover the mechanics of these implementations.

Static NAT With static NAT, a manual translation is performed by an address translation device, translating one IP address to a different one. Typically, static

TABLE 14-2 Common Address Translation Terms

Term	Definition
Inside	Networks located on the inside of your network
Outside	Networks located outside of your network
Local	The IP address physically assigned to a device
Global	The public IP address physically or logically assigned to a device
Inside local IP address	An inside device with an assigned private IP address
Inside global IP address	An inside device with a registered public IP address
Outside global IP address	An outside device with a registered public IP address
Outside local IP address	An outside device with an assigned private IP address

NAT is used to translate destination IP addresses in packets as they come into your network, but you can translate source addresses also. Figure 14-1 shows a simple example of outside users trying to access an inside web server. In this example, you want Internet users to access an internal web server, but this server is using a private address (10.1.1.1). This creates a problem, since if an outside user would put a private address in the destination IP address field, their ISP would drop this. Therefore, the web server needs to be presented as a having a public address. This is defined in the address translation device (in our case, this is a Cisco router).

TABLE 14-3 Common Address Translation Types

Translation Type	Explanation
Simple	One IP address is translated to a different IP address.
Extended	One IP address and one TCP/UDP port number are mapped to a different IP address and, possibly, port number.
Static	A manual address translation is performed between two addresses, and possibly port numbers.
Dynamic	An address translation device automatically performs address translation between two addresses, and possibly port numbers.
Network Address Translation (NAT)	Only IP addresses are translated (not port numbers).
Port Address Translation (PAT)	Many inside IP addresses are translated to a single IP address, where each inside address is given a different port number for uniqueness.

FIGURE 14-1 Static NAT example

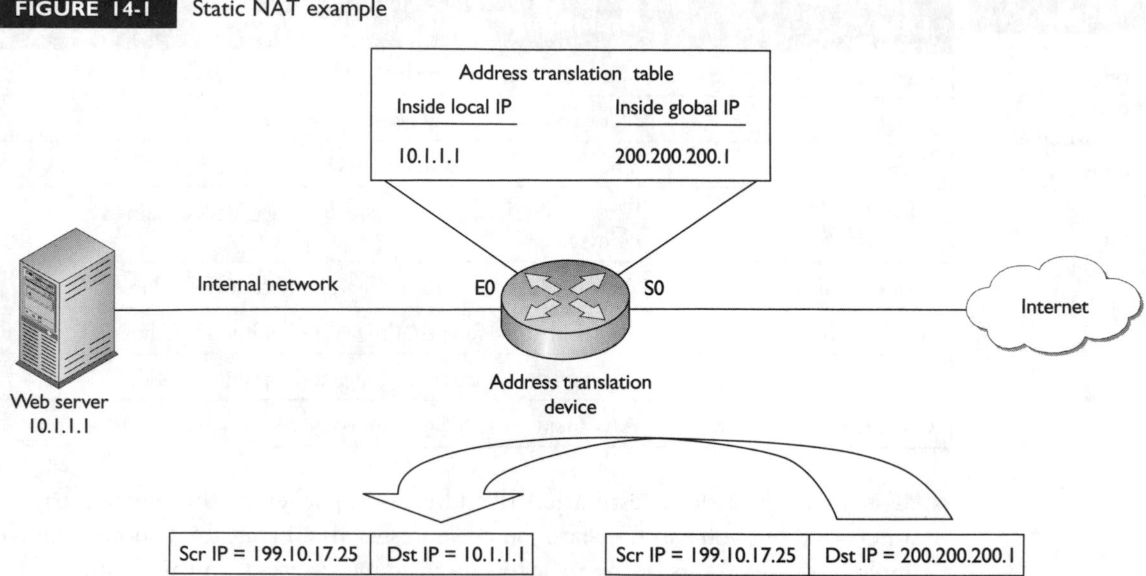

The web server is assigned an inside global IP address of 200.200.200.1 on the router, and your DNS server advertises this address to the outside users. When outside users send packets to the 200.200.200.1 address, the router examines its translation table for a matching entry. In this case, it sees that 200.200.200.1 maps to 10.1.1.1. The router then changes the destination IP address to 10.1.1.1 and forwards it to the inside web server. Note that if the router didn't do the translation to 10.1.1.1, the web server wouldn't know this information was meant for itself, since the outside user sent the traffic originally to 200.200.200.1. Likewise, when the web server sends traffic out to the public network, the router compares the source IP address to entries in its translation table, and if it finds a match, it changes the inside local IP address (private source address—10.1.1.1) to the inside global IP address (public source address—200.200.200.1).

Dynamic NAT With static address translation, you need to manually build the translations. If you have 1,000 devices, you need to create 1,000 static entries in the address translation table, which is a lot of work. Typically, static translation is done for inside resources that outside people want to access. When inside users access outside resources, dynamic NAT is typically used. In this situation, the address assigned to the internal user isn't that important, since outside devices don't directly access your internal users—they just return traffic to them that the inside user requested.

With dynamic NAT, you must manually define two sets of addresses on your address translation device. One set defines which inside addresses are allowed to be translated, and the other defines what these addresses are to be translated to. When an inside user sends traffic through the address translation device, say a router, it examines the source IP address and compares it to the internal local address pool. If it finds a match, then it determines which inside global address pool it should use for the translation. It then dynamically picks an address in the global address pool that is not currently assigned to an inside device. The router adds this entry in its address translation table, and the packet is then sent to the outside world. If no entry is found in the local address pool, then the address is not translated and forwarded to the outside world in its original state.

When returning traffic comes back into your network, the address translation device examines the destination IP addresses and checks them against the address translation table. Upon finding a matching entry, it converts the global inside address to the local inside address in the destination IP address field of the packet header and forwards the packet to the inside network.

Port Address Translation

One problem with static or dynamic NAT is that it provides only a one-to-one address translation. Therefore, if you have 5,000 internal devices with private addresses, and all 5,000 devices try to reach the Internet simultaneously, you need 5,000 public addresses in your inside global address pool. If you have only 1,000 public addresses, only the first 1,000 devices are translated and the remaining 4,000 won't be able to reach outside destinations.

To overcome this problem, you can use a process called *address overloading*. There are actually many terms used to describe this process, including Port Address Translation (PAT) and Network Address Port Translation (NAPT).

Using the Same IP Address With PAT, all machines that go through the address translation device have the same IP address assigned to them, and so the source port numbers are used to differentiate the different connections. If two devices have the same source port number, the translation device changes one of them to ensure uniqueness. When you look at the translation table in the address translation device, you'll see the following items:

- Inside local IP address (original source private IP)
- Inside local port number (original source port number)
- Inside global IP address (translated public source IP)

- Inside global port number (new source port number)
- Outside global IP address (destination public address)
- Outside global port number (destination port number)

One main advantage of NAT over PAT is that NAT will basically work with most types of IP connections. Since PAT relies on port numbers to differentiate connections, PAT works only with the TCP and UDP protocols; however, many vendors, including Cisco, also support ICMP with PAT using a proprietary translation method.

Example Using PAT Let's take a look at an example, shown in Figure 14-2, using PAT. In this example, both PCs execute a telnet to 199.199.199.1, and both of these connections use a source port number of 11,000. When these connections reach the address translation device, the translation device performs its PAT translation. For the first connection, say PC-A, the source IP address is changed to 200.200.200.7. Since this is the first connection, the source port number is left as is. When PC-B makes a telnet connection to the remote device, since it is using a source port number already in the table for a connection to the telnet server, the address translation device changes it from 11,000 to 11,001. Therefore, when traffic is sent from the telnet server to the inside PCs, the address translation device will be able to differentiate the two connections and undo the translation correctly by examining both the destination IP address and port number.

Since the port number in the TCP and UDP header is 16 bits in length, you can theoretically represent 65,536 internal machines with a single public IP address. However, in reality, this number is about 4,000 devices per public address. Note that you don't have to restrict yourself to one type of address translation process. For instance, you can use PAT for inside-to-outside connections and static NAT for outside-to-inside connections.

exam watch

PAT, or address overloading, allows you to use the same global IP address for all internal devices, where the source port is used (possibly changed), to differentiate among the different translated connections.

FIGURE 14-2 PAT example

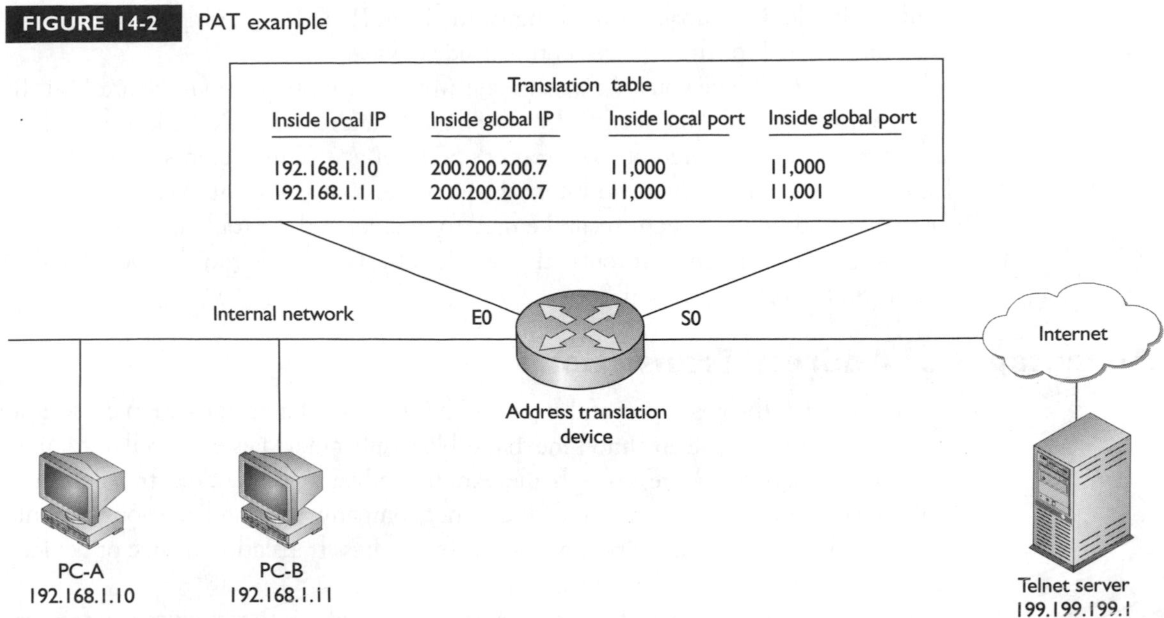

Port Address Redirection The last example showed PAT being carried out dynamically by the address translation device. There are situations, however, where this will not work. For instance, your ISP might assign you a single public IP address. You need to use this with PAT to allow inside users to access outside resources. However, you have a problem if you want outside users to access an internal service, such as a web server. Dynamic PAT, unfortunately, won't work in this situation.

> **exam watch** ***Port address redirection allows you to redirect application traffic directed to one address to a different address.***

However, there is another solution: static PAT. Static PAT is often called port address redirection (PAR). Let's look at a simple example to illustrate how PAR works. Assume that your ISP has assigned you a single public IP address: 199.199.199.1. You need to use this address for inside users to access the outside world, but you still need the outside world to access an internal web server. With static PAT, you set up your address translation device to look at not only the destination IP address (199.199.199.1), but also the destination port number (80 for a web server). You create a static PAT entry such that when the address translation device sees this combination of address and port number, the device translates it to the inside local IP address and, possibly, the port number used for the service on this inside device.

For example, assume you are given the network shown previously in Figure 14-1. In this example, your ISP has assigned you a single IP address, 200.200.200.1, and this address must be configured on your router's S0 interface. This presents a problem in this example, since you have an internal web server that you want external users to access. Port address redirection can be used to overcome this problem. You would set up a static PAT entry on your router that would take TCP traffic sent to 200.200.200.1 on port 80 to 10.1.1.1 on port 80.

Advantages of Address Translation

As mentioned at the beginning of this part of the chapter, address translation devices are typically used to give you an almost inexhaustible number of addresses as well as to hide your internal network addressing scheme. Another advantage of address translation is that if you change ISPs or merge with another company, you can keep your current scheme and make any necessary changes on your address translation device or devices, making your address management easier.

Another big advantage that address translation provides is that it gives you tighter control over traffic entering and leaving your network. For example, if you are using private addresses internally, all traffic entering and leaving must pass through an address translation device. Because of this restriction, it is much easier to implement your security and business policies.

Disadvantages of Address Translation

Even though address translation solves many problems and has many advantages, it also has its share of disadvantages. Here are the three main issues with address translation:

- Each connection has an added delay.
- Troubleshooting is more difficult.
- Not all applications work with address translation.

Remember the disadvantages and limitations of address translation.

Since address translation changes the contents of packets and, possibly, segment headers, as well as computing any necessary new checksum values, extra processing is required on each packet. This extra processing, obviously, will affect the throughput and speed of your connections. The more packets that pass through your address translation device needing translation, the more likely your users are to notice the delay. Therefore, choosing the appropriate product for address translation becomes very important.

Also, whenever problems arise with connections involving address translation, it is more difficult to troubleshoot them. When troubleshooting, it becomes more difficult to track down the real source and destination of a connection—you have to log into your address translation device and look at your translation tables. And if the packet is going through multiple layers of translation, possibly at both the source and destination sites, this can be a hair-pulling experience. Also, even though one of the advantages of address translation is that it hides your internal addressing scheme, it also creates security issues—an external hacker can more easily hide their identity by having their packets go through a translation device or multiple translation devices, trying to hide their true IP address.

Probably the most difficult issue with address translation is that not all applications will work with it. For instance, some applications embed IP addressing or port information in the actual data payload, expecting the destination device to use this addressing information in the payload instead of what is in the packet and segment headers. This can pose a problem with address translation, since address translation, by default, doesn't translate data payload information, only header information. Multimedia and NetBIOS applications are notorious for embedding addressing information in data payloads.

In some instances, certain vendors' address translation devices have the ability to detect this process for certain applications. For instance, Cisco routers and PIX firewalls support a fix-up process that addresses many NetBIOS and multimedia issues, including embedded addressing information. However, if your product doesn't support this feature, you'll need to disable address translation for the affected devices.

CERTIFICATION OBJECTIVE 14.02

Address Translation Configuration

The configuration of the different types of address translation, like NAT and PAT, is very similar. The following sections cover the configuration and verification of some of the types of address translation discussed so far.

NAT Configuration

As mentioned earlier, there are two types of NAT: static and dynamic. The configuration process is similar for the two types. Probably the most difficult process of configuring address translation is understanding the difference between the terms *inside* and *outside*. These terms refer to where your devices are located (inside) and where the external network (the Internet, for instance) is (outside). This is important when it comes to the configuration of address translation. In the IOS, there are two basic configuration steps that you must perform:

- Define the address translation type (*Global Configuration* mode commands).
- Define the location of devices (*Interface Subconfiguration* mode commands).

The following sections cover the configuration of both static and dynamic NAT.

Static NAT

As mentioned earlier in this chapter, static NAT is typically used when devices on the outside of your network want to access resources, such as web, DNS, and email servers, on the inside. Here are the two commands to define the static translations for NAT:

```
Router(config)# ip nat inside source static
                    inside_local_source_IP_address
                    inside_global_source_IP_address
Router(config)# ip nat outside source static
                    outside_global_destination_IP_address
                    outside_local_destination_IP_address
```

Remember how to create a static translation with the `ip nat inside|outside source static` command.

The **inside** and **outside** parameters specify the direction in which translation will occur. For instance, the **inside** keyword specifies that the inside *source* local IP addresses are translated to an inside global IP address. The **outside** keyword changes the outside *destination* global IP address to an outside local address.

After you configure your translations, you must specify which interfaces on your router are considered to be on the inside and which ones are on the outside. This is done with the following configuration:

```
Router(config)# interface type [slot_#/]port_#
Router(config-if)# ip nat inside|outside
```

Use the `ip nat inside|outside` Interface command to specify which interfaces are considered "`inside`" and which are "`outside`."

Specify **inside** for interfaces connected to the inside of your network and **outside** for interfaces connected to external networks.

Let's take a look a simple static NAT example. I'll use the network shown in

Figure 14-3 for this example. In this example, an internal web server (192.168.1.1) will be assigned a global IP address of 200.200.200.1.

Here's the configuration:

```
Router(config)# ip nat inside source static
                       192.168.1.1 200.200.200.1
Router(config)# interface ethernet 0
Router(config-if)# ip nat inside
Router(config-if)# exit
Router(config)# interface serial 0
 Router(config-if)# ip nat outside
```

The **ip nat inside source static** command defines the translation. The **ip nat inside** and **outside** commands specify what interfaces are on the inside (`E0`) and what interfaces are on the outside (`S0`). Note that any packets that don't match the address translation rule will pass between these two interfaces untranslated. If you want only translated packets to pass between these interfaces, you'll need to configure an appropriate ACL or ACLs.

14.01. The CD contains a multimedia demonstration of configuring static NAT on a router.

FIGURE 14-3 Network translation example

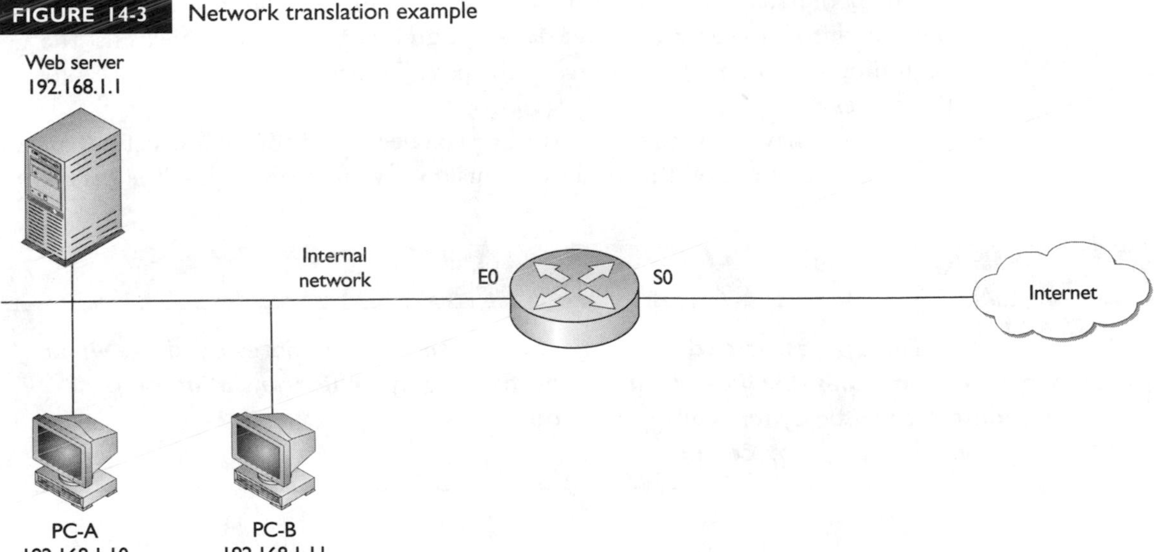

Dynamic NAT

When you are configuring dynamic NAT, you'll need to configure three things: what inside addresses are to be translated, what global addresses will be used for the dynamic translation, and what interfaces are involved in the translation. To specify what internal devices will have their source address translated, use the following command:

```
Router(config)# ip nat inside source
                      list standard_IP_ACL_#
                      pool NAT_pool_name
```

The **ip nat inside source list** command requires you to configure a standard IP ACL that has a list of the inside source addresses that will be translated—any addresses listed with a **permit** statement will be translated, and any addresses listed with a **deny**, or the implicit deny, statement will not be translated. Following this is the name of the address pool. This ties together the address pool you'll use that contains your global source IP addresses.

To create the pool of source inside global IP addresses, use this command:

```
Router(config)# ip nat pool NAT_pool_name
                     beginning_inside_global_IP_address
                     ending_inside_global_IP_address
                     netmask subnet_mask_of_addresses
```

The pool name that you specify references the inside addresses that will be translated from the **ip nat inside source list** command. Next, list the beginning and ending IP addresses in the pool, followed by the subnet mask for the addresses.

Once you have done this, the last thing you need to configure is which interfaces are considered to be on the inside and outside of your network. Use the **ip nat**

exam watch

The ip nat inside source list command specifies which internal addresses will be dynamically translated. The ip nat pool command specifies the global addresses to use when performing dynamic translation of local addresses.

inside and **ip nat outside** *Interface Subconfiguration* mode commands discussed earlier.

I'll use the network shown in Figure 14-3 to illustrate how dynamic NAT is configured. In this example, the two PCs will have dynamic NAT performed on them.

```
Router(config)# ip nat inside source list 1 pool nat-pool
Router(config)# access-list 1 permit 192.168.1.10 0.0.0.0
Router(config)# access-list 1 permit 192.168.1.11 0.0.0.0
Router(config)# ip nat pool nat-pool 200.200.200.2
                       200.200.200.3 netmask 255.255.255.0
Router(config)# interface ethernet 0
Router(config-if)# ip nat inside
Router(config-if)# exit
Router(config)# interface serial 0
Router(config-if)# ip nat outside
```

The **ip nat inside source list** command specifies the inside source IP addresses that will be translated. Notice that these are addresses in ACL 1—192.168.1.10 and 192.168.1.11. They are associated with the global address pool called *nat-pool*. The **ip nat pool** command specifies the global addresses that the inside source addresses will be translated to. And finally, `ethernet0` is specified as being on the inside and `serial0` is on the outside.

14.02. The CD contains a multimedia demonstration of configuring dynamic NAT on a router.

PAT Configuration

The last example showed an example of dynamic NAT. This section covers how to configure PAT on your router. This configuration, which is very similar to configuring dynamic NAT, requires three basic translation commands. The first thing you specify is which inside devices will have their source addresses translated. You'll use the same command as you used in dynamic NAT, but you'll add the **overload** parameter to specify that PAT is to be performed:

```
Router(config)# ip nat inside source
                       list standard_IP_ACL_#
                       pool NAT_pool_name overload
```

Next, you specify the global pool to use. Again, you'll use the same command as you used in dynamic NAT:

```
Router(config)# ip nat pool NAT_pool_name
                           beginning_inside_global_IP_address
                           ending_inside_global_IP_address
                           netmask subnet_mask_of_addresses
```

You can specify more than one address to use in PAT, or you can specify a single IP address (use the same address for the beginning and ending addresses). And last, you have to tell the IOS which interfaces are inside and outside, respectively, in terms of the **ip nat inside** and **ip nat outside** commands.

Let's use Figure 14-3 to illustrate how PAT is configured. In this example, only a single IP address is placed in the address pool (200.200.200.2):

```
Router(config)# ip nat inside source list 1 pool
                           nat-pool overload
Router(config)# access-list 1 permit 192.168.1.10 0.0.0.0
Router(config)# access-list 1 permit 192.168.1.11 0.0.0.0
Router(config)# ip nat pool nat-pool 200.200.200.2
                           200.200.200.2
                           netmask 255.255.255.0
Router(config)# interface ethernet 0
Router(config-if)# ip nat inside
Router(config-if)# exit
Router(config)# interface serial 0
Router(config-if)# ip nat outside
```

14.03. The CD contains a multimedia demonstration of configuring PAT on a router.

Load Distribution Configuration

Cisco routers support a process called *load*, or *traffic*, *distribution*. Load distribution allows you to distribute connection requests destined to a single IP address to multiple machines. For instance, you might have two web servers with the same content and want to split the incoming connections across both of these machines. Since both machines have *different* IP addresses, this creates a problem. Normally, a DNS server would send back just one address for a requested name resolution. You could solve this by using an enhanced DNS product that varies its replies among a group of addresses. The problem with this approach is that devices typically cache this information, and thus more traffic might be sent to one server than another.

A better choice is to use the load distribution feature in NAT. Set up your DNS server to send back a single IP address. Within your NAT configuration, you'll tell the router to round-robin between a range of internal addresses where this service is located. One problem with this feature is that it doesn't keep tabs on which services are available or not available, nor does it keep track of actual traffic loads on each of these internal devices—it load-balances on a connection-by-connection basis. Therefore, if you are concerned about these limitations, you'll want to purchase a true load balancing product.

The configuration of load distribution involves three steps. In the first step, you specify the internal IP addresses that are configured on the devices offering the service. This is done with the **ip nat pool** command:

```
Router(config)# ip nat pool pool_name
                          beginning_inside_local_IP_address
                          ending_inside_local_IP_address
                          prefix-length subnet_mask_bits
                          type rotary
```

First, you need to give the internal addresses a unique pool name. Following this are the beginning and ending internal addresses of the devices offering the same service. Following this, you need to configure the length, in bits, of the subnet mask of the location of these devices. And last, you have to specify the **type rotary** parameter to tell the IOS that you want to round-robin the assignment of connections to these internal devices. This causes the IOS to send the first connection request to the first address, the second request to the second address, and so on.

Next, you need to specify the global IP address that outside devices are using to reach the inside resource:

```
Router(config)# ip nat inside destination
                          list standard_ACL_# pool pool_name
```

This command requires you to specify a standard ACL number, which references the global IP address or addresses that will be redirected to internal machines. Second, you need to specify the pool name that needs to match the **ip nat pool** command. And last, you have to tell the IOS which interfaces are inside and outside, respectively, in terms of the **ip nat inside** and **ip nat outside** commands.

Let's take a look at an example configuration that uses load distribution. I'll use the network shown in Figure 14-4 to illustrate the configuration. In this example, there are two web servers with the same information on them: 192.168.1.1 and 192.168.1.2. They are represented as a single device with a global address of 200.200.200.1.

FIGURE 14-4 Load distribution example

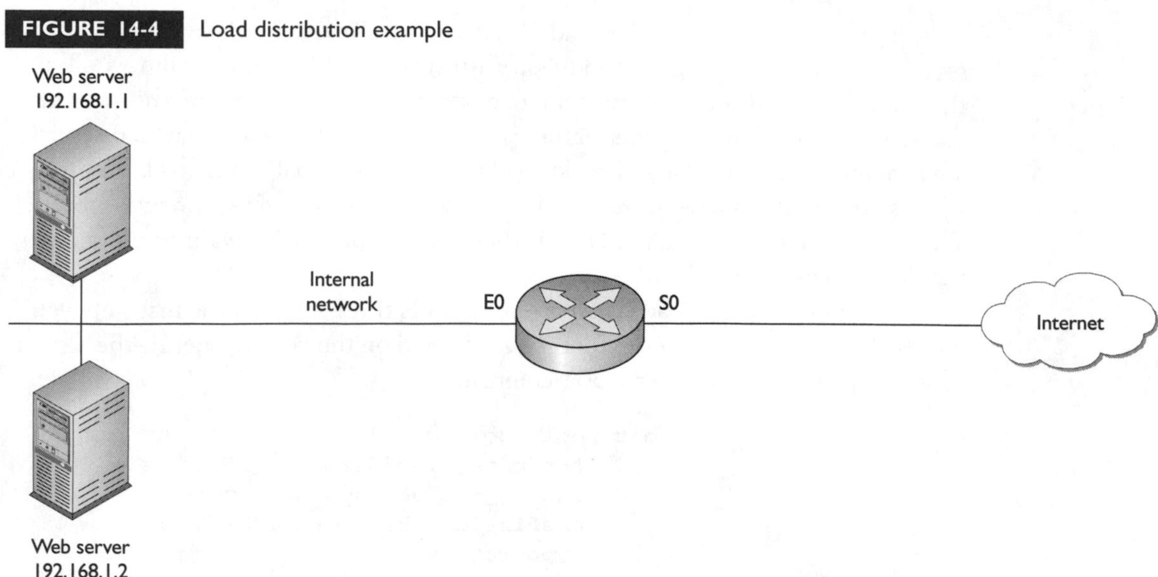

Here's the configuration:

```
Router(config)# ip nat pool inside-hosts
                192.168.1.1 192.168.1.2
                prefix-length 24 type rotary
Router(config)# ip nat inside destination list 1
                pool inside-hosts
Router(config)# access-list 1 permit 200.200.200.1
Router(config)# interface ethernet 0
Router(config-if)# ip nat inside
Router(config-if)# exit
Router(config)# interface serial 0
Router(config-if)# ip nat outside
```

14.04. The CD contains a multimedia demonstration of configuring load distribution on a router.

Address Translation Verification

Once you have configured address translation, there are many commands you can use to verify and troubleshoot the operation of address translation on your router. For instance, if you want to see the address translation on your router, use the **show ip nat translations** command:

```
Router# show ip nat translations
Pro  Inside global   Inside local   Outside local   Outside global
---  200.200.200.1   192.168.1.1    ---             ---
---  200.200.200.2   192.168.1.2    ---             –
```

In this example, two addresses are being translated: 192.168.1.1 to 200.200.200.1 and 192.168.1.2 to 200.200.200.2. Notice that no protocol is listed (`Pro`) or port numbers, indicating that this is NAT, not PAT.

Here's an example using PAT:

```
Router# show ip nat translations
Pro Inside global       Inside local       Outside local Outside global
tcp 200.200.200.1:1080 192.168.1.1:1080 201.1.1.1:23  201.1.1.1:23
tcp 200.200.200.1:1081 192.168.1.2:1080 201.1.1.1:23  201.1.1.1:23
```

In this example, both 192.168.1.1 and 192.168.1.2 are accessing the same outside device (201.1.1.1) using telnet. Notice that both also use the same source port number (1080 under the `Inside local` column). The IOS has noticed this and changed the second connection's source port number from 1080 to 1081.

14.05. The CD contains a multimedia demonstration of the `show ip nat translations` command on a router.

You can even see address translations statistics on your router with this command:

```
Router# show ip nat statistics
Total translations: 2 (0 static, 2 dynamic; 0 extended)
Outside interfaces: Serial0
Inside interfaces: Ethernet0
Hits: 98 Misses: 4
Expired translations: 1
Dynamic mappings:
-- Inside Source
access-list 1 pool nat-pool refcount 2
pool nat-pool: netmask 255.255.255.255
start 200.200.200.10 end 200.200.200.254
type generic, total addresses 12, allocated 1 (9%), misses 0
```

In this example, *hits* refers to the number of times the IOS looked into the translation table and found a match, while *misses* indicates the number of times the IOS looked in the table for a translation, didn't find one, and had to create one.

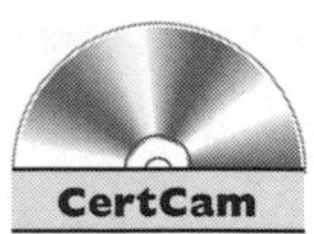

14.06. The CD contains a multimedia demonstration of the `show ip nat statistics` command on a router.

For dynamic entries in the translation table, you can clear all of the entries, or specific entries, using the following commands:

```
Router# clear ip nat translation *
Router# clear ip nat translation inside
                       global_IP_address local_IP_address
Router# clear ip nat translation outside
                       global_IP_address local_IP_address
Router# clear ip nat translation protocol inside
                       global_IP_address global_port
                       local_IP_address local_port
```

The first command clears all dynamic entries in the table. Note that to clear static entries, you need to delete your static NAT configuration commands from within *Configuration* mode.

14.07. The CD contains a multimedia demonstration of the `clear ip nat translation` command on a router.

Besides using **show** commands, you can also use **debug** commands for troubleshooting. The **debug ip nat** command, for instance, will show the translations the IOS is doing on every translated packet. This is useful in determining if the IOS is translating your packet and segment header addressing information correctly. Please note that on a busy network, this command will chew up a lot of CPU cycles on your router. Here's an example of this command:

```
Router# debug ip nat
05:32:23: NAT: s=192.168.1.10->200.200.200.2, d=201.1.1.1 [70]
05:32:23: NAT*: s=201.1.1.1, d=200.200.200.2->192.168.1.10 [70]
```

exam watch

Use the `show ip nat translations` command to display the router's translations. Use the `clear ip nat translations` command to clear dynamic translations from the translation table. The `debug ip nat` command shows the router performing address translation in a real-time fashion.

In the first line of this example, an internal machine (192.168.1.10) is having its address translated to 200.200.200.2 where the packet is being sent to 201.1.1.1. The second line shows the returning traffic from 201.1.1.1 and the translation from the global to the local inside address.

14.08. The CD contains a multimedia demonstration of the* `debug ip nat` *command on a router.

EXERCISE 14-1

Configuring Address Translation

These last few sections dealt with the configuration of address translation on IOS routers. This exercise will help you reinforce this material by configuring a simple static NAT translation. You'll perform this lab using Boson's NetSim simulator. After starting up the simulator, click the *LabNavigator* button. Next, double-click *Exercise 14-1* and click the *Load Lab* button. This will load the lab configuration based on Chapter 5's and 7's exercises.

1. On the 2500, configure a static route to 192.168.1.0/24, which is off of the 2600. View the routing table.

   At the top of the simulator in the menu bar, click the *eRouters* icon and choose *2500*. Configure the static route: **`configure terminal`**, **`ip route 192.168.1.0 255.255.255.0 192.168.2.1`**, and **`end`**. View the static route: **`show ip route`**. Make sure that 192.168.1.0/24 shows up in the routing table as a static route (`S`).

2. On the 2600, configure a static route to 192.168.3.0/24, which is off of the 2500. View the routing table.

   At the top of the simulator in the menu bar, click the *eRouters* icon and choose *2600*. Configure the static route: **`configure terminal`**, **`ip route 192.168.3.0 255.255.255.0 192.168.2.2`**, and **`end`**. View the static route: **`show ip route`**. Make sure that 192.168.3.0/24 shows up in the routing table as a static route (`S`).

3. From Host3, ping the `fa0/0` interface of the 2600. From Host3, ping Host1.

   At the top of the simulator in the menu bar, click the *eStations* icon and choose *Host3*. Ping the `serial0` and `fa0/0` interface of the 2600 router:

ping 192.168.2.1 and **ping 192.168.1.1**. The pings should be successful. Ping Host1: **ping 192.168.1.10**. The ping should be successful.

4. Check network connectivity between the two 2950 switches and the Host3.

   At the top of the simulator in the menu bar, click the *eSwitches* icon and choose *2950-1*. From the 2950-1 switch, ping Host3: **ping 192.168.3.2**. At the top of the simulator in the menu bar, click the *eSwitches* icon and choose *2950-2*. From the 2950-2 switch, ping Host3: **ping 192.168.3.2**. At the top of the simulator in the menu bar, click the *eStations* icon and choose *Host3*. From Host3, ping the 2950-1 switch: **ping 192.168.1.4**. From Host3, ping the 2950-2 switch: **ping 192.168.1.3**.

5. Set up a static route on the 2500 to reach 10.0.0.0/8, which are the global addresses behind the 2600. Remove the 192.168.1.0/24 static route.

   At the top of the simulator in the menu bar, click the *eRouters* icon and choose *2500*. On the 2500, set up a static route: **configure terminal** and **ip route 10.0.0.0 255.0.0.0 192.168.2.1**. Remove the old static route: **no ip route 192.168.1.0 255.255.255.0 192.168.2.1**. Exit *Configuration* mode: **end**. View the routing table: **show ip route**.

6. On the 2600 router, set up a static NAT translation for 2950-1 (10.0.0.1) and the 2950-2 (10.0.0.2). Configure `fa0/0` as the inside and `s0` as the outside for NAT. View your static translations.

   At the top of the simulator in the menu bar, click the *eRouters* icon and *2600*. Access *Configuration* mode: **configure terminal**. Set up static NAT statement on the 2600 router for 2950-1: **ip nat inside source static 192.168.1.4 10.0.0.1**. Set up static NAT statement on the 2600 router for 2950-2: **ip nat inside source static 192.168.1.3 10.0.0.2**. Specify **fa0/0** as the inside: **interface fa0/0**, **ip nat inside**, and **exit**. Specify s0 as the outside: **interface s0**, **ip nat outside**, and **end**. View the static translations: **show ip nat translations**.

7. Test the translation from Host3 by pinging the two switches with their global and local addresses.

   At the top of the simulator in the menu bar, click the *eStations* icon and choose *Host3*. From Host3, ping 2950-1's global address: **ping 10.0.0.1**. The ping should be successful. From Host3, ping 2950-1's local address: **ping**

192.168.1.4. The ping should fail (no route). From Host3, ping 2950-2's global address: **ping 10.0.0.2**. The ping should be successful. From Host3, ping 2950-2's local address: **ping 192.168.1.3**. The ping should fail (no route).

Now you should be more comfortable with configuring address translation on a router.

CERTIFICATION OBJECTIVE 14.03

Dynamic Host Configuration Protocol

The Dynamic Host Configuration Protocol (DHCP) allows devices to dynamically acquire their addressing information. DHCP, defined in RFC 2131, is actually based on BOOTP. It is built on a client/server model and defines two components:

- **Server** Delivering host configuration information
- **Client** Requesting and acquiring host configuration information

DHCP provides the following advantages:

- It reduces the amount of configuration on devices.
- It reduces likelihood of configuration errors.
- It gives you more control by centralizing IP addressing information.

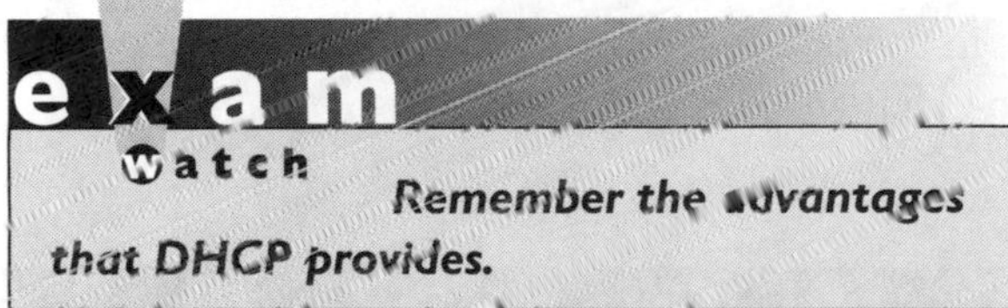

Remember the advantages that DHCP provides.

Most networks today employ DHCP because it is easy to implement and manage. Imagine you work for a company that is bought by another company and you must readdress your network, which contains 2,000 devices. If you have manually configured the IP addresses on these machines, then you must manually change each device's configuration. However, if you were using DHCP, you only have to change the configuration on the DHCP servers, and when the clients either reboot or must renew their addressing information, they'll acquire the addressing information from the new scheme.

DHCP Devices and Operation

As mentioned in the last section, DHCP contains two types of devices: servers and clients. IOS routers support both functions. Servers are responsible for assigning addressing information to clients, and clients request addressing information from servers. This section covers the interaction between these two types of devices.

A DHCP server can use three mechanisms, which are described in Table 14-4, when allocating address information. Most DHCP implementations use the dynamic allocation type.

When acquiring addressing information, a DHCP client goes through four steps:

1. A client generates a DHCPDISCOVER broadcast to discover who the DHCP servers are on the LAN segment.
2. All DHCP servers on the segment can respond to the client with a DHCPOFFER unicast message, which offers IP addressing information to the client. If a client receives messages from multiple servers, it chooses one (typically the first one).
3. Upon choosing one of the offers, the client responds to the corresponding server with a DHCPREQUEST message, telling the server that it wants to use the addressing information the server sent. If there is only one server and the server's information conflicts with the client's configuration, the client will respond with a DHCPDECLINE message.
4. The DHCP server responds with a DHCPACK, which is an acknowledgment to the client indicating that it received the DHCPREQUEST message and that the client accepted the addressing information. The server can also respond with a DHCPNACK, which tells the client the offer is no longer valid and the client should request addressing information again. This can happen if the client is tardy in responding with a DHCPREQUEST message after the server generated the DHCPOFFER message.

TABLE 14-4 DHCP Address Allocation Types

Allocation Type	Explanation
Automatic	Server assigns a permanent IP address to the client
Dynamic	Server assigns an IP address to a client for a period of time
Manual	IP address manually configured on the client, and DHCP is used to convey additional addressing information and verification

Remember the four steps that DHCP goes through when a client requests addressing information.

Remember that a DCHP server can assign an IP address; a subnet mask; a default gateway; DNS server, TFTP server, and WINS server addresses; and a domain name.

When a client shuts down gracefully, it can generate a DHCPRELEASE message, telling the server it no longer needs its assigned IP address. Most DHCP configurations involve a lease time, which specifies a time period that the client is allowed to use the address. Upon reaching this time limit, the client must renew its lease or get a new IP address.

DHCPOFFER server messages include the following information: IP address of the client, subnet mask of the segment, IP address of the default gateway, DNS domain name, DNS server address or addresses, WINS server address or addresses, and the TFTP server address or addresses. Please note that this is not an all-encompassing list.

DHCP Server Configuration

Cisco IOS routers can be DHCP servers. Please note, though, that this is not a full-functioning DHCP product and is typically used in small networking environments, such as SOHO or branch offices. Use the following configuration to set up a DHCP server:

```
Router(config)# [no] service dhcp
Router(config)# ip dhcp pool pool_name
Router(config-dhcp)# network network_number
                     [subnet_mask | /prefix_length]
Router(config-dhcp)# domain-name domain_name
Router(config-dhcp)# dns-server IP_address
                     [IP_address_2 . . . IP_address_8]
Router(config-dhcp)# netbios-name-server IP_address
                     [IP_address_2...IP_address_8]
Router(config-dhcp)# netbios-node-type node_type
Router(config-dhcp)# default-router IP_address
                     [IP_address_2...IP_address_8]
Router(config-dhcp)# lease days [hours][minutes] | infinite
Router(config-dhcp)# exit
Router(config)# ip dhcp ping timeout milliseconds
Router(config)# ip dhcp excluded-address beginning_IP_address
                     [ending_IP_address]
```

The **service dhcp** command enables and disables the DHCP server feature on your router. By default, this is enabled on your router. Precede the command with the **no** parameter to disable it. The **ip dhcp pool** command creates an addressing pool. The name you give this pool must be unique. Notice that when you execute this command, you are placed in *DHCP Subconfiguration* mode.

The **network** command specifies the range of IP addresses to be assigned to clients. You specify a network number followed by either a subnet mask or a slash and the number of networking bits in the network. If you omit the subnet mask value, it defaults to the subnet mask of the ClassA, B, or C network.

The **domain-name** command assigns the domain name to the client. The **dns-server** command allows you to assign up to eight DNS server addresses to the client. Separate each address from the next with a space. The **netbios-name-server** command allows you to assign up to eight WINS server addresses to the client. The **netbios-name-type** command assigns the node type to a Microsoft client. This identifies how Microsoft clients perform resolution. These types can be **b** (broadcast only), **p** (WINS only), **m** (broadcast, then WINS), or **h** (WINS, then broadcast). The **default-router** command allows you to assign up to eight default gateway addresses to the client for this range of addresses. The **lease** command specifies the duration of the lease. If you omit this, it defaults to one day. If you specify the **infinite** parameter, the IP address assigned to the client is assigned permanently.

The second to the last command in the preceding code listing is not done within *DHCP Subconfiguration* mode. The **ip dhcp ping timeout** command is used by the DHCP server to test if an available address the server has in its pool is or is not being used. Before a server will send an address in a DHCPOFFER message, it pings the address. This command is used to define how long the server should wait for a reply. By default, this is 500 milliseconds. If the server doesn't receive a reply in this time period, the server will assume the address is not being used and offer this to the client.

The **ip dhcp excluded-address** command excludes addresses from your network pool—these addresses are addresses that are already statically assigned to devices, perhaps servers, on the same segment as the client.

Let's take a look at a simple example of a DHCP server configuration. I'll use the network shown in Figure 14-5. The router in this example is the DHCP server, providing addresses for the 192.168.1.0/24 network.

Here's the configuration:

```
Router(config)# ip dhcp pool dhcppool
Router(config-dhcp)# network 192.168.1.0 255.255.255.0
```

```
Router(config-dhcp)# domain-name thisnetwork.com
Router(config-dhcp)# dns-server 192.168.1.2
Router(config-dhcp)# default-router 192.168.1.1
Router(config-dhcp)# lease 5
Router(config-dhcp)# exit
Router(config)# ip dhcp excluded-address 192.168.1.1
                                          192.168.1.2
```

The service dhcp command enables the DHCP server function on a router.

The pool, named *dhcppool,* includes all addresses in network 192.168.1.0/24 with the exception of the two excluded addresses: 192.168.1.1 and 192.168.1.2. The lease length was changed to five days.

14.09. The CD contains a multimedia demonstration of a DHCP server configuration on a router.

FIGURE 14-5 DHCP server example

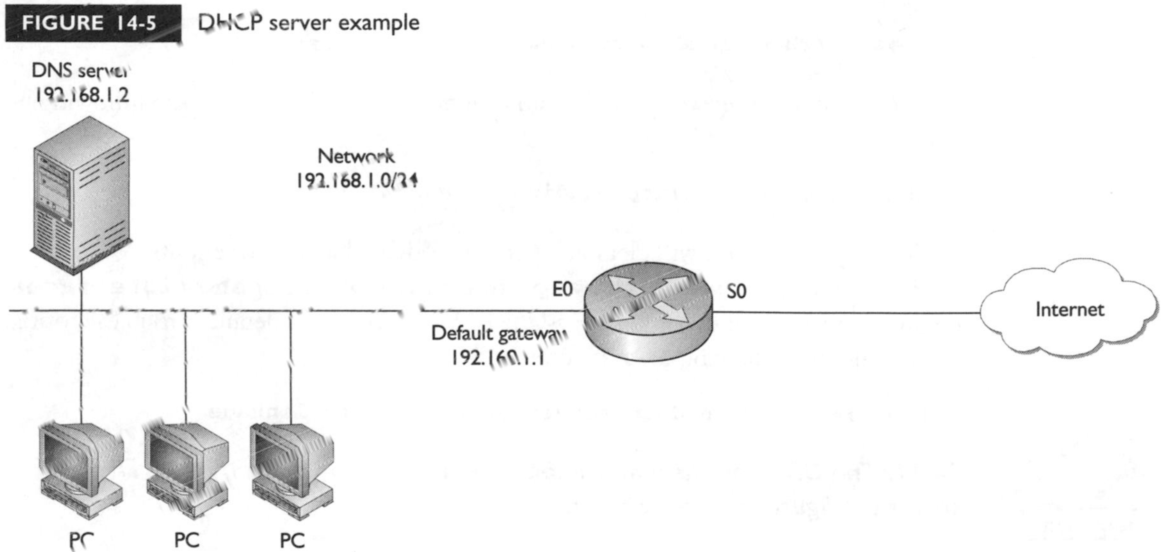

DHCP Client Configuration

You can configure an interface on your IOS router to use DHCP to *acquire* its IP address. This is commonly done if your router is directly connected to your ISP via a dialup, PPPoE, or cable modem connection and your ISP is assigning the addressing information to your router via DHCP. Here is the command to set up a DHCP client on your router:

Use the ip address dhcp command on a router's interface in order to use DHCP to acquire the router's IP address on the interface.

```
Router(config)# interface type [slot_#/]port_#
Router(config-if)# ip address dhcp
```

As you can see, this configuration is very easy.

14.10. The CD contains a multimedia demonstration of a DHCP client configuration on a router.

DHCP Verification

Once you have your DHCP server up and running, you can view the addresses assigned to clients with the following command:

```
Router# show ip dhcp binding [client_address]
```

On a DHCP server, you can clear an assigned client address with the following command:

```
Router# clear ip dhcp binding client_address | *
```

Entering an asterisk will clear all of the bounded addresses for clients.

If you are a client, use the **show ip interface brief** or **show interfaces** command to see your dynamically assigned address. For more detailed troubleshooting, you can use the following **debug** command:

```
Router# debug ip dhcp server events|packet|linkage
```

14.11. The CD contains a multimedia demonstration of verifying a DHCP server configuration on a router.

CERTIFICATION SUMMARY

Private addresses are defined in RFC 1918: 10.0.0.0/8, 172.16.0.0/16–172.31.0.0/16, and 192.168.0.0/24–192.168.255.0/24. If you use private addresses, you must have these translated to a public address before these packets reach a public network. Address translation is used when you don't have enough public addresses, you change ISPs but keep your existing addresses, you are merging companies with overlapping address spaces, or you want to assign the same IP address to multiple machines.

The term *inside local IP address* refers to packets with a private, or original IP address. The term *inside global IP address* refers to packets with a public, or translated, address. NAT translates one IP address to another where PAT (address overloading) translates many IP addresses to the same global address, where the source port numbers are changed to ensure the translation device can differentiate the connections. PAR redirects traffic destined to a port on one device to a different device.

Address translation allows access to an almost inexhaustible group of addresses and enables you to hide your internal network design from outsiders. It also gives you tighter control over traffic entering and leaving your network. However, address translation adds delay to your traffic, makes troubleshooting more difficult, and won't work with all applications, especially multimedia applications.

The **ip nat inside source static** command sets up static NAT. The **ip nat inside source list** and **ip nat pool** (add **overload** to do PAT) commands set up dynamic NAT or PAT. The **ip nat inside|outside** *Interface* commands define which interfaces are considered internal and external for address translation.

Use the **show ip nat translations** command to view the router's address translation table. The **clear ip nat translation** * command clears all dynamic address translation entries in the router's translation table. The **debug ip nat** command will show the translations the IOS is doing on every translated packet.

DHCP reduces the amount of configuration on devices, reduces the likelihood of configuration errors, and gives you more control of addressing by centralizing your addressing policies. A client goes through four steps when acquiring addressing information: DHCPDISCOVER, DHCPOFFER, DHCPREQUEST, and DHCPACK.

To enable the DHCP server function on a router, use the **service dhcp** command. Create your addressing policies with the **ip dhcp pool** command and create your address pool with the **network** command. To have the router act as a DHCP client, use the **ip address dhcp** *Interface* command.

TWO-MINUTE DRILL

Address Translation Overview

- RFC 1918 private addresses include 10.0.0.0/8, 172.16.0.0/16–172.31.0.0/16, and 192.168.0.0/24–192.168.255.0/24
- Reasons to use address translation include not having enough public addresses, changing ISPs, merging networks with overlapping addresses, and representing multiple devices as a single logical device. Disadvantages of address translation include connection delays, difficult troubleshooting, and that it doesn't work with all applications.
- An inside local IP address is a private address assigned to an inside device. An inside global IP address is a public address associated with an inside device.
- NAT does a one-to-one address translation. PAT translates multiple IP addresses to a single address, using the source port number to differentiate connections. Port address redirection is a form of static PAT, where traffic sent to a specific address and port is redirected to another machine (and possibly a different port). PAT can support up to 4,000 translations.

Address Translation Configuration

- To define inside and outside, use the **ip nat inside|outside** *Interface Subconfiguration* mode command.
- To configure static NAT, use the **ip nat inside|outside source static** command.
- To set up dynamic NAT, use the **ip nat inside source list** command, with a standard ACL specifying the inside local addresses. Add **overload** to this command to do PAT. Use the **ip nat pool** command to specify the global addresses.
- Load distribution allows you to distribute traffic sent to one IP address to multiple IP addresses.
- Use the **show ip nat translations** command to view the static and dynamic address translations. Use the **clear ip nat translation *** command to clear the dynamic translations from the address translation table. Use **debug ip nat** to see the actual translation process.

Dynamic Host Configuration Protocol

- ❑ Four steps occur when a client requests addressing information: a client generates a DHCPDISCOVER; servers respond with a DHCPOFFER; the client chooses one reply and responds to the server with a DHCPREQUEST; and the server acknowledges the request with a DHCPACK.
- ❑ To create a DHCP server pool, use the **`ip dhcp pool`** command. To specify the range of addresses, use the **`network`** command. Other commands include **`domain-name`**, **`dns-server`**, **`netbios-name-server`**, **`default-router`**, and **`lease`**. The default lease period is one day. The default ping timeout is 500 milliseconds.
- ❑ To acquire a DHCP address on a router's interface, use the **`ip address dhcp`** command.
- ❑ To view the assigned DHCP addresses, use the **`show ip dhcp binding`** command. To clear DHCP addresses on the server, use the **`clear ip dhcp binding`** * command.

SELF TEST

The following Self Test questions will help you measure your understanding of the material presented in this chapter. Read all the choices carefully, as there may be more than one correct answer. Choose all correct answers for each question.

Address Translation Overview

1. Which of the following is a private address?
   A. 192.169.7.17
   B. 172.32.28.39
   C. 10.1.256.8
   D. 172.16.255.89

2. Which of the following reasons might you need to use address translation?
   A. You have to use public addressing because your ISP didn't assign you enough private addresses.
   B. You are using private addresses but have changed ISPs, and your new ISP won't support these private addresses.
   C. You want to assign the same IP address to multiple machines so that users on the Internet see this offered service as a single logical computer.
   D. You are merging two companies that use different address spaces.

3. Private addressing is defined in RFC _________ (enter a number).

4. ___________ only translates one (and only one) IP address to another.
   A. NAT
   B. PAT
   C. PAR
   D. NAT and PAT

5. An _____________ is a public IP address associated with an inside device.
   A. Inside global IP address
   B. Inside local IP address
   C. Outside global IP address
   D. Outside local IP address

Address Translation Configuration

6. Which command is used to define the local addresses that are statically translated to global addresses?

A. `ip nat inside source static`

B. `ip nat inside`

C. `ip nat inside source list`

D. `ip nat pool`

7. Enter the router command to specify an interface to be considered as *outside* for address translation: ___________.

8. Enter the router command to view the address translation table: ___________.

9. When configuring the **`ip nat inside source`** command, which parameter must you specify to perform PAT?

A. `pat`

B. `overload`

C. `load`

D. `port`

10. Enter the router command to view, in real time, the address translations the IOS is performing: ___________.

11. Which router command clears all of the static translations in the address translation table?

A. `erase ip nat translation *`

B. `clear ip nat translation *`

C. `clear ip nat translation all`

D. None of these commands

12. ___________ allows you to distribute connection requests destined to a single IP address to multiple machines.

A. Traffic load

B. Traffic configuration

C. PAT

D. Load distribution

Dynamic Host Configuration Protocol

13. Which of the following is not an advantage of DHCP?

A. It allows for the use of private addressing.

B. It reduces the amount of configuration on devices.

C. It reduces likelihood of configuration errors.

D. It gives you more control by centralizing IP addressing information.

14. What command creates a DHCP address pool on a router?

A. `ip dhcp`

B. `ip pool dhcp`

C. `ip dhcp pool network`

D. `ip dhcp pool`

15. Enter the router command to have a router's interface acquire its IP address via DHCP: __________.

SELF TEST ANSWERS

Address Translation Overview

1. ☑ **D.** The address 172.16.255.89 is a private address.
   ☒ **A** and **B** are public addresses. **C** is an invalid address (256 is an invalid value).

2. ☑ **C.** You will need to use address translation (load distribution) if you want to assign the same IP address to multiple machines so that users on the Internet see this offered service as a single logical computer.
   ☒ **A** is not true, because it reverses the word public and private. **B** is not true, because it refers to private, not public addresses. **D** is not true, because it should say the same, not different, address spaces.

3. ☑ Private addressing is defined in RFC 1918.

4. ☑ **A.** NAT only translates one IP address to another.
   ☒ **B** and **D** are incorrect because PAT translates many addresses to one address. **C** is incorrect because PAT can translate a port number to another port number.

5. ☑ **A.** An inside global IP address is a public IP address assigned to an inside device.
   ☒ **B** refers to an inside private address. **C** refers to an outside public address. **D** refers to an outside private address.

Address Translation Configuration

6. ☑ **A.** The **`ip nat inside source static`** command configures static NAT translations
   ☒ **B** specifies an interface as being inside. **C** and **D** are used to configure dynamic NAT.

7. ☑ **`ip nat outside`**.

8. ☑ **`show ip nat translations`**.

9. ☑ **B.** Use the **`overload`** parameter with the **`ip nat inside source`** command to set up PAT.
   ☒ **A**, **C**, and **D** are invalid parameters.

10. ☑ **`debug ip nat`**.

11. ☑ **D.** The only way to remove static entries is to remove your static NAT commands from the router's configuration with the **`no`** parameter.
    ☒ **A** and **C** are invalid commands. **B** removes the dynamic entries from the address translation table.

12. ☑ D. Load distribution allows you to distribute connection requests destined to a single IP address to multiple machines.
☒ A and B are invalid terms. C refers to translating many addresses to a single address, changing the source port number to ensure uniqueness among connections.

Dynamic Host Configuration Protocol

13. ☑ A. Actually, DHCP allows for both private and public addressing—this is not an advantage of DHCP, just a function of it.
☒ B, C, and D are advantages of using DHCP.

14. ☑ D. The **`ip dhcp pool`** command creates a DHCP address pool.
☒ A, B, and C are invalid commands.

15. ☑ **`ip address dhcp`**.

15 WAN Introduction

CERTIFICATION OBJECTIVES

15.01 Wide Area Networking Overview

15.02 HDLC

15.03 PPP

✓ Two-Minute Drill

Q&A Self Test

The last few chapters introduced you to configuring IP features on your Cisco router. This chapter introduces you to wide area networking (WAN) concepts and some basic point-to-point configurations, including HDLC and PPP. The two chapters following this, Frame Relay and ISDN, focus on packet-switched and dialup connections, respectively.

CERTIFICATION OBJECTIVE 15.01

Wide Area Networking Overview

Typically, LAN connections are within a company and WAN connections allow you to connect to remote sites. Typically, you don't own the infrastructure for WAN connections—another company, such as a telephone company, provides the infrastructure. WAN connections are usually slower than LAN connections. A derivative of WAN solutions is the metropolitan area network (MAN). MANs sometimes use high-speed LAN connections in a small geographic area between different companies, or divisions within a company. MANs are becoming more and more popular in large cities and even provide connections over a LAN medium, such as Ethernet.

The most important factor in choosing a WAN service is cost.

One of the major factors when choosing a WAN or MAN provider is *cost*. These connections are billed in multiple ways: flat monthly lease cost, per-packet cost, per-minute cost, and many other methods. On top of this, you have many solutions to choose from to solve your WAN connection problems. In order to choose the right solution, you'll need to weigh your connection requirements, your traffic patterns, and the cost of the solution.

Equipment and Components

WAN connections are made up of many types of equipment and components. Figure 15-1 shows some of these WAN terms. Table 15-1 has a list of the terms and definitions.

It is important to remember the WAN terms in Table 15-1.

As you may recall from Chapter 2, a DCE terminates a connection between two sites and provides clocking and synchronization for that connection; it connects to a DTE. The DCE category includes equipment such as CSU/DSUs, NT1s, and modems. A DTE is an end-user device,

FIGURE 15-1 WAN terms

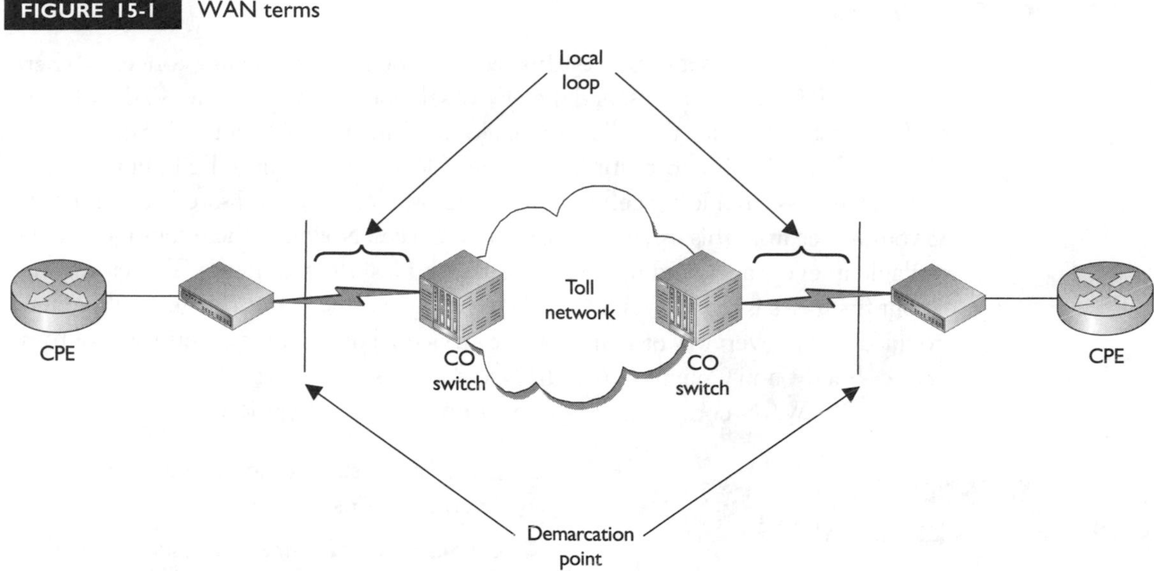

such as a router or PC, that connects to the WAN via the DCE equipment. In some circumstances, the function of the DCE might be built into the DTE's physical interface. For instance, certain Cisco routers can be purchased with built-in NT1s or CSU/DSUs in their WAN interfaces.

TABLE 15-1 WAN Terms and Definitions

Term	Definition
CPE (customer premises equipment)	This is your network's equipment, which includes the DCE (modem, NT1, CSU/DSU) and your DTE (router, access server).
Demarcation point	This is where the responsibility of the carrier is passed on to you; this could be inside or outside your local facility. Please note that this is a *logical* boundary, not necessarily a physical boundary.
Local loop	This is the connection from the carrier's switching equipment to the demarcation point.
CO (central office) switch	This is the carrier's switch within the toll network.
Toll network	This is the carrier's internal infrastructure for transporting your data.

Connection Types

As mentioned at the beginning of this section, you have two major concerns when choosing a WAN solution: cost and the type of solution. There are many WAN solutions to choose from, including the following: analog modems and ISDN for dialup connections, ATM, dedicated point-to-point leased lines (dedicated circuits), DSL, Frame Relay, SMDS, wireless (including cellular, laser microwave, radio, and satellite), and X.25. As you can see from this list, you have a lot of choices. Not all of these solutions will be available in every area, and not every solution is ideal for your needs. Therefore, one of your first tasks is to have a basic understanding of some of these services. Chapter 1 provided a brief overview of some of these services. This chapter covers some of these services briefly, and Chapters 16 and 17 expand on some of the others.

Typically, WAN connections fall under one of four categories:

Know about the four types of WAN connections: leased lines, circuit-switched connections, packet-switched connections, and cell-switched connections.

- *Leased lines*, such as dedicated circuits or connections
- *Circuit-switched connections*, such as analog modem and digital ISDN dialup connections
- *Packet-switched connections*, such as Frame Relay and X.25
- *Cell-switched connections*, such as ATM and SMDS

The following three sections will introduce you to these four connection types.

Leased-Line Connections

A leased-line connection is basically a dedicated circuit connection between two sites. It simulates a single cable connection between the local and remote sites. Leased lines are best suited when both of these conditions hold:

- The distance between the two sites is small, making them cost-effective.
- You have a constant amount of traffic between two sites and need to guarantee bandwidth for certain applications.

Even though leased lines can provide guaranteed bandwidth and minimal delay for connections, other available solutions, such as ATM, can provide the same features. The main disadvantage of leased lines is their cost—they are the most expensive WAN solution.

Leased lines use synchronous serial connections, with their data rates ranging from 2,400bps all the way up to 45Mbps, in what is referred to as a DS3 connection.

Remember that leased lines are used for short-distance connections and when you have a constant amount of traffic between sites with a need of guaranteed bandwidth.

A synchronous serial connection allows you to simultaneously send and receive information without having to wait for any signal from the remote side. Nor does a synchronous connection need to indicate when it is beginning to send something or the end of a transmission. These two things, plus how clocking is done, are the three major differences between synchronous and asynchronous connections—asynchronous connections are typically used for dialup connections, such as modems.

If you purchase a leased line, you will need the following equipment:

- **DTE** A router with a synchronous serial interface: this provides the data link framing and terminates the WAN connection.
- **DCE** A CSU/DSU to terminate the carrier's leased line connection: this provides the clocking and synchronization for the connection.

Figure 15-2 shows an example of the equipment required for a leased-line connection. The CSU/DSU is responsible for handling the physical layer framing, clocking, and synchronization of the connection. Data link layer protocols that you can use for

FIGURE 15-2 Leased line example

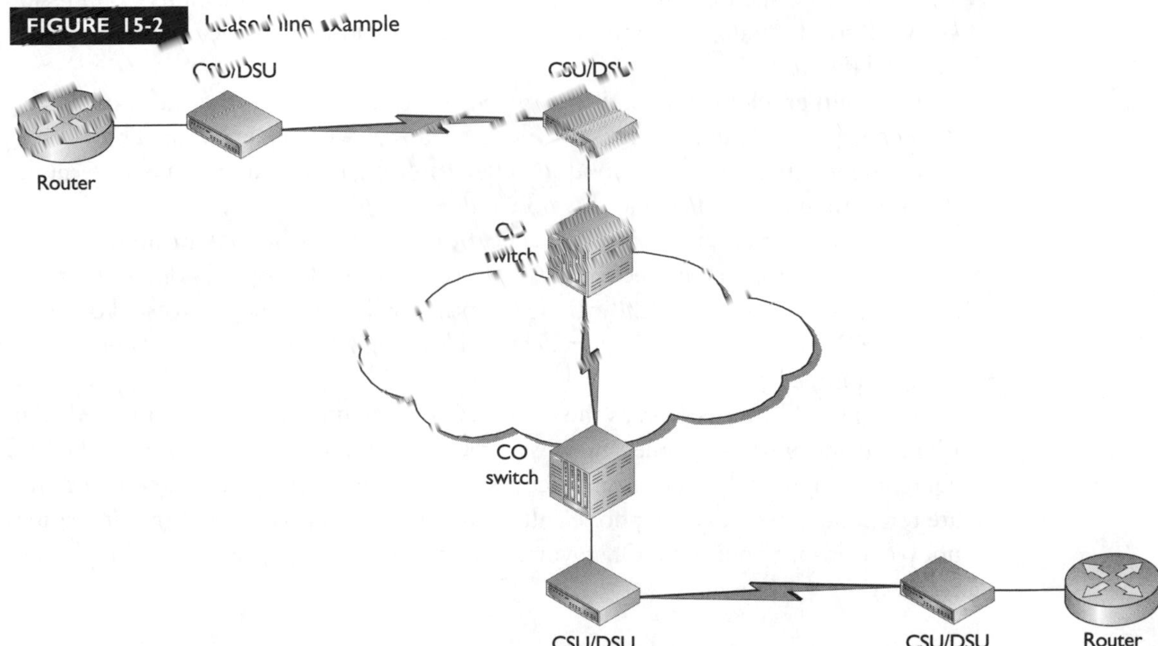

dedicated connections include PPP, SLIP, and HDLC. SLIP is rarely used and is restricted to IP traffic. SLIP has been replaced by PPP.

Circuit-Switched Connections

Circuit-switched connections are dialup connections, as are used by a PC with a modem when dialing up an ISP. Circuit-switched connections include the following types:

- **Asynchronous serial connections** These include analog modem dialup connections and the standard telephone system, which is commonly referred to as Plain Old Telephone Service (POTS) by the telephone carriers.
- **Synchronous serial connections** These include digital ISDN BRI and PRI dialup connections; they provide guaranteed bandwidth.

Analog connections are restricted by the FCC to 53Kbps.

Asynchronous serial connections are the cheapest form of WAN services but are also the most unreliable of the services. For instance, every time you make a connection using an analog modem, there is no guarantee of the connection rate you'll get. With these connections, the top connection rate in the U.S. is 53Kbps, but depending on the quality of the connection, you might get something as low as 300bps. The Federal Communications Commission (FCC) restricts analog data rates to 53Kbps or less. Other countries might support higher data rates.

The main problem with circuit-switched connections is that they are expensive if you need to make connections over long distances, with a per-minute charge that varies, depending on the destination. Therefore, the more data you have to send, the more time it will take, and the more money it will cost.

Asynchronous circuit-switched connections are typically used for home office and low-speed backup connections, as well as temporary low-speed connections for additional boosts in bandwidth when your primary link becomes congested or when it fails. ISDN (discussed in Chapter 17) provides a digital circuit-switched connection with guaranteed data rates.

With leased lines, as soon as the circuit is installed and you have configured your DTE, the line remains up unless there is a problem with the carrier's network or the DCE equipment. This is different from circuit-switched connections. These connections are temporary—you make a phone call to the remote DTE and when the line comes up, you transmit your data. Once you are done transmitting your data, the phone connection is terminated.

If you will be using a circuit-switched analog connection, you'll need this equipment:

- **DTE** A router with an asynchronous serial interface
- **DCE** A modem

If you will be using a circuit-switched digital connection, you'll need this equipment:

Remember that circuit-switched connections are typically used to back up primary connections, provide additional bandwidth boosts, and afford remote access to dialup users.

- **DTE** A router with an ISDN interface
- **DCE** An NT1 for a BRI or a CSU/DSU for a PRI

Figure 15-3 shows an example of an analog circuit-switched connection. With this connection, you'll typically use PPP or HDLC for the encapsulation: SLIP is rarely used.

Packet-Switched Connections

With leased lines and circuit-switched connections, a physical circuit is used to make the connection between the two sites. With a leased line, the same circuit path is always used. With circuit-switched connections, the circuit path is built every time a phone call is made, making it highly probable that the same circuit path will not be used for every phone call.

Packet-switched connections use logical circuits to make connections between two sites. These logical circuits are referred to as *virtual circuits (VCs)*. One advantage that

FIGURE 15-3 Analog circuit-switched connection

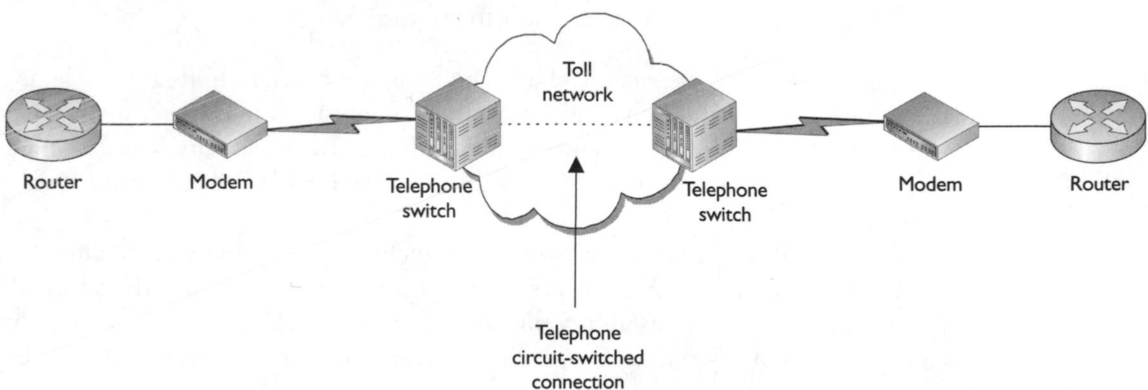

a logical circuit has over a physical one is that a logical circuit is not tied to any particular physical circuit. Instead, a logical circuit is built across any available physical connection. Another advantage of logical circuits is that you can build multiple logical circuits over the same physical circuit. Therefore, with a single physical connection to a carrier, you can connect to multiple sites. This is not possible with leased lines: for each location you want to connect to, you need a *separate* physical circuit, making the cost of the solution much higher that one that uses logical circuits. Technologies that use packet switching and logical circuits include ATM, Frame Relay, SMDS, and X.25. From a cost perspective, packet-switched solutions fall somewhere between circuit-switched solutions and leased lines.

The oldest of these four technologies is X.25, which is an ITU-T standard. X.25 is a network layer protocol that runs across both synchronous and asynchronous physical circuits, providing a lot of flexibility for your connection options. X.25 was actually developed to run across unreliable connections. It provides both error detection *and* correction, as well as flow control, at both the data link layer (by LAPB) and the network layer (by X.25). In this sense, it performs a function similar to what TCP, at the transport layer, provides for IP. Because of its overhead, X.25 is best delegated to asynchronous, unreliable connections. If you have a synchronous digital connection, another protocol, such as ATM or Frame Relay, is much more efficient.

Frame Relay is a digital packet-switched service that can run only across synchronous digital connections at the data link layer. Because it uses digital connections (which have very few errors), it does not perform any error correction or flow control as X.25 does. Frame Relay will, however, detect errors and drop bad frames. It is up to a higher-layer protocol, such as IP's TCP, to resend the dropped information.

If you are setting up a Frame Relay connection, you'll need the following equipment.

- **DTE** A router with a synchronous serial interface
- **DCE** A CSU/DSU to connect to the carrier

Figure 15-4 shows an example of a Frame Relay connection. In this example, the router needs only a single physical connection to the carrier to connect to multiple sites: this is accomplished via virtual circuits. Frame Relay supports speeds from fractional T1 or E1 connections (56–64Kbps) up to a DS3 (45Mbps). Frame Relay is discussed in Chapter 16.

ATM and SMDS are also packet-switched technologies that use digital circuits. Unlike Frame Relay and X.25, however, these services use fixed-length (53 byte) packets, called *cells*, to transmit information. Therefore, these services are commonly called cell-switched services. They have an advantage over Frame Relay in that they

FIGURE 15-4 Frame Relay packet-switched connection

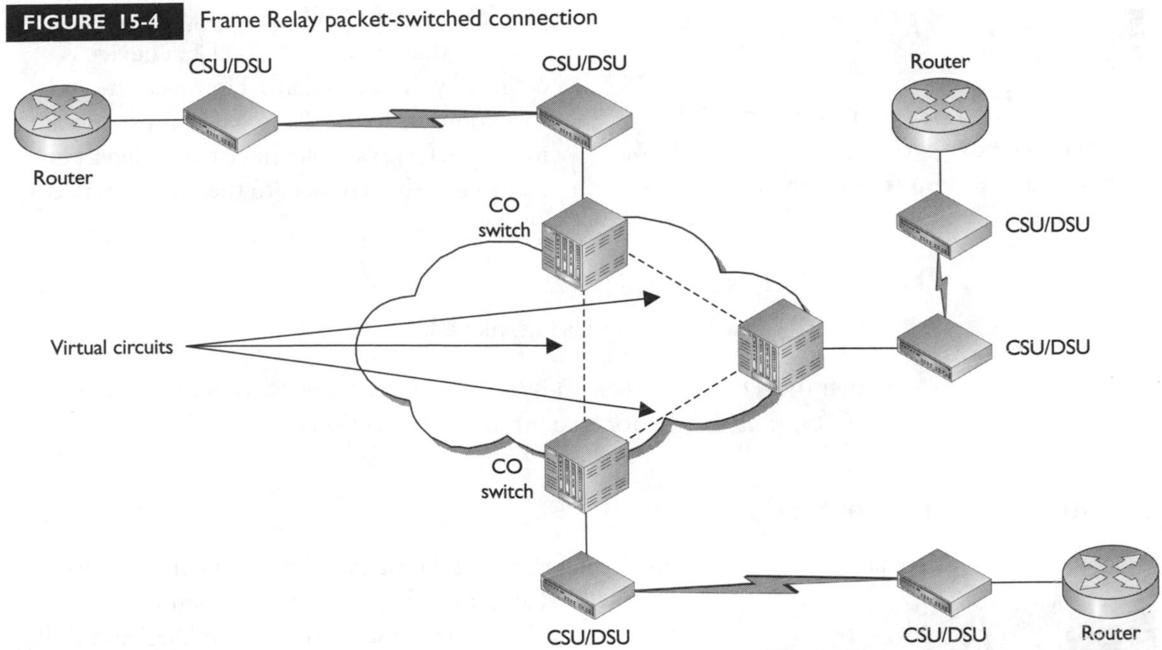

can provide guaranteed throughput and minimal delay for a multitude of services, including voice, video, and data. However, they do cost more than Frame Relay services.

> **exam watch**
>
> ***Remember that packet-switched and cell-switched services are typically used when a router has only a single WAN interface but needs to connect to multiple remote sites.***

SMDS, which was developed by BellCore, is precursor to ATM and has been replaced by the latter service. ATM (sort of an enhanced Frame Relay) can offer a connection guaranteed bandwidth, limited delay, limited number of errors, Quality of Service (QOS), and more. Frame Relay can provide some minimal guarantees to connections, but not the degree of precision that ATM can. Whereas Frame Relay is limited to 45Mbps connections, ATM can scale to very high speeds; OC-192 (SONET), for instance, affords about 10Gbps of bandwidth.

WAN Interfaces on Cisco Routers

Cisco supports a wide variety of serial cables for their serial router interfaces. Here are some of the cable types supported for synchronous serial interfaces: EIA/TIA-232,

Synchronous serial interfaces have either a DB-60 or DB-26 connector for connecting to Cisco routers.

EIA/TIA-449, EIA/TIA-530, V.35, and X.21. The end that connects to the DCE device is defined by these standards. However, the end that connects to the Cisco router is proprietary in nature. Cisco's cables have two different end connectors that connect to the serial interfaces of their routers:

- **DB-60** Has 60 pins
- **DB-26** Has 26 pins and is flat, like a USB cable

Note that these connectors are for synchronous serial connections. Cisco has other cable types, typically RJ-45, for asynchronous connections.

Encapsulation Methods

There are many different methods for encapsulating data for serial connections. Table 15-2 shows the most common ones. The following sections cover HDLC and PPP in more depth.

exam watch

Know the data link encapsulation types listed in Table 15-2.

TABLE 15-2 Common Encapsulation Methods

Protocol	Explanation
High-Level Data Link Control (HDLC)	Based on ISO standards, it is used with synchronous and asynchronous connections.
Synchronous Data Link Control Protocol (SDLC)	Used in IBM SNA environments, it has been replaced by HDLC.
Link Access Procedure Balanced (LAPB)	Used in X.25, it has extensive error detection and correction.
Link Access Procedure D Channel (LAPD)	It is used by ISDN to signal call setup and teardown of phone connections.
Link Access Procedure Frame mode bearer services (LAPF)	It is used in Frame Relay between a DTE and a DCE and is similar to LAPD.
Point-to-Point Protocol (PPP)	Based on RFC standards, PPP is the most common encapsulation used for dialup. It provides for authentication, handling multiple protocols, compression, and error detection.

CERTIFICATION OBJECTIVE 15.02

HDLC

Based on ISO standards, the HDLC (High-Level Data Link Control) protocol can be used with synchronous and asynchronous connections and defines the frame type and interaction between two devices at the data link layer. The following sections cover how Cisco implements HDLC and how it is configured on serial interfaces.

Frame Type

Cisco's implementation of HDLC is based on ISO's standards, but Cisco has made a change in the frame format, making it proprietary. In other words, Cisco's HDLC will work only if the remote end also supports Cisco's HDLC. Figure 15-5 shows examples of some WAN frame formats, including ISO's HDLC, Cisco's HDLC, and PPP. Notice that the main difference between ISO's HDLC and Cisco's frame format is that Cisco has a proprietary field. One of the problems with ISO's HDLC is that it does not define how to carry multiple protocols across a single link, as does Cisco's HDLC with the proprietary field. Therefore, ISO's HDLC is typically used on serial links where there is only a single protocol to transport. The *default* encapsulation on Cisco's synchronous serial interfaces is HDLC. Actually, Cisco supports only its own implementation of HDLC.

FIGURE 15-5 WAN frame types

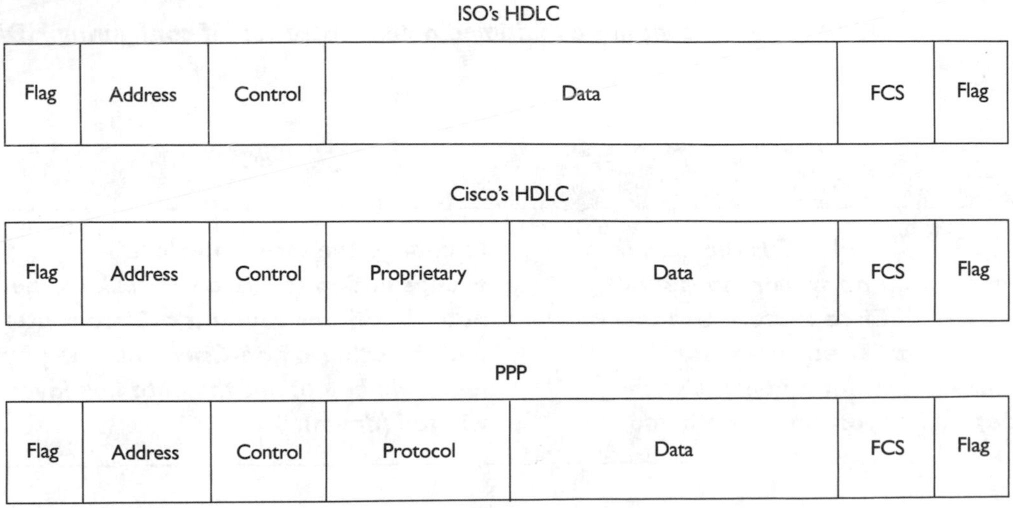

ISO's HDLC

Flag	Address	Control	Data	FCS	Flag

Cisco's HDLC

Flag	Address	Control	Proprietary	Data	FCS	Flag

PPP

Flag	Address	Control	Protocol	Data	FCS	Flag

Configuring HDLC

As mentioned in the preceding section, the default encapsulation on Cisco's synchronous serial interfaces is HDLC. You need to use the following configuration only if you changed the data link layer protocol to something else and then need to set it back to HDLC:

```
Router(config)# interface serial [slot_#/]port_#
Router(config-if)# encapsulation hdlc
```

Notice that you must be in the serial interface to change its data link layer encapsulation. If you had a different encapsulation configured on the serial interface, executing the preceding command would set the frame format to HDLC. Note that the other side must be set to Cisco's HDLC or the data link layer will fail on the interface.

After you have configured HDLC, use the **show interfaces** command to view the data link layer encapsulation:

```
Router# show interfaces serial 1
Serial1 is up, line protocol is up
  Hardware is MCI Serial
  Internet address is 192.168.2.2 255.255.255.0
  MTU 1500 bytes, BW 1544 Kbit, DLY 20000 usec, rely 255/255, load 1/255
  Encapsulation HDLC, loopback not set, keepalive set (10 sec)
  Last input 0:00:02, output 0:00:00, output hang never
  Last clearing of "show interface" counters never
  Output queue 0/40, 0 drops; input queue 0/75, 0 drops
<--output omitted-->
```

Notice in this example that the physical and data link layers are up and that the encapsulation is set to HDLC (`Encapsulation HDLC`).

15.01. The CD contains a multimedia demonstration of configuring HDLC on a router.

HDLC is the default encapsulation on synchronous serial interfaces of Cisco routers. Use the `show interfaces` command to see the encapsulation type. Use the `encapsulation hdlc` command to change the serial interface's encapsulation to Cisco's HDLC. Please note that if one router is a Cisco router and the other a non-Cisco one, the physical layer will be up, but the data link layer will fail (down).

CERTIFICATION OBJECTIVE 15.03

PPP

Where Cisco's HDLC is a proprietary protocol, PPP (the Point-to-Point Protocol) is based on a standard, defined in RFCs including 1332, 1661, and 2153. PPP works with asynchronous and synchronous serial interfaces as well as High-Speed Serial Interfaces (HSSI) and ISDN interfaces (BRI and PRI). The following sections offer an overview of PPP and how to configure PPP, including authentication.

PPP Components

PPP has many more features than HDLC. Like HDLC, PPP defines a frame type and how two PPP devices communicate with each other, including the multiplexing of network and data link layer protocols across the same link. However, PPP also

- Performs dynamic configuration of links
- Allows for authentication
- Compresses packet headers
- Tests the quality of links
- Performs error detection
- Allows multiple PPP physical connections to be bound together as a single logical connection

PPP has three main components:

- Frame format
- LCP (Link Control Protocol)
- NCP (Network Control Protocol)

Memorize the preceding list of features of PPP.

Each of these three components plays an important role in the setup, configuration, and transfer of information across a PPP connection. The following sections cover these components.

Frame Type

The first component of PPP is the frame type that it uses. The frame type defines how network layer packets are encapsulated in a PPP frame as well as the format of the PPP frame. PPP is typically used for serial WAN connections because of its open-standard character. It works on both asynchronous (modem) and synchronous (ISDN, point-to-point, and HSSI) connections. If you are dialing up to your ISP, you'll be using the PPP protocol. PPP's frame format is based on ISO's HDLC, as you can see in earlier Figure 15-5. The main difference is that the PPP frame has a protocol field, which defines the protocol of the network layer data that is encapsulated.

LCP and NCP

The second and third components of PPP are LCP and NCP. LCP, defined in RFCs 1548 and 1570, has as its primary responsibility to establish, configure, authenticate, and test a PPP connection. It handles all of the up-front work in setting up a connection. Here are some of the things that LCP will negotiate when setting up a PPP connection:

- Authentication method used (PAP or CHAP), if any
- Compression algorithm used (Stacker or Predictor), if any
- Callback phone number to use, if defined
- Multilink: other physical connections to use, if configured

There are three steps that LCP and NCP go through in order to establish a PPP connection:

1. Link establishment (LCP)
2. Authentication (LCP)
3. Protocol negotiation (NCP)

The first step is the link establishment phase. In this step, LCP negotiates the PPP parameters that are to be used for the connection, which may include the authentication method and compression algorithms. If authentication has been configured, the authentication type is negotiated. This can either be PAP or CHAP. These are discussed later, in the section "PPP Authentication." If authentication is configured and there is a match on the authentication type on both sides, then authentication is performed in the second step. If this is successful, NCP, in the third step, will negotiate the upper-layer protocols, which can include network layer protocols such as IP and IPX as well as data link layer protocols (bridged traffic, like Ethernet, and Cisco's CDP) that will be transmitted across the PPP link.

LCP is responsible for negotiating and maintaining a PPP connection, including any optional authentication. NCP is responsible for negotiating upper-layer protocols that will be carried across the PPP connection.

NCP defines the process for how the two PPP peers negotiate which network layer protocols, such as IP and IPX, will be used across the PPP connection. Once LCP and NCP perform their negotiation and the connection has been authenticated (if this has been defined), the data link layer will come up.

Once a connection is enabled, LCP uses error detection to monitor dropped data on the connection as well as loops at the data link layer. The Quality and Magic Numbers protocol is used by LCP to ensure that the connection remains reliable.

Configuring PPP

The configuration of PPP is as simple as that of HDLC. To specify that PPP is to be used on a WAN interface, use the following configuration:

```
Router(config)# interface type [slot_#]port_#
Router(config-if)# encapsulation ppp
```

As you can see, you need to specify the **ppp** parameter only in the **encapsulation** *Interface Subconfiguration* mode command. With the exception of authentication, other PPP options are not discussed in this book. These configuration commands are covered on Cisco's CCNP Remote Access exam.

15.02. The CD contains a multimedia demonstration of configuring PPP on a router.

Troubleshooting PPP

Once you have configured PPP on your router's interface, you can verify the status of the interface with the **show interfaces** command:

```
Router# show interfaces serial 0
Serial0 is up, line protocol is up
  Hardware is MCI Serial
  Internet address is 192.168.1.2 255.255.255.0
  MTU 1500 bytes, BW 1544 Kbit, DLY 20000 usec, rely 255/255, load 1/255
```

```
  Encapsulation PPP, loopback not set, keepalive set (10 sec)
  lcp state = OPEN
  ncp ccp state = NOT NEGOTIATED   ncp ipcp state = OPEN
  ncp osicp state = NOT NEGOTIATED   ncp ipxcp state = NOT NEGOTIATED
  ncp xnscp state = NOT NEGOTIATED   ncp vinescp state = NOT NEGOTIATED
  ncp deccp state = NOT NEGOTIATED   ncp bridgecp state = NOT NEGOTIATED
  ncp atalkcp state = NOT NEGOTIATED   ncp lex state = NOT NEGOTIATED
  ncp cdp state = OPEN
  Last input 0:00:00, output 0:00:00, output hang never
  Last clearing of "show interface" counters never
<--output omitted-->
```

exam watch

If one side is configured for PPP and the other side is configured with a different encapsulation type (like HDLC), the physical layer will be up, but the data link layer will be down.

In the fifth line of output, you can see that the encapsulation is set to PPP. Below this is the status of LCP (`lcp state = OPEN`). An `OPEN` state indicates that LCP has successfully negotiated its parameters and brought up the data link layer. The statuses of the protocols by NCP follow. In this example, only two protocols are running across this PPP connection: IP (`ncp icp state = OPEN`) and CDP (`ncp cdp state = OPEN`).

If you are having problems with the data link layer coming up when you've configured PPP, you can use the following **debug** command to troubleshoot the connection:

```
Router# debug ppp negotiation
PPP protocol negotiation debugging is on
Router# configure terminal
Enter configuration commands, one per line.  End with CNTL/Z.
Router(config)# interface serial 0
Router(config-if)# no shutdown
%LINK-3-UPDOWN: Interface Serial0, changed state to up
ppp: sending CONFREQ, type = 5 (CI_MAGICNUMBER), value = 4FEFE5
PPP Serial0: received config for type = 0x5 (MAGICNUMBER) value =
0x561036 acked
PPP Serial0: state = ACKSENT fsm_rconfack(0xC021): rcvd id 0x2
ppp: config ACK received, type = 5 (CI_MAGICNUMBER), value = 4FEFE5
ipcp: sending CONFREQ, type = 3 (CI_ADDRESS), Address = 192.168.2.1
ppp Serial0: Negotiate IP address: her address 192.168.2.2 (ACK)
ppp: ipcp_reqci: returning CONFACK.
ppp: cdp_reqci: returning CONFACK
PPP Serial0: state = ACKSENT fsm_rconfack(0x8021): rcvd id 0x2
ipcp: config ACK received, type = 3 (CI_ADDRESS), Address = 192.168.2.1
PPP Serial0: state = ACKSENT fsm_rconfack(0x8207): rcvd id 0x2
ppp: cdp_reqci: received CONFACK
%LINEPROTO-5-UPDOWN: Line protocol on Interface Serial0, changed state to up
```

In this example, **debug** was first enabled and then the serial interface was enabled. Notice that the two connected routers go through a negotiation process. They first verify their IP addresses, 192.168.2.1 and 192.168.2.2, to make sure they are not the same, and then they negotiate the protocols (`ipcp_reqci` and `cdp_reqci`). In this example, IP and CDP are negotiated and the data link layer comes up after the successful negotiation.

15.03. The CD contains a multimedia demonstration of troubleshooting PPP on a router.

exam watch

Use the `encapsulation ppp` command to change a serial interface's encapsulation to PPP. When you look at the output of the `show interfaces` command, any protocol listed as "`OPEN`" has been negotiated correctly. If you are having problems with the LCP negotiation, use the `debug ppp negotiation` command.

PPP Authentication

PPP, unlike HDLC, supports device authentication. You have two methods to choose from to implement authentication: the PPP Authentication Protocol (PAP) and the Challenge Handshake Authentication Protocol (CHAP). Both of these authentication methods are defined in RFC 1334; RFC 1994 replaces the CHAP component of RFC 1334. The authentication process is performed before the network and data link layer protocols are negotiated for the PPP connection by NCP. If the authentication fails, then the serial data link connection will not come up. Authentication is optional and adds very little overhead to the connection. As you will see in the following PAP and CHAP sections, the setup and troubleshooting of PAP and CHAP are easy.

PAP

Of the two PPP authentication protocols, PAP is the simplest, but the least secure. During the authentication phase, PAP goes through a two-way handshake process. In this process, the source sends its username (or hostname) and password, in clear text, to the destination. The destination compares this information with a list of locally stored usernames and passwords. If it finds a match, the destination sends back an *accept* message. If it doesn't find a match, it sends back a *reject* message. The top part of Figure 15-6 shows an example of PAP authentication.

FIGURE 15-6 PAP and CHAP authentication

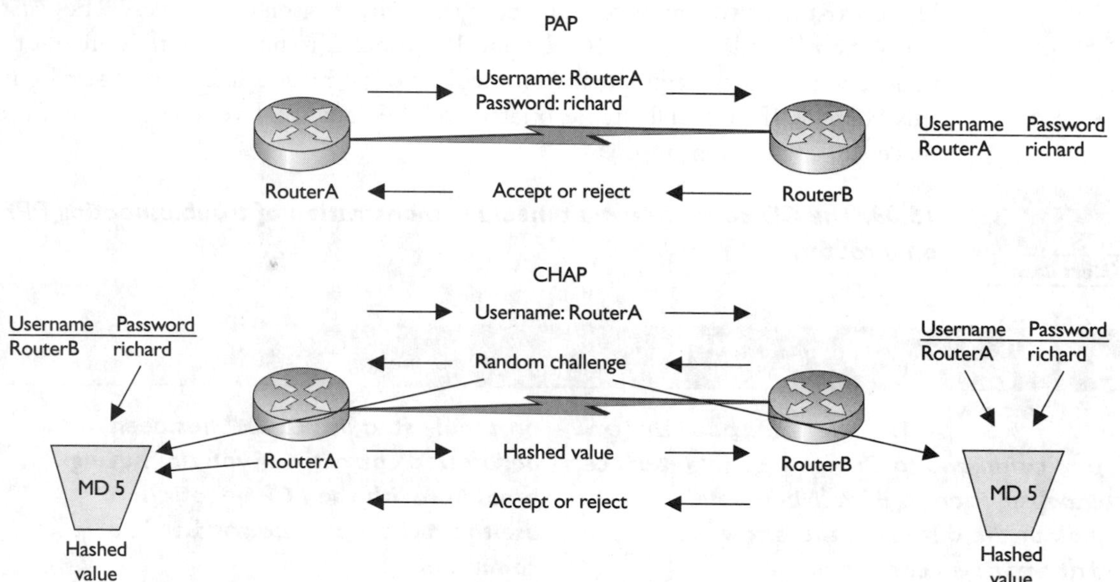

The configuration of PAP is straightforward. First, you need to determine which side will be the client side (sends the username and password) and which will be the server side (validates the username and password). To configure PAP for a PPP client, use this configuration:

```
Router(config)# interface type [slot_#]port_#
Router(config-if)# encapsulation ppp
Router(config-if)# ppp pap sent-username your_hostname
                         password password
```

The first thing you must do on the router's interface is to define the encapsulation type as PPP. Second, you must specify that PAP will be used for authentication and provide the username and password that will be used to perform the authentication on the server side. This is accomplished with the **ppp pap sent-username** command.

To configure the server side of a PPP PAP connection, use the following configuration:

```
Router(config)# hostname your_router's_hostname
Router(config)# username remote_hostname
                       password matching_password
Router(config)# interface type [slot_#/]port_#
Router(config-if)# encapsulation ppp
Router(config-if)# ppp authentication pap
```

The first thing you must do is to give your router a unique hostname. Second, you must list the remote host names and passwords these remote hosts will use when authenticating to your router. This is accomplished with the **username** command. Please note that the password you configure on this side must match the password on the remote side. On your router's WAN interface, you need to enable PPP with the **encapsulation ppp** command. Then, you can specify PAP authentication with the **ppp authentication pap** command.

The previous client and server code listings performs a one-way authentication—the client authenticates to the server and not vice versa. If you want to perform two-way authentication, where each side must authenticate to the other side, then configure both devices as PAP servers and clients.

15.04. The CD contains a multimedia demonstration of configuring PPP authentication using PAP on a router.

CHAP

One big problem with PAP is that it sends the username and password across the WAN connection in clear text. If someone is tapping into the WAN connection and eavesdropping on the PPP communication, they'll see the actual password that is being used. In other words, PAP is not a secure method of authentication.

CHAP, on the other hand, uses a one-way hash function based on the Message Digest 5 (MD5) hashing algorithm to hash the password. This hashed value is then sent across the wire. In this situation, the actual password is never sent. Anyone tapping the wire will not be able to reverse the hash to come up with the original password. This is why MD5 is referred to as a one-way function—it cannot be reverse-engineered.

CHAP uses a three-way handshake process to perform the authentication. The bottom part of Figure 15-6 shows the CHAP authentication process. First, the source sends its username (not its password) to the destination. The destination sends back a challenge, which is a random value generated by the destination. The challenge contains the following information:

- **Packet identifier** Set to 01 for a challenge, 02 for the reply to a challenge, 03 for allowing the PPP connection, and 04 for denying the connection
- **ID** A local sequence number assigned by the challenger to distinguish among multiple authentication processes
- **Random number** The random value used in the MD5 hash function
- **Router name** The name of the challenging router (the server), which is used by the source to find the appropriate password to use for authentication

Both sides then take the source's username, the matching password, and the challenge and run them through the MD5 hashing function. The source then takes the result of this function and sends it to the destination. The destination compares this value to the hashed output that it generated—if the two values match, then the password used by the source must have been the same as was used by the destination, and thus the destination will permit the connection.

The following configuration shows how to set up two-way CHAP authentication:

```
Router(config)# hostname your_router's_hostname
Router(config)# username remote_hostname
                      password matching_password
Router(config)# interface type [slot_#/]port_#
Router(config-if)# encapsulation ppp
Router(config-if)# ppp authentication chap
```

Notice that this is the same configuration as used with PPP PAP, with the exception of the omission of the sent username. The only difference is that the **chap** parameter is specified in the **ppp authentication** command.

Actually, here is the full syntax of the PPP authentication command:

```
Router(config-if)# ppp authentication
                      chap|pap|chap pap|pap chap
```

If you specify **pap chap** or **chap pap**, the router will negotiate both authentication parameters in the order that you specified them. For example, if you configure **chap pap**, your router will first try to negotiate CHAP; if this fails, then it will negotiate PAP.

15.05. The CD contains a multimedia demonstration of configuring PPP authentication using CHAP on a router.

Troubleshooting Authentication

To determine if authentication was successful, use the **show interfaces** command:

```
Router# show interfaces serial 0
Serial0 is up, line protocol is down
  Hardware is MCI Serial
  Internet address is 192.168.1.2 255.255.255.0
  MTU 1500 bytes, BW 1544 Kbit, DLY 20000 usec, rely 254/255, load 1/255
  Encapsulation PPP, loopback not set, keepalive set (10 sec)
  lcp state = ACKRCVD
  ncp ccp state = NOT NEGOTIATED   ncp ipcp state = CLOSED
  ncp osicp state = NOT NEGOTIATED   ncp ipxcp state = NOT NEGOTIATED
```

```
  ncp xnscp state = NOT NEGOTIATED   ncp vinescp state = NOT NEGOTIATED
  ncp deccp state = NOT NEGOTIATED   ncp bridgecp state = NOT NEGOTIATED
  ncp atalkcp state = NOT NEGOTIATED   ncp lex state = NOT NEGOTIATED
  ncp cdp state = CLOSED
  Last input 0:00:01, output 0:00:01, output hang never
<--output omitted-->
```

> **Remember how to use the *show interfaces* command when troubleshooting PPP connections.**

Notice the `lcp state` in this example: it's not `OPEN`. Also, notice the states for IP and CDP: `CLOSED`. These things indicates that there is something wrong with the LCP setup process. In this example, the CHAP passwords on the two routers didn't match.

Of course, looking at the preceding output, you don't really know that this was an authentication problem. To determine this, use the **`debug ppp authentication`** command. Here's an example of the use of this command with two-way CHAP authentication:

```
RouterA# debug ppp authentication
%LINK-3-UPDOWN: Interface Serial0, changed state to up
Se0 PPP: Treating connection as a dedicated line
Se0 PPP: Phase is AUTHENTICATING, by both
Se0 CHAP: O CHALLENGE id 2 len 28 from "RouterA"
Se0 CHAP: I CHALLENGE id 3 len 28 from "RouterB"
Se0 CHAP: O RESPONSE id 3 len 28 from "RouterA"
Se0 CHAP: I RESPONSE id 2 len 28 from "RouterB"
Se0 CHAP: O SUCCESS id 2 len 4
Se0 CHAP: I SUCCESS id 3 len 4
%LINEPROTO-5-UPDOWN: Line protocol on Interface Serial0, changed state to up
```

In this example, notice that both routers—RouterA and RouterB—are using CHAP for authentication. Both routers send a *CHALLENGE*, and both receive a corresponding *RESPONSE*. Notice the `I` and `O` following `Se0 CHAP:` This indicates the direction of the CHAP message. `I` is for in and `O` is for out. Following this is the status of the hashed passwords: `SUCCESS`. And last, you can see the data link layer coming up for the serial interface.

Here's an example of a router using PAP with two-way authentication:

```
RouterA# debug ppp authentication
%LINK-3-UPDOWN: Interface Serial0, changed state to up
Se0 PPP: Treating connection as a dedicated line
Se0 PPP: Phase is AUTHENTICATING, by both
Se0 PAP: O AUTH-REQ id 2 len 18 from "RouterA"
Se0 PAP: I AUTH-REQ id 3 len 18 from "RouterB"
```

```
Se0 PAP: Authenticating peer RouterB
Se0 PAP: O AUTH-ACK id 2 len 5
Se0 PAP: I AUTH-ACK id 3 len 5
%LINEPROTO-5-UPDOWN: Line protocol on Interface Serial0, changed state to up
```

In this example, notice that the authentication messages are different. The AUTH-REQ shows the server requesting the authentication from a router, and the AUTH-ACK acknowledges the successful password matching by a router. Notice that since both routers are requesting authentication, both routers are set up in server mode for PAP.

exam watch

PAP authentication sends the username and password across the wire in clear text. CHAP doesn't send the password in clear text—instead, a hashed value from the MD5 algorithm is sent. PAP uses a two-way handshake, while CHAP uses a three-way handshake. Use the `ppp authentication` command to specify which PPP authentication method to use. The `username` command allows you to build a local authentication table, which lists the remote names and passwords to use for authentication. The `debug ppp authentication` command can help you troubleshoot PPP problems—be familiar with the output of this command.

15.06. The CD contains a multimedia demonstration of troubleshooting PPP authentication on a router.

EXERCISE 15-1

Configuring PPP

These last few sections dealt with the configuration of PPP on IOS routers. This exercise will help you reinforce this material by configuring PPP and authentication. You'll perform this lab using Boson's NetSim simulator. After starting up the simulator, click the *LabNavigator* button. Next, double-click *Exercise 15-1* and click the *Load Lab* button. This will load the lab configuration based on Chapter 5's and 7's exercises.

1. Check network connectivity between the two routers.

   At the top of the simulator in the menu bar, click the *eRouters* icon and choose *2600*. From the 2600 router, verify the status of the serial interface:

show interface s0. Make sure the encapsulation is HDLC. From the 2600 router, ping the 2500: **ping 192.168.2.2**. The ping should be successful.

2. On the 2600 router, make sure its hostname is 2600. On the 2500 router, make sure its hostname is 2500.

   At the top of the simulator in the menu bar, click the *eRouters* icon and choose *2600*. On the 2600, examine the prompt. If the name of the router isn't *2600*, change it: **hostname 2600**. At the top of the simulator in the menu bar, click the *eRouters* icon and choose *2500*. On the 2500, examine the prompt. If the name of the router isn't *2500*, change it: **hostname 2500**.

3. On the 2600 router, set up PPP as the encapsulation on the `serial0` interface.

   At the top of the simulator in the menu bar, click the *eRouters* icon and choose *2600*. On the 2600, enter the serial interface: **configure terminal** and **interface serial 0**. Set up PPP as the data link frame type: **encapsulation ppp** and **end**. View the status of the interface: **show interface serial 0**. The physical layer should be up and the data link layer should be down—the 2500 still has HDLC configured. Also, examine the output of the **show** command to verify that the encapsulation is PPP.

4. On the 25000 router, set up PPP as the encapsulation on the `serial0` interface.

   At the top of the simulator in the menu bar, click the *eRouters* icon and choose *2500*. On the 2500, enter the serial interface: **configure terminal** and **interface serial 0**. Set up PPP as the data link frame type: **encapsulation ppp** and **end**. View the status of the interface: **show interface serial 0**. The physical *and* data link layers should be up (this should also be true on the 2600 router). Also check to make sure the encapsulation is PPP.

5. Set up PPP CHAP authentication on the 2600. Use a password of *richard*. Test the authentication.

   At the top of the simulator in the menu bar, click the *eRouters* icon and choose *2600*. Access *Configuration* mode: **configure terminal**. On the 2600, set up your username and password: **username 2500 password richard**. Enter the serial interface: **interface serial 0**. Set the authentication to CHAP: **ppp authentication chap**. Shut down the interface: **shutdown**. Bring the interface back up: **no shutdown**. Exit *Configuration* mode: **end**. Examine the status of the interface: **show interface serial 0**. The data link layer should be down, and the LCP should be `ACKRCVD`. Please note that you don't really need to bring the interface down and back up, because after a period of time, LCP will notice that authentication configuration and will perform it.

6. Set up PPP CHAP authentication on the 2500. Use a password of *richard*. Test the authentication. Test the connection.

   At the top of the simulator in the menu bar, click the *eRouters* icon and choose *2500*. Access *Configuration* mode: **`configure terminal`**. On the 2500, set up your username and password: **`username 2600 password richard`**. Enter the serial interface: **`interface serial 0`**. Set the authentication to CHAP: **`ppp authentication chap`**. Shut down the interface: **`shutdown`**. Bring the interface back up: **`no shutdown`**. Exit *Configuration* mode: **`end`**. Examine the status of the interface: **`show interface serial 0`**. The data link layer should come up and the LCP should be `OPEN`. IP and CDP should be the two protocols in an `OPEN` state. Ping the 2600: **`ping 192.168.2.1`**. The ping should be successful.

EXERCISE 15-2

Basic PPP Troubleshooting

This chapter dealt with HDLC and PPP. This exercise is a troubleshooting exercise and differs from the exercise you performed earlier in this chapter. In that exercise, you set up a PPP CHAP connection between the 2500 and 2600 routers. In this exercise, the network is already configured; however, there are three problems in this network you'll need to find and fix in order for it to operate correctly. All of these problems deal with connectivity between the 2500 and 2600 routers. You'll perform this exercise using Boson's NetSim simulator. You can find a picture of the network diagram for Boson's NetSim simulator in the Introduction of this book. The addressing scheme is the same. After starting up the simulator, click the *LabNavigator* button. Next, double-click *Exercise 15-2* and click the *Load Lab* button. This will load the lab configuration based on Chapter 5 and 7's exercises.

Let's start with your problem: the PPP data link layer between the 2500 and 2600 won't come up. Your task is to figure out what the three problems are and fix them. I recommend that you try this troubleshooting process on your own at first; if you experience difficulties, return to the steps and solutions provided here.

1. Examine the status of the serial interface on the 2600.

   At the top of the simulator in the menu bar, click the *eRouters* icon and choose *2600*. Examine `serial 0`: **`show interfaces serial 0`**. Note that the interface is *down* and *down*. This indicates a physical layer problem.

2. Check the status of `serial 0` on the 2500.

   At the top of the simulator in the menu bar, click the *eRouters* icon and choose *2500*. Examine the status of the interface: **`show interfaces serial 0`**. Notice that the interface is `administratively down`. Activate the interface: **`configure terminal`**, **`interface serial 0`**, **`no shutdown`**, and **`end`**. Examine the status of the interface: **`show interfaces serial 0`**. Notice that the status of the interface is `up` and `down`, indicating that there is a problem with the data link layer. Notice that the encapsulation, though, is set to PPP.

3. Check the 2600's serial encapsulation and the rest of its configuration.

   Examine the status of the interface: **`show interfaces serial 0`**. Notice that the status of the interface is `up` and `down`, indicating that there is a problem with the data link layer. Notice that the encapsulation, though, is set to PPP. Since both sides are set to PPP, there must be an authentication problem. Examine the 2600's active configuration: **`show running-config`**. CHAP is configured for authentication on `serial 0`. Notice, though, that the **`username`** has the 2600's, and not the 2500's. Fix this by doing the following: **`configure terminal`**, **`no username 2600 password cisco`**, **`username 2500 password cisco`**, and **`end`**. Reexamine the router's configuration: **`show running-config`**. Examine the status of the interface: **`show interfaces serial 0`**. The data link layer is still `down`, so there must be a problem on the 2500 router.

4. Access the 2500 router and determine the PPP problem.

   At the top of the simulator in the menu bar, click the *eRouters* icon and choose *2500*. Examine the active configuration: **`show running-config`**. The **`username`** command is correct, with the 2600's hostname and a password of *cisco*. However, there is a problem with the PPP authentication method on the serial interface: it's set to PAP. Fix this problem: **`configure terminal`**, **`interface serial 0`**, **`ppp authentication chap`**. Bounce the interface: **`shutdown`**, **`no shutdown`**, and **`end`**. Reexamine the router's configuration: **`show running-config`**. Examine the status of the interface: **`show interfaces serial 0`**. The data link layer should now be `up`.

5. Now test connectivity between the 2600 and 2500.

   At the top of the simulator in the menu bar, click the *eRouters* icon and choose *2600*. Test connectivity to the 2500: **ping 192.168.2.2**. The ping should be successful. If you want to allow connectivity for all devices, you'll need to add a static route on both the 2500 (to reach 192.168.1.0/24) and the 2600 (to reach 192.168.3.0/24).

Now you should be more comfortable with configuring PPP on a router.

CERTIFICATION SUMMARY

One of the major factors in choosing a WAN service is cost. The CPE is your WAN equipment. The demarcation point is the point where the carrier's responsibility for the circuit ends. The local loop is the connection from the demarcation point to the carrier's WAN switching equipment.

There are four main WAN connection categories. Leased lines include dedicated circuits, which are useful for short connections where you have constant traffic and need guaranteed bandwidth. Circuit-switched connections provide dialup capabilities, as are needed for analog modems and ISDN. These connections are mostly used for backup of primary connections and for an additional bandwidth boost. Packet-switched connections include Frame Relay and X.25. They are used to connect multiple sites together at a reasonable cost. If you need guaranteed bandwidth or need to carry multiple services, cell-switched services are a better solution; they include ATM and SMDS.

Cisco synchronous serial interfaces support DB-60 and DB-26 connectors. The default encapsulation on these interfaces is Cisco's HDLC. Cisco's HDLC and ISO's HDLC are not compatible with each other. Use the **encapsulation hdlc** command to change an interfaces encapsulation to Cisco's HDLC. The **show interfaces** command displays the data link layer encapsulation for a serial interface.

PPP is one of the most commonly used data link encapsulations for serial interfaces. It is an open standard. It defines three things: frame type, LCP, and NCP. When building a PPP connection, LCP takes place first, then authentication, and last NCP. LCP is responsible for negotiating parameters, setting up, and maintaining connections, which includes authentication, compression, link quality, error detection, multiplexing network layer protocols, and multilink. NCP handles the negotiation of the upper-layer protocols that the PPP connection will transport. To set up PPP as an encapsulation type on your serial interface, use the **encapsulation ppp** command. Use the **debug ppp negotiation** command to troubleshoot LCP and NCP problems.

There are two forms of PPP authentication: PAP and CHAP. PAP sends the password across the wire in clear text, while CHAP sends a hashed output value from the MD5 hash algorithm—the password is not sent across the connection. PAP goes through a two-way handshake, while CHAP goes through a three-way handshake. Authentication is optional but can be configured with the **ppp authentication pap | chap** *Interface* command. To build a local authentication table with usernames and passwords, use the **username** command. If you have authentication problems, troubleshoot them with the **debug ppp authentication** command.

TWO-MINUTE DRILL

Wide Area Networking Overview

- The CPE is your equipment. The demarcation point is the point where the carrier's responsibility ends. The local loop is the connection from the demarcation point to the carrier's equipment.
- Leased lines are dedicated circuits. Circuit-switched connections use analog modems or ISDN for dialup connections. Packet-switched services, such as ATM, Frame Relay, and X.25, use VCs for transmitting data. Of these, leased lines are the most costly. Packet-switched services are used when you need to connect a router to multiple destinations, but the router only has a single serial interface.
- Serial cables have either a DB-60 or DB-26 connector that connects to the serial interface of your Cisco router. The other end, which connects to the DCE device, is based on one of these standards: EIA/TIA-232, EIA/TIA-449, EIA/TIA-530, V.35, and X.21.

HDLC

- ISO's HDLC and Cisco's HDLC are not compatible. Cisco's frame format has a proprietary field that allows for the transport of multiple protocols. Cisco's HDLC is the default encapsulation on synchronous serial interfaces.
- To configure this frame format on an interface, use this command: **`encapsulation hdlc`**. Use the **`show interfaces`** command to verify your encapsulation.

PPP

- PPP is an open standard that provides dynamic configuration of links, authentication, error detection, compression, and multiple links.
- LCP sets up, configures, and transfers information across a PPP connection. NCP negotiates the data link and network protocols that will be transported across this link. The PPP frame format is based on ISO's HDLC.
- Use this interface command to specify PPP: **`encapsulation ppp`**. Use the **`show interfaces`** command to view the PPP status. `OPEN` indicates successful negotiation, and `CLOSED` indicates a problem. Use the **`debug ppp negotiation`** command for detailed troubleshooting of LCP and NCP.

- PAP uses a two-way handshake and sends the password across in clear text. CHAP uses a three-way handshake and sends a hashed value, which is created by MD5 by inputting a challenge, the hostname, and the password. To set up authentication, use the **ppp authentication chap|pap** command. Use the **debug ppp authentication** command to troubleshoot. CHALLENGE, RESPONSE, and SUCCESS messages are from CHAP, and AUTH-REQ and AUTH-ACK are from PAP.

SELF TEST

The following Self Test questions will help you measure your understanding of the material presented in this chapter. Read all the choices carefully, as there may be more than one correct answer. Choose all correct answers for each question.

Wide Area Networking Overview

1. The ________ is your network equipment, which includes the DCE (e.g., a modem) and the DTE (e.g., a router).
   A. Demarcation point
   B. Carrier switch
   C. Local loop
   D. CPE
2. The __________ is the point where the carrier's responsibility ends and yours begins.
   A. Local loop
   B. Demarcation point
   C. CPE
   D. Toll network
3. Which of the following is the most expensive type of WAN connection?
   A. Dedicated circuit connection
   B. Circuit-switched connection
   C. Packet-switched connection
4. Which of the following WAN categories does ISDN fall under?
   A. Dedicated circuit connection
   B. Circuit-switched connection
   C. Packet-switched connection
5. Which interface type is used to connect to the serial interface of a router?
   A. EIA/TIA-232
   B. V.35
   C. DB-60
   D. X.21

HDLC

6. Which frame field is different between ISO HDLC and Cisco's HDLC?
   A. Address
   B. Control
   C. Flag
   D. Proprietary
7. The default encapsulation on a synchronous serial interface is _________.
   A. HDLC
   B. PPP
   C. Neither HDLC nor PPP
8. Enter the router command to set the frame type of a serial interface to HDLC: _________.

PPP

9. PPP can do all of the following except ___________.
   A. Authentication
   B. Compression
   C. Quality of Service
   D. None of these
10. _________ negotiates the data link and network layer protocols that will traverse a PPP connection.
    A. LCP
    B. NCP
    C. CDP
    D. PAP
11. How many steps do LCP and NCP go through when setting up a connection?
    A. 1
    B. 2
    C. 3
    D. 4
12. Enter the router command to view the actual LCP and NCP setup process: __________.

13. When you have configured PPP on an interface and use the **`show interfaces`** command, what state indicates the successful negotiation of a network layer protocol?

   A. `ACK`

   B. `CHALLENGE`

   C. `CLOSED`

   D. `OPEN`

14. Which of the following is false concerning CHAP?

   A. It sends an encrypted password.

   B. It sends a challenge.

   C. It is more secure than PAP.

   D. It uses a three-way handshake.

15. When using debug with PAP, which of the following message types might you see?

   A. `AUTH-ACK`

   B. `SUCCESS`

   C. `CHALLENGE`

   D. None of these

A

SELF TEST ANSWERS

Wide Area Networking Overview

1. ☑ **D.** The CPE is your equipment that you use to connect to the WAN; it includes both DTE and DCE devices.
☒ **A** is the logical point where the carrier's responsibility stops and yours begins. **B** is the carrier's equipment that connects to the toll network. **C** is the connection between the demarcation point and the carrier's equipment.

2. ☑ **B.** The demarcation point is where the carrier's responsibility ends and yours begins.
☒ **A** is the connection between the demarcation point and the carrier's equipment. **C** is the equipment you use to connect to the WAN. **D** is the carrier's network used to connect your networks together.

3. ☑ **A.** The most expensive type of WAN connection is a leased line (dedicated circuit).
☒ **B** is the least expensive. **C** is somewhere between the cost of a leased line and a circuit-switched connection.

4. ☑ **B.** ISDN is a circuit-switched connection.
☒ **A** is a leased line. **C** includes ATM, Frame Relay, SMDS, and X.25.

5. ☑ **C.** The cable connected to the serial interface on a Cisco router uses either a DB-60 or DB-21 interface.
☒ **A**, **B**, and **D** are interfaces on the serial cable that connect to the DCE device, such as a modem or CSU/DSU.

HDLC

6. ☑ **D.** The proprietary field is unique between the Cisco HDLC frame format and ISO's.
☒ **A**, **B**, and **C** are in both frame formats.

7. ☑ **A.** HDLC is the default encapsulation on *synchronous* serial interfaces.
☒ **B** is not the default on any type of a serial interface. **C** incorrect is incorrect because it excludes HDLC.

8. ☑ **`encapsulation hdlc`**.

PPP

9. ☑ **C**. PPP does error detection and correction, but not Quality of Service.
☒ **A** and **B** are supported by PPP, and since there is an answer, **D** is incorrect.

10. ☑ **B**. NCP negotiates the data link and network layer protocols that will traverse a PPP connection.
☒ **A** sets up and monitors the PPP connection. **C** is a proprietary Cisco protocol that allows Cisco devices to share some basic information. **D** performs authentication for PPP.

11. ☑ **C**. LCP and NCP go through three steps: link establishment, authentication (optional), and protocol negotiation.

12. ☑ **`debug ppp negotiation`**.

13. ☑ **D**. `OPEN` indicates a successful negotiation of a network layer protocol in the **`show interfaces`** output.
☒ **A** is nonexistent. **B** shows up as a message type in the output of the **`debug ppp authentication`** command. **C** indicates an unsuccessful negotiation.

14. ☑ **A**. CHAP doesn't send the encrypted password—it sends a hashed value created from the MD5 algorithm.
☒ **B**, **C**, and **D** are true concerning CHAP.

15. ☑ **A**. `AUTH-ACK` is a PAP message from the output of the **`debug ppp authentication`** command.
☒ **B** and **C** are messages from CHAP authentication. **D** is incorrect because there is a correct answer.

16

Frame Relay

CERTIFICATION OBJECTIVES

16.01 Virtual Circuits (VCs)

16.02 Terminology and Operation

16.03 Frame Relay Configuration

16.04 Nonbroadcast Multiaccess

✓ Two-Minute Drill

Q&A Self Test

Chapter 15 introduced you to wide area networking and point-to-point connections using HDLC and PPP for a data link layer encapsulation. These protocols are common with leased lines and circuit-switched connections. This chapter introduces you to the next WAN topic: Frame Relay. Frame Relay is a data link layer packet-switching protocol that uses digital circuits and thus is virtually error-free. Therefore, it performs only error detection—it leaves error correction to an upper-layer protocol, such as TCP.

Frame Relay is actually a group of separate standards, including those from ITU-T and ANSI. Interestingly enough, Frame Relay defines only the interaction between the Frame Relay CPE and the Frame Relay carrier switch. The connection across the carrier's network is *not* defined by the Frame Relay standards. Most carriers, however, use ATM as a transport to move Frame Relay frames between different sites.

CERTIFICATION OBJECTIVE 16.01

Virtual Circuits (VCs)

Frame Relay is connection oriented: a connection must be established before information can be sent to a remote device. The connections used by Frame Relay are provided by virtual circuits (VCs). A VC is a logical connection between two devices; therefore, many of these VCs can exist on the same physical connection. The advantage that VCs have over leased lines is that they can provide full connectivity at a much lower price. VCs are also full-duplex: you can simultaneously send and receive on the same VC. Other packet- and cell-switching technologies, such as ATM, SMDS, and X.25, also use VCs. Most of the things covered in this section concerning VCs are true of Frame Relay as well as these other technologies.

Full-Meshed Design

As mentioned in the preceding paragraph, VCs are more cost effective than leased lines because they reduce the number of physical connections required to fully mesh your network, but still allowing a fully meshed topology.

Let's assume you have two choices for connecting four WAN devices together: leased lines and VCs. The top part of Figure 16-1 shows an example of connecting these devices using leased lines. Notice that to fully mesh this network (every device is connected to every other device), a total of six leased lines are required, including three serial interfaces on each router.

FIGURE 16-1 Leased lines and VCs

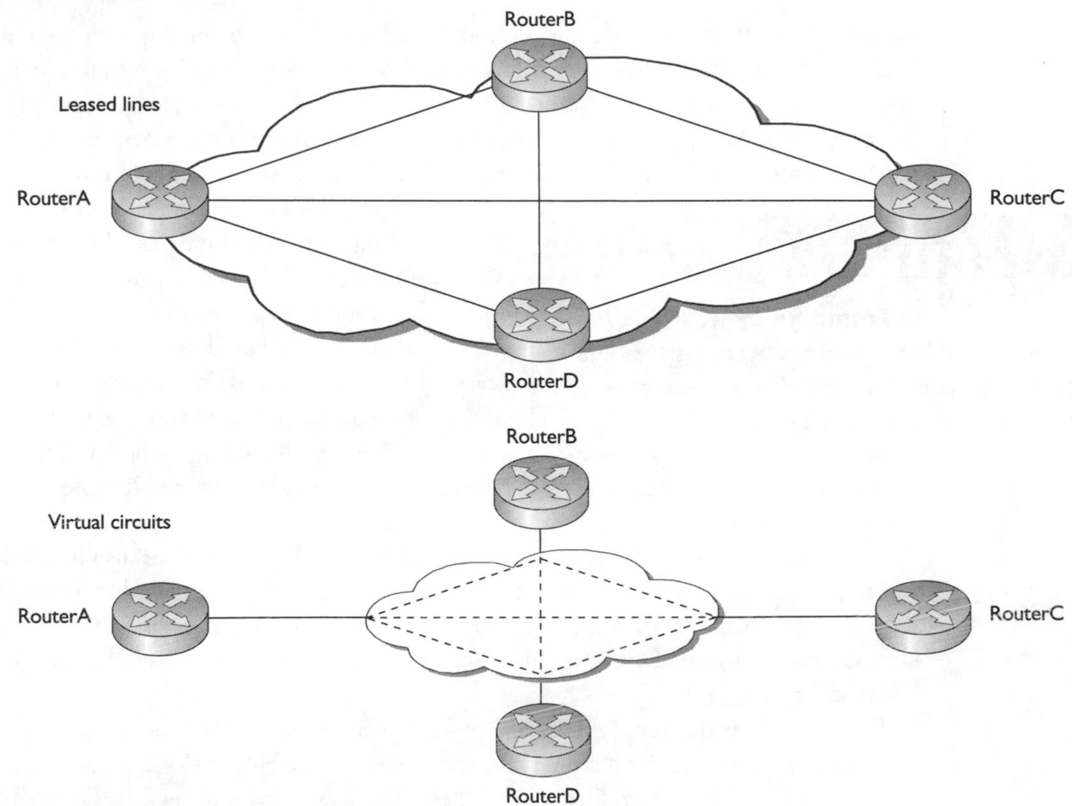

exam watch

Use this formula to figure out the number of connections needed to fully mesh a topology: (N*(N – 1))/2.

To figure out the number of connections required, you can use the following formula: (N*(N – 1))/2. In this formula, *N* is the number of devices you are connecting together. In our example, this was four devices, resulting in (4*(4 – 1))/2 = 6 leased lines. The more devices that you have, the more leased lines you need, as well as additional serial interfaces on each router. For instance, if you have ten routers you want to fully mesh, you would need a total of nine serial interfaces on each router and a total of 45 leased lines! If you were thinking of using a 1600, 1700, 2500, or even 2600 router, this would be unrealistic. Therefore, you would need a larger router, such as a 3600 or 7200, to handle all of these dedicated circuits. Imagine if you had 100 routers that you wanted to fully mesh: you would need 99 serial interfaces on each router and 4,950 leased lines! Not even a 7200 router can handle this!

Advantages of VCs

As you can see from the preceding section, leased lines have scalability problems. Frame Relay overcomes them by using virtual circuits. With VCs, you can have multiple logical circuits on the same physical connection, as is shown in the bottom part of Figure 16-1. When you use VCs, your router needs only a single serial interface connecting to the carrier. Across this physical connection, you'll use VCs to connect to your remote sites.

> **exam watch**
> ***Frame Relay with VCs is a good solution if your router has a single serial interface, but needs to connect to multiple WAN destinations.***

You can use the same formula described in the preceding section to figure out how many VCs you'll need to fully mesh your network. In our four-router example, you'd need 6 VCs. If you had 10 routers, you'd need 45 VCs; and if you had 100 routers, you'd need 4,950 VCs. One of the nice features of Frame Relay is that in all of these situations, you need only *one* serial interface to handle the VC connections. You could even use a smaller router to handle a lot of VC connections.

Actually, VCs use a process similar to what T1 and E1 leased lines use in sending information. With a T1, for instance, the physical layer T1 frame is broken up into 24 logical time slots, or channels, with 64Kbps of bandwidth each. Each of these time slots is referred to as a DS0, the smallest fixed amount of bandwidth in a channelized connection.

For example, you can have a carrier configure your T1 so that if you have six sites you want to connect to, you can have the carrier separate these time slots so that a certain number of time slots are redirected to each remote site, as is shown in Figure 16-2. In this example, the T1 has been split into five connections: Time slots 1–4 go to RemoteA, time slots 5–12 go to RemoteB, time slots 13–20 go to RemoteC, time slots 21–23 go to RemoteD, and time slot 24 goes to RemoteE.

As you can see from this example, this is somewhat similar to the use of VCs. However, breaking up a T1 or E1's time slots does have disadvantages. For instance, let's assume that the connection from the central site needs to send a constant rate of 128Kbps of data to RemoteE. You'll notice that the T1 was broken up and only one DS0, time slot 24, was assigned to this connection. Each DS0 has only 64Kbps worth of bandwidth. Therefore, unfortunately, this connection will become congested until traffic slows down to below 64Kbps. With this type of configuration, it is difficult to reconfigure the time slots of the T1, because you must also have the carrier involved. If your data rates change to remote sites, you'll need to reconfigure the time slots on your side to reflect the change as well as have the carrier reconfigure its side. With this process, adapting to data rate changes is a very slow and inflexible process. Even for slight data rate changes to remote sites, say, for example, a spike of 128Kbps to

FIGURE 16-2 Leased lines and time slots

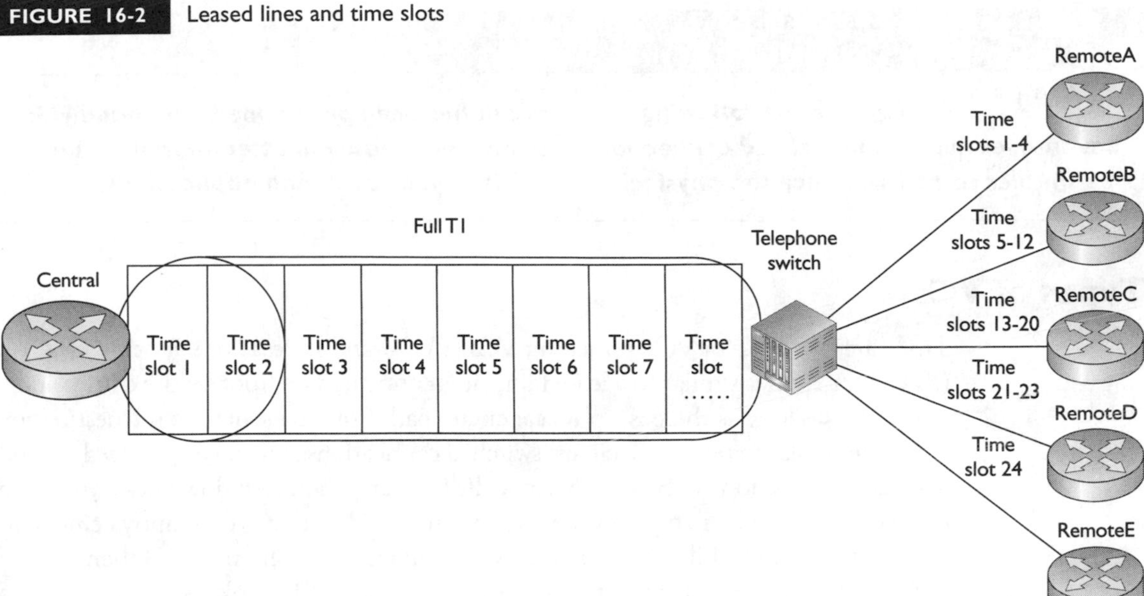

RemoteE, there will be a brief period of congestion. This is true *even if* the other time slots are empty—remember that these time slots are configured to have their traffic sent to a specific destination.

Frame Relay, using VCs, has an advantage over leased lines in this regard. VCs are *not* associated with any particular time slots on the channelized T1 connection. With Frame Relay, any time slot can be used to send traffic. This means that each VC to a destination has the potential to use the full bandwidth of the T1 connection, which provides you with much more flexibility. For example, if the RemoteE site has a brief bump in its traffic from 64Kbps to 128Kbps, and there is free bandwidth on the T1, the central router can use the free bandwidth on the T1 to accommodate the extra bandwidth required to get traffic to RemoteE.

Another advantage of Frame Relay is that it is much simpler to add new connections once the physical circuit has been provisioned. Let's use Figure 16-2 as an example. If these were leased-line connections, and you wanted to set up a separate leased line between RemoteA and RemoteB, it might take four–eight weeks for the carrier to install the new leased line! With Frame Relay and VCs, since these two routers already have a physical connection into the provider running Frame Relay, the carrier needs to add only a VC to its configuration to tie the two sites together—this can easily be done in a day or two. This fact provides a lot of flexibility to meet your network's requirements, especially if your traffic patterns change over time.

exam watch

VCs have the following advantages over a channelized connection: it's simpler to add VCs once the physical circuit has been provisioned, and bandwidth can be more easily allotted to match the needs of your users and applications.

Types of VCs

There are two types of VCs: *permanent* VCs *(PVCs)* and *switched* or *semipermanent* VCs *(SVCs)*. A PVC is similar to a leased line: it is configured up front by the carrier and remains up as long as there is a physical circuit path from the source to the destination. SVCs are similar to telephone circuit-switched connections: whenever you need to send data to a connection, an SVC is dynamically built and then torn down once your data has been sent. PVCs are typically used when you have data that is constantly being sent to a particular site, while SVCs are used when data is sent every now and then.

Cisco routers support both types of VCs. However, this book focuses on the configuration of PVCs for Frame Relay.

PVCs

A PVC is similar to a leased line, which is why it is referred to as a *permanent* VC. PVCs must be manually configured on each router and built on the carrier's switches before you can send any data. One disadvantage of PVCs is that they require a lot of manual configuration up front to establish the VC. Another disadvantage is that they aren't very flexible: if the PVC fails, there is no dynamic rebuilding of the PVC around the failure.

However, once you have a PVC configured, it will always be available, barring any failures between the source and destination. One of the biggest advantages that PVCs have over SVCs is that SVCs must be set up when you have data to send, a fact that introduces a small amount of delay before traffic can be sent to the destination. This is probably one of the main reasons that most people choose PVCs over SVCs for Frame Relay, considering that the cost is not too different between the two types.

SVCs

SVCs are similar to making a telephone call. For example, when you make a telephone call in the US, you need to dial a 7-, 10-, or 11-digit telephone number. This number is processed by the carrier's telephone switch, which uses its telephone routing table to bring up a circuit to the destination phone number. Once the circuit is built, the phone rings at the remote site, the destination person answers the phone, and *then* you can begin talking. Once you are done talking, you hang up the phone. This causes the carrier switch to tear down the circuit-switched connection.

SVCs use a similar process. Each SVC device is assigned a unique address, similar to a telephone number. In order to reach a destination device using an SVC, you'll need to know the destination device's address. In WAN environments, this is typically configured manually on your SVC device. Once your device knows the destination's address, it can forward the address to the carrier's SVC switch. The SVC switch then finds a path to the destination and builds a VC to it. Once the VC is built, the source and destination are notified about this, and both can start sending data across it. Once the source and destination are done sending data, they can signal their connected carrier switch to tear the connection down.

One advantage of SVCs is that they are temporary. Therefore, since you are using it only part of the time, the cost of an SVC is less than a PVC, since a PVC, even if you are not sending data across it, has to be sustained in the carrier's network. The problem with SVCs, however, is that the more you use them, the more they cost.

Compare this to making a long-distance telephone call where you are being billed for each minute—the more minutes you talk, the more expensive the connection becomes. At some point in time, it will be actually cheaper to use a fixed PVC than a dynamic SVC. SVCs are actually good for backup purposes—you might have a primary PVC to a site that costs X dollars a month and a backup SVC that costs you money only if you use it, and then that cost is based on how much you use it—perhaps based on the number of minutes used or the amount of traffic sent. If your primary PVC fails, the SVC is used only until the primary PVC is restored. In order to determine if you should be using an SVC or a PVC, you'll need to weigh in factors like the amount of use and the cost of a PVC versus that of an SVC given this level of use.

Another advantage of SVCs is that they are adaptable to changes in the network—if there is a failure of a physical link in the carrier's network, the SVC can be rebuilt across a redundant physical link inside the carrier's network.

The main disadvantages of SVCs are the initial setup and troubleshooting efforts associated with them as well as the time they take to establish. For example, in order to establish an SVC, you'll need to build a manual resolution table for each network layer protocol that is used between your router and the remote router. If you are running IP, IPX, and AppleTalk, you'll need to configure all three of these entries in your resolution table. Basically, your resolution table maps the remote's network layer address to its SVC address. Depending on the number of protocols that you are running and the number of sites that you are connecting to, this process can take a lot of time. When you experience problems with SVCs, they become more difficult to troubleshoot because of the extra configuration involved on your side as well as the routing table used on the carrier's side. Setting up PVCs is actually much easier. Plus, each time an SVC doesn't exist to a remote site, your router has to establish one, and it has to wait for the carrier switch to complete this process before your router can start sending its information to the destination.

exam watch

A PVC is similar to a dedicated leased line, while an SVC is similar to a circuit-switched connection, like ISDN. PVCs should be used when you have constant data being generated, while SVCs should be used when the data you have to send comes in small amounts and happens periodically.

Supported Serial Connections

A typical Frame Relay connection looks like that shown in Figure 16-3. As you can see in this example, serial cables connect from the router to the CSU/DSU and from the carrier switch to the CSU/DSU. The serial cables that you can use include the following: EIA/TIA-232, EIA/TIA-449, EIA/TIA-530, V.35, and X.25. The connection between the two CSU/DSUs is a channelized connection; it can be a fractional T1/E1 that has a single or multiple time slots, a full T1/E1 (a T1 has 24 time slots and an E1 has 30 usable time slots), or a DS3 (a T3 is clocked at 45Mbps and an E3 is clocked at 34Mbps).

FIGURE 16-3 Typical Frame Relay connection

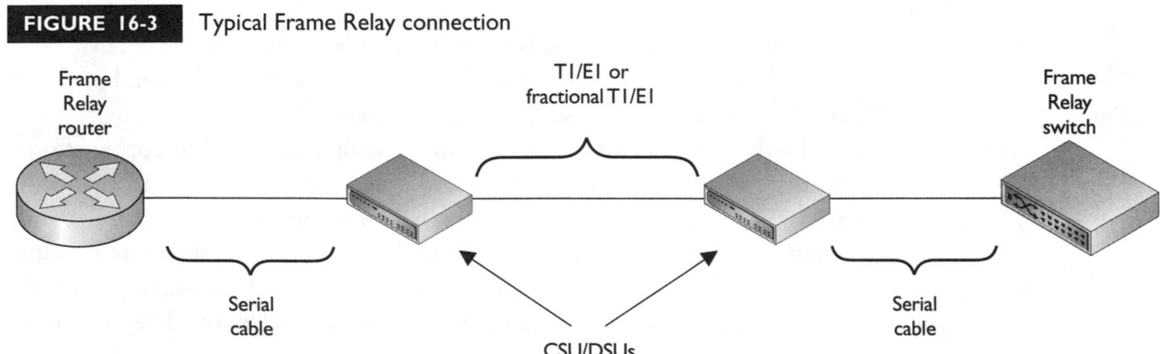

CERTIFICATION OBJECTIVE 16.02

Terminology and Operation

When compared to HDLC and PPP, Frame Relay is much more complex in operation, and many more terms are used to describe its components and operation. Table 16-1 contains an overview of these terms. Only the configuration of LMI is discussed in this book—the configuration of other parameters, such as B_C and B_E is beyond the scope of this book but is covered on the CCNP Remote Access exam. The following sections describe the operation of Frame Relay and cover these terms in more depth.

Remember the Frame Relay terms in Table 16-1.

TABLE 16-1 Common Frame Relay Terms

Term	Definition
LMI (local management interface)	This defines how the DTE (the router or other Frame Relay device) interacts with the DCE (the Frame Relay switch).
DLCI (data link connection identifier)	This value is used to uniquely identify each VC on a physical interface: it's the address of the VC. Using DCLIs, you can multiplex traffic for multiple destinations on a single physical interface. DLCIs are locally significant and can change on a segment-by-segment basis. In other words, the DLCI that your router uses to get to a remote destination might be 45, but the destination might be using 54 to return the traffic—and yet it's the *same* VC. The Frame Relay switch will do a translation between the DLCIs when it is switching frames between segments.
Access rate	This is the speed of the physical connection (such as a T1) between your router and the Frame Relay switch.
CIR (committed information rate)	This is the average data rate, measured over a fixed period of time, that the carrier guarantees for a VC.
B_C (committed burst rate)	This is the average data rate (over a period of a smaller fixed time than CIR) that a provider guarantees for a VC; in other words, it implies a smaller time period but a higher average than the CIR to allow for small bursts in traffic.
B_E (excessive burst rate)	This is the fastest data rate at which the provider will ever service the VC. Some carriers allow you to set this value to match the access rate.

TABLE 16-1 Common Frame Relay Terms *(continued)*

DE (discard eligibility)	This is used to mark a frame as low priority. You can do this manually, or the carrier will do this for a frame that is nonconforming to your traffic contract (exceeding CIR/B_C values).
Oversubscription	When you add up all of the CIRs of your VCs on an interface, they exceed the access rate of the interface: you are betting that all of your VCs will not run, simultaneously, at their traffic-contracted rates.
FECN (forward explicit congestion notification)	This value in the Frame Relay frame header is set by the carrier switch (typically) to indicate congestion inside the carrier network to the destination device at the end of the VC; the carrier may be doing this to your traffic as it is on its way to its destination.
BECN (backward explicit congestion notification)	This value is set by the destination DTE (Frame Relay device) in the header of the Frame Relay frame to indicate congestion (from the source to the destination) to the source of the Frame Relay frames (the source DTE, the router). Sometimes the carrier switches can generate BECN frames in the backward direction to the source to speed up the congestion notification process. The source can then adapt its rate on the VC appropriately.

LMI

LMI is used only locally, between the Frame Relay DTE (e.g., a router) and the Frame Relay DCE (e.g., a carrier switch), as is shown in Figure 16-4. In other words, LMI information originating on one Frame Relay DTE will *not* be propagated across the carrier network to a remote Frame Relay DTE: it is processed only between the Frame Relay DTEs and DCEs, which is why the word *local* is used in LMI. LMI is used for management purposes and allows two directly connected devices to share information about the status of VCs, as well as their configuration.

Three different standards are defined for LMI and its interaction with a Frame Relay DTE and DCE:

- ANSI's Annex D standard, T1.617
- ITU-T's Q.933 Annex A standard
- The *Gang of Four*, for the four companies that developed it: Cisco, DEC, StrataCom, and NorTel (Northern Telecom). This standard is commonly referred to as Cisco's LMI.

Because LMI is locally significant, each Frame Relay DTE in your network does not have to use the same LMI type. For example, Site 1 and Site 2, shown in Figure 16-4, might have a PVC connecting them together. The Site 1 router might be using ANSI for an LMI type, and the Site 2 router might be using the Q.933 LMI type. Even though they have a PVC connecting them, the LMI process is local and can therefore

FIGURE 16-4 LMI example

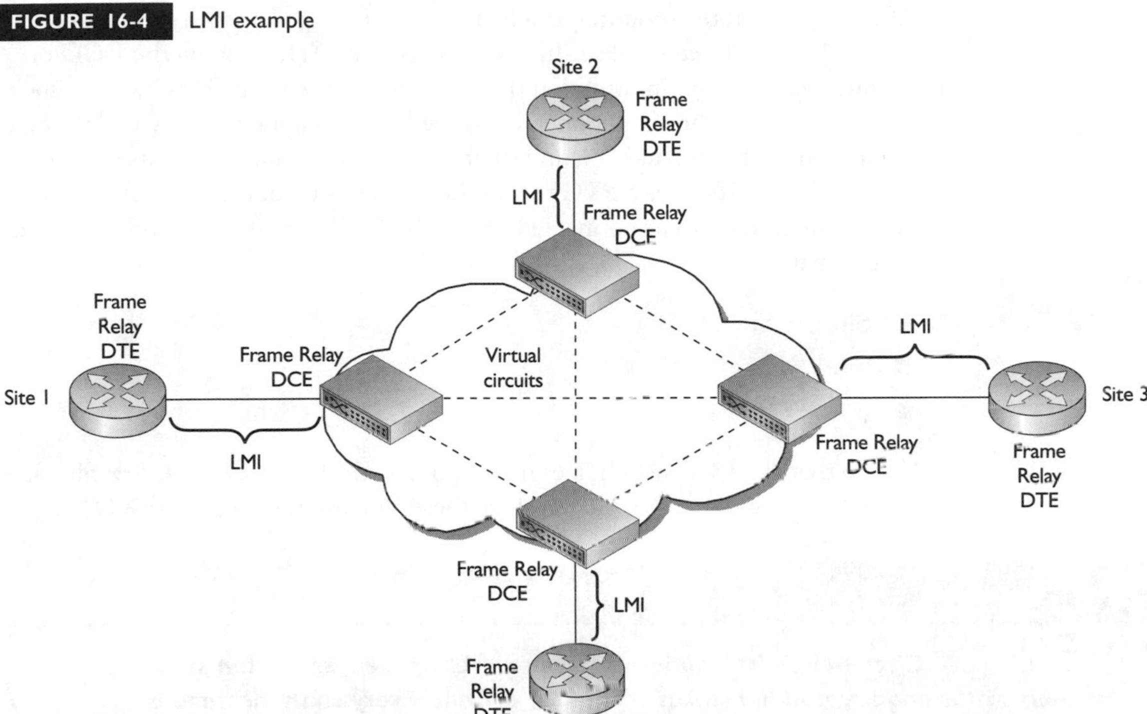

> **exam watch**
> ***LMI is local to the DTE and DCE and is not transmitted across the network. There are three LMI types: The Gang of Four (Cisco), ANSI's Annex D, and ITU-T's Q.933 Annex A.***

be different. Actually, the LMI type is typically dependent on the carrier and the switch that they are using. Most carrier switches support all three types, but some carriers don't. Likewise, those that do support all three might have standardized on a particular type. Cisco routers support all three LMI standards.

LMI's Functions

The main function of LMI is to allow the Frame Relay DTE and DCE to exchange status information about the VCs and themselves. To implement this function, the Frame Relay DTE sends an LMI *status enquiry* (query) message periodically to the attached Frame Relay DCE. Assuming that the DCE is turned on and the DCE is configured with the same LMI type, the DCE responds with a *status reply* message. These messages serve as a *keepalive* function, allowing the two devices to determine each other's state. Basically, the DTE is asking the switch "are you there?" and the switch responds "yes, I am." By default, only the DTE originates these keepalives; the DCE only responds.

After so many status enquiries, the Frame Relay DTE generates a special query message called a *full status update*. In this message, the DTE is asking the DCE for a full status update of all information that is related to the DTE. This includes such information as all of the VCs connected to the DTE, their addresses (DLCIs), their configurations (CIR, B_C, and B_E), and their statuses. For example, let's assume that Site 1 from Figure 16-4 has a PVC to all other remote sites and that it sends a full status update message to its connected DCE. The DCE responds with the following PVC information:

- Site1 → Site 2
- Site1 → Site 3
- Site1 → Site 4

Notice that the DCE switch does not respond with these VCs: Site 2 → Site 3, Site 3 → Site 4, and Site 2 → Site 4, since these VCs are not local to this DTE.

Cisco has default timers for their status enquiry and full status update messages. Status enquiry messages are sent every ten seconds, by default. Every sixth message is a full status update message.

LMI Standards

For the LMI communication to occur between the DTE and the DCE, the LMI information must use a VC, as must all other data. In order for the DTE and DCE to know that the Frame Relay frame contains LMI information, a reserved VC is used to share LMI information. The LMI type that you are using will determine the DLCI address that is used in the communication. Table 16-2 shows the DLCI addresses assigned to the three LMI types. DLCIs are discussed in more depth in the following section.

Memorize the DLCI numbers.

TABLE 16-2 LMI Addresses

LMI Type	DLCI #
ANSI Annex D	0
ITU-T Annex A	0
Gang of Four (Cisco)	1,023

DLCIs

Each VC has a unique *local* address, called a DLCI. This means that as a VC traverses various segments in a WAN, the DLCI numbers can be *different* for each segment. The carrier switches take care of converting a DLCI number from one segment to the number used on the next segment.

DLCI Example

Figure 16-5 shows an example of how DLCIs are used. In this example, there are three routers and three carrier switches. RouterA has a PVC to RouterB, and RouterA has another PVC to RouterC.

Let's take a closer look at the PVC between RouterA and RouterB. Starting from RouterA, the PVC traverses three physical links:

- RouterA → Switch 1 (DLCI 200)
- Switch 1 → Switch 2 (DLCI 200)
- Switch 2 → RouterB (DLCI 201)

FIGURE 16-5 DLCI addressing example

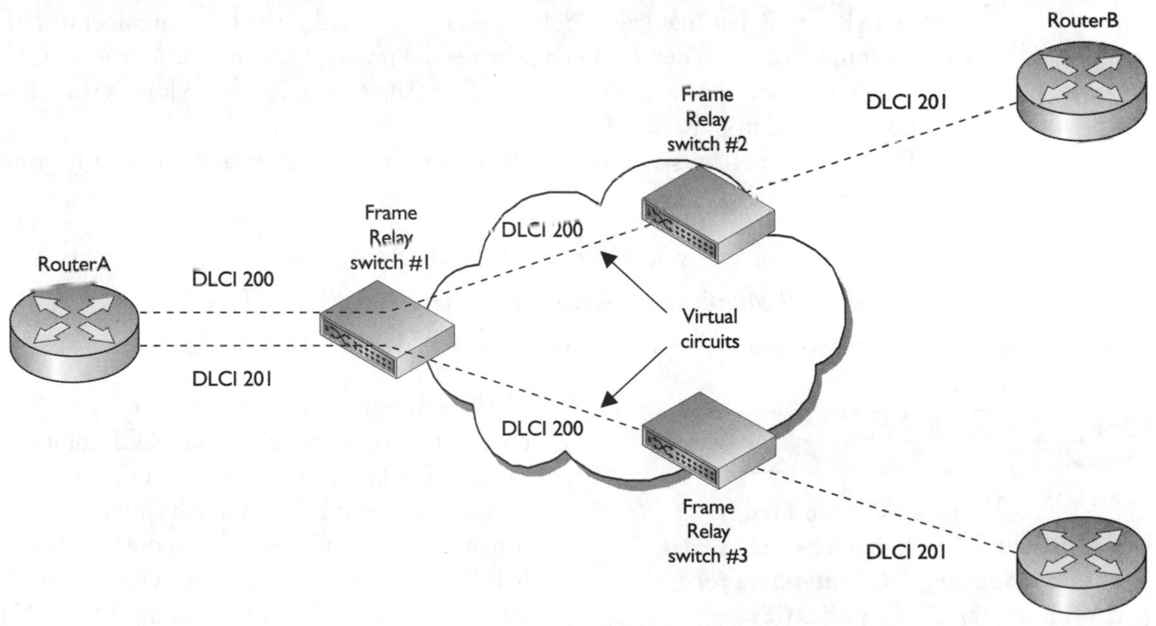

Note that DLCIs are locally significant: they need to be unique only on a segment-by-segment basis and do *not* need to be unique across the entire Frame Relay network. Given this statement, the DLCI number can change from segment to segment, and it is up to the carrier switch to change the DLCI in the frame header to the appropriate DLCI value for the next segment. This fact can be seen in this example, where the DTE segments have different DLCI values (200 and 201), but we're still dealing with the same PVC. Likewise, the DLCI numbers of 200 and 201 are used elsewhere in the network. What is important are the DLCIs on the same segment. For instance, RouterA has two PVCs to two different destinations. On the RouterA → Switch 1 connection, each of these PVCs needs a unique address value (200 and 201); however, these values do not have to be the same for each segment to the destination.

This can become confusing unless you look at the DLCI addressing from a device's and segment's perspective. As an example, if RouterA wants to send data to RouterB, it encapsulates it in a Frame Relay frame and puts a DLCI address of 200 in the header. When Switch 1 receives the frame, it looks at the DLCI address *and* the interface it was received on and compares these to its DLCI switching table. When it finds a match, the switch takes the DLCI number for the next segment (found in the same table entry), substitutes it into the frame header, and forwards the frame to the next device. In this case, the DLCI number remains the same (200). When Switch 2 receives the frame from Switch 1, it performs the same process and realizes it needs to forward the frame to RouterB, but that before doing this, it must change the DLCI number to 201 in the frame header. When RouterB receives the frame, it also examines the DLCI address in the frame header. When it sees 201 as the address, RouterB knows that the frame originated from RouterA.

This process, at first, seems confusing. However, to make it easier, look at it from the router's perspective:

- When RouterA wants to reach RouterB, RouterA uses DLCI 200.
- When RouterB wants to reach RouterA, RouterB uses DLCI 201.
- When RouterC wants to reach RouterA, RouterC uses DLCI 201.

DLCIs are locally significant. The carrier's switches take care of mapping DLCI numbers for a VC between DTEs and DCEs.

When the carrier creates a PVC for you between two sites, it assigns the DLCI number that you should use at each site to reach the other site. Certain DLCI numbers are reserved for management and control purposes, such as LMI's 0 and 1,023 values. Reserved DLCIs are 0–15 and 1,008–1,023. DLCI numbers from 16–1,007 are used for data connections.

Network and Service Interworking

As mentioned earlier in this chapter, Frame Relay is implemented between the Frame Relay DTE and the Frame Relay DCE. How the frame is carried across the Frame Relay carrier's network is not specified. In almost all situations, ATM is used as the transport. ATM, like Frame Relay, uses VCs. ATM, however, uses a different nomenclature in assigning an address to a VC. In ATM, there are two identifiers assigned to a VC: a virtual path identifier (VPI) and a virtual channel identifier (VCI). These two numbers serve the same purpose that a DLCI serves in Frame Relay. Like DLCIs, the VPI/VCI value is locally significant.

Remember the difference between Network and Service Interworking.

Two standards, FRF.5 and FRF.8, define how the frame and address conversion takes place:

- **FRF.5 (Network Interworking)** The two DTEs are Frame Relay and the carrier uses ATM as a transport.
- **FRF.8 (Service Interworking)** One DTE is a Frame Relay device and the other is an ATM device, and the carrier uses ATM as a transport.

Figure 16-6 shows an example of these two standards. FRF.5 defines how two Frame Relay devices can send frames back and forth across an ATM backbone, as is shown in Figure 16-6 between RouterA and RouterB. With FRF.5, the Frame Relay frame is

FIGURE 16-6 Network and service interworking example

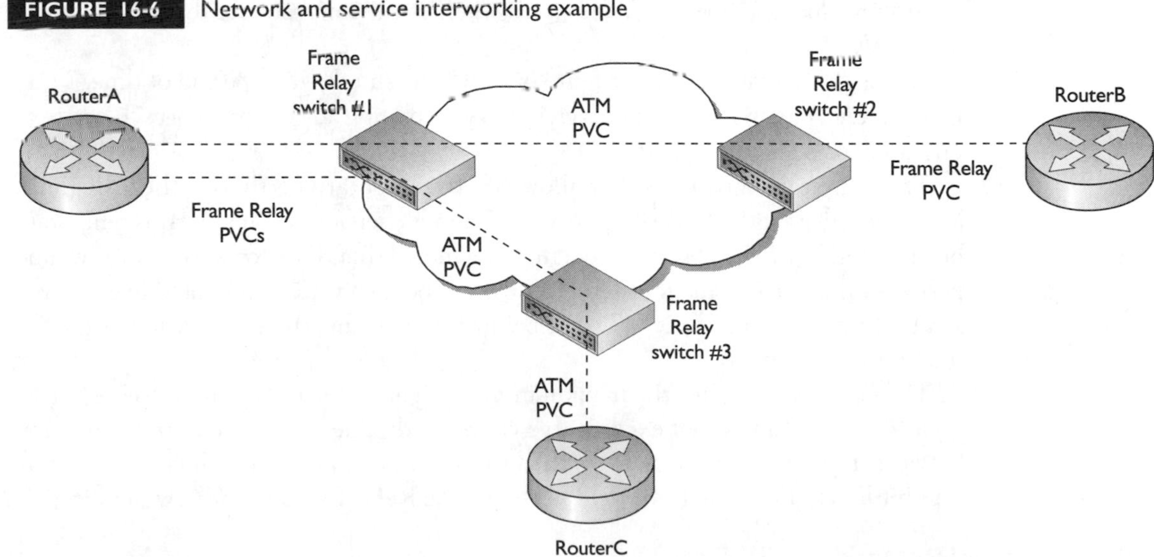

received by the connected switch. The switch figures out which ATM VC is to be used to get the information to the destination and *encapsulates* the Frame Relay frame into an ATM frame, which is then chunked up into ATM cells. When the ATM cells are received by the destination carrier switch, the switch reassembles the ATM cells back into an ATM frame, extracts the Frame Relay frame that was encapsulated, and then looks up the DLCI in its switching table. When switching the frame to the next segment, if the local DLCI number is different, the switch changes the DLCI in the header and recomputes the CRC.

The connection between RouterA and RouterC is an example of an FRF.8 connection. With FRF.8, one DTE is using Frame Relay and the other is using ATM. The carrier uses ATM to transport the information between the two DTEs. For example, in Figure 16-6, RouterA sends a Frame Relay frame to RouterC. The carrier's switch *converts* the Frame Relay frame into an ATM frame, which is different than what FRF.5 does. The switch then segments the ATM frame into cells and assigns the correct VPI/VCI address to the cells to get to the remote ATM switch. In this example, RouterA thinks it's talking to another Frame Relay device (RouterC). RouterC, on the other hand, thinks it's talking to an ATM device (RouterA).

VC Circuit Data Rates

Each data VC has a few parameters associated with it that affect its data rate and throughput. These values include the following: CIR (committed information rate), B_C (committed burst rate), B_E (excessive burst rate), and access rate. This section covers these four values and how the Frame Relay switch uses them to enforce the traffic contract for the VC.

CIR is the average contracted rate of a VC measured over a period of time. This is guaranteed rate that the carrier is giving to you, barring any major outages the carrier might experience in its network.

There are two burst rates that allow you to temporarily go above the CIR limit, assuming the provider has enough bandwidth in its network to support this temporary burst. B_C allows you to burst up to a higher average than CIR for a VC, but the time period of the burst is smaller than the time period that CIR is measured over. If you send information above the CIR, but below the B_C value, the carrier will permit the frame into its network.

The B_E value indicates the maximum rate you are allowed to send into the carrier on a VC. Any frames that exceeds this value are dropped. If you send traffic at a rate between B_C and B_E, the carrier switch marks the frames as discard eligible, using the one-bit Discard Eligible (DE) field in the Frame Relay frame header. By marking this bit, the carrier is saying that the frame is allowed in the network; however, as soon as the carrier experiences congestion, these are the first frames that are dropped. From the carrier's perspective, frames sent at a rate between B_C and B_E are bending the rules but will be allowed if there is enough bandwidth for them.

It is important to point out that *each* VC has its own CIR, B_C, and B_E values. However, depending on the carrier's implementation of Frame Relay, or how you purchase the VCs, the B_C and B_E values might not be used. In some instances, the B_C value defaults to the access rate—the speed of the physical connection from the Frame Relay DTE to the Frame Relay DCE. This could be a fractional T1 running at, say, 256Kbps, or a full T1 (1.544Mbps).

No matter how many VCs you have, or what their combined CIR values are, you are always limited to the access rate—you can't exceed the speed of the physical connection. It is a common practice to oversubscribe the speed of the physical connection: this occurs when the total CIR of all VCs exceeds the access rate. Basically, you're betting that all VCs will not simultaneously run at their CIRs, but that most will run below their CIR values at any given time, requiring a smaller speed connection to the carrier. There are two basic costs to a Frame Relay setup: the cost of each physical connection to the Frame Relay switch and the cost of each VC, which is usually dependent on its rate parameters.

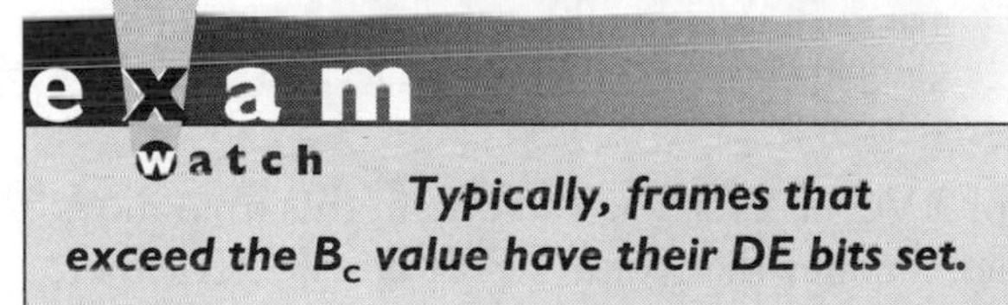

exam watch
Typically, frames that exceed the B_C value have their DE bits set.

Figure 16-7 shows an example of how these Frame Relay traffic parameters affect the data rate of a VC. The graph shows a linear progression of frames leaving a router's interface on a VC. As you can see from this figure, as long as the data rate of the VC is below the CIR/BC values, the Frame Relay switch allows the frames into the Frame Relay network. However, those frames (4 and 5) that exceed the BC value will have their DE bits set, which allows the carrier to drop these frames in times of internal congestion. Also, any frames that exceed BE are dropped: in this example, frames 6 and 7 are dropped.

Some carriers don't support B_C and B_E. Instead, they mark all frames that exceed the CIR as discard eligible. This means that you can send all your frames into the carrier network at the access rate speed and the carrier will permit them in (after marking the DE bit). All of these options and implementations can make it confusing when trying to find the right Frame Relay solution for your network. For example, one carrier might sell you a CIR of 0Kbps, which causes the carrier to permit all your traffic into the network but marks all of the frames as discard eligible. Assuming the carrier experiences no congestion problems, you're getting a great service. Of course, if the carrier is constantly experiencing congestion, you are getting very poor service, since some or most of your frames are dropped.

FIGURE 16-7 VC traffic parameters

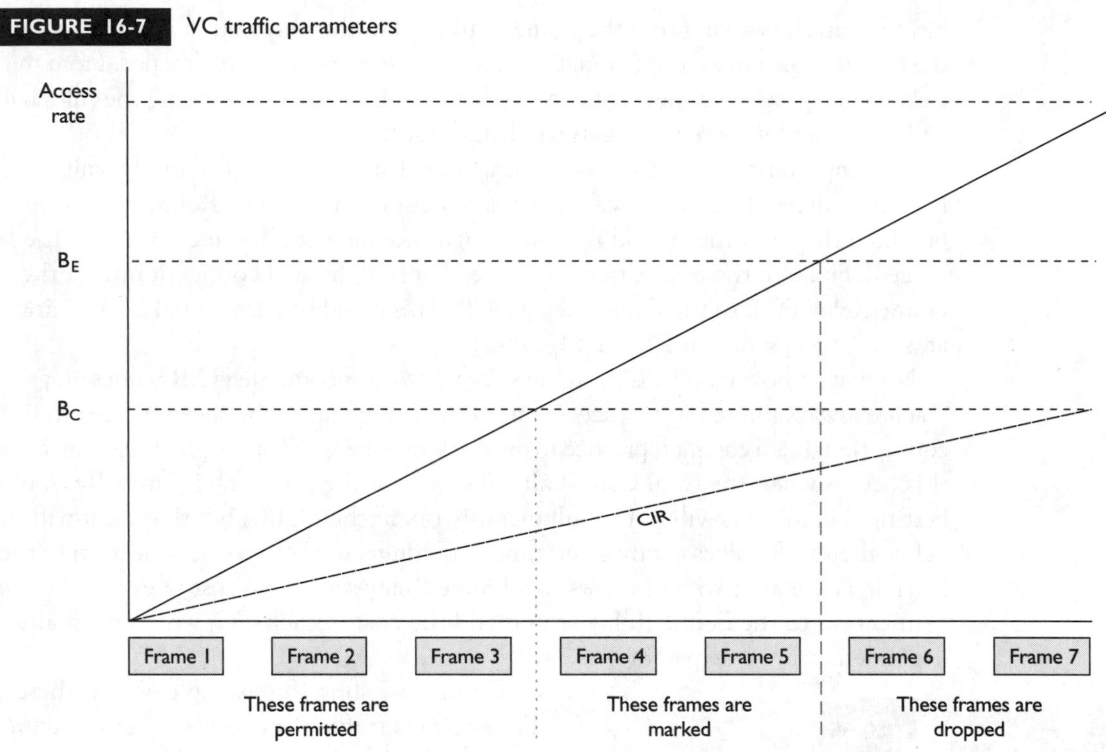

If you need a guaranteed rate for a VC or VCs, you can obtain this from most carriers, but you'll need to spend more money than for a CIR 0Kbps VC. The more bandwidth you require, the more expensive the circuit, since the carrier must reserve this bandwidth inside its network to accommodate your traffic rate needs.

And what makes this whole process complex is looking at your traffic rates for all your connections and try to get the best value for your money. Some network administrators oversubscribe their access rates, expecting that not all VCs will simultaneously send traffic at their CIR traffic rates. How Frame Relay operates and how your traffic behaves makes it difficult to pick the right Frame Relay service for your network.

Congestion Control

In the preceding section, you were shown how the different traffic parameters for a VC affect how traffic enters the carrier's network. Once this is accomplished, these values have no effect on traffic as it traverses the carrier's network to your remote site. Of course, this poses problems in a carrier's network—what if the carrier experiences congestion and begins dropping frames? It would be nice for the carrier to indicate to your Frame Relay devices that there is congestion and to have your devices slow the rates of their VCs before the carrier begins dropping your frames. Remember that Frame Relay has no retransmit option—if a frame is dropped because it has an FCS error or experiences congestion, it is up to the source device that *created* the frame to resend it.

To handle this problem, Frame Relay has a standard mechanism to signify and adapt to congestion problems in a Frame Relay carrier's network. Every Frame Relay frame header has two fields that are used to indicated congestion:

- Forward Explicit Congestion Notification (FECN)
- Backward Explicit Congestion Notification (BECN)

Figure 16-8 shows an example of how FECN and BECN are used. As RouterA is sending its information into the carrier network, the carrier network experiences congestion. For the VCs that experience congestion, the carrier marks the FECN bit in the frame header as these frames are heading to RouterB. Once the frames arrive at RouterB and RouterB sees the FECN bit set in the Frame Relay frame header, RouterB can send a Frame Relay frame in the reverse direction on the VC, marking the BECN bit in the header of the frame. With some vendor's carrier switches, to speed up the congestion notification process, the carrier switch actually generates a BECN frame in the reverse direction of the VC, back to the source, to indicate congestion issues. Once RouterA receives the BECN frames, it can then begin to slow down the data rate of the VC.

FIGURE 16-8 FECN and BECN illustration

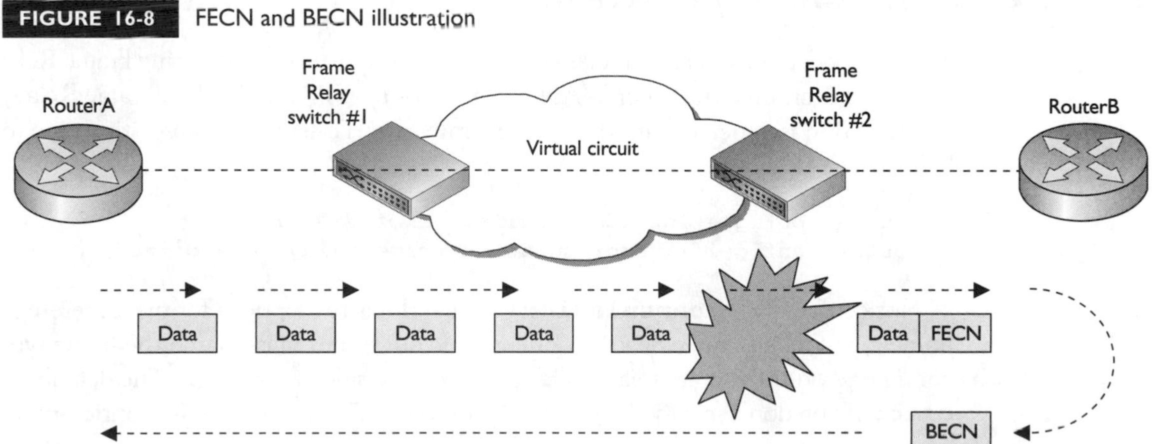

One of the main drawbacks of using the FECN/BECN method of congestion notification is that it is not a very efficient form of flow control. For example, the carrier might begin to mark the FECN bit in frames as they are headed to the destination to indicate a congestion problem. As the destination is responding to the source with BECN frames, the congestion disappears. When the source receives the BECN frames, it begins to slow down even though the congestion problem no longer exists. On top of this, there is no way of notifying the source or destination how much congestion exists—the source might begin slowing down the VC too slowly or too quickly without any decent feedback about how much to slow down. Because of these issues, many companies have opted to use ATM. ATM also supports flow control, but its implementation is more sophisticated than Frame Relay and allows VCs to adapt to congestion in a real-time fashion.

FECN is used to indicate congestion as frames go from the source to the destination. BECN is used by the destination (and sent to the source) to indicate that there is congestion from the source to the destination.

CERTIFICATION OBJECTIVE 16.03

Frame Relay Configuration

The remainder of this chapter focuses on the different ways of configuring Frame Relay on your router. Like the other WAN encapsulations, PPP and HDLC, Frame Relay's configuration is done on your router's serial interface. To set the encapsulation type to Frame Relay, use this configuration:

```
Router(config)# interface serial [slot_#/]port_#
Router(config-if)# encapsulation frame-relay [cisco|ietf]
```

Notice that the **encapsulation** command has two options for two different frame types. The frame type you configure on your router must match the frame type configured on the Frame Relay DTEs at the remote side of your VCs. The default is **cisco** if you don't specify the encapsulation type. This frame type is proprietary to

The encapsulation *frame-relay* command has two encapsulation types: *cisco* and *ietf*. The default is *cisco*. *ietf* is used for vendor interoperability.

Cisco equipment. In most instances, you'll use the standardized frame type (**ietf**). IETF has defined a standardized Frame Relay frame type in RFC 1490, which is interoperable with all vendors' Frame Relay equipment.

Once you have configured your frame type, use the **show interfaces** command to verify your frame type configuration:

```
Router# show interfaces serial 0
Serial 0 is up, line protocol is up
   Hardware is MCI Serial
   Internet address is 172.16.2.1, subnet mask is 255.255.255.0
   MTU 1500 bytes, BW 256 Kbit, DLY 20000 usec, rely 255/255, load 1/255
   Encapsulation FRAME-RELAY, loopback not set, keepalive set
   LMI DLCI    0, LMI sent 1107, LMI stat recvd 1107
   LMI type is ANSI Annex D
   Last input 0:00:00, output 0:00:00, output hang never
<--output omitted-->
```

Notice that the encapsulation type has been changed to *FRAME RELAY* in this example.

16.01. The CD contains a multimedia demonstration of changing the encapsulation type to Frame Relay on a router.

LMI Configuration

Once you have set the encapsulation on your serial interface, you need to define the LMI type that is used to communicate information between your router and the carrier's switch. Remember that LMI is a local process. What you configure on your router doesn't have to match what is on the remote routers: What has to match is what your carrier is using on their switch (the DTE to DCE connection).

Use this configuration to configure the LMI type:

```
Router(config)# interface serial [slot_#/]port_#
Router(config-if)# frame-relay lmi-type ansi|cisco|q933a
```

Note that the LMI type is specific to the entire interface, not to a VC. Table 16-3 maps the LMI parameters to the corresponding LMI standard.

TABLE 16-3 LMI Parameters

Parameter	Standard
`ansi`	ANSI's Annex D standard, T1.617
`cisco`	The gang of four
`q933a`	ITU-T's Q.933 Annex A standard

Starting with IOS 11.2, Cisco routers can autosense the LMI type that is configured on the carrier's switch. With this feature, the router sends a status enquiry for each LMI type to the carrier's switch, one at a time, and waits to see which one the switch will respond to. The router keeps on doing this until the switch responds to one of them. If you are not getting a response from the carrier, it is most likely that the carrier forgot to configure LMI on its switch.

Remember that a Cisco router generates an LMI status enquiry message every ten seconds. On the sixth message, the router sends a full status update query.

16.02. The CD contains a multimedia demonstration configuring the LMI type on a router.

Troubleshooting LMI

If you are experiencing LMI problems with your connection to the carrier's switch, you have three commands to assist you in the troubleshooting process:

- **`show interfaces`**
- **`show frame-relay lmi`**
- **`debug frame-relay lmi`**

The following sections cover each of these commands in detail.

The show interfaces Command

Besides showing you the encapsulation type of an interface, the **`show interfaces`** command also displays the LMI type that is being used as well as some LMI statistics, as is shown here:

```
Router# show interfaces serial 0
Serial 0 is up, line protocol is up
```

```
    Hardware is MCI Serial
    Internet address is 172.16.2.1, subnet mask is 255.255.255.0
    MTU 1500 bytes, BW 256 Kbit, DLY 20000 usec, rely 255/255, load 1/255
    Encapsulation FRAME-RELAY, loopback not set, keepalive set
    LMI DLCI    0, LMI sent 1107, LMI stat recvd 1107
    LMI type is ANSI Annex D
<--output omitted-->
```

Notice the two lines below the encapsulation. The first line shows the DLCI number used by LMI (0) as well as the number of status enquiries sent and received. If you re-execute the **show interfaces** command every ten seconds, both of these values should be incrementing. The second line shows the actual LMI type used (ANSI Annex D).

The show frame-relay lmi Command

If you want to see more detailed statistics regarding LMI than what the **show interfaces** command displays, then you can use the **show frame-relay lmi** command, shown here:

```
Router# show frame-relay lmi
LMI Statistics for interface Serial0
                        (Frame Relay DTE) LMI TYPE = ANSI
  Invalid Unnumbered info 0            Invalid Prot Disc 0
  Invalid dummy Call Ref 0             Invalid Msg Type 0
  Invalid Status Message 0             Invalid Lock Shift 0
  Invalid Information ID 0             Invalid Report IE Len 0
  Invalid Report Request 0             Invalid Keep IE Len 0
  Num Status Enq. Sent 12              Num Status msgs Rcvd 12
  Num Update Status Rcvd 2             Num Status Timeouts 2
```

With this command, you can see both valid and invalid messages. If the Invalid field values are incrementing, this can indicate a mismatch in the LMI configuration: you have one LMI type configured and the switch has another type configured. The last two lines of the output refer to the status enquiries that the router generates. The Num Status Enq Sent field is the number of enquiries your router has sent to the switch. The Num Status msgs Rcvd field is the number of replies that the switch has sent upon receiving your router's enquiries. The Num Update Status Rcvd are the number of full status updates messages the switch has sent. The Num Status Timeouts indicates the number of times your router sent an enquiry and did *not* receive a response back.

If you see the `Num Status Timeouts` increasing, but the `Num Status msgs Rcvd` is not increasing, this probably indicates that the provider forgot to enable LMI on their switch's interface.

16.03. The CD contains a multimedia demonstration of the `show frame-relay lmi` command on a router.

The debug frame-relay lmi Command

For more detailed troubleshooting of LMI, you can use the **debug frame-relay lmi** command. This command shows the actual LMI messages being sent and received by your router. Here's an example of the output of this command:

```
Router# debug frame-relay lmi
Serial0 (in): Status, myseq 290
RT IE 1, length 1, type 0
RT IE 3, length 2, yourseq 107, my seq 290
PVC IE 0x7, length 0x6, dlci 112, status 0x2 bw 0
Serial0 (out): StEnq, myseq 291, yourseq 107, DTE up
Datagramstart = 0x1959DF4, datagramsize = 13
FR encap = 0xFCF10309
00 75 01 01 01 03 02 D7 D4
```

In this output, the router, on `Serial0`, first receives a status reply from the switch to the two hundred ninetieth LMI status enquiry the router sent—this is the very first line. Following this on the fifth line is the router's two hundred ninety-first status enquiry being sent to the switch.

16.04. The CD contains a multimedia demonstration of the `debug frame-relay lmi` command on a router.

Use the `frame-relay lmi-type` command to specify the LMI type. Remember that Cisco routers can autosense the LMI type, so this command isn't necessary. The `show frame-relay lmi` command displays LMI interaction between the router and the switch. The `debug frame-relay lmi` command displays the actual LMI messages.

PVC Configuration

The preceding two sections showed you how to configure the interaction between your router (DTE) and the carrier's switch (DCE). This section expands upon this and shows you how to send data between two Frame Relay DTEs. As I mentioned earlier in the chapter, in order to send data to another DTE, a VC must first be established. This can be a PVC or an SVC. The CCNA exam focuses on PVCs, so I'll restrict myself to discussing the configuration of PVCs in this book.

One of the first issues that you'll have to deal with is that the router, by default, doesn't know what PVCs to use and which device is off of which PVC. Remember that PVCs are given unique locally significant addresses called DLCIs. Somehow the router has to learn the DLCI numbers and the layer-3 address that is at the remote end of the VC. You have two methods available to resolve this issue: manual and dynamic resolution. These resolutions map the layer-3 address of the remote Frame Relay DTE to the local DLCI number your router uses in order to reach this DTE. The following sections cover the configuration of both of these resolution types.

Manual Resolution

If you are using manual resolution to resolve layer-3 remote addresses to local DLCI numbers, then use the following configuration:

```
Router(config)# interface serial [slot_#/]port_#
Router(config-if)# frame-relay map protocol_name
                        destination_address local_dlci_#
                        [broadcast] [ietf|cisco]
```

The **frame-relay map** command is actually very similar to the X.25 map statement to resolve layer-3 addresses to X.25 SVC addresses. The *protocol_name* parameter specifies the layer-3 protocol that you are resolving, IP, IPX, or AppleTalk, for instance. If you are running two protocols between yourself and the remote DTE, such as IP and IPX, then you will need a separate **frame-relay map** command for each protocol and destination mapping. Following the name of the protocol is the remote DTE's layer-3 address (*destination_address*), such as its IP address. Following the layer-3 address is the local DLCI number *your* router should use in order to reach the remote DTE. These are the only three required parameters.

The other two parameters, the **broadcast** parameter and the frame type parameter, are optional. By default, local broadcasts and multicasts do not go across a manually resolved PVC. Therefore, if you are running RIP or EIGRP as a routing protocol, the routing updates these protocols generate will not go across the PVC unless you configure the **broadcast** parameter. If you don't want broadcast traffic going across a VC, then don't configure this parameter. If this is the case, then you'll need to configure static routes on both Frame Relay DTEs.

At the beginning of this objective, the text describes how to change the encapsulation type for Frame Relay frames with the **encapsulation frame-relay** command. This command allows you to specify one of two frame types: **ietf** or **cisco**, with **cisco** being the default. The problem with this command is that it specifies the same encapsulation on every VC. When doing manual resolution, you can specify the encapsulation for *each* VC separately. If you omit this, the encapsulation defaults to that encapsulation type on the serial interface.

Let's look at an example, shown in Figure 16-9, to illustrate how to set up manual resolution for a PVC configuration. Here's the configuration for RouterA:

```
RouterA(config)# interface serial 0
RouterA(config-if)# encapsulation frame-relay ietf
RouterA(config-if)# frame-relay lmi-type q933a
RouterA(config-if)# ip address 192.168.2.1 255.255.255.0
RouterA(config-if)# frame-relay map ip 192.168.2.2 103 broadcast
```

Here's the configuration for RouterB:

```
RouterB(config)# interface serial 0
RouterB(config-if)# encapsulation frame-relay ietf
RouterB(config-if)# frame-relay lmi-type ansi
RouterB(config-if)# ip address 192.168.2.2 255.255.255.0
RouterB(config-if)# frame-relay map ip 192.168.2.1 301 broadcast
```

exam watch

Use the frame-relay map command to configure manual resolution of PVCs. By default, broadcasts do not go across a manually resolved VC unless you use the broadcast parameter.

First, notice that the two routers are using *different* LMI types at each end. This is okay, since LMI is used only between the Frame Relay DTE and DCE devices. Second, notice that the DLCI numbers are different at each end. Again, remember that DLCI numbers are locally significant and do not have to be the same on all segments the VC traverses.

16.05. The CD contains a multimedia demonstration of configuring manual resolution for a PVC on a router.

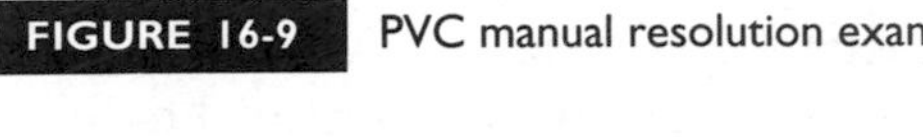
FIGURE 16-9 PVC manual resolution example

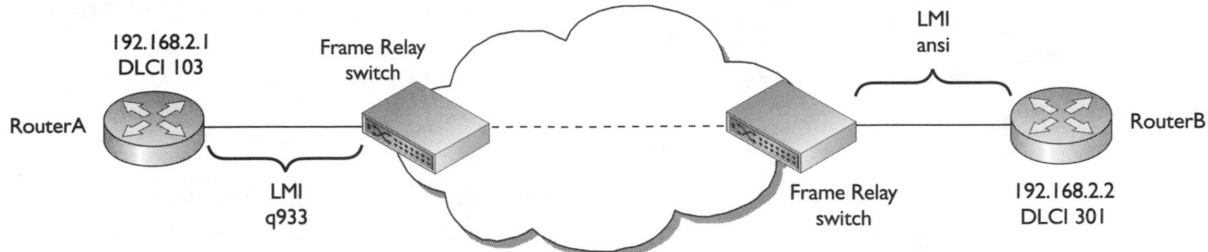

Dynamic Resolution

Instead of using manual resolution for your PVCs, you can use *dynamic* resolution. Dynamic resolution uses a feature called *inverse ARP*. This is something like a reverse ARP in TCP/IP. Inverse ARP allows devices to automatically discover the layer-3 protocol and address that are used on each VC.

Inverse ARP occurs every 60 seconds on VCs that are not manually configured. It occurs only on VCs that are in an *active* state. Recall from the LMI section that the state of the VCs is learned from the full status update message. For example, once the physical layer for the interface comes up, your router starts sending its LMI enquiries every ten seconds. On the sixth one, it sends a full status message, which requests the statuses of the VCs that the switch directs to this router's interface. In this example, it will take at least a minute before the router learns of the status of the VC.

Once the router sees an active status for a VC, it *then* does an inverse ARP on the VC if it is not already manually resolved with a **`frame-relay map`** command. This frame contains the layer-3 protocol and protocol address used by the router. When the frame arrives at the remote DTE, the device takes the protocol, layer-3 address, and local DLCI number and puts them in its VC resolution table. The remote DTEs do the same thing. Within a short period of time, your router will know the layer-3 addresses at the end of each of its dynamically resolved VCs. Once the router knows who is at the other end of the VC, your router can begin transmitting data to the remote DTE.

exam watch

Inverse ARP allows a router to send a Frame Relay frame across a VC with its layer-3 addressing information. The destination can then use this, along with the incoming DLCI number, to reach the advertiser.

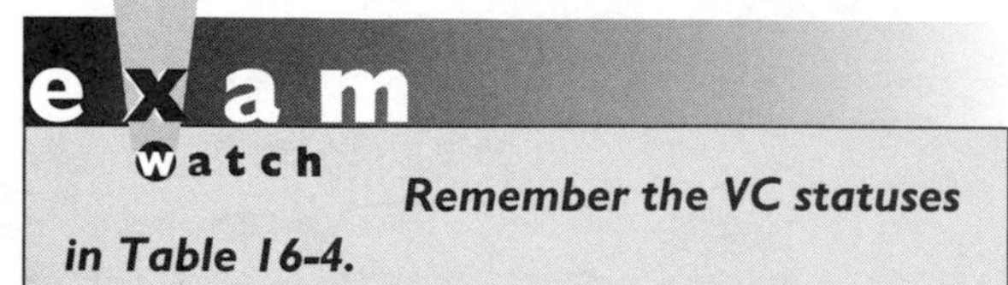

Remember the VC statuses in Table 16-4.

VC Status You already know about one of the states for a VC (active). There are three basic statuses for a VC, as shown in Table 16-4. In order for Inverse ARP to take place, the VC must have an active status.

Disadvantages of Dynamic Resolution Even though dynamic resolution requires no configuration on your router in order to work, it does have some disadvantages. First, one of the main problems of dynamic resolution is that in order for you to send data across the VC, you must wait until you learn the status of the VC and wait for the inverse ARP to occur. This process can sometimes take over 60 seconds, even if the data link layer is operational and the VC is in place. The advantage of manually resolved PVCs is that as soon as the data link layer is up, your router can immediately begin to send traffic to the destination router. Assuming that the Frame Relay switch replies to your router's first LMI enquiry, this can be less than a second before your router can begin transmitting information to the destination DTE. So even though the manual resolution process requires you to configure all of the manual resolution entries, many network administrators choose to do this so that data can begin to traverse the VCs as soon as the physical and data link layers are *up and up*.

The second disadvantage of dynamic resolution is that in some instances, with equipment from multiple vendors, you might experience problems with how different vendors implement inverse ARP. In this case, the dynamic resolution fails and you must resort to configuring manual resolution with the **`frame-relay map`** command. This might even be true between Cisco routers. I have experienced problems with routers running very old and new versions of the IOS trying to perform inverse ARP between them, and it failing. You could either use manual resolution or upgrade the IOS on the routers.

TABLE 16-4 VC Statuses

Status	Description
Active	The connection between both Frame Relay DTEs is up and operational.
Inactive	The connection between your Frame Relay DTE and DCE is up and operational, but there is something wrong with connection between your connected Frame Relay switch and the destination DTE.
Deleted	You are not receiving any LMI messages from the Frame Relay switch.

The third problem with dynamic resolution is that inverse ARP works only with the following protocols: AppleTalk, DECnet, IP, IPX, Vines, and XNS. If you have another protocol, you will need to configure manual resolution commands to solve your resolution problem.

Configuring Inverse ARP By default, inverse ARP is already *enabled* on your Cisco router. You can disable it or reenable it with the following configuration:

```
Router(config)# interface serial [slot_#/]port_#
Router(config-if)# [no] frame-relay inverse-arp
                        [protocol_name] [DLCI_#]
```

Without any options, the **frame-relay inverse-arp** command enables inverse ARP for all VCs on the router's serial interface. You can selectively disable inverse ARP for a particular protocol or VC (DLCI #). Use the **clear frame-relay-inarp** command to clear the Inverse ARP resolution table. To see the Inverse ARP statistics, use this command:

```
Router# show frame-relay traffic
Frame Relay statistics:
ARP requests sent 14, ARP replies sent 0
ARP request recvd 0, ARP replies recvd 10
```

Dynamic Resolution Example Previously, I showed you how to set up manual resolution for the VC connection shown in Figure 16-9. I'll use the same network, but instead implement dynamic resolution, to illustrate how this is set up on your router. In this example, I'll assume that your router is autosensing the LMI type. Here's the configuration for RouterA:

```
Router(config)# interface serial 0
Router(config-if)# encapsulation frame-relay ietf
Router(config-if)# ip address 192.168.2.1 255.255.255.0
```

Here's the configuration for RouterB:

```
Router(config)# interface serial 0
Router(config-if)# encapsulation frame-relay ietf
Router(config-if)# ip address 192.168.2.2 255.255.255.0
```

With autosensing of the LMI type, you don't need to configure the LMI type on the interface. And since you are using dynamic resolution with inverse ARP, which is enabled by default, you don't need any additional configuration on your router's serial interface. As you can see from the preceding code examples, the only thing you had to configure was the encapsulation type on the interface, making the setup of Frame Relay a simple and straightforward process.

16.06. The CD contains a multimedia demonstration of configuring dynamic resolution for a PVC on a router.

PVC Status Verification

To see all of the Frame Relay PVCs terminated at your router, as well as their statistics, use the **show frame-relay pvc** command. Optionally, you can look at just one PVC by following this command with the local DLCI number, as shown in this example:

```
Router# show frame-relay pvc 100
PVC Statistics for interface Serial0
                        (Frame Relay DTE) DLCI = 100,
    DLCI USAGE = LOCAL, PVC STATUS = ACTIVE, INTERFACE = Serial0
     input pkts 15          output pkts 26         in bytes 508
     out bytes 638          dropped pkts 1         in FECN pkts 0
     in BECN pkts 0         out FECN pkts 0        out BECN pkts 0
     in DE pkts 0           out DE pkts 0
     out bcast pkts 0       out bcast bytes 0
     pvc create time 00:22:01, last time pvc status
             changed 00:05:37
```

In this example, PVC 100's status is `ACTIVE`, which indicates that the PVC is operational between the two Frame Relay DTEs. You can also see traffic statistics for the PVC. In this example, 15 packets were received and 26 packets were transmitted on this PVC.

16.07. The CD contains a multimedia demonstration of using the show frame-relay pvc command on a router.

To see the VC resolution table, which maps layer-3 addresses to local DLCI numbers, use the **show frame-relay map** command:

```
Router# show frame-relay map
Serial0 (up): ip 192.168.2.2 dlci 32(0x20, 0x1C80), dynamic,
                        Broadcast, CISCO, status defined, active
```

In this output, there is one PVC with a DLCI of 32. At the end of this PVC is a router with an IP address of 192.168.2.2. Notice that this information was learned via inverse ARP (`dynamic`), that local broadcasts and multicasts are allowed, that the default frame type is **`cisco`**, and that the status of the VC is `active`. If you had configured manual resolution for this connection, the entry would have listed `static` instead of `dynamic`. Also, if the frame type was based on RFC 1490, the frame type would have been listed as `IETF`.

CertCam

16.08. The CD contains a multimedia demonstration of using the `show frame-relay map` command on a router.

exam watch

Use the `show frame-relay pvc` command to view the statuses of your VCs. Use the `show frame-relay map` command to view the manual or Inverse ARP mappings of layer-3 addresses to DLCIs.

EXERCISE 16-1

ON THE CD

Configuring Frame Relay

These preceding few sections dealt with the configuration of Frame Relay on a physical serial interface. This exercise will help you reinforce this material by configuring a simple Frame Relay connection. You'll use manual resolution with the VC. The DLCI number on both sides is 100. You'll perform this lab using Boson's NetSim simulator. You can find a picture of the network diagram for Boson's NetSim simulator in the Introduction of this book. After starting up the simulator, click the *LabNavigator* button. Next, double-click *Exercise 16-1* and click the *Load Lab* button. This will load the lab configuration based on Chapter 5's and 7's exercises.

1. On both routers, disable `serial0`—this is the dedicated point-to-point connection.

   At the top of the simulator in the menu bar, click the *eRouters* icon and choose *2600*. Execute the following: **`configure terminal`**, **`interface serial0`**, **`shutdown`**, and **`end`**. Use the **`show interfaces`** command to check the status of the interfaces. At this point, only the `fa0/0` interface on the 2600 should be enabled. At the top of the simulator in the menu bar, click the *eRouters* icon and choose *2500*. Execute the following: **configure terminal**, **interface serial0**, **shutdown**, and **end**. Use the **show interfaces** command to check the status of the interfaces. At this point, only the `e0` interface on the 2500 should be enabled.

2. Enable Frame Relay on the 2600. Enable the `serial1` interface. Use the Cisco frame type for Frame Relay. Set the LMI type to ITU-T. Assign the IP address. Verify the operation of LMI.

   At the top of the simulator in the menu bar, click the *eRouters* icon and choose *2600*. Enable the Frame Relay interface: **configure terminal**, **interface serial1** and **no shutdown**. Set the encapsulation and frame type: **encapsulation frame-relay**. Set the LMI type: **frame-relay lmi-type q933a**. Assign the IP address on the interface: **ip address 192.168.10.1 255.255.255.0**. Exit *Configuration* mode: **end**. Use the **show interfaces** command to verify that the interface is up and up and that LMI is functioning. Use the **show frame-relay lmi** command to make sure the router is sending and receiving LMI information.

3. Enable Frame Relay on the 2500. Enable the `serial1` interface. Use the Cisco frame type for Frame Relay. Set the LMI type to ITU-T. Assign the IP address. Verify the operation of LMI.

   At the top of the simulator in the menu bar, click the *eRouters* icon and choose *2500*. From the 2500 router, enable the interface: **configure terminal**, **interface serial1** and **no shutdown**. Set the encapsulation and frame type: **encapsulation frame-relay**. Set the LMI type: **frame-relay lmi-type q933a**. Assign the IP address on the interface: **ip address 192.168.10.2 255.255.255.0**. Exit *Configuration* mode: **end**. Use the **show interfaces** command to verify that the interface is up and up and that LMI is functioning. Use the **show frame-relay lmi** command to make sure the router is sending and receiving LMI information.

4. Set up manual resolution on the 2600 router. The DLCI number used locally is 100.

   At the top of the simulator in the menu bar, click the *eRouters* icon and choose *2600*. Enter the serial interface: **configure terminal** and

interface serial 1. Set up the manual resolution to *reach* the 2500 router: **frame-relay map ip 192.168.10.2 100**. Exit *Configuration* mode: **end**. View the resolution entry: **show frame-relay map**. View the PVC: **show frame-relay pvc**. The status of the VC should be ACTIVE.

5. Set up manual resolution on the 2500 router. The DLCI number used locally is 100.

   At the top of the simulator in the menu bar, click the *eRouters* icon and choose *2500*. Enter the serial interface: **configure terminal** and **interface serial 1**. Set up the manual resolution to reach the 2500 router: **frame-relay map ip 192.168.10.1 100**. Exit *Configuration* mode: **end**. View the resolution entry: **show frame-relay map**. View the PVC: **show frame-relay pvc**. The status of the VC should be ACTIVE.

6. On each router, set up a static route to the other router's remote network. View the routing table.

   At the top of the simulator in the menu bar, click the *eRouters* icon and choose *2600*. On the 2600, set up the static route to reach 192.168.3.0/24: **configure terminal** and **ip route 192.168.3.0 255.255.255.0 192.168.10.2**. Exit *Configuration* mode: **end**. View the routing table and look for the static route: **show ip route**. At the top of the simulator in the menu bar, click the *eRouters* icon and choose *2500*. On the 2500, set up the static route to reach 192.168.3.0/24: **configure terminal** and **ip route 192.168.1.0 255.255.255.0 192.168.10.1**. Exit *Configuration* mode: **end**. View the routing table and look for the static route: **show ip route**.

7. On the 2600, test the connection to the 2500. From Host-1, test the connection to Host-3.

   At the top of the simulator in the menu bar, click the *eRouters* icon and choose *2600*. On the 2600 router, ping the 2500's Frame Relay interface: **ping 192.168.10.2**. The ping should be successful. At the top of the simulator in the menu bar, click the *eStations* icon and choose *Host1*. On Host1, ping Host3: **ping 192.168.3.2**. The ping should be successful.

You should now be more familiar with setting up a basic manually resolved Frame Relay connection to a remote site.

CERTIFICATION OBJECTIVE 16.04

Nonbroadcast Multiaccess

Nonbroadcast multiaccess (NBMA) is a term used to describe WAN networks that use VCs for connectivity. In a broadcast medium in LAN environments such as Ethernet, every device is in the same broadcast domain—when a device generates a broadcast, every other device in the broadcast domain will see the segment, as is shown in the top part of Figure 16-10. As you can see in this example, RouterA generates one broadcast and the other two routers, RouterB and RouterC, receive it.

With WAN networks that use VCs, each device is connected to another device via a point-to-point VC—there can be only two devices connected to a VC. This poses a problem with NBMA environments.

FIGURE 16-10 Broadcast versus NBMA environments

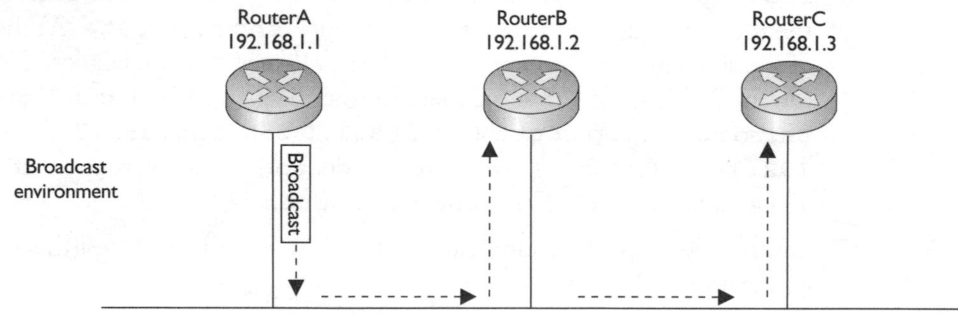

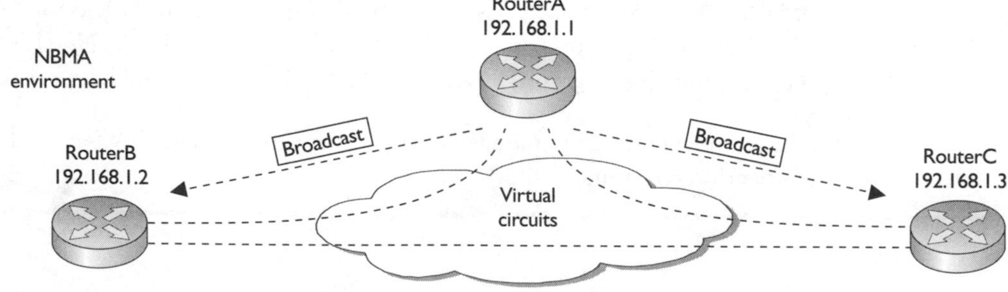

exam watch *An NBMA environment is an environment that allows access by multiple devices but doesn't support a traditional broadcast environment such as Ethernet or Token Ring.*

Topology Types

Before reading more about the issues of NBMA environments, consider some of the topologies you can use to connect your devices together using VCs. Table 16-5 contains the terms used to describe these various topologies. The bottom part of Figure 16-10 shows an example of a fully meshed network. In such a network, it is very easy to emulate a broadcast environment. In this environment, your router *replicates* the local broadcast across every VC in the subnet. For example, in Figure 16-10, when RouterA wants to send a local broadcast, it sends it across the two VCs to RouterB and RouterC. In a fully meshed environment, every device receives the original broadcast frame. This process is also true if RouterB or RouterC generates a broadcast.

Understand the topology types listed in Table 16-5.

Split Horizon Issues

The main problem of NBMA environments arises when the network is *partially* meshed for a subnet. This can create problems with routing protocols that support split horizon.

TABLE 16-5 NBMA Topology Types

Topology	Description
Fully meshed	Your router has VC connections to every other router.
Partially meshed	Your router has VC connections to some, but not all, of the other routers.
Point-to-point	Your router has a VC connection on only one other router (this is used to emulate leased lines/dedicated circuit connections).
Star	Your router has VC connections to some, but not all, of the other routers. This is sometimes called a *hub-and-spoke* topology, where the routers are partially meshed. Each remote site router has a connection to the central site router.

Recall from Chapter 9 that distance vector protocols like RIP and IGRP use split horizon to prevent routing loop problems. Split horizon states that if routing information is learned on an interface, this routing information will not be propagated out the same interface.

This is an issue with partially meshed networks that use VCs. For instance, two routers may be in the same subnet but not have a VC between them. With partially meshed networks, this can create routing issues. Let's look at Figure 16-11 to illustrate the problem. This figure shows a network where RouterA has a VC to the other three routers, but these three routers must go through RouterA to reach the other routers. The assumption here is that all of the routers are in the same subnet, and the three VCs terminated at RouterA are going into the same serial interface.

Let's look at this from a routing perspective, assuming that these routers are running RIPv1. RouterB, RouterC, and RouterD have no issues—they have only one VC apiece and can send and receive their routing updates on their VCs. However, RouterA has a problem disseminating routing information from RouterB, RouterC, or RouterD to

FIGURE 16-11 NBMA and split horizon issues

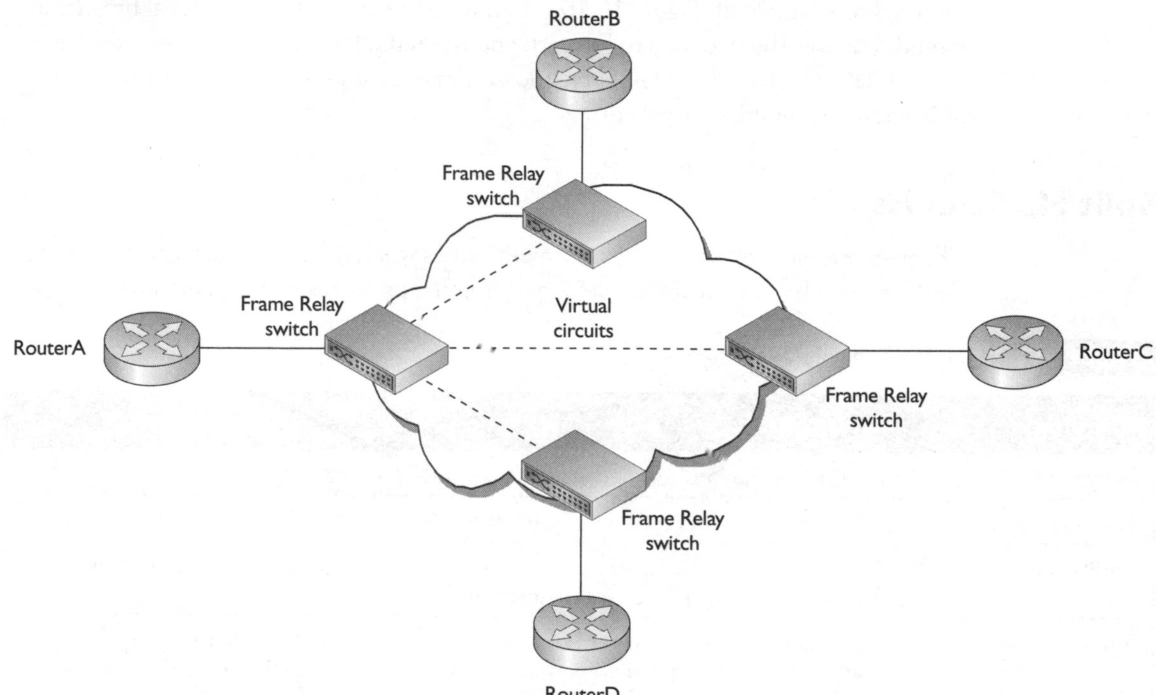

the others. For example, let's assume that RouterB generates a routing update. Since RouterB doesn't have a VC to RouterC and RouterD, it forwards the update to RouterA, in hopes that RouterA will forward this to the other two routers in the subnet. However, when RouterA receives the routing update from RouterB, RouterA can't forward this to RouterC and RouterD because of split horizon. Even though these two routers are off of different VCs than RouterB, they are off of the *same* physical interface. Therefore, by default, any routing information from these remote routers will not be propagated by RouterA to the other remote counterparts.

Figure 16-11 is a prime example of an NBMA environment. Even though it is possible to reach every router, even if it takes an extra hop, in the WAN network, broadcasts (and multicasts) don't function correctly.

Solutions to Split Horizon Problems

Given the preceding problem with routing protocols that use split horizon, there are solutions that you can use to overcome this issue:

- Create a fully meshed network.
- Use static routes.
- Disable split horizon.
- Use subinterfaces on RouterA and associate a single VC to each subinterface.

These solutions apply to any NBMA environment that uses VCs, including Frame Relay, X.25, SMDS, and ATM. In the following paragraphs, I'll deal with each of these solutions individually.

exam watch ***Remember the preceding solutions for overcoming split horizon in NBMA topologies. The preferred method is to use subinterfaces to deal with this problem.***

As to the first solution, if you fully mesh your WAN network, then you don't have to deal with split horizon problems with distance vector protocols: every router has a VC to every other router in the WAN. Therefore, when any router generates a routing update broadcast, the broadcast is replicated across every VC to all of the destination routers. The main problem with this solution is that to fully mesh your WAN network, you have to purchase a lot of VCs. In many cases, this doesn't make sense. For instance, in Figure 16-11, if most of the traffic is from RouterB, RouterC, and RouterD to RouterA, it makes no sense to pay extra money just to replicate the routing updates to the three unconnected routers.

The second solution has you configure static routes on RouterB, RouterC, and RouterD to solve your routing problems. This works fine if the number of networks and subnets these routers are connected to is small. But if these are major regional sites, with hundreds of networks, then setting up static routes becomes a monumental task. Not only does it take a lot of time to configure all of these routes, but you must also test and troubleshoot them, making this solution not very scalable.

The third solution has you disable split horizon on RouterA. Some layer-3 protocols allow you to disable split horizon, and some don't. And if the routing protocol allowed you to disable split horizon, it is an all or nothing proposition. In other words, Cisco doesn't let you enable or disable split horizon on an interface-by-interface basis. This can create problems if RouterA has multiple LAN connections. By disabling split horizon in this situation, you are allowing RouterB, RouterC, and RouterD to learn each other's routes, but you may be creating routing loops on the LAN side of RouterA.

Subinterfaces

The fourth solution is the *preferred* method for solving split horizon and routing problems in NBMA environments. Recall from Chapter 9 that a subinterface is a logical interface associated with a single physical interface. A physical interface can support many subinterfaces. Cisco routers treat subinterfaces just as they do physical interfaces. You can shut down a physical interface, shutting down all of its associated subinterfaces, or you can shut down a single subinterface while keeping the remaining subinterfaces operational.

When using subinterfaces in a Frame Relay environment, basically, you configure two commands on the physical (or major) interface:

- **`encapsulation frame-relay`**
- **`frame-relay lmi-type`**

All other configuration commands should be placed under the appropriate subinterface.

Overcoming Split Horizon Issues

By using subinterfaces, and placing each subinterface in a separate subnet, you make it *possible* for routing information received on one subinterface to be propagated to other subinterfaces on the same physical interface. Figure 16-12 shows an example of how subinterfaces can be used to overcome split horizon issues in a partially meshed NBMA environment. In this example, you create a separate subinterface on RouterA for each destination. Since RouterA is using a separate *subinterface* for each of these

FIGURE 16-12 Subinterfaces and split horizon

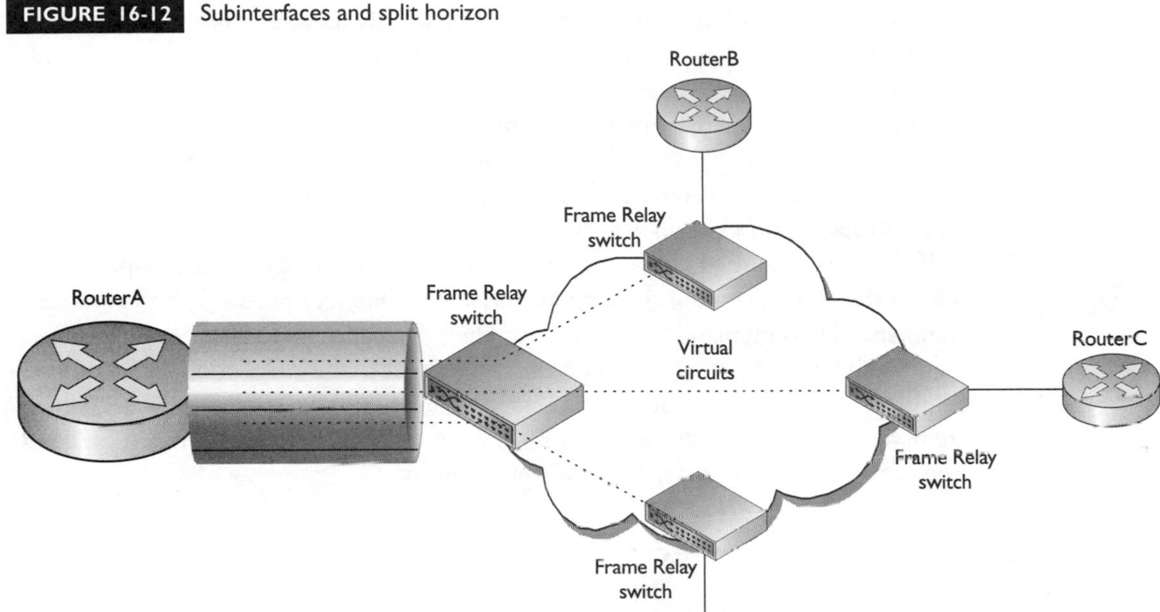

connections, a different subnet is used for each router-to-router connection. With this setup, if RouterB sent a routing update to RouterA, it would be processed on one subinterface and the routing information could be broadcast out the other two subinterfaces. This process allows you to overcome the split horizon problem.

The main problem with this solution is that for each subinterface on RouterA, you need a separate network or subnet number. Therefore, it is highly recommended that you use private IP addresses for these internal WAN connections.

Subinterface Types

As was described in Chapter 9, there are two types of subinterfaces: point-to-point and multipoint. Multipoint subinterfaces (subinterfaces with many VCs terminated on them) are good for fully meshed networks. If the WAN is fully meshed, the devices can be placed in the same subnet and thus require only one network number to address your devices. However, multipoint subinterfaces don't work well in partially meshed network designs. In this situation, they have problems with routing protocols that use split horizon.

Point-to-point subinterfaces work best in partially meshed environments or in environments where you need to simulate a leased-line connection. Point-to-point subinterfaces are used to overcome routing protocols that use split horizon. But like multipoint subinterfaces, point-to-point subinterfaces have their fair share of problems. In the biggest problem, each point-to-point subinterface requires a separate network or subnet number. If you have 200 subinterfaces on your serial interface, you need 200 subnets to accommodate your addressing needs.

If you are concerned about the addressing needs required of point-to-point subinterfaces, you can use the **ip unnumbered** *Interface Subconfiguration* mode command. This command *borrows* an IP address from another active interface on the router without your having to assign a different subnet to the connection. Most network administrators shy away from this command because it has its own set of issues, which are beyond the scope of this book. This command is covered further on the BSCI and Remote Access exams for the CCNP certification.

Creating Subinterfaces

To create a subinterface, use the following syntax:

```
Router(config)# interface serial [slot_#/]port_#.subinterface_#
                            point-to-point|multipoint
Router(config-subif)#
```

Subinterface numbers can range from 1 to 429,497,293. What number you choose as the subinterface number doesn't matter; it needs to be unique only among all of the subinterfaces for a given physical interface. The router uses this number to differentiate the subinterfaces for each physical interface. In IOS 11.3 and earlier, the interface type—**multipoint** or **point-to-point**—was optional. If you would omit the parameter, it would default to **multipoint**. Starting with IOS 12.0, this parameter is required—there is no default. And once you create a subinterface, notice that the prompt changed from `Router(config)#` to `Router(config-subif)#`.

Once you create a subinterface, you can delete it by prefacing the **interface** command with the **no** parameter. However, once you delete the subinterface, the subinterface still exists in the router's memory. To completely remove the subinterface, you need to save your configuration and reboot your router. Also, if you want to change the subinterface type from multipoint to point-to-point or vice versa, you must delete the subinterface, save your configuration, and reboot your router.

16.09. The CD contains a multimedia demonstration of creating subinterfaces on a router.

Configuring Frame Relay with Subinterfaces

When you are configuring Frame Relay with subinterfaces, you must associate your DLCI or DLCIs with each subinterface by using the **frame-relay interface-dlci** command:

```
Router(config)# interface serial [slot_#/]port_#.subinterface_#
                          point-to-point|multipoint
Router(config-subif)# frame-relay interface-dlci local_DLCI_#
```

If you have a point-to-point subinterface, you can assign only one VC, and thus one DLCI, to it. If it is a multipoint subinterface, you can assign multiple DLCIs to it. When creating your subinterfaces, it is a common practice to match the subinterface number with the DLCI number; however, remember that these two numbers have nothing in common and can be different. Also, make sure that you assign your layer-3 addressing to the subinterface and *not* the physical interface. The frame type and LMI type are, however, configured on the physical interface.

The **frame-relay interface-dlci** command uses dynamic resolution with inverse ARP. If you can't use inverse ARP, or don't want to, then use the **frame-relay map** command on the subinterface to perform manual resolution, like this:

```
Router(config)# interface serial [slot_#/]port_#.subinterface_#
                          point-to-point|multipoint
Router(config-subif)# frame-relay map protocol_name
                            destination_address local_dlci_#
                            [broadcast] [ietf|cisco]
```

Example Configuration with Multipoint Subinterfaces

This section offers an example of using multipoint subinterfaces on a router to set up Frame Relay connections. Let's use the network shown in Figure 16-13. In this example, I'll assume that LMI is being autosensed, and a single multipoint subinterface is used on RouterA.

Here's the configuration for RouterA:

```
RouterA(config)# interface serial 0
RouterA(config-if)# encapsulation frame-relay ietf
RouterA(config-if)# no shutdown
RouterA(config-if)# exit
RouterA(config)# interface serial0.1 multipoint
RouterA(config-subif)# ip address 192.168.1.1 255.255.255.0
RouterA(config-subif)# frame-relay interface-dlci 101
RouterA(config-subif)# frame-relay interface-dlci 102
```

FIGURE 16-13

Multipoint subinterface example

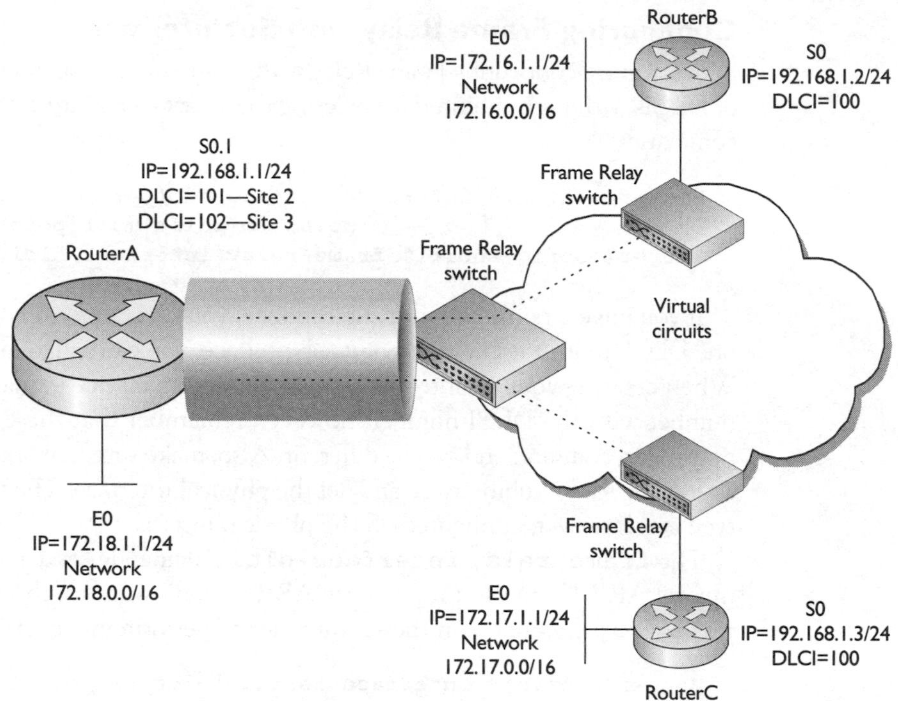

Since this is a partially meshed network, and you are terminating two VCs on the same subinterface, you need to do one of the following to solve split horizon issues: disable split horizon on RouterA or configure static routes on RouterB and RouterC.

In this example, you'll configure static routes. Here's the configuration for RouterB:

```
RouterB(config)# interface serial 0
RouterB(config-if)# encapsulation frame-relay ietf
RouterB(config-if)# ip address 192.168.1.2 255.255.255.0
RouterB(config-if)# no shutdown
RouterB(config-if)# exit
RouterB(config)# interface ethernet 0
RouterB(config-if)# ip address 172.16.1.1 255.255.255.0
RouterB(config-if)# no shutdown
RouterB(config-if)# exit
RouterB(config)# ip route 172.17.0.0 255.255.0.0 192.168.1.1
```

Notice in this example that you did not need to configure the DLCI number on the physical interface, since the router will learn this from the full status update via LMI. Also notice the static route on RouterB, which allows it to reach RouterC's network.

Here's the configuration for RouterC:

```
RouterC(config)# interface serial 0
RouterC(config-if)# encapsulation frame-relay ietf
RouterC(config-if)# ip address 192.168.1.3 255.255.255.0
RouterC(config-if)# no shutdown
RouterC(config-if)# exit
RouterC(config)# interface ethernet 0
RouterC(config-if)# ip address 172.17.1.1 255.255.255.0
RouterC(config-if)# no shutdown
RouterC(config-if)# exit
RouterC(config)# ip route 172.16.0.0 255.255.0.0 192.168.1.1
```

16.10. The CD contains a multimedia demonstration of setting up Frame Relay connections using multipoint subinterfaces on a router.

Example Configuration with Point-to-Point Subinterfaces

This section offers an example of using point-to-point subinterfaces on a router to set up Frame Relay connections. Let's use the network shown in Figure 16-14. In this example, I'll assume that LMI is being autosensed, and two point-to-point subinterfaces are used on RouterA.

The configurations on RouterB and RouterC are the same as before, with the exception that the static routes are not needed, since point-to-point subinterfaces are being used on RouterA and that RouterC will need a different IP address because of the two subnets (instead of one). The biggest difference is the configuration on RouterA, shown here:

```
RouterA(config)# interface serial 0
RouterA(config-if)# encapsulation frame-relay ietf
RouterA(config-if)# no shutdown
RouterA(config-if)# exit
RouterA(config)# interface serial0.1 point-to-point
RouterA(config-subif)# ip address 192.168.1.1 255.255.255.0
RouterA(config-subif)# frame-relay interface-dlci 101
RouterA(config-subif)# exit
RouterA(config)# interface serial0.2 point-to-point
RouterA(config-subif)# frame-relay interface-dlci 201
RouterA(config-subif)# ip address 192.168.2.1 255.255.255.0
```

In this example, subinterface `serial0.1` is connected to RouterB and subinterface `serial0.2` is connected to RouterC. Also notice that there is a different subnet on each subinterface. RouterB's configuration doesn't change, but you'll need

FIGURE 16-14

Point-to-point subinterface example

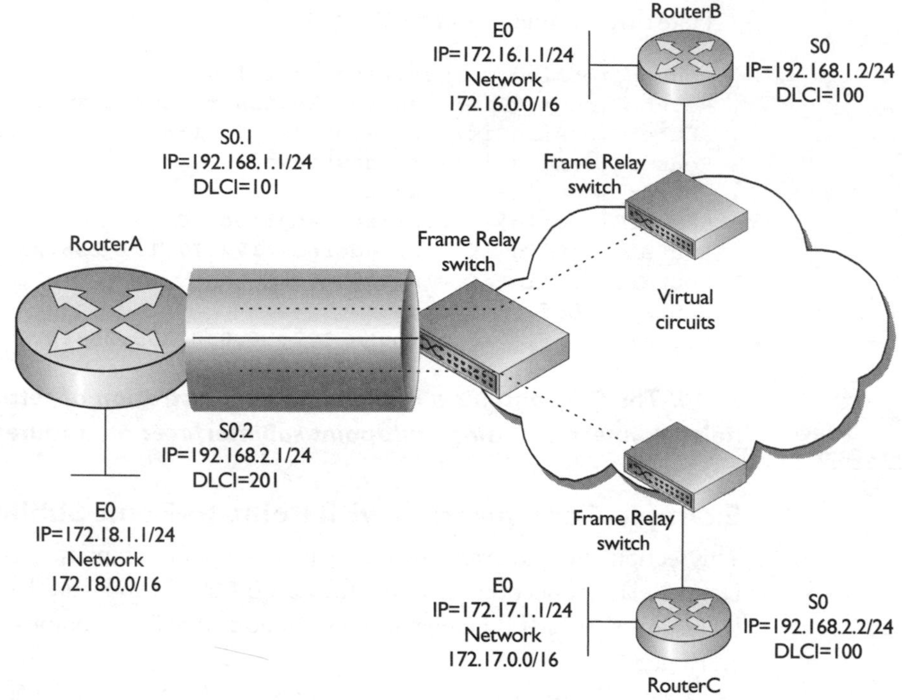

to configure 192.168.2.2 on RouterC's serial interface. One other item to point out is that if you are running a dynamic routing protocol like RIPv1 or IGRP, you could remove the static routes on RouterB and RouterC, since split horizon is solved by RouterA's configuration.

16.11. The CD contains a multimedia demonstration of setting up Frame Relay connections using point-to-point subinterfaces on a router.

exam watch

When configuring Frame Relay with subinterfaces, the Frame Relay encapsulation and LMI type go on the major (physical) interface. The IP address and DLCI number for the VC go on the subinterface. To specify the DLCI number, use the **`frame-relay interface-dlci`** ***command.***

EXERCISE 16-2

Configuring Frame Relay with Subinterfaces

These preceding few sections dealt with the configuration of Frame Relay using subinterfaces. This exercise will help you reinforce this material by configuring a simple Frame Relay point-to-point connection. This exercise builds upon the Exercise 16-1, moving the configuration from that exercise and placing it on a point-to-point subinterface. Also, inverse ARP is used to perform the resolution. You'll perform this lab using Boson's NetSim simulator. After starting up the simulator, click the *LabNavigator* button. Next, double-click *Exercise 16-2* and click the *Load Lab* button. This will load the lab configuration based on Exercise 16-1.

1. Remove the IP address on the physical interface of the 2600. Also remove the manual resolution command.

   At the top of the simulator in the menu bar, click the *eRouters* icon and choose *2600*. Remove the IP address on the interface: **configure terminal**, **interface serial1**, and **no ip address**. Remove the manual resolution command to reach the 2500 router: **no frame-relay map ip 192.168.10.2 100**. Exit *Configuration* mode: **end**. Use the **show interface serial1** command to verify the removal of the IP address and that the interface is up and up and that LMI is functioning. Use the **show frame-relay lmi** command to make sure the router is still sending and receiving LMI information. Make sure the resolution was removed: **show frame-relay map**. There should not be a manual resolution entry.

2. Remove the IP address on the physical interface of the 2500. Also remove the manual resolution command.

   At the top of the simulator in the menu bar, click the *eRouters* icon and choose *2500*. From the 2500 router, remove the IP address on the interface: **configure terminal**, **interface serial1**, and **no ip address**. Remove the manual resolution command to reach the 2600 router: **no frame-relay map ip 192.168.10.1 100**. Exit *Configuration* mode: **end**. Use the **show interface serial1** command to verify the removal of the IP address and that the interface is up and up and that LMI is functioning. Use the **show frame-relay lmi** command to make sure the router is still sending and receiving LMI information. Make sure the resolution was removed: **show frame-relay map**. There should not be a manual resolution entry.

3. Create a point-to-point subinterface on the 2600 router with a subinterface number of 100. Assign the DLCI to the subinterface. The DLCI number used locally is 100. Assign the IP address to the subinterface. Verify the configuration.

   At the top of the simulator in the menu bar, click the *eRouters* icon and choose *2600*. Create the subinterface: **configure terminal** and **interface serial 1.100 point-to-point**. Assign the DLCI: **frame-relay interface-dlci 100**. Assign the IP address: **ip address 192.168.10.1 255.255.255.0**. Exit *Configuration* mode: **end**. View the PVC: **show frame-relay pvc**.

4. Create a point-to-point subinterface on the 2500 router with a subinterface number of 100. On the 2500, create the subinterface: configure terminal, interface serial 1.100 point-to-point. The DLCI number used locally is 100. Assign the IP address to the subinterface. Verify the configuration.

   At the top of the simulator in the menu bar, click the *eRouters* icon and choose *2500*. On the 2500, create the subinterface: **configure terminal interface serial 1.100 point-to-point**. Assign the DLCI: **frame-relay interface-dlci 100**. Assign the IP address: **ip address 192.168.10.2 255.255.255.0**. Exit *Configuration* mode: **end**. View the PVC: show **frame-relay pvc**.

5. On the 2600, test the connection to the 2500. Verify the router's routing table. From Host1, test the connection to Host3.

   At the top of the simulator in the menu bar, click the *eRouters* icon and choose *2600*. On the 2600 router, ping the 2500's Frame Relay interface: **ping 192.168.10.2**. The ping should be successful. If it isn't, wait one minute and try again—the inverse ARP might be taking place. On Host1, ping Host3: **ping 192.168.3.2**. The ping should be successful.

Now you should be more familiar with configure Frame Relay with subinterfaces.

CERTIFICATION SUMMARY

Frame Relay uses VCs for connectivity. A VC is a logical connection between devices. There are two types of VCs: PVCs, which are similar to a leased line, and SVCs, which are similar to circuit-switched calls. VCs have advantages over leased lines in that once a physical connection is provisioned, it is very easy to add VCs as well as allocate bandwidth for users or applications by using VCs. If you want to fully mesh your Frame Relay routers, use this formula to figure out the number of required connections: (N*(N – 1))/2.

LMI defines how a Frame Relay DTE (router) interacts with a Frame Relay DCE (carrier switch). There are three types of LMI: Gang of Four, ANSI Annex D, and ITU-T Q.933 Annex A. LMI is local to two devices and is never forwarded through another device. By default, DTEs originate LMI messages. Cisco routers generate LMI messages every ten seconds, with a full status update occurring every sixth message. Each VC is given an address, called a DLCI. DLCIs are also locally significant and can change on a segment-by-segment basis. Carrier switches remap DLCI numbers in the Frame Relay header if there is a change from one segment to another. Carriers use two methods for transporting Frame Relay frames across their network. A Network Interworking connection uses ATM to transport Frame Relay frames between two Frame Relay devices. Service Interworking is used if one DTE is using Frame Relay and the remote DTE is using ATM.

There are many parameters that control the rate of traffic and congestion for a VC. CIR is the guaranteed average rate of a VC. B_C is a higher supported average rate, but measured over a shorter period than CIR. If frames exceed this rate, they are marked as discard eligible and are the first frames dropped by the carrier when the carrier experiences congestion problems. B_E is the maximum rate at which the carrier will service the VC; any data sent above this rate is dropped. Oversubscription is where the CIRs of all of your VCs exceed your access rate (physical line rate). You are betting that not all VCs will simultaneously run at their CIRs. FECN and BECN are used to indicate congestion from the source to the destination DTE.

There are two Frame Relay encapsulations: Cisco's and IETF's. Use the **`encapsulation frame-relay`** command to specify the encapsulation type. Cisco routers with IOS 11.2 or later can autosense the LMI type. To hard-code the LMI type, use the **`frame-relay lmi-type`** command. The **`show interfaces`** and **`show frame-relay lmi`** commands show the number of LMI messages sent and received.

There are two ways of performing layer-3 to DLCI resolution in your configuration: manually and dynamically. To specify a manually resolved VC, use the **`frame-relay`**

map command. Inverse ARP, which occurs every 60 seconds, allows you to dynamically learn the layer-3 addresses from each VC. Inverse ARP requires the VC to be in an active state, which indicates the VC is functioning between the two DTEs. If the VC is in an inactive state, the VC is functioning between the DTE and DCE, but there is a problem between the local DCE and the remote DTE. If the VC is in a deleted state, there is a problem with the VC between the local DTE and the local DCE. Use the **show frame-relay map** command to see your resolutions and the **show frame-relay pvc** command to view your PVCs.

NBMA environments have problems with distance vector routing protocols and split horizon when the network is partially meshed. To overcome split horizon, you can use any of the following solutions: fully mesh the network, use static routes, disable split horizon, or use subinterfaces. The recommended approach is to use subinterfaces. When configuring Frame Relay for subinterfaces, the encapsulation type and LMI type go on the main physical interface. All layer-3 addressing and the DLCI number for the VC (**frame-relay interface-dlci**) go on the subinterface.

TWO-MINUTE DRILL

Virtual Circuits

- Use this formula to figure out the number of connections required to fully mesh a network: (N*(N – 1))/2.
- VCs are not tied to any particular time slots on a channelized connection and are much easier to add or change than leased lines.
- A PVC is similar to a leased line and is always up. An SVC is similar to a telephone circuit-switched connection and is brought up when you have data to send and torn down when you are finished transmitting data. PVCs are best used if you have delay-sensitive information or you have data that you are constantly sending. SVCs are used when you occasionally need to send information or for backup purposes.

Terminology and Operation

- LMI defines how the Frame Relay DTE and DCE interact and is locally significant. There are three implementations of LMI: ITU-T Annex A, ANSI Annex D, and the Gang of Four. Cisco routers autosense LMI. By default, Cisco routers send out LMI queries every ten seconds, with a full status update every sixth query.
- DLCIs are used to locally identity a VC—they are the address of the VC. Since this number has only local significance, it can change on a hop-by-hop basis.
- The access rate is the physical speed of the line. CIR is the average data rate, over a period of time, of a VC. The committed burst rate is the average data rate, over a smaller period of time than CIR, for a VC. The excessive burst rate is the fastest rate at which a VC will be serviced by the carrier. A frame sent above the CIR/B_C values will have the discard eligibility bit set.
- Congestion experienced as frames go to a destination will have the FECN bit set. The destination will then send a frame with the BECN bit set back to the source, indicating congestion.

Frame Relay Configuration

- The **encapsulation frame-relay** command specifies the encapsulation type. There are two frame types: **cisco** and **ietf**; **cisco** is the default, but **ietf** is defined in RFC 1490.
- Use the **frame-relay lmi-type** command to hard-code the LMI type. As of IOS 11.2, Cisco routers autosense the LMI type. Use these commands to troubleshoot LMI: **show interfaces**, **show frame-relay lmi**, and **debug frame-relay lmi**.
- To configure a manually resolved PVC, use the **frame-relay map** command. If you omit the **broadcast** parameter, local broadcasts and multicasts won't traverse the VC. Inverse ARP is used for dynamic resolution. This occurs on a VC after the full status update is received and the VC is not already manually resolved.
- There are three statuses of VCs: active (the VC is up and operational between the two DTEs), inactive (the connection is functioning at least between the DTE and DCE), and deleted (the DTE/DCE connection is not functioning). To view a PVC, use the **show frame-relay pvc** command. To see the resolution entries, use the **show frame-relay map** command.

Nonbroadcast Multiaccess

- Partially meshed networks have VC connections to some, but not all, routers. A star (hub-and-spoke) topology is partially meshed. Partially meshed networks with VCs have problems with split horizon, which can be overcome by using one of the following solutions: use a fully meshed network, use static routes, disable split horizon, use subinterfaces.
- When using subinterfaces, the physical interface has the encapsulation and LMI type configured on it. Everything else is configured on the subinterface. When you delete a subinterface, save your configuration and reboot the router to remove it from RAM. Point-to-point subinterfaces should be used to solve split horizon problems.
- Use the **frame-relay interface-dlci** command to associate a VC to a particular subinterface.

SELF TEST

The following Self Test questions will help you measure your understanding of the material presented in this chapter. Read all the choices carefully, as there may be more than one correct answer. Choose all correct answers for each question.

Virtual Circuits

1. You have a total of five routers. ________ circuits are required to fully mesh the network, where every router needs ___________ interfaces.

A. 5, 5

B. 8, 4

C. 10, 5

D. 10, 4

2. A ___________ is similar to a telephone circuit-switched connection.

A. PVC

B. SVC

3. You have a 24-channel T1 connection to your router. How many VCs does this T1 support?

A. 1

B. 24

C. No limit

Terminology and Operation

4. _________ defines how the Frame Relay DTE and DCE interact with each other.

A. DLCI

B. CIR

C. LMI

D. PMI

5. The address of a Frame Relay VC is called a ___________.

A. Data link layer connection identifier

B. Data layer connection index

C. Data link connection index

D. Data link connection identifier

6. Frames sent above the __________ limit will have their __________ bit set.

   A. CIR, DE
   B. B_C, DE
   C. B_C, FECN
   D. CIR, FECN

7. When a carrier experiences congestion, it marks the ________ bit in the header of the Frame Relay frame.

   A. CIR
   B. DE
   C. BECN
   D. FECN

8. Annex A is which LMI standard?

   A. Cisco
   B. ITU-T Q.933
   C. ANSI

Frame Relay Configuration

9. Cisco routers generate LMI enquiries every ________ seconds and a full status update every __________ seconds.

   A. 10, 60
   B. 10, 6
   C. 60, 300
   D. 15, 60

10. Enter the router command to have the serial interface use a Frame Relay RFC 1490 frame type: ____________.

11. Enter the router command to set the LMI type to ITU-T Annex A: ____________.

12. When using the **show interfaces** command, which Frame Relay information can you not see?

    A. The DLCI number used for LMI
    B. The number of LMIs sent and received
    C. Statuses of PVCs
    D. The LMI type

13. Which Frame Relay command is used to manually resolve addresses?

A. `frame-relay interface-dlci`

B. `frame-relay map`

C. `frame-relay resolve`

D. `frame-relay lmi-type`

14. If you see a VC with an inactive status, this indicates ____________.

A. The connection between both Frame Relay DTEs is up and operational.

B. The connection between your Frame Relay DTE and DCE is up and operational, but there is something wrong with connection between your connected Frame Relay switch and the destination DTE.

C. You are not receiving any LMI messages from the Frame Relay switch.

Nonbroadcast Multiaccess

15. ________ topologies in NBMA environments do not have problems with split horizon.

A. Partially meshed

B. Fully meshed

C. Hub and spoke

D. Star

16. Enter the router command to create a multipoint subinterface on `serial0` with a subinterface number of 5: __________.

17. Enter the router command to associate DLCI 500 with a subinterface: ____________.

SELF TEST ANSWERS

Virtual Circuits

1. ☑ **D.** Use the (N*(N – 1)/2) formula for the number of circuits. You need a total of ten circuits and four interfaces on each router.
   ☒ **A** has the wrong number of circuits and interfaces. **B** has the wrong number of circuits. **C** has the wrong number of interfaces.

2. ☑ **B.** An SVC is similar to a telephone circuit-switched connection.
   ☒ **A** is similar to a leased line.

3. ☑ **C.** The number of VCs is not tied to any physical properties of a connection type. Remember that VCs are logical connections.
   ☒ **A** would be true if this were a leased line. **B** refers to the number of time slots in a T1 and has no effect on the number of VCs a connection can support.

Terminology and Operation

4. ☑ **C.** The local management interface (LMI) defines how the Frame Relay DTE and DCE interact with each other.
   ☒ **A** defines the local address of a VC. **B** defines the average traffic rate for a VC. **D** is a nonexistent acronym.

5. ☑ **D.** The address of a Frame Relay VC is called a data link connection identifier (DLCI).
   ☒ **A** and **B** include the term *layer*. **B** and **C** use the term *index*.

6. ☑ **B.** Frames sent above the B_C limit will have their DE bit set.
   ☒ **A** and **D** are incorrect because frames sent between CIR and B_C are okay. **C** and **D** specify FECN, which is used for flow control.

7. ☑ **D.** When a carrier experiences congestion, it marks the FECN bit in the header of the Frame Relay frame.
   ☒ **A** specifies the average rate of a VC. **B** is used to mark frames that exceed their allowable rate. **C** is marked by the destination device to indicate congestion, and is sent to the source device.

8. ☑ **B.** The LMI type Annex A is defined by ITU-T Q.933.
   ☒ **A** is the Gang of Four. **C** is Annex D.

Frame Relay Configuration

9. ☑ A. Cisco routers generate LMI enquiries every 10 seconds and a full status update every 60 seconds.
   ☒ B specifies the wrong update interval for the full update message. C has wrong values for both timers. D has a wrong value for the status enquiry timer.

10. ☑ **`encapsulation frame-relay ietf`**.

11. ☑ **`frame-relay lmi-type q933a`**.

12. ☑ C. When using the **`show interfaces`** command, you cannot see the statuses of the PVCs—you need to use the **`show frame-relay pvc`** command.
    ☒ A, B, and D can be seen in the output of this command.

13. ☑ B. The **`frame-relay map`** command is used to manually resolve layer-3 addresses to DLCIs.
    ☒ A associates a DLCI to a subinterface. C is a nonexistent command. D hard-codes the LMI type for the physical serial interface.

14. ☑ B. If you see a VC with an inactive status, this indicates that the connection between your Frame Relay DTE and DCE is up and operational, but there is something wrong with connection between your connected Frame Relay switch and the destination DTE.
    ☒ A is an active VC. C is a deleted VC.

Nonbroadcast Multiaccess

15. ☑ B. Fully meshed topologies in NBMA environments do not have problems with split horizon.
    ☒ A, C, and D have problems with split horizon.

16. ☑ **`interface serial0.5 multipoint`**.

17. ☑ **`frame-relay interface-dlci 500`**.

17

ISDN

CERTIFICATION OBJECTIVES

- 17.01 ISDN Introduction
- 17.02 ISDN Interface Configuration
- 17.03 Legacy Dial-on-Demand Routing
- 17.04 Dialer Profiles and DDR
- ✓ Two-Minute Drill
- Q&A Self Test

Chapter 15 introduced you to wide area networks and the first type of WAN connection: leased lines using HDLC and PPP. Chapter 16 introduced you to the second type of WAN connection: packet-switched connections using Frame Relay. This chapter introduces you to the third type of WAN connection: circuit-switched connections. Circuit-switched connections include analog and digital dialup connections. Analog connections use modems, while digital connections use ISDN and ISDN hardware for dialup connections. This chapter solely focuses on using ISDN for dialup. The hardware configurations for analog connections are different than for ISDN; however, the actual dialup commands are the same. Analog dialup is not covered in this book but is covered on Cisco's CCNP Remote Access exam.

CERTIFICATION OBJECTIVE 17.01

ISDN Introduction

The Integrated Services Digital Network (ISDN) is a group of standards that define how voice and data connections can be dynamically set up across digital circuits. Because ISDN uses digital circuits, it has the following advantages over analog connections:

- *ISDN sets up calls faster* Analog takes 30–60 seconds to complete a call, while ISDN takes only second or two.
- *ISDN has a guaranteed data rate* Analog provides no guarantee for bandwidth on a connection, whereas ISDN guarantees 64Kbps for each connection.
- *ISDN is more suitable to handle different types of services* Analog is not good at handling a mixture of voice, video, and data connections, whereas ISDN is.

ISDN is a better technology than analog modem dialup connections because of a faster setup time, guaranteed data rates, and multiple services are handled better.

This section discusses the types of connections used for ISDN as well as the standards ISDN uses to initiate phone connections. Out of all of the chapters in this book, as you will see, this chapter has the most acronyms, making it harder to learn.

ISDN Connections

Before I begin discussing ISDN itself, I first want to discuss the properties of the connection that ISDN uses. ISDN is a channelized service. *Channelized* services use a process called *time division multiplexing (TDM)* to create many logical channels on a single piece of wire. A channel is often referred to as a *time slot*.

Each channel, or time slot, is given its own amount of bandwidth and time on the wire, as is depicted in Figure 17-1. As you can see from the physical view of this figure, each channel is not simultaneously transmitting its information along with other channels. Instead, each channel must take its own turn in sending a small bit of information. All channels are given the same amount of bandwidth and time, and once all of the channels are given their chance to send information, the first channel begins again. Even if a channel doesn't have anything to send, a string of zeros is sent. The bottom part of Figure 17-1 shows a logical view of a TDM connection. From a user's perspective, it looks as if all channels are transmitting simultaneously.

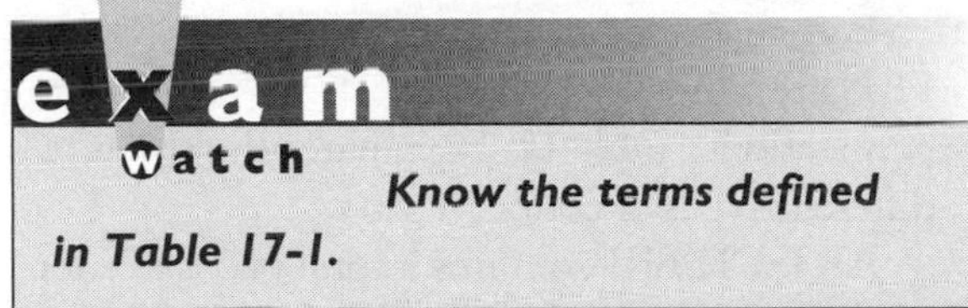

Table 17-1 has some common terms used when referring to channelized connections.

FIGURE 17-1 Physical and logical views of a TDM connection

Physical view

Time slot 1 | Time slot 2 | Time slot 3 | Time slot 4 | Time slot 5 | Time slot 6 | Time slot 7 | Time slot ....

Logical view

Time slot 1
Time slot 2
Time slot 3
Time slot 4
Time slot ....

TABLE 17-1 Channelized Connection Terms

Term	Definition
DS0	Is the smallest type of channelized connection, representing 64Kbps. Each channel in Figure 17-1 is a DS0.
DS1	Is a group of channelized connections. There are two basic types of DS1s: T1 and E1.
T1	Is a group of 24 DS0s that is common in North America. With its overhead, it has a clock rate of 1.544Mbps.
E1	Is a group of 32 DS0s that is common in Europe. It has a clock rate of 2.048Mbps.

ISDN supports two types of connections: Basic Rate Interface (BRI) and Primary Rate Interface (PRI). A BRI connection is somewhat of a fractional T1/E1 connection. PRIs are supported across both T1 and E1 connections. Table 17-2 compares the three different types of connections.

exam watch ***Definitely remember the information in Table 17-2. Each bearer channel, which is used for phone connections, only has 64Kbps of bandwidth.***

An ISDN BRI contains a total of 3 DS0s for 192Kbps of bandwidth. Two DS0s, called bearer channels, are used to make phone calls for voice, video, and data connections. The signaling channel contains one DS0 and is broken into two components: 16Kbps is used for signaling information (setting up and tearing down circuit-switched connections), and 48Kbps is used for frame synchronization, clocking, and physical layer framing.

There are two types of ISDN PRI connections: one for T1s and one for E1s. The PRI T1 uses 23 DS0s as bearer channels and 1 DS0 for signaling. The framing, clocking, and synchronization are built into the T1 frame structure and do not require a separate DS0 for these functions. A PRI E1 has a total of 32 channels, of which 30 DS0s are bearer channels; 1 DS0 is used for signaling; and 1 DS0 is used for framing, synchronization, and clocking. The signaling channel is comonly called the *D-channel.*

TABLE 17-2 ISDN Connection Types

Connection	Bearer Channel	Signaling Channel	Total Bandwidth
BRI	2 DS0s	1 DS0	192Kbps
PRI T1	23 DS0s	1 DS0	1.544Mbps
PRI E1	30 DS0s	1 DS0	2.048Mbps

ISDN Standards

It is difficult to learn how ISDN operates, in part because it is not a single standard, but a group of many different standards that work together to provide digital circuit-switched connections. Work on these standards began in the 1960s and was formally standardized in the early 1980s. ITU-T is responsible for developing and maintaining these standards, shown in Table 17-3.

exam watch

Q.921 is the signaling protocol used at layer-2 for the ISDN switch and the router (or other device) to communicate with each other. LAPD is the framing protocol used, which is based on ISO's HDLC frame format. Q.931 is the layer-3 protocol used to set up and tear down phone connections between ISDN end-point devices, such as routers.

One of the problems, sometimes, with ITU-T standards is that the standard is not exact in its description. For example, the Q series of standards that define how your device interoperates with the ISDN switch are not specific in how the interaction should occur. Therefore, many different types of ISDN switches exist with different flavors of the Q series of standards. To accommodate these different implementations, Cisco routers allow you to configure the switch type that you are connected to. This

TABLE 17-3 ISDN Standards

Type	Standard	Definition
Telephone standards	E.163	Defines the International telephone numbering plan
	E.164	Defines the International ISDN addressing
Terms, concepts, and interfaces	I.100	Defines the ISDN terms and concepts
	I.400	Defines the User-Network Interface (UNI) and its components
Signaling	Q.921	Defines Link Access Procedure on the D channel (LAPD), which is responsible for the data link layer (layer-2) connection between the router and the ISDN switch
	Q.931	Defines the network layer signaling (layer-3) used to set up and tear down phone connections

allows you to use the signaling protocol that your switch supports. As you will see later on in this chapter, this is one of the ISDN components that you must configure on your router.

Functional Groups and Reference Points

To help simplify the process for implementing ISDN, ITU-T's I standards define the ISDN components and relationships between the components. The components are called *function groups*. *Reference points* define the relationships between the components. The function groups and reference points can be seen in Figure 17-2. Table 17-4 defines the function groups found in Figure 17-2. Table 17-5 defines the reference points.

> **exam watch**
> ***Remember the function groups and reference points information in Tables 17-4 and 17-5 when preparing for the exam.***

Figure 17-2 and Tables 17-4 and 17-5 give a nice logical description of the components and

FIGURE 17-2 ISDN function groups and reference points

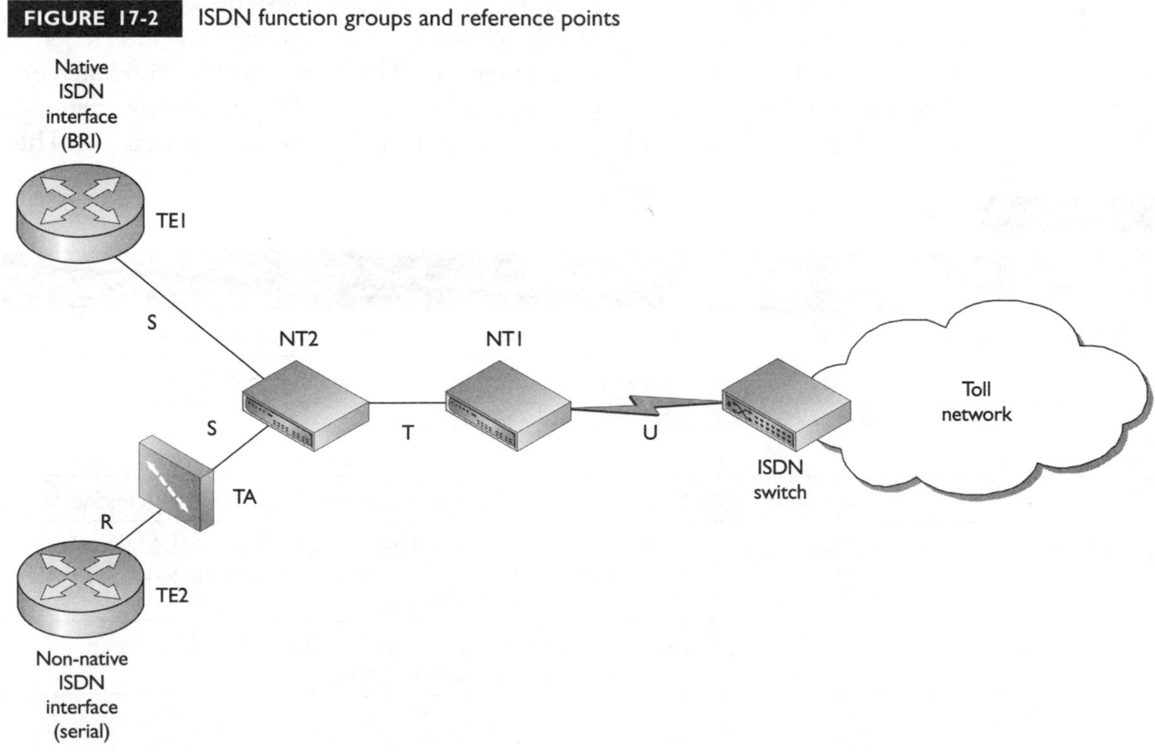

TABLE 17-4 ISDN Function Groups

Function Group	Definition
TE1 (Terminal Equipment 1)	Is an ISDN device with a native ISDN interface (such as a router with a BRI interface) that connects to an NT1 or NT2.
TE2 (Terminal Equipment 2)	Is an ISDN device with a non-native ISDN interface (such as a router with a serial interface) used for ISDN connectivity
TA (Terminal Adapter)	Connects a TE2 (non-native ISDN) to an NT2 or NT1
NT2 (Network Termination 2)	Connects multiple ISDN devices together, similar to a hub in Ethernet (the NT1 and NT2 are typically in the *same* physical chassis)
NT1 (Network Termination 1)	Connects your ISDN devices to the carrier network (converts ISDN four-wire connection to the carrier's two-wire connection)
LE (Local Exchange)	Provides a boundary between an NT1 located at the customer's site and the phone company's circuit-switched network. Note that this is not a physical device, but the phone company's network.

their interaction. In real life, however, ISDN isn't laid out so nice and neat. Let's look at a few examples to illustrate the physical connections that Cisco routers use for ISDN.

Cisco supports three types of BRI connections for their routers:

- Native ISDN interfaces with a built-in NT1
- Native ISDN interfaces without a built-in NT1
- Serial interfaces with an external terminal adapter and NT1

Cisco also supports two types of PRI connections for their routers:

- Native ISDN interfaces with an integrated CSU/DSU
- Native ISDN interfaces without an integrated CSU/DSU

TABLE 17-5 ISDN Reference Points

Reference Point	Definition
U	Defines the connection between an NT1 and an LE
T	Defines the connection between an NT2 and an NT1
S	Defines the connection between a TA/TE1 and an NT2
R	Defines the connection between a TE2 and a TA

The top part of Figure 17-3 shows an example of a router with a BRI interface and a built-in NT1. The S and T reference points are in the chassis of the router, and the R reference point is not included, since this is a native ISDN interface. The U reference point connects the router to the carrier. If you had a Cisco router with this type of interface, it would be labeled *U*. For a PRI U interface, the CSU/DSU is built into the PRI controller card.

The middle part of Figure 17-3 shows an example of a router with a BRI interface, but an external NT1. On a Cisco router, the BRI interface would be labeled *S/T*. In this situation, you would need to purchase an external NT1 device. The cable you would use would be UTP, with RJ-45 connectors. Here are the pinouts of this eight-pin cable: 1–2 unused, 3 TX+, 4 RX+, 5 RX–, 6 TX–, 7–8 unused. If you have a PRI S/T interface, CSU/DSU is not built into the physical interface: you will need to purchase this.

The bottom part of Figure 17-3 shows an example of a router with a serial interface that is used for an ISDN connection. By default, a serial interface doesn't understand an ISDN connection. A TA adapts the connection from an NT1 so that the serial interface can deal with ISDN. Typically, you would use a serial cable, such as an EIA/TIA-232, EIA/TIA-449, V.35, or X.21 cable, to connect the serial interface of the TA. Since this is a non-native interface, the R reference point defines the function between the router and the TA.

FIGURE 17-3 BRI router connections

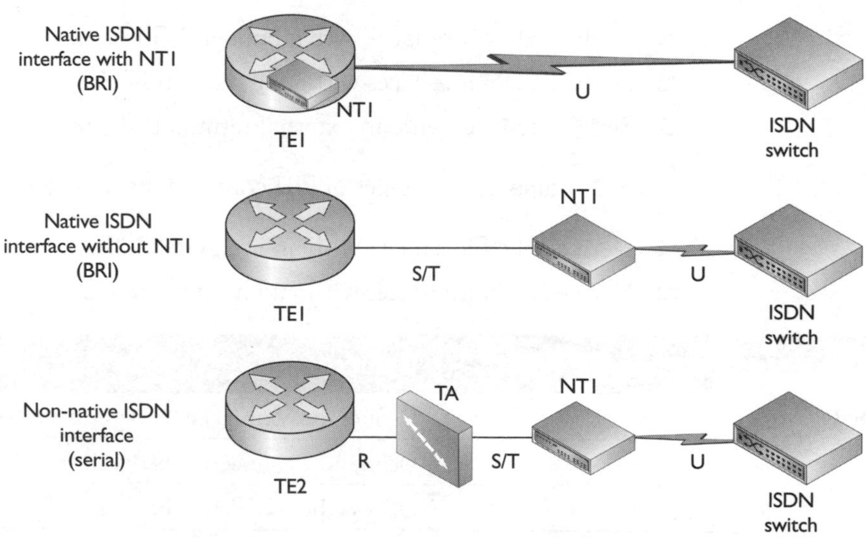

CERTIFICATION OBJECTIVE 17.02

ISDN Interface Configuration

Now that you have a basic understanding of the reference points and function groups of ISDN, let's talk about some of the basic ISDN configuration tasks you'll need to perform in order to interface your router with the ISDN switch. To initialize the connection between your router and the ISDN switch, you'll need to perform the following three steps:

1. Set up the ISDN switch type that the ISDN switch is using.
2. Optionally, specify the SPID or SPIDs (Service Profile Identifier) your carrier assigns to your BRI bearer (B) channels.
3. Verify your ISDN connection.

Switch Types

One of the first things you need to do is configure the ISDN switch type that your router is connected to. This can be configured at the *Global Configuration* or *Interface Subconfiguration* mode. If you define it globally, all of your ISDN interfaces will use the same switch type. You can override this on an interface-by-interface basis by configuring the switch type on a specific interface. Here is the configuration:

```
Router(config)# isdn switch-type ISDN_switch_type
-or-
Router(config-if)# isdn switch-type ISDN_switch_type
```

Prior to IOS 12.0, you could configure the switch type only globally. Starting in IOS 12.0, you can configure it at either location. Table 17-6 lists the ISDN switch types you can configure. Note that you must configure the correct switch type in order for your ISDN connection to function. In some cases, your provider might use one type of switch hardware but emulate a different switch type in software—you'll need to know what switch type the switch is emulating.

The isdn switch-type command can be used at Global or Interface Configuration mode. A switch type configured at Interface Subconfiguration mode overrides the global setting.

TABLE 17-6 ISDN Switch Type Parameters

Parameter	Connection	Description
basic-5ess	BRI	AT&T switch (used in North America)
basic-dms100	BRI	Nortel DMS-100 switch (used in North America)
basic-ni1	BRI	National ISDN 1 (used in North America)
basic-ni2	BRI	National ISDN 2 (used in North America)
basic-1tr6	BRI	(Germany)
basic-net3	BRI	(UK and parts of Europe)
basic-nwnet3	BRI	(Norway)
basic-nznet3	BRI	(New Zealand)
basic-ts013	BRI	TS013 and TS014 switches (Australia)
ntt	BRI	(Japan)
vn2	BRI	(France)
vn3	BRI	(France)
vn4	BRI	(France)
vn5	BRI	(France)
pri-4ess	PRI	AT&T switch (U.S.)
pri-5ess	PRI	AT&T switch (U.S.)
pri-dms100	PRI	NT switch (North America)
pri-nt	PRI	(Japan)
pri-net5	PRI	(Europe)

ISDN SPIDs

Service Profile IDs (SPIDs) are sometimes used by carriers on BRI connections that have a National ISDN-1 or Nortel DMS-100 switch. Because these two switches are typically used in North America, you will probably not have to worry about SPIDs from carriers elsewhere. SPIDs are used by the carrier to authenticate call requests and are used only on the local connection between your router and the ISDN switch. In this sense, they're like DLCIs—locally significant.

Based on the carrier's setup, you might be required to configure one or two SPIDs for your bearer channels before any type of phone call can be made by your router. Use the following configuration to define your SPIDs:

```
Router(config)# interface bri [slot_#/]port#
Router(config-if)# isdn spid1 spid_#_for_1st_BRI local_dial_#
Router(config-if)# isdn spid2 spid_#_for_2nd_BRI local_dial_#
```

SPID1 is for the first B-channel (B is short for bearer), and SPID2 is for the second B-channel. This number is normally your ten-digit telephone number plus some extra identifying digits. The local dial number is normally your seven-digit phone number (the three-digit local exchange number plus the four digits of your phone number). Your carrier will tell you whether you have to configure SPIDs or not and what you need to configure.

Use the isdn spid1|spid2 commands to assign SPIDs for National ISDN-1 and Nortel DMS-100 switches.

17.01. The CD contains a multimedia demonstration of configuring the ISDN switch type and SPIDs on a router.

PRI Commands

If you have a PRI interface, you'll need to configure some additional parameters before you can start making phone calls. After you have defined the ISDN switch type, you'll next need to configure the T1/E1 controller card and the serial interface associated with the controller card. The following two sections will show you the necessary configuration for your PRI connection.

Controller Card Configuration

Use the following configuration to set up your T1 or E1 PRI controller card:

```
Router(config)# controller t1|e1 [slot_#/]port_#
Router(config-controller)# framing esf|sf|crc4|nocrc4
Router(config-controller)# linecode ami|b8zs|hdb3
Router(config-controller)# clock source line
                          primary|secondary|internal
Router(config-controller)# pri-group timeslots [1-24|1-31]
Router(config-controller)# [no] shutdown
```

The physical framing used on the T1 or E1 is configured with the **framing** command. If you are configuring a T1 in North America, you'll typically use **esf** (Extended Super Frame); an E1 typically uses **crc4**. Following this is the line coding, which defines how 1's and 0's are physically represented on the wire. T1s typically use **b8zs**, and E1s use **hdb3**.

The **clock source** command defines how the router will acquire its clocking for synchronous digital connections. **primary** tells the router that the router will acquire clocking information from this line. **secondary** tells the router to use this interface as a backup source for acquiring the clocking. **internal** tells the router that it will provide clocking on the wire to the carrier—normally you don't use this third parameter in a production environment.

The **pri-group timeslots** command tells your router which time slot or time slots are going to be used for ISDN connections. You can purchase a fraction of the time slots if you don't need the full number of channels on a T1 or E1. This command tells the router which ones you are, and are not, using. Use the **shutdown** command to disable or enable the controller.

Here's a simple example of a router's configuration for a T1 PRI:

```
Router(config)# controller t1 0/0
Router(config-controller)# framing esf
Router(config-controller)# linecode b8zs
Router(config-controller)# clock source line primary
Router(config-controller)# pri-group timeslots 1-24
Router(config-controller)# no shutdown
```

Use the following command to verify the configuration of your controller card:

```
Router# show controllers t1|e1 [slot_#/port_#]
```

Here's an example:

```
Router# show controller t1 0
T1 0 is up.
  No alarms detected.
  Framing is ESF, Line Code is B8ZS, Clock Source is Line Primary.

  Version Info of slot 2:  HW: 2, Firmware: 14, NEAT PLD: 13,
NR Bus PLD: 19
  Data in current interval (476 seconds elapsed):
     0 Line Code Violations, 0 Path Code Violations
<--output omitted-->
```

Notice the first few lines of the display. In the first line, the physical layer is up. In the second line, no alarms are detected (the bottom part of the display shows the error statistics). The third line shows the configuration: the framing is ESF, line coding is B8ZS, and this line is the primary clock source.

Serial Interface Configuration

Once you have set up your T1 or E1 controller card, you can now proceed with the configuration of your serial interface. Actually, the configuration is not done on a *physical* serial interface, but a logical one that corresponds to the PRI-grouped time slots you created with the **pri-group timeslots** command. The main function of this interface is to tell the router which DS0 is being used as the D-channel (signaling). Use one of these two commands to set up the logical serial interface:

```
Router(config)# interface serial [slot_#/]port_#:23
Router(config)# interface serial [slot_#/]port_#:15
```

Use the same slot and port numbers that you used for the controller card configuration. Use the **23** parameter for a T1—this indicates that the last time slot is used for signaling. Use the **15** parameter for an E1—this indicates that the fourteenth time slot is used for signaling. Once you have created your logical serial interface, any dialup, encapsulation, or addressing commands, such as **encapsulation ppp** or **ip address**, are configured on the *logical* serial interface.

17.02. The CD contains a multimedia demonstration of configuring an ISDN PRI controller card and creating a logical ISDN PRI serial interface on a router.

Use the `controller` command to access your T1 or E1 controller for a PRI. The `pri-group` command specifies which DS0s the carrier has activated. To specify the signaling channel, use the `interface serial` command followed by the slot and port of the controller card, and then a colon and either 23 for a T1 or 15 for an E1.

Verifying Connections

Now that you have set up ISDN connectivity from your router to the ISDN switch, you will want to verify whether or not your router is communicating with the switch at both the physical and data link layers. Remember that the ITU-T Q.921 standard is used for communications at the data link layer. Here are the three commands that you'll use to verify that these two layers are functioning: **show interfaces**, **show isdn status**, and **debug isdn q921**. The following sections cover the use of these three commands.

The show interfaces Command

You have used the **show interfaces** command throughout this book to verify the status of the physical and data link layers. You can also use this command to verify the status of your ISDN connection:

```
Router# show interface bri [slot_#/]port_#[:1|2]
```

The **1** or **2** at the end of the command allows you to specify which B-channel you want to see. To view both B-channels, use this syntax:

```
Router# show interface bri [slot_#/]port_# 1 2
```

Here is an example of viewing the status of the first B-channel:

```
Router# show interface bri 0:1
BRI0:1 is up, line protocol is up
Hardware is BRI with U interface and external S bus interface
MTU 1500 bytes, BW 64 Kbit, DLY 20000 usec, rely 255/255,
     load 3/255
Encapsulation PPP, loopback not set, keepalive set (10 sec)
LCP Open, multilink Open
<--output omitted-->
```

17.03. The CD contains a multimedia demonstration of using the show interfaces bri command on a router.

The show isdn status Command

The **show isdn status** command gives you more detailed information about the status of the physical and data link layers than the **show interfaces** command:

```
Router# show isdn status
The current ISDN Switchtype = basic-ni1
ISDN BRI0 interface
    Layer 1 Status:
        ACTIVE
    Layer 2 Status:
        TEI = 64, State = MULTIPLE_FRAME_ESTABLISHED
        TEI = 65, State = MULTIPLE_FRAME_ESTABLISHED
    Spid status
TEI 64, ces = 1, state = 8 (established)
    Spid1 configured, spid1 sent, spid1 valid
Endpoint ID Info: epsf = 0, usid = 70, tid = 1
TEI 65, ces = 2, state = 8 (established)
    Spid1 configured, spid1 sent, spid1 valid
Endpoint ID Info: epsf = 0, usid = 70, tid = 2
    Layer 3 Status:
        No Active Layer 3 Call(s)
    Activated dsl 0 CCBs = 0
    Total Allocated ISDN CCBs = 0
```

In this example, layer-1 is `ACTIVE`. If there were a problem with the physical layer, it would say `DEACTIVATED`. To troubleshoot layer-1 problems, check the following:

- Check your cable and make sure the interface was activated with **no shutdown**.
- Call the carrier and verify that they have enabled their interface.

For layer-2 problems, you will see `NOT Activated` instead of actual TEI numbers if there is a problem. For an operational data link layer connection, you should see `MULTIPLE_FRAME_ESTABLISHED` as the state. If there is a problem with the data link layer, check the following:

- Verify that you have configured the correct ISDN switch type.
- If you are using SPIDs, verify their configuration.

Use the `show isdn status` command to verify your data link connection to the carrier's switch. Look for a `MULTIPLE_FRAME_ESTABLISHED` state.

The layer-3 status refers to whether or not there are any phone connections that are active. In this example, there are none.

17.04. The CD contains a multimedia demonstration of using the `show isdn status` command on a router.

The `debug isdn q921` Command

Use the **`debug isdn q921`** command for more detailed troubleshooting of the data link layer:

```
Router# debug isdn q921
May 23 11:19:12.106: ISDN BR0: TX ->  RRp sapi = 0  tei = 64 nr = 0
May 23 11:19:12.122: ISDN BR0: RX <-  RRf sapi = 0  tei = 64 nr = 2
```

In this example, you should see your router sending (`TX`) Q.921 frames to the switch as well as the switch's frames(RX). If you are seeing your router sending these frames but not receiving any responses back, check the switch type that you configured as well as your SPID values.

17.05. The CD contains a multimedia demonstration of using the `debug isdn q921` command on a router.

EXERCISE 17-1

Configuring ISDN Switch Connectivity

The last section dealt with setting up the ISDN connection between a Cisco router and a carrier's ISDN switch. This exercise will help you reinforce this material by configuring ISDN connectivity. You'll perform this lab using Boson's NetSim simulator. You can find a picture of the network diagram for Boson's NetSim simulator in the Introduction of this book. After starting up the simulator, click the *LabNavigator* button. Next, double-click *Exercise 17-1* and click the *Load Lab* button. This will load the lab configuration based on Chapter 5's and 7's exercises. The switch type used is Nortel DMS-100, and the two SPIDs are 4075551212 and 4075551213.

1. On the 2600 router, disable both the `serial0` and `serial1` interfaces. Verify your configuration.

   At the top of the simulator in the menu bar, click the *eRouters* icon and choose *2600*. Disable the interfaces: **`configure terminal`**, **`interface serial0`**, **`shutdown`**, **`exit`**, **`interface serial1`**, **`shutdown`**, and

end. Verify the status of the serial interfaces: **show interface s0** and **show interface s1**. Make sure that they have been administratively disabled.

2. On 2600 router, set the ISDN switch type. Set up the two SPIDs. Verify your configuration.

   On the 2600, set the ISDN switch type: **configure terminal** and **isdn switch-type basic-dms100**. Enter the BRI interface: **interface bri 0**. Assign your first SPID: **isdn spid1 4075551212**. Assign your second SPID: **isdn spid2 4075551213**. Enable the interface: **no shutdown**. Exit Configuration mode: **end**. View the status of the interface: **show interface bri 0**. The physical *and* data link layer should be up. Use the **show isdn status** command and check the Layer 2 Status, which should be MULTIPLE_FRAME_ESTABLISHED.

You should now be more comfortable with establishing ISDN connectivity to a carrier's ISDN switch.

CERTIFICATION OBJECTIVE 17.03

Legacy Dial-on-Demand Routing

The last section dealt with just the connection between the router and the ISDN switch (Q.921). The next two sections deal with how to have your router use its ISDN interface to establish a phone connection that can be used to transport data. Cisco uses the Dial-on-Demand Routing (DDR) feature to trigger phone calls, analog or digital, when it has *interesting* traffic to send to a remote destination. Interesting traffic is traffic that you define as important enough for the router to make a phone call. For example, you might not want ICMP to trigger a phone call, but telnet or FTP. Or perhaps traffic from particular subnet should trigger a phone call. As you will see, you have a lot of flexibility in defining what is interesting and what is not.

exam watch

DDR is best suited for the following areas: backing up a primary WAN connection; traffic that is low volume and periodic; or phone calls that are short and temporary.

Because the phone call the router is making might incur a toll charge, or a per-minute charge, you don't want your router to make unnecessary phone calls, or to keep these connections up indefinitely.

DDR is an excellent backup solution to other WAN connections, such as leased lines or Frame Relay. However, one thing to point out is that BRI and, especially, analog connections should be used to back up low-bandwidth primary connections.

Another thing to consider is that if you are using DDR, remember that analog connections take 30–60 seconds to establish, which might cause application timeout problems for you in any type of DDR scenario. Also consider that analog connections don't provide a guaranteed connection rate. The first time you connect, you might get a 48Kbps connection, and the second time, a 33.6Kbps connection—it all depends on the quality of the line and the modem that you are connecting to.

DDR Process

DDR goes through a four-step process when setting up a phone connection, which will then allow you to transfer data across it:

1. Your router receives a packet, and by checking its routing table, the router has determined that it needs to switch the packet out of the DDR interface.
2. Your router then determines whether or not the packet is *interesting*.
3. If the traffic is interesting and the phone connection hasn't been established yet, the router makes a phone call to establish the circuit-switched connection. If the packet isn't interesting and the DDR interface is not up, the router drops the packet; however, if the DDR connection has already been established, the router will allow both interesting and noninteresting traffic across the DDR circuit.
4. Once the circuit is up, the router will switch traffic out the DDR interface.

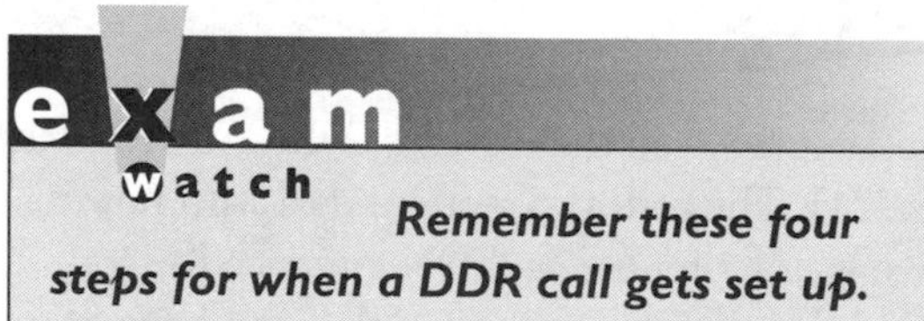

Remember these four steps for when a DDR call gets set up.

Legacy DDR Configuration

There are actually two ways of configuring DDR: legacy and profiles. This section covers the legacy, or old, method, and the last section in this book briefly covers profiles (the new method). In order for your router to perform the four steps covered in the earlier section "DDR Process," you will need to configure the commands in the following four corresponding steps:

1. Configure static routes for your traffic: for IP traffic, use the **ip route** command.
2. Define which traffic is interesting with the **dialer-list** commands.
3. Activate the **dialer-list** commands on the dialup interface with the **dialer-group** command.
4. Define the layer-3 address and phone number of the remote destination with the **dialer map** command.

There are other commands you can configure, but they are optional. First, you must define a static route to reach the destination. If you want the connection up only temporarily, then using a routing protocol like IP RIP or IGRP is out of the question—these send out periodic broadcasts that would keep a dialup link up indefinitely. The simplest solution is to use a static route. There are other options, such as snapshot routing, but these options are beyond the scope of this book. They are, however, covered on Cisco's CCNP Remote Access exam. Second, you'll use **dialer-list** commands to define what traffic is interesting (what traffic will trigger phone calls). Like ACL commands, these commands are dormant until you activate them. To activate them, as when activating ACLs, you'll apply them to your dialup interface with the **dialer-group** command. And last, you need to tell your router how to reach the destination specified in the static route—which phone number it should dial to make the circuit-switched connection. This is configured in the **dialer map** command.

Remember these four steps for configuring DDR; especially the commands associated with each step. The ip route and dialer list commands are Global Configuration mode commands and the dialer-group and dialer map are Interface Subconfiguration mode commands.

Configuring Static Routes

As mentioned in the last section, you want only specific traffic to trigger phone calls. What you don't want is unnecessary traffic triggering phone calls. For example, you probably don't want your routing protocol, IP RIPv1, for example, triggering phone calls every time it needs to send a routing update (which is every 30 seconds). This is especially true if there is a toll charge to make the phone call. One way of preventing this is to define a static route to define the remote destination(s), like this:

```
Router(config)# ip route IP_network_# subnet_mask
                    remote_router's_IP_address|router_interface
                    [administrative_distance]
```

If you have only one destination to reach off of the dialup interface, then you can specify your router's interface as the exit point. However, if the dialup interface is used to connect to multiple destinations, then specify the remote router's IP address instead.

If you are using DDR to back up a primary WAN connection, make sure that you set the administrative distance (AD) of the static route to a number *higher* than the routing protocol used across the primary connection. For example, let's assume that you are using RIP across the primary connection. Remember that the AD of a static route defaults to 0 or 1, depending on how you specify the destination. If you don't specify the administrative distance, then your router would use the dialup connection *instead* of the primary connection because the static route has an AD of 0 or 1, while RIP has an AD of 120. To fix this problem, make sure the static route for the backup connection has an AD higher than routing protocol, such as 121 in RIP's case. Let's take a look at an example, shown in Figure 17-4, to illustrate routing issues.

Assume the two routers in this example are running RIPv1. Here's RouterA's config:

```
RouterA(config)# ip route 172.16.3.0 255.255.255.0 172.16.2.2
RouterA(config)# router rip
RouterA(config-router)# network 172.16.0.0
RouterA(config-router)# exit
RouterA(config)# interface ethernet 0
RouterA(config-if)# ip address 172.16.1.1 255.255.255.0
RouterA(config-if)# exit
RouterA(config)# interface bri 0
RouterA(config-if)# ip address 172.16.2.1 255.255.255.0
```

In this example, a static route has been defined to reach 172.16.3.0/24. However, look at RIP's configuration closely. Remember that RIP is *classful*—this means that

FIGURE 17-4 Routing Issues with DDR

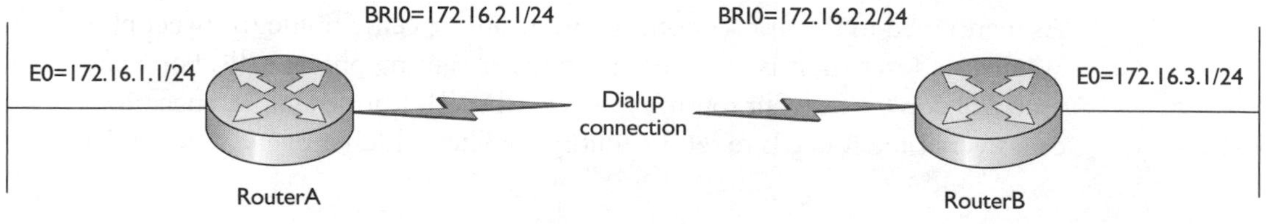

you specify the Class A, B, or C network number with the **network** statement and any interface associated with this network number will participate in the routing process. In this example, every interface associated with network 172.16.0.0/16 will participate in RIPv1. And since the BRI is being used for DDR to RouterB, the last thing you want is to have these routers dialing each other up every 30 seconds to share routing information.

Here are three solutions that you can use to prevent this problem from occurring:

- Make sure the network number of the DDR interface is not included in the **network** statement of your routing protocol. In this example, you could change the address on the BRI interface to a different network number.
- In your **dialer-list** configuration, exclude routing updates as interesting traffic (this is discussed in the next section).
- In your routing protocol's configuration, specify the DDR interface as passive. A passive interface will process received updates on the interface, but will not generate updates on it. To define the interface as passive, enter the *Routing Subconfiguration* mode for the routing protocol and configure this command: **passive** *interface_name*. The name of the interface is the name you use to access it, such as `bri0`.

There are other methods that you can use, but they are beyond the scope of this book.

17.06. The CD contains a multimedia demonstration of configuring a static route for DDR on a router.

Configuring Dialer Lists

Once you have taken care of your routing setup, you'll then need to use the **dialer-list** command to define what traffic is interesting:

```
Router(config)# dialer-list list_# protocol protocol_name
                     permit|deny [access-list ACL_#]
```

First, you must give the list a unique list number—this needs to be different from all of the other dialer lists on your router. Also, like an ACL number, this groups related dialer list entries together. Next, specify the protocol name, like **ip** or **ipx**, that is considered to be interesting traffic. Follow this with the action: **permit** means the traffic is interesting and **deny** means the traffic isn't interesting. If you don't specify an ACL number, which is optional, then all of the traffic for a particular protocol is included. If you specify an optional ACL number, only traffic specified in the ACL is included—this allows you to refine the criteria for traffic that is or isn't interesting. Any traffic specified with a **permit** parameter in the ACL is interesting. Note that there is an implicit deny at the bottom of the dialer list entries—any traffic that doesn't match the dialer list is deemed not interesting. Remember that uninteresting traffic will not trigger phone calls.

Here's a simple example of creating a dialer list:

```
Router(config)# dialer-list 1 protocol ipx permit
Router(config)# dialer-list 1 protocol ip permit
                        access-list 1
Router(config)# access-list 1 permit 172.16.1.0 0.0.0.255
```

In this example, there are two entries in the dialer list. The first entry specifies that all IPX traffic is interesting and will trigger phone calls. The second entry specifies that only traffic in ACL 1 is to be considered interesting. In this example, this is only traffic from devices with an address of 172.16.1.0/24. If you wanted to be more specific, you could have used an extended ACL instead of a standard one, like this:

```
Router(config)# dialer-list 1 protocol ip permit
                        access-list 100
Router(config)# access-list 100 permit tcp
                        172.16.1.0 0.0.0.255
                        172.16.3.0 0.0.0.255 eq smtp
Router(config)# access-list 100 permit tcp
                        172.16.1.0 0.0.0.255
                        172.16.3.0 0.0.0.255 eq telnet
```

In this example, anyone from 172.16.1.0/24 that sends e-mail to or telnets to 172.16.3.0/24 can trigger a phone call. Also, with dialer lists, you can mix and match the methods that you use to specify interesting traffic. In other words, a dialer list can include a standard ACL, an extended ACL, and all traffic for a protocol. Just remember to be as *specific* as you can about which traffic is considered interesting.

17.07. The CD contains a multimedia demonstration of creating a dialer list on a router.

Activating Dialer Lists

Once you have created your dialer list, it will not do anything until you activate it on your DDR interface with the **dialer-group** command:

```
Router(config)# interface type [slot_#/]port_#
Router(config-if)# dialer-group dialer_list_#
```

Here's a simple example:

```
Router(config)# dialer-list 1 protocol ip permit
Router(config)# interface bri0
Router(config-if)# dialer-group 1
```

Note that in this example, any type of IP traffic will trigger a phone call.

When initially setting up your DDR connection, you might want to allow any IP traffic to trigger a phone call. Then a simple ping should suffice to trigger a phone call. However, once you have the connection functioning, I highly recommend that you change this configuration to include extended and/or standard ACLs to define only necessary traffic as interesting.

There is one very important point to make about dialer lists and interesting traffic. First, only interesting traffic can trigger a phone call. However, once the phone connection has been established, *any* traffic can traverse the phone connection. In other words, a dialer list is *not* an ACL. A dialer list specifies only what traffic triggers phone calls. If you want to restrict traffic from traversing the DDR connection, configure an ACL and apply it to the DDR interface in the outbound direction.

Use the `dialer-list` command to specify which traffic should trigger phone calls. Activate your dialer list on an interface with the `dialer-group` command.

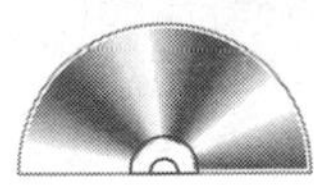

17.08. The CD contains a multimedia demonstration of activating a dialer list on a router.

Configuring Dialer Maps

Now that you have defined what traffic is interesting with your **dialer-list** commands and activated your dialer list on your router's interface with the **dialer-group** command, you are now ready to tell your router how to call the remote destination. To tell your router to make a phone call using legacy DDR, use the **dialer map** command:

```
Router(config)# interface type [slot_#/]port_#
Router(config-if)# dialer map protocol_name
                        address_of_destination_router
                        [name remote_router_name]
                        [speed 56|64] [broadcast]
                        destination_phone_number
```

The first thing you need to specify is the name of the layer-3 protocol and the remote router's layer-3 address. Optionally, you can specify the name of the router. This is used with PPP authentication and maps to a **username** command you have configured on your router. Typically, you'll use PPP as the encapsulation type for the interface, since this is almost a de facto standard for dialup connections.

Following the remote name is the speed of the connection. By default, ISDN BRI connections default to 64Kbps. However, some carriers, when they sell you a single-channel BRI, will clock you only 56Kbps worth of bandwidth. If this is the case, make sure that you change the speed to 56.

Also, by default, local broadcasts and multicasts will not traverse this connection. If you are running a routing protocol across this connection and want its broadcasts or multicasts to be sent across the connection, specify the **broadcast** parameter. Last, and most important, you need to specify the telephone number the router should use when dialing the destination.

exam watch

Be familiar with the syntax of the `dialer map` command and its parameters: the layer-3 protocol, the remote router's address, the remote's name, and the remote router's telephone number.

Here's an example of setting up PPP authentication and the destination's phone number:

```
RouterA(config)# username RouterB password richard
RouterA(config)# interface bri0
RouterA(config-if)# no shutdown
RouterA(config-if)# encapsulation ppp
RouterA(config-if)# ppp authentication chap
RouterA(config-if)# dialer map ip 172.16.2.2 name RouterB 14075551212
```

Notice the encapsulation was set to PPP and the authentication is CHAP. The **dialer map** command specifies the address of the remote router (172.16.2.2), its name (RouterB), and the phone number to dial in order to reach the destination. Since CHAP is being used, the name in the **dialer map** command tells the router which **username** command to use for PPP CHAP authentication. Before the phone call will be brought up by this router, the two routers will have to perform CHAP authentication—if this fails, the phone connection is terminated.

17.09. The CD contains a multimedia demonstration of configuring a dialer map on a router.

Configuring Optional Parameters

The DDR commands discussed so far are required to configure legacy DDR. The commands discussed in this section are optional. Once your router makes a phone call to the destination, any traffic (interesting and noninteresting) is allowed to traverse the connection. Of course, you don't want this connection to remain up indefinitely, especially if it is a toll call.

DDR connections have a default timeout of *120* seconds. As long as interesting traffic is crossing the connection, the timeout value is reset. Note that noninteresting traffic does *not* reset the timer. Once the timer reaches 0, the DDR connection is terminated—this is true even if noninteresting traffic is traversing the link. To change the idle timeout period, use this configuration:

```
Router(config)# interface type [slot_#/]port_#
Router(config-if)# dialer idle-timeout #_of_seconds
```

Specify the number of seconds a connection can remain idle (while no interest traffic is traversing it) before the connection is torn down. The connection idle timeout, however, can pose a problem if you have a single DDR connection, which is currently idle, and you have traffic that needs to trigger a phone call to a different destination. You can overcome this problem by defining a fast idle timer with the following command:

```
Router(config)# interface type [slot_#/]port_#
Router(config-if)# dialer fast-idle #_of_seconds
```

This timer specifies that after this number of idle seconds, if a new connection is required, the current connection is terminated and the new one is established (assuming no interesting traffic is traversing the currently active connection).

17.10. The CD contains a multimedia demonstration of configuring DDR idle timeouts on a router.

Another optional command is **dialer load-threshold**. This command allows you to perform load balancing across the two B-channels on your BRI. This feature is also referred to as *bandwidth on demand (BOD)*. For example, you might have a situation where your router makes a phone call on the first B-channel of your

DDR connections have a default idle timeout of 120 seconds (two minutes) if no interesting traffic is seen. Interesting traffic is defined with the `dialer-list` commands.

BRI and after a period of time, you exceed the 64Kbps bandwidth available on this channel. By default, your traffic would experience congestion and, in the worse case, would be dropped. To deal with this temporary burst of traffic, you can have your router bring up the second B-channel to handle the burst, and once the traffic falls back down to 64Kbps or lower, drop the connection on the second B-channel.

To configure this option, use the following configuration:

```
Router(config)# interface type [slot_#/]port_#
Router(config-if)# dialer load-threshold load
                     either|inbound|outbound
```

When specifying the load threshold value with the `dialer load-threshold` command, a value of 1 represents 1 percent, 128, 50 percent and 255, 100 percent for a load value.

The load threshold is specified as a number from 1 to 255. 1 represents 1 percent, 128, 50 percent, and 255, 100 percent load. In other words, this value is *not* a percentage. Once the load on the interface reaches this value, your router will bring up the second B-channel. You can measure the load in both directions (**either**), as traffic comes into the interface (**inbound**), or as traffic leaves the interface (**outbound**).

17.11. The CD contains a multimedia demonstration of configuring the DDR load threshold on a router.

Example Legacy DDR Configuration

To help you with understanding how all of the DDR components work together, let's take a look at a configuration example. I'll use the network shown in Figure 17-5. In this example, RouterA dials RouterB. I'll assume that CHAP is used for authentication and that only telnet traffic will trigger phone calls. Here's RouterA's configuration:

```
Router(config)# hostname RouterA
RouterA(config)# isdn switch-type basic-5ess
RouterA(config)# username RouterB password richard
```

```
RouterA(config)# ip route 192.168.3.0 255.255.255.0 192.168.1.2
RouterA(config)# dialer-list 1 protocol ip permit access-list 100
RouterA(config)# access-list 100 permit tcp any any eq telnet
RouterA(config)# interface bri0
RouterA(config-if)# no shutdown
RouterA(config-if)# encapsulation ppp
RouterA(config-if)# ppp authentication chap
RouterA(config-if)# ip address 192.168.1.1 255.255.255.0
RouterA(config-if)# dialer-group 1
RouterA(config-if)# dialer map ip 192.168.1.2 name RouterB 7247584321
```

This example shows that RouterA is connected to an AT&T 5ESS switch (**basic-5ess**). There is a static route pointing to RouterB's network (192.168.3.0/24). The dialer list specifies that any **permit** statements in ACL 100 will trigger traffic, which is only telnets. The dialer list is activated on the BRI interface with the **dialer-group** command. Also note that PPP and CHAP are enabled on the BRI interface.

The **dialer map** command specifies the phone number (724-758-4321) for RouterB (192.168.1.2, which ties back to the static route). The **name** parameter references the **username** command to use for CHAP authentication (the password is *richard*).

Please note that for ISDN, if one router is making a call and the other router is receiving it, you do not have to configure DDR on the second router—just your normal configuration. If you want two-way calling, you'll need to configure DDR on both routers. One problem with this approach, however, is that if both routers try to call each other simultaneously, you might get a busy signal or both B-channels might come up instead of one.

FIGURE 17-5 Legacy DDR example

Legacy DDR Verification

As you can see from the preceding example, the configuration is not too difficult. However, you have quite a few commands to configure; and if you forget a command, or misconfigure a command, tracking down the problem is not a simple process.

To see which DDR interface has made phone calls, as well as the status of the phone calls, use the **show dialer** command:

```
Router# show dialer
BRI0 - dialer type = ISDN
Dial String       Successes   Failures    Last called   Last status
7782002                   1          0    00:02:26        successful
0 incoming call(s) have been screened.
0 incoming call(s) rejected for callback.

BRI0:1 - dialer type = ISDN
Idle timer (120 secs), Fast idle timer (20 secs)
Wait for carrier (30 secs), Re-enable (15 secs)
Dialer state is data link layer up
Dial reason: ip (s=172.16.110.1, d=172.16.110.2)
Time until disconnect 52 secs
Connected to 7782002 (Router2)

BRI0:2 - dialer type = ISDN
Idle timer (120 secs), Fast idle timer (20 secs)
Wait for carrier (30 secs), Re-enable (15 secs)
Dialer state is idle
```

The show dialer command displays all active phone calls, while the show isdn active command displays only active ISDN calls.

From this output, you can see which phone numbers have been dialed, whether or not the phone calls were successful, the last time a remote router was called, and other statistics. For example, the phone number 778-2002 was dialed successfully one time a little bit over two minutes ago. Only the first B-channel was used with this connection (BRI0:1), which is currently up and will be disconnected in 52 seconds because no interesting traffic has gone across it in the last 68 seconds—the default idle timer is 120 seconds.

17.12. The CD contains a multimedia demonstration of using the show dialer command on a router.

To view only the active ISDN calls, use the **show isdn active** command:

```
Router# show isdn active
--------------------------------------------------------------
                  ISDN ACTIVE CALLS
--------------------------------------------------------------
History Table MaxLength = 320 entries
History Retain Timer = 15 Minutes
--------------------------------------------------------------
Call Calling Called  Duration   Remote Time until  Record Charge
Type Number  Number  Seconds    Name   Disconnect  Unit/Currency
---------------------------------------------------------------
Out          7782002 Active(12) RouterB       117           u(D)

---------------------------------------------------------------
```

In this output, there is only one active ISDN call. As shown by the `Call Type` (`Out`), this router initiated the connection. This connection has been up for 12 seconds, but for the last 3 seconds (120 – 117), no interesting traffic has traversed the dialup connection.

17.13. The CD contains a multimedia demonstration of using the `show isdn active` command on a router.

The **show isdn active** command shows only the active calls. To see calls the router either made or accepted previously, use the **show isdn history** command, shown here:

```
Router# show isdn history
 -------------------------------------------------------------
                    ISDN CALL HISTORY
--------------------------------------------------------------
History Table MaxLength = 320 entries
History Retain Timer = 15 Minutes
--------------------------------------------------------------
Call Calling Called  Duration   Remote Time until Record Charge
Type Number  Number  Seconds    Name   Disconnect Unit/Currency
--------------------------------------------------------------
Out          3590000        240 RouterB
In   3591111                 98 RouterC
--------------------------------------------------------------
```

In this example, this router made a phone call to 359-0000, which lasted 240 seconds. The second line shows that RouterC made a call to this router, and this call lasted 98 seconds.

17.14. The CD contains a multimedia demonstration of using the `show isdn history` command on a router.

Using debug for Troubleshooting

For detailed troubleshooting of DDR connections, you can use **`debug`** commands. The **`debug dialer`** command shows the DDR process of setting up or tearing down a connection:

```
Router# debug dialer
Dialing cause: BRI0: ip (s=192.168.1.1 d=192.168.11.25)
```

In this example, traffic from 192.168.1.1 triggered a phone call on BRI0. Therefore, this traffic from 192.168.1.1 must have been defined as interesting. If you are seeing a phone call triggered, then you have done everything correctly. If you are not seeing a phone connection being made, then examine the following:

1. Examine your routing table to make sure your router knows how to reach the destination (**`show ip route`**).
2. Verify that your DDR interface has been activated with the **`no shutdown`** command (**`show interfaces`**).
3. Check if you forgot to create or misconfigured your **`dialer-list`** commands.
4. Check if you forgot to activate the dialer list on your router's interface with the **`dialer-group`** command.

17.15. The CD contains a multimedia demonstration of using the `debug dialer` command on a router.

If you are having problems with ISDN making phone calls, you can use the **`debug isdn q931`** command to troubleshoot layer-3 ISDN DDR connections. This command will show the details of the setup and teardown of ISDN phone connections. Here is an example of the output of this command:

```
Router# debug isdn q931
RX <- SETUP pd = 8 callref = 0x06
 Bearer Capability i = 0x8890
 Channel ID i = 0x89
```

```
 Calling Party Number i = 0x0083, '4075551212'
TX -> CONNECT pd = 8 callref = 0x86
RX <- CONNECT_ACK pd = 8 callref = 0x06
```

In this example, a phone call was being made to 407-555-1212 and was successfully set up (`TX -> CONNECT` and `RX <- CONNECT_ACK`).

17.16. The CD contains a multimedia demonstration of using the `debug isdn q931` command on a router.

The `debug dialer` command displays when the router initiates and terminates any type of phone call. The `debug isdn q931` command displays the mechanics of setting up and tearing down ISDN phone calls.

Troubleshooting Steps

As you could see from the configuration section, there are many things that can go wrong with setting up a DDR connection. And with DDR, unfortunately, there isn't a single command on a router that will tell you the exact problem. Instead, you'll have to go through a handful of troubleshooting steps to determine what the problem is.

If your router is not making a phone call, then answer the following items:

- Is your router interacting with the ISDN switch?
  - Check the connection with the **`show isdn status`** command.
  - See if the router is sending and receiving Q.921 information with the **`debug isdn q921`** command.
  - Verify that your SPIDs are configured correctly with the **`show running-config`** command.
- Does your router have a static route pointing to the remote destination?
  - Use the **`show ip route`** command to examine your routing table.
- Is your dialer list configured correctly and activated?
  - Use the **`show running-config`** command to examine your **`dialer-list`** commands and if the DDR list has been activated on the dialup interface (**`dialer-group`**).

- Is your router attempting to dial the destination phone number?
  - Use the **debug dialer** command to see if the router is attempting to dial out.
  - Verify the phone number your router is dialing in the **dialer map** command.

If your router is actually dialing phone numbers, but the phone call is not completing, you should answer the following questions:

- For ISDN phone calls, is the phone connection being set up?
  - Check the ISDN connection setup with the **debug isdn q931** command.
- Is the encapsulation type the same on both ends?
  - Use the **show interfaces** command to check the encapsulation type (PPP or HDLC).
- If you are using PPP, is there a negotiation problem with the PPP parameters?
  - Use the **debug ppp negotiation** command to see if it is an LCP problem.
  - If you are using PAP or CHAP authentication, use the **debug ppp authentication** command to pinpoint authentication problems.

If the phone call is successfully set up, but the connection terminates prematurely, then answer the following questions:

- Have you defined your interesting traffic correctly with the **dialer-list** commands?
  - Use the **show dialer** command to check the status of the DDR connection.
  - If the DDR connection uses ISDN, use the **show isdn active** and **show isdn history** commands.
  - Check your dialer list configuration with the **show running-config** command.

Know how to use the correct command to troubleshoot specific DDR problems.

As you can see from these items, troubleshooting DDR is not a simple process.

CERTIFICATION OBJECTIVE 17.04

Dialer Profiles and DDR

With legacy DDR, the dialup interface must use the same configuration no matter what destinations it is connecting to. This can create issues when you have multiple destinations that you are connecting to. Plus, if your primary DDR interface fails, there is no simple alternative to using a backup DDR interface for dial-out connections. Dialer profiles solve this problem and provide the following enhancements:

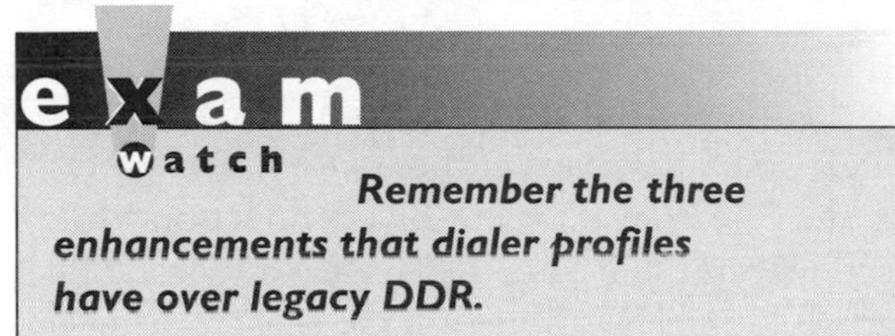

Remember the three enhancements that dialer profiles have over legacy DDR.

- Allows a physical interface to be shared by many logical DDR interfaces, which provides flexibility in how you set up and use your DDR connections.
- Allows you to share multiple dialup interfaces to back up multiple primary WAN circuits.
- Do not need a separate dialer map command for each protocol/destination combination, which reduces the complexity of your DDR configuration.

Dialer Profile Components

Dialer profiles contain two types of interfaces: logical DDR interfaces and physical interfaces. The *logical DDR* interfaces have the DDR configuration placed on them, while the *physical* interfaces have the physical properties and ISDN components (in the case of a BRI or PRI interface) configured on them. With dialer profiles, the logical interface performs the DDR function and chooses a physical interface to use to make the phone call. This enables you to group together a bunch of physical interfaces and allow a logical interface to use a free physical interface in the group to make a call. This provides you with a lot of flexibility and control over the use of your physical dialup interfaces.

Dialer profiles contain the following components:

- **Dialer interface** Contains the DDR configuration components, including the phone number to dial and the PPP authentication information to use. Multiple destinations can be called from the same dialer interface, but most administrators create a separate dialer interface for each destination.

- **Physical interface or interfaces** Contains the physical connection properties, such as the ISDN switch type, as well as which dialer interfaces are allowed to use it.
- **Dialer pool** Defines which dialer interfaces can use which physical interfaces.
- **Dialer map class (optional)** Defines call characteristics for a specific calling destination, which allows a single dialer interface to be configured correctly for multiple calling destinations.

Let's use Figure 17-6 to illustrate the use of these three components. There are three sites the router calls: Site1, Site2, and Site3. Each of these sites has different configuration characteristics: Site1 and Site2 have 64Kbps BRI connection while Site3 has only a 56Kbps BRI connection. Site1 and Site2 also have a 60-second idle timer, with a 10-second fast-idle timer, while Site3 has the default idle timer. One dialer pool has been configured with two BRI interfaces. The router will use this pool when connecting to any of three sites. Two dialer interfaces are set up that can use this pool of physical interfaces.

The first dialer interface, *Dialer interface 1*, has a configuration to dial to Site1. Notice that the map class called *Map one* specifies the configuration for the connection to Site1. *Dialer interface 2* is used to dial to two different sites: Site2 and Site3. When dialing to Site2, the *Map one* map class is used; when dialing to Site3, *Map two* is used.

FIGURE 17-6 Dialer profile components

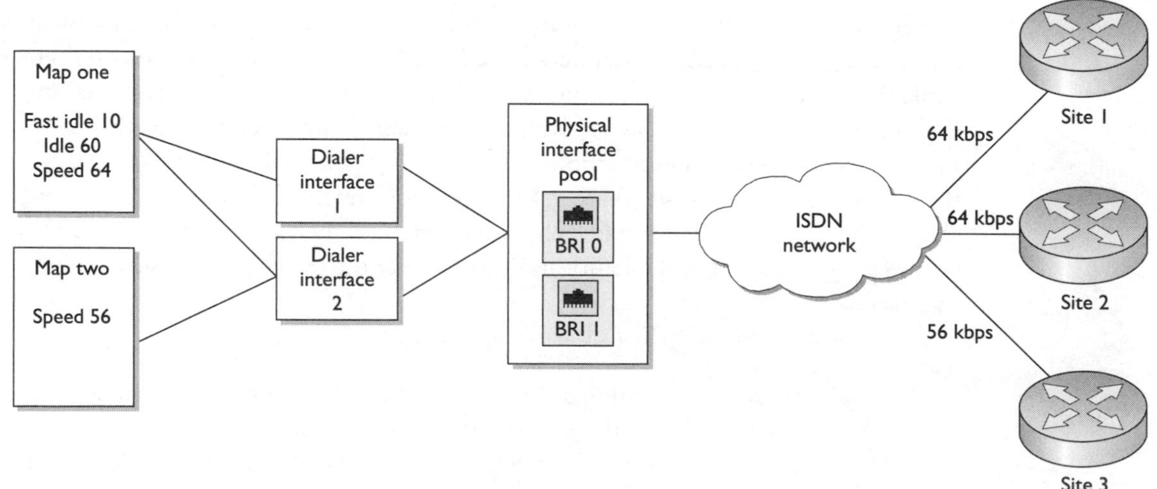

Notice that in this example that by separating the DDR components, you have a lot more flexibility when setting up connections using multiple physical interfaces and multiple destinations.

Configuring Dialer Profiles

Configuring dialer profiles is similar to configuring legacy DDR. With legacy DDR, the first two things you have to configure are your static routes and your dialer lists. This is also true with dialer profiles. You use the *same* commands for these two tasks. Once you have configured these two items, you are ready to proceed to configuring your dialer profile. Also, if you are using PPP authentication, you'll need to create your local database of usernames and passwords.

From this point onward, the configuration is different from a legacy configuration. With a legacy configuration, all of your DDR information is configured on the router's physical interface. With dialer profiles, the configuration is broken into at least two components: dialer interfaces, physical interfaces, and, optionally, map classes.

Dialer Interface Configuration

Dialer interfaces are logical interfaces on the router. They are like loopback interfaces, which were discussed in Chapter 11. To create a dialer interface's configuration, use the following:

```
Router(config)# interface dialer port_#
Router(config-if)# encapsulation ppp
Router(config-if)# ppp authentication
                        pap|chap|chap pap|pap chap
Router(config-if)# ip address IP_address subnet_mask
Router(config-if)# dialer remote-name name
Router(config-if)# dialer string phone_# [class map_name]
Router(config-if)# dialer pool pool_#
Router(config-if)# dialer-group dialer_list_#
```

The first thing you must do is to create your logical dialer interface with the **interface dialer** command. You must assign a port number to the interface, which is an arbitrary number. This number must be unique among all dialer interfaces. When you enter this command, you are taken into *Interface Subconfiguration* mode.

Once you are in *Interface Subconfiguration* mode, you need to specify the encapsulation type (**encapsulation ppp**) and, optionally, the authentication method to use (**ppp authentication**). You can also specify your layer-3 addressing, such as the IP address of the interface (**ip address**). Please note that the router treats the dialer interface like any other interface. When you create it, the dialer interface is automatically enabled.

You must specify the name of the remote router, even if you are not using PPP authentication. Use the **dialer remote-name** command to specify the name. If you don't enter this command, you will not be able to enter any other **dialer** commands on the interface.

Following this is the **dialer string** command. This command defines the phone number to call to reach the destination. With this command, you can point to an optional map class with the **class** parameter. If you don't specify a map class, the configuration parameters configured on the dialer interface are used. These parameters can include the idle timer (**dialer idle-timer**), the fast-idle timer (**dialer fast-idle**), and the speed of the ISDN connection (**dialer isdn speed**). You need to specify a map class only if the dialer interface is used to dial multiple locations, where these locations have different DDR configuration parameters.

The **dialer pool** command specifies which group of physical interfaces the dialer interface can use. The number you specify here must match the number used by the **dialer pool-member** command on the physical interface or interfaces you want the dialer interface to use. The pool number can range from 1 to 255.

Following this is the **dialer-group** command. Recall from the section "Legacy DDR Configuration" that this command activates a dialer list on the router's interface, which tells the router which traffic should trigger phone calls on this interface.

exam watch

Dialer profiles perform the DDR configuration under a logical dialer interface (`interface dialer`). All your DDR configuration is performed here. The `dialer remote-name` specifies the name of the remote router. The `dialer string` denotes the phone number to call. The `dialer pool`, specifies which physical interfaces the dialer interface can use.

Map Classes

If you specified a map class name in the **dialer string** command in the dialer interface configuration, you will need to create a corresponding map class. The function of a map class is to separate the configurations from the interface and centralize them under one set. You can then take this set and apply it to multiple interfaces. This reduces the amount of configuration that you have to perform and makes it easier to set up a consistent configuration. To create a map class, use these commands:

```
Router(config)# map-class dialer map_name
Router(config-map)# dialer isdn speed 56
Router(config-map)# dialer idle-timeout #_of_seconds
Router(config-map)# dialer fast-idle #_of_seconds
```

The name you specify with the **map-class** command must match the name specified in the **dialer string** command. When you execute this command, you are taken into *Map Subconfiguration* mode. The **dialer isdn speed** command allows you to specify the speed of the B-channel in an ISDN connection, which defaults to 64Kbps. You can set it to 56Kbps if your provider provides only 56Kbps B-channels or the remote side only supports 56Kbps connections. The **dialer idle-timeout** and **dialer fast-idle** commands were discussed in the section "Legacy DDR Configuration." Note that if these commands are configured in the map and also on the dialer interface, the map class name specified in the **dialer string** command supercedes the commands configured on the dialer interface.

Physical Interface Configuration

The last thing you must configure are your physical dialup interfaces. This book focuses on ISDN interfaces, so only these configurations are shown. There are basically four things you'll do on the physical interface: enable it, specify the encapsulation type (and the optional PPP authentication), and specify the DDR pool that the interface belongs to. Here are the commands you should use:

```
Router(config)# interface type [slot_#/]port_#
Router(config-if)# no shutdown
Router(config-if)# encapsulation ppp
Router(config-if)# ppp authentication
                        chap|pap|chap pap|pap chap
Router(config-if)# dialer pool-member pool_#
                       [priority priority_#]
                       [min-link #_of_B_channels]
                       [max-link #_of_B_channels]
```

The first thing you should do is to enable the physical interface with the **no shutdown** command. The second thing you must do is to configure the encapsulation type and authentication, if you're using PPP. Both PPP and HDLC are supported; however, almost everyone uses PPP. Since you probably don't know which authentication a dialer interface will use (one that is configured with PPP authentication), you probably want to specify both PAP and CHAP unless you've standardized on one authentication method.

The last thing you must do on the physical interface is to configure the **dialer pool-member** command. This command specifies which dialer interfaces (**dialer pool** command) can use this physical interface. If you want multiple physical interfaces to be in the same pool, then specify the pool number on the other physical interfaces with this command. The pool number can range from 1 to 255.

There are three optional parameters with this command. The **priority** parameter can have values from 1 to 255. This parameter prioritizes the interfaces in the same pool number: the higher the number, the higher the priority. If there is more than one physical interface in a pool, you can assign a priority to each interface. Then, when a dialer interface makes a phone connection using this pool, it will use the physical interface that has the highest priority that is currently available. If the physical interfaces have the same priority (the default), the dialer interface will use the physically lowest-numbered interface. An important item to point out about physical interfaces is that you can associated multiple pools to the same physical interface. This parameter can be used to avoid contention for physical interfaces, especially if there is more than one pool associated with a physical interface.

The **min-link** and **max-link** parameters specify how many B-channels are reserved on the physical interface for this pool. These parameters are typically used on a PRI connection. The **min-link** parameter specifies the minimum reserved channels, while the **max-link** command reserves the maximum number of B-channels for this pool. Here's a simple example to help explain the usage of these parameters:

```
Router(config)# interface serial0:23
Router(config-if)# no shutdown
Router(config-if)# encapsulation ppp
Router(config-if)# dialer pool-member 1 min-link 1 max-link 4
```

This example shows the configuration of a T1 PRI. In this example, pool 1 is associated with this interface. Pool 1 is allowed to use from one to four B-channels on this PRI: it is guaranteed at least one B-channel but can use up to four, if there are free channels. Another use of this command is to restrict the number of B-channels a dialer interface or interfaces can use—this is important if you have a limited number of B-channels and need to ensure that certain connections have access to your B-channels. If you don't specify minimum and maximum values, the interface can use any and all B-channels on the physical interface.

When configuring dialer profiles, don't configure any layer-3 addressing on your physical interfaces—this is done on the logical dialer interface. Also, use the `dialer pool-member` command to specify which dialer interfaces can use this physical interface—the pool numbers must match that configured with the `dialer pool` command under the logical dialer interface.

Verifying Your Dialer Profile Configuration

Once you have configured dialer profiles on your router, you can use the same exact commands to troubleshoot your dialup connections that you used in legacy DDR. The one exception to this is that since you are using a dialer interface to make the phone calls, specify the dialer interface, and not the physical interface, when troubleshooting and examining interface configurations. If no phone calls are being made, above all, make sure that the physical interface is enabled and is associated with the same pool number as the dialer interface.

Also, there is one additional command you can use to troubleshoot dialer profiles.

```
Router# show dialer interface bri|{serial:23|15} [slot_#/]port_#
```

This command shows DDR statistics for incoming and outgoing calls for the physical interfaces associated with the dialer interface. Here's an example:

```
Router# show dialer interface bri 0
BRI0   dialer type = ISDN
DIAL String     Successes     Failures   Last called   Last
status
0 incoming call(s) have been screened.

BRI0: B-Channel 1
Idle timer (120 secs), Fast idle timer (20 secs)
Wait for carrier (30 secs), Re-enable (15 secs)
Dialer state is data link layer up
Dial reason: ip (s=192.168.2.2, d=192.168.3.2)

Interface bound to profile Dialer1

Time until disconnect 102 secs
Current call connected 00:00:19
Connected to 7247584321 (RouterB)
```

```
BRI1: B-Channel 2
Idle timer (120 secs), Fast idle timer (20 secs)
Wait for carrier (30 secs), Re-enable (15 secs)
Dialer state is idle
```

In this example, `interface dialer 1` is using the first B-channel of `bri0`. The first B-channel is currently connected to RouterB, while the second B-channel is idle. The `Dialer state is data link layer up` message indicates that both the physical and data link layers are operational. If you see `Physical layer up`, this means that for PPP, LCP is operational, but NCP is not.

Dialer Profile Example

To help you understand the configuration using dialer profiles, let's take the legacy DDR example I showed earlier and convert this to use dialer profiles. The network this example uses was shown previously in Figure 17-5. The code configuration follows.

Here's RouterA's configuration:

```
Router(config)# hostname RouterA
RouterA(config)# isdn switch-type basic-5ess
RouterA(config)# username RouterB password richard
RouterA(config)# ip route 192.168.3.0 255.255.255.0 192.168.1.2
RouterA(config)# dialer-list 1 protocol ip permit access-list 100
RouterA(config)# access-list 100 permit tcp any any eq telnet
RouterA(config)# interface dialer 1
RouterA(config-if)# encapsulation ppp
RouterA(config-if)# ppp authentication chap
RouterA(config-if)# ip address 192.168.1.1 255.255.255.0
RouterA(config-if)# dialer remote-name RouterB
RouterA(config-if)# dialer string 7247584321
RouterA(config-if)# dialer pool 1
RouterA(config-if)# dialer-group 1
RouterA(config-if)# exit
RouterA(config)# interface bri0
RouterA(config-if)# no shutdown
RouterA(config-if)# encapsulation ppp
RouterA(config-if)# ppp authentication chap
RouterA(config-if)# dialer pool-member 1
```

This example shows that RouterA is connected to an AT&T 5ESS switch (**`basic-5ess`**). There is a static route pointing to RouterB's network (192.168.3.0/24). The dialer list specifies that any **`permit`** statements in ACL 100 will trigger traffic, which is only telnets. The dialer list is activated on the *dialer* interface with the **`dialer-group`** command. Also note that PPP and CHAP are enabled on the dialer *and* BRI interfaces.

Notice that the configuration is a little more complex than the legacy DDR configuration when you examine the configuration of the dialer and physical interfaces. The physical interface is assigned to pool 1, and the dialer interface references this pool. Also notice that all of the DDR commands are configured on the dialer interface. Typically, you use dialer profiles only when you have many destinations you need to call, and a limited number of physical interfaces. Legacy DDR is preferred when you have only one site you need to connect to off of the dialup interface.

17.17. The CD contains a multimedia demonstration of configuring dialer profiles on a router.

CERTIFICATION SUMMARY

ISDN provides digital circuit-switched connections. It has the following advantages over analog modems: fast call setup (one–two seconds), guaranteed data rate, and suitability for multiple services, such as data, voice, and video. A BRI has 2 bearer channels (64Kbps each) and a signaling channel (16Kbps). A T1 PRI has 23 bearer channels (64 Kbps each), and an E1 has 30 bearer channels (both have one signaling channel, but an E1 has an additional framing channel).

The Q.921 (layer-2) standard defines the interaction between the router and the ISDN switch, while the Q.931 (layer-3) standard defines the call setup and teardown process for ISDN phone calls. LAPD defines the framing used for layer-2.

A TE1 is an ISDN native interface, whereas a TE2 has a non-native interface and requires a TA. An NT1 connects your TE1/TE2 to the carrier's network—it converts an ISDN four-wire connection to the carrier's two-wire connection). The U reference point defines the connection between the NT1 and LE. The T reference point defines the connection between the NT1 and NT2. The S reference point defines the connection between the TA or TE1 to the NT2, and the R reference point defines the connection between the TE2 and the TA.

The **`isdn switch-type`** command specifies your ISDN switch type: this can be done from *Global Configuration* mode or *Interface Subconfiguration* mode. The National ISDN 1 and Nortel DMS-100 switches typically require you to configure SPIDs on your router. If you have a PRI T1 or E1, you must first configure your controller by going into *Controller Subconfiguration* mode (**controller**). Here you specify the line coding, framing, and which DS0s are used by the PRI. To specify which channel is the signaling channel, use the **interface serial** command. Use **15** for an E1 and **23** for a T1. The **show isdn status** command displays layer-2 ISDN information.

There are two methods for establishing a dialup connection: legacy DDR and dialer profiles. With legacy DDR, all dialup commands are configured on the physical dialup interface. With dialer profiles, the dialup commands are placed on a logical interface and you specify which physical interfaces the logical interface can use (**dialer pool** and **dialer pool-member** commands). For DDR, you need to specify a route (**ip route**) to the destination, what traffic will trigger a call (**dialer-list** and **dialer-group**), and how to reach the destination (**dialer map** with legacy and **dialer string** with profiles). Idle DDR connections will time out after not see any interesting traffic for a period of 120 seconds.

Use the **show dialer** and **show isdn active** to list your current ISDN phone connections. The **debug dialer** and **debug isdn q931** are helpful commands in troubleshooting the setup of ISDN phone calls.

TWO-MINUTE DRILL

ISDN Introduction

- A BRI has 2 B-channels (64Kbps each) and 1 D-channel (16Kbps), a PRI T1 has 23 B-channels and 1 D-channel, and a PRI E1 has 30 B-channels and 1 D-channel. Q.921 defines the connection between the router and the switch, and Q.931 defines how a phone connection is set up. LAPD is used as the ISDN frame type.
- A TE1 has a native ISDN interface. A TE2 has a serial interface and requires a TA. An NT2 connects multiple ISDN devices together, and an NT1 connects to the carrier, converting four-wire to two-wire. R is the connection between the TE2 and the TA. S is the connection between the TA/TE1 and the NT2. T is the connection between the NT2 and NT1, and U is the connection between the NT1 and LE.

ISDN Interface Configuration

- Use the **isdn switch-type** command to configure your ISDN switch type globally or on an interface. Use the **show isdn status** command to verify layer-1 and layer-2 connectivity.
- SPIDs are used by some switches to authenticate call requests; they are configured with the **isdn spid1|spid2** command.
- For PRI controllers, you must configure the following on the controller: **controller t1|e1**, **framing**, **linecode**, **clock source**, and **pri-group timeslots**. Then create the logical interface: **interface serial** *port_#*:**23|15**.

Legacy Dial-on-Demand Routing

- DDR is best suited for backup of primary WAN connections, when the traffic is low volume and periodic, and phone calls are short and temporary.
- You need to set up a static route and define interesting traffic (**dialer-list**). Activate the dialer list on the interface (**dialer-group**) and specify the dialing parameters (**dialer map**). The default idle timeout for interesting traffic is 120 seconds.

- The **show dialer** and **show isdn active** show current ISDN calls. Use the **debug dialer** command to see if your router is attempting to make phone calls.

Dialer Profiles and DDR

- Dialer profiles contain the following components: dialer interface, physical interface, dialer pool, and map classes (optional).
- Only the PPP encapsulation, authentication, and pool membership are configured on the physical interface (**dialer pool-member**).
- All DDR commands are configured on the logical dialer interface **dialer remote-name**, **dialer string**, **dialer pool**, **dialer group**. You must also assign the PPP encapsulation (and authentication) and the IP address to the dialer interface. Map classes can be used to group together common configuration parameters that are applied to dialer interfaces. To see which logical interfaces are associated with a physical interface, use the **show dialer interface bri0** command.

SELF TEST

The following Self Test questions will help you measure your understanding of the material presented in this chapter. Read all the choices carefully, as there may be more than one correct answer. Choose all correct answers for each question.

ISDN Introduction

1. What uses 64Kbps of bandwidth?

A. PRI

B. BRI

C. DS1

D. DS0

2. __________ defines LAPD, which is responsible for the data-link layer connection between the router and the ISDN switch.

A. Q.931

B. Q.921

C. I.921

D. I.931

3. The __________ reference point defines the connection between the NT2 and the NT1.

4. The __________ converts an ISDN four-wire connection to a two-wire connection.

ISDN Interface Configuration

5. Which router command specifies the ISDN switch the router is connected to?

A. `isdn switch-type`

B. `isdn connection-type`

C. `isdn spid1`

D. **`interface serial0:15`**

6. Which controller command specifies how ones and zeros are represented on a digital circuit?

A. `framing`

B. `linecode`

C. `clock source`

D. `interface`

7. Enter the PRI command that specifies time slots 1–24 are used on a T1 controller: ________.

8. Enter the router command that shows the status of the ISDN Q.921 connection between the router and the switch: ________

Legacy Dial-on-Demand Routing

9. Which of the following situations are best for DDR connections?
   A. Primary WAN connection
   B. A lot of constant traffic
   C. Long phone calls
   D. Backup connection

10. Which command defines interesting traffic?
   A. `dialer-group`
   B. `dialer-list`
   C. `dialer map`
   D. `dialer remote-name`

11. Enter the command to trigger phone calls on an interface for dialer list 1: ________.

12. An idle DDR connection will be torn down after ________ seconds of not seeing interesting traffic.

13. The **`dialer map`** command contains all of the following parameters except ________.
   A. Protocol name
   B. Remote router name
   C. Address of local router
   D. Speed of the connection

Dialer Profiles and DDR

14. Enter the router command to create a logical DDR interface with a port number of 0: ________.

15. Which of the following commands belongs on the physical interface when using dialer profiles?
   A. `dialer pool-member`
   B. `dialer-group`
   C. `ip address`
   D. `dialer string`

SELF TEST ANSWERS

ISDN Introduction

1. ☑ **D.** A DS0 uses 64Kbps of bandwidth.
☒ **A** and **C** use either 24 or 32 DS0s. **B** uses 3 DS0s.

2. ☑ **B.** Q.921 defines LAPD, which is responsible for the data-link layer connection between the router and the ISDN switch.
☒ **A** defines how layer-3 ISDN phone calls are set up. **C** and **D** are nonexistent standards.

3. ☑ The T reference point defines the connection between the NT2 and NT1.

4. ☑ The NT1 converts an ISDN four-wire connection to a two-wire connection.

ISDN Interface Configuration

5. ☑ **A.** The **`isdn switch-type`** command defines the switch type the router is connected to.
☒ **B** is an invalid command. **C** specifies the SPID for the first B-channel. **D** specifies the logical interface for an E1 PRI controller in port 0.

6. ☑ **B.** The **`linecode`** controller command specifies how ones and zeros are represented on a digital circuit.
☒ **A** specifies the controller's physical layer framing. **C** specifies how clocking is determined on the controller. **D** is not a controller command, but a global one.

7. ☑ **`pri-group timeslots 1-24`**.

8. ☑ **`show isdn status`**.

Legacy Dial-on-Demand Routing

9. ☑ **D.** DDR connections are best used as backup, or short, temporary connections.
☒ **A**, **B**, and **C** are suited for WAN services such as leased lines or packet-switched services.

10. ☑ **B.** The **`dialer-list`** command defines interesting traffic for DDR.
☒ **A** associates the interesting traffic with a DDR interface. **C** specifies how to reach the destination. **D** is a dialer profile command used to configure the remote device's name.

11. ☑ **`dialer-group 1`**.

12. ☑ An idle DDR connection will be torn down after *120* seconds of not seeing interesting traffic.

13. ☑ C. The **dialer map** command does not contain the local router's address, but the remote's.
☒ A, B, and D are part of the dialer map command.

Dialer Profiles and DDR

14. ☑ **interface dialer** 0.

15. ☑ A. The **dialer pool-member** command, along with the PPP configuration, is done on the physical interface.
☒ B, C, and D are done on the logical dialer interface.

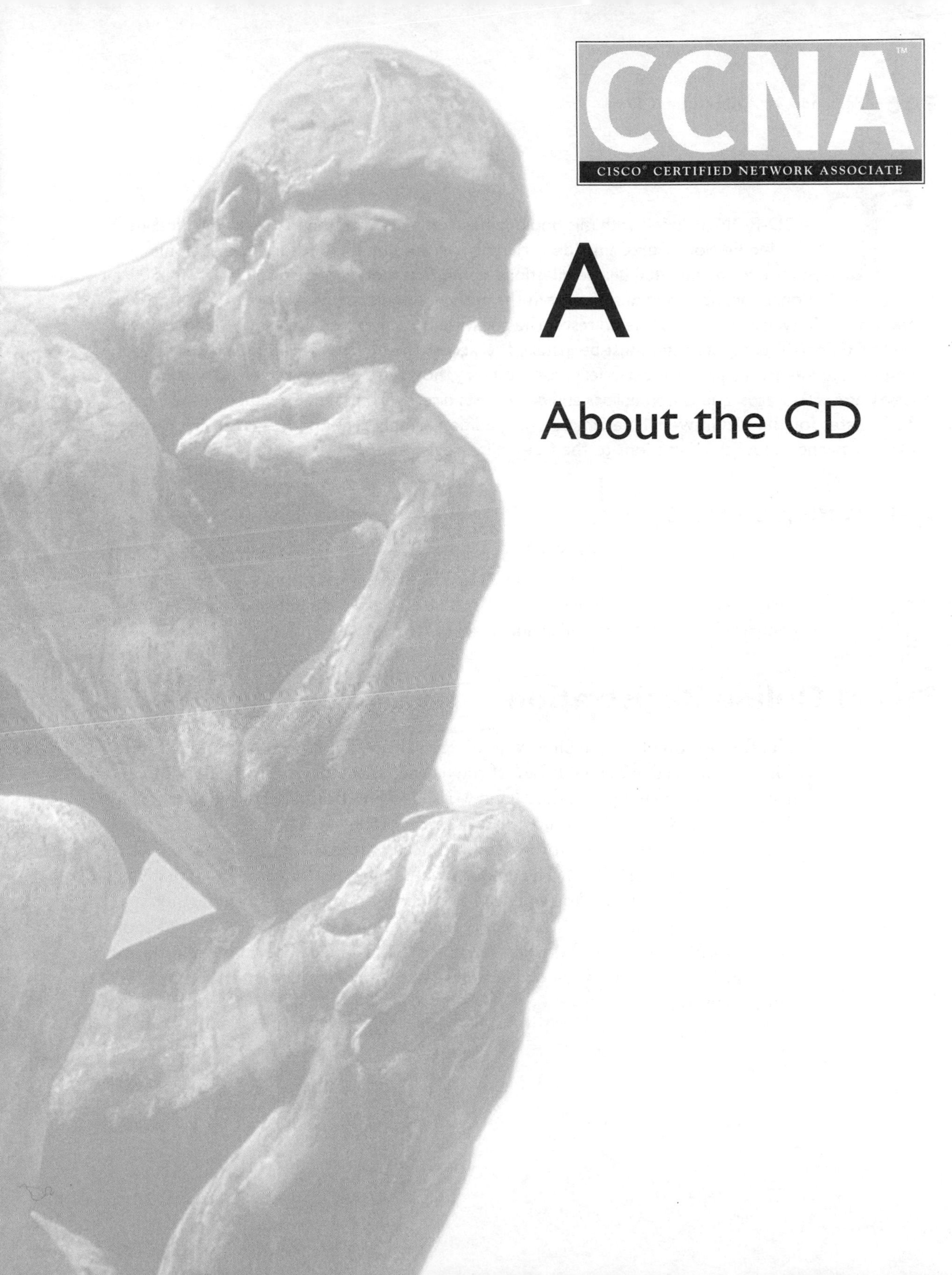

A

About the CD

The CD-ROM included with this book comes complete with the McGraw-Hill NetSim Learning Edition, CertCam video training narrated by the author, an electronic practice exam with 400 unique questions from the author, Flashcard software with 300 original additional questions and answers from the author, the electronic version of the book, and Boson Software utilities and demo tests. The software is easy to install on any Windows 98/Me/2000 Pro/XP computer and must be installed to access the McGraw-Hill NetSim Learning Edition and electronic practice exam features. You may, however, browse the electronic book, CertCams, Flashcards, and Boson utilities and demo tests directly from the CD without installation. To register for the McGraw-Hill NetSim Learning Edition, simply click the **Register** link on the Main Page and follow the directions to the free online registration.

System Requirements

Software requires Windows 98 or higher and Internet Explorer 5.0 or above and 120MB of hard disk space for full installation. The Electronic book requires Adobe Acrobat Reader version 5.0 or higher. To access the CertCams, you must have a Windows compatible sound card installed and enabled.

Boson Online Registration

The **Registration** link will allow you to access the McGraw-Hill NetSim Learning Edition and practice exam software. If you haven't selected the **Registration** link, the first time you attempt to run the McGraw-Hill NetSim Learning Edition or practice exam software you will be required to register the product.

Prior to registering the software, you will need to find the unique serial number included with the CD-ROM. The unique serial number is a 9-digit number that you'll find inside the CD sleeve. You will need to enter this number when you register.

Select the appropriate installation type, and then enter the unique serial code included with your CD-ROM when prompted and complete the online registration. Please make sure to use a valid e-mail address so that a confirmation registration code can be sent to you.

Installing and Running the McGraw-Hill NetSim Learning Edition and Practice Exam Software

If your computer CD-ROM drive is configured to auto run, the CD-ROM should automatically start up upon inserting the disk. If the auto run feature did not launch your CD, browse to the CD and Click on the "Setup" icon. From the opening screen you may install the McGraw-Hill NetSim Learning Edition or the practice exam software by selecting the **Install McGraw-Hill NetSim Learning Edition** or the **Install CCNA Study Guide Practice Exam** links. This will begin the installation process and create a program group named "Boson Software" in the START | PROGRAMS menu. To run the McGraw-Hill NetSim Learning Edition or the practice exam software use START | PROGRAMS | BOSON SOFTWARE. By default, most software will be installed to: C:\Program Files\McGraw-Hill CCNA Book\Flash Cards for CCNA

For information about customer support related to the content of the practice exam engine, see Customer Support at the end of the Appendix. Information about customer support for the Boson Software included on the CD is also listed below.

McGraw-Hill NetSim Learning Edition

The McGraw-Hill NetSim Learning Edition is an interactive network simulator that will allow you to simulate a wide variety of tasks as if you were working on a real network. Once you have installed the McGraw-Hill NetSim Learning Edition you may access it quickly through the CD launch page or you may also access it through START | PROGRAMS | BOSON SOFTWARE.

Practice Exam Software

The McGraw-Hill/Osborne practice exam provides you with a simulation of an actual CCNA exam. You have the option to customize your test-taking environment by selecting he number of questions, the type of questions, and the time allowed are to assist you in your studies. The exam engine also allows you to simulate a real test-taking environment. You also have the option to take exams by chapter or objective, and the option to take an open book exam, including hints, references, and answers. This practice exam has been created specifically for McGraw-Hill/Osborne, and is only available by purchasing a McGraw-Hill/Osborne book.

Electronic Book

The entire contents of the Study Guide are provided in PDF. Adobe's Acrobat Reader is used to read PDF files, which can be downloaded free of charge from www.adobe.com. Simply select the View Book in Electronic Format link from the main CD launch page.

CertCams

CertCam custom .AVI clips demonstrate how to perform complex configurations with IOS commands on Cisco routers and Catalyst switches. These clips walk you step-by-step through various system configurations. You can access the clips directly from the CertCam table of contents by selecting the View CertCam Index link on the Main CD launch page. Do not try to play the custom .AVI file clips without using the CDROM menu program. Each chapter that has CertCams in them references the appropriate link from this screen.

Flashcard Software

Included on the CD you can find a Flashcard quick study program for your PC, Pocket PC or Palm device. Click on Install Boson Flash Cards. Select the type of device you will be using (ie. Windows, PalmOS, or PocketPC). Finally, select Boson Flash Cards for CCNA: Windows, Palm, or PocketPC. To access the Flashcard software for Windows on your PC, use the START | PROGRAMS | MCGRAW-HILL | FLASH CARDS FOR CCNA menu to launch the card deck. To access the Flashcard software for PocketPC, use the START | PROGRAMS | MCGRAW-HILL | FLASH CARDS FOR CCNA. To access the Flashcard software for PalmOS, use the home button to access the McGraw-Hill FlashCards icon.

Boson Utilities and Boson Test Demos

We are happy to provide, by special arrangement with Boson Software, several free Network Utilities—among them a subnet calculator and a configuration register calculator—along with demos of Boson's own practice tests.

Help

Individual help features are also available through McGraw-Hill NetSim Learning Edition, the practice exam software, and the Flashcard software. Please review the Boson NetSim Learning Edition User's Guide for details on registration, and how-to directions on completing the practice labs.

Removing Installation(s)

For BEST results for removal of Windows programs, use the START | PROGRAMS | CONTROL PANEL | ADD/REMOVE PROGRAMS option to remove the McGraw-Hill NetSim Learning Edition or the practice exam software. You can also use the Add/Remove Programs Icon from your Control Panel, if available. For the PalmOS: APP | DELETE | MCGRAW-HILL FLASHCARDS. For the PocketPC: START | SETTINGS | SYSTEM | REMOVE PROGRAMS | FLASH CARDS.

Technical Support

For questions regarding the technical content of the book, electronic practice exam, the Flashcards, the electronic book, or the CertCams, please visit www.osborne.com <http://www.osborne.com> or email customer.service@mcgraw-hill.com <mailto:customer.service@mcgraw-hill.com>. For customers outside the 50 United States, email: international_cs@mcgraw-hill.com <mailto:international_cs@mcgraw-hill.com>.

Boson Software Technical Support

For technical problems with the software (installation, operation, and removing installations of the McGraw-Hill NetSim Learning Edition, the practice exam software, the Flashcard reader, the eBook reader, and the Boson Utilities and Test Demos), and for questions regarding the Boson Online Registration and Boson test demo content, please visit www.boson.com <http://www.boson.com> or email mcgraw@boson.com <mailto:mcgraw@boson.com> or follow the help instructions in the help features included with the McGraw-Hill NetSim Learning Edition or the practice exam software.

B

Exam Readiness Checklist

Exam Readiness Checklist

INTRO 640-821

Official Objective	Study Guide Coverage	Ch #	Beginner	Intermediate	Expert
Design and Support					
Use a subset of Cisco IOS commands to analyze and report network problems	Basic Switch Configuration Basic Router Configuration IOS Troubleshooting	5 5 6			
Use embedded layer-3 through layer-7 protocols to establish, test, suspend, or disconnect connectivity to remote devices from the router console	IOS Troubleshooting	6			
Determine IP addresses	Planning IP Addressing Figuring Out IP Address Components	3 3			
Implementation and Operation					
Establish communication between a terminal device and the router IOS, and use IOS for system analysis	Chassis Connections Cabling	4 4 4			
Manipulate system image and device configuration files	Connections Cables	4 4			
Perform an initial configuration on a router and save the resultant configuration file	Basic Router Configuration	5			
Use commands incorporated within IOS to analyze and report network problems	Basic Router Configuration IOS Troubleshooting	5 6			
Assign IP addresses	Basic Switch Configuration Basic Router Configuration	5 5			
Describe and install the hardware and software required to be able to communicate via a network	Chassis Router Hardware Components Router IOS Images	4 6 6			
Use embedded data link layer functionality to perform network neighbor discovery and analysis from the router	Basic Switch Configuration Basic Router Configuration IOS Troubleshooting	5 5 6			
Use embedded layer-3 through layer-7 protocols to establish, test, suspend or disconnect connectivity to remote devices from the router console	IOS Troubleshooting	6			

Exam Readiness Checklist

Official Objective	Study Guide Coverage	Ch #	Beginner	Intermediate	Expert
Technology					
Demonstrate the mathematical skills required to work seamlessly with integer decimal, binary and hexadecimal numbers and simple binary logic	IP Addressing Introduction	3			
Define and describe the structure and technologies of computer networks	Networks Topologies Network Types Hierarchical Network Model	1 1 1 2			
Describe the hardware and software required to be able to communicate via a network	OSI Reference Model Data Link Layer Network Layer Transport Layer Transferring Information Between Computers	2 2 2 2 2			
Describe the physical, electrical and mechanical properties and standards associated with optical, wireless, and copper media used in networks	OSI Reference Model	2			
Describe the topologies and physical issues associated with cabling common LANs	Topologies OSI Reference Model Data Link Layer	1 2 2			
Identify the key characteristics of common wide area networking (WAN) configurations and technologies, and differentiate between these and common LAN technologies	Networks Network Types Data Link Layer Wide Area Networking Overview	1 1 2 15			
Describe the purpose and fundamental operation of the Internetwork Operating System (IOS)	IOS Introduction	5			
Describe the role of a router in a WAN	Data Link Layer Network Layer	2 2			
Identify the major internal and external components of a router, and describe the associated functionality	Router Hardware Components	6			

Exam Readiness Checklist

Official Objective	Study Guide Coverage	Ch #	Beginner	Intermediate	Expert
Identify and describe the stages of the router boot-up sequence	Router Bootup Process	6			
Describe how the configuration register and boot system commands modify the router boot-up sequence	Router Bootup Process	6			
Describe the concepts associated with routing, and the different methods and protocols used to achieve it	Types of Routes Static Routes Dynamic Routing Protocols	9 9 9			
Describe how an IP address is associated with a device interface, and the association between physical and employ IP addressing techniques	Transferring Information Between Computers TCP/IP Protocol Stack IP Addressing Introduction Subnetting	2 3 3 3			
Employ IP addressing techniques	Planning IP Addressing Figuring Out IP Address Components Variable Length Subnet Masking Route Summarization	3 3 12 12			
Compare and contrast collision and broadcast domains, and describe the process of network segmentation	Data Link Layer Bridges and Switches	2 7			
Describe the principles and practice of switching in an Ethernet network	Data Link Layer Functions of Bridging and Switching	2 7			
Explain how collisions are detected and handled in an Ethernet system	Data Link Layer	2			
Explain the fundamental concepts associated with the Ethernet media access technique	Data Link Layer	2			
Describe how the protocols associated with TCP/IP allow host communication to occur	Transferring Information Between Computers TCP/IP Protocol Stack	2 3			
Describe the operation of the Internet Control Message Protocol (ICMP) and identify the reasons, types and format of associated error and control messages	TCP/IP Protocol Stack IOS Troubleshooting	3 6			
Describe the principles and practice of packet switching utilizing the Internet Protocol (IP)	TCP/IP Protocol Stack Types of Routes	3 9			

Exam Readiness Checklist

INCD 640-811

Official Objective	Study Guide Coverage	Ch #	Beginner	Intermediate	Expert
Planning and Designing					
Design or modify a simple LAN using Cisco products	Networks	1			
	Topologies	1			
	Network Types	1			
	Hierarchical Network Model	2			
Design an IP addressing scheme to support classful, classless, and private addressing to meet design requirements	IP Addressing Introduction	3			
	Subnetting	3			
	Planning IP Addressing	3			
	Variable Length Subnet Masking	12			
	Route Summarization	12			
Select an appropriate routing protocol based on user requirements	Types of Routes	9			
	Static Routes	9			
	Dynamic Routing Protocols	9			
Design a simple internetwork using Cisco products	Networks	1			
	Topologies	1			
	Network Types	1			
	Hierarchical Network Model	2			
	Cisco's Networking Products	4			
Develop an access list to meet user specifications	Access-List Overview	13			
	Types of Access-Lists	13			
	Placement of Access-Lists	13			
Choose WAN protocols to meet design requirements	Network Types	1			
	Wide Area Networking Overview	15			
Implementation and Operations					
Configure routing protocols given user requirements	IP Routing Protocol Basics	10			
	IP RIP	10			
	IP IGRP	10			
	OSPF	11			
	EIGRP	11			
Configure IP addresses, subnet masks, and gateway addresses on routers and hosts	Basic Switch Configuration	5			
	Basic Router Configuration	5			
Configure a router for additional administrative functionality	Basic Router Configuration	5			
	Address Translation Overview	14			
	Address Translation Configuration	14			
	Dynamic Host Configuration Protocol	14			

Exam Readiness Checklist

Official Objective	Study Guide Coverage	Ch #	Beginner	Intermediate	Expert
Configure a switch with VLANS and inter-switch communication	VLAN Overview	8			
	VLAN Connections	8			
	VLAN Trunk Protocol	8			
	1900 and 2950 VLAN Configuration	8			
Implement a LAN	IOS Basics	5			
	Basic Switch Configuration	5			
	Basic Router Configuration	5			
	1900 and 2950 Configuration	7			
Customize a switch configuration to meet specified network requirements	Basic Switch Configuration	6			
	1900 and 2950 Configuration	7			
Implement access lists	Basic Access-List Configuration	13			
	Wildcard Masks	13			
	Types of Access-Lists	13			
	Placement of Access-Lists	13			
Implement simple WAN protocols	HDLC	15			
	PPP	15			
	Frame Relay Configuration	16			
	Non-Broadcast Multi-Access	16			
	ISDN Interface Configuration	17			
	Legacy Dial-on-Demand Routing	17			
	Dialer Profiles and DDR	17			
Troubleshooting					
Utilize the OSI model as a guide for systematic network troubleshooting	OSI Reference Model	2			
	Data Link Layer	2			
	Network Layer	2			
	Transport Layer	2			
	IOS Troubleshooting	6			
Perform LAN and VLAN troubleshooting	IOS Troubleshooting	6			
	1900 and 2950 Configuration	7			
	1900 and 2950 VLAN Configuration	8			
Troubleshoot routing protocols	IOS Troubleshooting	6			
	Static Routes	9			
	IP RIP	10			
	IP IGRP	10			
	OSPF	11			
	EIGRP	11			

Exam Readiness Checklist

Official Objective	Study Guide Coverage	Ch #	Beginner	Intermediate	Expert
Troubleshoot IP addressing and host configuration	IOS Troubleshooting	6			
Troubleshoot a device as part of a working network	IOS Troubleshooting	6			
	1900 and 2950 VLAN Configuration	7			
Troubleshoot an access list	IOS Troubleshooting	6			
	Types of Access-Lists	13			
	Placement of Access-Lists	13			
Perform simple WAN troubleshooting	IOS Troubleshooting	6			
	HDLC	15			
	PPP	15			
	Frame Relay Configuration	16			
	Non-Broadcast Multi-Access	16			
	Legacy Dial-on-Demand Routing	17			
Technology					
Describe the Spanning Tree process	The Spanning Tree Protocol	7			
Evaluate the characteristics of LAN environments	OSI Reference Model	2			
	Data Link Layer	2			
	Network Layer	2			
	Transport Layer	2			
	Bridges and Switches	7			
	Functions of Bridges and Switches	7			
Evaluate the characteristics of routing protocols	Types of Routes	9			
	Static Routes	9			
	Router-on-a-Stick	9			
	Dynamic Routing Protocols	9			
	Problems with Distance Vector Protocols	9			
Evaluate rules for packet control	Access-List Overview	13			
Evaluate key characteristics of HDLC, PPP, Frame Relay, DDR, and ISDN technologies	Network Types	1			
	Wide Area Networking Overview	15			
	Virtual Circuits	16			
	Terminology and Operation	16			
	ISDN Introduction	17			

Glossary

802.1Q IEEE 802.1Q is a trunking standard. Unlike ISL trunks, where every frame traversing the trunk is tagged, or encapsulated, with an ISL header and a trailer, 802.1Q trunks support two types of frames: tagged and untagged. An untagged frame does not carry any VLAN identification information in it—basically, this is a simple Ethernet frame. 802.1Q tagging modifies the original Ethernet frame. A 4-byte field, called a tag field, is *inserted* into the middle of the original Ethernet frame, and the original frame's FCS (checksum) is recomputed in accordance with this change. Tagging is done in order to help other connected to switches to keep the frame in the source VLAN.

802.2 IEEE has split the data link layer into two components: MAC and LLC. The LLC, performed in software, is defined in 802.2 and is responsible for identifying the upper-layer protocol that is encapsulated. There are two implementations of LLC: SAP and SNAP. The MAC is performed in hardware. Examples of different types of MAC are 802.3 Ethernet and 802.5 Token Ring.

802.3 IEEE 802.3 defines how Ethernet is implemented. It is responsible for is defining the framing used to transmit information between two NICs. A frame standardizes the fields in the frame and their lengths so that every device understands how to read the contents of the frame. 802.3 has a length field, while Ethernet II has a type field. 802.2 LLC frames are encapsulated in an 802.3 frame before being set out of an Ethernet interface.

Access Layer The bottom layer of Cisco's 3-layer hierarchical model is the access layer. Actually, the access layer is at the periphery of your campus network, separated from the core layer by the distribution layer. The main function of the access layer is to provide the user his initial connection to your network. Typically, this connection is typically provided by a switch.

Access-Link Connection An access link is a connection to a device that has a standardized Ethernet NIC that understands only standardized Ethernet frames. In other words, we're talking about a normal NIC card that understands IEEE 802.3 and/or Ethernet II frames. Access-link connections can be associated only with one VLAN.

Access List (ACL) ACLs, known for their ability to filter traffic as it either comes into or leaves an interface, can also by used for other purposes, including the following: restrict telnet (VTY) access to the a router, filter routing information, prioritize WAN traffic with queuing, trigger phone calls with dial-on-demand routing (DDR), change the administrative distance of routes, and other things.

Address Overloading See *Port Address Translation*.

Access Rate This is the speed of the physical connection between your router and the Frame Relay switch (such as a T1).

Address Resolution Protocol (ARP) ARP is an Internet layer protocol that helps TCP/IP devices find other devices in the same broadcast domain. ARP uses a local broadcast to discover neighboring devices. Basically, ARP resolves a layer-3 IP address of a destination to the layer-2 MAC address of the destination.

Administrative Distance Administrative distance is a Cisco-proprietary mechanism used to rank the IP routing protocols. This is used as a tie-breaker if a router is learning the same route from two different routing protocols, like OSPF and EIGRP.

Advertisement Request An advertisement request message is a VTP message a VTP client generates. Clients don't store VLAN configuration information in NVRAM—instead, they learn this every time that they boot up.

Alternate Port State Alternate ports are new in Rapid STP (RSTP). An alternate port is a port that has an alternative path or paths to the root but is currently in a discarding state. When the root port fails, the switch can speed up convergence by using the alternate port.

Application Layer The seventh layer, or topmost layer, of the OSI Reference Model is the application layer. It provides the interface that a person uses to interact with the application.

Application-Specific Integrated Circuit (ASIC) ASICs are specialized processors that can do very few tasks but can do them extremely well. Processors, on the other hand, can perform many tasks, but are not necessarily optimized for these tasks. Many types of networking hardware, including switches, use ASICs.

Autonomous System (AS) An AS is a group of networks under a single administrative control, which could be your company's network, a division within your company, or a group of companies' networks.

Autosensing Autosensing is a mechanism that an Ethernet interface can use to figure out its configuration, which includes its duplexing and/or speed.

Backup Port State Backup ports are new in RSTP. A backup port is a port on a segment that could be used to leave a segment, although there is already an active designated port for the segment. When a designated port fails, a switch with a backup port can speed up convergence by using it.

Backward Explicit Congestion Notification (BECN) This value is set by the destination Frame Relay DTE in the header of the Frame Relay frame to indicate congestion (from the source to the destination) to the source of the Frame Relay frames. The source can then adapt its rate on the VC appropriately.

Bandwidth Domain All of the devices on the same layer-2 physical segment are said to be in the same bandwidth domain. The more devices you have on a physical segment, the less bandwidth each device has. You can use routers or switches to create separate bandwidth domains.

Basic Rate Interface (BRI) An ISDN BRI contains a total of three DS0s for 192Kbps of bandwidth. Two DS0s (64Kbps each), called bearer channels, are used to make phone calls for voice and data connections. The signaling channel contains one DS0 and is broken into two components: 16Kbps is used for signaling information (setting up and tearing down circuit-switched connections), and 48Kbps is used for synchronization, clocking, and physical layer framing.

Bits Binary represents protocol data units (PDUs) in bits. There are two bit values: on (1) and off (0), which are used by computers to encode information. Bits are physical layer PDUs.

Blocking State When STP is enabled, ports will go into a *blocking* state under one of three conditions: election of a root switch, when a switch receives a BPDU on a port that indicates a better path to the root than the port the switch is currently using to reach the root, and if a port is not a root port or a designated port. A port in a blocked state will remain there for 20 seconds by default. During this state, the only thing the port is doing is listening to and processing BPDUs on its interfaces.

Bridge A bridge solves layer-2 bandwidth and collision problems. It performs its switching function in software and supports only half-duplex connections. It typically supports 2–16 ports and performs store-and-forward switching.

Bridge (or Switch) ID Each layer-2 device running STP has a unique identifier assigned to it, which is then used in the BPDUs the layer-2 devices advertise. The Bridge ID has two components: the bridge's or switch's priority (2 bytes) and the bridge's or switch's MAC address (6 bytes).

Bridge Protocol Data Unit (BPDU) For STP to function, the switches need to share information with each other. BPDUs are sent out as multicasts every two seconds by default, and only other layer-2 devices are listening to this information. Switches use BPDUs to learn the topology of the network, including loops.

Broadcast A PDU sent to all devices. The destination MAC address denotes all devices on a segment (FFFF.FFFF.FFFF). A destination IP address of 255.255.255.255 is all devices.

Bus Topology A bus topology uses a single connection to connect all devices together. Certain media types, such as 10Base5 and 10Base2 Ethernet, use a bus topology.

Carrier Sense Multiple Access/Collision Detection (CSMA/CD) In an Ethernet environment, only one NIC can successfully send a frame at a time. All NICs, however, can simultaneously listen to information on the wire. Before an Ethernet NIC puts a frame on the wire, it will first *sense* the wire to ensure that no other frame is currently on the wire. The NIC must go through this sensing process, since the Ethernet medium supports *multiple access*—another NIC might already have a frame on the wire. If the NIC doesn't sense a frame on the wire, it will go ahead and transmit its own frame; otherwise, if there is a frame on the wire, the NIC will wait for the completion of the transmission for the frame on the wire and then transmit its own frame. If two or more machines simultaneously sense the wire and see no frame, and both place their frames on the wire, a *collision* will occur. The NICs, when they place a frame on the wire, will examine the status of the wire to ensure that a collision does not occur: this is the *collision detection* mechanism of CSMA/CD.

Challenge Handshake Authentication Protocol (CHAP) CHAP uses a three-way handshake process to perform the authentication for a PPP connection. First, the source sends its username (not its password) to the destination. The destination sends back a challenge, which is a random value generated by the destination. Both sides then take the source's username, the matching password, and the challenge and run them through the MD5 hashing function. The source will then take the result of this function and send it to the destination. The destination compares this value to the hashed output that it generated—if the two values match, then the password used by the source must have been the same used by the destination, and thus the destination will permit the connection.

Circuit-Switched Connection Circuit-switched connections are dialup connections. These include analog modem and digital ISDN dialup connections.

Classful Routing Protocols A classful routing protocol understands only class subnets. RIPv1 and IGRP are examples. A classful protocol does not send subnet mask information. RIP and IGRP can have subnet masks other than the default, but the subnet mask used must be the same for all subnets of a class address.

Classless Interdomain Routing (CIDR) CIDR is an extension to VLSM and route summarization. With VLSM, you can summarize subnets back to the Class A, B, or C network boundary. CIDR takes this one step further and allows you to summarize a block of contiguous Class A, B, and C networks. This is commonly referred to as *supernetting*. Today's classless protocols support supernetting. However, it is most commonly configured by ISPs on the Internet using BGP.

Classless Routing Protocols Classless routing protocols do not have any issues accepting routing updates with any bit value for a subnet mask, allowing nonconforming subnet masks, such as a default route. Classful routing can also accept a default route but requires the configuration of the **`ip classless`** command. However, this overrides the classful protocols' mechanics. Classless protocols include RIPv2, EIGRP, OSPF, IS-IS, and BGP.

Collision Domain All of the devices on the same layer-2 Ethernet physical segment are said to be in the same collision domain. The more devices you have on a physical segment, the more likely collisions will occur. You can use routers or switches to create separate collision domains. The terms collision domain and bandwidth domain are commonly used to refer to the same thing.

Command History By default, an IOS device will store the last ten commands that you executed. You can recall these commands by using either CTRL-P or the UP ARROW key. If you accidentally go past the command that you want to edit or reexecute, use CTRL-N or the DOWN ARROW key.

Command-Line Interface (CLI) The CLI provides a way for the user to interact with the operating system and the device's hardware components. This can be a text-based or GUI interface. A text-based interface has you type in commands on a command line. A GUI-based interface has you perform configuration tasks using a mouse and keyboard; you typically use such conventions as radio buttons, checkboxes, and pull-down options to select choices.

Committed Burst Rate (B_C) This is the average data rate (over a period of a smaller fixed time than CIR) that a provider guarantees for a Frame Relay VC; in other words, it's a smaller time period yet a higher average than CIR. This allows for small bursts in data streams.

Committed Information Rate (CIR) CIR is the average data rate, measured over a fixed period of time, which the carrier guarantees for a Frame Relay VC.

Common STP (CST) When one instance of STP is running for the switched network (all VLANs).

Configuration Mode *Configuration* mode in the IOS allows you to make configuration changes to a Cisco device, denoted by "(config)#" at the end of the prompt.

Connected Route A router will look at its active interfaces, examine the addresses configured on the interface and determine the corresponding network number, and populate the routing table with this information.

Content-Addressable Memory (CAM) Table A CAM table is an old bridging term that describes the table that holds the MAC addresses of devices and the ports off of which they reside. The layer-2 device uses this to make switching decisions. This is also referred to as a port address table.

Content Network (CN) CNs were developed to ease the access of users to Internet resources. CNs are aware of layers 4 through 7 of the OSI Reference Model and use this information to make intelligent decisions about how to obtain the information for the user or users.

Context-Sensitive Help The context-sensitive help feature of the IOS allows you to pull up help information concerning commands and parameters. Context-sensitive help is supported at all modes within the IOS, including *User EXEC*, *Privilege EXEC*, and *Configuration*. There are a variety ways to use this feature. If you are not sure what command that you need to execute, at the prompt, type in either the **`help`**

command or a **?**. The Cisco device will then display a list of commands that can be executed at the level in which you are currently located, along with a brief description.

Core Layer The core layer, as its name suggests, is the backbone of the network. It provides a very high speed connection between the different distribution layer devices. Because of the need for high-speed connections, the core consists of high-speed *switches* and will not, typically, perform any type of packet or frame manipulations, such as filtering or Quality of Service. Because switches are used at the core, the core is referred to as a layer-2 core. The traffic that traverses the core is typically to access enterprise corporate resources, such as the Internet, gateways, e-mail servers, and corporate applications.

Counting to Infinity One problem with a routing loop is the counting to infinity symptom. When a routing loops occurs, and a packet or packets are caught in the loop, they continuously circle around the loop, wasting bandwidth on the segments and CPU cycles on the routers that are processing these packets. To prevent packets from circling around the loop forever, distance vector protocols typically place a hop count limit on how far a packet is legally allowed to travel.

Crossover Cable An Ethernet crossover cable crosses over two sets of wires: pin 1 on one side is connected to pin 3 on the other and pin 2 is connected to pin 6. Crossover cables should be used when you connect a DTE to another DTE or a DCE to another DCE. Use a crossover cable to connect a hub to another hub; a switch to another switch; a hub to a switch; or a PC, router, or file server to another PC, router, or file server.

Customer Premises Equipment (CPE) This is your network's equipment, which includes the DCE (modem, NT1, CSU/DSU) and your DTE (router, access server). This is equipment located at your site, which connects to the carrier's WAN.

Cut-Through Switching With cut-through switching, the switch reads only the very first part of the frame before making a switching decision. Once the switch device reads the destination MAC address, it begins forwarding the frame (even though the frame may still be coming into the interface).

Data Communications Equipment (DCE) A DCE terminates a physical connection and provides clocking and synchronization of a connection between two sites. It connects to a DTE. The DCE category includes such equipment as CSU/DSUs, NT1s, and modems.

Data Link Connection Identifier A DLCI is used to uniquely identify each Frame Relay VC on a physical interface: they're the address of the VC. This gives you the ability to multiplex traffic for multiple destinations on a single physical interface. DLCIs are locally significant and can change on a segment-by-segment basis. The Frame Relay switch will do a translation between the DLCIs when it is switching frames between segments.

Data Link Layer The second layer in the OSI Reference Model is the data link layer. The data link layer provides for physical, or hardware, addresses. These hardware addresses are commonly called Media Access Control (MAC) addresses. The data link layer also defines how a networking device accesses the media that it is connected to by define the media's frame type. This includes the fields and components of the data link layer, or layer-2, frame.

Data Terminal Equipment (DTE) A DTE is an end-user device, like a router or PC, which connects to the WAN via the DCE equipment.

Datagram See *Packet*.

Default Route A default route is a special type of static route. Whereas a static route specifies a path a router should use to reach a specific destination, a default route specifies a path the router should use if it *doesn't* know how to reach a destination.

Demarcation Point This is where the responsibility of the carrier is passed on to you; it could be inside or outside your local facility. Note that this is a *logical* and not necessarily a physical boundary.

Designated Port With STP, each segment can have only one port on a single layer-2 device in a forwarding state, called a designated port. The layer-2 device with the best accumulated path cost will use its connected port to the segment as the designated port.

Designated Router (DR) An OSPF router will not form adjacencies to just any router. Instead, a client/server design is implemented in OSPF. For each network multi-access segment, there is a DR and a BDR as well as other routers. As an example, if you have ten VLANs in your switched area, you'll have ten DRs and ten BDRs. The one exception of a segment not having these two routers is on a WAN point-to-point link. When an OSPF router comes up, it forms adjacencies with the DR and the BDR on each multi-access segment that it is connected to. Any exchange of routing information is between these DR/BDR routers and the other OSPF neighbors on a segment (and vice versa). An OSPF router talks to a DR using the IP multicast address of 224.0.0.6. The DR and the BDR talk to all routers using the 224.0.0.5 multicast IP address.

Dial-on-Demand Routing (DDR) Cisco uses the DDR feature to trigger phone calls when a router has *interesting* traffic to send to a remote destination. Interesting traffic is traffic that you define as important.

Dialer Profiles Dialer profiles allow a physical interface to be shared by many logical DDR interfaces, which provides flexibility in how you set up and use your DDR connections. Dialer profiles are typically used when an interface has to handle many dialup connections with various configuration properties.

Discard Eligibility (DE) This is used to mark a Frame Relay frame as a low-priority frame. You can do this manually, or the carrier will do this for a frame that is nonconforming to your traffic contract (exceeding CIR/B_C values).

Distance Vector Protocols Distance vector routing protocols use the distance (metric) and direction (vector) to find paths to destinations. Sometimes these protocols are referred to as *routing by rumor*, since the routers learn routing information via broadcasts from directly connected neighbors, and these neighbors might have learned these networks from other neighboring routers. Some examples of IP routing protocols that are distance vector are RIPv1 and IGRP.

Distribution Layer The distribution layer, as opposed to the core and access layers, performs most of the connectivity tasks. Typically routers are used at the distribution layer to connect the access layers to the core. The responsibilities of the distribution layer include the following: containing broadcasts, securing traffic, providing a hierarchy through layer-3 logical addressing and route summarization, and translating between media types.

DIX See *Ethernet II*.

Dotted Decimal IPv4 addresses are 32 bits in length. However, to make the addresses readable, they are broken into four bytes (called octets), with a period (decimal) between each byte. So that the address is understandable to the human eye, the four sets of binary numbers are then converted to decimal. The format of this address is commonly called *dotted decimal*.

Duplex Duplexing refers to the method of transmitting and receiving frames. With a half-duplex configuration, an interface can either send or receive frames—it can't do both simultaneously. Half-duplex connections are used in shared environments: hubs, 10Base2 and 10Base5 cabling. With a full-duplex configuration, an interface can both send and receive simultaneously. Full-duplex connections are used in point-to-point connections. When enabled, full-duplexing causes the collision detection mechanism in the interface to be disabled.

Dynamic Host Configuration Protocol (DHCP) DHCP allows devices to dynamically acquire their IP addressing information. It is built on a client/server model and defines two components: Server (delivering host configuration information) and Client (requesting and acquiring host configuration information).

Dynamic Routing Protocols Dynamic routing protocols share network numbers a router knows about and reachability information concerning these networks.

Dynamic Trunk Protocol (DTP) The Dynamic Trunk Protocol (DTP) is used to dynamically form and verify a trunk connection between two Cisco switches. DTP is Cisco-proprietary and is supported on both 802.1Q and ISL trunks.

Dynamic VLANs With dynamic VLANs, the switch will automatically assign the port to a VLAN by using information from the user device, including its MAC address, IP address, or even directory information, such as usernames. The switch will then consult a policy server, called a VLAN Membership Policy Server (VMPS), which contains a mapping of device information to VLANs.

Enhanced IGRP (EIGRP) EIGRP is a Cisco-proprietary routing protocol for IP. It's actually based on IGRP, with many enhancements built into it. Because it has its roots in IGRP, the configuration is similar; however, it has many link state characteristics that were added to it to allow EIGRP to scale to enterprise network sizes. These characteristics include: Fast convergence, loop-free topology, VLSM and route summarization, multicast and incremental updates, and routing for multiple routed protocols (IP, IPX, and AppleTalk). EIGRP is a hybrid protocol.

Ethernet Ethernet is a LAN media type that functions at the data link layer. Ethernet uses the Carrier Sense Multiple Access/Collision Detection (CSMA/CD) mechanism to send information in a shared environment. Ethernet was initially developed with the idea that many devices would be connected to the same physical piece of wiring.

Ethernet II Ethernet II is one of the first Ethernet frame types. Digital, Intel, and Xerox (DIX) invented Ethernet. Ethernet II and 802.3 are very similar: they both use CSMA/CD to determine their operations. Their main difference lies the frames used to transmit information between NICs: Ethernet II does not have any sublayers and has a *type* field instead of a length field.

Excessive Burst Rate (B_E) This is the fastest data rate at which the provider will ever service a Frame Relay VC.

Extended Access List Extended ACLs can match on all of the following information: source *and* destination IP addresses, IP protocol (IP, TCP, UDP, ICMP, et cetera), and protocol information, such as port numbers for TCP and UDP, or message types for ICMP.

Exterior Gateway Protocol (EGP) An EGP handles routing between different autonomous systems. Today, there is only one active EGP: the Border Gateway Protocol (BGP). BGP is used to route traffic across the Internet backbone between different autonomous systems.

Extranet An extranet is an extended intranet, where certain internal services are made available to *known* external users or business partners at remote locations. The connections that are used by these external users and the internal resource are typically secured via a firewall and VPN.

Forward Explicit Congestion Notification (FECN) This value in the Frame Relay frame header is set by the carrier switch to indicate congestion inside the carrier network to the destination device at the end of the VC.

Forwarding State In STP, ports that are in a learning state after the forward delay timer expires are placed in a forwarding state. In a forwarding state, the port will process BPDUs, update its CAM table with frames that it receives, *and* forward user traffic through the port. Only root and designated ports will end up in a forwarding state.

Fragment-Free Switching Fragment-free switching is a modified form of cut-through switching. Where cut-through switching reads up to the destination MAC address field in the frame before making a switching decision, fragment-free switching makes sure that the frame is at least 64 bytes long.

Frame A frame is a PDU used at the data link layer. With IEEE, there are two PDUs used: one for LLC (802.2) and one for MAC (802.2 or 802.5).

Hardware Address See *Media Access Control (MAC) Address*.

Hierarchical Addressing Hierarchical addressing is used to set up a network so that routing information can be summarized. IP addresses are laid out such that as you go up each layer in the hierarchy, routes can be summarized into a smaller set of routes.

High-Level Data Link Control (HDLC) The HDLC protocol is based on ISO standards. It can be used with synchronous and asynchronous connections and defines the frame type and interaction between two devices at the data link layer. Cisco's implementation of HDLC is based on ISO's standards, but Cisco has made a change in the frame format, making it proprietary. In other words, Cisco's HDLC will work only if the remote end also supports Cisco's HDLC. The default encapsulation on synchronous serial interfaces on a Cisco router is Cisco's HDLC.

Hold-Down Timer In order to give routers running a distance vector protocol enough time to propagate a poisoned route and to ensure that no routing loops occur while propagation is occurring, a hold-down mechanism is used. During this period, the routers will freeze the poisoned route in their routing table for the period of the hold-down timer, which is typically three times the interval of the routing broadcast update.

Hub A hub is a physical layer device that provides a logical bus structure for Ethernet. A hub will take a physical layer signal from one interface and replicate that signal on all of its other interfaces.

Hybrid Routing Protocols A hybrid protocol takes the advantages of both distance vector and link state routing protocols and merges them into a new protocol. Typically, hybrid protocols are based on a distance vector protocol but contain many of the features and advantages of link state protocols. Examples of hybrid protocols include RIPv2 and EIGRP.

Implicit Deny With an ACL, if the router compares a packet to every statement in the list and does not find a match against the packet contents, the router will *drop* the packet. This is based on the invisible implicit deny statement at the end of every ACL.

Inside Global IP Address An inside device with an associated public IP address is called an inside global IP address.

Inside Local IP Address An inside device with an associated private IP address is called an inside local IP address.

Integrated Services Digital Network (ISDN) ISDN is a group of standards that define how voice and data connections can be dynamically set up across digital circuit-switched connections. Because ISDN uses digital circuits, it has the following advantages over analog: ISDN sets up calls in less than a second; provides a guaranteed data rate; and handles multiple services, like voice, video, and data.

Interswitch Link (ISL) ISL is a proprietary tagging method that Cisco developed to use for Ethernet and Token Ring trunk connections. ISL encapsulates the original frame by adding a 26-byte header and a 4-byte CRC trailer. The original Ethernet frame is placed between the header and the trailer. The VLAN tags are used by neighboring switches and other devices in order to maintain broadcast and subnet boundaries between multiple devices.

Interior Gateway Protocol (IGP) An IGP is a routing protocol that handles routing within a single autonomous system. IGPs include RIP, IGRP, EIGRP, OSPF, and IS-IS.

Interior Gateway Routing Protocol (IGRP) IGRP is a Cisco-proprietary routing protocol for IP. It is a distance vector protocol. IGRP uses triggered updates to speed up convergence and supports unequal-cost load balancing to a single destination. IGRP uses a composite metric, which includes bandwidth, delay, reliability, load, and MTU, when choosing paths to a destination.

Internet An internet exists where *unknown* external users can access internal resources in your network. In other words, your company might have a web site that sells various products, and you want any external user to be able to access this service.

Internet Control Message Protocol (ICMP) ICMP is used to send error and control information between TCP/IP devices. ICMP, defined in RFC 792, includes many different messages that devices can generate or respond to.

Internet Layer The Internet layer is a TCP/IP protocol stack layer and equates to the network (3) layer of the OSI Reference Model.

Internetwork Operating System (IOS) The IOS provides a function similar to that of Microsoft Windows XP or Linux: it controls and manages the hardware it is running on. Basically, the IOS provides the interface between you and the hardware, allowing you to execute commands to configure and manage your Cisco device.

Intranet An intranet is basically a network that is local to a company. In other words, users from within this company can find all of their resources without having to go outside of the company.

Inverse ARP Inverse ARP allows you to discover the layer-3 protocol address at the other end of a Frame Relay VC. This is something like a reverse ARP in TCP/IP.

Learning State In STP, from a listening state, a port moves into a learning state. During the learning state, the port is still listening for and processing BPDUs on the port; however, unlike when in the listening state, the port begins to process user frames: The switch examines the source addresses in the frames and updates its CAM table, but the switch is still not forwarding these frames out destination ports. Ports stay in this state for the length of the forward delay time (which defaults to 15 seconds).

Leased Line Leased lines are dedicated circuits or point-to-point connections in a WAN.

Legacy DDR Legacy DDR places the DDR configuration on a physical interface. Legacy DDR works fine if you have a small number of dialup connections that all have the same configuration properties.

Light-Emitting Diode (LED) Cisco uses LEDs to show the status of various physical components of its products. For instance, LEDs are commonly used to display the status of an interface. In Cisco's equipment, LEDs can change to various colors, such as green, amber, orange, red, or off, to indicate various states.

Link Control Protocol (LCP) LCP's primary responsibility is to establish, configure, authenticate, and test a PPP connection. Here are some of the things that LCP will negotiate when setting up a PPP connection: authentication method used (PAP or CHAP), compression algorithm used, callback phone number to use, and multilink.

Link State Advertisement OSPF routers use Link State Advertisements (LSAs) to communicate with each other. One type of LSA is a hello, which is used to form neighbor relationships and as a keep-alive function. Hellos are generated every ten seconds. When sharing link information (directly connected routes), links are sent to the DR (224.0.0.6) and the DR disseminates this to everyone (224.0.0.5) else on the segment.

Link State Protocols Link state protocols use an algorithm called the *Shortest Path First (SPF)* algorithm, invented by Dijkstra, to find the best layer-3 path to a destination. Whereas distance vector protocols rely on *rumors* from other neighbors about remote routes, link state protocols will learn the complete topology of the network: which routers are connected to which networks. OSPF is an example of a link state protocol.

Listening State After the 20-second blocking timer expires, a root or designated port in STP will move to a listening state. Any other port will remain in a blocked state. During the listening state, the port is still listening for BPDUs and double-checking the layer-2 topology. Again, the only traffic that is being processed in this state consists of BPDUs—all other traffic is dropped. A port will stay in this state for the length of the forward delay timer. The default for this value is 15 seconds.

Load Distribution Load distribution allows you to distribute connection requests destined to a single IP address to multiple machines.

Local Area Network (LAN) A LAN is used to connect networking devices together that are in a very close geographic area, such as a floor of a building, a building itself, or a campus environment.

Local Loop This is the connection from the carrier's switch to the demarcation point in a WAN connection.

Local Management Interface (LMI) LMI defines how the Frame Relay DTE, like a router, interacts with the Frame Relay DCE, a switch. LMI is local and is not sent to the destination DTE.

Logical Address The network layer is responsible for the logical address scheme. All layer-3 addressing schemes have two components: network and host (or node). Each segment (physical or logical) in your network needs a unique network number. Each host on these segments needs a unique host number from within the assigned network number. The combination of the network and host numbers assigned to a device provides a unique layer-3 address throughout the entire network.

Logical Link Control (LLC) See *802.2*.

Logical Topology A logical topology describes how devices communicate with each other across the physical topology.

Media Access Control (MAC) Address The data link layer uses MAC, or hardware, addresses for communication. For LAN communications, each machine on the same connected media type needs a unique MAC address. A MAC address is 48 bits in length and is represented as a 12-digit hexadecimal number. To make it easier to read, the MAC address is represented in a dotted hexadecimal format, like this: ffff.ffff.ffff.

Metric A routing protocol will use a measurement called a *metric* to determine which path is the best path. Examples of metrics include hop count, cost, bandwidth, and delay.

Metropolitan Area Network (MAN) A MAN is a hybrid between a LAN and a WAN. It connects two or more LANs in the same geographic area using high speed connections. Examples of a MAN would be the connection between two different buildings or offices in the same city.

Mode Button Certain Cisco products, such as the 1900 and 2950 Catalyst switches, have a MODE button that can be used to toggle the meaning of LED port statuses.

Multicast Frame With a multicast, the destination MAC address denotes a group of devices, which could include no device, some devices, or all devices.

Network A network is basically all of the components (hardware and software) involved in connecting computers together across small and large distances. The purpose of using networks is to provide easier access to information, thus increasing productivity for users.

Network Address Translation (NAT) NAT translates one IP address to another, typically private to public and vice versa.

Network Control Protocol (NCP) NCP defines the process for how the two PPP peers will negotiate which network layer protocols, such as IP and IPX, will be used across the PPP connection.

Network Layer The third layer of the OSI Reference Model is the network layer. The network layer provides for a logical topology of your network using logical, or layer-3, addresses.

Network Termination 1 (NT1) An NT1 connects your ISDN devices to the carrier network (converts an ISDN four-wire connection to the carrier's two-wire connection).

Network Termination 2 (NT2) An NT2 connects multiple ISDN devices together, much as a hub does in Ethernet.

Nonbroadcast Multiaccess (NBMA) Nonbroadcast multiaccess (NBMA) is a term used to describe WAN networks that use VCs for connectivity. With WAN networks that use VCs, each device is connected to another device via a point-to-point VC— only two devices can be connected to a VC. This poses a problem with partially-meshed NBMA environments where devices are located in the same subnet.

Open Shortest Path First The Open Shortest Path First (OSPF) protocol is a link state protocol that handles routing for IP traffic. It uses the SPF algorithm, developed by Dijkstra, to provide a loop-free topology. It also provides fast convergence with triggered, incremental updates via Link State Advertisements (LSAs). OSPF is a classless protocol and allows for a hierarchical design with VLSM and route summarization. It uses cost as a metric.

Open Systems Interconnection (OSI) Reference Model
The International Organization for Standardization (ISO), an international standards body, developed the Open Systems Interconnection (OSI) Reference Model to help describe how information is transferred from one machine to another: from when a user enters information using a keyboard and mouse to how it is converted to electrical or light signals to be transferred across an external medium. It is important to understand that the OSI Reference Model describes concepts and terms in a general manner, and that not every network protocol will fit nicely into the scheme explained in ISO's model (IP and IPX, for example, do not). Therefore, the OSI Reference Model is most often used as a teaching and troubleshooting tool.

Outside Global IP Address An outside device with a registered public IP address is called a device with an outside global IP address.

Oversubscription When you add up all of the CIRs of your VCs on an interface and they exceed the access rate of the interface, you have oversubscription; you are betting that all of your VCs will not run, simultaneously, at their traffic-contracted rates.

Packet A packet is a PDU used at the network layer. It is also referred to as a datagram in the TCP/IP protocol stack.

Packet-Switched Connection A packet-switched connection, such as Frame Relay and X.25, uses virtual circuits across the carrier's network to provide for WAN connections.

Path Cost In STP, path cost is what it costs to reach the root. When a BPDU comes into a port, the path cost value in the BPDU is incremented by the port cost of the incoming port. This value is incremented from layer-2 to layer-2 device. A path cost is basically the accumulated port costs from a switch to the root switch. The path cost value helps the layer-2 device figure out which ports should be root and designated ports.

Per-VLAN STP With PVST, each VLAN has its own instance of STP, with its own root switch, its own set of priorities, and its own set of BPDUs. Based on this information, each VLAN will develop its own loop-free topology.

Permanent Virtual Circuit (PVC) A PVC is similar to a leased line. PVCs must be manually configured on each router, and built on the carrier's switches before you can send any data. One disadvantage of PVCs is that they require a lot of manual configuration up front to establish the VC. Another disadvantage is that they aren't very flexible: if the PVC fails, there is no dynamic rebuilding of the PVC around the failure. However, once you have a PVC configured, it will always be available, barring any failures between the source and destination.

Physical Layer The first, or bottommost, layer of the OSI Reference Model is the physical layer. The physical layer is responsible for the physical mechanics of a network connection, which includes the following: type of interface used on the networking device, type of cable used for connecting devices together, the connectors used on each end of the cable, and the pinouts used for each of the connections on the cable.

Physical Topology A physical topology describes how devices are *physically* cabled together.

Point-to-Point Protocol (PPP) PPP is based on a set of WAN standards. PPP works with asynchronous and synchronous serial interfaces as well as High-Speed Serial Interfaces (HSSIs) and ISDN interfaces (BRI and PRI). PPP includes these features: It performs the dynamic configuration of links, allows for authentication, compresses packet headers, tests the quality of links, performs error detection, multiplexes network layer protocols across the same link, and allows multiple PPP physical connections to be bound together as a single logical connection.

Point-to-Point Topology A point-to-point topology has a single connection between two devices. In this topology, two devices can directly communicate with each other without interference from other devices.

Poisoned Route Route poisoning is a derivative of split horizon. With routing poisoning, when a router detects that one of its connected routes has failed, the router will *poison* the route by assigning an infinite metric to it. It is used by distance vector protocols to prevent routing loops.

Poison Reverse When a router advertises a poised route to its neighbors, its neighbors break the rule of split horizon and send back to the originator the same poisoned route, called a poison reverse. This ensures that everyone received the original update of the poisoned route. This process is used by distance vector protocols to prevent routing loops.

Port Address Redirection (PAR) Static PAT is often called port address redirection (PAR). An address translation device configured with PAR will take a packet destined to a certain destination address and port number and redirect it to another destination address and, possibly different, port number. This is different from NAT, which does only a one-to-one IP address translation.

Port Address Table See *Content-Addressable Memory (CAM) Table*.

Port Address Translation (PAT) Many inside IP addresses are translated to a single IP address, where each inside address is given a different port number for uniqueness.

Port-Based VLANs When you are dealing with static VLANs, you must manually assign a port on a switch to a VLAN. Such VLANs are typically called *port-based* VLANs.

Port Cost In STP, each port is assigned a cost that is inversely proportional to the bandwidth of the interface. The lower the port cost, the more preferred it is. When a BPDU comes into a port, the path cost value in the BPDU is incremented by the port cost of the incoming port. This helps the layer-2 device figure out which ports should be root and designated ports.

Power-On Self Test (POST) POST performs hardware tests when a Cisco device is booting up. These tests can include interfaces, ports, and memory components. For some components, if a failure occurs, the Cisco device will fail to boot up.

PPP Authentication Protocol (PAP) PAP is the simplest, but least secure, of PPP's authentication protocols. During the authentication phase, PAP will go through a two-way handshake process. In this process, the source sends its username and password, in clear text, to the destination. The destination compares this information with a list of locally stored usernames and passwords. If it finds a match, the destination sends back an accept message. If it doesn't find a match, it sends back a reject message.

Presentation Layer The sixth layer of the OSI Reference Model is the presentation layer, which is responsible for defining how information is presented to the user in the interface that they are using. This layer defines how text, graphics, video, and/or audio information is presented to the user.

Primary Rate Interface (PRI) There are two types of ISDN PRI connections: one for T1s and one for E1s. The PRI T1 uses 23 DS0s as bearer channels and 1 DS0 for signaling. The framing, clocking, and synchronization are built into the T1 frame structure and do not require a separate DS0 for these functions. A PRI E1 has a total of 32 channels: 30 DS0s are bearer channels; 1 DS0 is used for signaling; and 1 DS0 is used for framing, synchronization, and clocking.

Private IP Address RFC 1918 is a document that was created to address the shortage of IP addresses. When devices want to communicate with each other, each device needs a unique address. RFC 1918 has created a private address space that any company can use internally. These addresses include 10.0.0.0, 172.16.0.0–172.31.0.0, and 192.168.0.0–192.168.255.0. Private IP addresses are non–Internet routable. You must use address translation to translate a private address to a public one if you want to communicate with devices on a public network, like the Internet.

Privilege EXEC Mode *Privilege EXEC* mode provides high-level management access to the IOS, including all commands available at *User EXEC* mode. This mode is used for detailed troubleshooting and also is a stepping-stone to *Configuration* mode. If you see a "#" character at the end of the prompt information, then you know that you are in *Privilege EXEC* mode.

Protocol Data Unit (PDU) The term PDU is generically used to describe data and its overhead.

Q.921 Q.921 defines Link Access Procedure on the D channel (LAPD), which is responsible for the data link layer (layer-2) connection between the router and ISDN switch.

Q.931 Defines the network layer signaling (layer-3) used to set up and tear down ISDN calls.

Rapid Spanning Tree Protocol (RSTP) RSTP is an IEEE standard: 802.1w, which is interoperable with 802.1d and an extension to it. The problem with 802.1d is that it was designed back when waiting for 30 to 50 seconds for convergence wasn't a problem. However, in today's networks, this can cause serious performance problems for networks that use real-time applications, such as Voice over IP (VoIP). RSTP allows convergence to be almost instantaneous in most situations.

Ready/Not Ready Signals These signals can be used at the transport layer to implement flow control. With ready/not ready signals, when the destination receives more traffic than it can handle, it can send a *not ready* signal to the source, indicating that the source should stop transmitting data. When the destination has a chance to catch up and process the source's information, the destination will respond back with a *ready* signal. Upon receiving the ready signal, the source can resume the sending of data.

Reference Points ISDN uses references points to define the boundaries between ISDN components. R is the point between a TA and a TE2, S is the point between a TE2 or TE1 and an NT2, T is the point between an NT2 and an NT1, and U is the point between the NT1 and the local exchange.

Repeater A repeater is a physical layer device that will take a signal from one interface and replicate it to another. An Ethernet hub is an example of a repeater. Repeaters are typically used when you need to extend the distance of a cable.

Reverse Address Resolution Protocol RARP is sort of the reverse of an ARP. In an ARP, the device knows the layer-3 address, but not the data link layer address. With a RARP, the device doesn't have an IP address and wants to acquire one. The only address that this machine has is a MAC address. Common protocols that use RARP are BOOTP and DHCP.

Ring Topology A ring topology has device one connected to device two, device two connected to device three, and so on until the last device, which connects back to device one. Ring topologies can be implemented with a single ring or dual rings.

Rollover Cable A rollover cable is used for console connections and looks like an Ethernet CAT-5 cable; however, this cable is proprietary to Cisco and will not work for other types of connections. The rollover cable has 8 wires inside its plastic shielding and two RJ-45 connectors at each end. Each side of the rollover cable reverses the pins compared to the other side: pin 1 on one side is mapped to pin 8 on the other side; pin 2 is mapped to pin 7, and on and so forth.

Root Bridge or Switch When STP is running, a spanning tree is first created. Basically, a spanning tree is an inverted tree. At the top of the tree is the root bridge. From the root bridge, there are branches (physical Ethernet connections) connecting to other switches, and branches from these switches to other switches, and so on. The layer-2 device with the lowest Bridge ID (bridge priority + MAC address) is elected as the root.

Root Port In STP, each nonroot switch needs to select a single port it will use to reach the root switch. Typically, this is the port that has the best accumulated path cost to the root.

Router Routers function at the network layer. Because routers operate at a higher layer than layer-2 devices and use logical addressing, they provide many more advantages. Routers perform the following functions: define logical addressing schemes, contain broadcasts and multicasts, find layer-3 paths to destinations, connect different media types, switch packets on the same interface using VLANs, and use advanced features such as filtering and Quality of Service.

Router-on-a-Stick A router-on-a-stick is a router with a single trunk connection to a switch; it routes between the VLANs on this trunk connection.

Routing Information Protocol (RIP) IP *RIP (Routing Information Protocol)* comes in two different versions: 1 and 2. Version 1 is a distance vector protocol. Version 2 is a hybrid protocol. RIPv1 uses local broadcasts to share routing information. These updates are periodic in nature, occurring, by default, every 30 seconds. Both versions of RIP use *hop count* as a metric, which is not always the best metric to use. To prevent packets from circling around a loop forever, both versions of RIP use counting to infinity, placing a hop count limit of 15—any packet that reaches the sixteenth hop will be dropped. Instead of using broadcasts, RIPv2 uses *multicasts*. And to speed up convergence, RIPv2 supports *triggered* updates. RIPv1 is classful, and RIPv2 is classless.

Routing Table Routers will use network numbers to make routing decisions: how to get a packet to its destination. They will build a routing table, which contains path information. This information includes the network number, which interface the router should use to reach the network number, the metric of the path, and how the router learned about this network number.

Runtless Switching See *Fragment-Free Switching*.

Segment A segment is a PDU used at the transport layer.

Service Access Point (SAP) The LLC performs its multiplexing by using SAP identifiers. When a network layer protocol is encapsulated in the 802.2 frame, the protocol of the network data is placed in the SAP field. The destination uses this to determine which layer-3 protocol should process the frame.

Service Profile Identifiers (SPIDs) SPIDs are sometimes used by carriers on ISDN BRI connections that have a National ISDN-1 or Nortel DMS-100 switch. SPIDs are used by the carrier to authenticate call requests and are used only on the local connection between your router and the ISDN switch.

Session Layer The sixth layer of the OSI Reference Model is the session layer. The session layer is responsible for initiating the setup and teardown of connections. In order to perform these functions, the session layer must determine whether or not data stays local to a computer or must be obtained or sent to a remote networking device.

Spanning Tree Protocol The main function of STP is to remove layer-2 loops from your topology. DEC originally developed STP; IEEE took the initial implementation of STP and enhanced it (802.1d).

Split Horizon Split horizon states that if a neighboring router sends a route to a router, the receiving router will not propagate this route back to the advertising router on the same interface. It is used by distance vector protocols to prevent routing loops.

Standard IP Access List (ACL) Standard ACLs allow you to match packets based on only the source IP address.

Star Topology A star topology contains a central device that has many point-to-point connections to other devices. Star topologies are used in environments where many devices need to be connected together, but where a full mesh is cost-prohibitive.

Static Route A static route is a route that is manually configured on the router.

Static VLANs See *Port-Based VLANs*.

Sticky Learning Sticky learning is a port security feature that allows the switch to dynamically learn which MAC addresses are off of which ports, and then set up permanent CAM table entries for these.

Storage Area Network (SAN) SANs provide a high-speed infrastructure to move data between storage devices and file servers. This infrastructure can be dedicated to just these devices, or it can include other devices. Typically, fiber channels are used for the connections.

Store-and-Forward Switching Store-and-forward switching is the most basic form of switching. Here, the layer-2 device must pull in the entire frame into the buffer of the port and check the CRC of the frame before that device will perform any additional processing on the frame.

Straight-Through Cable An Ethernet straight-through cable has pin 1 on one side connected to pin 1 on the other side, pin 2 to pin 2, and so on. A straight-through cable is used for DTE-to-DCE connections. A DTE is a router, PC, or file server, and a DCE is a hub or switch.

Subinterface A subinterface is a logical interface associated with a single physical interface. A physical interface can support many subinterfaces. Cisco routers treat subinterfaces just as they do physical interfaces. You can shut down a physical interface, shutting down all of its associated subinterfaces, or you can shut down a single subinterface while keeping the remaining subinterfaces operational.

Subnet Mask When dealing with TCP/IP addresses, there are actually three components to the address: a network component, a host component, and a *subnet mask*. The function of the subnet mask is to differentiate between the network address, the host addresses, and the directed broadcast address for a network or subnet.

Subnetwork Access Point (SNAP) There are two frame types supported by 802.2: SAP and SNAP. One of the issues of the original SAP field in the 802.2 SAP frame is that even though it is eight bytes in length, only the first six bits are used for identifying upper-layer protocols, which allows up to 64 protocols. Back in the 1980s, there were many more protocols than 64, plus there was expectation that more protocols would be created. SNAP overcomes this limitation without having to change the length of the SAP field. To indicate a SNAP frame, the SAP fields are set to hexadecimal AA, the control field is set to 0x03, and the OUI field is set to 0x0. The *type* field identifies the upper-layer protocol that is encapsulated in payload of the 802.2 frame. AppleTalk is an example of a protocol that uses an 802.2 SNAP frame.

Subset Advertisement When a server responds to a VTP client's or VTP server's request, it generates a subset advertisement. A subset advertisement contains detailed VLAN configuration information, including the VLAN numbers, names, types, and other information.

Summary Advertisement A summary advertisement is generated by a switch in VTP server mode. Summary advertisements are generated every five minutes by default, or when a configuration change takes place on the server switch. Unlike a subset advertisement, a summary advertisement contains only summarized VLAN information.

Supernetting See *Classless Interdomain Routing (CIDR)*.

Switch A switch is a layer-2 device that is used to solve bandwidth and collision problems. Switches perform their switching in hardware called ASICs. All switches support store-and-forward switching. Some switches also support cut-through and fragment-free switching. Switches typically support both half- and full-duplexing. Switches come in many sizes, and some have over a hundred ports.

Switched Virtual Circuit (SVC) SVCs are similar to making a telephone call. Each SVC device is assigned a unique address, similar to a telephone number. In order to reach a destination device using an SVC, you'll need to know the destination device's address. In WAN environments, this is typically configured manually on your SVC device. Your device sends the SVC address to the carrier switch, which sets up the connection. Once you are done with the circuit, your device signals the carrier switch to tear it down. SVCs are used for intermittent data or for backup purposes.

Symbolic Translation If the CLI parser cannot find the actual command that you entered, the IOS will assume that you are trying to telnet to a machine by that name and will attempt a DNS resolution of the name to an IP address.

System Configuration Dialog When a router boots up, runs its hardware diagnostics, and loads the IOS software, the IOS then attempts to find a configuration file in NVRAM. If it can't find a configuration file to load, the IOS will then run the *System Configuration Dialog*, commonly referred to as *Setup* mode, which is a script that prompts you for configuration information. The purpose of this script is to ask you questions that will allow you to set up a basic configuration on your router.

Terminal Adapter (TA) A TA connects a TE2 (nonnative ISDN interface, like serial) to an NT2 or NT1.

Terminal Equipment 1 (TE1) A TE1 is an ISDN device with a native ISDN interface (such as a router with a BRI interface) that connects to an NT1 or NT2.

Terminal Equipment 2 (TE2) A TE2 is an ISDN device with a nonnative ISDN interface (such as a router with a serial interface) used for ISDN connectivity.

Time Division Multiplexing (TDM) Channelized services, such as a T1 or E1, use a process called TDM to create many logical channels on a single piece of wire. A channel is often referred to as a timeslot. Each channel or timeslot is given its own amount of bandwidth and time on the wire. Each channel does not simultaneously transmit its information along with other channels. Instead, each channel must take its own turn in sending a small bit of information. All channels are given the same amount of bandwidth and time, and once all of the channels are given their chance to send information, the first channel begins again.

Transmission Control Protocol (TCP) TCP's main responsibility is to provide a reliable logical connection between two devices within TCP/IP. It can uses windowing to implement flow control so that a source device doesn't overwhelm a destination with too many segments.

Transmission Control Protocol/Internet Protocol (TCP/IP) TCP/IP is a standard that includes many protocols. It defines how machines on an internetwork can communicate with each other. It was initially funded by and developed for DARPA. Originally designed in RFC 791, it has become the de facto standard for networking protocols. The Internet uses TCP/IP to carry data between networks, and most corporations today use TCP/IP for their networks.

Transparent Bridge or Switch The term *transparent* appropriately describes a transparently bridged network—the devices connected to the network are unaware that the bridge, or switch, is a part of the network and is forwarding frames to the destination. Basically, transparent bridge networks physically look like a bunch of stars connected together. However, transparent bridges give the appearance to connected devices that every device in the broadcast domain is on the same logical segment.

Transport Layer The fourth layer of the OSI Reference Model is the transport layer, which is responsible for the actual mechanics of a connection. It can provide both reliable and unreliable delivery of data on a connection. For reliable connections, the transport layer is responsible for error detection and correction: when an error is detected with the sending of information, the transport layer will resend the data. For unreliable connections, the transport layer provides only error detection—error correction is left up to one of the higher layers (typically the application layer).

Trunk Connection Trunk connections are capable of carrying traffic for multiple VLANs. In order to support trunking, the original Ethernet frame must be modified to carry VLAN information. This is to ensure that the broadcast integrity is maintained.

Unicast Frame With a unicast, the destination MAC address denotes a single device.

User Datagram Protocol (UDP) UDP provides an unreliable connection at the transport layer. UDP doesn't go through a three-way handshake to set up a connection—it just begins sending its information. Likewise, UDP doesn't check to see if sent segments were received by a destination; in other words, it doesn't have an acknowledgment process. Typically, if an acknowledgment process is necessary, the application layer, will provide this verification.

User EXEC Mode *User EXEC* mode provides basic access to the IOS, with limited command availability (basically simple monitoring and troubleshooting). If you see a ">" character at the end of the prompt information, then you know that you are in *User EXEC* mode.

Variable-Length Subnet Masking (VLSM) VLSM allows you to have more than one mask for a given class of address, albeit a Class A, B, or C network number. Classful protocols such as RIPv1 and IGRP do not support VLSM. To deploy VLSM requires a routing protocol that is classless, such as BGP, EIGRP, IS-IS, OSPF, or RIPv2. VLSM provides two major advantages: more efficient use of addressing and the ability to perform route summarization.

Virtual Circuit (VC) A VC is a logical connection between two devices. Therefore, many of these VCs can exist on the same physical connection. The advantage that VCs have over leased lines is that they can provide full connectivity at a much lesser price than using leased lines.

Virtual LAN (VLAN) A VLAN is a group of networking devices in the same broadcast domain. VLANs are not restricted to any physical boundary in the switched network, assuming that all the devices are interconnected via switches and that there are no intervening layer-3 devices. Logically speaking, VLANs are also subnets.

VLAN Trunk Protocol (VTP) The VLAN Trunk Protocol (VTP) is a proprietary Cisco protocol used to share VLAN configuration information between Cisco switches on trunk connections. VTP allows switches to share and synchronize their VLAN information, which ensures that your network has a consistent VLAN configuration.

Virtual Private Network (VPN) A VPN is a special type of secure network. A VPN is used to provide a secure connection across a public network, like an internet. Extranets typically use a VPN to provide a secure connection between a company and its known external users or offices.

VTP Client Mode A VTP client switch cannot make changes to its VLAN configuration itself—it requires a server switch to tell it about the VLAN changes. When a client switch receives a VTP message from a server switch, it incorporates the changes and then floods the VTP message out its remaining trunk ports. An important point to make is that a client switch does not store its VLAN configuration information in NVRAM—instead, it learns this from a server switch every time it boots up.

VTP Pruning VTP pruning is a Cisco VTP feature that allows your switches to dynamically delete or add VLANs to a trunk, creating a more efficient switching network.

VTP Server Mode A switch configured in VTP server mode can add, modify, and delete VLANs. A VTP server switch, when making a change, propagates the VTP message concerning the change on all of this trunk ports. If a server switch receives a VTP update message, it will incorporate the update and forward the message out its remaining trunk ports.

VTP Transparent Mode A switch configured in VTP transparent mode can add, modify, and delete VLANs. Configuration changes made to a transparent switch affect only *that* switch, and no other switch in the network. A transparent switch ignores VTP messages—it will accept them on trunk ports and forward them out its remaining trunk ports, but it will not incorporate the message changes.

Virtual Terminal (VTY) A VTY is a logical line on a Cisco device, which is used to manage telnet connections.

Wide Area Network (WAN) A WAN is used to connect LANs together. Typically, WANs are used when the LANs that need to be connected are separated by a large distance. Where a corporation provides its own infrastructure for a LAN, WANs are leased from carrier networks, such as telephone companies. There are four basic types of connections, or circuits, used in WAN services: circuit-switched, cell-switched, packet-switched, and dedicated connections.

Wildcard Mask When dealing with IP addresses in ACL statements, you can use wildcard masks to match on a range of addresses instead of having to manually enter every IP address that you want to match on. A wildcard mask is *not* a subnet mask. Like an IP address or subnet mask, a wildcard mask consists of 32 bits. With a wildcard mask, a 0 in a bit position means that the corresponding bit position in the address of the ACL statement *must* match the bit position in the IP address in the examined packet. A 1 in a bit position means that the corresponding bit position in the address of the ACL statement does *not* have to match the bit position in the IP address in the examined packet. OSPF **`network`** statements also use wildcard masks.

Windowing TCP and other transport layer protocols allow the regulation of the flow of segments, ensuring that one device doesn't flood another device with too many segments. TCP uses a sliding windowing mechanism to assist with flow control. For example, if you have a window size of 1, a device can send only one segment, and then it must wait for a corresponding acknowledgment before receiving the next segment.

INDEX

A

B

C

T

INTERNATIONAL CONTACT INFORMATION

AUSTRALIA
McGraw-Hill Book Company
Australia Pty. Ltd.
TEL +61-2-9900-1800
FAX +61-2-9878-8881
http://www.mcgraw-hill.com.au
books-it_sydney@mcgraw-hill.com

CANADA
McGraw-Hill Ryerson Ltd.
TEL +905-430-5000
FAX +905-430-5020
http://www.mcgraw-hill.ca

GREECE, MIDDLE EAST, & AFRICA (Excluding South Africa)
McGraw-Hill Hellas
TEL +30-210-6560-990
TEL +30-210-6560-993
TEL +30-210-6560-994
FAX +30-210-6545-525

MEXICO (Also serving Latin America)
McGraw-Hill Interamericana Editores
S.A. de C.V.
TEL +525-1500-5108
FAX +525-117-1589
http://www.mcgraw-hill.com.mx
carlos_ruiz@mcgraw-hill.com

SINGAPORE (Serving Asia)
McGraw-Hill Book Company
TEL +65-6863-1580
FAX +65-6862-3354
http://www.mcgraw-hill.com.sg
mghasia@mcgraw-hill.com

SOUTH AFRICA
McGraw-Hill South Africa
TEL +27-11-622-7512
FAX +27-11-622-9045
robyn_swanepoel@mcgraw-hill.com

SPAIN
McGraw-Hill/
Interamericana de España, S.A.U.
TEL +34-91-180-3000
FAX +34-91-372-8513
http://www.mcgraw-hill.es
professional@mcgraw-hill.es

UNITED KINGDOM, NORTHERN, EASTERN, & CENTRAL EUROPE
McGraw-Hill Education Europe
TEL +44-1-628-502500
FAX +44-1-628-770224
http://www.mcgraw-hill.co.uk
emea_queries@mcgraw-hill.com

ALL OTHER INQUIRIES Contact:
McGraw-Hill/Osborne
TEL +1-510-420-7700
FAX +1-510-420-7703
http://www.osborne.com
omg_international@mcgraw-hill.com

LICENSE AGREEMENT

THIS PRODUCT (THE "PRODUCT") CONTAINS PROPRIETARY SOFTWARE, DATA AND INFORMATION (INCLUDING DOCUMENTATION) OWNED BY THE McGRAW-HILL COMPANIES, INC. ("McGRAW-HILL") AND ITS LICENSORS. YOUR RIGHT TO USE THE PRODUCT IS GOVERNED BY THE TERMS AND CONDITIONS OF THIS AGREEMENT.

LICENSE: Throughout this License Agreement, "you" shall mean either the individual or the entity whose agent opens this package. You are granted a non-exclusive and non-transferable license to use the Product subject to the following terms:

(i) If you have licensed a single user version of the Product, the Product may only be used on a single computer (i.e., a single CPU). If you licensed and paid the fee applicable to a local area network or wide area network version of the Product, you are subject to the terms of the following subparagraph (ii).

(ii) If you have licensed a local area network version, you may use the Product on unlimited workstations located in one single building selected by you that is served by such local area network. If you have licensed a wide area network version, you may use the Product on unlimited workstations located in multiple buildings on the same site selected by you that is served by such wide area network; provided, however, that any building will not be considered located in the same site if it is more than five (5) miles away from any building included in such site. In addition, you may only use a local area or wide area network version of the Product on one single server. If you wish to use the Product on more than one server, you must obtain written authorization from McGraw-Hill and pay additional fees.

(iii) You may make one copy of the Product for back-up purposes only and you must maintain an accurate record as to the location of the back-up at all times.

COPYRIGHT; RESTRICTIONS ON USE AND TRANSFER: All rights (including copyright) in and to the Product are owned by McGraw-Hill and its licensors. You are the owner of the enclosed disc on which the Product is recorded. You may not use, copy, decompile, disassemble, reverse engineer, modify, reproduce, create derivative works, transmit, distribute, sublicense, store in a database or retrieval system of any kind, rent or transfer the Product, or any portion thereof, in any form or by any means (including electronically or otherwise) except as expressly provided for in this License Agreement. You must reproduce the copyright notices, trademark notices, legends and logos of McGraw-Hill and its licensors that appear on the Product on the back-up copy of the Product which you are permitted to make hereunder. All rights in the Product not expressly granted herein are reserved by McGraw-Hill and its licensors.

TERM: This License Agreement is effective until terminated. It will terminate if you fail to comply with any term or condition of this License Agreement. Upon termination, you are obligated to return to McGraw-Hill the Product together with all copies thereof and to purge all copies of the Product included in any and all servers and computer facilities.

DISCLAIMER OF WARRANTY: THE PRODUCT AND THE BACK-UP COPY ARE LICENSED "AS IS." McGRAW-HILL, ITS LICENSORS AND THE AUTHORS MAKE NO WARRANTIES, EXPRESS OR IMPLIED, AS TO THE RESULTS TO BE OBTAINED BY ANY PERSON OR ENTITY FROM USE OF THE PRODUCT, ANY INFORMATION OR DATA INCLUDED THEREIN AND/OR ANY TECHNICAL SUPPORT SERVICES PROVIDED HEREUNDER, IF ANY ("TECHNICAL SUPPORT SERVICES"). McGRAW-HILL, ITS LICENSORS AND THE AUTHORS MAKE NO EXPRESS OR IMPLIED WARRANTIES OF MERCHANTABILITY OR FITNESS FOR A PARTICULAR PURPOSE OR USE WITH RESPECT TO THE PRODUCT. McGRAW-HILL, ITS LICENSORS, AND THE AUTHORS MAKE NO GUARANTEE THAT YOU WILL PASS ANY CERTIFICATION EXAM WHATSOEVER BY USING THIS PRODUCT. NEITHER McGRAW-HILL, ANY OF ITS LICENSORS NOR THE AUTHORS WARRANT THAT THE FUNCTIONS CONTAINED IN THE PRODUCT WILL MEET YOUR REQUIREMENTS OR THAT THE OPERATION OF THE PRODUCT WILL BE UNINTERRUPTED OR ERROR FREE. YOU ASSUME THE ENTIRE RISK WITH RESPECT TO THE QUALITY AND PERFORMANCE OF THE PRODUCT.

LIMITED WARRANTY FOR DISC: To the original licensee only, McGraw-Hill warrants that the enclosed disc on which the Product is recorded is free from defects in materials and workmanship under normal use and service for a period of ninety (90) days from the date of purchase. In the event of a defect in the disc covered by the foregoing warranty, McGraw-Hill will replace the disc.

LIMITATION OF LIABILITY: NEITHER McGRAW-HILL, ITS LICENSORS NOR THE AUTHORS SHALL BE LIABLE FOR ANY INDIRECT, SPECIAL OR CONSEQUENTIAL DAMAGES, SUCH AS BUT NOT LIMITED TO, LOSS OF ANTICIPATED PROFITS OR BENEFITS, RESULTING FROM THE USE OR INABILITY TO USE THE PRODUCT EVEN IF ANY OF THEM HAS BEEN ADVISED OF THE POSSIBILITY OF SUCH DAMAGES. THIS LIMITATION OF LIABILITY SHALL APPLY TO ANY CLAIM OR CAUSE WHATSOEVER WHETHER SUCH CLAIM OR CAUSE ARISES IN CONTRACT, TORT, OR OTHERWISE. Some states do not allow the exclusion or limitation of indirect, special or consequential damages, so the above limitation may not apply to you.

U.S. GOVERNMENT RESTRICTED RIGHTS: Any software included in the Product is provided with restricted rights subject to subparagraphs (c), (1) and (2) of the Commercial Computer Software-Restricted Rights clause at 48 C.F.R. 52.227-19. The terms of this Agreement applicable to the use of the data in the Product are those under which the data are generally made available to the general public by McGraw-Hill. Except as provided herein, no reproduction, use, or disclosure rights are granted with respect to the data included in the Product and no right to modify or create derivative works from any such data is hereby granted.

GENERAL: This License Agreement constitutes the entire agreement between the parties relating to the Product. The terms of any Purchase Order shall have no effect on the terms of this License Agreement. Failure of McGraw-Hill to insist at any time on strict compliance with his License Agreement shall not constitute a waiver of any rights under this License Agreement. This License Agreement shall be construed overned in accordance with the laws of the State of New York. If any provision of this License Agreement is held to be contrary to law, ovision will be enforced to the maximum extent permissible and the remaining provisions will remain in full force and effect.